MW01148549

ALTAR
AND
CHURCH

CULTORIBUS
SACRAE LITURGIAE

Stefan Heid

ALTAR
AND
CHURCH

Principles of Liturgy from Early Christianity

The Catholic University of America Press
Washington, D.C.

SCHNELL + STEINER

Cover:

Zechariah and the Angel at the altar of the Temple (Lk 1:11), Pericopes of Henry II, c. 1002–1012, Staatsbibliothek München Clm. 4452, fol. 149v.

Despite intensive efforts, it was not possible to identify the rights holders
of the images in all cases. Justified claims are settled within the framework of the usual agreements.

English translation copyright © 2023
Schnell und Steiner
Originally published as Altar und Kirche : Prinzipien christlicher Liturgie
(Regensburg: Schnell und Steiner, 3rd., revised edition 2023).

The paper used in this publication meets the minimum requirements of American
National Standards for Information Science—Permanence of Paper for Printed Library Materials, ANSI Z39.48-1992.

North American printing information:

Cataloging-in-Publication Data is available from the Library of Congress

ISBN: 978-0-8132-3743-5

Translation from the German: Susan Johnson

Carbon neutral
Print product
ClimatePartner.com/10951-2310-1001

European printing information:

Bibliographic information published by the Deutsche Nationalbibliothek:
The Deutsche Nationalbibliothek lists this publication in the Deutsche Nationalbibliografie;
detailed bibliographic data are available on the Internet at: https://dnb.de.

first edition 2023
© 2023 Verlag Schnell & Steiner GmbH, Leibnizstr. 13, 93055 Regensburg, Germany
Cover Design: Anna Braungart, Tübingen
Layout: typegerecht berlin
Print: Gutenberg Beuys Feindruckerei GmbH, Langenhagen, Germany

ISBN 978-3-7954-3845-6

Further information about our publications can be found under:
www.schnell-und-steiner.de

CONTENTS

PREFACE

Whereas developments in technology replace outdated methods with better ones and then the old ones are never needed again, the Church must always look at her history in order to remain up to date. The Church cannot simply reinvent herself or renew herself at will, but must trust in her origins, in Scripture and Tradition. The *communio* of faith has from the very beginning taken place and been renewed in worship, primarily in the celebration of the Eucharist.

This leads us to the central themes of the present book: the early Christian altar and church building. The word "principles" in the subtitle is meant here in a double sense: on the one hand, it is about the beginnings of the liturgy and, on the other hand, it is about its principles, i.e. those things that are so fundamental and important for Christian worship that up to the Middle Ages they were found in all churches and to this day continue to exert an influence, especially in the communities of the East. In many cases, however, the praxis has meanwhile diverged a long way from what it once was and is now increasingly subject to ideological decisions.

The early Christian altar is not a bad starting point for getting to the bottom of things. Why and since when has the altar been used? Is it an authentic element of worship or an aberration of the times? Is it possible that the simple meal table of the house churches was how it began? And anyway, who is allowed to erect an altar? What is its function in the church space? Since the Second Vatican Council, there has been a blossoming of altar building in the Catholic world, one that paradoxically enough goes hand in hand with an unheard-of destruction of historical altars. How is this to be explained?

In order to ascertain how things began, it is necessary to take a careful look at numerous textual and pictorial sources, both at difficult, cumbersome texts and at those that it is all too easy to imagine one has understood. The sources must be allowed to speak for themselves, to say what they really want to say without being told what they mean. It is worth taking trouble over details, too, as this opens up new ways of seeing the most important motives and forms of the Christian worship of God, as well as a new understanding of the real conditions in situ of building a community.

I would like to thank Susan Johnson for the translation of *Altar und Kirche: Prinzipien christlicher Liturgie*, 3rd revised edition (Regensburg: Verlag Schnell & Steiner, 2023) into English and the copyeditor Gregory Black. Quotations from German sources have been translated ad hoc into English unless a published translation is available, in which case this is noted.

Stefan Heid

I. PROLOGUE

Altars are indispensable furnishings for the offering of sacrifices: from time immemorial, condensation points of the sacred and catalysts of cult. That is already true of the ancient Greeks and Romans, to remain just within the European cultural sphere. But the altar is also the central item of furniture in every ecclesial space, thus making it a distinctive Christian hallmark. This applies to all the major religious communities, whether Eastern Catholic, Orthodox or Roman Catholic. The Lutheran Reformation, too, adopts the altar, stressing the centrality of the high altar and not infrequently re-orchestrating it by decorating it with imagery that brings out the connection between the meal and the sacrifice on the cross. The prayers at the altar continue to be said facing the altar. Only the Reformed (Calvinists, Zwinglians) break with the tradition and consciously use ordinary tables. Under their influence, liturgy and cult are more and more eclipsed in the Neo-Protestantism of the nineteenth and twentieth centuries in favour of a religion of moralizing bourgeois sermons. Even though altars are still to be found in many Lutheran churches, they are in reality a traditional element that has simply been left behind.

With the above-mentioned exceptions, the altar dominates every church. In 315, one of the main orations given at the consecration of the new cathedral at Tyre (Lebanon) – probably by Bishop Eusebius of Caesarea – is a panegyric on the "great temple" that culminates with "the great and august and unique altar" at which Jesus himself as the High Priest offers up the sacrificial offerings.[1] A few centuries later, in around 400, John Chrysostom, as patriarch of Constantinople, asks the rich landowners to erect churches with the "altar of God" on their vast estates.[2] So the altar suffices to turn a hall into a church: no altar, no church. Many voices since the third century could be cited that name altar and church, the terms in the title of the present book, in one breath.[3]

---

1 Euseb. hist. eccl. 10,4,68 (SC 55, 102 f.).
2 Joh. Chrys. in act. apost. hom. 18,4 (PG 60,147)
3 Cypr. ep. 70,2 (CSEL 3,2, 768): *qui nec altare habuit nec ecclesiam*. Orig. in Iesu Nav. hom. 2,1 (SC 71, 116): *ecclesias exstrui, altaria [...] respergi*. Ibid. 9,1 (244): *in hoc aedificio ecclesiae oportet esse et altare*.

Ibid. 10,3 (276): *ad ornatum quoque altaris vel ecclesiae aliquid conferant*. Hieron. ep. 60,16,3 (CSEL 54, 571): *subversae ecclesiae, ad altaria Christi stabulati equi*. Euseb. laud. Const. 16,10 (GCS Euseb. 1, 253). Cf. Prud. peristeph. 10,46–50 (CCL 126, 332).

But did Jesus want this? Is it still genuine Christianity? Or do we not instead have to accuse the Church of breaking with her origins? In this connection, people are fond of using the telling phrase "Constantinian shift", which they claim to have led at the beginning of the fourth century to the secularization and paradoxically also the sacralization of the Church. They argue that with Emperor Constantine's conversion, on the one hand the spirit of this world entered Christianity and, on the other, the fragrance of sanctity and mystery began to rise up in the halls of the Christians. Does this mark the beginning of something completely new? Since when have there been churches and altars anyway? And what significance do altars and sacred spaces have for Christian worship?

1. ABSENCE OF CULT IN EARLY CHRISTIANITY

Current research is in virtually complete ecumenical agreement that the original, true Christianity knew neither altars nor sacred spaces and in fact expressly rejected them as a matter of principle. Hence, in the beginning there were just tables of some kind or other at the gatherings, possibly dining tables, which were used, as the case may be, for the celebration of the Eucharist or for other kinds of meals. The Protestant New Testament scholar Peter Lampe writes in his influential book on the Christians in the city of Rome in the first two centuries (1987):

> In view of the concurrence of archaeological and literary evidence, we may conclude that, in the first two centuries, there were no 'house churches' in the sense of specific rooms permanently set aside for worship in secular houses. Positively speaking, the Christians of the first and second centuries celebrated their liturgy in rooms that were used in everyday life. This means that the rooms used for Sunday worship had no special immoveable cultic equipment.[4]

Nothing different is to be found in the handbook written by the Catholic Church historian Alfons Fürst:

> Rather than in sacred, consecrated temples, the Christians celebrated their worship in quite ordinary rooms and buildings. Nor was there an altar or any divine images. The tables for the Eucharist had neither the form nor the function of altars (in antiquity mostly

---

4   LAMPE 2003, 368. To be noted here is the narrow use of the term "house church" to refer to a prayer room located in a "house".

rectangular blocks of stone on which burnt offerings were sacrificed; for offerings of food and drink tables were used). The Christians used ordinary movable tables, which are likely to have been made as a rule of wood. The 'church' was not the dwelling of the deity but rather the meeting room of the community [...] which for that very reason is called 'church' [...]. It was only over the course of centuries that, under the influence of pagan cultic ideas, [...] sacrality was attributed to the Christian meeting rooms. [...] With the understanding of the Eucharist as a sacrifice, the table increasingly became an 'altar', albeit without taking on the form of a pagan altar. The eucharistic meal in private houses turned into the ecclesial cult in a sacred building.[5]

For both of these authors it is a matter of certainty that the Christian movement began more as one of philosophy and ethics, and at all events not as a religion in the way this was understood in antiquity. Hence it had neither cult nor sacrifice.[6] It was, in their view, only in the course of foreign infiltration by the dominant Greek culture that in the third century Christianity was distorted into a priestly religion. Now sacrifices and altars began to be spoken of. The break and the real fall are thus located at the afore-mentioned "Constantinian shift", when, although with the conversion of Constantine and the onset of mass baptisms shortly afterwards the former paganism was ousted from the public sphere, it was nonetheless resurgent in an altered form, precisely in Christianity.[7]

This all sounds fine and plausible. But if you take a step back, you soon notice that this view of the early Church is typically modern. What lies behind it is the naïve hope that there once existed a flawless primitive Christianity which began, as it were, as the fundamentalist revival movement of the itinerant preacher Jesus, sealed off from any harmful outside influence. Only later, spoilt by its success, did this movement com-promise itself and become infected by pagan ideas. This or something like it is how, for example, North American sects imagine the beginnings of Christianity to have been. In Europe, Rousseau already longed for the *religion pure* of the Gospel and pure primitive

5 A. FÜRST, Die Liturgie der Alten Kirche (Münster 2008) 65 f. Already DEICHMANN 1964, 56: "For many generations the Christian cultic building was secular. The community could and was permitted to gather in any room for the Eucharist and common prayer. In these assembly rooms any table could serve for the Eucharist; there was no altar. This was the nature of the so-called house-churches in the early Christian period." KLAUCK 1981, 77: "Parallel to the transition from private house to cultic build-ing, a further development took place during the same period, namely that leading from the dining and family table around which the house commu-nity gathered to the sacred one reserved solely for the priest."

6 DE BLAAUW 2008, 261 f.; JUDGE 2008, 417 f., 421. More balanced on the New Testament understand-ing of cult is B. NEUNHEUSER, Storia della liturgia attraverso le epoche culturali (Tivoli ²1988) 23 f.

7 SOTIRA 2013, 20.

Christianity as an alternative to Roman Catholicism.[8] In this current, French Calvinism combines in the Prussian Union (1817) with German Lutheranism, which now intensifies its *sola scriptura* into a hostility towards visual images and cult:[9] only the word of Sacred Scripture is still to count – burn the images and get rid of the rites!

In a secularized form, this ideal of purity lives on in university theology, which champions the ideal of a noble and primitive Jesuanic Christianity, claiming that this conclusion is based on objective research and scientificity. The primitive Christianity of a Jesus or Paul is imagined to be correspondingly "puritanical". The influential German Liberal Protestantism of an Albrecht Ritschl (1822–1889) (Bonn) or Adolf Harnack (1851–1930) (Berlin) attaches to the kind of Christianity deviating from this which began to emerge from the third century onwards the label of "Early Catholicism" (*Frühkatholizismus*) and ascribes to it grave aberrations associated with key terms such as sacerdotal hierarchy, dogmas, sacraments, the cult of saints and the sacrificial cult. Thus, so the argument goes, in the third century a Catholicism *avant la lettre* took shape, displaying all the evil characteristics of later denominational Catholicism.

This theory of decline and Hellenization has long since become the standard repertoire and hermeneutic key of historical and theological scholarship. It has established itself to such an extent that in both Protestant and Catholic research it counts as certain that in the first and second centuries there was no altar and naturally no sacred room for worship either; indeed, that it is impossible for the two of them to have existed. It was only in the third century, so the argument goes, that pagan ideas gradually seeped into Christianity, as a result of which the Christians erected altars and understood the meals they had hitherto celebrated to be sacrifices. But it was only with Emperor Constantine that this process was carried to extremes and rendered irreversible.

The first Catholic theologian to enthusiastically embrace this opinion was the Augsburg priest Franz Wieland, who studied Christian archaeological evidence at the Campo Santo Teutonico in Rome. This work produced four studies published between 1906 and 1912 on the early Christian altar and sacrifice which came to the firm con-

---

8 Cf. H. Maier, Revolution und Kirche. Zur Frühgeschichte der Christlichen Demokratie (Freiburg i.Br. ⁵1988) 117, 127.

9 G. A. M. Rouwhorst, Which Religion is Most Sacrificial? Reflections on the Transformations of Sacrifice in Early Christianity and Rabbinic Judaism, in: A. Houtman et al. (eds.), The Actuality of Sacrifice. Past and Present (Leiden 2014) 261–274. On the alleged early Christian iconophobia in Adolf Harnack and Theodor Klauser see Finney

1994, 7–10. The interpretation of early Christianity still prevailing among liberal Protestant theologians in Berlin (Andresen 1975, 6) is viewed critically by C. Markschies, Hellenisierung des Christentums. Sinn und Unsinn einer historischen Deutungskategorie (Leipzig 2012). See in general C. Jäggi, Sakralität im Protestantismus, oder: Wo steckt das Heilige nach der Reformation?, in: A. Beck / A. Berndt (eds.), Sakralität und Sakralisierung (Stuttgart 2013) 53–70.

clusion that up to the third century neither existed.[10] Wieland's abolition of the early Christian altar is based on this premise: "Since the concept of altar is always correlated to the respective concept of sacrifice, it is of crucial importance to know the primitive Church's understanding of the Eucharist."[11] So the theologian Wieland concludes from early Christian theology that there cannot have been an altar. He thinks he knows that into the third century the Eucharist was not a sacrifice but rather a meal with "thanksgiving" (eucharist): people ate together and gave thanks to God at the same time, that was all. No sacrificial gifts were offered up; rather, the thanksgiving was understood as a spiritual sacrifice. If there was no sacrificial act, then there was no altar either but rather just an "in itself insignificant meal table."[12] It was only at the turn of the third century that an innovation occurred when the offering up of material gifts began to be spoken of.[13]

With this scenario, Wieland makes the development of the altar fit perfectly into the chronological framework of liberal Protestant theology. In fact, it does at first sight seem for theological but also for archaeological and literary reasons impossible to accept the existence of an early Christian altar before the third century: after all, are not ancient altars imagined to be solid blocks of stone dripping with animal blood standing outside temples in the open air (Fig. 1; below Figs. 4, 6, 19, 119, 128)? Is it not evident that such altars of slaughter and holocaust are totally unfit for the Lord's Supper? Do not the early writers of the Church quite rightly insist on speaking of the eucharistic "table" (Gk. τράπεζα / Lat. *mensa*) even though they do occasionally already use the term "altar" (Gk. θυσιαστήριον / Lat. *altare*)?[14] Is it not only after the Constantinian shift that the "table" turns into the "*sacred* table" as a kind of compromise formula enabling a continued avoidance of the unloved word "altar" yet still sacralising the table? And even if there is talk of the "altar", does this not have to be understood purely symbolically, as a metaphor for Christ slaughtered on the Cross or in general as the Christian life of sacrifice?[15]

One is automatically inclined to answer all these questions in the affirmative. Nevertheless Wieland's studies met with criticism[16] and were even placed on the Index of For-

10 WIELAND 1906; *id.* 1908; *id.* 1909; *id.* 1912. On the person Franz Wieland see HEID / DENNERT 2012, 1321; J. SCHEPERS, Streitbare Brüder. Ein parallelbiographischer Zugriff auf Modernismuskontroverse und Antimodernisteneid am Beispiel von Franz und Konstantin Wieland (Paderborn 2016).
11 WIELAND 1906, 3.
12 WIELAND 1912, 30. Cf. RAUSCHEN 1910, 75–77.
13 WIELAND 1912, 10–22, 29. Also in the same vein: Theologisches Wörterbuch zum Neuen Testament 3 (1938) 189 f. On Wieland's concept of sacrifice see

MOLL 1975, 30–33.
14 WIELAND 1912, 29.
15 Theologians consistently share this opinion, but so do archaeologists, e.g. GUIDOBALDI 2001, 173. Cf. JUDGE 2008, 424 f.
16 DÖLGER 1930, 161: "But Wieland did not grasp the true content of several important texts." His main opponent was, however, the Jesuit Emil Dorsch, who offered a polemical but nonetheless often accurate response to Wieland.

Fig. 1: Sacrificed ram on an altar, Rome, 2nd century AD.; Royal Collection, British Museum 1963,1029.2; photo: © Royal Collection Trust.

bidden Books in 1911.[17] This immediately triggered the accusation that with this measure the Vatican wanted to put an end to free research. That made the censured Wieland even more interesting, and consequently his basic theses, much to the annoyance of the Vatican, have gained acceptance everywhere.[18] On the Protestant side, by contrast, it led to a sense of being vindicated since Martin Luther had already rejected the Sacrifice of the Mass. Wieland received, as it were, the highest accolade when Adolf Harnack drew a magisterial line under the debate:

17　H. Wolf (ed.), Systematisches Repertorium zur Buchzensur 1814–1917. Indexkongregation (Paderborn 2005) 750 f.; *id.* (ed.), Römische Bücherverbote. Edition der Bandi von Inquisition und Indexkongregation 1814–1917 (Paderborn 2005) 547–550.

18　D. Burkard, Der Schatten des "Modernismus" auf dem *Campo Santo Teutonico*?, in: S. Heid / K.-J. Hummel (eds.), Päpstlichkeit und Patriotismus. Der *Campo Santo Teutonico*: Ort der Deutschen zwischen Risorgimento und Erstem Weltkrieg (1870–1918) (Freiburg i.Br. 2018) 359–415, here 384–395. Wieland found his most influential supporter in the Bonn professor Theodor Klauser (1894–1984). On his person see Heid / Dennert 2012, 738–740.

The crucial point is: in the first two centuries there was no real Christian altar; the 'sacred' altar only developed gradually in the course of the 3rd century, indeed the idea that it is permanently sacred and not just at the moment of the sacrificial act was probably not arrived at much before the time when the altar was linked to the *memorial* of a martyr or saint. Now as long as there was no altar in the specific sense, there were also no 'sacred' churches.[19]

All that dates from a good century ago, and yet it is still mainstream, whether in academic research or in its pastoral popularisation. The author of the present study holds a different view on the essential points because he is convinced that the research has manoeuvred itself into a blind alley. A science that is committed in a good Protestant sense to the Word alone and finds everything external, graspable and sensual suspect blocks its view of the real world. It is utterly incapable either of appreciating the pagan religiosity of Rome with its realism, formalism and ritualism[20] or of building a bridge to the liturgy of nascent Christianity. The great religious phenomena and upheavals of late antiquity ultimately remain foreign to it. This should be contrasted with, to suggest just one example, the case of Franz Joseph Dölger (1879–1940),[21] who spent his whole life researching the academic field of antiquity and Christianity and, precisely because his spiritual home was in Catholicism, possessed a deep insight into the complex realities of sacrality and rituality in late antiquity. This is not meant in any way to claim that it is possible to draw seamless conclusions from present-day Catholicism about the past.[22] And yet: when historical research also concerns itself with religious imagination and respect for traditions, their denominational provenance does in fact become relevant.

2. THE MEAL TABLE AT THE RECLINING MEAL

As far as the early Christian altar is concerned, the generally accepted opinion can be outlined as follows: Jesus was not a priest and therefore did not offer any sacrifices. When he took meals among his friends or with sinners, these were normal meals at normal dining tables. The so-called Last Supper before the Crucifixion was, as the name Last *Supper* reveals, merely a meal to satisfy hunger. Since it was at such a meal that

19 HARNACK 1924, 612 f.
20 Theodor Mommsen judged the ancient Roman religion to be cold and decadent; SCHEID 2009, 19–21.
21 S. HEID, Franz Joseph Dölger, in: HEID / DENNERT 2012, 427–429.
22 See the illuminating analysis of the Catholic and Protestant images of history in RATZINGER 1966, 10–15.

Jesus instituted the Eucharist with bread and wine, this action, too, so the thinking goes, can only have taken place at a normal dining table (cf. Lk 22:21: τράπεζα).[23] And since the Christians continued to celebrate their community Eucharist as a Lord's Supper in remembrance of Jesus, they for a long time also continued to use such a table. When, for practical reasons, the Eucharist was later separated from the communal meal, the form of the dining table (made of wood) was retained for the Eucharist. It was only with the inception of church-building at the end of the third century and above all in the post-Constantinian period that more sturdy tables were erected, which were, so to speak, sacredly charged by being treated like altars.[24]

The Christian persecutions are also popularly cited in support of this narrative. It is claimed that Christians went into hiding and improvised their worship in small groups using the private city residences (*domus*) of wealthy Christian families (below Fig. 10).[25] Since such houses continued to serve their families as living quarters, there were no rooms reserved in them exclusively for worship. In practice, they would set up a horse-shoe-shaped couch (*stibadium*) (Fig. 2) in the dining room or three individual sofas placed in a semicircle (*triclinium*); in the middle stood the dining tables (Fig. 3).[26] The source that is quoted to support this claim is a single reference in the Acts of Thomas (third century) which speaks of the table adjacent to a triclinium being used for a blessing of bread, an action that can probably be interpreted as a Eucharist.[27] Alfred Stuiber concludes from this that rooms were made available by wealthy Christians on an ad hoc basis for the celebration of the Eucharist and that a random table was used.[28]

23 NUSSBAUM 1961b, 19.
24 This view has meanwhile become virtually canonical and is widespread in all the handbooks, encyclopaedias and other publications: KIRSCH / KLAUSER 1950, 334f.; NUSSBAUM 1965, 377; WESSEL 1966a, 111f.; SAXER 1994b, 241f.; BROX 1995, 119f.; SAHAS 1997, 40; SMITH 2003, 177f.; CLAUSSEN 2010, 26; BUTZKAMM 2011, 149–152; SOTIRA 2013, 16; RAMISCH 2018, 25f. BRAUN 1924a, 1, 3: "For the formal development of the altar, at all times up to the present it is not the sacrificial character of the Eucharist but rather its meal character that has been decisive. Whatever form the stipes of the altar was given, the whole thing was always a table." In the meantime even archaeologists share this view: DUVAL 1992, 171: "It is quite clear that the Christian altar is directly derived from the Roman dining-table (*mensa*)"; similarly DUVAL 2005, 11. GUIDOBALDI 2001, 172: The Christian altar is not derived from the pagan altar but from the triclinium table. DE BLAAUW 2008, 373: the term "*thysiastérion*" in Eusebius' sermon at the consecration of the cathedral at Tyre and "*altare*" in the Roman churches' reports of the Constantinian donations (in the *Liber Pontificalis*) show "how the meal table of the Christian Eucharist also took on the character of a sacrificial table". Similarly DEICHMANN 1964, 56; J. A. IÑIGUEZ, El altar cristiano 1 (Pamplona 1978) 17; A. GERHARDS, Der christliche Altar. Opferstätte oder Mahltisch?, in: A. GERHARDS / K. RICHTER (eds.), Das Opfer (Freiburg i.Br. 2000) 272–285, here 275; RIESNER 2007, 169.
25 BOUYER 1993, 43f. It is frequently alleged that the Church as an institution did not possess any property rights; PECKLERS 2013, 28.
26 On the dining room in houses in late antiquity see EEECAA 2, 649f.; I. BALDINI LIPPOLIS, La *Domus* tardoantic. Forme e rappresentazioni dello spazio domestico nelle città del mediterraneo (Bologna 2001) 79–83.
27 Acta Thomae 49 (LIPSIUS / BONNET 1903, 165f.); 131–133 (238–240).

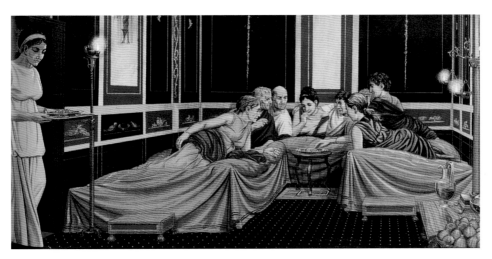

Fig. 2: Sigma meal on a stibadium; CONNOLLY / DODGE 1998, Fig. 149.

Whether he was right to do so is open to question. The Acts of Thomas is, after all, a novel-like text that portrays a fanciful image of the apostolic period. In addition, it is the only source that refers to tables being used simultaneously for sacred and profane purposes. The claim that random dining tables were used for the Eucharist therefore stands on very shaky legs. A popular counter-argument is that everyday matters are not reflected in literature, meaning that the use of dining tables for the Eucharist was so banal and widespread that it was not even mentioned. Such an argument *e silentio* does not, however, work because it is possible to prove anything and everything in this manner. The historian must instead be able to provide a sufficient number of positive proofs. And then it will become clear that it is not Eucharist-dining tables that predominate in early Christian literature but rather sacred tables or altars (below chapter II).

Nor has archaeology to date discovered any private triclinium (with a dining table) that can be proved to have served as a location for the celebration of the Eucharist.[29] Unfortunately the lack of evidence occasionally tempts researchers to embellish their speculations all the more elaborately. You can find in the research an astonishing knowledge of the interior design and furnishings of private Christian houses as well as of the purported eucharistic celebrations in the triclinia located in these houses.[30] The Christians are, for example, claimed to have been able to celebrate their worship in the

28 STUIBER 1978, 308; THÜMMEL 1999a, 490. Even MAZZA 2005, 59 still relies on this unique text to uphold the assertion of the use of profane moveable tables.

29 BOUYER 1993, 45.

30 ALIKIN 2010, 53 f.

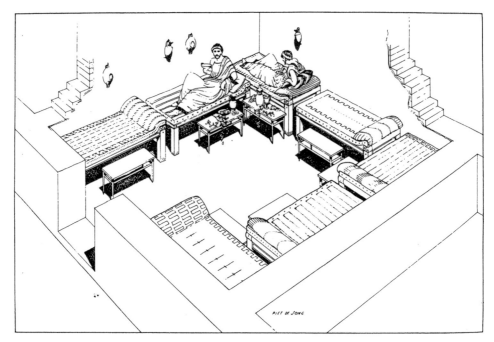

Fig. 3: Reconstruction of a banqueting room with seven *klínai*; KLINGHARDT 1996, Fig. 9.

personal, intimate atmosphere of an *ecclesiola*.[31] The head or lady of the house, members of an apparently wealthy, respectable people, would offer themselves to preside at the celebration.[32] Since reclining diners lie on their stomachs and cannot easily get up, they have need of servants (slaves) to wait on them. At a reclining meal, the servers approach the table from the open side at the front, the edge of which can be flat. It is from this necessity, such scholars conclude, that the office of deacon (servant at table, cf. Acts 6:2) came about.[33]

Not only the notion of domestic celebrations of the Eucharist at the dining table but also the closely associated idea of domestic churches (below chapter III, 1) are pure wishful thinking. This requires close examination: what is problematic is not the idea of reclining meals as such, nor can eucharistic celebrations within the framework of reclining meals be completely ruled out, to begin with at least. The problem is rather that people today immediately associate reclining meals with profane dining tables. That is, however, jumping the gun. To be sure, the Christians did not have any altars for sacri-

31 PECKLERS 2012, 28.   33 WIELAND 1906, 37, 46.
32 See below p. XXX n. 7.

ficial slaughter such as were used in other religions. But to conclude from this that the Eucharist was simply a meal and therefore only used dining tables is neither theologically nor historically compelling. Nor is this fact disguised by the statement – for its part a theological one – that the Eucharist is (as a meal?) in every respect so unique that no analogous Jewish or pagan cultic practices exist.[34]

In fact, the opposite is likely to be true. Jewish as well as pagan religious practice knows meal events at which sacrificial tables are also used alongside dining tables. In ancient society, a sophisticated, formal meal always also possesses religious-ritual elements for which a sacred table is used. Why then should the Christians not adopt this practice for their celebration of the Eucharist since it is a celebration, too? After all, it is for them not just any meal but rather an elevated meal with ritual elements. For the Eucharist there can certainly be no question of using an altar of sacrificial slaughter, but such altars do not play any role at ancient banquets either. For the latter, special cultic furniture is used for the ritual elements, above all sacred tables (Gk. ἱερὰ τράπεζα / Lat. *mensa sacra*). Such tables played a role in both pagan and Jewish antiquity in combination with communal meals. This then opens up a new approach to the Christian altar from the perspective of religious history.

This much is clear: there is no simple either-or of Eucharist or meal, altar or dining table. Such a narrowing down to bipolar alternatives does not do justice to the religious horizon of antiquity. Certainly, early Christianity rejected the pagan altar of animal sacrifices. But the alternative for the Eucharist is not a profane dining table.[35] Rather, there is a third variant, one that lends itself perfectly to the eucharistic blessing of bread and wine: the sacred table.

There are numerous testimonies in texts and images that refer to sacred tables in antiquity. In principle, an ordinary table was ruled out for a cultic or sacrificial act. Consequently two main types of furniture developed: alongside the sacrificial altars there were sacred tables. The two pieces of furniture had a similar function in the ancient sacrificial cult and ultimately became interchangeable; accordingly, sacred tables can be referred to as "altars" and vice versa: altars as "tables".[36] Within the same cult, at one moment a "holy table"[37] and at the next an altar will serve the same needs.[38] How closely the two pieces of furniture belong together is seen in the solid sacrificial altars on which are depicted sacred tables (Fig. 4).[39]

---

34 WIELAND 1906, 3.

35 E.g. BRAUN 1924a, 49 f.

36 For example, in Ez 39:20 and 44:16 LXX the "table" of God in the Jerusalem Temple is an altar of sacrificial slaughter. Comprehensively on the altar of antiquity ThesCRA 4; on the sacred table see ibid. 5, 230–240; GOUDINEAU 1967; SIEBERT 1999, 98–102.

37 KRUSE 1932, 946.

38 REISCH 1894, 1676; KIRSCH / KLAUSER 1950, 312 f., 319. For a sacred table used as an altar see e.g. DE GRÜNEISEN 1911, 221; MATZ 1969, Supplement 105.

39 A further example: ThesCRA 5, Plate 49, No. 822.

Fig. 4: Funerary altar of Amemptus with a frontal relief showing a sacred table with cult instruments lying on it, c. 41 AD; Musée du Louvre MA 488; photo: bpk-Bildagentur.

Fig. 5: Temple of the God Dagon in Ashdod with two sacrificial altars and a sacred table (1 Sam 5:1–5) in a fresco of the synagogue at Dura Europos (before 256/257), National Museum in Damascus; photo: Alamy Stock Photo.

In spite of many similarities, there are also differences: whereas the frequently solid altars serve predominantly for animal sacrifices, the lighter tables are used for bloodless sacrifices; for example, for the offering not of animals but rather of food and drink, or they are used as places to set down the sacrificial gifts and cultic instruments. Altars and sacred tables, as *res sacrae*, are surrounded in equal measure with an aura of sanctity.[40] Sacred tables belong to the sacrificial cult just as much as proper altars do, except that they are preferred for some functions[41] (Fig 5; above Fig. 4, below Figs. 9, 24). At such tables, the cultic servants perform their duties standing,[42] just as the altar is likewise approached standing (Heb 10:11); only rarely does anyone sit. Sacred tables are placed next to the altars[43] in temples and in front of images of the gods, but also in private houses.[44] They are consecrated together with the altar and temple.[45]

40 On the sanctity of the altar in antiquity see REISCH 1894, 1688–1691.
41 Seminally MISCHKOWSKI 1917.
42 W. HELBIG / H. SPEIER, Führer durch die öffentlichen Sammlungen klassischer Altertümer in Rom 2 (Tübingen ⁴1966) 182 No. 1372. See further I. KRAUSKOPF, in: ThesCRA 5, 239, No. 559.
43 In the frescoes of the synagogue at Dura Europos

the showbread table is depicted standing next to the two altars in the Jerusalem Temple. For altar and mensa see also N. ZIMMERMANN / S. LADSTÄTTER, Wandmalerei in Ephesos von hellenistischer bis in byzantinische Zeit (Wien 2010) 126 Fig. 226.
44 MISCHKOWSKI 1917, 6 f.
45 SIEBERT 1999, 98–102, esp. 98 f.

Immolation altars and sacred tables thus belong to the same cultic context. However, that does not mean that because they rigorously rejected altars for sacrificial slaughter the Christians did not want sacred tables either. After all, the immolation altar is from its very design intended exclusively for animal sacrifice. And, of course, Christians do not sacrifice either animals, meat or entrails (above Fig. 1). By contrast, sacred tables are veritably ideal cultic furnishings for Christian worship, with its offering of bread and wine. It is from such sacred tables that the Christian altar has to be derived[46] – or put differently – within the religious horizons of antiquity, the table for the celebration of the Eucharist is nothing other than the Christian variant of the ancient sacred table.

One must not imagine the Christian adaptation of the ancient sacred table to have consisted in the Christians taking a piece of pagan cultic furniture that had previously

---

46 Illustrative images of ancient sacred tables: Thes-CRA 2, Plate 103, Fig. 224; Plate 104, Fig. 269; Plate 106, No. 332; Plate 108; No. 390. NUSSBAUM 1961, 20 addresses sacred tables but then insists on focussing completely on meal tables. At the end (p. 36), he returns to the sacrificial table but without drawing the appropriate conclusions. Similarly BRAUN 1924a, 23. THÜMMEL 1999a, 490 f. would like to derive the altar not from sacred tables but from banqueting tables. However, banqueting tables may also have served as sacred tables.

served for offering sacrifices to Jupiter, Venus or some other deity and using it for the Eucharist. It is more likely that they purchased a suitable table at an appropriate shop (selling sacred furnishings), which was, as long as it had never been used, still profane. In just the same way, rich Christians would have no compunction about buying sarcophaguses at pagan shops for their burials. Alternatively, they might not have bought a sacred table at all but instead made their own altar, modelling it on such tables. Whatever the case, it was only at the moment when Christian worship was first celebrated at a piece of furniture that it became a sacred table. This table, which could just as easily have ended up as a "table of Jupiter" or "of Diana" – that is, as a "table of demons" – now became a "table of the Lord" (1 Cor 10:21) and was henceforth reserved exclusively for the "Lord's Supper" (1 Cor 11:20).

As has already been indicated, in antiquity the sacred table also plays a role at communal meals, which leads us, as far as Christianity is concerned, to take a look at the celebration of the Eucharist. Franz Wieland assumes that, on account of the Last Supper, the eucharistic table was a normal dining table, an assumption that has to date tied down all subsequent research. However, no matter what concrete form the Last Supper may have taken,[47] one thing is clear: even at such meals there were sacred tables for cultic acts. The Christians did not celebrate the Last Supper as an evening meal to satisfy their physical hunger (*coena*). The Lord's commission to "do this in remembrance of me" applied solely to the rite of bread and cup (1 Cor 11:24 f.). They ate their fill at home before they came to the community gathering (1 Cor 11:22, 34).

That explains why, despite its containing certain meal elements, the community gathering is seen by Paul as only embodying a cultic act in the rite of bread and cup.[48] Already in the New Testament (the Gospels, Paul, Letter to the Hebrews), this double rite displays all the characteristics of a sacrificial act analogous to the Old Testament cult.[49] At reclining meals it was normal for the tables to be changed over for the individual courses[50] as well as for the concluding act of sacrifice.[51] The same is to be assumed for Christian eating habits: they did not celebrate the "Lord's Supper" (1 Cor 11:20) or its sacred double rite (1 Cor 11:23–25) at the ordinary food tables but rather fetched in a special table, Paul's so-called "table of the Lord" (1 Cor 10:21).

---

47 Cf. MEYER 1989, 65–68.

48 KLAUCK 1982, 295; MEYER 1989, 75 f.

49 Did. 14 (SC 248, 192). This sacrifice can only refer to the Eucharist (Did. 9). Cf. FERGUSON 1997, 1015; JUDGE 2008, 424; LEONHARD / ECKHARDT 2010, 1074 f.; WEIDEMANN 2014, 51–53; DALY / NESSELRATH 2015, 176. RAUSCHEN 1910, 93 f. sees correctly that already the Apostolic Fathers and Apologists and then also Irenaeus, Clemens, Ter-

tullian and Cyprian all call the celebration of the Eucharist the sacrifice of the Christians.

50 Changing the tables is more practical and requires fewer staff than serving the individual vessels of food.

51 Fresco of a young woman engaged in sacrifice carrying a table, from Pompei: A. MAIURI, La peinture romaine (Geneva 1953) 86.

Such a process of fetching in a cultic table during a common meal is recorded by the Jewish writer Philo of Alexandria (first century).[52] He refers to the so-called showbread table of the Jerusalem Temple as the "table for thanksgiving for mortal things, for loaves and libations are placed upon it" (cf. Nm 4:7).[53] Further, he calls the showbread table a "holy table" (ἱερὰ τράπεζα), thus making it into a sacred table.[54] In general, the "holy table" is for Philo the table upon which the flesh that has previously been offered on the "altar" is laid. In this way, the symposium of those offering the sacrifice comes to partake at the altar and to share table fellowship using it.[55] Obviously, the showbread table in the temple was for Philo one of those "holy tables" from which sacrificial offerings were eaten within the framework of a cultic meal.[56]

It gets even more interesting when Philo comes to speak of the ritual reclining meals of the special Jewish group known as the Therapeutae. A number of them carry the "pure table" (Lev 24:6) for the "most holy food"; namely, leavened bread with salt, into the meeting room, in remembrance of the "holy table" in the pronaos of the temple in Jerusalem.[57] It is at this table that the "presider" appears to stand when performing the cultic acts; at all events, he rises shortly before the table is carried in, whereas the others all remain reclining.[58] He probably stands at the table with his eyes and hands lifted up to heaven in prayer.[59] The table that has been brought in is no everyday table; rather, it is reserved, as a "pure" and "holy" table, for the cultic act. The fact that it is seen in analogy to the showbread table of the Jerusalem Temple confirms once more that it is a sacred table. Since it takes several people to carry it, it must have been pretty solid, too.

The same thing, i.e. the sacred table at the reclining meal, also exists in Roman religious culture. Here, at a private banquet the traditional sacrifice is offered to the domestic deities (*lares*) or to the genius of the master of the house after the actual meal but before the drinking session (symposium) begins. The sacrifice takes place as soon as the food tables of the two courses (*mensa prima* and *secunda*) have been cleared away (*mensis remotis*) and the participants have washed their hands. The table sacrifice is a ritual act that is performed at its own altar or sacred table. Standing on the sacred table are now the vessels containing the food offerings. This is why the sacrifice takes place at the end of the meal. Only when the company have consumed their own food do they

52 Cf. I. HEINEMANN, Therapeutai, in: Paulys Real-Encyclopädie der Classischen Altertumswissenschaft, 2nd series 5a (1934) 2321–2346, here 2332. Against this KLINGHARDT 1996, 191f.
53 Philo. quis rer. div. 226.
54 Philo. spec. leg. 1,172; 2,161; vit. cont. 81; quis rer. div. 175; spec. leg. 1,118.
55 Philo. spec. leg. 1,220f.
56 Cf. Philo. somn. 1,51; quis rer. div. 175.
57 Philo. vit. cont. 73, 81; KLAUCK 1982, 184–187. Against this congr. erud. 168: gilt table in the Holy of Holies. Cf. LEONHARD / ECKHARDT 2010, 1060.
58 Philo. vit. cont. 80, 82.
59 Cf. ibid. 66f.

offer up the share of it set aside for the gods. They rise to pray as they do so.[60] So it is quite clear that the sacred table has nothing to do with the dining tables carried out into the kitchen. On no account do people eat and sacrifice at the same triclinium table. It is possible for large trays to be brought in for the various courses at ancient meals and to be placed on the triclinium table one after the other.[61] But it goes without saying that a tray is not used for the table sacrifice, which would make the meal table and the sacrifice table the same, but instead, a separate table is fetched for it. This is also the case in the worship community at Corinth in Paul's time, where there is a separate "table of the Lord" (i.e. not just a tray).

This does not exhaust the examples that can be cited from antiquity. A corresponding way of proceeding is also to be observed at the banquet held by the Roman Arval Brethren in honour of the *Dea Dia*. Once the tables are cleared away, the magister and brothers rise for the handwashing. Then they lie down on the couches (κλίναι), which are now spread with covers as a sign of the special sacredness of what is happening. Strictly speaking, the priests do not in fact perform the sacrifice lying down since there are sons of senators serving them who carry their offerings of incense and wine to the altar (*ara*).[62] A similar scenario can also be assumed for the mystery cult of Mithras. The furnishings of the cave-like worship rooms suggest that one participant would perform the sacrifice standing at the altar placed in front of the cultic image while the other participants reclined on benches to the right and left of it (Fig. 6).[63]

---

60 Vössing 2004. For the food sacrifice in the domestic cult *mensae sacrae* are used; J. Marquardt, Römische Staatsverwaltung 3 (Leipzig ²1885) 166 f. Tertullian is still familiar with the practice of standing up to pray after handwashing at the communal meals of the Christians: Tert. apol. 39,18 (153): *Post aquam manualem* [...] *provocatur in medium Deo canere* [...]. *Aeque oratio convivium dirimit.* Trad. Apost. 25 (FC 1, 276): participants at the meal standing up to pray *post cenam*. See also Dölger 1936, 116–137.
61 See below p. 435 n. 101.
62 Scheid 199, 536–540.
63 A fresco at the Barberini mithraeum might allow the conclusion that instead of a solid altar a sacred table was used, at which the priest likewise performed the ritual act (Pecklers 2012, 22 Fig. 2; Della Portella 2000, 38 f.). A good overview of the Mithraic sacrifice and meal is offered in Klauck 1982, 138–149. The nature of the sacrificial act in the Mithraea is disputed; V. Huet / F. Prescendi, in: ThesCRA 1, 194 f. On altars, cultic tables and sacrificial meals see J. P. Kane, The Mithraic cult meal in its Greek and Roman environment, in: J. R. Hinnells (ed.), Mithraic Studies 2 (Manchester 1975) 313–351. V. Huet, in: ThCRA 2 (Los Angeles 2004) 272 f. and R. L. Gordon, Mithras, in: RACh 24 (2012) 964–1009 only touch in passing on the sacrificial acts (and altar) in Mithraism.

Fig. 6: Mithraeum beneath the church of *San Clemente* in Rome; left and right the reclining benches, in the middle the altar, mid-3rd century AD; photo: Alamy Stock Photo.

SUMMARY

The view that has been posited in the literature for a century now and greeted with a broad consensus among scholars argues that early Christianity only mutated into a religion as a secondary development when, in the third and fourth centuries, it donned new clothes alien to it incorporating the transferable components of sanctity, sacrifice and altar. However, this view is based on a nineteenth-century ideological-theological premise that culminates in liberal Protestantism. It is time to emancipate ourselves from it and take an unimpeded look at the beginnings of the Christian altar. A first step consists in seeing not so much the (immolation) altar but rather the sacred table as the item of cultic furniture that was widely used in antiquity in both Jewish and pagan religious praxis and in putting the Christian altar in this context.

It immediately suggests itself that, in the cultures of both the Latin West and the Greek East, from the second half of the first century on the Christians used separate cultic tables for the Eucharist at their communal meals and that these tables were quite in line with the pagan tradition.[64] This then lends a new plausibility and significance to those texts which, as early as the first and second centuries, speak of a table or altar in connection with the Eucharist and often tend to be dismissed as metaphorical or infelicitously formulated. At the same time, Christianity emerges once more not as an anti-religion but rather as an integral, albeit always critical, part of the social and religious culture of late antiquity.

---

64 On the Greek libation offering after the meal see
  KLINGHARDT 1996, 101–111.

II. ORIGINS

The altar as a sacred table

The disputes in their current form over whether the Eucharist is a sacrifice or a meal cannot be traced back to the early Church. Such an either/or dichotomy did not arise back then. You can tell this precisely from the cultic furniture that was used, namely a table, but a table that was an altar: a sacred table, a *mensa sacra*. There are statements to be found in the earliest Christian writings that converge to a high degree in pointing to the use of sacred tables for the Eucharist. These texts will be presented below in chronological order.

1. "TABLE OF THE LORD"

The first relevant text – written only two decades after Jesus's death – comes from Paul. And, as is so often the case, we have a conflict to thank for the valuable historical traces it has left behind, in this case in the First Letter to the Corinthians (c. 55/56). The apostle is on a missionary journey when he hears of a vexing situation relating to the "Lord's Supper" (1 Cor 11:20) in the Greek port city of Corinth. There is discord among the local Christians and strife at their gatherings (1 Cor 11:17–34).[1] One of the sources of this tension is the fact that some Christians are eating flesh that has been sacrificed to idols, i.e. the flesh of animals that have been slaughtered during the celebration of pagan sacrifices. Some of their fellow religionists are annoyed that Christians, of all people, are eating such flesh. In chapter 10 of his letter to the Christians in Corinth Paul states his position on this matter, and in so doing also gives us an insight into the earliest Christian cultic practice:

> 14 Therefore […] flee from the worship of idols. […] 16 The *cup of blessing* (ποτήριον τῆς εὐλογίας) that we bless, is it not a sharing in the blood of Christ? The bread that we break, is it not a sharing in the body of Christ? 17 Because there is one bread, we who are many

---

1 K. Vössing, Das "Herrenmahl" und 1 Cor. 11 im Kontext antiker Gemeinschaftsmähler, in: JbAC 54 (2011) 41–72.

are one body, for we all partake of the one bread. 18 Consider the people of Israel according to the flesh; are not those who eat the sacrifices partners in the *altar* (θυσιαστήριον)?
19 What do I imply then? That food sacrificed to idols is anything, or that an idol is anything? 20 No, I imply that what pagans sacrifice, they sacrifice to demons and not to God.
I do not want you to be partners with demons. 21 You cannot drink the *cup of the Lord*
(ποτήριον κυρίου) and the cup of demons. You cannot partake of the *table of the Lord*
(τράπεζα κυρίου) and the table of demons. 22 Or are we provoking the Lord to jealousy?
(1 Cor 10:14 – 22).

This is the first mention of the eucharistic "table" by an author of the Church. One is
immediately inclined to take it to be an ordinary table. For the word "altar" is not used
until a few decades later in another New Testament epistle, the Letter to the Hebrews,
and might there indicate a new linguistic usage (below chapter II, 2). From this, Franz
Wieland concludes that Paul is thinking neither of a Christian altar nor of a sacrifice
in connection with "table" but merely of the communion with God that is established
through consuming the Body ("table") and Blood ("cup") of Christ.[2] Similarly, Enrico
Mazza infers from Paul's choice of words in speaking of the Lord's *Supper* and a spiritual
food (1 Cor 11:20) that the table in question is a profane dining table.[3]

But this is far from doing justice to the text. First it is necessary to understand the
historical situation. Among the Christians in Corinth there is no agreement on whether
it is permitted to eat flesh that has been sacrificed to idols, i.e. flesh coming from pagan
animal sacrifices. After all, in antiquity the sacrificed flesh was by no means destroyed
but rather consumed by the people participating in the sacrifice or elsewhere (cf. Hos
8:13). At high feasts there are such large quantities of flesh that it is given cheaply to
the people because it cannot be stored for long. Such high-quality goods – sacrificial
animals must be without blemish – are bought at temple markets (1 Cor 10:25) or consumed in temple restaurants (1 Cor 8:10). The wealthy inhabitants of Corinth do not
want to forego these practices and therefore maintain that the flesh is unobjectionable
(1 Cor 10:19 f., 23). In fact, according to pagan law the sacrificial flesh can be, as it were,
profaned through the laying on of hands before it gets to the market.[4] The Christians
in Corinth may possibly also be invoking the practice of the diaspora Jews, who allow

---

2   WIELAND 1908, 32 – 37; *id.* 1909, 9 – 16. L. GOP-
    PELT, in: Theologisches Wörterbuch zum Neuen
    Testament 8 (Stuttgart 1969) 214: "This linguistic
    borrowing (from Mal 1:7, 12) does not make the
    table an altar for Paul, and the comparison with the
    cultic meal does not give the Lord's Supper a sacri-
    ficial character." J. BEHM, in: Theologisches Wör-
    terbuch zum Neuen Testament 3 (Stuttgart 1938)

184: "In the remarks about the Lord's Supper in 1
Cor 10:11 not the slightest grounds are to be found
for supposing 'that the celebration of the Eucharist
is according to Paul a sacred sacrificial meal.'"

3   MAZZA 2005, 57 f. WHITE 1996, 107: "Paul presup-
    poses that the gathering was held around the com-
    mon table."

4   SCHEID 2009, 87.

meat offered to idols to be consumed (1 Cor 10:18)[5] because idols do not really exist (1 Chr 16:26). Paul only half agrees with this: the gods of the pagans may be spurious, but there are nonetheless demons behind their sacrificial cult (1 Cor 10:20). Sacrifices are offered to demons at the "table of demons" (1 Cor 10:21), which is here undoubtedly a sacrificial altar (1 Cor 10:18).[6] Therefore, even though eating flesh sacrificed to idols would not bring Christians communion with the gods, it would still make them partners with demons (1 Cor 10:20 f.), which he does not regard as making matters any better.

The conflict probably breaks out in Corinth because a number of people have brought flesh offered to idols along with them to the community gathering. Thus it comes about that Paul compares two cultic acts: the Eucharist (1 Cor 10:16) with the sacrifice of the Jews (1 Cor 10:18) and of the pagans (1 Cor 10:20), in which sacrifice and meal are to be seen as integral parts of every sacrificial act (cf. 1 Cor 8:10).[7] This is an important point: in neither case is the meal seen in contradistinction to the sacrifice, as if eating were something profane and only sacrificing something sacred. On the contrary, eating belongs inseparably to the ancient sacrificial cult. Whoever eats shares in the altar (1 Cor 10:18); that is, in the sacrifice. By speaking of eating the Eucharist within the context of Jewish and pagan sacrificial meals, Paul is in any event ascribing a cultic character to the Eucharist.[8]

The Eucharist is also a cultic action in the way it proceeds, namely with a blessing and a breaking of bread. Above all, mention of the Blood of Christ brings to mind a cultic food consumed with a cultic drinking vessel in a way that we are familiar with from pagan sacrifices (1 Cor 10:21).[9] If, then, the sacrificial food on the pagan altar or table is sacred – admittedly in a demonic sense – then the Christian food must be so even more since it really does grant a sharing in the Body and Blood of Christ, doing so to such a degree that those receiving Communion form one single body (of Christ) (1 Cor 10:17). Indeed, this food is so extraordinary that receiving it unworthily can lead to death (1 Cor 11:30).

If the Eucharist is a cultic food, then the cultic furniture is indispensable to it: that is, the "table of the Lord" (1 Cor 10:21), on which the cup and the bread are prepared (1 Cor 10:16). What belongs to the Jewish (and pagan) sacrifice, on the other hand, is the "altar" that the sacrificial offering lies on (1 Cor 10:18) and which, in the case of the pagan altar, Paul calls "the table of demons" from which one eats (1 Cor 10:21). Wieland stumbled over this, thinking that the "table" of the Christians was a normal dining table and not an altar since, so he surmised, Paul would otherwise have spoken of the "altar".[10] He is

5   As a rule, 1 Cor 10:18 is in the modern commentaries applied to the Jewish temple cult.
6   KLAUCK 1982, 270.
7   Cf. ABYNEIKO 2014, 51 f. On the sacrificial meal see KLAUCK 1982.
8   ÖHLER 2014, 498 f.
9   ThesCRA 5, 354–357.
10 WIELAND 1909, 16.

only able to level this charge against Paul because he fails to recognise that in antiquity the terms "altar" and "table" could be used synonymously.[11] This actually already follows from Paul's use of the term "table of demons" (1 Cor 10:21) when he is undoubtedly referring to a sacrificial altar (1 Cor 10:18).

It is also important to note that in antiquity the food was not offered up and eaten at the same table during the sacrifice. The sacrificial food is not eaten *at* the altar but rather *from* the altar. The same goes analogously for the sacred table – for the very reason that it is not an ordinary dining table that you sit at. This is the background to Paul's saying that you cannot "partake" of both the "table of demons" and the "table of the Lord" (1 Cor 10:21; cf. 1 Cor 10:18; Heb 13:10).

Paul's argumentative context, namely his desire to settle disputed cultic questions, therefore suggests that the table used by the Christians for their eucharistic worship is a sacred table. This view is supported by an observation made by Dieter Böhler: Paul is not the first to use the syntagma "table of the Lord" (τράπεζα κυρίου); he in fact borrowed it from the Septuagint, the Greek translation of the Old Testament.[12] The expression is found there twice in Malachi (Mal 1:7, 12 LXX; see also Ez 44:15 f. LXX).[13] Yet the prophet also calls the "table of the Lord" an "altar" (θυσιαστήριον) (Mal 1:7 LXX). So Malachi is talking about a sacred or sacrificial table. It serves for the incense offering (Mal 1:10), which is always accompanied by an offering of flour and wine (Nm 15:4 f.).

This "table of the Lord" or "altar" in Malachi is taken up by Paul: however, for him the "Lord" is not Yahweh but Christ. Therefore the "table *of the Lord*" is for him the eucharistic table, and is so on account of the sacrifice of flour and wine offered on it. The gift of bread and wine at the Eucharist is that "pure offering" that is offered "in every place" – including Corinth (1 Cor 1:2) – "in my [Yahweh's] name" (Mal 1:11 LXX).[14] Undoubtedly, Paul understands the "table of the Lord" in Corinth to be a true sacred or sacrificial table,[15] and does so irrespective of whether and how he understands the Eucharist as an act of sacrifice. All that matters is that he sees the eucharistic food analogously to the sacrificial food on Malachi's altar table. Hence it is unacceptable to try to contort the Corinthian "table of the Lord" into a "slightly metaphorical table of the Lord's Supper".[16]

Finally, there is the question of how one must imagine that the Lord's Supper was concretely celebrated (1 Cor 11:20) and how the sacred table was used. First of all, the

---

11 KLAUCK 1982, 269 f.
12 BÖHLER 2013, 109–114; *id.* 2022, 27–33. BARTH 1999, 173 f. KLAUCK 1982, 270 n. 189 recognises the connection to the "table of the Lord" in Malachi, yet far underestimates its significance for the interpretation of Paul.
13 A. MEINHOLD, Maleachi = Biblischer Kommentar Altes Testament 14,8 (Neukirchen-Vluyn 2006)

104–106. Ez 40:42 (LXX) speaks in a comparable way of "tables" of hewn stone for the burnt offering (cf. Ez 44:15 f.).
14 Did 14 (SC 248, 192) applies Mal 1:11 about one hundred times to the Eucharist. ÖHLER 2016a, 499 f.: Eucharist as sacrifice in 1 Cor.
15 LANG 2022, 46 f., 71.
16 So KLAUCK 1982, 270.

Lord's Supper is a typically semi-ritual meal at which people eat and a religious act is performed. Paul is still familiar with the practice of combining the core eucharistic rite with a meal, something he admittedly does not approve of on account of abuses (1 Cor 11:20–22). The participants lie on benches or sit (1 Cor 14:30) and consume ordinary food. Then follows the actual Eucharist, the core rite of which is the parallelised blessing of bread and wine based on the so-called Last Supper of Jesus with his disciples (1 Cor 11:23–26: twice repeated "do *this* in remembrance of me").[17]

The exegetes argue over whether the rite of bread and cup took place in Corinth as a discrete rite "after supper" (1 Cor 11:25) or whether the blessing of the bread took place first, followed by the communal meal and then finally the blessing of the cup.[18] To my mind, the first variant, namely the twofold eucharistic act following the meal, is to be preferred. In Corinth the people all come to the assembly bringing their food with them and immediately start to eat without waiting for the rest, so that one is already drunk before another has ever taken a bite (1 Cor 11:21, 33). Evidently some participants then consume the eucharistic food in an inebriated state as if it were quite ordinary fare (Cor 11:27–29). From that it can be concluded that there was no set beginning to the gathering but that the participants turned up in dribs and drabs. Only when all are present can the blessing of the bread and cup take place so that the whole community can really form one body (1 Cor 10:17). This means that even though it was only the blessing over the cup that Jesus spoke "*after* the meal" (1 Cor 11:25), both blessings in fact have to wait until after the meal.

Accordingly, the sequence of the Eucharist at Corinth will have to be imagined as follows: the aforementioned "table of the Lord", together with the bread and cup, is only brought in at the end of the meal once the food tables have been cleared away. The presider approaches the table, blesses the eucharistic food and distributes it from this table, thus allowing those present to participate in the table of the Lord (1 Cor 10:21), a table from which no food other than this eucharistic food has ever been served. And precisely that is the striking factor, the one that makes it possible for Paul to argue with good reason that you cannot eat from this special table of the Lord and at the same time from the sacrificial tables of demons. But even if the rites of bread and cup did take place separately – in fact particularly then – the two acts will have been performed at a special table, the "table of the Lord", so as to underline the sacred oneness of the twofold act.

---

17 Lang 2022, 23: "The formulaic way in which Paul presents Jesus's sayings at the Last Supper suggests their liturgical use".

18 The first variant is the majority view; on the second see Klinghardt 1996, 276–371; Messner 2001, 165–168; *id.* 2003, 420 f. It is, however, unconvincing that it is necessary to strain the interpretation of *two* terms (προλαμβάνειν and ἐκδέχεσθαι).

What is crucial for the Corinthian celebration of the Eucharist is its visible ritualization through a table, and not, for instance, the question of how the blessing of the bread and cup fitted into the course of the Last Supper. After all, for this double rite Paul mentions only the *one* "table of the Lord" at which both acts of blessing take place, whereas the rest of the meal requires a number of tables depending on how many participants are present.[19]

2. "WE HAVE AN ALTAR"

The second witness to the early Christian altar is the Letter to the Hebrews, the author of which is unknown. The letter is generally located in Italy or Rome (Heb 13:24) and dated to the end of the first century.[20] The Age of the Apostles is already past (Heb 2:3; 13:7, 17). On the other hand, the famous Jewish Temple in Jerusalem still seems to be in use (Heb 8:4; 9:8–10; 10:1 f.). This favours an early dating (before the destruction of the Temple in 70 A.D.).[21] The letter must be addressed to a specific community, albeit one without a name and impossible to localise,[22] and it deals with a concrete crisis in the life of the community, not an abstract or universal one. In spite of its glorious past (Heb 10:32–34; cf. 6:10, 12), the local community in question is in danger of apostasy (Heb 4:6; 6:6; 10:26). Apparently some of the baptized have gone over to Jewish practices and are promoting them among their fellow Christians (Heb 13:9). The letter wants to preserve the community from further apostasy (Heb 3:12; 4:1; 10:23, 35, 38 f.; 12:15, 25) and pulls out all the theological and rhetorical stops to do so. The lamentable apostasy is connected with the participation of Christians in Jewish cultic meals (Heb 12:16). It is about "gifts and sacrifices" (at the Jerusalem Temple?), more specifically "food and drink" (Heb 9:9 f.). By contrast, the letter warns against "food" that has not benefited the vagabonds (cf. Heb 13:9). It points to the better "altar" of

19 Failure to pay attention to these circumstances in my view argues against the explanation of the Corinthian community gathering in KLING-HARDT 1996, 269–371, who assumes an integrated meal-Eucharist, which means that the one "table of the Lord" and "cup of blessing" cannot actually exist.

20 Basic reading LANE 1991. On the following HEID 2015a.

21 R. BURNET, La finale de l'épître aux Hébreux. Une addition Alexandrine de la fin du IIᵉ siècle? in: Revue Biblique 120 (2013) 423–440. With similar

argumentation (still-existent worship in the Jerusalem Temple) ZIEGLER 2007, 84 dates the First Epistle of Clement to between 63 and 70 and regards it as possible that its author was the same as that of Hebrews (ibid. 97). An early dating (66/67) and a homiletic character are also advocated by BARTH 1999, 53–55 and VANHOYE 2015, 1, 15. See also VIELHAUER 1975, 239–243 (homiletic character) und FELD 1985, 14–18 (early dating).

22 A local church (Heb 13:12, 14: the people of a city; cf. 11:10, 16; 12:22) – not vagabonds (cf. Heb 13:9) – led by "leaders" (Heb 13:7, 17, 24).

the Christians, from which the Judaizers (those who "officiate in the tent") are not permitted to eat (Heb 13:10).[23]

A detailed analysis of that part of the text in which the "altar" (θυσιαστήριον) of the Christians is mentioned is absolutely essential.

> [7] Remember your leaders, those who spoke the word of God to you; consider the outcome of their way of life, and imitate their faith. [8] Jesus Christ is the same yesterday and today and for ever. [9] Do not be carried away by all kinds of strange teachings; for it is well for the heart to be strengthened by grace, not by food, which have not benefited those walking around. [10] *We have an altar* (θυσιαστήριον) *from which those who officiate in the tent (tabernacle) have no right to eat.* [11] For the bodies of those animals whose blood is brought into the sanctuary by the high priest as a sacrifice for sin are burned outside the camp. [12] Therefore Jesus also suffered outside the city gate in order to sanctify the people by his own blood. [13] Let us then go to him outside the camp and bear the abuse he endured. [14] For here we have no lasting city, but we are looking for the city that is to come. [15] Through him, then, let us continually offer a sacrifice of praise to God, that is, the fruit of lips that confess his name. [16] Do not neglect to do good and to share what you have, for such sacrifices are pleasing to God. [17] Obey your leaders [...] (Heb 13:7–17).

The lexical meaning of the word (θυσιαστήριον) is clear: an altar for sacrifice. So it is a physical altar of the Christians ("*We* have an altar") that is being referred to. This altar competes with the altar of the Jews even if the latter is not expressly mentioned. Nevertheless it is clear: the Jews (those who officiate in the tent) have their altar from which they eat; the Christians, on the other hand, have theirs (Heb 13:10). Basically the Letter to the Hebrews does not say anything different from what Paul has already said: there is the "altar" from which the Jews eat (1 Cor 10:18; cf. Rv 11:1) and the "table of the Lord" from which the Christians eat (1 Cor 10:21). One cannot eat from both altars. To be sure, Paul only inveighs against the pagan "tables of demons" (1 Cor 10:21) and here, the Letter to the Hebrews makes the matter very clear: the Jewish sacrificial foods are as taboo for Christians as are the pagan foods.

What is interesting for the altar question here is precisely the concrete detail given about the event: "eating from the altar" is permitted for some and not for others. That,

---

23 The "servants of the tent" (= those who officiate in the tent/tabernacle) recall the Levites of the Old Testament, who are assigned the task of serving in the Tent of Meeting and at the altars (θυσιαστήριον) (1 Ch 6:33; Heb 7:11–13). They have the right to eat the unleavened food offerings from the altar of the Tent of Meeting (Lv 6:7–11). The interpretation of the servants of the tent in Heb 13:10 as the presiders at Christian worship (WECKWERTH 1963, 229–331) is completely erroneous.

after all, means that every altar is exclusive, including that of the Christians. "Church fellowship" is altar fellowship. Unlike the otherwise high theology of the Letter to the Hebrews, this is quite simple and possible for every believer to comprehend: everyone must know from which altar he or she eats. The altar is subject to sanctions. It is a canonical entity: it "communicates" and "excommunicates". Apostates and Judaizers are not allowed to eat from the altar of the Christians (anymore) because they have their own altar. This refers both to the Jerusalem altar and to the sacred tables at which Jewish circles in the diaspora celebrate sacrificial meals (modelled on the Temple) (Heb 13:9).[24] One must at all events envisage a Jewish altar or sacred table from which Judaizing Christians receive food.[25]

Observations to date suggest that the "altar" in Hebrews should be seen as denoting the same piece of cultic equipment that Paul calls the "table of the Lord". Calling the eucharistic table an "altar" (θυσιαστήριον) makes its sacredness as a sacrificial table unmistakably clear. Nevertheless most scholars are reluctant to see the "altar" in Hebrews as a sacred table.[26] The reason for this may be that they associate the word "altar" exclusively with one for slaughtering animal sacrifices (above Figs. 1, 4; below Figs. 119, 128). But θυσιαστήριον can also mean the holy table. This then removes a second misgiving, namely that it is impossible to imagine eating from an altar (on which sacrificial animals are slaughtered). It may also be that the formulation in the singular – "We (Christians) have *an* altar" – has led to its being assumed to be merely a metaphor. The singular can be explained by positing that the author must have based the letter on the concrete situation of one particular community meeting for worship (Heb 10:25), which would have had only one altar.

Instead of simply accepting what is given, the exegetes perform veritable contortions in order to avoid the conclusion that the "altar" in Hebrews is actually an altar. Franz Wieland wants to see it as Christ crucified on Golgotha,[27] an interpretation that is prob-

---

24 Thurén 1973, 105–176; Galley 1987–1988, 81; Weidemann 2014, 372.

25 Philo. ad Gaium 156: The Jews offer pious gifts ("sacrifices") from their first fruits. For (incense-?) altars in synagogues see Goodenough 1964, 26 f.; *id.* 1953, Fig. 593; ANRW 2,16,1 (1978) 601. On the altar of incense see Gäbel 2006, 257–263. There is a suspicion that older references to altars in rabbinic literature fell prey to censorship. Valerius Maximus (c. 14–37): *Iudaeos quoque, qui Romanis tradere sacra sua conati erant, idem Hispalus urbe exterminavit arasque privatas et publicis locis abiecit* (Stern 1976, 358). T. L. Donaldson, Judaism and the Gentiles (Waco / Tex. 2007) 376–379 views the mention of the altars in Valerius Maximus as

a misunderstanding. Jewish altars (in synagogues) are spoken of in Iren. adv. haer. 4,18,2 (SC 100,2, 598) and Min. Fel. 33,2 (CSEL 2, 46). Cf. ibid. 10,4 (14): *templis aris victimis caerimoniisque coluerunt.* The Therapautae around Alexandria are familiar with cultic meals having tables and altars; Philo. vit. cont. 80 f.

26 All the same, Rauschen 1910, 83 f. against Wieland sees the table of the Eucharist in Heb 13:10 as being called an altar and compared with the Jewish sacrificial table. The same direction is now being taken above all by Weidemann 2014, 371–377.

27 Wieland 1906, 25, 39; *id.* 1908, 37–41; *id.* 1909, 16–34. Stuiber 1978, 309 understands the altar as "Jesus' work of salvation in his death on the Cross."

ably inspired more by the patristic topos of the altar of the Cross[28] than by the biblical text. Georg Gäbel assumes that Heb 13:10 is speaking of the *heavenly* altar in contrast to the earthly Jerusalem altar.[29] Knut Backhaus does not even want to consider a heavenly altar but instead sees in the altar "the cross standing before the sanctuary of the divine presence or […] the High Priest in his self-giving."[30] For him the expression "We *have* an altar" indicates the present possession of salvation and is to be understood as analogous to "We *have* […] a high priest" (Heb 8:1).[31] But why should the High Priest on the Cross be referred to with an abstruse altar metaphor for which there is absolutely no preparation in the preceding text?

A close exegesis of the text is helpful if we want to escape from the metaphor trap. Backhaus rightly recognises that the *Sitz im Leben* of the Letter to the Hebrews is the communal Lord's Supper.[32] In concrete terms, the Letter to the Hebrews is, according to its style and construction, a sermon given at the community gathering (Heb 10:25) after the Old Testament readings (Heb 1:1; 2:1).[33] This reveals the celebration of the liturgy to be the appropriate horizon of understanding. The letter is not for private reading but is instead read aloud to a largish audience. The community hears the text only once, the sentences following each other in sequence from beginning to end, and the meaning is constructed solely in this direction; the letter cannot be interpreted backwards. It is of further significance that the theological passages end in the middle of chapter 10 and that then paraenetic sections begin. The concluding chapter, chapter 13, to which the passage referring to the altar belongs, is concerned with concrete community life.

So if the *Sitz im Leben* of the Letter to the Hebrews is the community gathering, one wonders why the faithful should understand the words "we have an altar" in any way other than literally, especially since eating is concretely mentioned in the same sentence (Heb 13:10). There is nothing here to suggest a metaphorical use since it is merely describing a cultic action that is common in antiquity; namely, consuming the sacrificial food from the altar. Even if the preacher were to have a theological meta-

28 (Ps.-) Aug. serm. 366,6 (PL 39, 1649); Joh. Chrys. cruc. et latr. 1 (PG 49, 400); Leo. serm. 55,3 (CCL 138A, 325); 59,5 (356); 64,3 (391); then also in the Tridentine decree on the Sacrifice of the Mass: see H. Denziger / P. Hünermann, Compendium of Creeds, Definitions, and Declarations on Matters of Faith and Morals, Latin-English (San Francisco ⁴³2012), Nos. 1740, 1743.
29 Gäbel 2006, 457 f.
30 Backhaus 2009a, 470.
31 This is unconvincing because the Christians really do "have" a High Priest, who is now enthroned in heaven. The "have" in Heb 13:14 is even more real: the Christians do at present "have" here (in Rome?) a concrete city, but not a lasting one; therefore they are looking for the (heavenly) city that is to come (Heb 13:14).
32 Backhaus 2009b, 59–61.
33 Galley 1987–1988. Cf. Feld 1985, 21 f.

phor in mind, this is nevertheless attached to a concrete piece of furniture that his listeners can see in front of them when they are gathered for the cultic meal. This item of furniture is quite naturally called an "altar" because this nomenclature is familiar to the audience.

Those exegetes who regard the altar as simply a metaphor also have to spiritualize the concept of "to eat" from it, too.[34] Strictly speaking, it would in fact be the eating that is the actual metaphor, which makes the matter even more abstruse. Backhaus thinks that "to eat" from the altar refers to "enjoying the fruit of salvation won on the Cross, tasting the eschatological gift."[35] But would anyone who read or heard the Letter to the Hebrews ever have come up with such an idea? Backhaus himself speaks of a "somewhat unusual metaphor".[36] However, the problem only arises when he understands the word "altar" as a metaphor and not in its lexical meaning, i.e. an altar at which people do in fact eat (cf. 1 Cor 10:18).[37]

In its totality, the Letter to the Hebrews very concretely depicts the ecclesial-sacramental situation of the community.[38] It speaks of Communion (Heb 6:4), baptism (Heb 6:2, 4; 10:22, 32), and finally the altar (Heb 13:10). The letter does consistently draw a contrast between itself and the Old Testament according to the pattern of heavenly versus earthly, but in so doing its aim is simply to emancipate itself from the Jewish religion, not to dissipate the ecclesial reality in metaphors and symbols. One must resist any spiritualizing tendency in Hebrews and instead try to unearth the reality that lies behind it. Even when the exegetes emphasize the theologizing tendency of the epistle, arguing that it does not permit any real cult but rather only a spiritual Christianity, they cannot deny that a metaphor requires a correlate in reality.[39] If everything were purely spiritual, metaphors would say nothing, or put differently: those who maintain that blood, flesh, water and altar are metaphors will be unable to avoid talking about the ritual reality behind them.

---

34 A false interpretation of Heb 13:9 according to WIELAND 1909, 18, 21 also leads to this slippery slope. In no way is Hebrews warning here in general against cultic meals as if it also rejected the Eucharist along the lines of "grace, not food!"

35 BACKHAUS 2009a, 470. Cf. STUIBER 1978, 309.

36 BACKHAUS 2009a, 470.

37 Correctly E. Dorsch (in WIELAND 1908, 40); BARTH 1999, 51 f. If a spiritual altar really were what was meant here, this could have been expressed more simply: "We have an altar that those who officiate in the tent have no right to *approach*"

(instead of "eat from"). For while the high priests *approach* the offering (Heb 9:7 f.; 10:1), the Christians, through Jesus' blood, have confident access to the heavenly sanctuary (Heb 10:19, 22; cf. 4:16; 6:19 f.; 12:22).

38 The sacramental-cultic background of Hebrews is stressed, with good reasoning, against the spiritualizing exegetes in FELD 1985, 93–97.

39 ROLOFF 1981, 407: "The difficult passage in Heb 13:10 appears to be speaking of a Christian altar, albeit probably in a figurative-metaphorical sense."

This ritual reality is the reason that Hebrews distinguishes meticulously between the Body and Blood of Christ when speaking of his salvific death on the Cross (Heb 2:14; 10:19 f.; 13:11 f.; cf. 7:15). For what lies behind it is the cultic act of the new covenant, at which bread and wine are eaten and drunk. As already stated, the Letter to the Hebrews is directed against those who participate in Jewish cultic meals. In the eyes of the letter, they have fallen away from both baptism and Eucharist (Heb 6:4), taken the Blood of the covenant to be "normal" blood (Heb 10:29) and sold their birthright for a single meal (Heb 12:16).[40]

This polemic against those "who have spurned the Son of God and esteemed as ordinary the blood of the covenant by which they were sanctified, and outraged the Spirit of thanksgiving (χάρις)"[41] (cf. Heb 10:29)[42] is perplexing. For if the Christians who have been received into the community through baptism (Heb 10:26: received the knowledge of the truth) and Communion (Heb 10:29: sanctified by the blood[43]) take the covenantal and sacrificial Blood of the Son of God (Heb 10:26) to be "ordinary" blood, then a ritual-cultic interpretation is inevitable[44] in that a transformation through an act of blessing is implied.

Far more important for a cultic-religious interpretation of the Eucharist is the fact that the apostates make themselves guilty of a veritable cultic offence. In the Old Testament already, offences against "the altar (θυσιαστήριον) of the Lord your God" (Dt 16:21 LXX) had to be authenticated by two to three witnesses. This is now also the case when Judaizers are being convicted of outrages against the Christian altar (Heb 10:28 = Dt 17:6 LXX). This is made even more evident by the divine curse that the Letter to the Hebrews then utters over the apostates (Heb 10:30). The curse is carefully chosen from the book of Deuteronomy (Dt 32:35 f. LXX). There it is directed against the heathen gods, their grapes of poison and their bitter clusters (Dt 32:32 f. LXX) at their sacrificial meals and

---

40 See the following footnote.

41 A sign of cultic terminology: χάρις is regularly translated with "grace". That can hardly be correct here. Rather, it is likely to refer to the εὐ-χαρισ-τία (eucharistia = "thanksgiving"). Whoever spurns the eucharistic blood commits an offence against the "spirit of thanksgiving". Heb 12:14–16 refers to participating in worship: "Pursue peace (kiss of peace) with everyone, and the holiness (through the blood of the covenant: Heb 10:29) without which no one will see the Lord. See to it that no one fails to obtain the grace of God; that no root of bitterness (cf. Dt 32:32 LXX: cluster of bitterness) springs up and causes trouble (Dt 29:17 LXX), and through it many become defiled. See to it that no one becomes like Esau, a fornicator (i.e. apostate)

and profane person, who sold his birthright for a single meal" (Heb 12:14–16). Did. 4 (FC 1, 220): the peace and the Eucharist. 1 Cor 10:30: χάρις (thankfulness) and εὐχαριστεῖν (give thanks). For the contrasting of "ordinary" food with "blessed" eucharistic food see Iustin. apol. 1, 66,2 (SC 507, 306).

42 Cf. Trad. Apost. 37 (FC 1, 294): *Corpus enim est Christi edendum credentibus et non contemnendum*. The Body of Christ is spurned (καταπατήσας), for example, when it is given to unbelievers.

43 Sanctification through the Blood of Christ, see Heb 10:10.

44 Support for a Eucharistic interpretation of Heb 10:29 is also expressed by Betz 1955, 108 f.

offering of libations (Dt 32:38 LXX). The Letter to the Hebrews applies this to the Jews, who ridicule the wine of the gentiles, namely the Christians (Heb 10:29 f.).[45] This makes it clear that Hebrews relates the Blood of the covenant to the Eucharist as the cultic meal of the Christians which is performed with wine.

So Hebrews is really not about high theology but is rather based on concrete events in the community: certain Christians have consumed the useless Jewish sacrificial foods (Heb 9:9; 13:9; cf. 10:26, 29) instead of the useful eucharistic food (Heb 9:14). The food and drink of the old covenant, which "cannot perfect the conscience of the worshipper" (Heb 9:9), is contrasted with the Blood of the spotless self-sacrifice of Christ, which will "purify our conscience […] to worship[46] the living God" (Heb 9:14).

The reproaches are aimed at those Christians who might be participating in Jewish sacrificial meals (Heb 10:26; cf. 12:16; 13:9)[47] instead of the Christian gathering (Heb 10:25; cf. 12:14). If their transgression is intentional and attested (Heb 10:26, 28), the ecclesiastical penalty (Heb 10:29) of excommunication[48] remains (Heb 12:17; cf. 3:11, 16–19; 4:3, 5 f.; 6:6, 8; 10:26–31). The excommunicated are no longer admitted to the altar (Heb 13:10; cf. 12:15 f.). On the other hand, the faithful Christians, i.e. the assembled hearers of the Word of God (Heb 12:19, 25) and of the sermon (Heb 6:9; 10:39) "have come to Mount Zion and to the city of the living God, the heavenly Jerusalem, and to innumerable angels in festal gathering, and to the assembly of the firstborn who are enrolled in heaven (those who have not sold their right as firstborn for a meal – Heb 12:16) […] and to Jesus, the mediator of a new covenant, and to the sprinkled blood" (Heb 12:22–24). Even if the heavenly dimension dominates here, this is after all what is owed to the rhetorical hyperbole aimed at making clear to the hearers why no one is any longer admitted to Communion (of the "sprinkled blood") or permitted to approach (the altar) who has even once eaten of the Jewish sacrifices. For what the Christians eat from their own altar is just too overwhelming and incomparable to allow this.

It is therefore logical that the sermon of Hebrews speaks of the altar on which those foods lie, of which only Christians are permitted to eat (Heb 13:10). It immediately goes on to speak of the Blood and Body of Christ (Heb 13:11 f.). This must be understood sacramentally: here those "foods" are being talked about that are useful and can be received only from the altar of the Christians: flesh and blood. Now it could be objected that the preacher seemingly leads his hearers away from this altar in that they are to go outside the gate (Heb 13:12) of the city (Heb 13:14) in order to get to Christ (Heb 13:13). That is

---

45 See also Dt 32:35 and Heb 8:13.

46 The term λειτουργεῖν used here means, as in Heb 9:9, service of the cult.

47 On such meal celebrations see O. Michel, der Brief an die Hebräer (Göttingen 1957) 496–503.

48 Roloff 1981, 407 on Heb 13:10: the provision for exclusion in sacred law (*sakralrechtlich*). Weidemann 2014, 373.

indeed a difficulty or ambiguity that the preacher manoeuvres himself into. For while Christ offers his Blood at the altar (Heb 7:13) in the (heavenly) Jerusalem Temple inside the city (Heb 9:7, 12; 10:19 f.), he offers his Body (on the altar of burnt offering) outside the city gate (Heb 13:11).[49]

The difficulty is mitigated when one recognises that the burning of the animal carcasses outside the city is not just a matter of disposing of carcasses, but rather an act of sacrifice in itself (Lv 4:21):[50] instead of the previous burnt offerings, it is the Body of Christ that is sacrificed (Heb 10:5–10). Thus, when Christians are called on to go outside the city, in a certain sense they do not leave the altar, but go from one altar to another. Nevertheless, the difficulty remains that here the image of two altars is evoked: one inside the city, the other outside. The preacher leaves this unresolved since the two biblical altars are actually not important at all. In the end, what counts is the real Christian altar, a single one that, as it were, combines the two Old Testament altars when the Blood and Flesh of Christ come together on it.

In my opinion, the Letter to the Hebrews is shaped throughout by one idea: Christ standing as High Priest at the altar. The attractiveness of this idea has to do with the ecclesial reality that the rite over bread and wine is performed at an altar. A priest always performs the sacrifices (at the altar) in a standing position (Heb 10:11). Christ is a high priest "in things relating to God" to atone for sins through gifts and sacrifices (Heb 2:17; 5:1; 7:25, 27). Although Christ comes from a tribe from which no member has ever previously served at the altar (Heb 7:13), for him the sacred law was changed (Heb 7:12, 18 f.) by appointing him a priest (for the altar) (Heb 7:16) according to the order of Melchisedek (Heb 5:6, 10; 6:20; 7:17). Melchisedek is introduced as the archetype of Christ because he sacrificed bread and wine (Gn 14:18). Christ thus corresponds to the profile of a priest who is there solely to offer gifts and sacrifices.

The priest must necessarily have something to offer (Heb 8:3; 5:1). This statement implies an altar on which to place the offerings. Christ, as the High Priest in the heavenly sanctuary, offered his Blood as an immaculate sacrifice (Heb 9:14; 13:11). Unquestionably, he offered himself only once (Heb 9:26), but he now appears "in the presence of God

---

49 It is not that the remark about the separation of sacrificial blood and animal bodies (Heb 13:11) is intended to decode a prior altar metaphor in accordance with Jesus's death on the Cross (this WIELAND 1908, 39; *id.* 1909, 17 f.); rather, it serves to justify the ecclesial penalty of excommunication theologically, i.e. in accordance with scripture. The contrast between the altar of the Christians and that of the Jerusalem Temple is made concrete through the spatial distance of the sanctuary ("tent") from the suburb (outside the camp). Only in this way does it become clear why the servants of the tent cannot eat from the altar of the Christians: the altar that the Christians have does not stand in the temple but outside Jerusalem. Since those who officiate in the tent are in the tent, they cannot be at the altar outside the city.

50 The difficulties that THURÉN 1973, 78–81 and other interpreters have with the burning stem from their failure to understand the quality of burning as a sacrificial act.

on our behalf" (Heb 9:24). He is able to save those who approach God "through him" since he at all times makes intercession for them (before God) (Heb 7:25). "Through him" the hearers of the Letter to the Hebrews, after leaving the camp, should now at all times offer the sacrifice of praise to God (Heb 13:15).

Remarkably often Christ is portrayed as the High Priest who stands "before God" and "in the sight of God". This has to do with the fact that the priest stands upright when offering the sacrifice and looks beyond the altar to God (below chapter IV, 4d). On the other hand, when it says that Christ, after his sacrifice, has taken his seat forever at the right hand of God (Heb 1:3, 8, 13; 8:1; 10:12; 12:2, following Ps 110:1), this implies that Father and Son are seated side by side. This thus also brings up Christ's function as ruler, while standing before God expresses his function as priest. Both functions continue.[51] Although Christ is seen as the one seated in heaven, he is still also the one standing at the altar.

As already mentioned, the preacher's call to go out of the camp (Heb 13:13) marks the transition to the celebration of the Eucharist, which now takes place at the community's own altar. Something similar is said in an earlier passage: "Let us therefore approach the throne of thanksgiving (χάρις) with boldness, so that we may receive mercy and find grace (χάρις) to help in time of need"[52] (Heb 4:16). This was preceded by the admonition to remain faithful (Heb 4:14); that is, not to participate in the Jewish cultic meals (Heb 9:9; 13:9; cf. 10:26, 29). Instead one should approach the "throne of thanksgiving".[53] This consciously evokes the image of the altar,[54] at which thanks are given in a standing position. The call to approach "the throne of thanksgiving" is indeed founded on the fact that the High Priest (Christ) is appointed (there) in order to offer atoning gifts and sacrifices for humanity "in relation to God" (Heb 5:1). In another passage as well, the preacher calls on the baptized to "approach" (Heb 10:22), which in the context of a community gathering can once more only refer to the altar. Here again, the reason is that there is a high priest available who is placed "over the house of God" (Heb 10:21).

51 The Letter to the Hebrews does not intend to say that Christ's priesthood – and thus his standing at the altar – has ceased (Heb 5:6, following Ps 110:4), but merely that he made a one-time sacrifice of his life (Heb 10:12).
52 Cf. Ps 103:27: food in due season.
53 This expression is regularly translated as "throne of grace", but in the context this makes less sense than a cultic reference, as in Heb 10:29 (see above n. 41).
54 Throne as altar see Rv 2:13: "Satan's throne" – an altar in Pergamon? The altar as the throne of the deity see MISCHKOWSKI 1917, 10 f. A contrasting interpretation is offered by O. WISCHMEYER, Offenbarung 2,13 f. Der Thron des Satans und Metaphern des Bösen im Neuen Testament, in: T. KHIDESHELI / N. KAVVADAS (eds.), Bau und Schrift (Münster 2015) 97–110, who adduces substantial grounds for seeing "Satan's throne" as a polemical code for Pergamon as Satan's dwelling place because Antipas was martyred there. Altar as Christ's *Bema* (seat) see Joh. Chrys. in Eph. hom. 3,4 (PG 62, 28).

It therefore comes as no surprise when the Letter to Hebrews concludes by inviting its listeners to go outside the camp (Heb 13:13) to celebrate the Eucharist: "Through him, then, let us continually offer a sacrifice of praise to God, that is, the fruit of lips that confess his name. Do not neglect to do good and to share what you have, for such sacrifices are pleasing to God" (Heb 13:15 f.).[55] This marks the transition from the liturgy of the word and the sermon to the Eucharist. This transition is also indicated by the "Amen" with which the sermon concludes (Heb 13:21). Thus the focus shifts automatically to the altar at which the actual Eucharist will now be celebrated.

This is all the more the case because the "sacrifice of praise" that is now to be offered – the thanksgiving (Eucharist)[56] – is not a purely verbal act. Jukka Thurén and, with additional arguments, Robert Abyneiko have pointed out that the Letter to the Hebrews speaks throughout of the sacrificial service of the old covenant and with the "sacrifice of praise" also makes a connection to the sacrificial praxis of the Old Testament. There the "sacrifice of praise" was not a purely spiritual act of praise, but rather a concrete sacrifice with a sacrificial meal.[57] One can also ask why Hebrews comes to speak of the "sacrifice of praise" at this particular moment if it is not on account of the "altar" in which the Christians participate (Heb 13:10). In the Old Testament, altars are erected so as to call upon the name of the Lord (Gn 12:8; 13:4; 26:25);[58] here in the Letter to the Hebrews, Christians should now offer the sacrifice of praise and confess the name of God – undoubtedly at an altar (Mal 1:11 f.). The "fruit of the lips" of the sacrifice of praise and the "giving of fellowship" ("partners in the altar" [1 Cor 10:18]) are concrete actions that are carried out: the real fruits and gifts offered by the faithful on the altar for the Eucharist and for feeding the poor correspond to the spiritual fruits of offering praise.[59]

So there is nothing that would go against understanding the "altar" of Hebrews as a real altar table,[60] especially as Heb 10:10–12 can only be formulated in this way if the Eucharist is, by analogy with the animal bodies of the Jerusalem Temple cult, a sacrificial body, namely the sacrificial Body of Christ. Having seen this correctly, Thurén calls for "the Lord's Supper to be seen as the genuinely Christian sacrificial meal".[61] The "altar" is in his view to be related to eating the Body of Christ and thus to the Christian liturgy.[62] It is thus all the more surprising that Thurén then, at the last moment, slides back into thinking in metaphors and categorically rejects the idea of a real altar.

55 Cf. Wieland 1908, 105–107; id. 1909, 20.
56 Weidemann 2014, 376.
57 Thurén 1973, 77, 80; Abyneiko 2014, 55–60.
58 Böhler 2013, 110 f.
59 Cf. Thurén 1973, 80, 153–163.

60 Theologisches Wörterbuch zum Neuen Testament 3 (Stuttgart 1938) 182 n. 12.
61 Thurén 1973, 204.
62 Ibid. 76.

Here Hans-Detlof Galley is more consistent. He, too, relates the altar in Hebrews to the celebration of the Eucharist and says: "For Hebrews, every table from which the community receives the Lord's Supper is removed from the profane (10:29) and becomes an altar."[63] So he acknowledges a Christian altar but then gets bogged down in the traditional Protestant understanding of the Lord's Supper, according to which bread and wine become only temporarily the Body and Blood of Christ, which means that whatever table is used only becomes an altar for the duration of the Eucharist. However, in view of what was common religious practice in antiquity, for the Letter to the Hebrews every altar will be a *res sacra*.

The Letter to the Hebrews talks about a piece of furniture that is indispensable for the celebration of the Eucharist. This so-called altar will have had the form of a table. The faithful receive the Eucharist exclusively from this table. With this, Hebrews confirms what Paul already knows: the Eucharist cannot be celebrated without the "table of the Lord" or the "altar". For the Eucharist is eaten exclusively from this altar. The bread and cup must be placed visibly on the altar in order to become the sacred food of the Christians. If the Eucharist is a cultic act, then the table is an integral part of this cultic act. It is consequently a sacred table. It is subject to sacred law. For this table is in competition with other, namely Jewish, sacred tables. No one who participates in the Jewish meals is still allowed to eat from the altar of the Christians. So the uniqueness of the altar also has something to do with keeping watch over who participates in the Eucharist.[64]

3. SERVANTS AT GOD'S ALTAR

Neither the table in Paul nor the altar in the Letter to the Hebrews is an outlier; rather, they converge in a series of further statements by early Church writers. Among these is the First Epistle of Clement (c. 96 or c. 64–70),[65] which was composed in Rome and addressed to the Christian community in Corinth. With the Epistle of Clement this Greek city comes into focus once more and, perhaps more importantly, so does the Christian community in the capital city of Rome that was its origin. The epistle talks about the altar, initially in the Old Testament context:

> Whosoever will candidly consider each particular, will recognise the greatness of the gifts which were given by him (Jacob). For from him [have sprung] all the priests and Levites

63 GALLEY, 1987–1988, 82, who further concludes from Heb 13:9 that the Lord's Supper is here no longer linked to a common meal (ibid. 81). The same position is proposed by VANHOYE 2015, 224–226.

64 On name-checking, see below p. 100 n. 154.
65 ZIEGLER 2007, 84. Recently a dating of around 120 has also been proposed; KRITZINGER 2016, 28.

who minister at *the altar of God* (τῷ θυσιαστηρίῳ τοῦ θεοῦ). From him also [was descended] our Lord Jesus Christ according to the flesh. From him [arose] kings, princes, and rulers of the race of Judah.[66]

Franz Wieland is of the opinion that 1 Clement distinguishes between the old and new covenants, which means that there is only an Old Testament "altar of God" and not a Christian one.[67] The passage quoted would seem to confirm this. Although the broader context deals with a comparison between the Old Testament cultic regulations and the situation in the Christian community in Corinth, the question is to what extent this comparison evidences the existence of a full-blown Christian cult with altar and sacrifice.

Horacio E. Lona, like Wieland, believes that the statements about the Old Testament cultic regulations cannot be in any way related to the content and form of Christian worship. The Epistle of Clement is solely concerned with the formal aspect that order must prevail: the order of worship must be maintained in the community in Corinth just as much as it was in the Old Testament.[68] What the Christian worship concretely looks like is not, according to Lona, at issue. But such a view is not convincing because it assumes a pure formalism and ultimately fails to take the pragmatism of the text into consideration.

First of all, it should be taken seriously that the author of the epistle is well informed, possibly even having personal knowledge, about the community in Corinth.[69] His intention is to restore ecclesiastical order among the overseers (ἐπίσκοποι) – i.e. the presbyters[70] – and the deacons after some of the presbyters had apparently inflicted lasting damage on the city's community, which then also affected their worship.[71] So the core issue is discipline. That is why the letter appeals to Old Testament cultic regulations, intending them to endow his call for discipline with the highest authority. But if these cultic regulations had in no way born any resemblance to the concrete worship in Corinth,[72] the Corinthians would have shrugged their shoulders and asked what the defunct cult of the Old Testament had to do with them – and the author could have spared himself the letter. Instead, the epistle blurs the boundaries between Old Testament and Christian worship, right down to the terminology,[73] in order to use this convergence to lend added emphasis to his admonition. He picks out what is useful to him from the Old Testament,

66 1 Clem. 32,1 f. (SC 167, 150).
67 WIELAND 1908, 42 f.
68 LONA 1998, 435–437.
69 1 Clem. 1,2 (SC 167, 100) speaks of a visit to Corinth. LONA 1998, 120 baselessly regards this as an invention.
70 1 Clem. 47,6 (SC 167, 178); 54,2 (186); 57,1 (190).
71 Ibid. 42,4 f. (SC 167, 168–170).
72 Thus WIELAND 1908, 43.

73 Two examples: in the Jerusalem Temple cult, the "priests" are allotted their "proper place" (1 Clem. 40,5 [SC 167, 166]); likewise the Christian "presbyters" have a "place" appointed to them (44,5 [174]). The high priest and the other "liturgists" of the Jerusalem Temple perform a "service" (liturgy) (40,5 [166]; 41,2 [168]), just as the Christian "presbyters" fulfil their "service" (liturgy) (44,6 [174]).

which he summarizes appositely in his own words in order that the Corinthians will not be left with any back doors or excuses.

But now let us follow the train of thought in detail, starting from the above quotation. The readers in Corinth really have it rubbed in their noses: "Whosoever will candidly consider each particular." The remarks about Jesus, the priests and Levites are not made just for their own sake, but are meant to strike home with the rebellious presbyters in Corinth. This is then repeated: "These things therefore being manifest to us, and since we look into the depths of the divine knowledge,"[74] and put concretely: "*we* must do all things in [their proper] order, which the Lord has commanded us to perform at stated times. He has enjoined offerings [to be presented] and service (προσφοραὶ καὶ λειτουργίαι) to be performed [to Him], and that not thoughtlessly or irregularly, but at the appointed times and hours."[75] What is important is that the "Lord" giving the commands here is the God of the old covenant and of Jesus Christ. What "the Lord" decrees in the old covenant is not a superseded regulation meant for the Jews, but continues to apply with respect to his Son and the Christians.

These ordinances also include regulations stipulating by whom and where the cult is to be performed.[76] The remarks concerning the personnel and place of the cult are aimed at the worship of Christians ("we").[77] The epistle then continues, first of all regarding the personnel of the cult: "For his own peculiar cultic services (liturgies) are assigned to the high priest, and their own proper place is prescribed to the priests, and their own special ministrations (διακονίαι) devolve on the Levites. The layman is bound by the laws that pertain to laymen."[78] This is largely the language of the Old Testament, with one significant exception: the term "layman" is not found in either the Septuagint or the New Testament.[79] It is a Christian neologism that points to a corresponding linguistic usage in Rome or Corinth. In any case, the passage is specifically aimed at the situation in Corinth. Why else would the epistle have gone into the subject of the laity?[80]

So the whole passage about high priests, priests, Levites and laity *also* refers to Christian worship. Already in the earlier remark that Jesus Christ is "the High Priest of all *our* offerings (προσφοραί),"[81] what the Epistle of Clement is talking about is nothing other than the Christian sacrificial ministry,[82] which now has to be reorganised in Corinth.

---

74 1 Clem. 40,1 (SC 167, 166).
75 Ibid. 40,1 f. (SC 167, 166).
76 Ibid. 40,3 (SC 167, 166).
77 Otherwise WIELAND 1908, 43.
78 1 Clem. 40,5 (SC 167, 166).
79 SC 167, 166 f. n. 5.
80 Laypeople were apparently involved in electing the presbyters in Corinth, and were possibly also

among the troublemakers; cf. 1 Clem. 44,3 (SC 167, 172); 47,6 (178).
81 1 Clem. 36,1 (SC 167, 158).
82 Ibid. 35,12–36,2 (SC 167, 158–160) stands in a liturgical context (sacrifice of praise, prayer gesture of fixing the gaze on heaven, initiation ["taste the immortal knowledge"], cf. Heb 6:4). Otherwise WIELAND 1909, 44 f.

Christ the High Priest presides over the celebration,[83] and in addition there are functions (as servants of the altar) allotted to the priests; that is, the presbyters, and to the Levites; that is, the deacons.[84] The sentence that follows confirms that it is the personnel of Christian worship who are being referred to: "Let each one of us, brethren, be well pleasing to God in his own rank, and have a good conscience, not transgressing the appointed rules of his ministration."[85]

There follow regulations regarding the place where the cult is to be celebrated:

> Not in every place, my brethren, are the daily sacrifices offered or the free-will offerings, or the sin-offerings and trespass-offerings, but only in Jerusalem; and there also the offering is not made in every place, but *before the temple at the altar,* and the offering is first inspected by the High Priest and the cultic ministers [liturgists] already mentioned. Those therefore who do anything contrary to that which is agreeable to his will suffer the penalty of death. You see, brethren, that the more knowledge we have been entrusted with, the greater also is the risk we incur.[86]

Here too, as the last sentence shows, it is about greater knowledge. The insubordinate presbyters of Corinth should finally realise that the regulations of the Old Testament also determine the order of Christian worship. But now it might also appear that the whole thing is only about the Jerusalem Temple cult, and that the liturgical "ministers already mentioned" have nothing to do with the Christian cult after all. Once again, textual pragmatics are helpful here. The letter is addressed to the local church in Corinth, which is a single church.[87] If, in case of further disobedience, the insubordinate presbyters should leave the city,[88] the local community's jurisdiction with respect to them extends only up to the city boundary. Hence the comparison is concretely between the sacred jurisdiction of the Jerusalem Temple and the order of worship for the whole city of Corinth.[89] The aim of the letter is to preserve the unity of the city's community, and here the circumstances in Jerusalem are an exact match for those in Corinth. Just as in Jerusalem there is only one Temple and one altar (Rv 11:1), so in Corinth, too, there is only one place of assembly with a place of sacrifice; only there are the city's clergy permitted

---

83 In 1 Clem. 61,3 (SC 167, 200) and 64 (202) Christ is called within one and the same prayer both "High Priest" and "presider" (cf. WIELAND 1909, 45). In Euseb. hist. eccl. 10,4,68 (SC 55, 102), Christ himself still stands (beside the bishop) at the altar.

84 1 Clem. 40,5 (SC 167, 166).

85 Ibid. 41,1 (SC 167, 166).

86 Ibid. 41,2–4 (SC 167, 166–168): […] ἔμπροσθεν τοῦ ναοῦ πρὸς τὸ θυσιαστήριον […].

87 Ibid. prooem. (SC 167, 98).

88 Ibid. 54,2 (SC 167, 186).

89 This follows from a second observation: 1 Clem. 41,3 (SC 167, 168) is evidently already familiar with the downfall of the temple in Jerusalem (in 70 A.D.) and openly threatens the insubordinate presbyters in Corinth with the same fate of death as the Jews suffered then. If he nevertheless speaks of the sacrifices at the altar of the Jerusalem Temple in the present tense, this is precisely because in so doing he is in fact referring to the Christian sacrifices.

to perform the liturgy. On the other hand, the traditional presbyters seem to have been ousted by the emergence of a competing place of worship.[90]

In the end, one cannot help but wonder why the Epistle of Clement is so certain that its argumentation using the Jerusalem Temple cult and the altar there will bring the Corinthians to order. The basic requirement will certainly be that the Corinthians, too, are convinced that there must be only one place of worship in their city. For what the presbyters are arguing about is the presidency at the Eucharistic celebration of the whole community. Furthermore, the author of the letter is apparently certain that the Old Testament–based cultic understanding of the Eucharist and the Church's ministries is accepted in Corinth. Otherwise he would not have based the core statements of his epistle on this being the case. Perhaps terms that have already taken on a Christian colouring such as "temple" (ναός) (for the assembly room), "altar" (θυσιαστήριον) (for the sacrificial table), "priest" (ἱερεύς) (for the presbyters) and "Levite" (λευΐτης) (for the deacons) do not yet belong to the general vocabulary of either Rome or Corinth. But the issue that lies behind all this, namely the unity of worship and the sacrificial ministry at an appropriate sacred table, are basic coordinates of community life, points at which conflicts cannot arise but within the framework of which they can also be overcome.

The congregation in Corinth is undoubtedly familiar with a sacred table. It is therefore not by chance that in the middle of its remarks about the offices of episcope and deacon the Epistle of Clement quotes Moses's selection of priests for cultic ministry by placing their staffs or rods on the "table of God" in the Tent of Meeting.[91] He also mentions the "sacrifices" of Cain and Abel, and thinks that although both offered their "gifts" rightly, it was in not dividing the gifts rightly that the sin of Cain lay.[92] When the epistle then states that it is a sin to eject from the episcopate those presbyters who have offered their "gifts" in a blameless and holy manner,[93] this shows that here again the Eucharist is being seen as the celebration of a sacrifice.

4. ONE ALTAR – ONE CUP

The use of sacred terminology such as "temple" and above all "altar" for the purpose of crisis management in the community sets a precedent, one that has already been taken up by Bishop Ignatius of Antioch, who is known to have been familiar with the Epistle of Clement. His interest is above all in a honing down to *one* temple, *one* bishop, *one* altar.

90 1 Clem. 41,2 (SC 167, 166–168); cf. ibid. 44,3–6 (172–174). Correctly Wieland 1909, 47 f.
91 1 Clem. 43,2 (SC 167, 170).
92 Ibid. 4,2–4 (SC 167, 104).
93 Ibid. 44,4 (SC 167, 172). Misunderstood grammatically by Wieland 1909, 49 f.

In around 110/20 he writes seven letters to various communities in Asia Minor and to the Christian community in Rome.[94] In the Syrian city of Antioch, Ignatius was condemned to be killed by lions (*ad bestias*) on account of his faith; but the punishment was to be carried out in Rome. When he wrote his letters, he was already on the journey to Italy.

In five letters alone, Ignatius mentions the "altar" (θυσιαστήριον) a total of six times, each time in connection with Christian worship. In light of the texts we have presented so far and in view of Ignatius's practised use of language, it should be beyond doubt that in around 100 A.D. the use of altars is something that is taken for granted in the Christian communities of Asia Minor and Rome. The research, however, does not like to admit this and remains suspicious precisely because Ignatius speaks throughout of the "altar" and never of the "table".

Some scholars do not rule out the possibility that one or the other of the texts treated below might perhaps indeed be speaking of a real Christian altar.[95] But most of them follow Wieland, who vehemently rejects a Christian altar in the case of Ignatius, too. He restricts the concept of "altar" to use for sacrificial slaughter, which is naturally unthinkable for Christian worship. Furthermore, according to Wieland, Ignatius does not know of any oblation of gifts;[96] rather, he maintains, Ignatius calls the Eucharist a gift of God, which comes from God and therefore is not offered by man.[97] For this reason, he concludes, Ignatius uses the non-Christian term "altar" simply as a metaphor, for instance as an image for the unity of the Church or even for Christ. For him no kind of relationship between the "altar" and the Christian eucharistic table exists.[98]

But can it really be that the Bishop of the Syrian capital turns pagan altars into a metaphor for the Church and for Christ? In view of the harsh criticism of the Apologists against

---

94 The authenticity of Ignatius's letters continues to be both disputed and defended to the point of exhaustion in the research. I myself support the majority view, which regards the Middle Recension as containing authentic writings from the first third of the second century. On the discussion see W. Pratscher (ed.), Die Apostolischen Väter (Göttingen 2009) 104–129. W. R. Schoedel, Polycarp of Smyrna and Ignatius of Antioch, in: ANRW 2,27,1 (Berlin / New York 1993) 272–358: c. 105 to 135; C. Munier, Où en est la question d'Ignace d'Antioche? Bilan d'une siècle de recherches 1870–1988, in: ANRW 2,27,1 (Berlin / New York 1993) 359–484: first third of the second century H.-U. Weidemann, Die Pastoralbriefe, in: Theologische Rundschau 81 (2016) 353–403, here 376, quotes Annette Merz: "The Ignatian epistles (of the so-called Middle Recension) are 'with a probability bordering on certainty not forgeries.'" The forgery

hypothesis of Otto Zwierlein, according to which the Ignatian epistles date from the end of the second century, is based on a philological constructivism which leaves any historical context out of consideration; Heid 2011.
95 Braun 1924a, 30–32.
96 Wieland 1908, 44–50; *id.* 1909, 51–61.
97 Ign. ad Smyrn. 7,1 (SC 10³, 160); Wieland 1908, 78 f.
98 Wieland's interpretation is shared by most other expositors, e.g. Thümmel 1999a, 491 n. 13; R. Kieffer, La demeure divine dans le temple et sur l'autel chez Ignace d'Antioche, in: M. Hengel *et al.* (eds.), Die Stadt Gottes (Tübingen 2000) 287–301. Leonhard / Eckhardt 2010, 1076: "'Altar' oder 'Tempel' als Bild für die Gemeindeversammlung." Schoedel 1990, 109, 201, 244 sees only a symbolic use in the word "altar".

the pagan altars of immolation (below chapter IV, 1), that is highly questionable. Added to this, there is the matter of textual pragmatics. The Ignatian letters are, like the Letter to the Hebrews before them, designed to be read aloud at the liturgical gathering. They are therefore not received by theologians at their desks, to whom talk of the altar will possibly appear to be abstract, leading them to philosophize about whether it could be a metaphor. Instead, the hermeneutic context is the concrete worship of the community: Ignatius is alluding more or less explicitly to the current worship situation of his addressees when he speaks of the "altar". If he is using the word "altar" naturally and knows his hearers to have the eucharistic table in front of their eyes at that moment, then there are two possibilities: either the hearers understand the eucharistic table metaphorically as an altar or it really is for them an altar in the sense of a sacred table. There is every indication that the "altar" in the second sense had long since been adopted into Christian language usage.

In fact, Ignatius uses the word "altar" in the same way throughout. To be sure, the meaning can also extend into the symbolic-metaphorical, but the point of reference is always the table that serves for the celebration of the Eucharist at the community gathering and which is univocally termed an altar.

In his letter to the Christians in *Rome*, this altar is for Ignatius at the same time an image of martyrdom:

> Grant me no more than to be a drink-offering poured out to God while there is still an *altar* (θυσιαστήριον) prepared, so that having formed a chorus in love you can sing praises to the Father in Christ Jesus.[99]

He is speaking here of his own impending martyrdom in that the being "poured out" can only be referred to the shedding of his blood. In this sense, the "prepared altar" can also be understood as a metaphorical image for his imminent martyrdom. At first sight it seems as if Ignatius were comparing his blood sacrifice with a pagan sacrificial rite – for instance, in the imperial cult[100] – at which wine is poured out on the altar.[101] The idea would thus be that through his martyrdom at the hands of the persecutors of Christians Ignatius wanted to be sacrificed, as it were, on an altar to idols. Nevertheless, such a comparison would actually be pretty peculiar for a bishop. Furthermore, the drink offering could theoretically also refer to Jewish rites (e.g. Nm 28 f.). The choir, too, could also in principle allude to a pagan or Jewish choir that performed during sacrifices,[102]

---

99 Ign. ad Rom. 2,2 (SC 10³, 128): Πλέον μοι μὴ παράσχησθε τοῦ σπονδισθῆναι θεῷ, ὡς ἔτι θυσιαστήριον ἕτοιμόν ἐστιν, ἵνα ἐν ἀγάπῃ χορὸς γενόμενοι ᾄσητε τῷ πατρὶ [...].

100 Brent 1999, 232.

101 Wieland 1908, 48 f.

102 Wieland 1906, 43; *id.* 1908, 49; Brent 1999, 233–235. "Choir" frequent in the LXX.

but Ignatius speaks unambiguously of the Christians forming a choir. So what is being talked about is a Christian choir (in divine worship).[103]

The crucial way of approaching a Christian interpretation of the "altar" is to look at the Pauline background of the drink-offering metaphor.[104] For Paul's Letter to the Philippians says in reference to the martyrdom of the Apostle (Ph 1:13, 17, 20; cf. 2 Tm 4:6): "But even if I am being poured out as a libation over the sacrifice and the offering of your faith, I am glad" (Ph 2:17). Here Paul draws an analogy between his imminent martyrdom and the community's celebration of the Eucharist: the martyr's drink offering relates to the Blood of the Eucharistic cup.[105] So the drink offering in Ignatius has nothing to do with pagan rites but refers to the Eucharistic Blood. The "altar" here is nothing other than the eucharistic table. Once again, the pragmatics of the text is important. The letter is read aloud at the worship gathering. So the altar really is prepared; the cup with Christ's Blood is standing on the altar[106] and the choir is singing. Just as the faithful in Rome celebrate their blood Eucharist, so they should also allow the martyr Eucharist of Ignatius, that is, his martyrdom.[107] For the metaphor of martyrdom as a drink offering at the altar, Ignatius is able to start from the table of the Eucharist, which is for him a real altar.[108]

Furthermore, in his letter to the Christians in *Philadelphia* Ignatius calls the eucharistic table an altar without any hint of metaphor:

> Take heed, then, to partake of the *one* Eucharist. For (there is only) *one* flesh of our Lord Jesus Christ, and *one* cup (ποτήριον) for the union of His blood, *one altar* (θυσιαστήριον) as *one* bishop, along with the presbytery and deacons.[109]

The context of the letter is the liturgical gathering: the congregation in Philadelphia assembled round the eucharistic table with the bishop and clergy – the collegial "presbytery" – which receives the Body and Blood of the Lord. In this gathering there is but *one* flesh, *one* cup, *one* altar and *one* bishop. It is indisputable that the "altar" here

---

103 So also Ign. ad Eph. 4,1 f. (SC 10³, 72). Cf. WIELAND 1909, 59.

104 Not seen by WIELAND 1908, 48 f.; *id.* 1909, 58 f.; BRENT 1999, 232.

105 The cup is, like the drink offering, a symbol of martyrdom: Mt 20:23, 28; 26:39.

106 The cup with the Blood on the altar see Ign. ad Philad. 4 (SC 10³, 142–144).

107 S. HEID, in: GNILKA 2015, 97 f. See also R. D. STEFANUT, Eucharistic Theology in the Martyrdom of

Ignatius of Antioch, in: Studia Patristica 65 (2013) 39–47.

108 THURÉN 1973, 85 n. 300.

109 Ign. ad Philad. 4 (SC 10³, 142–144): Σπουδάσατε οὖν μιᾷ εὐχαριστίᾳ χρῆσθαι· μία γὰρ σάρξ τοῦ κυρίου ἡμῶν Ἰησοῦ Χριστοῦ καὶ ἓν ποτήριον εἰς ἕνωσιν τοῦ αἵματος αὐτοῦ, ἓν θυσιαστήριον, ὡς εἷς ἐπίσκοπος ἅμα τῷ πρεσβυτερίῳ καὶ διακόνοις. Altar at Ignatius see BARTH 1999, 55–64.

refers to the eucharistic table.[110] The objection is raised, however, that this table is only being called a (pagan) "altar" by way of a comparison so as to thus emphasize the uniqueness of the table in the same way as the uniqueness of Christ's Blood is expressed through the one cup. This is unconvincing. It is absolutely impossible for a pagan altar to stand for unity since inside and in front of the temples and in the graveyards there are countless altars to all kinds of deities. Unique is precisely what the altar in antiquity is not; it is plural since every god is due his own altar. At best the Jewish altar in Jerusalem could stand for unity, for although there are many altars there for burnt, sin and incense offerings, there is only one main altar at the Temple.[111] Whatever the case may be, there was no need to try to use the "altar" as a metaphor for unity. After all, Ignatius need only have spoken of the "*one* table" since there was just one single "table of the Lord" in every worship community. That makes the eucharistic table an eminently suitable symbol of unity. So the fact that Ignatius calls this table an altar has nothing to do with a metaphor. Rather, it is simply a use of language familiar to both him and his addressees not requiring any explanation: the eucharistic table simply is an altar.[112] On it are laid the sacrificial offerings of Christ's Body and Blood. This altar is thus an image for the unity of the local church, which gathers with its bishop around the one altar.

Every Christian community in a town possesses just one episcopal altar. That is something that Ignatius takes so much for granted as a visible and incontrovertible fact that it becomes the point of departure for further catechetical remarks. He states that the *one* altar is a symbol of there being *one* community (i.e. the local church) in that this community literally *is* the altar. Ignatius is on several occasions using the word θυσιαστήριον in this sense when he uses the formulations "within the altar" and "outside the altar", for example in his letter to the Christians in *Ephesus*:

> If anyone is not within the *altar* (θυσιαστήριον), he is deprived of the "bread of God" (Jn 6:33). For if the prayer of one (person) or another (person) possesses such power, how much more that of the bishop and the whole Church![113]

110 SAHAS 1997, 40. Cf. RAUSCHEN 1910, 84 against Franz Wieland.

111 1 Clem. 41,2 (SC 167, 168).

112 It is beyond me how SCHOEDEL 1990, 315 can cast doubt on this simple fact. He invokes the other altar passages in Ignatius, but that simply defers the decision.

113 Ign. ad Eph. 5,2 (SC 10³, 72–74): ἐὰν μή τις ἦ ἐντὸς τοῦ θυσιαστηρίου, ὑστερεῖται τοῦ ἄρτου τοῦ θεοῦ. Εἰ γὰρ ἑνὸς καὶ δευτέρου προσευχὴ τοσαύτην ἰσχὺν ἔχει, πόσῳ μᾶλλον ἥ τε τοῦ ἐπισκόπου καὶ πάσης τῆς ἐκκλησίας; Not very convincing is the commentary by SCHOEDEL 1990, 109.

Ignatius knows that his audience is the local community of Ephesus gathered around their bishop for the Eucharist,[114] a group that he also calls a "choir".[115] But is the "altar" mentioned in such a liturgical context really an altar or is the normal table just being called an altar here in order to make it into a metaphor for the unity of the Church? The second option might be indicated by the strange formulation "within the altar" as it does not seem to work for a table. So it appears unlikely that Ignatius was thinking of the Jewish showbread table on which the "bread of God" was laid (cf. Ex 25:30).[116]

The formulation "within the altar" therefore makes Wieland think of an altar for sacrificial slaughter, which, being made of solid stone, to his way of thinking symbolizes unity.[117] So in this case the eucharistic table would not really be an altar but would instead merely be the subject of comparison with a pagan altar. But what on earth would impel Ignatius to adduce of all things an altar of sacrificial slaughter as a metaphor for the unity of the Church when there is in any case a plurality of pagan altars? Should one then translate the word θυσιαστήριον here as "altar space",[118] which would make the altar area of the Christian meeting place an image for the worshipping community?

All of these deliberations fall into the error of not taking Ignatian realism seriously. The faithful do not *form* an altar or altar space in the metaphorical sense; rather, they *are* the particular altar (τὸ θυσιαστήριον) that is standing in front of them. This concrete altar represents the unity of the community. Here the formula applies: *lex orandi – lex credendi*. Liturgical praxis allows conclusions to be drawn about the practice of faith. At the *one* altar of the community stands the *one* bishop. This one altar points to the united local church. If all of the believers together *are* the one altar, then the individual believer is naturally *within* the altar. For not every individual can be an altar, since there is only one single altar. Furthermore, the expression "within the altar" is no longer in any way strange if the altar table is completely covered with a cloth and is therefore cubic in shape.

This interpretation is confirmed by another passage in the Letter to the *Trallians*, in which Ignatius once again talks about unity:

[You will avoid heresy] if you are not puffed up, and continue in intimate union with Jesus Christ our God, and the bishop, and the enactments of the apostles. He that is within the

---

114 Ign. ad Eph. 5,3 (SC 10³, 74).
115 Ibid. 4,2 (SC 10³, 72).
116 Philo. quis rer. div. 226 calls the showbread table of the Jerusalem Temple the "table for thanksgi-

ving (eucharist) for mortal things since loaves and libations are placed upon it" (cf. Nb 4:7).
117 Wieland 1908, 47.
118 Klauck 1989. Cf. Thurén 1973, 84 f.

altar (θυσιαστήριον) is pure, but he that is outside the *altar* (θυσιαστήριον) is not pure; that is, he who does anything apart from bishop, and presbytery, and deacons, such a man is not pure in his conscience.[119]

Here, too, the idea is that the faithful either *are* the altar (are inside) or *are not* (are outside). The identification of the faithful with an altar rules out the possibility that Ignatius is thinking of a pagan altar. Rather, Ignatius is visualizing the eucharistic table around which the Trallian community is gathered when his letter is read out.

A different direction is taken by the letter to the Christians in *Magnesia*. Ignatius urges them not to do anything without the bishop and the presbyters:

As therefore the Lord did nothing without the Father, [...] so neither do anything without the bishop and presbyters. Neither endeavour that anything appear blessed that you do by yourselves in private; but in the assembly,[120] (let there be) *one* prayer, *one* supplication, *one* mind, *one* hope, in love and in undefiled joy – that is Jesus Christ, than whom nothing is more excellent. All of you, as you come together into *one* temple of God, as (you come together) at *one* altar, (so you come together) at *one* Jesus Christ.[121]

The last sentence poses problems with its sparse formulation. It is translated as a rule as if it contained no more than a comparison: Christ is "so to speak" (ὡς) identified with temple and altar: "All come together to the One Jesus Christ, as (if) to One temple, as (if) to One altar."[122] Real things are said not to be what Ignatius had in mind here. In fact he does use the temple (of God) elsewhere as an image for the individual faithful and can thus also speak of many temples of God.[123] But only in the Letter to the Magnesians is the *one* altar used alongside the *one* temple. Would the temple comparison not have sufficed if it had been just a matter of a metaphor for Christ?

119 Ign. ad Trall. 7,1f. (SC 10³, 116): [...] Ὁ ἐντὸς θυσιαστηρίου ὢν καθαρός ἐστιν· ὁ δὲ ἐκτὸς θυσιαστηρίου ὢν οὐ καθαρός ἐστιν· τοῦτ᾽ ἔστιν ὁ χωρὶς ἐπισκόπου καὶ πρεσβυτερίου καὶ διακόνων πράσσων τι, οὐ καθαρός ἐστι τῇ συνειδήσει. Here altar, bishop, presbytery and deacons are used without an article. However, the meaning is always *the* altar, *the* bishop, *the* presbytery and *the* deacons (see below n. 121). The commentary by Schoedel 1990, 244f. is superficial.

120 On ἐπὶ τὸ αὐτό see below Subject Index and Iustin. apol. 1,67,3 (SC 507, 308), Fischer 1986, 167 n. 23 and Boguniowski 1987, 138–159.

121 Ign. ad Magn. 7,1f. (SC 10³, 100): Ὥσπερ οὖν ὁ κύριος ἄνευ τοῦ πατρὸς οὐδὲν ἐποίησεν, [...] οὕτως μηδὲ ὑμεῖς ἄνευ τοῦ ἐπισκόπου καὶ τῶν πρεσβυτέρων μηδὲν πράσσετε· μηδὲ πειράσητε εὔλογόν τι φαίνεσθαι ἰδίᾳ ὑμῖν, ἀλλ᾽ ἐπὶ τὸ αὐτὸ μία προσευχή, μία δέησις, εἷς νοῦς, μία ἐλπὶς ἐν ἀγάπῃ, ἐν τῇ χαρᾷ τῇ ἀμώμῳ, ὅ ἐστιν Ἰησοῦς Χριστός [...]. Πάντες ὡς εἰς ἕνα ναὸν συντρέχετε θεοῦ, ὡς ἐπὶ ἓν θυσιαστήριον, ἐπὶ ἕνα Ἰησοῦν Χριστόν [...].

122 Wieland 1908, 44; id. 1909, 56f.

123 Ign. ad Eph. 9,1 (SC 10³, 76); 15,3 (ibid. 84); ad Philad. 7,2 (ibid. 146–148).

If the word order of the Greek original is taken into account, the sentence in question can also be translated differently: "All of you, when you come together in *one* temple of God, when (you come together) at *one* altar, (you thus come together) with *one* Jesus Christ." Now the words take on a tangible meaning: the Christian worship room is called a "temple" and the sacrificial table an "altar". But can that not also apply to the Jerusalem Temple and its altar? There is no denying that Old Testament cultic terminology is being used here (Rv 11:1: the temple of God and the altar). But Ignatius is concerned with the concrete worship gathering in Magnesia[124] at which his letter will be read;[125] he explicitly opposes private gatherings without the bishop.[126] So what lies behind his sketchy formulations is the thinking that just as only one temple and one (main) altar stand in Jerusalem, so in Magnesia, too, there is but one Christian temple and in this temple one altar where the bishop is. All other gatherings are illegal.

When the Christians in Magnesia come to the "altar" in their "temple", then they come together with *one* Christ. Here Christ is understood as the High Priest. At the altar of the Christians stands Christ himself. That is one more reason Ignatius speaks of a Christian altar. For as the High Priest in the Holy of Holies,[127] Christ is someone sacrificing at the altar. It is astonishing how very similar Ignatius's trains of thought here are to those he had already developed in the First Epistle of Clement, which was addressed to the quarrelling community in Corinth (above chapter II, 3).

Ignatius is an important witness in documenting the way of speaking about the Christian "altar" that had gained currency in Antioch, Asia Minor and Rome at the beginning of the second century. He no longer has to explain this terminology: it is by now established usage thanks to a worship praxis that has, as the First Epistle of Clement attests, already become traditional. At every gathering of the local church with its bishop, bread and cup stand on a table referred to exclusively as an "altar" by Ignatius. This altar can for him become an epitome of Church unity.

---

124 THURÉN 1973, 86: "Here the 'altar' is to be found in the concrete Eucharistic Sunday worship of the community."

125 "Rather let there be one prayer in the community." A (worship) gathering presided over by the bishops and clergy is also spoken of Ign. ad Magn. 4 (SC 10³, 96); 6,1 (SC 10³, 98); 7,1 (SC 10³, 100).

126 Ign. ad Magn. 4 (SC 10³, 96); 7,1 (100).

127 Ign. ad Philad. 9,1 (SC 10³, 150).

5. SACRALITY OF THE ALTAR TABLE

As far as the development of the Christian altar is concerned, ever since Franz Wieland the research has adhered to a three-stage model. According to this model, the table used by the Christians for the Eucharist was and at first remained an ordinary dining table. Only in the third century was it so-to-speak temporarily sacralised into an "altar" for the duration of the worship: outside the celebration "it was inconsequential and paid no further attention."[128] In the third phase, from the fourth century on, a consecration took place in the sense of its being specially prepared (e.g. through anointing), which turned the table permanently into a sacred altar.[129] Wieland thinks that whenever the texts talk of a "table" – and that is the case from Paul onwards (1 Cor 10:21) – they are referring to a profane piece of furniture. When, for example, in a letter dating from the mid–third century Dionysius of Alexandria refers to the "table" instead of the "altar", this is said to show that it is only in the liturgy itself that the table is called an "altar" and is something holy.[130] Accordingly, a table can be sometimes sacred, sometimes profane; a table can be an altar, yet not an altar.[131]

These are untenable theological constructions. In reality, the word "table" always has a context. In his letter, Dionysius is talking about the "table" in the context of the Eucharist and says that from this table "the holy food" and "the holy" are received.[132] What is profane about this? According to Wieland's logic, Dionysius would, moreover, have to speak of "bread" and "wine" instead of "holy food" outside the Eucharistic celebration.

But Wieland wants at all costs to turn the altar into an inconsequential piece of furniture, so irrelevant that one could have even done without it.[133] He reads this into the depictions of reclining meals to be found in the catacombs, which he interprets as Eucharists, and in which the table is occasionally absent (Fig. 7; below Fig. 127). One could, however, add that, conversely, there are also pictures displaying several tables, which makes them appear correspondingly more insignificant. But apart from the absurdity of such sophistry, the number of tables in these pictures is anyway irrelevant since what they depict is always funeral banquets, never Eucharistic celebrations.

Contrary to what Wieland is willing to admit, one gets the impression that already for Paul, the Letter to the Hebrews, and Ignatius the "table of the Lord" or "altar" on the one hand represents something unique and indispensable, but on the other, not a

---

128 Wieland 1908, 100; *id*. 1906, 114–127; *id*. 1909, 104; *id*. 1912, 32.

129 Wieland 1912, 39–41. Cf. Braun 1924a, 169–174; Dölger 1930, 180–182; Kirsch / Klauser 1950, 352.

130 Wieland 1906, 120.

131 Cf. ibid. 119: "So we are faced with the curious fact that the third-century Church has an altar and has none. How might this phenomenon be explained?"

132 Euseb. hist. eccl. 7,9,4 (SC 41, 175).

133 Wieland 1906, 141.

Fig. 7: Funerary banquet (probably with bread, fish and wine) in the *Cappella Graeca* in the Catacomb of Priscilla, 3rd century, according to Wilpert a "rappresentazione eucaristica"; photo: PCAS.

completely different and striking innovation since it fits in with the general use of sacred tables. On the basis of an already well-established praxis, the "table of the Lord" or "altar" can serve the community in solving internal disputes (against the "table of demons", the Judaizers, and the forming of groups), and as a habitually used piece of cultic furniture it is already charged with symbolism (as a sign of unity).

So everything boils down to understanding the Christian altar from the perspective of the sacred table and thus from within the religious horizon of late antiquity. Accordingly, a eucharistic table is permanently sacred on account of its cultic use. One can speak here of sacrality through use – but certainly not in the sense that a profane table only becomes an altar for the duration of the Eucharist. Rather, its first-time use turns a table suitable for the Eucharistic cult into a *res sacra* in an unspectacular but permanent way.[134] Lasting sacrality does not depend on a formal act of consecration but happens *ipso facto* through being put to religious use.

---

134 This requires neither a solemn first use, nor ex- piatory acts (cf. Ex 29:36), nor anointings (cf. Ex 29:36; Nm 7:1), nor a dedication feast (cf. 2 Chr 7:9).

Wieland states correctly that the celebration of the Eucharist makes the altar into an altar, but the sentence that follows – "Where the Eucharist is not, the table is not an altar"[135] – is superfluous, unprovable and, into the bargain, senseless in the context of late antiquity. The sacrality of the eucharistic table is not diminished by its being used sporadically or moved. There is hardly any doubt that in the third century the table was occasionally set up specially for the celebration of the Eucharist. But why should that prove its profanity?[136] The texts speak of setting up the *altar* for the very reason that it remains an altar outside the liturgy, too. As an item of cultic furniture it is stored in a safe place and definitely not used in between as a kitchen table.

In a seminal essay titled "The Holiness of the Altar and its Justification in Christian Antiquity", (1930) Franz Joseph Dölger demonstrated that already in the third century, i.e. before the Constantinian shift, Christian altars and eucharistic tables were considered sacred objects.[137] An archaeological find in Megiddo, south of Nazareth, might confirm this in a spectacular way if the worship room there really does turn out to date from the third century (before 230 or after 250) (Fig. 8; below Fig. 18).[138] It is a richly appointed building in an otherwise modest civil settlement of a Roman military camp. The oratory measures 5 x 10 m and lies on the north-south axis. It has a large mosaic floor and in the middle stone blocks that apparently formed the base of a solid table.[139] Directly next to this there is a donation inscription: "The God-loving Akeptous has offered the table to (the) God Jesus Christ as a memorial."[140] Reiner Sörries sees "table" here as pointing to a mobile table altar that has not been preserved.[141] But why should one speculate about a table that has not been preserved when it is possible that the blocks of stone next to the inscription are precisely what the inscription indicates: the base of an altar? A floor inscription also enforces a fixed point of reference. It makes no sense to record the donation of a table to God in the mosaic if the object in question is not permanently standing there. The offering to God (προσήνικεν [...] Θεῷ) expresses what is essentially a consecration. "Table" must therefore be understood here as being synonymous with sacred table.

The early textual sources, too, reveal more about the permanence of the cultic pur-

135 WIELAND 1906, 121.

136 Ibid. 122 f.

137 DÖLGER 1930, 161–183. On the sacrality of Christian cultic equipment and rooms in the third century see also B. A. STEWART, Priests of my People. Levitical Paradigms for Early Christian Ministers (Frankfurt a.M. 2015). BRAUN 1924ab does not concern himself with the question of sacrality.

138 TEPPER / DI SEGNI 2006; RIESNER 2007; MELL 2011, 22 f. Doubts regarding the dating are ex-

pressed by ADAMS 2013, 96–99. BRANDENBURG 2017b, 45 upholds the dating even "if the dating on the basis of, for instance, the form of the donation inscription may seem a little early."

139 SHALEV-HURVITZ 2015, 29 f.

140 Προσήνικεν Ἀκεπτοῦς ἡ φιλόθεος τὴν τράπεζαν Θεῷ Ἰησοῦ Χριστῷ μνημόσυνον. TEPPER / DI SEGNI 2006, 36.

141 R. SÖRRIES, Spätantike und frühchristliche Kunst (Köln 2013) 66 f.

Fig. 8: Floor mosaic of the Oratory at Megiddo near Nazareth with the altar base in the middle; to the right of it the donation inscription for the altar, 3ʳᵈ century; Tepper / Di Segni 2006, 32.

pose of the eucharistic table than would seem at first sight to be the case. As far as the "table of the Lord" in Paul's writings is concerned (above chapter II, 1), there are a few further observations to be made here. This table is certainly not a profane table, for example the table of a triclinium, since Paul is not talking about profane meals: rather, the whole passage deals with the worship of God or gods as well as with sacrificial or cultic meals (1 Cor 10:18–20) and not with common meals for satisfying hunger, which should instead be held at home (1 Cor 11:22, 34). Therefore the "table of the Lord" (1 Cor 10:21 = Mal 1:7, 12 LXX) has, as in Malachi, the character of an altar (θυσιαστήριον).

Paul speaks not only of the "table of the Lord" but also of the "cup of the Lord" (1 Cor 10:21; 11:27). These two objects are what matters to him – the objects through which the Body and Blood of Christ are communicated to the worshippers, who drink from the cup and partake of the table (1 Cor 10:21). Without the cup and without the table the Eucharist is inconceivable.[142] For the question of their sacrality it is important that, regardless of the size of the gathering, Paul speaks of *one* table (1 Cor 10:16–18) and *one*

142 Similarly then in Ign. ad Philad. 4 (SC 10³, 142).

cup of the Eucharist, whereas at the satiating meal everyone eats his or her own food, apparently all eating from their own tables (1 Cor 11:21). At the daily meals for the care of widows there is also a "waiting at the tables" (Acts 6:1 f.) inasmuch as the number of tables depends on the numbers of the needy. By contrast, for the Eucharist no additional tables whatsoever are set up to match a growing number of participants.[143] The exclusiveness of the eucharistic table and cup is indicative of their being genuine cultic instruments. This can be compared to the sacrificial bowl (*patera*) and jug (*guttus*) used in the pagan cult; both, together with the altar, belong so exclusively to sacrificial service that they are often depicted on the sides of the altars.

The chalice has a sacred value; Paul calls it the "cup of blessing" because it is blessed during the ritual (1 Cor 10:16). By analogy the "table of the Lord" is a "table of blessing", even if this is not explicitly stated. But the blessing assumed to be performed over the bread must at the same time bless the table on which the bread lies. That will also be the reason why both of these cultic instruments belong to the Lord, and do so permanently: "of the Lord" is to be understood as a genitive of possession.[144] These are consecrated objects, i.e. table and cup may only be used to serve the cult of the Christian God. If the eucharistic table and cup had been used in between for normal meals as well, it would have been inappropriate to speak of the "table of the Lord" and the "cup of the Lord".

In antiquity an altar is reserved for a particular god, to whom alone sacrifices are allowed to be offered, and it bears an inscription to this effect.[145] The altar (*ara*) is considered to be the inalienable possession of the deity.[146] We can recall the curious case of the altar dedicated "to an unknown god" in Athens (Acts 17:23) and the "Altar of Victory" in the Roman Senate House (Curia). It is a sacrilege to offer sacrifices on an altar to a god to whom it is not dedicated, which leads to a multiplication of altars. Hence Cyprian says that when the Christians remove the altar of the Lord, the pagans erect their altars there with the corresponding statues of deities.[147] Because there are many deities there are also many altars, which are often erected next to each other.[148]

Accordingly, the Christian altar is used exclusively for the ritual worship of the Christian God. Paul wants to strengthen this exclusivity: just as the cup and table belong exclusively to God, so the Christians should belong exclusively to God and participate only

---

143   Otherwise Kopeček 2006, 194 f.

144   Cf. R. Kühner / B. Gerth, Ausführliche Grammatik der griechischen Sprache 2,1 (Hannover / Leipzig ³1898) 332. In Ez 44,16 LXX God speaks of "my sanctuary" and "my table". Also the "church of God" in Corinth is naturally always the church of God (1 Cor 1:2), not just when it comes together for the Lord's Supper (1 Cor 11:22).

145   On the exclusivity of the altars see Reisch 1894, 1642. Since, however, it was possible for an altar to be dedicated to several related deities, Paul was quite justified in speaking of the "table of demons".

146   Scheid 2014, 29 f.

147   Cypr. ep. 59,18 (CSEL 3,2, 688).

148   On the multiplicity of altars see Scheid 2014, 30 – 33.

in his cup and table. The argument culminates in the sentence: "Or are we provoking the Lord to jealousy?" (1 Cor 10:22). God's jealousy is provoked when the exclusiveness of his cup and his table is ignored. Evidently Paul is counting on his readers' sacred fear. The "table of the Lord" of which someone "partakes" (1 Cor 10:21) is different from yet similar to a table of demons and to the "altar" of the Temple in Jerusalem; that person may also become a "partner" (1 Cor 10:18) in these. The thinking behind this is that on the table of demons (1 Cor 10:21), the Jerusalem altar (1 Cor 10:18; cf. 9:13) and the table of the Lord (1 Cor 10:21) there lie foods that are either good or bad by virtue of the nature of the table: the table in a certain way infects what lies on it.

The haptic moment is so important that the table is sufficient as a distinguishing feature of the foods. For this reason, not only the unworthy eating of the Flesh and Blood is subject to sanctions (1 Cor 11:27, 34), but ultimately also the table: whoever does not eat exclusively from the "Lord's table" incurs punishment (1 Cor 10:22). The sacredness of the Lord's table is thus not diminished at all, but rather increased as compared to the "table of demons". What Paul does not say is that the Lord's table, unlike the table of demons, is an ordinary dining table; on the contrary, he depicts the table as being something very special, even more exclusive than the table of demons. The same exclusiveness is also to be found in the Letter to the Hebrews, in the First Epistle of Clement, and in Ignatius (above chapter II, 2 – 4).

It can be assumed that contact with holy things plays a role in the effective sacralization of a cultic object. In antiquity the table itself apparently becomes the seat of the deity if it has the image of the god on it.[149] Above all, the holiness of the altar results from its contact with sacrificial flesh and blood.[150] The same idea holds sway in Judaism: whatever is touched by the sacrificial flesh becomes holy (Lv 6:27 LXX). Blood is the sanctifying substance par excellence with which altars are sprinkled (Ex 24:6). Conversely, the altar can sanctify the offerings (Mt 23:19). The Christians do not fundamentally reject such ideas; they can continue to work in a different way.[151] The Letter to the Hebrews is aware that in the old covenant the cultic instruments are purified by the sprinkling of blood (Heb 9:19–22) and regards this as necessary (Heb 9:23). For the author of Hebrews, the Blood of Christ is cleansing and sanctifying blood (Heb 9:13 f.; cf. 7:26). The altar itself (Heb 13:10), or the throne of grace (thanksgiving) (Heb 4:16) on which the Body and Blood of Christ "are enthroned", is made sacred through touching the sacrificial offerings.

For Ignatius of Antioch, too, what matters is the visible presence of bread and wine on the altar table. For the Bishop's prayer extends only to the altar:

---

149 MISCHKOWSKI 1917, 11.
150 ZIEHEN 1950, 326.

151 Prud. c. Symm. 1, 398 f. (FC 85, 136); Isid. etym. 15,4,2 (LINDSAY 1911b, 167); ZIEHEN 1950, 326.

If anyone is not within the *altar* (ἐντὸς τοῦ θυσιαστηρίου), he is without the "bread of God" (Jn 6:33). For if the prayer of one (person) or another (person) possesses such power, how much more that of the bishop and the whole Church![152]

The expression "within the altar" makes sense when the altar table is covered with a cloth. It is, of course, above all the altar slab on which the sacrificial offerings lie that is meant here. Only when someone is within the altar does the bread of God transformed by the power of prayer lie on it, and in this respect he is not "without the bread". Here Ignatius is thinking of physical contact: through the power of the bishop's words of consecration and the prayer of the Church, the bread lying on the altar becomes the "Bread of God". The altar itself is sacralised, i.e. purified, through physical contact with the offerings:

> He that is within the *altar* is pure, but he that is outside the *altar* is not pure; that is, he who does anything apart from bishop, and presbytery, and deacons, such a man is not pure in his conscience.[153]

Naturally the altar is something pure for Ignatius. With it he associates the purity of conscience of the faithful. But to what does the altar owe its purity? Presumably to the holy offerings lying on it! They are pure, otherwise Ignatius would not have described his martyrdom in Eucharistic terminology as "pure bread" and a sacrifice for God.[154] Through the physical contact of the altar-*mensa* with the pure offerings the altar itself becomes pure.

Very much along the same lines as the Letter to the Hebrews, Origen says (c. 240) that "altars are not sprinkled with the blood of sheep, but consecrated through the precious blood of Christ."[155] He argues biblically here: both the Old Testament altar and the Christian altar are holy because of blood: in Old Testament times it was the blood of animal sacrifices, now it is the Blood of Christ. Wieland is correct in assuming that for Origen the Christian altar is a table. But he draws the wrong conclusion from this; namely, that a table can only be sacred during the celebration of the Eucharist.[156] In reality, though, Origen could not have expressed his conviction of the lasting sacrality of the Christian altar table more strongly than by comparing it with the Old Testament altar. For the sprinkling of blood irreversibly turns an altar into a sacrosanct cultic object.

---

152 Ign. ad Eph. 5,2 (SC 10³, 72–74). Text see above n. 113.

153 Ign. ad Trall. 7,2 (SC 10³, 116). Text see above n. 119.

154 Ign. ad Rom. 4,1 f. (SC 10³, 130). Antiquity, too, used "pure loaves" for sacrifices (e.g. Herodotus 2,40,2).

155 Orig. in Iesu Nav. hom. 2,1 (SC 71, 116); DÖLGER 1930, 176.

156 WIELAND 1909, 104.

The same argument also works the other way around in that the Christian altar is holy precisely because it is *not* touched by any (animal) blood. On this, Clement of Alexandria (c. 150–215) states:

> But although there has been much talk of the very ancient altar at Delos being holy and it has been told that Pythagoras, too, approached only this one altar because it was undefiled by blood and death, when we say that a *truly sacred altar* is the just soul and the incense rising from it as holy prayer, they will not believe us?[157]

Pointing to the altar of Delos, the only pagan altar not to be the site of animal sacrifices, Clement claims that an altar is holy as long as it is not defiled through bloody sacrifices. Holiness therefore comes from contact of the sacrificial material with the altar. Clement spiritualizes the truly holy altar, turning it into the soul, but his categories undoubtedly also apply to the Christian altar, which he explicitly mentions in the same context.[158] It is only the fact that bread and wine lie on this altar, not bloody sacrifices, that makes Clement think of the altar at Delos at all.[159] According to this logic, the Christian altar is immaculate and holy (cf. Mal 1:7, 12 LXX) precisely because it is touched only by bread and wine. Methodius of Olympus († c. 311/12) also speaks of the bloodless and therefore holy and pure altar.[160]

The Jewish practice according to which only flawless, perfect objects may be sacrificed also belongs in this context. Here the "Lord's table" spoken of by Malachi and subsequently by Paul comes up once again: only "pure" offerings should be sacrificed on it (Mal 1:11). The prophet scolds those priests who defile the "Lord's table" by laying polluted bread on it and sacrificing sick and lame animals (Mal 1:7 f. 12 f. LXX). The First Epistle of Clement applies an examination of the offerings specifically to the Christian gifts offered on the altar by priests and deacons.[161] The Didache (= The Lord's Teaching Through the Twelve Apostles) (c. 100) follows Malachi (Mal 1:11, 14) in speaking of the purity of the Christian sacrifice, which is out of the ordinary and thus sacred.[162] Speaking

---

157 Clem. Alex. strom. 7,6,32,5 (SC 428, 118–120). Text see below p. 175 n. 62.

158 See preceding footnote.

159 It needs to be examined whether the floor mosaics in churches that depict the Peaceful Kingdom (*Tierfrieden* – cf. Is 11:6–9), which are most often to be located in front of the altar, have anything to do with the idea of the bloodless sacrifice inasmuch as the animals no longer have to fear ritual slaughter. Cf. R. WISSKIRCHEN, Zum "Tierfrieden" in spätantiken Denkmälern, in: JbAC 52 (2009) 142–163 with a different interpretation.

160 Method. Olymp. symp. 5,6,126 (SC 95, 158). Con-

stant. Aug. or. ad coet. sanct. 12,5 (FC 55, 174): the pure, unbloody sacrifice of the Christians.

161 1 Clem. 41,2 (SC 167, 168). Cf. Past. Herm. 68,5 (SC 53², 264): Examination of the staffs on the altar (θυσιαστήριον).

162 Did. 14 (SC 248, 192). H. VAN DE SANDT, Why does the Didache Conceive of the Eucharist as a Holy Meal?, in: *Vigiliae Christianae* 65 (2011) 1–20, here 20 on Did. 14: "suggest that the Eucharist table is compared to the temple altar." In Heb 13:10 the altar itself enters the sanctified sphere of serving the Christian cult (Heb 13:12). WEIDEMANN 2014, 374 f.

of the "pure altar" (Ignatius) also points in the same direction. Finally, Justin (c. 150) sees the "pure sacrifice" (Mal 1:11) as being fulfilled in the Eucharistic gifts.[163] So the altar must be preserved from any kind of taint. Its purity is watched over by God himself. This sentiment is expressed in Polycarp's Epistle:

> Teach the widows to be discreet as respects the faith of the Lord, praying continually for all, being far from all slandering, evil-speaking, false-witnessing, love of money, and every kind of evil; knowing that they are the *altar of God* (θυσιαστήριον θεοῦ), and he examines everything as to its blamelessness, and that nothing is hid from him, neither reasonings, nor reflections, nor any one of the secret things of the heart.[164]

The altar possesses powers that it can pass on. In the Jewish understanding, whoever touches the most holy altar of sacrifice becomes himself holy (Ex 29:37).[165] Swearing an oath with one hand on the altar (Ex 17:15 f.; cf. Mt 23:18–20) is a custom to be found among both pagans and Christians.[166] Dölger states quite correctly that the touching of the altar by simple believers for the purposes of an oath does not express disrespect but, on the contrary, great respect for the altar.[167] Apparently a special strength goes out from touching the altar. This is also indicated by the ancient practice of resting one's right hand on the sacred table during certain sacrificial acts (Fig. 9). And there is in fact repeated evidence that only one hand rather than two was raised in prayer[168] or that one hand was placed on the altar.[169]

This may possibly live on in the Christian rite.[170] Gregory of Nyssa († c. 394) says that the "holy table", the "spotless altar" which has received God's blessing can no longer be touched by everyone, but only reverently by the priest.[171] The same is true of asylum, which in the narrower sense refers to the altar: anyone who holds on to the altar enjoys God's protection.[172] According to John Chrysostom († 407), the bishop

---

163 See below p. 170 n. 29.

164 Polyc. ad Phil. 4,3 (SC 10³, 208).

165 NEUSNER 2001, 247.

166 Polyc. ad Phil. 4,3 (SC 10³, 208).

167 DÖLGER 1930, 166 f. Swearing with a hand on the altar: Greg. Tur. hist. Franc. 3,14; 4,46; 5,3, 32. Oath at the altar: Ps.-Athan. in nativ. praec. 1 (PG 28, 908C). Pagan altars: handshake over an altar: JbAC 2012, Taf. 1–2.

168 C. SITTL, Die Gebärden der Griechen und Römer (Leipzig 1890) 187–189; F. HEILER, Das Gebet (München ⁵1923) 102; DÖLGER 1943, 464; *id.* 1972, 314; G. NEUMANN, Gesten und Gebärden in der griechischen Kunst (Berlin 1965) 78–81.

169 SITTL 1890, 192, 318.

170 This could be indicated in Ambr. exam. 6,9,69 (CSEL 32,1, 257): *manus est quae praeclaris eminet factis, quae conciliatrix divinae gratiae sacris infertur altaribus.*

171 Greg. Nyss. in diem lum. (PG 46, 581C); this is confirmed by Joh. Chrys. in act. apost. hom. 9,6 (PG 60, 84). DÖLGER 1930, 167. Greg. Naz. or. 18,22 (PG 35, 1012A): cleansing of the holy table from something unholy (unclean hands?).

172 DÖLGER 1930, 170.

Fig. 9: Sacrifice to Hygieia/Salus, the goddess of good health, whose statue stands on the sacred table; relief in the Capitoline Museums, Empire; photo: D-DAI-ROM 31.1 548.

not only raises his hands in prayer at the altar, but also touches the table, whereupon spiritual springs gush forth to transform bread and wine.[173] It is interesting to learn in this context of Nonna, the mother of Bishop Gregory of Nazianz († 390), who once stood praying in the church, apparently with her hands and eyes turned upwards. For then God speaks to her from above and invites her to come to the altar. When she

173 Joh. Chrys. cat. bapt. 2,4,26 (FC 6,1, 286).

then steps up to the altar, she lays one hand on it and raises the other in prayer.[174] The Roman liturgy is acquainted with the gesture of blessing in which the priest touches the altar with one hand. The 1962 Missal still instructs the priest: *Cum seipsum signat, semper sinistram ponit infra pectus: in aliis benedictionibus cum est ad altare, et benedicit oblata, vel aliquid aliud, ponit eam super altar, nisi aliter notetur* (When he signs himself with the cross, he always places his left hand on his chest; at the other blessings on the altar, when he blesses the gifts or something else, he places his left hand on the altar if no other direction is given). This is the case, for example, during the five prayers of blessing that the priest says on Palm Sunday over the palms while resting his left hand on the altar.[175] Holiness as it were flows from the mensa into the person praying and strengthens his or her prayer.

In the fourth century, the Donatists in Numidia cut down the wooden altars of the Catholics because they thought that these had been profaned by being touched by unholy priests and were consequently no longer usable.[176] This tells us indirectly that the Donatists regarded the altars as sacred objects. At the same time it expresses the conviction that a priest touching the mensa with his hand can possibly defile it. This seems to confirm that the priest used to touch the altar slab at least from time to time while praying.

Optatus of Milevis (c. 365) thinks it a sacrilege to destroy an altar at which for many long years "holy sacrifices have been offered"[177] and on which the Body and Blood of Christ have lain[178] or "dwelt".[179] For him, too, the altar slab was certainly particularly holy[180] because holiness emanated from the Eucharistic gifts. John Chrysostom says the same thing: the Christian altar of stone is awful and admirable on account of the sacrifice that is laid upon it; it is holy and venerable as soon as it has received the Body of Christ. Indeed, it is then itself Christ's Body.[181] Although it seems that Chrysostom only ever considers the altar to be holy when the Body of Christ is lying on it, it is nevertheless clear that he is here following the ancient thinking according to which the altar is and remains sacred through contact with the sacrifice.[182] For the altar is no "simple table".[183] The precise thing that the formal consecration of the altar that was already appearing in the East in the mid–fourth century is not is a spiritualization of the sacrality of the

---

174 Dölger 1930, 169 n. 25.

175 Hartmann 1940, 782. Extraordinary form of the Roman Rite, but before the reform of the liturgy for Holy Week and Easter under Pius XII.

176 Opt. Mil. 6,1,1–11 (SC 413, 160–166); Dölger 1930, 171.

177 Opt. Mil. 6,1,4 (SC 413, 152).

178 Ibid.. 6,1,2 (SC 413, 160–162). Dölger 1930, 173.

179 Opt. Mil. 6,1,4 (SC 413, 162).

180 Cf. Agnell. Lib. Pont. Rav. 24,64 (FC 21,1, 286): *mensa vero desuper est sancta ara.*

181 Joh. Chrys. in 2 Cor. hom. 20,3 (PG 61, 540).

182 Joh. Chrys. in 1 Cor. hom. 36,5 (PG 61, 343); Dölger 1930, 177 f. Cf. van de Paverd 1970, 54 f.

183 Joh. Chrys. comm. in Matth. 82,2 (PG 58, 740).

altar through "mere" words of blessing; rather, it is an intensified concretisation of this sacrality in the anointing of the altar mensa (cf. Ex 40:10). A non-concrete and intangible sacrality is quite unthinkable in antiquity. The anointing is presumably intended to enable the mensa to receive the divine gifts.[184]

One particular feature of later times also deserves mention. When Optatus of Milevis says that the sanctity of the altar permeates everything, even extending to the base on which the altar stands,[185] he is saying that the altar table, even without relics, sanctifies the whole space between the top slab and the base slab. This is referring precisely to that sacred interior space of the altar which was at that time called the *confessio* and which was especially charged with meaning, above all through having relics deposited in it. Pope Gregory the Great (590–604) tells of miraculous dust coming from the base of an altar[186] which the priest (not a layman) collects. This is likely to have been a *stipes* or table altar.

In the Eastern churches there was a prohibition against washing wooden and stone altars,[187] and there were special rules about how the sanctuary and the area around altar were to be swept. The cleaning water was to be disposed of in a river. This measure indirectly confirms that the dust was considered sacred.[188] It can be assumed that it was also kept by the faithful as eulogia or as a blessing water. Archaeologically, at least, there are water channels (so-called ϑάλασσα) preserved in the ground in Byzantine churches leading away from the altar and occasionally ending in a container. These could have been used to produce such blessing water.

It is frequently alleged that the sacrality of an object depends on its shape (angular versus round) or its material (stone versus wood). Hence, so it is claimed, the early use of wooden tables for the Eucharist indicates a profane meal situation. These are unfounded assertions. For in antiquity it was neither its shape nor the material it was made of that determined the sacredness of an altar or table but rather its use. It is astonishing what was used as an altar! This ranged from a rickety iron tripod to a stone column and a wooden table to an altar made of a solid block of stone. Even the sacred tables of antiquity and Christianity can vary greatly in shape and material without losing any of their sacredness.

184 Dölger 1930, 180 f.
185 Opt. Mil. 6,1,10 (SC 413, 166).
186 Greg. I dial. 3,17,3 (SC 260, 338).
187 Dölger 1930, 170 f.
188 Can. Hippol. arab. 29 (Riedel 1900, 219 [PO 31, 400]): "They should cast the dust that is swept from the holy place into a surging river." Basil. can.

96 (Riedel 1900, 272): "The earth that is swept from the altar should be thrown into the water of a flowing river." On the cleaning of churches and altars see also Joh. Chrys. in Eph. hom. 3,5 (PG 62, 30). Greg. Naz. or. 18,10 (PG 35, 996C) speaks of the "divine floor" around the altar.

Certainly, an altar of immolation is more likely to be thought of as being made of stone.[189] John Chrysostom's remark that the stone altar is awe-inspiring[190] could also lead one to assume that only a stone altar was sacred. Synodal resolutions stipulating that it is only permitted to anoint an altar made of stone might point in this direction as well.[191] But resolutions of this kind date from the sixth century, when complex liturgical altar consecrations[192] and an elaborated sacred law already existed. In reality, even a wooden table used for the Eucharist was not a profane item of furniture.

The two North Africans, Cyprian († 258) and Augustine († 430), speak of the *mensa*, with which one can easily associate a wooden table. But from these same bishops we have clear acknowledgements of the holiness of this (wooden) altar, which they just as easily call an altar (*altare*) because the sacrifice (*sacrificium*) is offered at it to God.[193] Cyprian carries the sacrality of the table to extremes when he calls the altar erected against sacred law (*contra fas*),[194] for example by an anti-bishop, "profane"; at it "sacrilegious sacrifices" are offered.[195] For him such an altar is therefore an ordinary table. The altar of the legitimate bishop, on the other hand, is "divine".[196] It is not impossible that at that time the initial erection of an altar was already associated with some kind of consecration.[197]

Nevertheless, it is often claimed that in North Africa mobile wooden tables were what was normally used, which points to the original use of dining tables for the Eucharist. Above all the archaeologist Stéphane Gsell popularised the idea of mobile wooden altars in North Africa.[198] In the meantime, it is known that fixed installations of altars made of stone were the rule there, too,[199] even if archaeological evidence of structurally fixed altars is only available from the end of the fourth century onwards.[200] The trend from wooden to stone altars observed in all ecclesiastical regions – with regional variations from the fourth to the sixth century – has nothing to do with a late sacralisation of the

---

189 Eger. itin. 4,2 (CCL 175, 42).

190 Joh. Chrys. in 2 Cor. hom. 20,3 (PG 61, 540). Cf. VAN DE PAVERD 1970, 54.

191 Conc. Epaonense a. 517, can. 26 (CCL 148A, 30). Stone altar see also Balai (BKV Ausgewählte Schriften syr. Dichter 65).

192 L. KOEP, *Consecratio* I, in: RACh 3 (1957) 269–283, here 278 f.

193 Cypr. ep. 59,18 (CSEL 3,2, 688): *Domini altare.* Ep. 63,5 (704): *Sed et per Salomonem spiritus sanctus typum dominici sacrificii ante praemonstrat, immolatae hostiae et panis et vini sed et altaris et apostolorum faciens mentionem […] mactavit suas hostias, miscuit in cratera vinum suum et paravit suam mensam.* Aug. serm. 310,2

(PL 38, 1413): *in eodem loco mensa Deo constructa est, et tamen mensa dicitur Cypriani, non quia ibi est unquam Cyprianus epulatus […], sed in qua sacrificium Deo […] offeratur.*

194 Cypr. ep. 73,2 (CSEL 3,2, 780).

195 Ibid. 68,2 (CSEL 3,2, 745).

196 Ibid. 72,2 (CSEL 3,2, 776): *altare unum adque divinum.*

197 Cf. DÖLGER 1930, 182.

198 Cf. F. BARATTE, Charles-Emile-Stéphane Gsell, in: HEID / DENNERT 2012, 1, 622 f. Wooden altar e.g. Aug. ep. 185,7,27 (PL 33, 805).

199 DUVAL 2005, 7; *id.* 1972, 1150, 1154.

200 DE BLAAUW 2008, 374.

altar; instead, it affects the whole of the liturgical interior decoration of the churches and has to do with changing tastes and modernisation.[201] For example, wooden cancelli and ambos, which can hardly be called sacred objects, were replaced by installations made of stone and marble. At all events, Gregory of Nyssa states explicitly about the altar – he seems to be thinking of a box-shaped altar here – that stone is the normal building material. It is God's blessing alone that makes it a "holy table" and "flawless altar".[202] Only indirectly can a connection be made between the replacement of wooden mensas with stone altars and their sacred character; instead, theft-proof stone altars were preferred for depositing relics in.[203] But the relics merely reinforced the already-given sacredness of the altars.

There are further reasons why the material the altar is made of does not allow any conclusions to be drawn about its sacredness. Like dining tables, sacred pagan tables could be made of wood, stone or marble.[204] And statues of gods could be made of stone, wood, ivory or some other material, too. No one would have considered a wooden god less worthy of worship than a marble god. In addition to this, no one knows for certain what material and shape the Christians preferred for their altars in the first three centuries. What is probably the oldest preserved altar, namely that at Megiddo, dates from the middle of the third century and is made of stone (*stipes* altar).[205] Optatus of Milevis shows that for Donatists and Catholics alike wooden altars were sacred objects that must never be destroyed.[206] Finally, it should be taken into account that altar tables have – since the fourth century at the latest – been covered with cloths, so that the material they are made of is no longer recognisable (below Fig. 42). Such altar cloths are later imitated as permanent coverings, for example when wooden altars at least are sometimes covered with silver or other metals.[207]

201 Cf. de Blaauw 2008, 374, 378.

202 Greg. Nys. in diem lum. (PG 46, 581C).

203 Cf. de Blaauw 2008, 373 f. Different Jansen 2015, 120.

204 Reisch 1894, 1663 f.; ThesCRA 5 (Los Angeles 2005) 231 f.

205 See above p. 56 f.

206 Opt. Mil. 6,1,11 (SC 413, 166).

207 Cf. Method. Olymp. symp. 5,6,126 (SC 95, 158). Altar made of bronze or gold: PG 55, 431.

SUMMARY

The question of the origin of the Christian altar leads to the reality in antiquity of sacred tables. Paul speaks of the "table of the Lord", the Letter to the Hebrews of "altar", and Ignatius of Antioch six times likewise of "altar". In each case the context is Christian community worship and the Eucharist. Textual sources from the first and second centuries leave scarcely any room for doubt that from Antioch to Rome, from Syria to Italy, special sacred tables, called in antiquity "tables" or "altars", were in use for the Eucharist. At the same time as they criticised pagan sacrifices and altars, the Christians established their own cultic practice, among the instruments of which was included, alongside the cup, also the sacred table. As far as cultural history is concerned, this is modelled on the evening banquet of antiquity, which is combined with a food sacrifice and for which similar tables are used. The eucharistic table becomes a *res sacra* through the (first) cultic act performed at it and is dedicated exclusively to sacrificing to the Christian God. The table in itself is something special and holy because it comes into contact with the sacrificial offerings.

Nascent Christianity stands more in the Jewish than the pagan tradition. It is possible that the Christian altar is more closely related to the temple and the synagogue than has hitherto been recognised. The texts in Paul, Hebrews, and Ignatius give us a sense of this. At all events, the Christian altar is not – viewed ideally – derived from the altar of immolation for animal sacrifices but rather from the showbread table of the Jerusalem Temple, which was a sacred table on which the food offerings were laid. The relationship between the showbread table and the Eucharist needs to be reconsidered.[208] One can also ask oneself whether there is not a connection between the Christian altar and the synagogue in that in the latter the Torah scroll is spread out on a table and read aloud from there.[209] In late antiquity, the synagogue at Sardis had a magnificent solid marble table standing in front of the apse for this purpose.[210]

---

208 Böhler 2022, 25 f, 32. Cf. M. Barker, Temple Themes in Christian Worship (London 2007).
209 My thanks to Winfried König (Cologne) for pointing this out. Cf. R. Bauckham / S. De Luca, Magdala as we now know it, in: Early Christian-ity 6 (2015) 91–118, here 111; de Blaauw 2008, 251 f. Fig. 3 (Synagogue of Sardis); I. Elbogen, Der jüdische Gottesdienst in seiner geschichtlichen Entwicklung (Hildesheim 1995) 473.
210 Katz 2006, 534.

III. UNITY

House Churches *versus* Bishop's Church

The question of the early Christian altar is closely related to the problem of the so-called house churches. Today the term "house church" will perhaps be associated with the situation in countries like China where state persecution means that Christian communities can only practise their faith in secret and with a number of people in their homes. In free countries, the idea of house churches is associated with the hope that if a large number of families pass on their faith to the next generation in their homes, this will serve to build up the community. Although most people are not aware of it, such ideas are connected with a recent theory in theological science that can be called the house-church theory.

1. THE FALLACY OF HOUSE CHURCHES

The house-church theory says that nascent Christianity spread in the cities in the private homes of wealthy Christians where the Eucharist was celebrated within the family circle. This celebration of the Eucharist is imagined to have taken place in the dining room (triclinium) at a dining table. As has already been stated, a formal reclining meal in antiquity could certainly be accompanied by ritual acts at a sacred table (above chapter I, 2). So even if house churches are supposed to have existed – for which there is no evidence – this in no way excludes the possibility that the Christians also had altars or sacred tables at their gatherings in addition to dining tables. But first of all there is another consequence, one that is much more significant: an unlimited multiplicity of house churches in a city would also imply a large number of sacred tables. Altars would be, as it were, mass goods, which would then imply a certain arbitrariness.

However, the texts we have looked at so far and other evidence all point in a different direction: the altar is something unique, something embodying authority. The First Letter to the Corinthians, the Letter to the Hebrews and the epistles of Ignatius already indicate that only *one* table is ever used for the celebration of the Eucharist (above chapter II, 1–4). The table or altar is always spoken of in the singular. In no case are additional tables set up when a larger number of people attend the Eucharist. The sacred "table of the Lord" (1 Cor 10:21) is clearly not capable of being multiplied. The rule is: each community has only one altar. Studies have so far delimited this rule by committing themselves to the house-church theory and then concluding: *one* house church – *one* altar. The assumption was that the communities that gathered in private houses for the Eucharist were small, at most twenty to forty people,[1] so that each house church needed only one table. If the community grew, then a new house church was established. With a multiplicity of worshipping communities in the cities, each group could thus gather around its table as the symbol of unity. However, in reality the principle of unity is devalued by this since there are now many house communities and tables in every city.[2] This makes the tables arbitrary and profane again – and that is precisely what the proponents of the house-church theory emphasize.

In truth, they are missing the point here. The house-church theory actually obstructs the view of the early Christian church structure and hence also of the function of the church building and altar. Therefore it is vital to scrutinize the house-church theory by examining its roots. Recently, L. Michael White (1990, 1996), Bradley Blue (1994) and Roger W. Gehring (2004) have argued, from an archaeological and New Testament perspective, that the first two centuries of Christianity must be regarded very much as "the age of house churches".[3] Marlis Gielen writes in the *Lexikon für Theologie und Kirche*: "Up to the middle of the 3rd century AD, the life of the community took place exclusively in private houses, so community was always *house* community."[4] Jochen Wagner, too, sees the house churches as the existential formula of the early Church: "The ancient οἶκος was thus the place where the communities were founded, the site of their worship gathering as well as accommodation for legations and missionaries. The house [...] was the social model for the communities, the infrastructure of the nascent Church."[5] Accordingly, the archaeologists hunt sedulously for house churches, discussing which wall remains in Rome or Pompeii that they might be found in, and even the artwork that might possibly have decorated them.[6]

Despite all the differences in detail, the house-church model implies that the earliest Christian mission began diffusely in the cities and was successful precisely among wealthy citizens, who converted to each preacher's variant of the new faith and placed their city residences at his disposal for their meetings. Here, a new community cell then grew up with its own worship services. The rich head of the house, whether male (*pa-*

---

1 Cf. Nussbaum 1965, 377.
2 Leclercq 1907, 3185; Palazzo 2008, 74 f.
3 Rordorf 1964, 111.

4 Gielen 1995, 1216.
5 Wagner 2011, 33; cf. 48.
6 Balch 2008, 14–16.

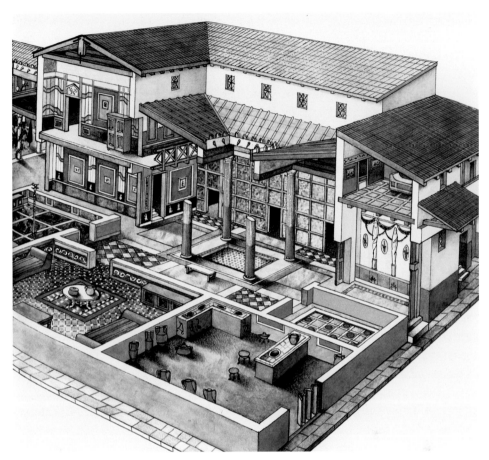

Fig. 10: Private city residence in the Roman style (*domus romana*), dining room on the left; Liberati / Bourbon 1996, 65.

terfamilias/οἰκοδεσπότης) or female (*matrona*), also presided at the house liturgy.[7] The same thing could happen here and there in different districts of the city. The result was the development of a plural community and decentralized building activity.[8] All this nowadays goes under the heading of house-church Christianity with its associations

---

7   Meyer 1989, 79; Bowes 2008, 49 f.; Alikin 2010, 69 f.; Wagner 2011, 49; Ebner 2012, 179–186. Particularly in the teaching on ecclesiastical offices, house churches are assumed without question; e.g. Zeller 2002, 187 f.

8   Meyer 1989, 77 is convinced: "The setting for the celebration of the Lord's Supper in primitive Christianity was the community gatherings […], more specifically in the small *house communities* or in the *local community* comprising several house communities."

of domesticity, familiarity and privacy as well as the architectural concepts of a *domus romana*, i.e. the standard Roman private town house (Fig. 10).[9]

The assumption is that every city had a number of private residences, each of which served a group of believers as a place of assembly and worship without losing its character as a family home. The fact is, however, that despite an intensive search, archaeologists have not found a single building that might fit the description of a house church that is given above. The proponents of the house-church theory try to explain this by asserting that private city residences became meeting places for Christian groups without being structurally altered for this purpose. So the triclinium was not converted for the Eucharist or provided with an altar, but instead family meals were held there as well as worship and *agape*. This means that if the house churches were not altered during the phase of mixed profane and sacred use, then it is basically impossible to verify their existence archaeologically.[10] With such arguments, the proponents of the house-church theory divest themselves of any burden of proof and can resign themselves to never being able to discover house churches as they understand them by means of archaeology.[11]

All the more notice was taken of news of the discovery (1920) and excavation (up to 1939) of the ecclesiastical building complex at Dura Europos on the Euphrates, which they claimed in their initial euphoria to be monumental proof that early Christianity spread in the cities in private homes (Fig. 11). In the meantime, people have become distinctly more cautious. Hence we must take a closer look at what Dura really does prove and what it does not.

The building existed for only a short time, between 232/33 and 256/57. It is correct that it was a Christian meeting place in the garrison town of Dura Europos, with its approximately six to eight thousand inhabitants.[12] This is clear from the presence of a baptistery with Old and New Testament frescoes. However, during its Christian use the building was no longer a family residence at all, but served exclusively for Christian worship.[13] There were no longer any residential units, the cistern was sealed, and the latrine was put out of use.[14] The triclinium was deprived of its function and expanded into a hall for the celebration of the Eucharist.[15]

9 On the *domus romana* see MARQUARDT 1886, 213–250; BOWES 2010; CLARKE 2014; SESSA 2018, 84–124.

10 Cf. WHITE 1997, 25; LICCARDO 2005, 25; DOIG 2009, 4.

11 Cf. WAGNER 2011, 31; LAMPE 2003, 368 f.

12 J. GUTMANN, Dura-Europos, in: RBK 1 (1966) 1217–1240.

13 KRAELING 1967, 155; APOLLONJ GHETTI 1978, 503 f.; WHITE 1990, 120 f; BRENK 2003, 69; ADAMS 2013, 89–95; CANTINO WATAGHIN 2014, 586; BRANDT 2016, 17 f.; CIANCA 2018, 91. DE BLAUUW 2008, 285, on the other hand, is of the opinion that the complex probably still served as a dwelling house even after its conversion. There is, however, no evidence to support this.

14 BRENK 2003, 66–68.

15 Although it is not certain that the large room was used for the celebration of the Eucharist, most scholars rightly assume this to have been the case.

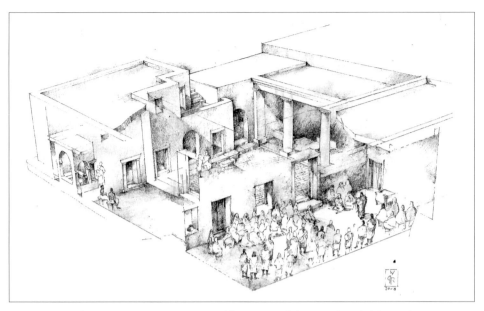

Fig. 11: Church of Dura Europos, Reconstruction of the rooms and their uses by Wladek Prosol; Peppard 2016, 18 Fig. 1.4.

So there can be no question of a mixed use, i.e. both profane and sacred.[16] Although the complex had an ascending staircase, this did not lead to an upper floor with apartments, but, in keeping with how all the houses in the city were built, only onto the roof terrace.[17] A mixed use could at best be assumed before the building's conversion, but there is no indication that it was ever inhabited by Christians before it was converted. But this still does not make the supporters of the house church abandon their theory, and now they claim that Dura Europos proves at least that the church buildings were originally private dwellings, which once – and this is to them the important point – served as a refuge for smallish worship communities.[18] But this remains pure speculation: historiography without sources – as is the statement by Hans-Josef Klauck that "what is present suffices, combined with the written evidence, to validate the existence

16 Even if such a mixed use is repeatedly postulated, for example by Larson-Miller 2006, 16, who speaks of the "division between the remaining private space of the domestic use of the building and the 'public' Christian space."

17 Here Bowes 2008, 49 f. is mistaken. See also Süssenbach 1977, 112.

18 Klauck 1981, 80; W. Gessel, Hauskirche I. Historisch-theologisch, in: LThK³ 4 (1995) 1217 f., here 1217; Stewart 2015, 105. Also Mell 2011, 39 maintains erroneously that with Dura Europos it is possible to provide archaeological proof of the institution of the house church in a private house.

of house churches."[19] L. Michael White is likely to be correct in assuming that from 180 to 200 onwards the Christians had exclusive church rooms (he speaks of "house of the church" = *domus ecclesiae*).[20] There is, however, no proof of his further assumption that such church buildings took the place of private "house churches", so that several church rooms would be expected in every city.[21]

Gisela Cantino Wataghin summarizes the findings with the statement that from an archaeological point of view the "house churches" prove to be in every respect a modern invention. She suggests that in cases like Dura Europos one should speak simply of "churches".[22] For this, it is best to use the Latin term *domus ecclesiae* (church building), which implies neither a specific architecture nor a private status. An instructive comment on this is made by the pagan Porphyry of Tyre (c. 270), according to which Christians erect "very large buildings (οἶκοι)" in which they gather to pray even though they could in fact pray at home in their "private houses" (οἰκίαι).[23] So the prayer houses in which the Christians gather have nothing to do with their private houses. Dura Europos is so far the only church to which an ordinary Roman private house was converted.[24] Otherwise, for the third century one can still point to the oratory at Megiddo near Nazareth (above Fig. 8, below Fig. 18), which is architecturally just a hall (with neither a baptistery nor other worship rooms).

The house-church theory is based on the assumption that Christianity had not only profane but also plural, some say "democratic" beginnings.[25] Christianity, they say, emerged in private circles here and there in the cities. Each householder determined the faith and liturgy of his household community. This led to plural Christianities. The three-tier structure of offices – bishop, presbyters and deacons – that became established throughout the Church from between 90/100 and 150/80 can then be explained sociologically as corresponding to the functions of the house church.[26] Only gradually did the leaders of the various house churches grow together into a unified

19 KLAUCK 1981, 77.
20 WHITE 1990, 4, 118 f.
21 Ibid. 111.
22 CANTINO WATAGHIN 2014, 584–593; SESSA 2009; BRANDT 2016, 15. Cf. WHITE 1990, 111–123. Those who excavated Dura Europos already speak of the church: C. HOPKINS, The Christian Church, in: M. I. ROSTOVTZEFF (ed.), The Excavations at Dura-Europos (New Haven 1934) 238–253. So also BRANDENBURG 2013, 13 f. Yet there is time and again talk of the "house churches of Dura Europos", e.g. YASIN 2012, 937; PEPPARD 2016, 17 f.

The term "house church" can be accepted at most as a – highly contaminated – linguistic convention for pre-basilica worship; CHAVARRÍA ARNAU 2009, 48. Along these lines GAMBER 1968a.
23 Porphyr. adv. Christ. frgm. 76 (HARNACK 1916, 93). SÜSSENBACH 1977, 111 groundlessly considers this passage to be an interpolation.
24 BRENK 2003, 65; MACMULLEN 2009, 3.
25 GEHRING 2004, 27. SNYDER 2003, 299: "It must be stated that the pre-Constantinian Church was remarkably democratic."
26 WAGNER 2011, 49. Cf. CATTANEO 2017, 82 f.

presbyterium and, in the latter half of the second century, for practical reasons, seek a superordinate leader, namely the bishop.[27] In principle, this follows a very schematic interpretive model already established by Jerome: at the beginning, all presbyters were equal; only in order to avoid divisions did they elect from their midst a bishop as a superordinate authority.[28]

But how likely is such a scenario? If it is merely a question of whether a college of presbyters acting and celebrating the Eucharist together elects a leader and calls him a bishop, then this is easily conceivable. But if it is a question of several house-church presbyters in a city first functioning autonomously in their respective congregations and then at some point handing over their power to a central bishop, then it is quite inconceivable. For the fact is that in the second and third centuries the bishop everywhere possessed sole authority over the Christians of his city. How could there have been autonomous house churches before this? If such house churches had ever existed, why did no presbyter in the third and fourth centuries ever question the oppressive authority of the bishop, using the original autonomy of the house churches as an argument? Has it ever been seen in Church history that independent religious groups – call them house churches, sects or denominations – at some point unanimously joined together in a city, renounced their independence and looked for a boss who now decided everything and even claimed sole responsibility over the money? And is this exactly what is supposed to have happened in the case of the house churches, silently and simultaneously, in every city in the world? Is it not instead both psychologically and sociologically always the case that in the beginning there is unity, which then disintegrates through strife and resentment?[29]

In addition, there is the following objection: if there were numerous house churches in every city, then these house churches must all have had their own liturgical books for their autonomous liturgy – and there were quite a lot of these. For in practice every house church had to possess the books of the Holy Scriptures of the Old Testament. After all, the Old Testament was quite simply the text and prayer book of the first Christians. But is it conceivable that every house church possessed a copy of the complete set of Old Testament books, or at least of the Pentateuch, which is in itself extremely substantial? What might that have cost? How many decades might it have taken for

---

27 ZELLER 2002, 187 f. Whether the house churches belonged to the sub-unit of the city's total community is a matter of dispute among the adherents of the house-church theory; GIELEN 1995, 1216.

28 Hieron. ep. 146,1,6 (CSEL 56,1, 310); comm. in Tit. 1,5 (CCL 77C, 14). BARLEA 1975, 160 f. Cf. U. DELL'ORTO / S. XERES (eds.), Manuale di Storia della Chiesa 1 (Lavis 2018) 81 f.

29 On the apostolic and thus uniform origin of the city communities see ZIZIOULAS 2001, 59 – 68.

each house church to acquire such a library of hundreds of scrolls? Or are people going to try to claim that the reason why Marcion did away with the Old Testament was that the house churches could not afford it? The true scenario will have been that the cost of acquiring the sacred books – which on account of their frequent use and being read in public had to be of high quality and to have an easily legible script – was something the Christians took upon themselves to procure only once in every city; this will then have been for the central act of worship of the city's entire community, which joined together to pay for them. Despite this, there will naturally still also have been individual biblical books circulating in private hands, especially among philosophers (apologists) and theological teachers.[30]

In the end, the question of whether or not such a thing as house churches ever existed is simply a matter of calculations. Take Rome, for example: according to current archaeological knowledge, there are an impressive 1,790 *domus* spread throughout the city.[31] Traditionally, researchers have reckoned that there were twenty-five house churches in the third century.[32] If each comprises twenty to forty people, this yields a total of five hundred to one thousand Christians. One could further speculate that two dozen rich Christians headed these house churches and celebrated the liturgy in spacious halls with many people.[33] On the other hand, the rule of thumb for reclining meals is: "seven a symposium, nine a pandemonium" or "seven guests a meal, nine an ordeal".[34] In this case, one would have to expect a hundred house churches or more. But whether it was twenty-five or one hundred, the chances of finding archaeological evidence of one of these house churches in one of the 1,790 *domus* must be fairly high. So why has not a single one been found? While there are generally no written sources for house churches, from about 200 onwards the texts do speak of large meeting rooms or church gatherings, and surprisingly only ever of one per city (below chapter III, 2). Finding the one large place of assembly in a city from the pre-Constantinian period is therefore far less likely than coming across one of the many house churches. After all, in Dura Europos the bishop's church was found, but not any house churches; nor were any found in Rome. This archaeological deficit in Rome is detrimental to the house-church theory.

It is not only fundamental considerations of this kind that cast doubt on the house-church theory. Its central defect is the lack of any evidence at all in the written sources.

---

30 HARNACK 1912 sees the spread of the biblical books too optimistically. Cf. WRIGHT 2017.

31 GUIDOBALDI 1993, 75. This number applies to the time of Constantine.

32 Occasionally Rome's 25 titular churches are cited in support of this conjecture: LP 3,1 (DUCHESNE 1886, 122): *Hic ex praecepto beati Petri XXV presbiteros ordinavit in urbe Roma.* Ibid. 6,2 (126): *Hic titulos in urbe Roma dividit presbiteris.*

33 So GUIDOBALDI 1993, 75.

34 DÖLGER 1943, 587.

There is not a single contemporary text that clearly speaks of house churches. House churches in the sense outlined above thus turn out to be a veritable scientific delusion, a paper construct that belongs in the wastepaper basket. And that is exactly where it has been sent by Georg Schöllgen (1988) and, particularly vigorously, by Edward Adams (2013).[35] Even if new defenders of the house churches keep on appearing, they do not present any better arguments, but merely pile further hypotheses onto an already shaky edifice. So although Roger W. Gehring assembles every mention of a house in the New Testament into a grand picture of early Christian mission history, he nevertheless fails to provide any compelling evidence.[36] Nor is it any help to try to explain away the "low number [!] of mentions (of house churches) in the New Testament" by contending that Paul sacrificed them to his theological concept of unity.[37] You cannot do both: make Paul the key witness for house churches (see below) and at the same time make him their betrayer! However, some people are evidently disinclined to bid farewell to an historical narrative that has long since laid claim to canonical validity and has calamitously found its way into all the handbooks and encyclopaedias on Church history and archaeology.[38]

To avoid any misunderstandings: it goes without saying that the early Christians, too, lived in houses and not in caves. Of course, the New Testament writings mention houses and also residential dwellings any number of times. Of course, Christians met up in private houses and prayed together. Of course, there were wealthy Christians who could afford their own homes and welcomed Christians there (Rm 16:5; 1 Cor 16:15, etc.). Even bishops can be heads of households (*paterfamilias*) (1 Tm 3:5). Of course, the apocryphal literature is full of encounters of the apostles with householders. Of course, the apostles and missionaries preached in houses (Acts 5:42), schools (Acts 19:9) and barns,[39] just as Jesus frequented the homes of wealthy families such as those of Matthew the tax collector (Mt 9:10) and his friends in Bethany (Jn 11:20). And Paul undoubtedly endeavoured to win whole "houses" for the Christian faith.[40]

But there is nothing to support the claim that the Eucharist was celebrated in such private houses. Jesus did not celebrate the Last Supper in the house of a family with

---

35 Schöllgen 1988; Adams 2013.

36 Gehring 2004. Similarly Mell 2011, 37–51. In my opinion, some people rely too heavily on the translations of the Pauline texts produced by proponents of the house-church theory. Hence, in spite of many good observations, the theory of sacred house churches in Cianca 2018, 22–27 is left hanging in the air.

37 Wagner 2011, 39 f.

38 E.g. Quacquarelli 1977, 239; K.-H. Bieritz / C. Kähler, Haus III. (Altes Testament / Neues Testament / Kirchengeschichtlich / Praktisch-theologisch), in: TRE 14 (1985) 478–492, here 484 f.; Dassmann 1986, 891–894; Osiek 2002, 97–100; Liccardo 2005, 22 f.; de Blaauw 2008, 283 f.; Metzger 2015, 190–195, 309–328; Kritzinger 2016, 24–27. Öhler 2016a shows the weaknesses of the house-church theory yet still speaks of "the role of house churches as pillars of early Christianity." Cf. *id.* 2016b, 539.

39 Cf. Leppin 2018, 122 f.

40 Gielen 1986, 118.

whom he was friendly, but rather in a specially rented upper room (Mk 14:14 f.). Paul also held the (eucharistic) assembly in Troas in a (rented) upper room (Acts 20:7 f.). A private house is probably the precise place where the gathering for the Lord's Supper in Corinth was *not* held (1 Cor 11:22; 14:35); rather, it took place in premises belonging to the community. Nor did any persecutors drive the Christians into the seclusion of small groups, private houses, and catacombs. The myth of the "church of the catacombs" and clandestine services in private houses was put about by the Roman legend-writers of the fifth and sixth centuries and to this day still has its adherents among, of all circles, the scientific community. In reality, no one prevented the Christians from going openly and honestly from all parts of the city to the bishop's central act of worship.[41]

To this extent, there is no evidence for the theory that church- and worship-centres developed from private houses in the various parts of the city and that the house church was the matrix of primitive Christian mission, identity and liturgy. In any case, we need to take a closer look at what the claim that the Eucharist was celebrated in a private city residence means and can actually say. Naturally, a (former) city residence may have served the bishop as a place of worship. But those who gathered there were not a private, select circle, but rather members of the whole city community (local church), i.e. from among all the Christians irrespective of rank, nation and age. This was already true in the earliest, apostolic period. For the very fact that there was no house-church structure in the early Church, but instead everyone across all the social strata came together for a single act of worship, explains the social tensions that already appeared in Paul's time at the community's worship in Corinth.[42] Viewed in this light, it is coincidental and immaterial whether or not the meeting takes place in a private house. A rented or purchased hall is equally possible. On the other hand, no support is to be found in the texts for intimate group Eucharists.[43]

This is not the place to present and refute all the arguments of the proponents of the house-church theory, even though they keep on citing the same texts and differ only in the boldness of their deductions. Basically, they model their image on isolated and ambiguous statements from the Acts of the Apostles which suggest that the Christian mission began in Jerusalem in the "houses" where they celebrated the Eucharist at the same time as the main evening meal.[44] Something similar is suggested by the Revised

---

41 There is authentic evidence for the public nature of churchgoing. See below p. 114 f.

42 Cf. Jas 2:2: "For if a person with gold rings and in fine clothes comes into your assembly, and if a poor person in dirty clothes also comes in [...]"

43 Despite his balanced approach, Messner 2003a, 360 f., 421 also seems to espouse the idyll of a house-church liturgy.

44 Wieland 1906, 28–31; Saxer 1988, 168; Neunheuser 1988, 37; Wagner 2011, 40 f.

Standard Version Catholic Edition (RSVCE), which translates the verse in question as: "Day by day, attending the temple together and breaking bread in their homes, they partook of food with glad and generous hearts" (Acts 2:46).[45] But in what houses, when "all who owned lands or houses sold them" and gave the proceeds to the apostles (Acts 4:34 f.)? And does the "breaking of bread" (Acts 2:42) here, at least inclusively, also mean the Eucharist since Jesus "broke bread" at the last meal in Jerusalem (Mt 26:26) and the Risen Lord "took bread, blessed and broke it" at Emmaus (Lk 24:30)? This cannot be ruled out as Acts also speaks of meeting "to break bread" on Sundays (Acts 20:7).[46]

But Luke scarcely envisages a primitive community in Jerusalem spread out across worship held in houses. His ideal goes in exactly in the opposite direction: "the whole group of those who believed were of one heart and soul" (Acts 4:32) and gathers with one accord "at home/in a house" (κατ᾽ οἶκον) – not "in their homes" – just as they all meet in the temple (Acts 2:46; 5:42).[47] What is meant by the latter is a gathering within the temple precincts, for example in Solomon's Portico (Acts 3:11; 5:12). Accordingly, the assembly "at home/in a house" can refer to a spacious private house with a garden.[48] If the thousands of newly converted Christians (Acts 2:41) make it seem unrealistic for them to assemble in a single building, this is surely only due to a narrow understanding of house. In any case, Luke is not thinking of a multiplicity of house churches, but rather of a single, relatively large house in Jerusalem (cf. Acts 12:12 f.),[49] in which the upper room might then also possibly be found (Acts 1:13; 2:1), which likewise served as a meeting place and held 120 people (Acts 1:15). It is quite astonishing for Marcel Metzger to know that this number is to be understood purely symbolically because a hall in Troas similar to the upper room holds scarcely more than twenty people.[50] In this, he underestimates the architectural skills of antiquity.[51] It is correct that apart from this large house in Jerusalem there was another circle that gathered around James (Acts 12:17). But whether this was a "household", as is claimed,[52] and whether a separate eucharistic community was formed there, are matters of pure speculation. Luke himself rather assumes a single worship community in Jerusalem. Accordingly, he speaks of "the church in Jerusalem", to which "all", including the apostles, belong (Acts 8:1; cf. 5:11),[53] just as there is only one local community each in the mission cities

45 καθ᾽ ἡμέραν τε προσκαρτεροῦντες ὁμοθυμαδὸν ἐν τῷ ἱερῷ, κλῶντές τε κατ᾽ οἶκον ἄρτον, μετελάμβανον τροφῆς ἐν ἀγαλλιάσει.
46 Cf. Nussbaum 1996 (1974), 122f., 126; Lang 2022, 30.
47 Schöllgen 1988, 79; Zizioulas 2001, 91f. Cf. Boguniowski 1987, 18–29.
48 Cf. Öhler 2017.
49 Cf. Klauck 1981, 48f.
50 Metzger 1998, 28f.
51 Correctly Gehring 2004, 65f.
52 Cf. Mell 2011, 39.
53 On the structure of the primitive community in Jerusalem, but without any discussion of its worship, see Riesner 2012.

of the diaspora.[54] In Miletus, Paul meets "the elders of the (local) church" of Ephesus (Acts 20:17) and reminds them that in Ephesus he taught them "publicly and in houses (κατ᾽οἴκους)" (Acts 20:20). With this he is saying no more and no less than that he preached equally in public places and in private rooms. There is no mention of a house church or multiple house churches.[55]

It is necessary to distinguish from the Acts texts that do not contain any indication of house churches four passages in the Pauline epistles which do seem to speak explicitly of house churches, enabling L. Michael White to say: "If the house church setting was basic to the social fabric of Paul's mission, it was also the center of assembly and worship within the local group."[56] Of course, if the antecedent clause falls, then the consequent clause falls, too. This means that if the house-church theory collapses, then there is no longer any point in asserting the existence of a private house-church liturgy either. And indeed, there is not a single passage in which Paul mentions house churches, so the whole theory collapses completely as there is no evidence for house churches outside Paul either. Hence it is vitally important to look closely at these four passages and thus put an end to the spectre of house churches once and for all.

In Paul's letters the phrase ἡ κατ᾽οἶκον ἐκκλησία is found four times (Rm 16:5; 1 Cor 16:19; Col 4:15; Phlm 2), but is not used by any other writer:

1. Ἀσπάσασθε […] καὶ τὴν κατ᾽οἶκον αὐτῶν ἐκκλησίαν (Rm 16:5).
   RSVCE: Greet also the church in their (= Prisca's and Aquila's) house.
2. ἀσπάζεται ὑμᾶς ἐν κυρίῳ πολλὰ Ἀκύλας καὶ Πρίσκα σὺν τῇ κατ᾽οἶκον αὐτῶν ἐκκλησίᾳ (1 Cor 16:19).
   RSVCE: Aquila and Prisca, together with the church in their house, send you hearty greetings in the Lord.
3. Ἀσπάσασθε […] καὶ Νύμφαν καὶ τὴν κατ᾽οἶκον αὐτῆς ἐκκλησίαν (Col 4:15).
   RSVCE: Give my greetings […] to Nympha and the church in her house.
4. Παῦλος […] Φιλήμονι […] καὶ τῇ κατ᾽οἶκόν σου ἐκκλησίᾳ (Phm 1 f.).
   RSVCE: Paul […] to Philemon […] and the church in your house.

In its interpretation of the four passages, the Revised Standard Version Catholic Edition follow the standard exegetical commentaries[57] – with dire consequences. For it is on

---

54 Acts 13:1 (Antioch); 14:21–23 (Derbe, Lystra, Iconium, Antioch); 14:27 (Antioch); 16:14 f. (cities of Lycaonia); 18:22 (Caesarea); 20:17 (Ephesus).

55 Differently WIELAND 1906, 32; GEHRING 2004, 143 f.

56 WHITE 1996, 107.

57 E.g. SCHLIER 1977, 443.

these four Pauline passages alone that the whole theory of house churches or house communities is based, a theory that now enjoys the widest authority as a result of how the passages are translated into various vernacular languages. This lays a false trail. For the texts yield nothing of the kind. The term "house church" or "house community" does not appear in either Acts or Paul or anywhere else in the New Testament. But if the term is absent, then so is the thing itself: the New Testament does not refer to any house churches![58]

The seemingly unambiguous term "house church" or "house community" (house church/church in the household, *casa-chiesa/chiesa domestica*, *Hauskirche*, etc.) is a recent academic coinage,[59] and, what is more, a quite audacious translation of the expression ἡ κατ᾿ οἶκον ἐκκλησία, which then tends to be labelled as the Pauline house-church formula. This suggests that the house church is an institution to be taken for granted and one that already has its own "formula". Instead of just "house church", others translate the expression with "the church in/at their/her/your house"[60] or "the church that meets in their house". They think that each of the cities of the Pauline mission had several such house churches or house communities with their own worship services. Although Ioannis Zizioulas wants to retain the unity of the city's Eucharist, he nevertheless claims, based on the house-church formula, that at the time this central service was celebrated exclusively in Christian houses.

Zizioulas and Marlis Gielen before him are right in saying that for Paul there is only one local community that meets within a city for common worship (below chapter III, 2).[61] It is not even out of the question that it might meet in the house of a rich Christian. But the supposed house-church formula is in itself no proof of such a local community, nor of there being many particular communities, and certainly not of a celebration of the Eucharist since not one of the four passages contains any mention of a worship gathering.[62] Therefore, and also from looking at the closer context, one must

---

58 SCHLOEDER 2012, 14.
59 SESSA 2009, 90 f.
60 WHITE 1990, 4.
61 GIELEN 1986; *id.* 2019; ZIZIOULAS 2001, 49–52. Even if one wanted to go against all probability and stick to the idea of a house church, all that could be found in Paul would be at most one ἐκκλησία κατ᾿ οἶκον per city. Rm 16:5; 1 Cor 16:19; Col 4:5; Phlm 2. This is confirmed by the plural in Acts 8:3 and 20:20. GIELEN 1986, 121; SCHÖLLGEN 1988, 78; ZIZIOULAS 2001, 90 f.
62 Cf. GIELEN 1986, 120 f.; SCHÖLLGEN 1988, 79. MESSNER 2003a, 360 sees correctly that ἐκκλησία

in the so-called house-church formulae also means the gathering (not necessarily the community), but he fails to draw the right conclusions and thinks that the Eucharist was celebrated in these houses. There is no evidence to support the consistent association of the Pauline "house churches" with the celebration of the Eucharist (e.g. BOGUNIOWSKI 1987, 50; ZIZIOULAS 2001, 90 f.); there at best the speculation that the "Lord's Supper" in Corinth (1 Cor 11:20) took place in a "house church" (e.g. WHITE 1990, 107–109; *id.* 2016, 467), but that, too, is no more than a construction (see below p. 98 f.).

instead assume that what Paul means by ἐκκλησία in the passages in question is not the "church" (or community) at all.[63] After all, in everyday language ἐκκλησία – in a similar way to συναγωγή – is first of all and before taking on any religious colouring simply the "assembly",[64] both the city assembly as well as just a gathering of people whose scope is, if necessary, specified by an attribute.[65] And indeed, why should Paul not occasionally retain the profane usage of ἐκκλησία in his letters?

So Paul uses ἐκκλησία in different ways: one time for "church", another time for just an "assembly".[66] In the first case, by analogy with the civic assembly of the polis,[67] he means the entirety of the Christians in a city when he speaks of, for example, the ἐκκλησία (singular) at Cenchreae and in Corinth and of the ἐκκλησία of the Laodiceans and the Thessalonians (Rm 16:1; 1 Cor 1:2; 10:32; Col 4:16; 1 Thes 1:1). His letters are thus not addressed to private individuals, but rather to the ἐκκλησία of the respective city, namely to the assembly of the local community in which these very letters are to be read. When he has the cities of a whole region in mind, he speaks appropriately of "the churches" in the plural: "of the Gentiles" (Rm 16:4), "of Galatia" (1 Cor 16:1; Gal 1:2), "of Asia" (1 Cor 16:19), "of Macedonia" (2 Cor 8:1) and "of Judea" (1 Thes 2:14).[68] The ἐκκλησία is thus for Paul first of all and fundamentally the (worship) assembly of the whole local church, i.e. of all the baptised in a city. This is clearly a case of ecclesiological terminology.

In two of the four passages containing a "house-church formula" Paul also speaks first of such an ἐκκλησία as a local church, but then immediately afterwards of the ἐκκλησία κατ᾽οἶκον (Rm 16:4 f.; 1 Cor 16:19). Here the change of meaning of ἐκκλησία is obvious, namely the change from ecclesiastical to everyday usage. To indicate this change, Paul adds two attributes to ἐκκλησία: κατ᾽οἶκον and a possessive pronoun. It now refers to a mere assembly, and specifically to the ἐκκλησία-assembly in a private house. This conjures up the idea of the community of a grand household: the head of the house and his wife, the clients, slaves, freed men and women and the *familiares*.[69] The fact that all four references are greetings might support this: Paul is either greeting a household or send-

---

63 This mistake is also made by Klauck 1981, 21 and frequently; he is then followed by many others: Lampe 2003, 193, 398 and frequently; Bogunio-wski 1987, 50–62; Brent 1995, 398; Oberlinner 2007, 304 f.; Penna 2009, 191; Alikin 2010, 49–51; Mell 2011, 42; Wagner 2011, 35–37; Adams 2013, 18–21.

64 F. Montanari, The Brill Dictionary of Ancient Greek (Leiden / Boston 2015) 632; cf. Mohrmann 1962, 161; Gielen 1986, 119. White 1997, 28

sees correctly that *ecclesia* is originally simply the gathering, not necessarily the Christian gathering, but fails to apply this insight to the alleged house churches in Paul; White 1990, 104–110.

65 Cf. gielen 1986, 119.

66 Long 2018, 204.

67 Cf. Peterson 2010.

68 See below p. 96.

69 Hitherto I have advocated above all for this possibility: Heid 2019a, 82; *id.*, 2019c, 7 f.

ing greetings from one. This is a matter of courtesy and has nothing to do with whether the members of the household are Christians or pagans.

But there is another way of understanding the ἐκκλησία κατ᾽οἶκον, one that leads in a somewhat different direction and is actually more likely. According to this reading, Paul is greeting not so much a stable household community as rather his missionary co-workers who are guests of a Christian householder.[70] Paul was not a lone missionary, but was, as it were, his own logistics enterprise. He had numerous co-workers and engaged in an extensive and expensive correspondence and travel activity. He and his co-workers were constantly on the move, and a good deal of their travelling also has to do with the contact via letter between the local churches. He writes his letters during his extended stays in various cities in Greece and Asia Minor. Paul, his co-workers and the other missionaries depend on the hospitality of local Christians (according to Jesus's missionary method: Lk 10:1–7). Paul seems to refer to such groups of missionaries lodging in a house as ἐκκλησία κατ᾽οἶκον.

This is most clearly seen in the Letter to the Romans. Paul sends greetings from Corinth, which is where he writes the letter, from "all the ἐκκλησίαι of Christ" (Rm 16:16) "to all God's beloved in Rome, who are called to be saints" (Rm 1:7). These are not private greetings; here Paul is conveying the greetings of the local churches of the mission territories in Greece and Asia Minor (the churches of the Gentiles in Rm 16:4) to the local church in Rome. This is intended to flatter the Romans: all the cities of the eastern orbit send their greetings to the capital! Then, at the end of the letter, there are again greetings to the Christian community of Rome, this time from individuals, namely his missionary companions: from Timothy, Lucius, Jason and Sosipater, as well as from his scribe Tertius (Rm 16:21 f.) and finally from Gaius, of whom Paul says that he (in his house) in Corinth "is host to me and to the whole ἐκκλησία": Γάϊος ὁ ξένος μου καὶ ὅλης τῆς ἐκκλησίας (Rm 16:23).[71] This is not a matter of "eucharistic" hospitality, as if Gaius had invited the entire local Christian community (ὅλης τῆς ἐκκλησίας) to the Eucharist, but rather a matter of civic hospitality: for weeks Gaius has apparently hosted Paul's entire missionary team (ὅλης τῆς ἐκκλησίας), i.e. the assemblage of those who are passing through Corinth with Paul.[72] Since Paul and his company stayed for many weeks and Gaius apparently did not ask for any money (cf. 1 Cor 9:1–18; 2 Thes 3:9), his hospitality

---

70 Paul does actually prefer to greet only the Christians in a house (Rm 16:11).

71 Ξένος is here manifestly not the "guest" but rather the "host", as practically all commentators see correctly. Only KLOPPENBORG 2017 sees it differently.

72 SCHLIER 1977, 451. This removes the need for other more complicated interpretations, e.g. that of ADAMS 2013, 27–29.

is specifically praised – also in order to commend similar hospitality to the Romans when his missionary teams come to Rome.

This offers a key to understanding the supposed house church (ἐκκλησία κατ᾽ οἶκον) in Rm 16:5. First of all, it is important to note that this verse is found within a particular section, namely Rm 16:1–15, which is a greeting. It is normally supposed that Paul is asking the Christians in Rome to greet certain members of their community or of the house churches there in his name.[73] Since Paul had never been to Rome, it is assumed that he knew most of these people from his own missionary work in the East. But that would be very strange: so many Romans are supposed to have met and helped Paul in his missions and are now all back living in Rome? An argument against this is the fact that they would then hear the greetings themselves when the letter was read out (during worship) and would, as it were, have to pass them on to themselves.[74] On closer inspection, however, it becomes clear that Paul is not asking the Roman Christians to greet the list of members of the community *from him* at all. Rather, he is urging the Roman community to "welcome" (ἀσπάζεσθαι) guests from outside, namely his missionary helpers (Rm 16:1–7, 13 f.) when they arrive in Rome from Greece or Asia Minor. Paul wants to impress the Christians of the capital with his long list: look, I have all these co-workers and fellow campaigners, both men and women – including whole groups of people (Rm 16:10 f., 13 f., 15) – in my mission cities, and they are all setting off for Rome!

This is the context into which the greetings to the ἐκκλησία κατ᾽ οἶκον (Rm 16:5) fit. Hence they do not refer to the house community, but to the missionary team sent by Paul who lodge in a house. First of all, Paul uses ἐκκλησία for the city community or local church at the beginning of the list of greetings when he speaks of the "ἐκκλησία in Cenchreae" (Rm 16:1) and of "all the ἐκκλησίαι of the (regions of the) Gentiles" (Rm 16:4). This is the immediate context of the sentence "Greet Prisca and Aquila, who work with me in Christ Jesus […]. Greet also the ἐκκλησία in their house (καὶ τὴν κατ᾽ οἶκον αὐτῶν ἐκκλησίαν)" (Rm 16:3–5). Prisca and Aquila also help Paul as missionaries, accompanying him to the various cities over a long period of time. They continue to own a house in Rome. Both now want to travel to Rome for a time. And because they have their house there, they make it available to the other participants in the journey. The "ἐκκλησία in their house" is thus a temporary house community, namely the group of all those guests who accompany Prisca and Aquila to Rome. It is Paul's wish that when both the couple and their guests attend the worship of the whole community in Rome, they will be formally welcomed by the Christians there.

---

73 Schlier 1977, 442.   74 Ibid. 443.

Prisca and Aquila not only own a house in Rome, but have meanwhile settled in Ephesus. The missionaries likewise stay in their house there: Apollos (Acts 18:26) and Paul along with his co-workers (Acts 18:19–21; 1 Cor 16:17). In the literature, this house, too, is often styled a house church, but there are no grounds for this. What it says in the greetings addressed to the "church of God in Corinth" (1 Cor 1:2) at the end of the First Letter to the Corinthians, which was itself written in Ephesus, is merely: "The ἐκκλησίαι of Asia send greetings. Aquila and Prisca, together with the ἐκκλησία in their house, greet you warmly in the Lord" (1 Cor 16:19). Here, too, two uses of the word ἐκκλησία are directly juxtaposed. First, it is clearly the local church that is meant, but then it is the gathering of the missionaries – Paul's co-workers (1 Cor 16:17) – in the house of Aquila and Prisca.

In the Letter to the Colossians, too, the alleged house-church formula is encountered in the concluding list of greetings. Once again, there is an announcement that several of Paul's co-workers will be arriving in Colossae (Col 4:8–10). It can also be assumed that the other persons who seem to be known to the Christians in Colossae will be arriving soon (e.g. Epaphras – Col 4:12). Then follows the sentence: "Give my greetings to the brothers in Laodicea, and to Nympha and the ἐκκλησία in her house" (Col 4:15). Laodicea, like Colossae and Hierapolis, belongs to Epaphras's mission territory (Col 4:13). There seems to be regular contact between Colossae and Laodicea, so Paul can assume that his greetings will soon reach Laodicea. There, however, he distinguishes two addressees of his greetings: the "brothers in Laodicea" and the ἐκκλησία in the house of Nympha. What is meant by the "brothers in Laodicea" (cf. Col 1:2) is the local church, the "ἐκκλησία of the Laodiceans" (Col 4:16), from which the ἐκκλησία in the house of Nympha clearly has to be distinguished. It is therefore unacceptable to claim that the local church of Laodicea gathered for worship in the house of Nympha. Rather, it has to be assumed that, as in the other cases, Nympha's house was a mission station. Epaphras and his co-workers probably stayed there during their visits. Such visits are linked to the correspondence. For Paul writes: "And when this letter has been read among you (in Colossae), have it read also in the ἐκκλησία of the Laodiceans; and see that you read also the letter from Laodicea" (Col 4:16). The letters are therefore read out to the whole local community (in its worship) – by no means just to a house community.

The fourth alleged house-church formula is in the Letter to Philemon. Here it is found in the list of addressees: "Paul […], to Philemon our dear friend and co-worker, to Apphia our sister, to Archippus our fellow-soldier, and to the ἐκκλησία in your house" (Phlm 1 f.). It is clear that Philemon owns a house in Colossae (cf. Col 4:9). But is this a house church? There is no indication of that. Instead, we once again have to assume that it refers to a company of missionaries residing there temporarily. For Onesimus himself is one of Paul's co-workers on his missionary journeys, which means that he only uses his house in Colossae intermittently (Phlm 1; Col 4:9). Then or on other occasions he apparently puts it at the disposal of missionary friends (Phlm 2; Col 4:8 f.).

So there is much to suggest that the ἐκκλησία κατ᾽οἶκον is to be sought very specifically in the historical setting of Paul's mission and refers to a temporary house community of missionaries. That then explains why this linguistic usage disappears with the end of the Pauline mission. Although it is conceivable that the Christians of Rome or Colossae met together for the Eucharist in the houses that Paul greets, there is no proof that this was ever the case. In no way do the texts provide any grounds for speaking of a house-community substructure in the local churches with autonomous worship and community centres – that is to say, "house churches".

If Paul's wording itself does not support the idea of house churches, then other considerations, too, should long since have raised doubts as to the existence of such institutions. It is, for example, striking that none of the early writers, beginning with Paul, gives any indication of what is to happen if the worship gathering becomes too large. They do not set an upper limit, yet one would quickly be reached at a reclining meal in a house church for reasons of space.[75] There is never any mention of a growing house church having to be divided into further house churches. The authors take it for granted that in any case only one "table of the Lord" or "altar" is used irrespective of the number of participants. Especially in view of the tensions and factions in Corinth (1 Cor 1:11 f.), Paul could easily have told those who were not happy with an all-too- modest Lord's Supper to move to another house church. But all he says is that the insatiable should eat at home and then come together for the Lord's Supper ἐπὶ τὸ αὐτό (in one place) (1 Cor 11:22; 14:23). So it appears that there is only one opportunity to partake of the "Lord's Table".[76] The Letter to the Hebrews, too, sees the exclusive right as lying with the "altar", from which the Judaizers who participate in Jewish cultic meals are not permitted to eat (Heb 13:10). Why does the Letter to the Hebrews not simply say that those who do not wish to renounce Jewish cultic meals should look for another house church, one that is more liberal? Ignatius says even more bluntly that it is only from the one altar that one receives a share in God's bread, indeed in God himself.[77] So every table or altar fellowship tries to preserve its unity without ever thinking of dividing into smaller groups.

The pre-Constantinian church authors, too, remain persistently silent about house churches. But if Paul and the Acts of the Apostles do, as is claimed, almost systematically bind the early Christian mission to a network of private houses, why do we never

---

75 MESSNER 2003a, 361 limits the number of participants to fifteen for a triclinium; if more were present, several reclining groups would have to be set up. This would amount to perhaps a few dozen people.

76 GIELEN 1986, 114.
77 Ign. ad Eph. 5,2 (SC 10³, 72–74); ad Trall. 7,1 f. (116).

hear anything about this in the later literature?[78] Did the entire body of apocryphal and Church literature from the First Letter of Clement right down to Origen engage in a conspiracy of silence about these once flourishing institutions?[79] Are the bishops from Ignatius of Antioch[80] to Eusebius of Caesarea supposed to have exercised some kind of blanket censorship?[81] Did they, despite all their immense biblical and historical knowledge, omit to mention the house churches? The reason for their silence is simple: house churches never existed. Furthermore, by then the connotation of the word ἐκκλησία was almost exclusively that of "church", so that the Pauline formula ἐκκλησία κατ᾽οἶκον no longer made any real sense. Although Origen († c. 254), in his commentary on the Letter to the Romans, still understands the supposed house-church formula (Rm 16:5) in its proper sense, i.e. as meaning just the household consisting of masters and servants, later authors clearly have considerably more problems with it. [82]

However, the absence in any shape or form of house churches in the early Christian literature does not deter the proponents of the house-church theory.[83] They point out that since Origen,[84] anyway since Eusebius of Caesarea († 339), the use of language has changed and now one speaks of the οἶκος ἐκκλησίας / *domus ecclesiae* instead of the ἐκκλησία κατ᾽οἶκον and means with this the house churches.[85] But that is just another dubious hypothesis. There were no "house churches" for Paul, and so it is impossible to draw a line from the Pauline ἐκκλησία κατ᾽οἶκον to the later use of the word οἶκος

78 KLAUCK 1981, 62; SCHLOEDER 2012, 14.

79 Against WIELAND 1906, 67–69 the Apocryphal Acts of the Apostles do not have any house churches, and the Philopatris dialogue does not produce anything either. Cf. KLAUCK 1981, 72 f.

80 On Ignatius's alleged battle against house churches (KRITZINGER 2016, 32; KLAUCK 1981, 62) see below p. 99 f.

81 The well-known passage Euseb. mart. Pal. 13,1 (SC 55, 170) is translated incorrectly by A. BIGELMAIR (BKV Euseb. 1, 308): "so that they converted houses into churches." The correct translation is: "so that they erected buildings for the church assemblies" (cf. SC 55, 170). Orig. in Ex. hom. 12,2 (SC 321, 358) does not offer much either: *ecclesia* for the worship room and *dominica domus* for the whole complex of annexe rooms? There is no indication whatsoever that Origin is referring to "private houses with multiple rooms" – so FRANK 1997, 123 and ZELLER 2002, 330. Trad. Apost. 35 (FC 1, 292); 41 (298): are church and place of catechesis identical?

82 Orig. comm. in Rom. 16,5 (FC 2,5, 246): [*hospitalitas*] *non solum in voluntate et proposito dominorum, sed et grato ac fideli constitit ministerio famulorum. idcirco omnes, qui ministerium istud*

cum ipsis [*dominis*] *fideliter adimplebant*, '*domesticam eorum' nominavit* 'ecclesiam'. Instead of *ecclesia domestica* the Greek original undoubtedly had ἡ κατ᾽οἶκον ἐκκλησία. Rufinus's Latin translation follows the Greek text faithfully, but the result is to make it incomprehensible since *ecclesia*, unlike ἐκκλησία, has the established meaning of "church". Later Greek commentators interpret the ἐκκλησία κατ᾽οἶκον as if Paul were calling the house community in question, on account of their virtue, a quasi "church of its own"; Joh. Chrys. in Rom. hom. 30,3 (PG 60, 664); CRAMER 1967, 343.

83 The texts cited by MELL 2011, 50–53 in support of house churches in the second and third centuries have no value whatsoever as evidence.

84 Orig. in Ex. hom. 2,2 (SC 321, 76): *domos ecclesiae faciant*. The Greek original has unfortunately not survived, so the passage remains uncertain.

85 Euseb. hist. eccl. 7,30,19 (SC 41, 219); 8,13,13 (SC 55, 31); 9,9,11 (67). In vit. Const. 3,43,3 (SC 559, 404) the term sounds too banal to him, so that he adds the attribute "holy" to it. Even later witnesses for the *domus ecclesiae*: Chrom. Aquil. tract. in Math. 19,4 (CCL 9A, 289); Gaud. Brix. serm. 2,11 (CSEL 68, 26); 4,10 f. (41).

ἐκκλησίας. And there is no question of being unable to translate οἶκος ἐκκλησίας as "house church". The only permissible translation is "church house" or "church building".[86] It is certainly not as if this were a case of an older way of speaking or even a memory of actual "house churches" from apostolic times.[87] Although it is seemingly just a matter of switching round two words, there is a world of difference between "house church" and "church house"! There never were house churches, but there were church buildings; hence an historical evolution from house churches to church buildings can be ruled out.[88] Even if Eusebius speaks of the confessors in the copper mines in Palestine converting "houses" (οἶκοι) into churches (ἐκκλησίαι),[89] such formulations do not display any connection with alleged house churches in the New Testament. What is more, the house terminology from Paul to Eusebius does not permit any conclusions to be drawn with respect to architecture.[90] The term "house" is not limited to the standard-design private Roman city residence (domus romana).

2. ONE CHURCH PER CITY

If there were no house churches in the aforesaid sense, then what was there? This question has been left unspoken in the background in our deliberations so far. Can one reject the house-church theory even though there appears to be no alternative? After all, Christianity must somehow have organised itself in the cities and developed a community life. First, we have to dispose of the false implications of the house-church theory. For if the construct of house churches goes, then the connection between private and community life goes with it. Then there is nothing left to prevent us from assuming that people lived at home but went elsewhere for their church gathering. What is ultimately at stake is where the Christians gathered for worship. Even without the house-church theory, Edward Adams assumes several places of worship in every city. He runs through the possibilities of shops, workshops, warehouses, barns, hotels, inns and bathhouses being used as meeting places.[91] Several such localities might have served for worship in a city. With this, Adams retains the idea of plurality.

---

86 Kraeling 1967, 127 f. rightly avoids the term "house church" and speaks instead of the "house of the church".
87 Differently J. E. Stambaugh, The Functions of Roman Temples, in: ANRW 2,16,1 (1978) 554–608, here 602.
88 Differently White 1990, 111; Kritzinger 2016, 144.

89 See above n. 81.
90 Bartelink 1971, 115 f.; Duval 2000, 372; de Blaauw 2010b, 22; Sotinel 2010c, 2.
91 Adams 2013, 137–156. Essentially in agreement with him Kloppenborg 2019, 97–123. Cf. Schöllgen 1988, 80; Wieland 1906, 69–71; Kritzinger 2016, 142 f.

This opens up a wide range of speculations, and one might think that in each city it was a matter of chance which variant was chosen depending on social, economic and religious circumstances. And yet there was not just a free play of forces. Those dynamics that moved in the direction of a unified church structure must not be overlooked. Nor can this tendency towards unity be overestimated. A Christianity that was diffusing privately would have petered out before society in late antiquity had even noticed it. There is, on the other hand, much to support the assumption that a missionary Christianity immediately penetrated the cities as an identifiable entity. Those it was engaging with were the urban population, and in this dynamic the Christians presented themselves in their worship as a whole community, certainly not as one that withdrew into the private family sphere. Even though there may have been private Christian circles, it is impossible to see how these could ever have developed into a direction-determining force or have even remotely constituted an alternative to the collective worship of the local church.

The most important argument in support of this scenario is the observation that not a single text from the first three centuries contains evidence of a plurality of locations in a city for the celebration of the Eucharist. Rather, it must be assumed that there was only one location in every city where the Eucharist was celebrated. The cities of Rome and Alexandria, exceptional as they are on account of their size, do not really constitute exceptions here, but are instead special cases (below chapter III, 4).

Of course, the uniqueness of a city's location for the Eucharist is closely related to the episcopal structure of the local churches: every bishop claimed for his city the right to gather all the Christians together for the Eucharist. Nowadays the objection is quickly raised that the bishops were the very people who rewrote Church history to suit their own purposes. They wanted to assert their government over the city and thus caused all traces of church plurality and deviating Christianities to vanish. But this objection, justified though it may be, does not get us anywhere. For the opposite of a (supposed bishop's) lie is not yet the truth. If we do not want to engage in sourceless history, the only option is to question, analyse and evaluate the available texts and finally to draw up from them a balance of probabilities.

Ioannis Zizioulas has already drawn attention to the early Church's principle of the unity of the local church, according to which all the Christians of a city would ideally celebrate the Eucharist at a single altar together with the presbyterium (college of priests) and the bishop.[92] This, and not the house churches, constitutes the ecclesial structural principle as such. This basic principle of Church and liturgy is no abstraction *post fes-*

---

92 ZIZIOULAS 2001 assumes the ecclesiological principle, but does not provide the historical evidence that it was everywhere the case in reality.

tum, but is already expressly formulated by Bishop Ignatius of Antioch (c. 110/20).[93] According to this principle, there is – in a city – only *one* bishop, *one* presbyterium and *one* altar for the (Sunday) Eucharist (above chapter II, 4). One must take Ignatius at his word since the historical facts confirm what he says: up to the fourth century, there is in every city just one large hall (within a building complex) for the celebration of the Eucharist. At the latest from the second century on, this hall functioned as a sacred space exclusively for worship and was equipped with an altar (below chapter IV, 2).[94] In principle, then, there is only one altar in every episcopal city. There is, in fact, no historical evidence that the presbyters had the authority to celebrate the Eucharist independently in the first few centuries. Rather, they always worked for the local church under the supervision of the bishop, baptising and assisting at the bishop's Eucharist. It was only in the post-Constantinian period that this principle fell out of use, but even in the fourth century it was still the exception for presbyters to preside at the Eucharist.[95]

The objection is immediately raised against the one-church principle that it is unrealistic to imagine that by the third and fourth centuries there would still have been room for all the Christians of a city in a single house of God.[96] But are the premises on which such doubts are based correct? First of all, all the figures regarding the population of a city, the percentage of Christians and the number of churchgoers are highly speculative. They would therefore be an unreliable reason to exclude the possibility that a single church building could have been enough for the Christians of a city in the third century. Other considerations sound a further note of caution. If a city's churchgoers were allegedly unable to fit into a single house of God, how many (smaller) churches or even house churches, whose triclinium could seat only two to three dozen people, must there have been instead? Why is it that there are not at least two or three such micro-meeting places to be found in a single late antique city, but always only one church, namely that of the bishop? According to Eusebius, churches at the turn of the third and fourth centuries could hold many hundreds, possibly up to a thousand people.[97] Why shouldn't that be enough for Sunday worship?

Everything here depends on the number of churchgoers. According to a thesis put forward by Ramsay MacMullen, only a small number of Christians – perhaps only five percent – attended the bishop's service.[98] The high church attendance of the nineteenth and twentieth centuries should not lead one to assume that in the early Church all the baptised attended Sunday Mass. If today, despite intensive pastoral care, only five per-

93 Zizioulas 2001, 110–118.
94 Heid 2017a. Differently Harnack 1924, 613.
95 Barlea 1975, 181.
96 Robinson 2017, 230.
97 See below p. 126.

98 MacMullen 2009, 111–114. Cf. Robinson 2017, 226 f. There is no need to pursue any further how MacMullen arrives at his numbers. They are certainly based on false assumptions.

cent still go to church, why should it have been different back then?[99] The Christians came from paganism, where people participated in this or that public sacrifice at irregular intervals. They were in no way accustomed to going to church every week; this had to be painstakingly taught to them. In a city of five thousand inhabitants at the beginning of the third century, ten percent might have been Christians, i.e. five hundred people; this means that with an assumed five percent being churchgoers, there would have been 25 people attending the Eucharist. In Rome, there might have been 350.[100] And even for a later period, exaggerated numbers should not be assumed. Hence there is no statistical reason to reject the principle of one city – one church building.

The urban environment of the early Christian mission also suggests the one-church principle. Christianity was organised in cities and structured itself as a territorially circumscribed community.[101] The social unit of a city also forms the ecclesial matrix of the Christian community. Nothing was more obvious than to understand the Christians of a city as a single Christian community with a single altar for the celebration of the Eucharist. In this sense it is true: it is the city walls that make the Christian,[102] with the corporate unity of the Christians being established by the bishop. By the middle of the third century at the latest, in most provinces of the Roman Empire there was a bishop residing in every town, however small, that had Christians.[103]

The monepiscopate has existed since the second century. In Antioch it already obtained in around 100, in Asia Minor in the first half of the second century, and in Rome and other cities not until the second half of the second century. But this staggered inception does not necessarily mean that urban Christianity had previously disintegrated into autonomous Christianities and independent worship circles. It was not the monepiscopate that first led to the formation of a strictly closed local community.[104] Rather, prior to the monepiscopate it will have been assumed that the presbyters formed the governing body of a local church (cf. Acts 14:23; Ti 1:5).[105] Everything

---

99 Cf. Heb 10:25. Tert. or. 19,1 (CCL 1, 267): *Similiter et de stationum diebus non putant plerique sacrificiorum orationibus interveniendum.*

100 Based on the contestable numbers put forward by Bodel 2008, 183.

101 Robinson 2017 questions the "urban thesis" using a more sociological approach (a calculation of the Christian proportion of the population). Nevertheless, our historical knowledge of church organisation is concentrated on the cities. Scarcely anything reliable is known about the situation in the countryside in the pre-Constantinian period. Christian communities with their own liturgy in the cemeteries are coming into vogue among researchers (Robinson 2017, 227 f., 231), but here,

too, very little is known. In addition, the suburb forms a social unit with the city.

102 On a quite different context see P. Courcelle, *Parietes faciunt christianos?*, in: Mélanges d'archéologie, d'épigraphie et d'histoire offerts à J. Carcopino (Paris 1996) 241–248; Cantino Wataghin 2014, 575 f.

103 Harnack 1924, 457.

104 Differently Harnack 1910, 76.

105 For Rome see M.-Y. Perrin, in: Pietri 2003, 674 f. A college of presbyters in no way rules out an internal hierarchy. On the contrary, the monepiscopate, too, for a long time retained a presbyteral-collegial structure.

indicates that they acted as a close-knit college (*presbyterium*), i.e. were responsible for the whole city and ensured the effective (jurisdictional and liturgical) unity of the city's Christianity.[106] In any case, the presbyteral constitution does not in any way imply a number of places of worship, as if every presbyter were the leader of a house church. There is nothing to justify trying to trace back the profile of the presbyter as *paterfamilias* (as depicted in the Pastoral Epistles [1 Tm 3:4]) to the alleged house-church structure of early Christianity.[107] The biblical text is simply drawing on domestic concepts to present an ethics of office.[108]

Even though Adolf Harnack also subscribes to the house-church theory, he still notices how unconvincing it is. He says that the house churches were merely tolerated by the church leaders and that it is unclear how an affective and effective unity of the city community could be maintained in the context of a house-church structure.[109] That is precisely the point: Why should a church unity ever have arisen out of a multiplicity if the unity did not exist to begin with and therefore lacked all legitimacy? And then later: How could the Christians have spoken of *the* Church of Jesus Christ and its unity if they did not actually experience a visible united community in their own city? The factual unity that existed in the second and third centuries could only have existed under the communication conditions of the day if there had been a physical-topographical unity, i.e. if people met regularly in the cities for a single service of common worship, even if not all the baptised participated in it (cf. Heb 10:25).

Once the myth of house churches has been exploded, this has consequences for the development of the Church and of the liturgy. A Christianity that spread via private city residences would have relied primarily on rich citizens who could afford such houses.[110] Such a Christianity would have gone down in history as the religion of the rich and would probably soon have disappeared. House churches would also have dragged the bishop's administration into a maelstrom of property and legal issues. The claim that the Christians, as a *religio illicita*, could not acquire corporate property and thus had to rely on the use of private houses does not improve anything. First, such a view is outdated insofar as the Church could very well acquire property.[111] Second, if the Christians did

---

106 FRANK 1997, 100 f.
107 Correctly GIELEN 1986, 124. ALIKIN 2010, 51 f., on the other hand, sees the *Sitz im Leben* of the Pastoral Epistles as lying in the house churches. Similarly SAXER 2003, 281: "The author [of the Pastoral Epistles] was therefore thinking, on the one hand, of a family-type community, one of the house communities mentioned in the letters, and, on the other hand, of the co-existence of several such communities in the same city."
108 Differently BOWES 2008, 50–52. Cf. DASSMANN 1986, 894–897.
109 HARNACK 1924, 457 f., 612.
110 Cf. SAXER 2003, 286; BOWES 2008, 49.
111 BOWES 2008, 64.

depend on rich people, then was it not better to settle for *one* rich person who had enough money to provide a large hall in which everyone could come together: poor and rich, women and men? In fact, the Christians did form a community that cut across all classes and held together despite various differences.[112] This was, crucially, due to the unity of the place of eucharistic worship: *one* city – *one* altar.

It is of great importance for the development of early Christian liturgy that when the concept of house churches is abandoned, this at the same time renders the idea obsolete that there were private worship services in which every *paterfamilias* created his own liturgy according to his ability. When Romano Penna says that for Paul the only location of church and worship was the house, and that the Christian cultus was a house and family cultus or absolutely not a cultus at all,[113] this must be vigorously contradicted since there is neither any reliable evidence nor any likely scenario at all for a eucharistic house-church liturgy. And yet the house-church theory is trotted out over and over again to bolster the notion of privately founded, liturgically independent worship centres and to claim that these were finally suppressed by the bishops.[114] Of course the Christians used to pray at home, but they never claimed to be able to replace the episcopal community liturgy with such prayer. On the contrary, the fundamental principles of Christian liturgy are its episcopal and public nature. The Christian liturgy in its highest form, the celebration of baptism and of the Eucharist, belongs in the tradition of public worship, not of mystery cults. It did not develop from private house communities, but has from the start possessed a strong element of unity in that there is always only a single cultus in a city and thus also only one kind of liturgy, the episcopal liturgy.

The cliché of a catacomb church hiding in private circles must finally be banished from the repertoire of historians. The public nature of worship accords with the Christian self-understanding as church (ἐκκλησία).[115] Everyone could know where the Christians met and what they were doing. Addressing the pagans in around 150, Justin states that there is only one place of worship in every city and that the same liturgy is always celebrated there, which he then goes on to describe with respect to the Eucharist and baptism.[116] How could he know this if countless house churches existed with a corresponding number of varieties of worship? But Justin was well aware that the services he had experienced in the cities of Palestine, Asia Minor and Italy were always the same. A central liturgical celebration quickly develops impressive forms requiring a differ-

112 SMITH 2003 confines the idea of social unity sociologically to the idea of a meal. He speaks of a "banquet ideology" in Paul (ibid. 175).
113 PENNA 2009, 195.
114 BOWES 2008, 71.
115 MESSNER 2003a, 354 f., 360.
116 Iustin. Apol. 1, 67,3 (SC 507, 308).

entiated worship staff. The personnel structure of the local church in the ranks of dea-
con-presbyter-bishop grew out of this central worship and was fully developed by the
second century.

The unity of the urban worship community and the restriction to a single location
and altar are furthermore important instruments of securing the authority of the presbyterium and the bishops. Their concern is not pastoral ministry to a district of the city
through an ever-expanding network of churches, but rather, quite the opposite – an in-
sistence on the one church assembly at the one altar – no matter how large the community becomes. The monepiscopate is defined topographically: in a city there is only one
bishop,[117] indeed only one bishop is permitted, as the Council of Nicaea (325) admon-
ishes (Can. 8: μὴ ἐν τῇ πόλει δύο ἐπίσκοποι ὦσιν). What this means in concrete terms is
that the ecclesiastical jurisdiction of the bishop encompasses the urban area (including
the suburbs).[118] Interestingly, the size of the city does not make any difference here: not
even in Rome is there more than one bishop even though they could have invoked the
fact that they had two apostles – Peter and Paul – in support of having more than one.[119]
But if the unity rule applies to bishops, why should it be different with the altars? Is it
not, then, an inevitable conclusion that only one altar exists for the episcopal Eucharist,
no matter how large a city is?

Before the single-church principle is demonstrated in detail in the following chapter
using topographical and chronological sources, three fundamental exceptions need to
be addressed which at the same time confirm the validity of this principle. First, there
is the evident case of a plurality of churches in certain cities that are suffering from a
church schism. For the flip side of the principle of unity is the splitting off of schismatic
groups. Historically, the Novatians and Donatists were the first groups to set up a count-
er-hierarchy with their own altar in every city in the third and fourth centuries. Such
secessions did not happen because the worshipping community had become too large
and these groups had, so to speak, won themselves the right to their own parish church
through sheer defiance, but rather because they rejected the local bishop and elected
their own. Significantly enough, the apostates only ever erected just one altar, so that
there was a maximum of two churches in a city until another group possibly split off.
Bishop Cyprian of Carthage states his claim quite plainly in these cases that the heretics
possess neither a church nor an altar.[120] Of course they do, but he denies the sacrality of

---

117 HARNACK 1910, 77. Hieron. Ep. 146,1,3 (CSEL
56,1, 309): *ne quis contentiose in una ecclesia
plures episcopos fuisse contendat.*

118 On later episcopal governance of the city see RAPP
2005, 274–289.

119 Under Bishop Victor of Rome (189–199) there was

an antipope Natalius, who broke with the Church
but was then reconciled with it; Euseb. hist. eccl.
5,28,10–12 (SC 41, 76 f.).

120 Cypr. Ep. 70,2 (CSEL 3,2, 768): *qui nec altare
habuit nec ecclesiam.*

illegitimate altars: for him they are just tables,[121] and the churches of the schismatics do not deserve the name "church". Constantine's Edict against the Heretics of 25 September 326 reveals that in various cities the Novatians, Valentinians, Marcionites, Paulians and Montanists held their meetings in their own churches. Their "houses of prayer" were now confiscated and made over to the respective Catholic bishops.[122] The edict also says that instead of going to their own meetings, the sectarians should rather go to the "catholic church" for the proper worship of God, which is sure to mean the bishop's church. This indicates a single place of worship in a city. However, the use of churches formerly used by sects by the Catholics was bound to undermine the ecclesial principle of unity. Sadly, no more detailed information has been preserved on these events. But the question arises of how these churches were incorporated by the bishops into the existing pastoral and liturgical system.[123]

The second exception is double-churches, which had existed since Constantinian times, e.g. in Aquileia and Trier. One can speak just as well of co-cathedrals. If an older church became too small, it was not necessarily demolished, but instead a larger church was built next to it. This does not, however, alter the fact that both churches are reserved solely for episcopal worship. It is always the bishop who celebrates the Eucharist there, or his representative. There can be no question of a parish church system.

The third exception is the graveyard or cemetery churches. In the first few centuries of the spread of Christianity in the cities, life was ordered in such a way that the city of the living was to be strictly separated from the city of the dead (necropolis): between the two lay the city wall (below Figs. 14, 15). The ancient and also the Christian cemeteries always extended along the roads leading out of the cities. The bishops exercised ecclesiastical jurisdiction not only over the urban area, but also over the suburbs (*suburbium*) if church cemeteries were located there.[124] It was in such cemeteries that the martyrs of the Decian, Valerian and Diocletian persecutions were buried. From the middle of the third century on, a lively veneration of the martyrs undoubtedly took place at their graves. Nevertheless, right on into the Constantinian period no churches are to be expected in the cemeteries; but after that they are. But here, too, it is always the bishop who presides at the liturgy. The unity of the city's worship is preserved even though there may now be other altars outside the city in the cemetery churches. The cemetery churches are no more parish churches than the co-cathedrals are, but rather station churches: there it is

121 Ibid. 68,2 (CSEL 3,2, 745); ep. 73,2 (780).
122 Euseb. Vit. Const. 3,64 f. (SC 559, 448 – 452). Dörries 1954, 82 – 84; Dassmann 1986, 893.
123 As a rule, the bishops tried to push the sectarians

out into the suburban churches. Theodoret. Hist. eccl. 5,33,3 – 5 (SC 530, 464 – 466).
124 Zizioulas 2001, 94 – 98; Gutsfeld 2003.

the local bishop who celebrates the liturgy, or a presbyter representing him. As with the Sunday Mass inside the city, in principle all the city's Christians must participate in the station masses, too.

3. PUTTING IT TO THE TEST

In the following, we shall look at all the available textual sources from the first four centuries that speak of Christian places of worship in individual cities or various regions which have hitherto been read by researchers as if it were to be taken for granted that several places of worship existed within a city.[125] In almost every case, it is possible to counter this assumption and uphold the validity of the principle of unity outlined above. The few special cases that do exist can be explained by local circumstances.

For *Asia Minor* (western Turkey), we have the seven letters of the seer John and the letters of the apostle Paul. John (end of the first century?) assumes in his Revelation (Apocalypse) that there is only one "(local) church" (ἐκκλησία) in each of the cities of Ephesus, Smyrna,[126] Pergamum, Thyatira, Sardis, Philadelphia and Laodicea (Rv 1:4; 2:1, 8, 12, 18; 3:1, 7, 14). The German *Einheitsübersetzung* of the New Testament here translates ἐκκλησία throughout as "*Gemeinde*" (in Ephesus, etc.), thus suggesting house communities, while the RSVCE has "church" throughout. But there is only ever one ἐκκλησία spoken of per city. John thinks in terms of cities: all the Christians of a city belong to the ἐκκλησία. There is no reference to multiple "*Gemeinden*" or "churches" in any of the seven cities. The letters are read in the respective local churches and brought to the ears of the Christians there (Rv 1:3 f.; 2:7, 11, 17, 29; 3:6, 13, 22). The obvious assumption is that there is only one worship assembly in each city and that John wishes to address this audience.

Paul reflects the same ecclesiology, according to which there is only one "(local) church" in every city: he never addresses his letters to part of a community, but always to all the Christians of a city (Rm 16:1; 1 Cor 1:2; 10:32; 16:1, 19; Col 4:16; Phil 1:1; 1 Thes 1:1).[127] His description of the Lord's Supper in Corinth is significant: there "the whole church" (ἡ ἐκκλησία ὅλη) comes together (1 Cor 14:23), more specifically "the

---

125 On the following HEID 2018.
126 Cf. Clem. Alex. Quis div. salv. 42,3 (SC 537, 210): the "church" assembled in Smyrna c. 100 under the presidency of the bishop (so SC 537, 210 n. 1).

127 BATIFFOL 1910, 74 f.; SCHÖLLGEN 1988, 79; ZIZIOULAS 2001, 46 f.; KLOPPENBORG 2019, 290–292.

church of God that is in Corinth (1 Cor 1:2) comes together" (ἐπὶ τὸ αὐτό) (1 Cor 11:20; 14:23)[128] "in the church assembly" (ἐν ἐκκλησίᾳ) (1 Cor 11:18, 22; cf. Acts 11:26),[129] and explicitly does not do so in a private dwelling (1 Cor. 11:22, 34; 14:35: οἰκία, οἶκος); rather, they go from their private homes to the liturgical gathering.[130] The significance of the celebration of the Lord's Supper for the unity of the community in Christ, which is constituted by partaking of the one bread (1 Cor 10:16 f.), also requires theologically that all the members of the community come together.[131] So, there are evidently not six or more house churches in Corinth, as has been strongly speculated,[132] but just this one assembly of the whole city community.[133]

This is supported by further observations: the First Letter to the Corinthians is dated around 55, i.e. only two decades after Easter. At that time, it is more likely that a central Christian community has developed in Corinth rather than a multitude of small, uncoordinated house churches. The long list of charisms (1 Cor 12:28–31; 14:26–40)[134] presupposes for Corinth a church made up of a large number of members, presumably one to two hundred persons.[135] For reasons of space alone, this hardly suggests a reclining meal; in fact, Paul speaks of the participants sitting (1 Cor 14:30). He now also says explicitly that the charisms, such as prophecy and tongues, burst forth when "the whole church comes together" (1 Cor 14:23). Furthermore, the tensions in the community between various groups ("I belong to Paul", or "I belong to Apollos", or "I belong to Cephas" [1 Cor 1:12]) are in no way tensions between house churches; in that case they would have avoided each other! Rather, the conflicts exist and are painfully perceived because all the people come together in the same worship service (1 Cor 11:18).[136] Besides, Paul would not have written such a fundamental treatise as First Corinthians for a small house church. For in it he authoritatively sets out the rules ordering the already large church in Corinth, which is proud of its apostolic foundation.

---

128 ἐπὶ τὸ αὐτό in the NT always means "in one place", i.e. not, for example, "for the same activity"; see 1 Cor 7:5; Mt 22:34; Lk 17:35; Rev 1:15; 2:44.

129 The sevenfold συνέρχεσθαι (1 Cor 11:17 f., 20, 33 f.; 14:23, 26) is an ancient specialist term for the city assembly; KLAUCK 1982, 287.

130 For Paul, the "church" is concretely the eucharistic assembly; ZIZIOULAS 2001, 48 f.

131 MESSNER 2003a, 360.

132 WHITE 1990, 105; id. 1996, 105; id. 2016, 467; ROBINSON 2017, 229. Also KLAUCK 1982, 290 f. superfluously assumes several house churches although he recognises "that in spite of this there continued to be a gathering of all the members of the community in one place." Similarly PENNA 2009, 191 f.; MELL 2011, 42 f.

133 Basically recognised correctly by GIELEN 1986, 114; KLINGHARDT 1996, 364; ADAMS 2013, 24–30. Differently WIELAND 1906, 31 f.; WAGNER 2011, 43; KRITZINGER 2016, 25.

134 The same worship gathering is to be assumed for 1 Cor 11 and 14; MESSNER 2003a, 423.

135 It is hard to understand why MESSNER 2003a, 360 correctly assumes a unified act of worship for the city community in Corinth, yet speaks ibid. 421 of a small group of a few dozen persons.

136 FILSON 1939 fails to recognize this. KLAUCK 1981, 38 f. sees the contradiction and therefore postulates for Corinth both worship in house churches as well as a gathering of the whole community (on Sundays).

The purpose of the letter is not to admonish quarrelling house churches. Otherwise Paul would at least have had to add: "Present this letter to all the house churches as well." This is an important point since an equivalent request in 1 Thes 5:27 is cited to claim that a multitude of house churches existed in the Pauline mission cities.[137] What it says in the First Letter to the Thessalonians is: "I solemnly command you by the Lord that this letter be read to all of them" [all the brothers]. This, though, gives no indication whatsoever of the existence of any house churches. For the letter is addressed "to the church of the Thessalonians," i.e. to the one assembly of the city's community.[138] First of all, of course, the letter arrives to the "presiders" (cf. 1 Thes 5:12). These are then without fail to read it aloud at the common worship where all the brothers gather. After that, the letter was then shared with other local churches (not house churches), as is evident from the letter addressed to the Christians in the city of Colossae (Phrygia) in Asia Minor (Col 1:2), which states, "And when this letter has been read among you, have it read also in the church of the Laodiceans; and see that you read also the letter from Laodicea" (Col 4:16).[139]

But back to Corinth. For the First Letter of Clement, too, which was sent from Rome to Corinth at the end of the first century (above chapter II, 3), all the believers of a city, whether in Rome or in Corinth, form the community of the local church, which is thus defined topographically.[140] The unity of the urban church is realised in the liturgy. All are to gather together "conscientiously" and "in harmony" in the same place (ἐπὶ τὸ αὐτό) for prayer and to sing God's praises "as with one mouth".[141] With this, the letter takes up a Pauline formula which the apostle has already used with reference to the worship gathering "in the same place" in Corinth (1 Cor 11:20; 14:23). So there is only a single worship location there even around the year 100. As is well known, the Letter of Clement presupposes a presbyteral constitution since it does not yet seem to be familiar with a monepiscopate. This does not mean, however, that the presbyters led

---

137 WAGNER 2011, 45.

138 Accordingly 1 Thes 2:14 speaks of "the churches of God in Christ Jesus that are in Judea" because this region has several cities with Christian communities.

139 ZIZIOULAS 2001, 46.

140 1 Clem. prooem. (SC 167, 98): "The church of God which sojourns at Rome, to the church of God sojourning at Corinth. Ibid. 42,4 (168): through countries and cities the apostles have appointed bishops and deacons. Ibid. 44,3 (172): "the whole church" means precisely that of Corinth. Ibid. 54,2 f. (186): anyone who is insubordinate should

leave the city. Although LONA 1998, 61 f. says that the Roman community is not a unified entity, he significantly enough does not speak of house churches. Ibid. 440 does admittedly state: "Towards the end of the first century the worship gathering took place in private houses."

141 1 Clem. 34,7 (SC 167, 156). Cf. 40,2 f. (166). LONA 1998, 373: "The text does not contain any discernible evidence of a eucharistic gathering." That may be true, but what is meant is undoubtedly a worship gathering, and the most obvious thing to think of here, too, is the Eucharist.

their own "house churches" in the various districts of Corinth.[142] Rather, they formed a college that worshipped together with the faithful. In the building used for this purpose there were apparently permanently installed seats for the clergy. The Letter of Clement speaks of a "place now appointed" for the presbyter-episcopes – probably elevated seats inside the church (episcope = over-seer) – from which they may not be expelled.[143] It does not talk of seats in the plural but only of one clergy seat. This means that the presbyters in Corinth celebrated their worship together in a single meeting place of the city community and at a single sacrificial table.

Bishop Ignatius of Antioch (c. 110/20) is even clearer (above chapter II, 4): in the cities of Asia Minor to which he addresses his letters (Ephesus, Magnesia, Tralles, Philadelphia, Smyrna), but also in his Syrian home city of Antioch and in Rome, there is for him only one church community,[144] one worship service, one bishop who presides at the worship, one "temple of God" and one altar. What is important here is that from the outset the entire college of priests – the "presbyterium" – is part of the bishop's worship.[145] There is no tendency towards division among the bishop's clergy. If Ignatius repeatedly calls for unity, this is not in order to bring presbyters into line who might be leading independent house churches and are to be forced under episcopal authority.[146] His addressees are rather precisely those faithful who attend the bishop's worship service at which his letter is read out but who are endangered by religious persuasions (heresies) that wish to draw them away from the bishop and his presbyterium.[147] For this reason the faithful are urged not to stay away from the bishop's worship service and to continue to come to the assembly (ἐπὶ τὸ αὐτό).[148] They are not to meet privately, but rather to do everything in common with the bishop and the presbyterium.[149]

---

142 Differently Lampe 2003, 398 f.

143 1 Clem. 44,4 f. (SC 167, 172); Kritzinger 2016, 116.

144 Ign. ad Eph. prooem. (SC 10³, 66); ad Magn. prooem. (SC 10³, 94); ad Trall. prooem. (SC 10³, 110); ad Rom. prooem. (SC 10³, 124); ad Polyc. 7,1 (SC 10³, 178); Polyc. ad Phil. prooem. (SC 10³, 202).

145 Ign. ad Eph. 2,2 (SC 10³, 70); ad Magn. 6,1 f. (98); ad Trall. 2,2 (112); 13,2 (122); ad Smyrn. 8,1 (162). On the college of priests of the city of Ephesus see also Harnack 1985, 13*.

146 There are no house churches in Ignatius's epistles. Ign. ad Eph. 9,1 (SC 10³, 76); 16,1 (84) merely uses the house metaphor. On the other hand, Leppin 2018, 186: "He [Ignatius] is familiar with house churches, but he is envisaging supra-house structures."

147 Against Schoedel 1990, 380 Ign. ad Smyrn. 6,1 (SC 10³, 160) does not attest to worship conducted by presbyters in competition with the bishop but rather to a schismatic-heretical group. Cf. Schöllgen 1988, 79. Otherwise, too, Ignatius warns of heresies from outside whenever he calls for unity with the bishop and presbyterium: ad Eph. 6,2–7,2 (SC 10³, 74–76), ad Magn. 8,1 (SC 10³,100), ad Trall. 6,1 f. (SC 10³, 116), ad Philad. 6,1 (SC 10³, 144).

148 Ign. ad Eph. 5,3 (SC 10³, 74).

149 Ign. ad Magn. 7,1 (SC 10³, 100); ad Trall. 7,2 (SC 10³, 116); ad Philad. 7,1 (SC 10³, 146).

There is no conclusive evidence in Ignatius for partial communities.[150] If separatists were to have their own altar and celebrate the Eucharist without the consent of the bishop – of which, however, not a single concrete case is mentioned[151] – then it is simply not a legitimate altar since the only one of these is that of the Catholic community.[152] If there had been services led by presbyters to which the faithful migrated, Ignatius would undoubtedly have explicitly rebuked them for this. It is true that a celebration of the Eucharist by a presbyter, i.e. without a bishop, is mentioned once in Smyrna, but this is not a general authorisation at all but merely an emergency decree in the case of the bishop's absence. Permission is required for every case in which a presbyter celebrates that "proper Eucharist" over which the bishop otherwise presides. For nothing of what belongs "in the church assembly" (εἰς τὴν ἐκκλησίαν, singular!) may be done without the bishop or without his permission. Where the bishop (or exceptionally his representative) is, there the faithful must gather.[153]

Ignatius even wants to have the participants in the (eucharistic) assembly checked by name: all are to come, without exception.[154] This only makes sense if there is a single place of worship and people do not have the option of choosing this or that house church. Nor is there even the slightest need for presbyteral house churches,[155] for even baptism and the love feast (*agape*) may only be held in the presence of the bishop.[156] All the same, there are Christians in Smyrna in Asia Minor who hold their own worship services and stay away from the episcopal Eucharist and common prayer.[157] They are probably Gnostics. It is not, however, said that there were several such dissenting groups, nor is their activity connected with private houses or even house churches. Certainly, Ignatius does know "houses", i.e. families he is friendly with, in Smyrna.[158] However, these have nothing to do with the separate Gnostic groups, and they undoubtedly attend the central episcopal service; otherwise Ignatius would not have been friends with them.

All in all, Ignatius is *the* Church Father who shows the ecclesial principle of unity to be a genuine ecclesial norm which does not remain just a principle but essentially also corresponds to the praxis. Accordingly, in wide regions from Antioch to Italy, there can only have been one episcopal altar in each city.

---

150 Schöllgen 1988, 80.

151 Differently Dassmann 1986, 892 f.

152 Wieland 1909, 55 sees this but misunderstands it.

153 Ign. ad Smyrn. 8,1 (SC 10³, 162).

154 Ign. ad Eph. 20,2 (SC 10³, 90); ad Polyc. 4,2 (SC 10³, 174). Cf. Wieland 1906, 34. The same kind of check is also demanded by the Synod of Elvira (see below n. 327).

155 Differently Schoedel 1990, 380; Kritzinger 2016, 32.

156 Ign. ad Smyrn. 8,2 (SC 10³, 162). The agape is scarcely the Eucharist; differently Schoedel 1990, 382.

157 Ign. ad Smyrn. 6,1–9,1 (SC 10³, 160–162).

158 Ibid. 13,1 f. (SC 10³, 166–168); ad Polyc. 8,2 (SC 10³, 180).

This is confirmed by other sources for what is modern-day eastern Turkey. Around 235, an earthquake in some places in *Cappadocia* and *Pontus* set off a wave of hatred against the Christians, whose "churches" were persecuted and burned down.[159] Precisely this dual use of "church" in the sense of local church, which is persecuted, and assembly building, which is set on fire, reveals that each town has only one church. In around 240, Gregory Thaumaturgus built a church in his episcopal city of Neocaesarea in Pontus, no doubt because the previous church building was destroyed by the earthquake. As later described by Gregory of Nyssa, this church is likely to have been the only one in the city.[160]

A statement made by Bishop Firmilian of Caesarea in Cappadocia, writing in 256 to Bishop Cyprian of Carthage, also fits into this picture: there is no forgiveness in the assemblies of the Anabaptists (Novatians) but only in the bishops' churches. But the heretics, in opposition to the one Catholic Church of the bishops, usurped the priesthood[161] and erected "profane altars".[162] It is true that altars are spoken of here in the plural, but Firmilian is not talking about just one city but rather about all the episcopal cities in which the Novatians seceded. This is a polemic against Pope Stephen in Rome, whose recognition of heretical baptism inevitably led him to establish many church buildings (with baptisteries) by recognising the churches of the Novatians.[163] This does not necessarily describe the real situation in Rome, which Firmilian hardly knew. He is only painting a picture of the disastrous consequences of Roman dogmatics. In his eyes, the recognition of heretical baptism destroys what applies in Cappadocia and should also apply to Rome; namely, the principle of ecclesial unity with only "one Catholic Church" and one altar in every episcopal city.[164]

For the period of Diocletian's persecution of the Christians (303–305), Lactantius attests to a single (episcopal) church in Nicomedia (*Bithynia*)[165] and in Heraclea (*Thrace*).[166] In around 315–340, the senator Eugenius, during his time as bishop of Laodicea (*Phrygia*), "rebuilds the whole church from the foundations."[167] This is apparently the

159 Orig. comm. ser. in Matth. 39 (GCS Orig. 11, 75): *in locis quibusdam* [...] *persecutiones passae sunt ecclesiae et incensae sunt.* Cf. Molthagen 1975, 55.
160 Greg. Nyss. vit. Greg. Thaum. (PG 46, 924BC).
161 Cypr. [Firmilian.] ep. 75,16 (CSEL 3,2, 820f.). What is meant by the churches of the bishops is certainly the church buildings that stand on the apostolic rock. Ep. 75,17 (821).
162 Ibid. 75,16 (CSEL 3,2, 821): *altaria profana.*
163 Ibid. 75,17 (CSEL 3,2, 821): *multas alias petras inducat et ecclesiarum multarum nova aedificia constituat, dum esse illic baptisma sua auctoritate defendit.*
164 It apparently also remains the same under the great Cappadocian bishop Basil († 378). Cf. Gain 2001, 1020–1022.
165 Lact. mort. pers. 12,2f. (SC 39, 91); div. inst. 5,2,2 (SC 204, 134). On 23 February 303, the church in the immediate vicinity of the imperial palace in Nicomedia was destroyed. Molthagen 1975, 102, 105f.
166 Dölger 1950, 175f., 190.
167 Guyot / Klein 1993, 256–259; Calder 1920; Dresken-Weiland 2005–2006.

only church in the city. It is the bishop's church, whose predecessor was probably destroyed in the Diocletian persecution.[168] The synod in Cappadocian Neocaesarea (c. 314–319) assumes only one church in an episcopal city.[169]

Basil of Caesarea († 379) complains that the metropolitan of Gangra and other "Arian" bishops amnestied by Emperor Julian the Apostate (361–363) in 361 returned to their dioceses, overthrew the altars of the Nicene bishops there and set up their own instead.[170] Corresponding actions took place the other way round, too.[171] It is true that altars are spoken of in the plural here, but there is no explicit mention of several altars in one city. Rather, the statement must be seen as relating to the bishop's church in each of the cities of the ecclesiastical province of Gangra. Nevertheless, it would also not be surprising if at this time, in the second half of the fourth century, some cities already possessed two or three church buildings.

The same goes for the following episodes. People have wanted to conclude from a sermon by Basil of Caesarea in honour of the martyr Gordius which speaks of the destruction of Caesarea's Christian "prayer houses" and "altars" that there were several churches there.[172] But this is by no means necessarily so since Basil was preaching the sermon in the suburban church of Gordius and would therefore mention the martyrs' churches. Thus there may still have been a single altar inside the city at that time.

During the time of Emperor Julian, martyrs' churches with altars were built near the temple of Apollo at Didyma in a suburb of Miletus.[173] These, too, were evidently located outside the city.[174]

In a funeral oration for his sister Gorgonia, which he apparently delivered in the episcopal church of Iconium in around 370,[175] Gregory of Nazianzus († c. 390) says that, in despair over her grave illness, she "threw herself before the altar" at night in supplication, finally resting her head on the altar, and was healed.[176] On account of the night hour, it is sometimes thought that this must have taken place in her private oratory.[177] In the late fourth century, there may of course have been private chapels, but these do not in any case affect the ecclesial principle of unity. All the same, a careful interpretation helps us gain a better understanding of the local circumstances. Once again, everything points to the fact that in Iconium there is only the bishop's church. In a private chapel,

---

168 Alongside it, there may already have been a (suburban) martyr's church; CALDER 1920, 58.

169 Can. 13 (JOANNOU 1962, 81).

170 Basil. ep. 226,2 (PG 32, 845AB).

171 Ibid. 251,3 (PG 32, 936B).

172 Basil. hom. 18,2 (PG 31, 496A). Cf. LECLERCQ 1907, 3185.

173 Sozom. hist. eccl. 5,20,7 (SC 495, 206–208).

174 W. MÜLLER-WIENER, Milet, in: RBK 6 (2005) 362–377, here 372.

175 Cf. J. A. McGUCKIN, St Gregory of Nazianzus. An intellectual biography (New York 2001) 166. A bishop was present at the sermon (SC 405, 60).

176 Greg. Naz. or. 8,18 (SC 405, 284).

177 SC 405, 285 n. 2. But there is no mention of this, nor of the episode's having taken place in private so that hitherto no one had known about it.

Gorgonia could have rested her head on the altar at any time, so why at night? It is also uncertain whether private oratories possessed altars.[178] Furthermore, the congregation prayed publicly for her health,[179] i.e. in a church. What is special here is precisely that Gorgonia goes to the church at night in order to pray alone at the altar. As a person of public interest, she is allowed to do so. In addition, Gregory mentions that Gorgonia gave votive offerings to many "temples", most especially to the church in which he is now delivering her funeral oration.[180] She very probably made these gifts to this church on account of her healing there. So everything supports the idea that "the altar" of her healing stands in Iconium's only church, namely the bishop's church in which her brother is preaching. The other "temples" to which Gorgonia made gifts could have been anywhere; she will certainly have remembered the bishop's church of her father Gregory the Elder in Nazianzus.

In Cilician Sebaste, too, there was still only one church and one altar in 375.[181]

Even *Constantinople* (Fig. 12)[182] possessed only the bishop's church *Hagia Eirene*, which had probably already existed in pre-Constantinian times (the "Old Church") and was then rebuilt.[183] In a letter to Eusebius of Caesarea, Emperor Constantine († 337) announces his intention to build several churches in the city of Constantinople since – after its elevation to capital of the Eastern Empire in 330 – the number of Christians living there had grown considerably.[184] Apparently, up to then there was only the church of *Hagia Eirene*, which was then given the status of a second cathedral when the nearby "Great Church" (later *Hagia Sophia*) was added as a palace and bishop's church; this was probably begun under Emperor Constantine, although the church was not consecrated until around 360.[185] From then on, the two churches formed a single church complex.[186] As early as the Constantinian period, another building was erected in the city centre, the Church of the Holy Apostles. Here, however, two buildings must be distinguished. Initially there was no church there, only a mausoleum. To all appearances, this was an *Apostoleion* with the cenotaphs of twelve apostles and no altar. When, from 337 on, this central building then served as a mausoleum for the city's founder, Constantine, an altar

---

178 Cf. Geront. vit. Melan. 5 (SC 90, 134). In Greg. Nyss. vit. Macr. 31 (SC 178, 244) it is not clear whether an oratory or a church is meant; anyway, there is no mention of the altar.

179 Greg. Naz. or. 8,17 (SC 405, 284).

180 Ibid. 8,11 (SC 405, 268).

181 Basil. ep. 244,7 (PG 32, 921A); 250 (932A); 251 (937A).

182 M. RESTLE, Konstantinopel, in: RBK 4 (1990) 366–737, here 367–377; BERGER 2006, 449; BOWES 2008, 106 f.

183 Its altar in the year 335 is mentioned in Socr. hist. eccl. 1,37,7 (SC 477, 254).

184 Euseb. vit. Const. 4,36,1 (SC 559, 496).

185 T. F. MATHEWS, The Early Churches of Constantinople. Architecture and Liturgy (London 1971) 11.

186 E. RUSSO, Costantino da Bisanzio a Costantinopoli, in: Acta ad Archaeolgiam et Artium Historiam Pertinentia 29 (2017) 73–112, here 107 f.

was placed in the centre of the room opposite the imperial sarcophagus, possibly only for the commemoration of the dead emperor. It is an altar endowed by the emperor for the sole purpose of his being prayed for at the masses that would take place there after his death.[187] Even in pagan antiquity, imperial mausoleums were at the same time cult rooms in which sacrifices were made to the genius of the emperor. One can even ask whether what Constantine intended with the altar is a kind of Christianised imperial cult.[188] In any case, Constantine's mausoleum is not a proper church and is hardly suitable for worship services of any size. This defect was only remedied by Constantine's son Constantius II, who had the Church of the Holy Apostles built in the form of a cruciform basilica on the site of the spacious portico enclosing the mausoleum (consecration with the deposition of relics around 356/57 and again in 370).[189] The location of the mausoleum within the city walls in fact violates ancient custom, but Constantine calls himself "Bishop (in charge of affairs external to the Church)" and also claims special powers as *Pontifex Maximus*.[190] In addition, the new Church of the Holy Apostles is likely to have served from the start as the burial place of the bishops,[191] which thus episcopally sanctions the breaking of sacred law.

All in all, Eusebius's statement that Constantine embellished Constantinople with numerous prayer houses and large churches in honour of the martyrs in the suburbs and in the city itself[192] is not necessarily incorrect. But it undoubtedly creates a grandiose impression that conceals a much more modest reality. Constantinople celebrated the feasts of two historical martyrs on 11 and 19 May.[193] The Church of St Mokios was located outside the Constantinian city walls and existed from 402 at the latest.[194] Although the Church of St Akakios lay outside the old city of Byzantium on the southern coast of the headland, it was inside the Constantinian city wall, and existed from 359 at

187 Euseb. vit. Const. 4,60,2 (SC 559, 526). De Blaauw 2006, 169 notes correctly that the mausoleum becomes a church secondarily through the altar. See also the altar in the mausoleum of St Helena in Rome in SS Marcellino e Pietro: LP 34,26 (Duchesne 1886, 182): *altarem ex argento purissimo* […] *ante sepulchrum beatae Helenae Augustae*; cf. Diefenbach 2007, 168–171. Recently also F. Coarelli, Mauseolei imperiali tardoantichi. Le origini di un tipo architettonico, in: O. Brandt et al. (eds.), *Acta XVI congressus internationalis archaeologiae christianae* 1 (Città del Vaticano 2016) 493–508; V. Fiocchi Nicolai, Le aree funerarie cristiane di età costantiniana e la nascita delle chiese con funzione sepolcrale, in: ibid. 619–670, here 633.

188 Imperial cult still in the fifth century see D. Boin, Late antique *divi* and imperial priests of

the late fourth and early fifth centuries, in: M. R. Salzmann et al. (eds.), Pagans and Christians in Late Antique Rome (Cambridge 2016) 139–161.

189 Thus, plausibly, C. Mango, Constantine's Mausoleum and the Translation of Relics, in: Byzantinische Zeitschrift 83 (1990) 51–62.

190 Cf. Herrmann 1980, 378f.

191 Socr. hist. eccl. 1,40,2 (SC 477, 262); Sozom. hist. eccl. 2,34,6 (SC 306, 384); J. F. Baldovin, The Urban Character of Christian Worship (Rome 1987) 292–297.

192 Euseb. vit. Const. 3,48,1 (SC 559, 412).

193 Thus the Syrian calendar (c. 362): Maximos (= Mokios?) on 11 May, Hesychios (= Akakios?) on 19 May.

194 R. Janin, La géographie ecclésiastique de l'empire byzantin (Paris 1953) 367–371.

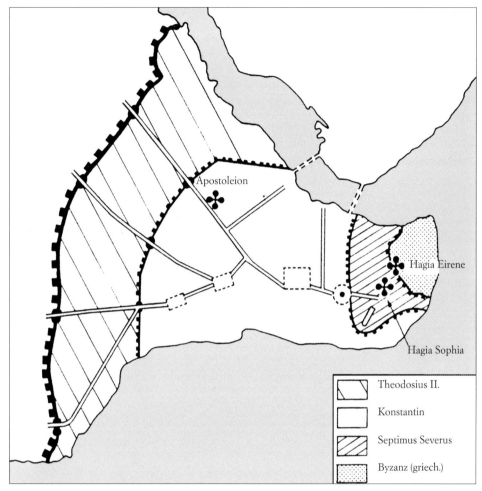

Fig. 12: Map of Constantinople, 4th / 5th century; FRASCHETTI 2002, 19 Fig. 4.

the latest.[195] According to a thoroughly credible tradition, both churches were erected by Constantine. This would mean that the one-church principle was already broken in Constantine's time, not by the Church of the Holy Apostles, but by the Martyrium of St Acacius. However, two qualifications must be added: first, it is by no means certain that the aforementioned martyrium possessed an altar from the start, and second, it was only later and by chance that it came to be located within the city as a result of the extension of the city wall.

195 Ibid. 18 f. According to the Synaxarion of Constantinople, the feast day of this church is 7–8 May;
this may be a later development than that represented in the Syrian calendar.

On the other hand, the church of Paulos (only later so named), whose location is not certain, was built in the early 340s and was used by the followers of the Arian Makedonios. In it, Makedonios was elected anti-bishop. The church therefore had a cathedra and altar and belonged to a schismatic community. It was not by chance that it later became the burial place of the Orthodox bishop Paulos and thus a regular bishop's church.[196] Gregory of Nazianzus, who resided in Constantinople in 379–381 as a kind of Catholic anti-bishop, possessed only a makeshift chapel in a private house.[197] At that time, there were already several churches in the city, but they were all in the hands of the Arians.[198]

There are several testimonies for *eastern and western Syria*, but they cannot always be localised with certainty. The Didache (c. 100) assumes a local or urban Christianity (in Syria),[199] with apparently only one common Sunday Eucharist being celebrated in each place.[200] The Chronicle of Edessa (sixth century) reports, on the basis of older documents, that in 201 a great flood destroyed "the sanctuary of the Christian church".[201] According to this, there was only one church in Edessa.[202] In any case, there is no mention of further churches there before 379.[203]

The community described in the so-called *Traditio Apostolica* at the beginning of the third century, which can perhaps likewise be located in Syria, has only one church space in the city where all the faithful, priests and deacons gather daily for prayer and catechesis[204] and where the bishop celebrates the Eucharist on Sundays.[205] One passage states:

> The deacons and presbyters shall meet daily at the place which the bishop appoints for them. […] When all have come, they shall teach all those who are assembled in the church.[206]

196 SC 516, 110 n. 1 and 2. Socr. hist. eccl. 2,12,2 (SC 493, 50); 5,9,2 (SC 505, 172); Sozom. hist. eccl. 7,10,4 (SC 516, 110).
197 FC 22, 18; van de Paverd 1970, 412.
198 Sozom. hist. eccl. 7,5,1 (SC 516, 86).
199 Did. 12,2f. (SC 248, 188).
200 Did. 4,3 (SC 248, 158); 4,14 (164); 9,5 (176); 14,1 (192). In line with this, in every place (i.e. in every city) and at all times (only) one sacrifice should be offered, cf. Did. 14,3 (SC 248, 192).
201 Chron. Edess. (CSCO 2 / Syr. 2, 3): *in templum* (h.e. partem ecclesiae ubi populus locum habebat) *aedis sacrae Christianorum*.
202 The church was located within the city walls; Leppin 2018, 125.
203 E. Kirsten, Edessa, in: RACh 4 (1959) 552–597, here 577.
204 Trad. Apost. 35 (FC 1, 292); 39 (296); 41 (298–300). Ibid. 40 (298): the bishop is responsible (alongside the city church) for the cemeteries.
205 Trad. Apost. 8 (FC 1, 236): the deacons serve the (local) church in God's sanctuary at the celebration of the Eucharist. Ibid. 21 (266): at the baptismal Eucharist (at Easter) all the people gather. Ibid. 22 (272): on Sundays the bishop delivers the Eucharist to "all the people".
206 Trad. Apost. 39 (FC 1, 296).

When Peter Lampe concludes from this that there is still no central location where the monarchical bishop resides, but that he changes his location for every gathering,[207] then this looks more like a misunderstanding. For here, as elsewhere, there is only ever talk of *the* church in the singular. Before the clergy go together to this church to instruct the faithful, they assemble at another location outside the church which appears not to be fixed, so this is not a religious meeting. The evident purpose of it can only be for the bishop's daily business meeting with the presbyters, in which the deacons are also expressly meant to participate.

A further text from Syria, the *Didascalia*, describes the circumstances of a city community in the middle of the third century. It too knows only the bishop's church.[208] On the one hand, this "house (of the Lord)" is so large that it offers ample space for laity and the quite large number of clergy; on the other hand, if the worship is well attended, the faithful have to sit or stand in cramped conditions.[209]

The already-mentioned Christian meeting place in Dura Europos on the Euphrates (from 232/33 to 256/57) dates from approximately the same time. It is regarded as the only undisputed example of a house church in which a Roman private house with its various rooms was converted in such a way as to henceforth serve exclusively for cultic purposes, i.e. for baptism and the celebration of the Eucharist.[210] What Dura Europos is not is precisely a house church in the sense of a private residence that would have served as a kind of community centre and place of worship at the same time. Rather, it is simply a church building (*domus ecclesiae*). In addition, the archaeologists have been unable to find any other Christian place of worship in the city. Nor is such a thing to be expected since the church has a baptistery and is therefore likely to be the bishop's church.[211] Consequently, all the Christians of Dura Europos gather there for worship. The large hall (5 × 13 m) has room for about sixty-five to seventy-five people, depending on whether you think of them lying on mats or standing.[212] It might be objected that this is not enough space for an urban Christian community. But first, the prayer room of the only synagogue in Dura Europos was only slightly larger (7 × 13 m), and second, simply nothing is known about the number of Christians (and Jews). There is no evidence

207 LAMPE 2003, 406.
208 ACHELIS / FLEMMING 1904, 267, 272. Didasc. syr. 12 (FUNK 1905, 158) speaks of *episcopi* and *ecclesiae*, the parallel text of the Const. Apost. 2,57,1 f. (FUNK 1905, 159) of a bishop and a church of God. Both texts mean the local bishop and local church. There is no idea of there being a number of churches in a city. The Syriac *Didascalia* seems not to use the word "church" for the church building; VOELKL 1954, 114.
209 Didasc. syr. 12 (ACHELIS / FLEMMING 1904, 68–70).
210 BRENK 2003, 65; MACMULLEN 2009, 3.
211 Even if it was not a bishop's church (cf. NUSSBAUM 1965, 32), it was still the central Catholic church.
212 KRAELING 1967, 19 and SNYDER 2003, 132: 65–75 persons. MACMULLEN 2009, 3 and PEPPARD 2016, 17: seventy-five persons.

whatsoever for the assumption that the church building did not suffice for the worship of the Christians of Dura Europos.

For the West Syrian metropolis of Antioch, the statements of Bishop Ignatius are once more pertinent to the second century (above chapter II, 4). What he writes in his seven letters to the various local churches in Asia Minor and to the community in Rome leaves no doubt that in his home city of Antioch, too, there is only one church space with one altar. As late as the middle of the third century only one "church", also called "church house" (ὁ τῆς ἐκκλησίας οἶκος), is attested there, over which the bishops Domnus and Paul of Samosata argued until the imperial decision of 270.[213] If there had been several churches, they would probably not have had to fight over the church.

A passage from the Pseudo-Clementines may also belong to the same period. It speaks of a certain Theophilus who transformed his town house (*domus*) in Antioch into a very large basilica, called a "church", in which a cathedra was erected for the apostle Peter so that the people might meet there daily.[214] According to this, there was a single church space in Antioch, too, which had room for all the Christians of the city even though this church was originally a private house. This legend is probably attached to what was at that time the bishop's church of the city. It was indeed said of the so-called Ancient Church of Antioch that it had apostolic origins. It had been destroyed in the Diocletian persecution and rebuilt around 313–324. It seems to have been the bishop's church.[215] It was then replaced in this function by the Great Church that Emperor Constantine started to have built in 327, but which was only completed under his son Constantius II (337–361).[216] The new cathedral had probably not yet been consecrated when the Synod of Antioch of 341 decreed in Canon 5 that a presbyter who had fallen out with the bishop and held his own assembly for which he erected "another altar" was to be excommunicated along with his followers, clergy and laity alike.[217] "Another altar" is probably to be understood in the sense of a second altar alongside that of the bishop. Thus, in Antioch there was still only the altar of the Ancient Church, which as a second church later became the co-cathedral.

---

213 Euseb. hist. eccl. 7,30,10. 19 (SC 41, 217. 219); JUDGE 2008, 428. Possibly also to be applied to Antioch is Euseb. hist. eccl. 6,34 (SC 41, 137); AUBÉ 1881, 470 f.

214 Ps.-Clem. recogn. 10,71,2 f. (GCS PsClem. 2, 371): *Theofilus* [...] *domus suae ingentem basilicam ecclesiae nomine consecraret, in qua Petro apostolo constituta est ab omni populo cathedra.* Cf. 4,6 (149): the *domus* of Maro in Tripoli in which Peter preaches holds five hundred men. WIELAND 1906, 70 wants to read a house church in Tripoli into rec-

ogn. 6,15,4–6 (GCS PsClem. 2, 196), which, however, the text does not actually yield. All the same, a single worship service is assumed here for the local *ecclesia*, namely that of the bishop.

215 ELTESTER 1937, 273.

216 Ibid. 254.

217 Const. Apost. 8,47 = Can. Apost. 31 (SC 336, 282): [...] θυσιαστήριον ἕτερον πήξῃ [...]. Translation according to C. STEPHENS, Canon Law and Episcopal Authority. The Canons of Antioch and Sardica (Oxford 2015): "If a presbyter or deacon,

As far as *Palestine* and *Lebanon* are concerned, in around 180 Hegesippus speaks of the "churches" over which the descendants of the Lord's brother Jude presided.[218] However, this does not refer to a specific city, for example Jerusalem, but rather to the "entire church".[219] So the idea is that they led the Christian communities in the cities of a wider region.[220] In Palestinian Caesarea in the mid–third century there seems to have been only the bishop's church.[221] This is also confirmed by Origen: a priest since 232, he speaks several times in his sermons in Caesarea, which he undoubtedly held in the bishop's church, of the church (*ecclesia*) as a church building – and this for him necessarily possesses an altar.[222] He speaks of the church in the singular, to which the faithful come, in which they adorn the altar and where they have themselves blessed by the priests (*sacerdotes*).[223] So what he has in mind is the episcopal Mass celebrated in the company of the presbyterium. When he speaks of churches in the plural, he is referring to the whole world. For example, Jerusalem and the altar of the temple there were destroyed while churches with altars were now being built by the Gentiles.[224] In the same way, the whole globe is full of "church buildings" (*domus ecclesiae*).[225] In one sermon he speaks of the "holy places" entrusted to the priests in the cities and suburbs.[226] But here he refers exclusively to the Old Testament (Nm 35,1 f.?).

In Tyre in Lebanon, too, there appears to be only the altar of the bishop's church.[227] In any case, the new cathedral consecrated around 314–321 was built over its destroyed predecessor building. Further north lies Heliopolis. Eusebius recounts that Constantine erected a very large church there (after 324), also called a prayer house, as well as an

---

despising his bishop, separates from the church, forms a separate community, erects an altar, and refuses to listen to the warnings of his bishop, and does not intend to listen or obey his summons, repeated a first and second time, he will be completely deposed, without the hope of remission or the ability to recover his status. If he continues to cause troubles and seditions in the church, he shall be returned to order, like a seditious person, by the civil power."

218 Euseb. hist. eccl. 3,20,6 (SC 31, 124).

219 Ibid. 3,32,6 (SC 31, 144).

220 For Hegesippus, the church structure consists of local churches each with a president-bishop: Euseb. hist. eccl. 4,22,2–4 (SC 31, 200). The choice of the word "president" points to the episcopal cathedra in the church building.

221 Euseb. hist. eccl. 7,15,1–5 (SC 41, 189 f.); DÖLGER 1930, 163. For a short period of time two bishops presided over "the same church" (of Caesarea);

Euseb. hist. eccl. 7,32,21 (SC 41, 227). That is obviously a special case and does not imply two Christian communities, each with its own church. Practically nothing is known about cultic buildings in Caesarea before Constantine; ELLIGER 2001, 1054 f.

222 See above p. 9 n. 3.

223 Orig. in Jesu Nav. hom. 10,3 (SC 71, 276): *ut ad ecclesiam veniant et inclinent caput suum sacerdotibus […], ad ornatum quoque altaris vel ecclesiae aliquid conferant.* Orig. in Gen. hom. 10,3 (SC 7², 264): *ad ecclesiam convenitis.*

224 Orig. in Jesu Nav. hom. 2,1 (SC 71, 116): *Cum vero videris introire gentes ad fidem, ecclesias exstrui, altaria […].*

225 Orig. in Ex. hom. 2,2 (SC 321, 76).

226 Orig. in Lev. hom. 11,1 (SC 287, 142).

227 Euseb. hist. eccl. 10,4,68 (SC 55, 102). Eusebius speaks of the "sole altar" of the new cathedral in Tyre.

episcopal residence. The church was designed to be large because the emperor was hoping for numerous conversions among the city's population. So there was no thought of building further churches later on. Eusebius also assigns the priests and deacons (of the city) to the Constantinian "Church of God" as serving clergy. Consequently, he is not thinking of parishes or small churches, but only of a central city clergy at the cathedral. This also becomes clear from the context, where Eusebius claims that the church was the first church in the city altogether.[228]

Even more telling is Bishop Cyril of Jerusalem (Fig. 13). In 348 he instructs the catechumens that when they arrive in other cities, they are not to ask simply for "the Lord's house" (τὸ κυριακόν) or "the church" (ἡ ἐκκλησία), since this is also what the heretics call their dens, but to ask instead for "the Catholic church".[229] Cyril thus shows himself convinced that each town has only one church building belonging to the Catholic Church, but possibly other churches belonging to Christian sects.[230] The one Catholic church can, of course, only be the bishop's church. Cyril's own cathedral church in Jerusalem is the complex donated by Emperor Constantine and comprising the Church of the Holy Sepulchre together with the Basilica of the Invention of the Holy Cross, the Golgotha and the Sepulchre Rotunda. In later times it probably possessed several altars,[231] but not necessarily in Cyril's time, as the Basilica of the Invention of the Holy Cross alone was considered a church space (with an altar).[232]

One statement of Cyril's, however, has given the impression that in Jerusalem at least there was an additional Catholic church. He says that "here, in Jerusalem" there is the "Upper Church" (ἡ ἀνωτέρα ἐκκλησία). It stands where the Holy Spirit descended on the apostles,[233] and that is where Pentecost is said to have occurred (Acts 2:1–4). The expression "Upper Church" might be taken as a common term used locally in the sense of "the upper church". If this were the case, then there would be at least two churches in Jerusalem: the "lower" bishop's church in the city centre and the "upper" church – outside the city proper – on Mount Zion.[234] This is, however, very unlikely because then his own episcopal city of all places would constitute an exception to what Cyril told the catechumens. If a late

228 Euseb. vit. Const. 3,58,1–3 (SC 559, 430–432).

229 Cyrill. Hier. cat. 18,26 (Rupp 1860, 328).

230 Licinius does order the Christians to no longer gather in the "city prayer houses", but this is addressed to the whole Eastern Empire and also includes the non-Catholic churches; Euseb. vit. Const. 1,53,2 (SC 559, 256).

231 Paulin. Nol. ep. 31,6 (FC 25,2, 742): *condita in passionis loco basilica, quae auratis corusca laquearibus et aureis dives altaribus.* This letter dates from 403.

232 Cf. Heid 2001a, 46.

233 Cyrill. Hier. cat. 16,4 (Rupp 1960, 208–210). J. Wilkinson, Egeria's Travels (Warminster ³2002) 10. Cyril speaks twice of the "Upper Church", i.e. this was what it was called, not because it was located on the upper floor but because seen from the city it lay up above on Mount Zion.

234 So C. Kopp, Die Heiligen Stätten der Evangelien (Regensburg 1959) 379. Cf. G. Röwekamp, in: FC 68, 314 n. 784.

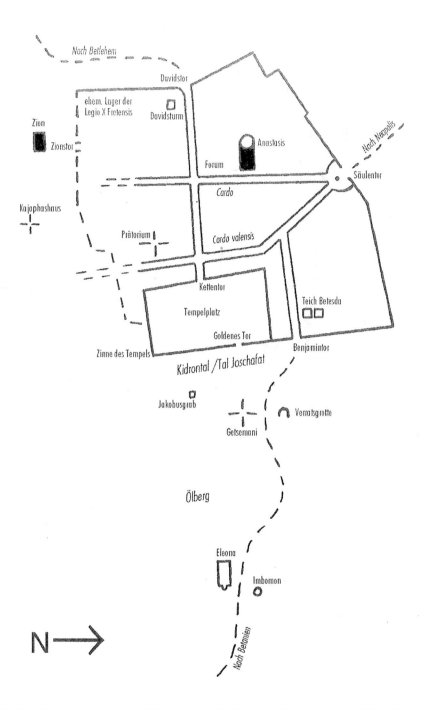

Fig. 13: Map of Jerusalem at the time of Bishop Cyril (mid-4th century); G. RÖWEKAMP, in: FC 20, 365.

statement by Epiphanius of Salamis is to be trusted, a worship space had already existed for a long time on Mount Zion, but more probably a chapel, possibly on an upper floor.[235] But would Cyril really compare the huge complex of his bishop's church and a little chapel like "the Upper Church"? To be sure, Cyril is also familiar with ἐκκλησία[236] as a term for the church building alongside κυριακόν.[237] However, ἐκκλησία also means, as he himself states, the "assembly".[238] Now, according to Acts, the apostles gathered in an "upper room" after the Ascension (Acts 1:13 f.). With this in mind, Cyril speaks of ἡ ἀνωτέρα τῶν ἀποστόλων ἐκκλησία. This does not mean "the upper church of the apostles"; no church ever bore this title in Jerusalem. Rather, the whole expression must be translated as "the upper place of assembly of the apostles". The "upper" refers to the upper room where the apostles regularly gathered (Acts 1:13). In Cyril's day, no second church existed on Mount Zion, but only a place of remembrance of the apostles' assembly at Pentecost. It was only later that a church was built there, as the pilgrim Egeria (381–384) testifies.[239]

A similar picture can be painted for the trading city of Gaza. Before Bishop Porphyry (c. 400), it had a single church, the Eirene (Peace), plus martyrs' churches outside the city.[240] One statement by the church historian Sozomen (fifth century), who was particularly familiar with Gaza, is revealing. He recalls the time when Gaza and the nearby port city of Maiuma (Constantia) were not yet administratively united. From this time it is possible to explain why both places have a bishop and their own altar offerings (θυσιαστήρια), which are measured according to the original city areas and their respective surrounding countryside.[241] It is clear that the altar offerings refer to each bishop's altar, besides which there seem to be no other altars. The contributions paid by the faithful living within the circumscribed boundaries are called altar offerings here because they are probably placed on the altar.

A meaningful picture already emerges of *North Africa* in the second and third centuries which supports the single-church principle – even if researchers still tend to work with the cliché of private houses or house churches, especially for the large city of Carthage.[242] Winfried Elliger, for example, claims that even in the time of Bishop Cyprian († 258) there was no specific church space in the city, but that they used the *tablinium* or the *oecus* (*triclinium*) of the private houses, where the altar, cathedra and pulpit stood.[243] The

235 Epiph. mens. et pond. 14 (PG 43, 261A). Epiphanius († 403) here speaks unambiguously of a small "church of God" at the time of Emperor Hadrian, but the idea that this was a specially built church is not credible. The mere fact that it is supposed to have been small – because the upper floor itself was the church? – indicates that it was a mere memorial site.

236 Cyrill. Hier. cat. 14,6 (Rupp 1860, 114).

237 Dölger 1950, 166 f.

238 Cyrill. Hier. cat. 18,22–26 (Rupp 1860, 324–330).

239 A hypothetical reconstruction of the Mount Zion church in J. Wilkinson, Gerusalemme la città santa (Rome 1981) 144 Fig. 38.

240 G. Downey, Gaza, in RACh 8 (1972) 1123–1134, here 1131.

241 Sozom. hist. eccl. 5,3,8 (SC 495, 106).

242 E.g. Burns / Jensen 2014, 87.

idea of celebrating the Eucharist in the dining rooms of the house churches seems to be supported by a more recent theory, according to which Tertullian of Carthage († after 220) only knew the full celebration of the Eucharist in the context of the Mediterranean *cena*. This symposium-type Eucharist was, though, the central, i.e. the only, celebration of the Christians in Carthage.[244]

Whatever the case may be, whether many house churches or a central mass meal, nothing about it is to be found in Tertullian. The latter is not acquainted with an agape-Eucharist, but distinguishes two types of events celebrated by the Christians that possibly take place on the same day but at different times. In the evening there is the reclining meal,[245] which for logistical reasons is only possible in a smallish circle. This agape is also called the "supper of God" (*cena Dei*) and the "banquet of the Lord" (*convivium dominicum*). This sounds unusual to us today since the terms "supper" (*coena*) and "banquet" (*convivium*) tend to make us think of the Eucharist. But for Tertullian, it is precisely not the Eucharist but rather the agape that is linked to Jesus's Last Supper. The Eucharist, on the other hand, he calls the "sacrament of the Eucharist" (*eucharistiae sacramentum*). It takes place in the morning[246] and is attended by the whole community (*ecclesia*).[247]

---

243 ELLIGER 2004, 269.

244 KLINGHARDT 1996, 514–516; LEONHARD / ECK-HARDT 2010, 1081 f. Cf. ROUWHORST 2015, 61 f.; MESSNER 2003a, 434.

245 It is exactly this distinction between Eucharist and evening agape that is meant in Tert. ux. 2,8,8 (CCL 1, 394): *In ecclesia dei pariter utrique, pariter in convivio dei*. Tert. ux. 2,4,2 (CCL 1, 388 f.): *convivium dominicum*. This is precisely about the *nocturnae convocationes*, more specifically the *sollemnia Paschae* and the *convivium dominicum*. The latter can likewise only refer to the evening agape, i.e. the *cena* or the *convicium*; apol. 39,16 f. (CCL 1, 152); spect. 13,4 (239): *cena Dei*. Cf. Trad. Apost. 27 (FC 1, 280): *cena dominica*. This is confirmed by the suspicion with which the pagans view the (night-time!) *convivium dominicum*; this is exactly what is said of the agape, which is accused of being intemperate (Tert. apol. 39 contradicts this). The fact that the agape takes place in the evening is also clear from Tert. ieiun. 17,3 (CCL 2, 1276) and Act. Perp. et Fel. 17,1 (BASTI-AENSEN 1995, 138).

246 DEKKERS 1948, 242–245. According to Tert. or. 19,1–3 (CCL 1, 267 f.) the *sacrificium* celebrated at *the ara Dei* takes place in the morning. Tert. cor. 3,3 (CCL 2, 1043): *Eucharistiae sacramentum*

[…] *etiam antelucanis coetibus*. This must apply to the complete celebration of the Eucharist (differently LEONHARD / ECKHARDT 2010, 1083). For what point would there have been in merely distributing the Eucharist in the morning, and what is more, just the remains of the agape-Eucharist from the evening before (so also BURNS / JENSEN 2014, 239, 242)? Only at the *eucharistiae sacramentum* is there mention of "presidents" (cor. 3,3 [CCL 2, 1043]: *praesidentes*), not at the agape, which were likely to have been less coordinated by the Church. A further reason why the evening agape cannot be linked to the Eucharist is that Communion takes place *ante omnem cibum*, which therefore means in the early morning (eucharistic fast); Tert. ux. 2,5,3 (CCL 1, 389); WIELAND 1906, 107. Finally, BURNS / JENSEN loc.cit. 240 recognise correctly that Tertullian never speaks of the Eucharist in connection with the evening banquet.

247 Tert. cor. 3,3 (CCL 2, 1043): *Eucharistiae sacramentum, et in tempore victus et omnibus mandatum a domino, etiam antelucanis coetibus nec de aliorum manu quam praesidentium sumimus.* KLINGHARDT 1996, 516 thinks that cor. 3,3 depicts a morning celebration of the Eucharist, "but not as a central meal celebration". This is precisely why his thesis that the Lord's Supper por-

Tertullian does not say where the agapes are held, who organises them (the bishop?) or whether several take place in different places. However, since the contemporaneous *Traditio Apostolica* likewise distinguishes between the (morning[248]) Eucharist and the "Lord's Supper" (*cena domini*), and since this semi-ritual reclining evening meal is presided over by the bishop,[249] it will also be assumed for Tertullian that there is only one evening meal at the bishop's residence or with the bishop. On the other hand, the "church assemblies" (*ecclesiae*) for the Eucharist described by Tertullian take place in the "house of God" (*domus Dei*).[250] There, the church assembly meets under the overseer (*antistes*), and there, too, a baptistery is to be found.[251] At the worship, the people and (all) the priests are present, the latter sitting together.[252] There is apparently only this one worship space, even when the congregation grows larger.[253] Tertullian, in whose time the number of Christians in Carthage was estimated at between one and several thousand (out of a population of about one hundred thousand),[254] mentions the concern of some Christians that the pagans might take action against them because they all "converge on the church assembly" at the same time and in large numbers.[255] This supports the idea

trayed by Tertullian (apol. 39) is the Eucharist is untenable. He also neglects the considerations of liturgical pragmatics: according to Tertullian, the Eucharist is celebrated by a priest standing at the altar. How could that be compatible with a meal Eucharist? Saxer 1994a, 310, fails to recognise that for Tertullian Eucharist and banquet (*cena Dei, convivium*) are two different things. A double celebration is likely already to have been the practice in Asia Minor at the beginning of the second century. Plin. ep. 10,96,7 (Schuster 1933, 364) distinguishes between the morning meeting of the Christians on a certain fixed day and a further gathering to eat on the same day, during which only ordinary food was eaten. Apparently, Pliny distinguishes the Sunday Eucharist in the morning from the evening agape. It is highly unlikely, though, that that "certain fixed day" would mean just Easter (so Klinghardt 1996, 327 n. 86).

248 It probably took place in the morning on account of the prescribed eucharistic fast; Trad. Apost. 36 (FC 1, 292).

249 Trad. Apost. 26 f. (FC 1, 278–280): *Et cum cenant, qui adsunt fideles sument de manu episcopi paululum panis […], quia eulogia est et non eucharistia […]. Catecuminus in cena dominica non concumbat. Per omnem vero oblationem memor sit qui offert eius qui illum vocavit.* W. Geerlings, in: FC 1, 193: "The clearly implemented separation of common meal and celebration of the Eucharist

[…]" Lietzmann 1926, 197 f. For Klinghardt 1996, 513, on the other hand, the *Traditio Apostolica* describes the Eucharist as an evening meal for satisfying hunger.

250 Tert. ux. 2,8,3 (CCL 1, 392): *Sordent talibus ecclesiae: difficile in domo dei dives.* Idol. 7,1 (CCL 2, 1106): *in ecclesiam venire, de adversaria officina in domum dei venire.*

251 Tert. cor. 3,2 (CCL 2, 1042): *Denique, ut a baptismate ingrediar, aquam adituri ibidem, sed et aliquanto prius in ecclesia sub antistitis manu, contestamur nos renuntiare diabolo et pompae et angelis eius.* The *antistes* appears to belong to a college of *praesidentes*; ibid. 3,3 (1043).

252 Tert. exh. cast. 7,3 (CCL 2, 1024 f.): *Differentiam inter ordinem et plebem constituit ecclesiae auctoritas et honor per ordinis consessus sanctificatos deo. Ubi ecclesiastici ordinis non est consessus […].*

253 Dassmann 1986, 898.

254 Schöllgen 1985, 298. This number, too, renders obsolete the thesis propounded by Leonhard / Eckhardt 2010, 1083. How are one thousand Christians supposed to organise an agape meal every evening?

255 Tert. fug. 3,2 (CCL 2, 1139): *simul convenimus et complures concurrimus in ecclesiam.* This statement falls within Tertullian's Montanist period, but he is certain to have continued to participate in Catholic worship. Schöllgen 1985, 308 f. also assumes this. See also below n. 402.

of a central Catholic worship service for which, towards the end of the second century, it was possible that a large, elaborate building had to be erected.[256] At all events, Tertullian does not speak, as is repeatedly claimed, of eucharistic celebrations in private houses, which were allegedly presided over by laypersons.[257]

On the other hand, a great many heretics who distanced themselves from their own founders (e.g. Valentine, Marcion) "have not even churches (*ecclesiae*). Motherless, houseless, creedless, outcasts, they wander about in their own essential worthlessness."[258] This means that in Carthage the tightly organised Valentinians and Marcionites each have their own meeting place (*ecclesia*) with a fixed address (*sedes*), but many small groups are, as it were, invisible. They do not formally split off from their mother sect and do not have their own place of worship, but gather here or there.[259] On no account does Tertullian say that in Carthage there were innumerable church buildings on both the Catholic and the heretical side. For the fixed seat (*sedes*), in connection with the metaphor of the mother, implies unity: every major sect – no different from the Catholic Church – possesses just one single meeting place.

Even half a century after Tertullian, Bishop Cyprian of Carthage assumes that the entire local congregation gathers for worship in one room.[260] At no point is there any mention of (house) churches that are independently looked after by the presbyters. It does state that the presbyters also celebrate the Eucharist without the bishop, but apparently only in emergency situations, for example in the prisons.[261] However, during

---

256 SCHÖLLGEN 1985, 309 on Tert. apol. 39,14 (CCL 1, 152). However, I share the doubts of SCHÖLLGEN loc.cit. 308 that Tert. adv. Val. 3,1 (CCL 2, 754): *Nostrae columbae etiam domus simplex, in editis semper et apertis et ad lucem*, is speaking of this church building.

257 Cf. Tert. exh. cast. 11,1 f. (CCL 2, 1031): [...] *Stabis ergo ad dominum cum tot uxoribus, quot in oratione commemores? et offeres pro duabus et commendabis illas duas per sacerdotem de monogamia ordinatum* [...]. This is not referring to a celebration of the Eucharist by laypersons; rather, the layperson offers his oblation through the priest. So there is no suggestion of house-church worship here either. Over and over again, people use Tert. exh. cast. 7,3 (CCL 2, 1024 f.) (e.g. BURNS / JENSEN 2014, 239, 245 f., 260) to claim lay Eucharists, but here Tertullian is styling the layman a priest in order to be able to impose the same sexual morality on him (CAMELOT 1970, 16 nm. 49 speaks of "sophism"). Nevertheless, he makes a strict distinction between laity and ordained clergy and accuses the heretics of giving layper-

sons priestly tasks; praescr. haer. 41,8 (CCL 1, 222): *et laicis sacerdotalia munera iniungunt.*

258 Ibid. 42,10 (CCL 1, 222): *Plerique nec ecclesias habent, sine matre, sine sede, orbi fide, extorres quasi sibilati vagantur.* Cf. DÖLGER, 1930, 48 f.; id. 1934, 229. Euseb. vit. Const. 3,66,3 (SC 559, 454) still says that in the Constantinian period heretics and schismatics gained their fatherland again, recognised their mother the Church and returned to her.

259 Tert. praescr. haer. 42,6 (CCL 1, 222): *scismata apud haereticos fere non sunt quia, cum sint, non parent.*

260 RENAUD 1971, 9–11, 13. BURNS / JENSEN 2014, 251: "no evidence of private or household celebrations." Cypr. or. dom. 4 (CSEL 3,1, 269): *in unum cum fratribus convenimus et sacrificia divina cum Dei sacerdote celebramus.* Here the *in unum* [*locum*] takes up the ἐπὶ τὸ αὐτό (see below Subject Index).

261 Cypr. ep. 5,2 (CSEL 3,2, 479) at the time of the Decian persecution. RENAUD 1971, 56 f. PALAZZO 2008, 75 here assumes the use of portable wooden altars.

the Valerian persecution of the Christians public meetings are banned, meaning that no services of any kind can take place, not even in the prisons.[262] Vincenzo Monachino sums up for the fourth century what can equally well be said about the preceding period in Carthage: the presbyters are strictly attached to the episcopal administration. They form his advisory body and represent the bishop, if necessary, at the celebration of the Eucharist and the administration of penance.[263]

When Cyprian speaks of baptism "in the church", he does not mean by this an abstract concept but rather the concrete bishop's church, for example that in Carthage.[264] Here, pastoral care is centrally organised: everything takes place in the (one) church at the (one) altar of Bishop Cyprian; both baptism and the Eucharist are linked to this place.[265] He can therefore say in a way what everyone understands: there can be no baptism outside the Church for those who are baptised in the Church.[266] Cyprian thus knows of only one church building in his own episcopal city and in the cities of his diocese to which the baptismal candidates come. These are the bishop's churches with baptisteries. Those who are baptised outside these churches have to be rebaptised.[267] Now one might think that although Cyprian mentions only one baptistery, there could well have been other churches without a baptistery. However, another statement speaks against this. For alongside the baptisms "outside the Church", he also deplores sacrilegious celebrations of the sacrifice "outside (the Church)". He emphasises that there is only one altar at which it is permitted to sacrifice.[268] In the dispute over heretical baptism, it becomes clear that in every city there is only one church,[269] namely the Catholic bishop's church, which has a baptistery and an altar.[270] The heretics are simply not Christians because they do not come into the church of the Catholic bishop.[271] The latter, for his part, must not admit

262 Molthagen 1975, 87–92, 96.
263 Monachino 1947, 158.
264 On sacred space in Cyprian see Stewart 2015, 171–174.
265 Cypr. ep. 70,2 (CSEL 3,2, 768): *porro autem eucharistia est unde baptizati unguntur oleum in altari sanctificatum. sanctificare autem non potuit olei creaturam qui nec altare habuit nec ecclesiam. unde nec unctio spiritalis apud haereticos potest esse, quando constet oleum sanctificari et eucharistiam fieri apud illos omnino non posse.*
266 Ibid. 73,2 (CSEL 3,2, 779): *quod si in ecclesia baptizatos rebaptizandos foris extra ecclesiam […].*
267 Ibid. 72,1 (CSEL 3,2, 775): *eos qui sunt foris extra ecclesiam tincti […], quando ad nos adque ad ecclesiam quae est una venerint, baptizari oportere.*

268 Ibid. 72,2 (CSEL 3,2, 776): *contra altare unum adque divinum sacrificia foris falsa ac sacrilega offerre.*
269 Cf. ibid. 72,2 (CSEL 3,2, 776): *rebelles contra ecclesiam steterint.* This one church he also calls a *domus fidei*: ibid. 72,2 (777).
270 Conc. Carth. a. 256, 1 (Mansi 1, 952C): *Ego unum baptisma in ecclesia sola scio, et extra ecclesiam nullum. […] sacerdotium administrat profanus, ponit altare sacrilegus.* Ibid. 33 (958C): *privatus fons noster est, intelligant cuncti ecclesiae nostrae adversarii […]. Nec duobus populis salutarem aquam tribuere potest ille, qui unius gregis pastor est.*
271 Ibid. 24 (Mansi 1, 956E–957A): *Haeretici Christiani sunt, an non? Si Christiani sunt, cur in ecclesia Dei non sunt?* So asks Secundinus, the bishop

those into the house of God (*domus Dei*), whom he must even refuse entry into his private house.[272]

Cyprian and all the North African bishops defend an ecclesial principle that has been traditional at least since Ignatius of Antioch, but which also makes sense in the face of separatist movements. For example, the schismatic priest and anti-bishop Novatian went against ecclesial norms and erected his own altar (*altare conlocare*) so as to be able to offer the eucharistic sacrifice. For Cyprian, however, there can only be one altar and the only person entitled to erect it is the (rightful) bishop. When he asks rhetorically whether he must resign his altar and cathedra now that Novatian has erected his altar and cathedra in Carthage,[273] he undoubtedly really only possessed one cathedra and one altar.[274] He does not recognise the schismatic houses of God as places of worship.[275]

The Novatian schism is not the only problematic case in Carthage. A certain Fortunatus also tried to establish himself as an anti-bishop because he found Cyprian to be too strict with those who had lapsed from faith during the persecution. For Cyprian, this Fortunatus is of course "outside the Church",[276] especially because he tries to expel Cyprian and his presbyters and take over the bishop's church. He wants Cyprian's priests – his clergy (*clerus noster*) – to leave their venerable seats in the church and remove the altar of the Lord.[277] Hence there is only this one altar in Carthage around which the bishop and his clergy gather. Every bishop has, so to speak, his altar. The priests also participate in the episcopal Eucharist at this altar. The new priests are taken into service, Cyprian says, in order to "serve the altar and the sacrifices".[278] Again, he speaks in the singular of the altar of the bishop's church,[279] not of altars of house churches.

---

of a North African city. There would be no point in this question if *ecclesia* here meant the universal Church. The "church of God" is the church building of the Catholics as opposed to that of the heretics.

272 Ibid. 81 (Mansi 1, 965A): *Quomodo admitti tales in domum Dei possunt, qui in domum nostram privatam admitti prohibentur.*

273 Cypr. ep. 73,2 (CSEL 3,2, 780): *quia et honorem cathedrae sacerdotalis Novatianus usurpat, num idcirco nos cathedrae renuntiare debemus? et quia Novatianus altare conlocare et sacrificia offerre contra fas nititur, ab altari et sacrificiis cessare nos oportet, ne paria et similia cum illo celebrare videamur?*

274 There is no knowledge of Cyprian having erected a second altar in Carthage on his own authority.

275 Cypr. ep. 68,2 (CSEL 3,2, 745); 69,8 (757); 73,2 (780). Conc. Elib. can. 22 (Vilella / Barreda 573): *si quis de catholica ecclesia ad haeresem transitum fecerit.*

276 Cypr. ep. 59,18 (CSEL 3,2, 687): *extra ecclesiam constituti.*

277 Ibid. 59,18 (CSEL 3,2, 687 f.): *quid superest quam ut ecclesia Capitolio cedat et recedentibus sacerdotibus ac Domini altare removentibus in cleri nostri sacrum venerandumque congestum simulacra adque idola cum aris suis transeant.*

278 Ibid. 1,1 (CSEL 3,2, 465): *quando singuli divino sacerdotio honorati et in clerico ministerio constituti non nisi altari et sacrificiis deservire.*

279 Ibid. 1,2 (CSEL 3,2, 467): *sacerdotes et ministros Dei altari eius et ecclesiae vacantes.*

The whole controversy turns on the unity of the local church. Cyprian excommunicates both those who have lapsed from the faith during the persecution and the schismatics. Because there is only one bishop's church in the city, when he says that someone is excluded from the church, this formulation simply describes the fact that the person concerned is no longer allowed to enter the bishop's church. Excommunication is not a bureaucratic act by which one learns that one no longer belongs to the community of the universal Church; rather, it means being prohibited from entering the church of the local bishop for the celebration of the Eucharist and from receiving Communion there. Cyprian complains about the lax presbyters of the anti-bishop, who give the greeting of peace to the apostates who are outside the Church and offer fellowship to those who are not permitted to receive Communion (in the bishop's church), simply so that those who are outside do not knock on the doors of Cyprian's church and return to it.[280] In fact, however, those who have lapsed during the persecution are running back to the Church every day, knocking on the door there and causing strife inside among the people of God (gathered for worship), which Cyprian is hardly able to settle.[281] Fortunatus and Felicissimus, too, are no longer "in the Church", and they do not even dare to come or to approach the threshold of the church (of Carthage), but stay outside in the provinces.[282]

So there is no doubt what Cyprian means when he states quite unequivocally in a letter to his community in Carthage that there is only one church, only one cathedra and only one altar.[283] Just by way of confirmation, let us quote another of Cyprian's letters. It is addressed to a neighbouring bishop in whose city consecrated virgins, a deacon, and other men had allegedly sinned with each other. Apparently, there was a scandal in the church when the bishop "held back" the deacon and the other men,[284] which must probably mean from entering the church. Thereupon unpleasant scenes took place in the

---

280 Ibid. 59,13 (CSEL 3,2, 682): […] *ne pulsetur ad ecclesiam Christi, sed sublata paenitentia* […] *despectis episcopis* […] *pax a presbyteris verbis fallacibus praedicetur, et ne lapsi surgant aut foris positi ad ecclesiam redeant, communicatio non communicantibus offeratur?* The *ecclesia Christi* is here not abstract at all but would distinguish the church building of the Catholics, i.e. Cyprian's episcopal church, from the church building of the anti-bishop Fortunatus, which Cyprian naturally does not recognise as a church.

281 Ibid. 59,15 (CSEL 3,2, 684f.): *remeant cotidie adque ad ecclesiam pulsant* […]. […] *superbi sic ad ecclesiam remeant, ut bona intus ingenia corrumpant. vix plebi persuadeo, immo extorqueo, ut tales patiantur admitti.*

282 Ibid. 59,16 (CSEL 3,2, 686): […] *ut etsi in ecclesia essent, eici tales de ecclesia debuissent ?* […] *nec audent venire aut ad ecclesiae limen accedere, sed foris per provinciam circumveniendis fratribus et spoliandis pererrant.*

283 Ibid. 43,5 (CSEL 3,2, 594): *Deus unus est et Christus unus et una ecclesia et cathedra una* […]. *aliud altare constitui aut sacerdotium novum fieri praeter unum altare et unum sacerdotium non potest.* The *sacerdotium* is the episcopal office, here specifically Cyprian's priestly office in Carthage. Clearly only one altar in Carthage also ibid. 66,5 (730): *sit antistes et rector altari eorum pariter et plebi restitutus.*

284 Ibid. 4,4 (CSEL 3,2, 475): *abstinendo diaconum* […], *sed et ceteros.*

church in front of the horrified congregation.[285] Cyprian now gives his advice on how the "servants of God" – deacon and virgins – can be readmitted. For now, they remain "thrown out" of the church, where they do not survive. For outside the "house of God", the church, there is no salvation.[286] This alludes to the Eucharist, which only exists in the church and without which the servants of God must so to speak starve. On the other hand, those who confess their sins can return to the church.[287]

Cyprian's remark is also revealing in that not all the brothers can take part in the bishop's evening meal (*cena*, *convivium*), a semi-ritual meal with "sacrificed" mingled wine. For this reason, he says, the Eucharist (*sacramentum*) is celebrated early in the morning.[288] Only part of the community participated in the meal for reasons of space – probably because it was a reclining meal – and it was celebrated outside the church. But this in no way means that they spread out over various households in the city;[289] rather, all those invited would gather in a dining room in the bishop's house or in a private house in the presence of the bishop.[290] On the other hand, for the celebration of the Eucharist in which "our people" and "the whole brotherhood" participate,[291] the bishop's church must have served as a larger assembly room. In addition to the spatial separation of the *coena* and the Eucharist, there is also the temporal one: since it is hard to celebrate mass immediately after the evening meal at which heavy wine is drunk, the Eucharist is moved to the early morning.[292] So in the fifty years since Tertullian, nothing has changed in Carthage as regards the way the Eucharist and the agape are handled.

---

285 Ibid. 4,5 (CSEL 3,2, 477): *nec sacerdotes Dei ** aut per ecclesiam scandalo se et fratribus offerant.*

286 Ibid. 4,4 (CSEL 3,2, 477): [...] *dum de ecclesia eiciuntur. neque enim vivere foris possunt, cum domus Dei una sit et nemini salus esse nisi in ecclesia possit.*

287 Ibid. 4,4 (CSEL 3,2, 476): *postea exomologesi facta ad ecclesiam redeat.* [...] *numquam a nobis admitti in ecclesiam posse.*

288 Ibid. 63,16 (CSEL 3,2, 714): [...] *quod etsi mane aqua sola offerri videtur, tamen cum ad cenandum venimus, mixtum calicem offerimus? sed cum cenamus, ad convivium nostrum plebem convocare non possumus, ut sacramenti veritatem fraternitate omni praesente celebremus.* Fundamental DEKKERS 1948, 246–249. Cf. KLINGHARDT 1996, 516f.; LEONHARD / ECKHARDT 2010, 1083; MESSNER 2003a, 434; *id.* 2006, 69–71.

289 BURNS / JENSEN 2014, 247, 251, 259 postulate, without any evidence: "evening supper at which Christians gathered in smaller groups", "evening *convivia*, presumably in private homes".

290 The situation is probably similar to that in the *Traditio Apostolica*, where the episcopal *coena* appears to take place alternately in the various houses since the participants are supposed to pray for the person who has invited them into his house; Trad. Apost. 27 (FC 1, 280). Thus, here as there, the church is not used for the agape. Interestingly, the church complex at Dura Europos does not have a kitchen and the latrine was put out of use in the alterations (BRENK 2003, 66–68). This makes it likely that a celebration of the ordinary evening meal there can be ruled out.

291 Cypr. ep. 63,16 (CSEL 3,2, 714). Text above n. 288. The fact that the entire people participated in the Eucharist but only a few in the agape is confirmed in Trad. Apost. 22 (FC 1, 272): *omni populo*, or ibid. 26 (278): *qui adsunt fideles.* ALIKIN 2010, 143f.

292 Cypr. ep. 63,15 (CSEL 3,2, 713): *nisi si in sacrificiis matutinis hoc quis veretur, ne per saporem vini redoleat sanguinem Christi.* Ibid. 63,16 (714): *nos autem resurrectionem Domini mane celebramus.*

By 303, the *Basilica Novarum* already exists in Carthage. But this church is located outside the city in the "new cemeteries" (*novae areae*).[293] Optatus of Milevis, speaking at a great temporal distance about the consecration of Caecilianus as bishop in 312/13, seems to be familiar with only one church in Carthage, namely the bishop's church, which he calls a *basilica* and *ecclesia*.[294] It is only from the middle of the fourth century onwards that a multiplicity of churches is to be expected. In the fifth and sixth centuries, there are about twenty churches in Carthage in the possession of the Catholics, Donatists, and Arians (Vandals).[295]

Continuing in North Africa, two consular and administrative documents dealing with a dispute between Catholics and Donatists in around 315–320 mention ecclesiastical buildings in the episcopal cities of Cirta and Abthugni.[296] They refer to the situation during the Diocletian persecution (303). Researchers like to count these texts on the side of the house-church theory since they mention the *domus* in Cirta,[297] citing the church complex in Dura Europos as a comparable case. The buildings in Cirta and Abthugni are indeed likely to have been extensive and to have possessed integrated or independent church spaces.[298] What is important, though, is that in Cirta and probably also in Abthugni there was only one church (*basilica*, *ecclesia*), namely the bishop's church.[299] In the case of Cirta, this is certain because the Donatists successfully occupied the "basilica of the Catholic Church" there and Emperor Constantine had no choice but to finance a new basilica for the Catholics in 330.[300] There are further reports of the destruction of the basilicas in the episcopal cities of Furnos and Zama.[301] Here, too, this certainly refers just to the bishop's churches. In no case is there any mention of decentralised community halls or house churches.[302]

---

293 Saxer 1980a, 186; Burns / Jensen 2014, 135. Cf. A. Schwarze, Untersuchungen über die äußere Entwicklung der afrikanischen Kirche mit besonderer Verwertung der archäologischen Funde (Göttingen 1892) 34 f.

294 Opt. Mil. 1,19,2 f. (SC 412, 212).

295 Elliger 2004, 270; Burns / Jensen 2014, 90, 134.

296 The Cirta documents (CSEL 26, 185–197) were written c. 320, those of Abthugni (ibid. 197–204) c. 315.

297 [Opt. Mil.] gesta apud Zenoph. (CSEL 26, 186): *ad domum, in qua Christiani conveniebant.* Ibid. (195): *in casa maiore.*

298 Duval 2000, 353–395. On Dura Europos see ibid. 359 f.

299 [Opt. Mil.] gesta apud Zenoph. (CSEL 26, 185): *semper civitas nostra unam ecclesiam habet.* Ibid. (193): *in basilica.* [Opt. Mil.] act. purg. Fel. (ibid. 199): *mittunt in domo episcopi Felicis […]. sic*

Galatius nobiscum perrexit ad locum, ubi orationes celebrare consueti fuerant. inde cathedram tulimus.

300 Constant. Aug. ep. de basilica cath. (CSEL 26, 215).

301 [Opt. Mil.] act. purg. Fel. (CSEL 26, 199).

302 Duval 2000, 111–114, 373–382, 397 f. concludes from the mention of a *casa maior* in Cirta, which she interprets as the bishop's church, that *casae minores*, i.e. smaller places of worship, also existed. This is fraught with many uncertainties: 1. the textual tradition is disputed (ibid. 373); 2. the *casa maior* could be the larger church of an episcopal double-church complex; 3. it is not clear whether the *casa maior* is a church at all; 4. both the *casa maior* (if it is not a bishop's church) and the presumed smaller churches could be located in the cemeteries; 5. the cathedra in the *casa maior* (ibid. 375) can be a mobile, ad hoc chair; and 6.

As late as Easter 407, Augustine († 430) says that in his episcopal city of Hippo Regius – which numbered perhaps thirty to forty thousand inhabitants[303] – there was only permitted to be one altar, namely that of his church. The Donatists split the church by erecting a second altar within the city.[304] So Hippo possesses a single Catholic altar, which accordingly stands in the *Basilica Maior* or *Basilica Pacis*, Augustine's episcopal church. Of course, this does not exclude the possibility of a double-cathedral such as existed in many other cities. Augustine mentions, for example, an "ancient other church", but it is by no means certain that this was located within the city.[305] Othmar Perler considers the *Basilica Leontiana*, which Augustine mentions on several occasions, to be the first, "ancient" cathedral of Hippo, dating from the first half of the fourth century and still in use when the *Basilica Maior* was built.[306] But even its location within the city is not conclusive.[307]

Hippo Regius possesses a number of martyrs' churches that are scarcely possible to locate archaeologically but which, based on the general practice, can be assumed to be found outside the city in the cemeteries.[308] The same is conceivable for the *Basilica Leontiana*. If Augustine celebrates the Ascension there several times,[309] this could indicate a kind of station church outside the city, just as in Jerusalem Christ's Ascension was celebrated on the Mount of Olives. Furthermore, in Hippo Augustine opposes the drinking parties that took place in the cemetery churches in honour of the martyrs.[310] In 395 – still as a presbyter – he objects to the debauchery on the feast day of Leontius (4 May). Even though Augustine does not give the latter the title of martyr, he is undoubtedly venerated as such since the Donatists also celebrate his feast.[311] However, whereas the Catholics cel-

---

Duval herself says that *casa* is never used to mean a church (hence even less so *casae minores* for small churches!) and that, furthermore, in the text the church is called a *basilica* and *domus* (ibid. 377, 379f.).

303 VAN DER MEER 1951, 42.

304 Aug. in ep. Joh. ad Parth. 3,7 (PL 35, 2001): *Si ergo non a nobis eximus, in unitate sumus: si in unitate sumus, quid faciunt in hac civitate duo altaria?* ROETZER 1930, 85.

305 Aug. ep. 99,1. 3 (CSEL 34, 535): *antiqua alter ecclesia* (the Basilica Leontiana?). The letter talks about two *domus* (*eam, quam dare possumus* […], [*eam,*] *quam* […] *dare non possumus*), both of which are immediately adjacent to a church: the one next to Augustine's episcopal church (*quae nostris adhaeret parietibus*), the other on estates (*praedia*) and directly adjacent *antiquae alteri ecclesiae*. It is thus more likely that the second

church lies outside the city. Differently DUVAL 1991, 460; LANCEL 2004–2010, 355.

306 PERLER 1955, 341 f.; so also LANCEL 2004–2010, 355. C. LAMBOT, Les sermons de Saint Augustin pour les fêtes de Paques, in: Revue des Sciences Religieuses 30 (1956) 230–240, here 234–238 identifies the Leontiana with the Basilica Maior.

307 Cf. J.-P. CAILLET, *Basilica*, in: Augustinus-Lexikon 1 (1986–1994) 608–614, here 613; DUVAL 1991, 459 f. VAN DER MEER 1951, 42 speaks of churches, among them the Leontiana, in the "outlying districts".

308 LANCEL 2004–2010, 355.

309 PERLER 1955, 306.

310 Aug. ep. 22,3. 6 (CSEL 34, 57. 58 f.). The meals for the dead took place in the church: ibid. 29,5 (117).

311 Ibid. 29,11 (CSEL 34, 121); cf. SAXER 1980a, 177. Differently PERLER 1955, 301.

ebrate Leontius in the eponymous basilica,[312] the Donatists hold their revels in their city church. Since the feast day is on the day of Leontius's burial (*dies depositionis*), the church bearing his name is likely also to be the site of his tomb and therefore to lie outside the city gates in one of the cemeteries.[313] This is suggested by the fact that Augustine, the local bishop Valerius and the clergy "went out" – from the city to the *Basilica Leontiana* – and after the service "went back" – from the basilica to the city.[314] From Augustine's remark in his sermon that you could hear the carousing of the Donatists in their church at the same hour, people have concluded that the *Basilica Leontiana* lay in the immediate proximity of the Donatist cathedral inside the city.[315] But this is by no means certain. It is also possible to understand the text in such a way that Augustine was merely informed when he was preaching in the *Basilica Leontiana* that the Donatists were holding their "usual revelry".[316] In addition to this, in his fight against the carousing on the feast of Leontius, Augustine points to similar abuses in the martyrs' churches outside the gates of Rome, particularly in *San Pietro in Vaticano*.[317] All this leads one to assume that the *Basilica Leontiana* was a cemetery church – built by Leontius during his lifetime – in which Leontius was later venerated as a martyr. In this way it would remain true that in the fifth century there was still only one Catholic church in the city of Hippo.

For *Italy*, it will be enough to look more closely at Milan (for Rome, see below chapter III, 4). All the information about church buildings in Milan goes back to statements made by Ambrose (bishop 374–397) in the controversy with the Arians, although these were not always entirely clear.[318] Vincenzo Monachino thought that when Ambrose became bishop in 374, there were three basilicas, the *Vetus* and the *Portiana*, both outside the city walls, and the *Nova* inside the city.[319] In the meantime, however, it is generally assumed –

312 Aug. serm. 262,2,2 (PL 38, 1208). Aug. ep. 29,6 (CSEL 34, 118) probably means the Leontiana when it says: *totum tam magnae basilicae spatium turbis epulantium ebriorumque complerent.*

313 Aug. serm. 262,2,2 (PL 38, 1208): *Conditoris basilicae hujus sancti Leontii hodie depositio est.* Augustine must presumably have held this sermon in the Basilica Leontiana on the date of Leontius's death because it is his burial church. Differently PERLER 1955, 304.

314 Aug. ep. 29,11 (CSEL 34, 121): *usque ad horam, qua cum episcopo egrederemur* [...]; *nobisque egressis* [...]. [...] *nobisque cum episcopo recedentibus.*

315 LANCEL 2004–2010, 355; BURNS / JENSEN 2014, 155.

316 Aug. ep. 29,11 (CSEL 34, 121): *habui brevem sermonem quo gratias agerem deo, et quoniam in* *haereticorum basilica audiebamus ab eis solita convivia celebrata, cum adhuc etiam eo ipso tempore, quo a nobis ista gerebantur, illi in poculis perdurarent* [...]. Correctly PERLER 1955, 305.

317 Aug. ep. 29,9 f. (CSEL 34, 120).

318 H. SAVON, Ambroise de Milan (Paris 1997) 193–222; DASSMANN 2004, 95–98. The Arians lay claim first of all to the suburban Basilica Portiana and then, probably not by chance, to the Basilica Nova Maior, i.e. the larger of the two cathedral basilicas (St Tecla), which had been erected and restored by the Arian bishop Auxentius (355–374). The episode of the virgin fleeing *ad sacrosanctum altare* happened certainly in the cathedral of Ambrose himself; Ambr. virg. 1,11,65 (PL 16, 218A). The same goes for the flight of Cresconius *ad altare Domini*; Paulin. vit. Ambr. 34 (PL 14, 39A).

including for archaeological reasons – that the *Basilica Vetus* is in fact the old bishop's church inside the city (*Santo Stefano*), which might well date from Constantinian times. A few decades later, the considerably larger *Basilica Nova* was erected not far away, i.e. likewise within the city.[320] The terms Old and New Basilica in themselves indicate that these are the only two church buildings in the city. Both function as bishop's churches, thus forming a kind of double-cathedral. In Milan, the dominance of this church complex is particularly striking in that Ambrose, finding the two basilicas (*Santo Stefano, Santa Tecla*) already there, does not build any other church within the city, only suburban ones (Fig. 14).[321] The liturgical functions of the presbyterium remain surprisingly unremarkable in his writings – for example in *De officiis* on the duties of priests. There is confirmation, however, that the bishop always presides at the liturgy and that the presbyters merely assist him at the Eucharist and at baptism or represent him in his absence. The same is likely to apply to the liturgical ministries in the cemetery and martyrs' churches.[322]

In *Spain*, the Synod of Elvira takes place at the beginning of the fourth century, attended by numerous bishops and priests from the peninsula. The synod several times uses *ecclesia* in the singular to mean a church building.[323] The singular indicates that in each of the cities there is only the bishop's church (*ecclesia catholica*[324]), in which stand the cathedra[325] and the baptismal font.[326] Canon 21 does, in fact, speak of the city church, whose clergy supervise the regular church attendance of the faithful and the catechumens.[327]

For *Gaul*, only Bishop Irenaeus of Lyons (c. 200) needs to be mentioned here.[328] He speaks of the "altar" (in the "house of God") in the singular and links it to the priestly ministry of Jesus's disciples, i.e. the apostles.[329] Elsewhere, he concerns himself with the bishops appointed by the apostles, with whom one must be in communion. The heretics, on the

319 Monachino 1947, 3. Otherwise good observations ibid. 3–5.

320 EEECAA 2, 141.

321 H. Leppin *et al.*, Mailand, in: RACh 23 (2010) 1156–1202, here 1188–1200; S. Lusuardi Siena et al., Le chiese di Ambrogio e Milano. Ambito topografico ed evoluzione costruttiva dal punto di vista archeologico, in: P. Boucheron / S. Gioanni (eds.), La memoria di Ambrogio di Milano (Rome 2015) 31–86.

322 Monachino 1947, 20–22.

323 Conc. Elib. 36 (Vilella / Barreda 2002, 574): *placuit picturas in ecclesia esse non debere*. Cf. ibid. 29, 38, 52, 56; Voelkl 1954, 115 n. 81.

324 Conc. Elib. 22 (Vilella / Barreda 2002, 573).

325 Ibid. 58 (Vilella / Barreda 2002, 577).

326 Ibid. 48 (Vilella / Barreda 2002, 576).

327 Ibid. 21 (Vilella / Barreda 2002, 573): *si quis in civitate positus tres Dominicas ad ecclesiam non accesserit, pauco tempore abstineatur [, ut correptus esse videatur]*. Similarly ibid. 45 (575): *qui aliquando fuerit catecuminus et per infinita tempora numquam ad ecclesiam accesserit*, and ibid. 46 (575): *si quis fidelis apostata per infinita tempora ad ecclesiam non accesserit*.

328 On the topographical classification of city (the bishop's church) and suburb (the martyrs' churches) in fourth- to sixth-century Gaul see B. Beaujard, Le culte des saints en Gaule. Les premiers temps. D'Hilaire de Poitiers à la fin du VIᵉ siècle (Paris 2000), esp. Table 8.

329 Iren. adv. haer. 4,8,3 (SC 100,2, 472).

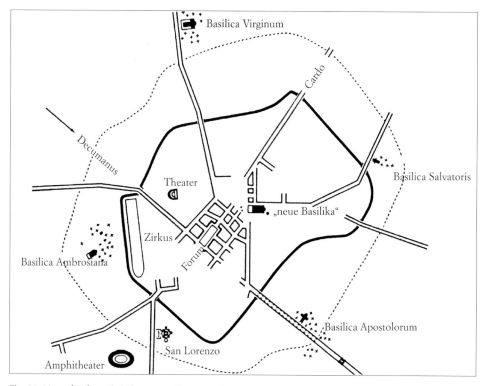

Fig. 14: Map of Milan, 4th / 5th century; Fraschetti 2002, 17 Fig. 3.

other hand, separate themselves from them and "gather together in whatever place". They bring strange fire, i.e. alien doctrines, to the "altar of God".[330] One might think that the dissenters set up their own altars in their meeting places. But it is more likely that Irenaeus intends to say that they separate themselves from the mother church, where alone the "altar of God" stands, after they have tried to spread their teachings there.

The Emperor Diocletian's edict of the year 303 persecuting the Christians demands the razing of their churches (ἐκκλησίαι).[331] A corresponding decree by Constantius Chlorus demands the demolition in the West of the *conventicula*,[332] which means the same thing, namely church buildings. The word conventicle might mislead one into thinking of small house churches,[333] but the word itself simply means the "meeting places" of the

---

330 Ibid. 4,26,2 (SC 100,2, 718): *Et haeretici quidem alienum ignem afferentes ad altare Dei.*

331 Euseb. hist. eccl. 8,2,4 (SC 55, 7); Molthagen 1975, 105 f.

332 Lact. mort. pers. 15,7 (SC 39, 94): *conventicula id est parietes.* See further Ammian. Marc. 27,3,13 (Seyfarth 1986, 60): *in basilica Sicinini, ubi ritus christiani est conventiculum.*

Christians. Nothing is said about the type and size of the buildings. At the beginning of the fourth century, the Christian Arnobius, too, speaks of the *conventicula* of the Christians that were torn down by their persecutors stating that in them the highest God is worshipped.[334] These are already fairly impressive cult buildings, otherwise they would not have to be demonstratively torn down. Galerius's Edicts of Toleration in 311 and 313 permitted the re-establishment of the *conventicula* everywhere in the Empire and speak of the *loca ad quae antea convenire consueverant*.[335] Neither of these decrees implies a plurality of city churches since the measures affect the provinces as a whole and probably include not only the city churches but also the cemeteries.

Even in Eusebius's panegyric on the consecration of the cathedral in Tyre (c. 314–321), there is nothing to suggest that there are or were other "churches" in the city besides this bishop's church;[336] on the contrary: the bishop's church destroyed in the persecution is rebuilt on the same site so that all the Christians of the city can again gather "in the same place" (ἐπὶ ταὐτόν).[337]

If there is ideally only one place of assembly in each city, it can be assumed that these buildings had to be enlarged in the course of the third century at the latest, when there was a long period of peace from 260 to 303. Eusebius, with a view particularly to the eastern half of the empire, does indeed speak of thousands taking part in the services, of countless Christians assembling in every city and of splendid gatherings being celebrated in the houses of prayer. Since the old buildings were no longer sufficient on account of the growing number of believers, new, spacious churches were built from scratch in all the cities.[338] This building boom has been interpreted to mean that larger church halls were erected in place of the numerous *domus ecclesiae* in the cities.[339] But there is absolutely no need for Eusebius to be understood in this way.[340] In fact, it is hard

---

333 Cf. WIELAND 1906, 74 f.

334 Arnob. adv. nat. 4,36 (CSEL 4, 171): *cur immaniter conventicula dirui, in quibus summus oratur deus.* Even in the fourth century, people still speak of conventicles, Ambrosiast. ad Ephes. 4,12 (CSEL 81,3, 100): *at ubi autem omnia loca circumplexa est ecclesia, conventicula constituta sunt et rectores et cetera officia ecclesiis sunt ordinata.*

335 Lact. mort. pers. 34,4 (SC 39, 118); 48,7 (133). VOELKL 1954, 108 f.; MOLTHAGEN 1975, 118–120; DUVAL 2000, 397 f.

336 Euseb. hist. eccl. 10,4,14 (SC 55, 85) mentions the destruction of many "churches" and "buildings", but that does not refer just to Tyre; cf. ibid. 10,4,20 (87). The comparison of the cathedral in Tyre with the Jerusalem Temple suggests that there was only this one church there.

337 Euseb. hist. eccl. 10,4,28 (SC 55, 90).

338 Ibid. 8,1,5 (SC 55, 4): πῶς δ'ἄν τις διαγράψειεν τὰς μυριάνδρους ἐκείνας ἐπισυναγωγὰς καὶ τὰ πλήθη τῶν κατὰ πᾶσαν πόλιν ἀθροισμάτων τάς τε ἐπισήμους ἐν τοῖς προσευκτηρίοις συνδρομάς; ὧν δὴ ἕνεκα μηδαμῶς ἔτι τοῖς πάλαι οἰκοδομήμασιν ἀρκούμενοι, εὐρείας εἰς πλάτος ἀνὰ πάσας τὰς πόλεις ἐκ θεμελίων ἀνίστων ἐκκλησίας. MOLTHAGEN 1975, 101 f.

339 WHITE 1990, 127 f.

340 Cf. the mistranslation by G. BARDY, in: SC 55, 4: "et dans chaque ville, on faisait sortir du sol de vastes et larges églises." Euseb. comm. in Ps. 83,4 (PG 23, 1008A) speaks of the altars erected throughout the whole oecumene after the persecutions.

to imagine that the cities were filled with churches already in the third century. In that case, a number of smaller churches would have sufficed in order to remedy the lack of space. But what Eusebius has in mind is large church halls that may possibly hold a thousand people and take the place of the buildings that preceded them; he is only interested in the bishop's churches.

This is also how Rufinus sees it in his translation of Eusebius's *Ecclesiastical History* (c. 401) when he adds that the size of the churches was so enormous that their dimensions approached those of cities.[341] What Rufinus will have had specifically in mind is the episcopal double-church in his home town of Aquileia. It is hard to imagine that several such church complexes would have been built in one city. Hence Eusebius, too, will be understood as saying that there was, and was allowed to be in a city only the bishop's church, which was able to accommodate all the Christians of that city.[342]

The development of adapting the episcopal worship spaces to suit the growing urban communities continued into Constantinian times, as is shown by the examples of Aquileia, Milan, Verona, Salona, Geneva and Trier, places where archaeology has brought large episcopal church complexes to light.[343] It is, after all, significant that the oldest and often the only monumental evidence brought to light by Christian archaeology in the cities throughout the entire early Christian oecumene is the cathedral complexes.[344] This is no coincidence and is echoed in the written sources. Eusebius speaks of a decree issued by Emperor Constantine in 324 instructing him to restore and extend the existing church buildings in the churches of his diocese or, if necessary, to erect new ones. Equivalent letters were sent to all the leading bishops.[345] There is no mention here of a proliferation of churches. It is rather to be assumed that the emperor had in mind only those bishop's churches that were either in a ruinous state, had grown too small, or had been destroyed in the Diocletian persecution[346] and therefore had to be rebuilt. Since Constantine evidently assumed that the Christians of a city gathered together with the

341 Rufin. hist. eccl. 8,1,6 (GCS Euseb. 2,2, 739): *cottidie orationum domus dilatarentur, ita ut amplitudo earum concludere instar urbium videretur.*

342 This was, for example, the case in Aquileia. The church of St Hilarius as the second church inside the city is likely not dated from before the fifth century; C. Jäggi, Aspekte der städtebaulichen Entwicklung Aquileias in frühchristlicher Zeit, in: JbAC 33 (1990) 158–196, here 178 f.

343 Cantino Wataghin 2014, 594–604.

344 See the comprehensive volume by G. Cerulli Irelli, Il mondo dell'Archeologia Cristiana (Rome 2018).

345 Euseb. vit. Const. 2,45,1 (SC 559, 314–316); 2,46,3 f. (316–318). Cf. 3,1,4 (350). Dörries 1954, 55. When there is talk of those presiding over the churches – bishops, priests and deacons – this does not refer to church buildings but rather to the local churches. Cf. vit. Const. 3,58,3 (SC 559, 432): Constantine builds the first church in Baalbek (Heliopolis), namely the cathedral, for bishop, priests and deacons. Therefore it remained true here as well: one city – one church – one cathedra – one clergy.

346 Euseb. vit. Const. 1,13,2 (SC 559, 196–198); 3,1,4 (350); hist. eccl. 8,2,4 (SC 55, 7); theoph. syr. 3,20 (GCS Euseb. 3,2, 134*).

bishop for the Eucharist, this meant that there was now above all a greater need for space, something to which particular attention was to be paid when undertaking these measures.[347] Successive double-church complexes also ultimately served the need for expansion of the bishop's church in many cities, with a smaller and, later, a larger space existing side by side. These are de facto co-cathedrals.

There is in principle a further consideration to be taken into account for episcopal building complexes. If at a bishop's church or within the bishop's house there is another hall (possibly with an apse) which has no liturgical facilities, then it could have served as a classroom for the catechumens (*catechumeneum*), as a hall for the daily audience (*audientia episcopalis*) or as a triclinium for the evening agape presided over by the bishop. Such meals were charitable in nature and were counted among the bishop's duties. They were not simple evening meals to which anyone at all was invited, but quasi-cultic meals in which the clergy also participated. Such meals, which included prayers, readings and blessings, recalled Jesus's Last Supper. Since they fell out of use in the fourth century, such spaces could subsequently have been used as second churches or for other purposes.

In conclusion, there is one more query to be put to the proponents of the house-church theory, for whom it is to be expected that the crucial period of Christianity's liberation and expansion at the turn of the third and fourth centuries will usher in the final demise of the supposedly once autonomous private community centres. In the understanding of these proponents, the bishops consolidate their power by ensuring that they alone build their cathedrals and by allowing the previous house churches to die out. As part of the same process, the once autonomous presbyters, the house-church fathers, are deprived of their powers and are now no longer allowed to celebrate the Eucharist themselves, but are now assigned to merely assisting at the Mass celebrated by the bishop. But if this really was how things happened, wouldn't it be a complete mystery why the presbyters put up with it without a word of complaint? For in the sources there is not the slightest indication that this exorbitant shift of power in favour of the bishop's worship service in the city ever led to any protests. Nor is there any mention of the sad demise of the house churches and their centuries-old worship communities. Is such a complete blackout in the tradition plausible? Must we not instead conclude quite soberly that in reality such house churches never existed?

---

347 This is the reason that Eusebius says that the emperor expects that "pretty nearly all mankind would henceforth attach themselves to the service of God"; Euseb. vit. Const. 2,45,1 (SC 559, 314–316).

4. ROME AND ALEXANDRIA

At least in the relatively large cities, and even more so in the mega-cities of antiquity, the research has ruled out the possibility that the Christians were able to meet on Sundays to celebrate the Eucharist all together.[348] There were, it says, simply no adequate facilities for such mass gatherings. This leaves no alternative but to assume that the Christians gathered in private house churches,[349] which were replaced in the course of the third century by church buildings (*domus ecclesiae*). Only recently, for example, Ramsay MacMullen once more declared himself convinced in the case of Rome that, based on first-century texts – he is thinking of the Letter to the Romans – there is no doubt that such house churches existed up to the end of the persecutions, even though all attempts to support this position with archaeological evidence have so far come to nothing.[350]

Behind the house-church theory lies a sociological concept. For the hypothesis of a fragmented Christianity seems to be especially attractive when applied to Rome and Alexandria on account of the social and ethnic differences and the (consequent) presence of sectarian groups, which can be conveniently distributed among individual house churches. Peter Lampe has published a study on Rome along these lines which many consider authoritative. In it he draws a picture for the first and second centuries of a theologically plural Christianity divided into house churches.[351]

In my opinion, these are experimental games staged too easily according to sociological categories. A multitude of private and semi-private associations existed in antiquity, especially cult communities that were socially open.[352] Of course, Christianity in Rome was diversified, but certainly not necessarily in such a way that individual groups of different ethnicities and theologies led isolated lives of their own.[353] In reality, these diversifications are in fact experienced as discord and strife precisely because they are not parallel, autonomous, isolated Christianities. If this were the case, nothing would have been handed down about such groups among the writers in the main church because they would never have come into contact with them. In fact, however, such writers engage in intensive discussions of special doctrines. But not a single text is to be found – not even among the so-called sects – that would claim that a multiplicity of Christianity is right and a plurality of autonomous groups is the royal road. On the contrary, the

348 HARNACK 1924, 612.
349 Ibid.
350 MACMULLEN 2009, 87.
351 LAMPE 2003 (orig. 1987). The study's massive methodological and factual errors are revealed by SCHÖLLGEN 1989. Despite this, BRENT 1995, 398–405 adopts Lampe's theses and outlines an image of a "house community" of Hippolytus in Rome. Likewise LEPPIN 2018, 240: "Even inside a large city like Rome several communities existed alongside each other."
352 KLOPPENBORG 2019, 29, 81, 85–87.
353 ROBINSON 2017, 114 f. sees the Christian communities more as a linguistic and cultural mix.

need for church unity is not even questioned by the sects, let alone by the rest of the Christian population. This unity – not always easy to achieve – is experienced, but where concretely? In common worship!

Against the background of the knowledge assembled so far about the churches in Asia Minor, Syria, Palestine, North Africa, Spain and Gaul, it can be assumed that large cities do not differ from the smaller episcopal cities with regard to the ecclesial principle of unity. However, when faced with increasing membership, the bishops in the large cities have to be inventive and seek practical solutions.

a. Rome

In around the year 55, the apostle *Paul* wrote a letter from Corinth, where he was residing at the time, addressed "to all God's beloved in Rome" (Rm 1:7). This is the famous Letter to the Romans, which is not a short occasional letter, but rather a theological tract of considerable length. The letter gives an impression of the special closeness and unity of the Roman Christians.[354] Their faith is proclaimed throughout the world (Rm 1:8). Paul wants to travel there, see them and find comfort among and with them (Rm 1:10–12). Paul greets individually the household of Prisca and Aquila (Rm 16:5) and mentions further Christian groups in Rome (Rm 16:10 f.; cf. 16:14 f.); it is perfectly understandable that in this large city there are a number of circles of Christians that feature family bonds. But none of this is evidence of house churches in the sense of autonomous worship communities in private urban residences, as much of the research assumes.[355] If, however, the construct of private house churches is dropped because Paul never speaks of any such thing in his various letters (above chapter III, 1), then for Rome, too, nothing remains but to assume that a centralised service took place in a fairly large meeting place.

Against this assumption, the argument is advanced that Paul addresses his letter "to all [...] in Rome" (Rm 1:7) without referring to the Christians of Rome as a "church", thus assuming a centralised gathering.[356] Such reasoning is surprising. For how is the letter

354 HARNACK 1924, 839. On the following HEID 2016a.

355 TABBERNEE 2014, 396 f. believes he has discovered at least seven independent worship communities in Rm 16. For several house churches with eucharistic celebrations see WIELAND 1906, 31 f.; HARNACK 1924, 839; PADOVESE 2000, 74; SAXER 2003, 286; PENNA 2009, 190 f.; WAGNER 2011, 41 f.; VORHOLT 2012, 211; LEAL 2018, 69–72. Correctly, on the other hand, SCHÖLLGEN 1988, 78 f.; ADAMS

2013, 30–33. When Paul speaks of the "churches of the Gentiles" (Rm 16:4), he means by this the churches of the diaspora. The "church in their [Prisca's and Aquila's] house" (Rm 16:5) remains in the singular, i.e. it is not known whether further (purported) house churches existed in Rome or whether the entire church of Rome gathered only in the house of the couple Prisca and Aquila.

356 GEHRING 2004, 146.

supposed to reach "all [...] in Rome" if not by being read out in the church assembly? The people met for worship, and did so every Sunday, which meant that the letter could be read out and interpreted in sections. Given its size, this will have taken months. It is inconceivable that, instead of this, it could have done the rounds of house churches like a circular letter; in that way it would have taken many years to read. In order to speed this up, the letter would have had to be copied for each house church – but who had the time and money for that? And further: in view of a largely illiterate population, much time would have been wasted on such a major epistle as the Letter to the Romans if it were not read out in small chunks and explained immediately. Are we then to assume that in every house church there was someone who could read and someone else who had enough theological knowledge to interpret the letter? How many theologians were there in Rome? Are we really to believe that the proclamation and interpretation of an apostle's letter was left to some or other house fathers and mothers? Such a major letter from the hand of the apostle himself was *the* sensation, a tremendous honour for Rome. It demanded the collective attention of all; no one wanted to miss its being read out. If the letter was meant to have been circulated from house church to house church, why does Paul not mention this explicitly? Instead, the only conceivable solution is that the Roman Christians were organised in their entirety and that the Roman church was already just as consolidated as that in Corinth.

The already-mentioned *First Letter of Clement*, which was written in Rome, offers even clearer support for the idea of a single celebration of the Eucharist by the entire Roman community since its call for all the presbyters in Corinth to worship in unity undoubtedly applies to Rome as well (above chapter II, 3).

The *Shepherd of Hermas*, written in around 140/50 and likewise in Rome, deserves special attention. Hermas apparently had private visions urging him to call the Roman community to repentance and to obtain the presbyters' permission for this. He is to relate the visions "in this city, along with the presbyters who preside over the church (ἐκκλησία)".[357] This makes it clear, first, that the presbyters in Rome form a college which presides over the whole local church, and second that this college must possess a meeting place where the faithful of the city can assemble with it. For this reason, Hermas speaks in the singular of the "sanctuary" (ἁγίασμα)[358] and "house of God" (οἶκος τοῦ θεοῦ),[359] apparently meaning by this the assembly room expressed in terms echoing the

357 Past. Herm. 8,3 (SC 53², 96). ἐκκλησία is here both the church assembly and the local church.
358 Ibid. 10,1 (SC 53², 102). "Sanctuary" fits better than "altar", cf. Clem. Alex. strom. 4,4,15,6 (SC 463, 82); 4,6,30,1 (106). Differently Brox 1991, 116. In the *Acts of Marinos the Martyr* the altar is

referred to c. 260–268 as ἁγίασμα; Dölger 1930, 163 f.
359 Past. Herm. 90,1 (SC 53², 318); 90,9–91,1 (322). Here, too, the term ἐκκλησία occurs (= church assembly of Rome), which is now identified with the tower. The οἶκος τοῦ θεοῦ is therefore in all prob-

Jerusalem Temple (Ex 25:7, 1 Chr 22:19; 28:10 LXX etc.). There the "presbyters" take their seats on a common bench (συμψέλιον),[360] where, due to their leadership function, they "preside"[361] over the "church (assembly)" (ἐκκλησία) of the city of Rome. The fact that the individual seats of the presbyters are allocated on the right and left according to their rank makes it clear that this is a kind of sigma-shaped synthronos in the Christians' meeting room. A similar seating arrangement – twenty-four thrones of the presbyters around the main throne, in front of which stands an altar – is already encountered in the Apocalypse of John (Rv 4:4; 8:3). It is to be assumed that there is also an altar in the church space described by Hermas since he speaks in the singular of "the altar of God" (τὸ θυσιαστήριον τοῦ θεοῦ), to which the prayers of the faithful ascend.[362] Everything, then, suggests that the presbyters celebrate the Eucharist together and do not scatter among supposed house churches for the Sunday service. It is even striking that the author Hermas is himself a householder, i.e. owns a city residence,[363] but does not know of either one or several "house churches" in Rome. Despite his concern for the Christian way of life of his own people, he does not hold any religious gatherings in his house. It is therefore impossible to understand how Norbert Brox wants to read into the *Shepherd of Hermas* a fractionisation of the Roman city church into house churches.[364] Instead, Stephan Zorell is correct when he writes: "As the number of believers gradually increased, the need seems to have been met at first by increasing only the number of clergy, not the number of churches."[365]

The Christian philosopher *Justin*, who was familiar from his own experience with the ecclesiastical situation in Palestine, Asia Minor and Rome, wrote in his *Apology* in around 150 an extremely important, even crucial, sentence:

> And on the day called Sunday, *all* who sojourn in the cities or in the country gather together *to one place* (ἐπὶ τὸ αὐτό).[366]

---

ability also a building (tower = church) because Hermas here speaks of the excommunication of those who must do penance before they "will enter the house of God." On the ecclesial nature of penance in Hermas see B. Poschmann, *Paenitentia secunda* (Bonn 1940) 189–202.

360 Past. Herm. 9,7–10,4 (SC 53², 100–102). On the presbyters' bench see also ibid. 17,7 (124) and Kritzinger 2016, 116.

361 Past. Herm. 8,3 (SC 53², 96). The presiders are those who are also referred to as "pre-leaders" (προηγούμενοι) and "first seated on the cathedra" (πρωτοκαθετρίται); ibid. 17,7 (124). This could be understood as a precursor of the monepiscopate

in the sense that in each case a *Primus inter pares* presided in the college of presbyters.

362 Past. Herm. 42,2 f. (SC 53², 190).

363 Ibid. 66,3 (SC 53², 256).

364 Brox 1991, 536. So also M. Grundeken, Community Building in the *Shepherd of Hermas* (Leiden / Boston 2015) 154. Wagner 2011, 285–292, proceeds in the context of the *Shepherd of Hermas* from the unproven premise of "communities" in Rome, but often speaks just of "the community".

365 Zorell 1902, 76.

366 Iustin. apol. 1, 67,3 (SC 507, 308): πάντων κατὰ πόλεις ἢ ἀγροὺς μενόντων ἐπὶ τὸ αὐτὸ συνέλευσις γίνεται.

In the overall context, Justin speaks unambiguously of the celebration of the Eucharist as he knows it, one must assume, from his sojourns in the eastern and western regions of the Church. The widespread way of celebrating the Eucharist no longer has anything to do with an agape or with a reclining meal.[367] Justin describes only the standard sacramental celebration consisting of the liturgy of the word and the rite of bread and cup. Furthermore, in the sentence quoted above the city reference is remarkable: Justin speaks of those "who sojourn in the cities". Here, too, he does not have a specific city in mind, but claims to describe a general practice. Alongside the cities, he mentions the countryside ("those who sojourn [...] in the country"). This probably means the countryside surrounding the cities (*suburbium*). So according to this, the urban and rural populations meet on Sundays to worship together.[368]

The eucharistic gathering takes place only on Sunday, not on weekdays, and always "in the same place" (ἐπὶ τὸ αὐτὸ). So there is a clear definition of time and place. The phrase "in the same place" in Christian usage refers to the (worship) gathering of all the Christians of a city.[369] Justin, too, undoubtedly means here a single assembly room for the celebration of the Eucharist, for he wants to emphasise that all the Christians of a city, even those from the surrounding area, come together in a single place. In order to prevent any doubts from arising about the unified worship, Justin adds elsewhere that "Sunday is the day on which we all hold our common assembly."[370] This would make little sense if several services took place in a city. It is obvious that the place of assembly, whose exact location Justin does not specify, is not somewhere out in the country, but – at least for Sunday worship – inside the city.

So all the Christians of a city and its surrounding area come together on Sundays at a place inside the city. This perichoresis between city and countryside is not as unusual as it seems. In Rome, for example, on the feast days of the martyrs, people met at the cemeteries outside the gates of the city (*suburbium*), which meant that the inhabitants went out to the cemeteries. In the case of the tombs of Peter and Paul, this is to be assumed from as early as the second century,[371] and even more so for the graves of the martyrs of the Decian persecution from the second half of the third century onwards. So the system works in both directions: it is always all the Christians of the *urbs* and the *suburbium* who gather, either in the city or in one of the cemeteries. Justin probably emphasises the fact of a single assembly because he wants to dispel any impression among the pagan

367 Messner 2003a, 432.
368 Zorell 1902, 76.
369 Acts 2:1, 44, 47; 1 Cor 11:20; 14:23; 1 Clem. 34,7 (SC 167, 156); ep. Barn. 4,10 (SC 172, 102); Ign. ad Eph. 5,3 (SC 10³, 74); Orig. orat. 31,5 (GCS Orig.

2, 398). Cf. Rordorf 1964, 114; Boguniowski 1987, 138–159; *id*. 1988.
370 Iustin. apol. 1, 67,8 (SC 507, 310): κοινῇ πάντες τὴν συνέλευσιν ποιούμεθα.
371 S. Heid, in: Gnilka 2015, 81–108.

readers of his *Apology* that the Christians held clandestine celebrations and did immoral things at them.[372]

Justin assumes without exception that there was only one place of worship per city. Another passage points in the same direction. There, he compares the baptism and subsequent procession of the neophytes to the worshipping community with the ritual washings of the pagans before they enter a temple to perform the sacrificial acts.[373] So Justin seems to assume, by analogy with the temples, a church complex with separate rooms for baptism and Eucharist. This in no way conjures up the idea of private house churches, but rather suggests a public cultic space, perhaps comparable to Dura Europos.

Justin does not explicitly mention Rome in his remarks on the Sunday Eucharist, but he doesn't exclude the city in which he was probably staying when he wrote the *Apology*.[374] This is all the more significant since, due to its size, several places of worship would be expected there. Wouldn't it then have been imperative for Justin to say that everywhere, just not in Rome, people met in a single place? Since he does not give any indication of an exception, it must be concluded that Rome, too, had just one Sunday service. Nevertheless, due to a series of misinterpretations, Peter Lampe assumes that Christianity in Rome divided up into house churches and that Justin's *Apology* must be interpreted accordingly.[375] For this, he relies on the Acts of Justin Martyr, which recount his trial and violent death in Rome. They are used by researchers as a prime text to support the idea that a series of house churches existed in Rome with their own eucharistic celebrations.[376] But this conclusion is anything but reliable. For the Acts of Justin Martyr have a split textual tradition and date back only to the third century. Hence, for methodological reasons, the authentic *Apology* (c. 160) must be accorded precedence. But even for the third century, the Acts yield little on the question of house churches because although they do speak of meeting places, there is no clear connection to the celebration of the Eucharist. Therefore, there is nothing for it but to conclude with Georg Schöllgen that the Acts of Justin Martyr are "certainly no evidence for house churches" in Rome.[377] Of course, there may nevertheless have been several meeting places groups of Christians in Rome used during the week (e.g. for prayer, catechesis, receiving portions of food), but on the Lord's Day they all attended the bishop's Mass together.

372 Cf. Iustin. apol. 1, 26,7 (SC 507, 200).
373 Ibid. 1, 62,1 (SC 507, 292–294).
374 Cf. SCHÖLLGEN 1988, 29 f.
375 LAMPE 2003, 365. Thus already KLAUCK 1981, 70.

376 For example, WHITE 1996, 110; SAXER 2003, 319; ALIKIN 2010, 52.
377 SCHÖLLGEN 1988, 79. Cf. HEID 2016a, 273–275.

Researchers also like to point to the heretical groups that existed in the capital as implying that they had their own worship services. In principle this is conceivable, but even that does not prove the existence of house churches. These groups came into conflict with the "presbyters" of Rome, and these conflicts were permanent. If heretics could simply have withdrawn into their house churches, no permanent conflict would have been expected. Such a possibility of withdrawing evidently did not exist. Irenaeus complains that the Valentinians, Marcionites, Cerinthians and Gnostics consider themselves wiser than the presbyters,[378] so it appears that they quarrel with the presbyters. They themselves presumably do not belong to the hierarchy and, at least in the second century, do not yet celebrate their own Eucharist.[379] In fact, the heretical groups are not described in the early texts as autonomous worship circles, but rather as philosophical schools. Their teachers enter into opposition to the presbyter-bishops of the local churches on an intellectual level,[380] but do not yet see themselves as anti-bishops. Instead, they attempt to be present at the centralised services of the presbyters in order to win new followers for their own circles there. What would they have gained by cutting themselves off? And the other way round: Why should Justin and Irenaeus get upset about the sects if they led a separate life? It is in the dynamic of sects that their followers participate in the centralised services of the mainstream church.[381] In fact, it is said of Cerdo that under Bishop Hyginus (138–142?) he "often came to church and (often) made the profession of faith." Here "church" must surely mean the centralised episcopal worship gathering. There Cerdo had, on the one hand, occasionally spread secret doctrines and, on the other hand, made a profession of faith. In the end, he is convicted (in the church) of false teachings and separates himself from the assembly of the brothers, i.e. from the centralised worship community.[382]

If it is then said that Cerdo's successor Marcion unfolded his greatest influence under Bishop Aniket (155–166?),[383] then this is perhaps not a merely chronological statement, but rather an indication of the actual influence Marcion exercised over the Roman com-

---

378 Iren. adv. haer. 3,2,2 (SC 211, 26): *dicentes se non solum presbyteris sed etiam apostolis exsistentes sapientiores.* Tert. praesc. haer. 41,4 (CCL 1, 221): *Omnes tument, omnes scientiam pollicentur.*

379 Tert. praescr. haer. 41 (CCL 1, 221 f.) speaks with polemical exaggeration of officeholders and priestly functions among the heretics, but exactly how this is to be understood remains unclear.

380 Iren. adv. haer. 3,3,1 (SC 211, 30): *in omni Ecclesia* […], *ab apostolis instituti sunt episcopi in Ecclesiis.* In Irenaeus, "church" is always the local episcopal church; ibid. 3,3,2 (32): church of Rome. Ibid. 3,3,4 (38): church of Smyrna.

381 Tert. praescr. haer. 41,3 (CCL 1, 221): *Pacem quoque passim cum omnibus miscent.* Ibid. 42,1 (222): *hoc sit negotium illis, non ethnicos convertendi sed nostros evertendi.* Cf. Euseb. hist. eccl. 5,15 (SC 41, 45); 6,2,14 (86).

382 Iren. adv. haer. 3,4,3 (SC 211, 50): *saepe in Ecclesiam veniens et exhomologesim faciens* […], *modo quidem latenter docens, modo vero exhomologesim faciens, modo vero ab aliquibus traductus in his quae docebat male et abstentus est a religiosorum hominum conventu.*

383 Iren. adv. haer. 3,4,3 (SC 211, 50–52): *Marcion autem illi succedens invaluit sub Aniceto.*

munity. At all events, he tries to buy himself into the "church" of Rome with two hundred thousand sesterces.[384] This, and even more so the fact that the whole sum is later paid back to him again, shows that the church of Rome has a central financial administration. After all, the very thing that Marcion did not do was to give the money to various house churches, something that would have given him easier access to Christian circles. And the presbyters did not allow the money to trickle away into the house churches either – there are no house churches, only the centralised worship service of the presbyters. That is also why Marcion can be excommunicated in 144 (? The date is uncertain). Excommunication means exclusion from worship, but it can only be imposed if there is a common worship service of the entire Roman congregation and a centralised jurisdiction, not with a ragged worship landscape split up into house churches. Whether Marcion immediately set about organising his own church with its own services is doubtful. His followers did not wear a mark of Cain on their foreheads and will have continued to try to remain present in the services of the main church in order to promote themselves.

Tertullian of Carthage, too, is well aware (c. 203) that the sectarians recite the creed in the church, but interpret its words differently.[385] This is not a private event, but takes place before the forum of the city community,[386] i.e. in the bishop's worship service. Tertullian cites as an example the Roman bishop before whom all say the creed.[387] Michel-Yves Perrin is therefore correct in saying that the presbyter-led second-century community of Rome was by no means already breaking up into a large church and smaller sects. Rather, despite considerable doctrinal differences and disputes, it behaved as a unit. He consequently rejects the theory that before the establishment of the monepiscopate the Roman community had broken up into a multitude of house churches or schools.[388]

Of course, the Christians in Rome also met privately in houses.[389] This applies, for example, to Justin's school of philosophy and to other elite circles (Novatians, Valentin-

384 References in HARNACK 1985, 25f., 17*, 24f.*. Harnack saw this quite differently in 1870 in order to prove that Marcion in Rome was long since no longer a "Katholiker"; F. STECK, Adolf Harnack: Marcion. Der moderne Gläubige des 2. Jahrhunderts, der erste Reformator. Die Dorpater Preisschrift (1870) (Berlin / New York 2003) 113f.

385 Tert. praescr. haer. 26,10 (CCL 1, 208): *ut alium Deum in ecclesia dicerent.*

386 Ibid. 20,5 (CCL 1, 202): *Et perinde ecclesias apud unamquamque civitatem condiderunt.* The "churches" here are certainly not house churches since what follows deals with the apostolic churches of Corinth, Philippi, Ephesus and Rome (ibid. 20,6; 27,1–4; 36,1f.). Ibid. 30,2 (210): *eccle-*

siam Romanensem. Ibid. 32,2 (213): *Smyrnaeorum ecclesia […], sicut Romanorum.*

387 Ibid. 30,2 (CCL 1, 210): *in catholicae primo doctrinam credidisse apud ecclesiam Romanensem sub episcopatu Eleutheri.*

388 M.-Y. PERRIN, in: PIETRI 2003, 682–685, referring to SCHÖLLGEN 1988. See also C. DELL'OSSO, Viele Christentümer? Ein Einspruch, in: RQ 110 (2015) 145–156.

389 Iustin. dial. 47,2 (MARCOVICH 1997, 147) speaks of there being Christians who would not spend time in a house with Christians who come "from the circumcision". LAMPE 2003, 365 reads this as evidence of house churches. This says a great deal about how he handles sources.

ians, Marcionites, Paulians, Montanists, etc.). Alongside these, there also seem to have been decentralised meeting places that could only have existed in contact with Church leadership. In his description of the celebration of the Eucharist, Justin tells of a strange procedure which he observes in general in all cities, but which has a special relevance for Rome – at the end of the "president's" celebration of the Sunday Eucharist, the eucharistic gifts (bread, wine and water) are carried by the deacons to "those who are absent".[390] This short note sounds inconsequential; it could be misunderstood as a kind of Communion for the sick. However, it might in fact conceal a key piece of information for understanding how the Roman church was organised.

First of all, what is described here is not an unusual custom at meals in antiquity. It was a common practice then to send portions of food from the sacrificial meals to those who were absent, with both food (bread, meat) and drink (wine) being sent.[391] Analogously, the practice arose among the Christians of sending portions of the Eucharist as a sign of unity and fellowship. If Justin regards this sending of portions of the Eucharist to be a general practice, this is most easily explained by the unity of the city's worship service: precisely because there are no house churches or decentralised services but only a centralised (presbyteral or episcopal) liturgy, it has to be guaranteed through portions of food so that all who wish to can preserve their unity with this liturgy and thus with the bishop or presbyterium. This becomes all the more imperative in a city as large as Rome, where it is clear that not everyone who wants to is able to attend the centralised episcopal service.

The distribution of food portions gives rise to a number of reflections. Just think of all the bother: not only do considerable quantities of bread, wine and water have to be consecrated at the centralised celebration of the Eucharist, they also have be transported for miles. The fact that specific officeholders, namely deacons, are entrusted with this task shows how seriously it is taken. Another reason for this is, of course, to ensure that the Eucharist is not distributed to the excommunicate. This requires clerical control, which is possibly connected with bureaucracy. Furthermore, the distribution certainly does not take place individually, for how would the deacons have known from Sunday to Sunday who was absent from the main service and where they lived? It is also inconceivable that deacons went from house to house with considerable quantities of bread, wine and water. Finally, Justin gives the impression that the deacons left the centralised service immediately after Communion so they would still to be able to deliver the gifts round the city on Sunday.[392] Thus, the eucharistic celebration is likely to have taken place

---

390 Iustin. apol. 1, 65,5 (SC 507, 304); 67,5 (310).

391 A. Stuiber, Apophoreton, in: RACh Suppl. 1 (2001) 514–522, here 516 f. Cf. Nussbaum 1996 (1974) 134 f.

392 Iustin. apol. 1, 65,5 (SC 507, 304).

in the morning.[393] Nevertheless, it is scarcely possible to visit all the absentees in their homes within the space of a few hours. It must therefore be assumed that each deacon was assigned a specific collection location in the city, where he probably distributed the food to the faithful during a short service after they had recited a creed by way of a check.[394]

If these reflections are correct, then there are decentralised meeting points in various parts of Rome (as well). However, no eucharistic celebrations (and therefore no baptisms) take place there since no presbyters are involved, only deacons, who cannot preside at a Eucharist. Without a celebration of the Eucharist, there is also no Offertory and hence probably no collection either. The collection locations are thus financially dependent and are drip-fed from the centralised worship service. So these halls will have been modest and not have had an altar. The organisationally complex procedure of distributing the Eucharist is under the direction of the leading presbyter (bishop).[395] The decentralised gatherings are therefore decidedly dependent institutions that do not suggest autonomous house churches. In any case, the distribution of the Eucharist in the city area strongly reinforces the impression that the ecclesial principle of unity is to be upheld here at all costs: in a city of whatever size, there must be only one place for the Eucharist and one altar. Those who cannot personally participate in the centralised Eucharist must receive the sacramental gifts from this celebration by other means.

In his *Apology*, Justin does not describe a house-church liturgy, but rather the centralised celebration of the Eucharist for which all Christians come together from town and country "in the same place" (ἐπὶ τὸ αὐτό). Interestingly, in the context of the liturgy he always speaks only of the "presider"[396] and the deacons as the acting persons. From this point of view, too, there is little doubt that Justin is not describing a house-church liturgy. For this would mean that every house church had several deacons. But deacons

393 This is also suggested by the sun and Resurrection symbolism; Iustin. apol. 1, 67,8 (SC 507, 310–312). There may possibly also have been an evening gathering; cf. ibid 1, 26,7 (200).

394 It is by no means certain that all the portions are consumed together at that time; it is also possible that the faithful took some of them home with them to eat during the week.

395 Euseb. hist. eccl. 5,24,15 (SC 41, 71) on (the Roman presbyter = bishop) Victor (189–199?) and his predecessor. MONACHINO 1947, 281 and LAMPE 2003, 382 f., 387 interpret the passage as if in the second century the bishops of Rome distributed the portions of eucharistic food to all the presbyters of Rome, who, for their part, celebrated the Eucharist in various churches of the city. But here presbyter refers exclusively to bishop, and there is no mention of city communities, only of dioceses (παροικίαι). The Easter practice only differs between the Western dioceses and those of Asia Minor, not within Rome itself, where the leading presbyters do not permit any deviations; HEID 2019c. See also N. PAXTON, The eucharistic bread. Breaking and commingling in early Christian Rome, in: Downside Review 122 (2004) 79–93, here 84.

396 This is an officeholder whose office authorises him to celebrate the Eucharist; MESSNER 2003a, 431 n. 448. ZIEGLER 2007, 266 thinks that it always refers to the same person, de facto the bishop.

have always been attached to the bishop, and in Rome their number is limited to seven citywide.[397] Justin mentions the deacons only in their function as bearers of the portions of the Eucharist. At no point does he mention the presbyters, but they must have existed. For both the First Letter of Clement (c. 96) (above chapter II, 3) and the Shepherd of Hermas (140/50) (above p. 130 f.) indicate that in Rome the presbyters were present at the community's centralised eucharistic celebration. Whether the monepiscopate already existed in Rome or the presbyters administered the church of Rome collegially, in either case the presbyters celebrated the service together and left the distribution of the food portions to the deacons.

As late as around 200, there seems to have been only the one bishop's church in Rome. Several texts confirm this. The *Muratorian Fragment* deals with those sacred writings that are allowed to be read in the church of Rome. These permitted writings are read "in the church to the people". Since the cathedra is mentioned immediately before this comment about reading, it must be talking about a bishop's church with the appropriate seat of honour for the presider.[398] If other church spaces had existed, it would have been imperative for the text to mention them so as to ensure that no unauthorised texts were read in these churches either.

In addition, *Irenaeus of Lyons* writes in around 200 that, in spite of a simmering conflict over the correct date of Easter, Bishop Anicetus (c. 155–166) "conceded the administration of the eucharist in the church" to Bishop Polycarp of Smyrna, who was residing in Rome at the time.[399] This can scarcely mean that Anicetus gave the Eucharist to his brother bishop during the service. That would not have been worth mentioning since Rome and the local churches of Asia Minor were in communion with one another.[400] Rather, the permission concerned something special, namely that Polycarp was allowed to preside at the Eucharist in Anicetus's church instead of the local bishop. "Church" accordingly means the bishop's church of Rome. The fact that there was a uniform praxis for Easter and fasting in Rome, as Irenaeus testifies, also speaks in favour of a single location for the Eucharist. Contrary to what is frequently asserted, Irenaeus is not aware of a community of exiles from Asia Minor in Rome who deviated from the episcopal celebration and celebrated Easter on 14 Nisan.[401]

Finally, *Hippolytus of Rome*, c. 200–204, in his commentary on Daniel, speaks in general terms of the persecutors of the Christians insidiously waiting for the moment when all the Christians had gathered for prayer "in the house of God" and then drag-

397 This is documented from the mid–third century onwards, but the tradition is certain to be far older.
398 LIETZMANN 1921a, 8–10.
399 Euseb. hist. eccl. 5,24,17 (SC 41, 71): ἐκοινώνησαν ἑαυτοῖς, καὶ ἐν τῇ ἐκκλησίᾳ παρεχώρησεν ὁ Ἀνίκητος τὴν εὐχαριστίαν τῷ Πολυκάρπῳ.
400 Euseb. hist. eccl. 5,24,15 (SC 41, 71).
401 Euseb. hist. eccl. 5,23 f. (SC 41, 66–71). On the question of the Quartodecimans in Rome see HEID 2019c.

ging some of them before the court.[402] He thus assumes that there is only one church in a city – even in Rome – and that this location is known to the authorities. A few years later, Hippolytus, now an anti-bishop, speaks of Victor (c. 189–199) as "the bishop of the church",[403] by which he means the local church of Rome.[404] Hippolytus compares the "school" (of bishop Callistus [217–222], whom he does not recognise) with the (other) "sects" of the "church" (in Rome).[405] He does not speak of the church building itself, but he says that the followers of the (pseudo-)bishop Callistus call themselves the "Catholic Church" and that some prefer to meet at their place rather than at his, i.e. Hippolytus's.[406] It also says that former members of various sects defected to Callistus and filled his "school".[407] The word διδασκαλεῖον used here means the place where the pupils gather round the teacher and "fill" the hall. This means that Hippolytus is aware of only one bishop's church in Rome, which he admittedly does not recognise; he himself, of course, as an anti-bishop, also has a church building.[408]

An *anonymous work* about the past of the Roman priest Novatian leads as far back as the middle of the third century.[409] The intention is to show that once, when he was still a presbyter of the church of Rome, this over-strict priest was by no means so hard on sinners. For he had, it says, learned "in the house of God" of many and grave crimes that had happened in the past "in the church",[410] and had wept over the transgressions of others as his own "in the one house, that is, the Church of Christ."[411] The "one house" here cannot be merely metaphorically the church community[412] since it emphasizes the

402 Hippol. comm. in Dan. 1,21,2f. (GCS Hippol. 1,1², 48). See above n. 255.

403 Hippol. ref. 9,12,10 (MARCOVICH 1986, 352).

404 Cf. ibid. 9,12,15 (MARCOVICH 1986, 353): here, the "churches" means the non-Roman local churches. MARCOVICH offers an unnecessary alternative reading, namely "church" (applied to Rome).

405 Ibid. 9,12,20f. (MARCOVICH 1986, 354).

406 Ibid. 9,12,25 (MARCOVICH 1986, 356).

407 Ibid. 9,12,21 (MARCOVICH 1986, 354). Hippolytus, too, has "ejected from the church" a number of people who then go to the school of Callistus.

408 Next in chronological order after Hippolytus, there is a note to be mentioned in the *Historia Augusta* which appears to be evidence of a house church in Rome during the time of Alexander Severus (222–235) (DAL COVOLO 1988). But since this work dates from the fourth or fifth century – but also on account of the text itself – this work must be discarded as completely unproductive for addressing this question.

409 CCL 4, 134f. HARNACK 1895, esp. 15.

410 Anon. ad Novat. 14,1 (CCL 4, 148): *haeretice Novatiane, qui post tot et tanta in ecclesia a quibusdam retro voluntate commissa crimina, quae et tu ipse in domo Dei priusquam apostata esses cognoveras.*

411 Ibid. 13,8 (CCL 4, 147): *iste Novatianus [...], qui semper in domo una, id est Christi ecclesia, proximorum delicta ut propria fleverit, onera fratrum, sicut apostolus hortatur, sustinuerit, lubricos in fide caelesti allocutione corroboraverit.*

412 Ibid. 1,7 (CCL 4, 138): *[...] id est Christi ecclesia perseverant; in qua domo si perseverasses, Novatiane, vas forsitan et pretiosum fuisses [...]* does not contradict this. For here, too, the author is thinking of the bishop's church. If Novitian had remained there, he might have had a career as a bishop ahead of him. But things turned out differently: ibid. 2,6 (139): *Illic impudenter et sine ulla ordinationis lege episcopatus appetitur, hic autem propriis sedibus et cathedrae sibi traditae a Deo renuntiatur.* Cf. HARNACK 1895, 11, 25, 28.

public confession of guilt, which could only have taken place in a liturgical setting in front of the bishop. So at that time there was one single church building in Rome, namely that in which the bishop's cathedra stood.[413] And this is also the place of worship that Cyprian is thinking of when he writes to the confessor Bishop Lucius (253–254) that he has returned from exile to the church and the people of Rome in order to approach the altar of God and prepare the people for martyrdom.[414] Clearly, then, Cyprian assumes that all the Christians of the city gather for the Eucharist at the service celebrated by the bishop of Rome.

A much-discussed statement made by the Roman *bishop Cornelius* in a letter to his Antiochian brother bishop Fabius (251) belongs to the same period. At that time there were posts in Rome for forty-six presbyters, seven deacons, seven subdeacons and forty-two acolytes who were financed by the church community.[415] Researchers suggest that the forty-six presbyters were intended for service in the supposed house churches or *domus ecclesiae* – about twenty in number.[416] One does indeed wonder what else forty-six presbyters had to do. However, it is by no means certain that the main task of the presbyters at that time lay in the liturgy. There were certainly plenty of other tasks for them in looking after the faithful, church administration, and charitable works. In the liturgy, their competence must have been somewhat modest: "The presbyters were simply the assistants of the bishop in his worship activities in the cathedral; without him, without his special commission, nothing was allowed to be undertaken."[417]

When the aforementioned statistics regarding church personnel are weighed up carefully, they do not support the idea of house churches at all. First of all, there are only seven deacons. This number is obviously connected with the seven deacons in the Acts of the Apostles (Acts 6:3) and probably also with Rome's seven ecclesiastical administrative districts.[418] It is, on the other hand, erroneous to assume that each house church or each *domus ecclesiae* had its own deacon. The number of forty-two acolytes can probably be explained by their being attached to the seven regions, so that each region had six acolytes. The office of acolyte seems altogether to be a Roman invention.

---

413 See the preceding footnote.

414 Cypr. ep. 61,1 f. (CSEL 3,2, 695 f.): [...] *ut ad ec-clesiam maior rediret.* [...] *sed magis crevit sacer-dotalis auctoritas, ut altari Dei adsistat antistes qui ad confessionis arma sumenda et facienda martyria non verbis plebem sed factis cohortetur.*

415 Euseb. hist. eccl. 6,43,11 (SC 41, 156). HARNACK 1924, 860 f. It is important to note that Cornelius is not describing the actual numbers of clergy but the number of posts. The numbers are therefore not random but allow conclusions to be drawn

about the structure of the church; S. HEID, *Hic fecit ordinationes. Die Weihestatistiken des Liber Pontificalis und die Kirchenorganisation Roms*, in: K. HERBERS / M. SIMPERL (eds.), Das Buch der Päpste – Liber pontificalis. Ein Schlüsseldokument europäischer Geschichte (Freiburg i.Br. 2020) 157–217.

416 HARNACK 1924, 857–860; LAMPE 2003, 361; BRENT 1995, 398–400; THOMPSON 2015, 21–24.

417 ZORELL 1902, 76.

418 HARNACK 1924, 843–849; PIETRI 1997, 181 f.

This apparently indispensable, full-time ministry is best explained by Rome's adherence to the centralised episcopal Sunday Eucharist. According to Justin's testimony (c. 160), deacons still distributed the food portions to those who were absent, apparently directly following the Sunday liturgy. The presbyters had nothing to do with this. A century later, due to the limited number of deacons (seven) and the increased number of believers, this arrangement appears no longer to have been possible. In order nevertheless to ensure the distribution of the food portions, and probably also so that the deacons can stay at the bishop's liturgy, acolytes now take what is later called the *fermentum*, namely the eucharistic gifts from the bishop's Mass, to the absent faithful.[419]

In the middle of the third century, too, there are no eucharistic celebrations outside the bishop's Mass. The Christians go to the bishop's service for their Sunday Eucharist; otherwise they receive portions of the Eucharist at certain decentralised locations.[420] Such rooms and halls (owned by the Roman church) will have existed as they did in Justin's time, but now in all seven regions of the city. Although the deacons are now relieved of the rite of *fermentum*, it is hardly likely that delivering the Eucharist is left entirely to the lower clergy. The acolytes are more likely only to be responsible for the transport. In the halls, they can be assumed to have been received by the presbyters, who will meanwhile have gone there after the bishop's Mass. The presbyters will then have held a kind of service of the word before distributing the *fermentum*.[421] However, it is only outside the city – and this is of central significance – that they have the right to celebrate the Sunday Eucharist independently. They were only given the right to celebrate the Eucharist inside the city in the course of the fifth century at the earliest.[422] Their main task remains to assist at the bishop's centralised Sunday liturgy, and in connection with this task falls to them another task connected with the *fermentum*. So now as before they do not to lead house churches and are also not pastors of parishes;

---

419 There can be scarcely any doubt that a connection existed considerably earlier between *fermentum* and the office of acolyte. Innoc. I ep. ad Decent. 8 (FC 58,2, 496): *fermentum a nobis confectum per acolitos accipiunt*. If it is said at the time of Damasus (366–384) that Tarcisius carried Christ's sacraments on him (*Christi sacramenta gerentem*) (FERRUA 1942, 117), then he evidently did so officially, i.e. as an acolyte. The legend of Pope Stephen does in fact call Tarcisius an acolyte; Vit. Steph. (MOMBRITIUS 1910, 2, 500).

420 This is not intended to claim that these locations were not churches or that they are in any way connected to the later titular churches. Cf. SAXER 1989, 928.

421 It is not necessarily the case that the faithful consumed the Eucharist immediately. They possibly kept it at home and consumed some of it every day; Trad. Apost. 37 (FC 1, 294). See below p. 461.

422 Innoc. I ep. ad Decent. 8 (FC 58,2, 496) still does not allow the titular presbyters to celebrate the Eucharist autonomously (see below n. 550). The emancipation of the titular presbyters in the fifth century is probably connected with the daily celebration of the Eucharist becoming customary; cf. S. HEID, Celibacy in the Early Church (San Francisco 2000) 234.

rather, they act as a college that is in close contact with the bishop without having an independent role as liturgists.[423]

The rooms for the distribution of the *fermentum* probably still do not possess an altar since no celebration of the Eucharist takes place there. On the other hand, they will hardly have done without a table upon which to set down the eucharistic species. Whether such rooms already have the format of churches and can be considered sacred spaces is questionable, even if it is in the nature of things that they will be used more and more for other acts of worship as well. In the end, however, they will have remained of secondary importance. Neither an archaeological nor a literary memory of them has survived.

Here we must briefly mention the founding rector of the Pontifical Institute for Christian Archaeology, Johann Peter Kirsch (1861–1941). In the 1920s and '30s, he placed the focus of the Institute's research on proving the existence of predecessor buildings under Rome's city churches, the so-called titular churches. It was there, he believed, that he was most likely to find older worship spaces. And older building structures from pre-Constantinian times were in fact uncovered under various titular churches.[424] Although Kirsch did not see them as private house churches, he did regard them as pre-basilical church buildings (*domus ecclesiae*), near which the dwellings of the presbyters would also have been located. This gave rise to the impression that as early as the third century the presbyters already exercised a real pastoral function (as do present-day parish priests) at these predecessors of the titular churches.[425] But Kirsch was too optimistic. In the meantime, we know that no archaeological evidence of house churches or even Christian meeting and worship spaces has as yet been discovered for pre-Constantinian Rome. The fact that houses or similar predecessor buildings are found under the early Christian churches means little. For in Rome practically every building, whether public or private, stands on late antique walls. From the end of the fourth century, numerous private city residences passed into the possession of the Roman church, thus offering the clergy the opportunity to build (titular) churches there.[426] But in no case has it been proved that these houses previously belonged to Christians and, above all, that eucha-

423 [Cypr.] ep. 8,3 (CSEL 3,2, 488): *et presbyteri et tota ecclesia*. An interesting case is the community in the Syrian *Didascalia*. ACHELIS / FLEMMING 1904, 272: "The community is not so large that it requires more than one house of God [!]. Since the bishop regularly leads the worship there, the presbyters did not have an independent role as preachers and liturgists. They only appeared together as a college [...]. They form an honorary council which only comes into operation on special occasions."

424 KIRSCH 1918. S. HEID, Johann Peter Kirsch, in: HEID / DENNERT 2012, 732–735.

425 MONACHINO 1947, 328.

426 C. MACHADO, Between Memory and Oblivion. The end of the Roman *domus*, in: R. BEHRWALD / C. WITSCHEL (eds.), Rom in der Spätantike (Stuttgart 2012) 111–138, here 124–130.

ristic worship was once celebrated there: not under San Clemente nor under Santa Pudentiana, Santi Giovanni e Paolo or San Martino ai Monti.[427]

If it has hitherto proved impossible to discover any archaeological evidence in Rome of a pre-Constantinian church space, where then did the centralised episcopal Sunday Mass take place? We are left with speculations, but there are three suggestions. The traditional solution is to think of a stable centralised seat with a cathedral, for example on the Aventine. Adolf Harnack, on the other hand, believes that each bishop chose as his official seat the church where he had resided before his election as a presbyter.[428] This therefore presupposes several churches in pre-Constantinian or at the latest Constantinian times. Ulrich Stutz contemplates the idea that the bishop celebrated in all the churches of the city in turn.[429]

The last two suggestions are purely stop-gap solutions. For if Harnack and Stutz really are thinking of a centralised episcopal service, then a considerable number of possible places must be assumed for it. Did Rome have a dozen large churches in which the Roman bishops could hold worship services for the city? In view of the absence of archaeological finds, this seems too bold an assumption. A more likely proposal is that there was a single large church space, plus the quite modest rooms for the distribution of the *fermentum*. Even the logistics of the distribution of the food portions assumed by Justin can best be implemented if there is a centralised celebration of the Eucharist at an unchanging location in the city, with additional smaller decentralised rooms. What point would there be in constantly changing where the bishop celebrates? The bond of communion was in any case guaranteed by the *fermentum*.

The preferred thesis is therefore that there was a centralised seat of the Roman bishop with a church (*domus ecclesiae*). It is interesting in this context that Cornelius in his aforementioned letter to Fabius also speaks of fifty-two full-time exorcists, lectors and *ostiarii* in the service of the Roman church. This is difficult to explain without the existence of a prestigious episcopal church whose gates were guarded by the *ostiarii*. A clue

---

427 Kirsch 1918 was refuted by Apollonj Ghetti 1978 and Pietri 1997, 1, 127–145 (originally 1978). See White 1997, 5; Liccardo 2005, 36–38; Bowes 2008, 73 f.; Krönung 2008; de Blaauw 2010b, 22–24; Adams 2013, 99–104; Brandenburg 2013, 12. Yet Kirsch's thesis is still tenaciously adhered to in one way or another by Kraeling 1967, 128–137; Quacquarelli 1977, 241 f.; Klauck 1981, 78; White 1990, 22–24; *id.* 1996, 111–115; Osiek 2002, 95; Snyder 2003, 140–155; Bowes 2008, 65–71; Alikin 2010, 54; Pecklers 2012, 28–30.

428 Harnack 1924, 836–840.

429 U. Stutz, Review of J. P. Kirsch, Die römischen Titelkirchen und die Verfassung der stadtrömischen Kirche unter Papst Fabian, in: Zeitschrift der Savigny-Stiftung für Rechtsgeschichte, 40 kanon. Abt. 9 (1919) 288–312, here 299–301. He is followed by C. G. Fürst, *Cardinalis*. Prolegomena zu einer Rechtsgeschichte des römischen Kardinalskollegiums (München 1967) 16. The purported titular church in which the 340/341 synod assembled is not, as Stutz 1919, 296 maintains, referred to as a church but merely as a place of assembly.

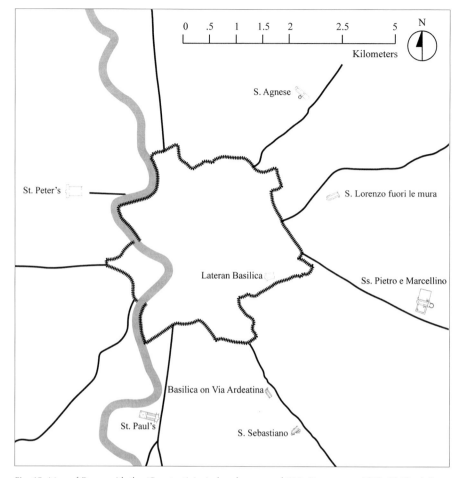

Fig. 15: Map of Rome with the (Constantinian) churches around 330; CAMERLENGHI 2018, 33 Fig. 1.8.

to this could also be provided by the *Historia Augusta*. It quotes a letter from Emperor Aurelian (270–278) to the Roman Senate in which the emperor contrasts the "temple of all gods" with the/a "church of the Christians".[430] Apparently, Aurelian has two specific buildings in Rome in mind as the main places of worship for the two religions.

It is also significant that after the end of the Diocletian persecution of the Christians (303–305) and the defeat of his rival Maxentius at the Milvian Bridge, Emperor Con-

---

430 Hist. Aug. vit. Aurel. 20,5 (PASCHOUD 2002, 32): *Miror vos, patres sancti, tamdiu de aperiendis Sibyllinis dubitasse libris, proinde quasi in Christianorum ecclesia, non in templo deorum* *omnium tractaretis.* MOHRMANN 1962, 160 attributes the quotation to the author, not to Aurelian, thus dating it to around 330.

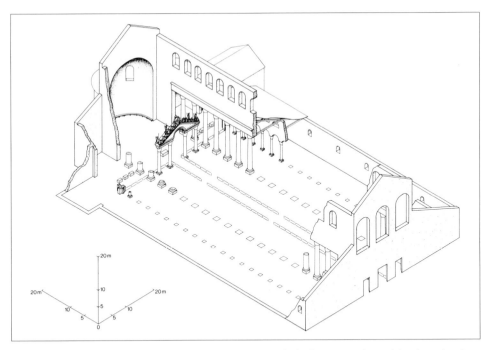

Fig. 16: Reconstruction of the Constantinian Lateran Basilica with the fastigium in front of the chancel and the seven silver altars for the offerings in the transept; DE BLAAUW 1994, Fig. 2.

stantine founded a huge bishop's church for Rome, the Lateran Basilica. It is, however, the only church within the city and has to suffice for Bishop Sylvester and the entire Christian community of Rome (Fig. 15). The nearby church of *Santa Croce in Gerusalemme* for the emperor's mother Helena does not count here because it is a private palace chapel.[431] All that is important here is that there is no mention of house churches that possibly claimed support from the emperor. The only person Constantine has contact with is Bishop Sylvester. Neither of them is contemplating building parish churches. Instead, the Lateran Basilica was designed from the start to be large enough to accommodate the entire Christian population of Rome (Fig. 16).[432] It appears that, as was already the case in Justin's day, they had only the one episcopal celebration of the Eucharist. It is

431 Constantine similarly erects one church each in Ostia (SS Peter and Paul), Albano (John the Baptist), Capua (Church of the Apostles) and Naples.

432 Of course, one should not fall prey to any misconceptions here. The church had a capacity of ten thousand faithful, but there was certainly never any idea of actually filling it. Its size was also due to the need of both the emperor and the bishop to hold official functions in a prestigious setting, and its length was intended to be conducive to a solemn entry. The congregation were concentrated – primarily for acoustic reasons – in the area at the front.

all the more astonishing that this principle was upheld as the Lateran lies on the outskirts of the city and demands an unreasonably long walk of most city dwellers.[433] But there are in fact bishop's churches on the periphery of other cities, too, without any evidence for the time being that other churches existed in the city centre.[434] The furnishings of the Lateran Basilica also support the idea of a unified service: it is given seven side altars for the offerings of the city's seven church regions, evidently because the seven regions do not have their own eucharistic celebrations in their parts of the city on Sundays.

The fact that Constantine built only the Lateran Basilica is no coincidence, but rather intentional, for he certainly did not lack the money for further churches. After all, he and his successors had several martyrs' churches built outside the gates of the city in the cemeteries (*San Pietro, San Paolo, San Sebastiano, Sant'Agnese, San Lorenzo fuori le mura, Santi Marcellino e Pietro*).[435] They too are of considerable size and yet do not compete with the Lateran because they are not used for Sunday Mass but only on the feast days of the martyrs. The *suburbium* belongs to the city and thus to the jurisdiction of the bishop. These are not churches for the rural population or regional pastoral centres. Rather, all these churches serve the entire Christian population of the city for the martyrs' feasts. They do not minister only to the Christians of the neighbourhoods closest to them since the martyrs belong, as it were, to everyone. In that sense, not only Peter and Paul, but all the martyrs of Rome are the patron saints of the city.

Even if the faithful may have to walk several kilometres from the city centre to the martyrs' churches, this is nothing out of the ordinary for Romans since the Lateran itself also lies on the outskirts. However, while in general the location of the bishop's church is a matter of chance – donations, property ownership, etc. – the suburban martyrs' churches obey a fixed law: they are always located near the martyrs' graves, i.e. in

433 Even so, additional churches are then established in Rome in the fourth century, and possibly still in Constantine's day, because in the long run the peripheral location of the Lateran really was inconvenient.

434 On Arles see M. Heijmans, Topographie des groupes épiscopaux urbains – Arles, in: *Acta XV congressus internationalis Archaeologiae Christianae* 1 (Città del Vaticano 2013) 623–631. On Aosta see R. Perinetti, La cattedrale di Aosta (IT). La topografia urbana antecedente la costruzione del complesso episcopale, in: *Acta XV congressus internationalis Archaeologiae Christianae* 1 (Città del Vaticano 2013) 637–648. On Barcelona see J. Beltrán de Heredia, Topografía de los grupos episcopales urbanos – Barcelona, in: *Acta XV congressus internationalis Archaeologiae Christianae* 1 (Città del Vaticano 2013) 649–664.

On Geneva see C. Bonnet, Le groupe épiscopal de Genève après trente ans de recherches, in: *Acta XV congressus internationalis Archaeologiae Christianae* 1 (Città del Vaticano 2013) 665–674. On Trier see W. Weber, Die Trierer Domgrabung 2,2 (Trier 2017); A. Paranou, Hypothesen zur Entstehung und Funktion der Doppelbasilika in Trier, in: *Acta XVI congressus internationalis archaeologiae christianae* 1 (Città del Vaticano 2016) 563–582. On Salona see N. Cambi, Salona, in: A. di Berardino (ed.), Nuovo dizionario patristico e di antichità cristiane 3 (Genova / Milano 2008) 4669–4672. See the overview in Testini 1989, esp. 37.

435 Aiello 2012 intends to minimise Constantine's church-building activity in Rome. This provocative thesis has given rise to numerous dissenting voices.

cemeteries. Hence their number varies according to the number of holy sites. Martyrs' churches are *lieux de mémoire* and serve to commemorate specific heroes of Christianity whose graves, according to Roman burial law, cannot be moved. A martyr can therefore only be celebrated at his or her grave. This makes every martyr's church both unique and indispensable. Its exclusive right is reflected in the fact that on the respective feast day – the day of the death or burial of the martyr in question – the bishop comes and celebrates the liturgy there together with all the faithful (station liturgy).

For the Constantinian period, the Roman festival calendar from the year 336 has been preserved (*depositio martyrum*), which names the impressive total of thirty-one martyrs' feasts during the course of a year on which the bishop travels from the Lateran – since he has resided there – to the catacombs. In this respect, Rome is undoubtedly unique: it boasts more martyrs under the emperors Decius, Valerian and Diocletian than any other city. It must be assumed that from as early as the mid–third century onwards the bishops regularly visited the martyrs' and bishops' tombs outside the city gates.[436] So the cemeteries and catacombs are already legitimised as locations for episcopal worship alongside the assumed bishop's church inside the city when Constantine builds the great basilicas there. The calendar for the year 336 thus bears witness to a first type of papal stational liturgy in Rome.[437] The martyrs' churches are under the jurisdiction of the bishop, which he exercises through the liturgy celebrated there. So the very fact that these churches are located outside the gates of the city confirms the principle: one city – one bishop – one Eucharist.

b. Alexandria

On account of its size and tradition, the Egyptian city of Alexandria is most comparable to Rome. Here, too, the size of the city led to special forms of the relationship between centralised episcopal worship and decentralised assemblies.

Clement of Alexandria (c. 150–215) offers an image of the church that is shaped by the city: in a city there is a single congregation ("church") and a bishop with his clergy; the bishop presides over the church assembly.[438] Only that place of assembly in which the

436 S. Heid, in: Gnilka 2015, 185–188. Cf. Commod. instr. 2,13[17],19 (CCL 128, 52): *Si refrigerare cupis animam, ad martyres i!* This could refer to the *Triclia* of San Sebastiano.
437 Cf. Coll. Avell. 1,12 (CSEL 35, 4): *per coemeteria martyrum stationes.* In Rome, a distinction has to be made between a first type of stational liturgy (the martyrs' liturgy in the cemeteries/catacombs in the fourth and fifth centuries) and the classical medieval type (in the titular churches, from the sixth century on).
438 Clem. Alex. quis div. salv. 42,2f. (SC 537, 208–210); strom. 3,18,108,2 (GCS Clem. Alex. 2, 246). Cf. Dölger 1950, 188.

Eucharist is celebrated in accordance with the Church's regulations is a "church".[439] This means that Clement can only be thinking of the episcopal Eucharist. When heretical leaders ("Sophists") glory in "being at the head of a school rather than presiding over a church",[440] they are deliberately placing themselves in opposition to the bishops, not to presbyters of some kind or others who preside over house churches or smaller churches. Furthermore, in view of the many altars of the pagans, Clement speaks in the singular of "the altar that is with us here".[441] When he speaks shortly afterwards of the only altar on Delos which is undefiled by the offering of bloody sacrifices, this reinforces the assumption that in Alexandria he knows only the altar of the bishop's church.[442]

Clement uses the word "church" (ἐκκλησία) to mean a Christian assembly room.[443] He does not seem to be familiar with a plurality of churches in one city. In those places where he speaks of "churches" in the plural, he is more likely to be thinking of the assemblies of the faithful, not necessarily of a plurality of assembly rooms.[444] This is not contradicted by his assertion that the true Gnostics, i.e. the Christians, do not pray in a "selected sanctuary" but everywhere. This does not mean that there were churches everywhere in Alexandria. Rather, Clement is polemicising against pagan temples and festivals, so what he wants to say is that the Christians do not pray *like the pagans* in the temples of the gods.[445]

What *Origen of Alexandria* (first half of the third century) means by "church" is all the Christians of a city, i.e. the local church (e.g. in Corinth, Ephesus, Pergamum).[446] The Christians gather for prayer "in the same place" (ἐπὶ τὸ αὐτό).[447] This means Origen was probably thinking of the bishop's service. There are in any case no references in Origen to decentralised places of assembly. According to a late testimony, he for years interpreted Sacred Scripture in Alexandria on Wednesday and Friday "in the church".[448] On these days, however, no Eucharist was celebrated,[449] since daily celebration did not emerge until the fifth century.[450] At the Eucharist, it would have been the bishop who

---

439 Clem. Alex. strom. 1,19,96,1 f. (SC 30, 121).

440 Ibid. 7,15,92,7 (SC 428, 282): αὐχοῦσι προῖστασθαι διατριβῆς μᾶλλον ἢ ἐκκλησίας.

441 Ibid. 7,6,31,8 (SC 428, 116): τὸ παρ᾽ ἡμῖν θυσιαστήριον ἐνταῦθα. WIELAND 1906, 110 incomprehensibly does not see in this any "material equipment […] that could have counted as an altar in the church of Alexandria."

442 Ibid. 7,6,32,5 (SC 428, 118–120).

443 Ibid. 1,15,66,2 (SC 30, 98): what the Christians nowadays called "church" was, he says, anticipated in the "common hall" of the Pythagoreans.

444 Clem. Alex. paed. 3,11,80,1 (SC 158, 154) and ibid. 3,11,81,2 (156) is translated correctly here by C.

Mondésert und C. Matray with "assemblées". What Strom. 8,7,22,3 (GCS Clem. Alex. 3, 93) is talking about is profane "assemblies".

445 Clem. Alex. strom. 7,7,35,3 (SC 428, 130).

446 Orig. c. Cels. 3,30 (SC 136, 72); CAMELOT 1970, 8.

447 Orig. orat. 31,5. 7 (GCS Orig. 2, 398. 400). Cf. in Luc. hom. 23,7 f. (SC 87, 320–322); in Hier. hom. 5,16 (SC 232, 322–324).

448 According to the late testimony of Socr. hist. eccl. 5,22,46 (SC 505, 228). Cf. MARTIN 1989, 1142 n. 35.

449 Socr. hist. eccl. 5,22,45 (SC 505, 228).

450 M. E. JOHNSON, Liturgy in Early Christian Egypt (Cambridge 1995) 17.

preached – on no account a layman like Origen.[451] Thus, the two fast days were the only possibility for him. For this reason alone, it must be assumed that Origen did not expound the scriptures in some small city gathering, but rather in the bishop's church.

Dionysius, a pupil of Origen, was the bishop of Alexandria from 248 to c. 265 and left behind fragments of correspondence. According to this correspondence, the state authorities are aware of the assemblies of the bishop and his clergy both in the city and in the cemeteries.[452] All the places of assembly are under the jurisdiction of the bishop.[453] In the city itself there is apparently only the bishop's church. For Dionysius affirms that, despite his exile in Cephro, he is spiritually present in the city of Alexandria at the visible assembly of the faithful – meaning the worship gathering.[454] A letter from Dionysius to Bishop Sixtus II of Rome points in the same direction. According to this, there seems to be only one meeting place of the brethren in Alexandria, where the bishop presides at the celebration of the Eucharist as well as at baptism; it is also where the eucharistic "table" (τράπεζα) is to be found.[455]

Under the aforementioned Dionysius, Alexandria probably possessed a bishop's church (not localised),[456] which may well already have been replaced by the later bishop Theonas (282–300) under Emperor Aurelian (270–275) with a second, larger church (the Church of St Theonas on the northwestern edge of the city). This was then extended under Bishop Alexander (312–328). It is certainly the scene of an appearance by the desert father Anthony to inveigh against the Arians (c. 337/38). "All the people in the city ran together to see Anthony" and came "into the church".[457] This church must therefore already have been of considerable size. Nevertheless, it was evidently soon no longer able to hold the entire community, so that around 340 the construction of a significantly larger church was begun at a different location, but once again on the outskirts of the city (in the former temple district of the Kaisareion, opposite the eastern harbour).[458] The fact that two or three successive bishop's churches were built with ever larger dimensions points to the tradition of the one episcopal service for everyone.[459]

---

451 It is a matter of debate how Origen's alleged preaching activity in Alexandria fits into the context of his lay preaching in Caesarea and the conflict that arose over this preaching with the Alexandrian bishop. Cf. A. Fürst, Origenes (Stuttgart 2017) 8 f.

452 Euseb. hist. eccl. 7,11,10 (SC 41, 181).

453 Ibid. 7,13 (SC 41, 188). The bishop of Alexandria sees to the burial of the martyrs in the cemeteries; ibid. 7,11,24 (185).

454 Ibid. 7,11,12 (SC 41, 182). In the same way, he gathers a new "church" around him in Cephro. Ibid. 7,11,17 (183) speaks of meetings of the faithful with the bishop in places located in the surroundings of Alexandria.

455 Ibid. 7,9 (SC 41, 174 f.).

456 Seeliger / Krumeich 2007, 54 would like to see in the *Domus Dionysii* or the *Dominicum Dionysii* a "house church" or episcopal palace chapel. But this is unclear and speculative.

457 Athan. vit. Anton. 70,1 f. (SC 400, 316–318).

458 Seeliger / Krumeich 2007, 45–55; Martin 1984, here 213 f., 217 f.; *id.* 1989, 1136 f.

459 With R. C. Mortimer, against Brakmann 1979, 147.

Later sources from the fourth and fifth centuries claim that there were several churches in Alexandria at the beginning of the fourth century. This is interesting in that this circumstance is specially explained on every mention, apparently because it is unusual. The time in question is that of the presbyter Arius (c. 310–320). It is said to have been common at the time for the presbyters themselves to run the churches (ἐκκλησίαι) in the various parts of town. This claim is indirectly justified by the size of the city since a single bishop alone could not cope with all the demands of pastoral care.[460] But this is about the gatherings of the faithful and the sermons of the presbyters, not eucharistic celebrations. These gatherings are more likely to be limited to the Liturgy of the Hours, a sermon and baptismal catechesis.[461] If Stefan Klug thinks that in the third century the church of Alexandria consisted of several individual communities, each led by presbyters,[462] then this is open to interpretation. In any case, the presbyters do not seem to have had eucharistic and baptismal rights.

The Oxyrhynchus Papyri mention in the time of the Diocletian persecution (5 February 304) "the former church of the village of Chysis near Oxyrhynchus". The original order for the confiscation of church property mentioned only "the church", but it turned out to be abandoned or destroyed. Thus, the mention of "the church" at the beginning of the fourth century indicates that there was probably just this church.[463] A few years later, in peacetime (315 or later), a military text listing guard districts mentions "the northern church" and "the southern church" in Oxyrhynchus. As their names indicate, the two buildings lie in the northern and southern parts of the city. Although the editors of the papyrus have added a question mark querying whether the term ἐκκλησία really refers to churches,[464] there is no reason why this should not be the case.[465] But then the question arises as to whether there were more churches and what their relationship was to the bishop's church that undoubtedly existed (churches of special groups?).

460 Sozom. hist. eccl. 1,15,12 (SC 306, 188–190); Epiph. pan. 69,1,2 (GCS Epiph. 3, 152). Kirsch 1918, 181 f.; Martin 1989, 1135; Metzger 2015, 224.

461 Sozom. hist. eccl. 1,15,11 (SC 306, 188): ἐκκλησιάζειν. Epiph. pan. 69,2,5 (GCS Epiph. 3, 154): κατὰ τὴν εἰθισμένην σύναξιν τὸν αὐτῷ πεπιστευμένον λαὸν διδάσκων. The synaxis is the liturgical assembly, for example for the Liturgy of the Hours, not necessarily for the celebration of the Eucharist. Cf. Martin 1989, 1140, 1142.

462 S. Klug, Alexandria und Rom. Die Geschichte der Beziehungen zweier Kirchen in der Antike (Münster 2014) 65.

463 P.Oxy. XXXIII.2673: L. H. Blumell / T. A. Wayment (eds.), Christian Oxyrhynchus. Texts, Documents and Sources (Waco 2015) 411–421. Cf. M. Choat / R. Yuen-Collingridge, A Church with No Books and a Reader Who Cannot Write. The Strange Case of P.Oxy. 33.2673, in: Bulletin of the American Society of Papyrologists 46 (2009) 109–138, here 113, 116, 119; A. M. Luijendijk, Greetings in the Lord. Early Christians and the Oxyrhynchus Papyri (Harvard 2008) 203 f.

464 P.Oxy. XLIII verso, 1,10; 3,19: Grenfell / Hunt 1898, 89.

465 Luijendijk 2008, 19 f.; Blumell / Wayment 2015, 408–411.

Between 351 and 353, Athanasius (bishop 328–373) celebrated Easter with all the Christians of the city in the above-mentioned, still incomplete, "great church" of the Kaisareion before it was possible to consecrate it with imperial permission. This in itself makes clear that in principle all the faithful of the city are supposed to participate in the bishop's liturgy. In order to justify why he was celebrating in an unfinished church, Athanasius claims that the city at the time had only a few extremely confined church spaces. He explicitly mentions the Church of Theonas, but this again only brings a bishop's church into the picture.[466]

Taking all the testimonies together, it is possible to say that in Alexandria in around 300 presbyters probably gathered the faithful with episcopal permission in decentralised churches for the Liturgy of the Hours, the Liturgy of the Word and sermons.[467] These churches are modest institutions that in no way challenged the unified episcopal worship. Annick Martin rightly assumes that the presbyters of Alexandria were late in receiving the right to celebrate the Sunday Eucharist themselves, perhaps, as in Rome, not until the fifth century.[468] Therefore these churches – perhaps unlike the older bishop's churches – would initially still not have had an altar. In retrospect they are called churches, but originally they may have been regarded as prayer houses. Whether there was a rite in Alexandria comparable to the Roman *fermentum* is not known.

The so-called *Canons of Hippolytus*, a Church Order from the years 336–340, are controversial, as it is not clear whether they are premised on the situation in the Egyptian province or are to be located in the city of Alexandria.[469] Annick Martin comes down on the side of Alexandria.[470] It is in any case clear that these canons have a city community in mind with a bishop and clergy.[471] It speaks of the (episcopal) "church" in every place[472] and of the "whole people", namely the local community.[473] These gather, for example, at the consecration of a bishop for a single service with bishop and presbyters.[474] Consequently, there must be a church building that can accommodate the entire

---

466 Athan. apol. ad Const. 14, 16 (SC 56², 114–116, 120). MARTIN 1989, 1137; METZGER 2015, 225f. The Christians offered to gather for the Paschal Feast, if need be, outside the city "in desert places". On the *suburbium* see MARTIN 1989, 1135, 1139; differently BRAKMANN 1979, 144.

467 Eusebius speaks in his *Church History* several times of the churches and *paroikíai* of the bishops of Alexandria, but this is unlikely to refer to the city's presbyter churches and more likely to mean the enormous Alexandrine diocese; cf. MARTIN 1989, 1136 n. 8. SEELIGER / KRUMEICH 2007, 49–53 are aware of only episcopally founded sacred buildings from c. 324 onwards. More opti-

mistic MARTIN 1984, 214–216; *id.* 1989, 1138f. Cf. BRAKMANN 1979, 144.

468 MARTIN 1989, 1140, 1142.

469 BRAKMANN 1979 opts for the first possibility. Apparently Athan. vit. Anton. 2,1–3,1 (SC 400, 132–134) assumes that in Anthony's central Egyptian hometown there was only one church.

470 MARTIN 1989, 1136 n. 8.

471 Can. Hippol. arab. 9 (PO 31, 360–362); 23 (390).

472 Ibid. 3 (PO 31, 352).

473 Ibid. 2 (PO 31, 348): the bishop is chosen by the "whole people".

474 Ibid. 3 (PO 31, 350–352). Cf. ibid. 19 (382): gathering of the "whole people" at Easter.

local community. Further, the Church Order says that the baptismal candidates "come to the church",[475] meaning the church building. There is evidently only the one "church" in which all the clergy and the "whole people" gather daily for morning prayers[476] and where the faithful make their (votive) offerings.[477] It is here, too, that what appears to be the only altar stands.[478] Like the bishops, the presbyters, too, are also ordained for the local church.[479] They must participate in the bishop's service every Sunday.[480] It is not completely out of the question that other church spaces exist besides the cathedral. Indeed, one canon speaks of sermons "in a church".[481] While there is only one celebration of Mass with the bishop and clergy, this could point to sermon services held by the presbyters in other city churches.

5. ITINERANT EPISCOPAL ALTAR?

Our observations so far might shed some light on the question of mobile altars. The fact that mobile eucharistic furniture existed is often used by researchers as an argument for its profanity: the early Church, they say, only used mobile and thus allegedly profane dining tables as eucharistic furniture. Franz Wieland, for example, is certain that:

> Although the communion table had already been accorded the dignity and veneration of something sacred from the third century onwards, throughout this century it was nevertheless only considered an 'altar' for as long as the respective celebration lasted. Outside of this time it was insignificant and no notice was taken of it. There was no 'altar', i.e. in the sense of a permanent and fixed sanctum in the temple.[482]

It was possible for such a link between mobility and profanity to arise because at that time a distinction was made in canon law between an *altare fixum* and an *altare portatile*. According to this, the mobile altar was used in the event that no consecrated altar was available in a church.[483] The historical argument in support of the purported connection between mobility and profanity is the assertion that the congregations initially just used alternating, profane spaces for their services and only later had fixed

475 Ibid. 10 (PO 31, 362).
476 Ibid. 21 (PO 31, 386).
477 Ibid. 32 (PO 31, 404); 36 (408).
478 Ibid. 29 (PO 31, 398).
479 Ibid. 4 (PO 31, 354).
480 Ibid. 37 (PO 31, 410) together with 30 (402).
481 Ibid. 26 (PO 31, 394). But one important MS reads "in the church"; furthermore, the same canon then speaks again of "the church", likewise ibid. 27 (394).
482 Wieland 1912, 32. Similarly *id.* 1906, 119 f.
483 Braun 1924a, 42–45.

meeting places, so that then altars came into use.[484] Other researchers cling to the connection between mobility and profanity even when it has to be assumed that genuine places of worship existed. Willy Rordorf, for example, says of the church at Dura Europos from the mid–third century: "A mortared-in altar has not been found in Dura-Europos. So it seems that an ordinary table served the purposes of an altar."[485] But why should the altar that was no longer discovered when the worship space was excavated 1,700 years later have been profane just because it was not found? Furthermore, the church at Dura Europos (like the neighbouring synagogue) was deliberately abandoned when it became necessary to reinforce the city wall against an imminent Sassanid attack. All the furnishings were carefully removed before it was filled in,[486] including the altar – and this because it was sacred and needed for the celebration of the Eucharist in another, provisional hall.[487]

The association of mobility with profanity is a modern construct. Antiquity knew no such connection. Movable sacred tables and altars were just as holy as fixed ones.[488] Portable tripods were full sacrificial altars.[489] The practice among the Jews and Romans of bringing sacred tables to banquets for the ritual food or the table sacrifice is also revealing.[490] The table for the bread of the Presence and the altar of the burnt offering of the Israelites were already carried through the desert (Ex 25:28; 27:7), undoubtedly without losing their holiness (Ex 29:37). The Romans certainly had no intention of profaning the showbread table from the Jerusalem Temple when they carried it in triumph through Rome; rather, they wanted to incorporate it as sacred booty into the temple treasure of Jupiter. Nor did it in any way detract from the sacredness of the statues of the gods of antiquity when they were carried around in solemn processions.

There is no reason to query that the Christians had mobile altars – made of wood. When Ignatius of Antioch prays that he would like to be sacrificed to God "while an altar is still prepared",[491] this can be understood as referring to a mobile altar.[492] But the mobile altar here, too, is still called an "altar". The Christians adopt the pagan language

---

484 WIELAND 1912, 32; BRAUN 1924a, 55 f, 65–71, 101–109; FRANK 1997, 123; ZELLER 2002, 330. DEICHMANN 1964, 58 is of the opinion that it was only during the course of the fourth century that the table occasionally used for the Eucharist became a fixed altar intended exclusively for the Eucharist.
485 RORDORF 1964, 122.
486 MELL 2011, 23.
487 This is a similar case to Megiddo, where the floor

was sealed and the altar slab removed. See below p. 184.
488 REISCH 1894, 1648–1650, 1685.
489 SIEBERT 1999, 93–98. Movable altars for animal sacrifice among the Romans see Prud. peristeph. 10,916 (CCL 126, 361).
490 See above p. 23 f.
491 Ign. ad Rom. 2,2 (SC 10³, 128).
492 But it might also be referring to altar decoration. Altar decoration see REISCH 1894, 1687.

usage in which the "setting up" of an altar can equally mean fixing it permanently[493] or installing it temporarily.[494] When it comes to mobile altars in church spaces, they are certainly always installed in the same place. In the church at Dura Europos, there is a special podium by the east wall on which a mobile altar may well have stood, which, like the holy scriptures, was taken to safety.[495]

Regional differences must also be taken into account here. The Syrian *Didascalia* dating from the third century speaks at all events of the "altar of God" which is immovable, firmly founded in one place and stationary in that place.[496] Such clear words force one to rule out a mobile altar.[497] In Palestine, too, altars probably belonged to the immovable furnishings of the churches around the mid–third century.[498]

Archaeological findings may indicate a partial mobility of the altars. Sometimes four postholes are found in the ground or in a floor slab in which stood either a wooden or a stone table with four legs[499] (below Figs. 42, 50). The function of the holes was to anchor the table firmly but tables that were actually movable were fixed in this way. The floor slab was considered an integral and therefore equally holy part of the altar. The partial mobility of the altar can be imagined as resembling that of the cathedra. Roman officials had the chair (*sella curulis*) carried behind them for use at off-site appointments. But normally it stood in their official seat. It is no coincidence that it is Cyprian of Carthage († 258) who knows of the mobility not only of the altar but also of the bishop's cathedra.[500] When, from the third century onwards, the bishops also held their own courts (*audientia episcopalis*) and sat in the bishop's chair for this purpose,[501] they probably

493 Cf. a pagan altar inscription in BUCHOWIECKI 1967, 585. Cf. Lact. div. inst. 1,20,33 (CSEL 19, 77): *ara posita est.* Symm. or. 2,32 (MGH.AA 6,1, 330): *illis singula templa fundantur et sua cuique locantur altaria.* The erection of altars see also *Thesaurus Linguae Latinae* 1 (1900) 1725, line 59; ibid. 1725, lines 78 f. On mensa see ibid. 8 (1966) 743 f.

494 Theod. de situ terrae sanctae 12 (CCL 175, 120): *ponitur altaris* here clearly means a temporarily installed altar. Likewise *Thesaurus Linguae Latinae* 1 (1900) 1727, line 20; ibid. 2 (1906) 382, lines 60–63.

495 LANG 2003, 72; BRENK 2003, 67; MACMULLEN 2009, 3. 5. In any case, the altar was removed before the church was filled in. RIESNER 2007, 160 expresses the not very convincing opinion that a 1,00 × 1,50 m. podium cannot have supported an altar and that it is more likely to have been a podium for a seat. Since at the time the priest did not genuflect at the altar, the podium was large enough for both altar and priest.

496 Didasc. syr. 15 (ACHELIS / FLEMMING 1904, 77); BRAUN 1924a, 56; DÖLGER 1930, 164 f. The idea that the *Didascalia* did not here assume a fixed church altar (cf. WIELAND 1906, 118 f.; MESSNER 2003a, 365) is erroneous.

497 M. METZGER, in: SC 329, 80.

498 Cf. DÖLGER 1930, 163 f. See also the prayer house in Megiddo (third century?) above p. 56 f.

499 KIRSCH / KLAUSER 1950, 338. Cf. Athan. hist. Arian. 56 (PG 25, 760D); Basil. ep. 226,2 (PG 32, 845AB).

500 Cypr. ep. 68,2 (CSEL 3,2, 745) on Novitian: *profanum altare erigere et adulteram cathedram conlocare.* Ep. 69,8 (757): *cathedram sibi constituere.* Wooden, mobile episcopal throne see Athan. hist. Arian. 56 (PG 25, 760D). On the cathedra as *sella curulis* in Cyprian see BRENT 2010, 61–63. Altar as official insignia METZGER 2015, 263.

501 HERRMANN 1980, 78–86, 205–231; RAPP 2005, 242–252; KRITZINGER 2016, 118 f.

needed mobile cathedras (*sedes*) which they could set up either in the basilica or in the audience hall as needed. In the church, a sufficiently large podium was enough to set it up on. Here too, as with the altar, the chair was not arbitrary just because it was portable; it remained the bishop's sacrosanct chair of office. For a long time, the pope's equipment in the Lateran included a mobile cathedra.[502]

Cyprian is rightly cited as the most important witness to altar tables which were set up (*conlocare*)[503] and equally also removed as needed.[504] He speaks of a great assembly of faithful and priests for which the altar was set up (in the church): *altari posito*.[505] The sacred aura of the altar is quite intentional here: it is meant to make the disputing parties curb their emotions in its presence.[506] When Cyprian speaks of the altar, it goes without saying that he is referring to the one at which he himself celebrates. Hence it belongs to the bishop's church. Elsewhere, Cyprian lets it be understood that the altar is to be taken to a place of safety if the need arises in order to protect it from being profaned by unbelievers.[507]

This situation remained unchanged until the time of Constantine. Caecilianus, the Catholic bishop of Carthage beginning in 311/12, is regarded by the Donatists as an apostate. Therefore, in their eyes, he sacrilegiously erects the altar at which he celebrates false sacred rites and fake mysteries.[508] Interestingly, he erects "a/the altar". So it is not a matter of Caecilianus's being accused of building churches and erecting altars everywhere. Rather, it can only be the bishop's altar that is meant here, which is obviously mobile. From a Catholic perspective, Optatus of Milevis (c. 365) writes about Caecilianus's consecration as bishop: the church of Carthage is crowded with people, the bishop's cathedra is occupied, "the altar in its place" (*erat altare loco suo*), at which Cyprian, Carpoforius and Lucilianus have already sacrificed.[509] But immediately afterwards, "altar against altar" is erected (*altare contra altare erectum*) by a group of Christians and an illegitimate episcopal consecration, namely that of the Donatist bishop Majorinus, is performed.[510] The circumstances described here force one to conclude that since the

502 OR XI,99 (ANDRIEU 1948, 446): *conpositam sedem in ecclesia*.
503 Cypr. ep. 73,2 (CSEL 3,2, 780): *altare conlocare*. WIELAND 1906, 122f.
504 Cypr. ep. 59,18 (CSEL 3,2, 688): *recedentibus sacerdotibus ac Domini altare removentibus*.
505 Ibid. 45,2 (CSEL 3,2, 600).
506 DÖLGER 1930, 162f.
507 Cypr. ep. 59,18 (CSEL 3,2, 687). BRAUN 1924a, 55; DÖLGER 1930, 161–163. Such a profanation see Marcellin. et Faustin. lib. prec. 20,76 (CCL 69,

378): *ipsum altare Dei de dominico sublatum in templo sub pedibus idoli posuerunt*. The Alexandrine priest Macarius was accused in 335 of breaking the chalice, overturning the altar and burning the books during a celebration of the Eucharist; FC 58,1, 106f. n. 119, 110, 112, 118.
508 Pass. Saturnini 19 (PL 8, 702B): *erigit altare sacrilegus, celebrat sacramenta profanus*.
509 Opt. Mil. 1,19,2f. (SC 412, 212).
510 Ibid. 1,19,4 (SC 412, 214).

time of Cyprian the same mobile altar has been used in Carthage that is normally set up in the bishop's church.[511]

Optatus also speaks of movable wooden altars and complains that the Donatists are initially not content simply to remove the altars of the Catholics, but also destroy them;[512] later they are satisfied with just removing them.[513] So although the altars are in principle movable – they can be carried away – they normally stand in their fixed place in the church.[514] Already in pagan antiquity, a cult is established by the erection of a sacred table and possibly ended by forcibly removing or overturning it.[515] This is also what the Donatists do with Catholic altars. Unfortunately, Optatus does not give any indication of which churches the altars were removed from. But their destruction is connected with the atrocities associated with the return of the exiled Donatist bishops and the restoration of their church structure under Emperor Julian the Apostate in 361.[516] It may therefore be assumed that these acts of destruction mainly affected the bishop's churches of the North African cities.

For the fifth century, two further testimonies from Africa can be considered. In North Africa, Augustine speaks in a sermon of the "altar that is now placed on the ground in the church".[517] His aim is to establish a connection between the altar "set up on earth" and the heavenly altar at which Christ stands. This points to a table altar that is in principle mobile. Whether Augustine always celebrated at such an altar cannot be determined.

Around 412, an unlawful consecration takes place in the castle of the village of Hydrax in Cyrenaica (Egypt), which has been destroyed by an earthquake. Bishop Paul of Erythron consecrates a tiny room with an altar that has been brought in.[518] It is interesting that the altar itself is apparently not consecrated. It is sufficient to cover it with the "mystical (altar) cloth" for the celebration of the Eucharist. One must assume that the

---

511 BRAUN 1924a, 68 says quite rightly that it is not possible to tell directly from Optatus how the altar was set up. Nevertheless, its mobility follows from the fact that it is the same altar that was already used by Cyprian.

512 Opt. Mil. 6,1,1 (SC 413, 164): *Quid enim tam sacrilegum quam altaria Dei […] radere, removere.* Ibid. 6,1,8 (164): *Si suffecerat removere, non licuit frangere.*

513 Ibid. 6,1,11 (SC 413, 166).

514 The same goes for those "holy tables" that the barbarians carried off from the Kyrenaika in 412 and used for distributing sacrificial meat; Synes. catast. (PG 66, 1569C).

515 SIEBERT 1999, 101 with a reference to MISCHKOWSKI 1917, 8–10.

516 B. KRIEGBAUM, in: S. DÖPP / W. GEERLINGS (eds.), Lexikon der antiken christlichen Literatur (Freiburg i.Br. ³2002) 527.

517 Aug. serm. 351,4,7 (PL 39, 1543): *Ad hoc enim altare, quod nunc in Ecclesia est in terra positum, terrenis oculis expositum, ad mysteriorum divinorum signacula celebranda.*

518 Synes. ep. 67 (PG 66, 1420CD); B. BOTTE / H. BRAKMANN, Kirchweihe, in: RACh 20 (2004) 1139–1169, here 1147 f.

bishop did not leave the altar in this abandoned fort but took it back to his episcopal church.

This raises the question of the itinerant episcopal altar. Éric Palazzo thinks that the principle of the *one* altar pronounced by Ignatius of Antioch subsequently led to the abolition of mobile altars.[519] It is also possible to see it exactly the other way round, especially as Ignatius himself possibly assumed the existence of a mobile altar:[520] the principle of a single episcopal altar requires it to be mobile. If the bishop celebrates outside his cathedral, he has to take the cathedral altar with him or to have a mobile substitute altar ready at hand. For what happens when – at the latest from the third century on – the Eucharist is also celebrated in cemeteries at the tombs of martyrs? In Rome, after the Decian persecution of the Christians (250–251), there began to be gatherings at the martyrs' graves[521] in which, to all appearances, the bishop participated.[522] It is hard to imagine that he did not celebrate the Eucharist on this occasion.[523] So how can the principle of one altar be upheld now? Possibly such station masses are the reason for making use of mobile altars or for taking the altar of the bishop's church to wherever the bishop is celebrating. In a letter to Bishop Cornelius of Rome (251–253), Cyprian speaks in such a matter-of-fact way of the bishop's altar being carried away by the priests[524] that it seems he assumes the situation in Rome to be similar to that in Carthage.

For Carthage, at any rate, it is easily conceivable that the altar goes with the bishop, so to speak, when he celebrates the Mass outside his church. In this sense, the bishop would be the "rector" of the altar:[525] he gives instructions as to where it is to be placed. Afterwards, it is returned to its location in the bishop's church. If there really were decentralised, presbyter-run prayer rooms in Rome and Alexandria in the third century where the Eucharist was not normally celebrated, then it is quite conceivable that the bishop occasionally celebrated there at his own altar brought from the episcopal church.[526]

In the case of the synchronous double-church of Aquileia (built by Bishop Theodore around 313–319, later enlarged), it might be that the episcopal altar was initially movable and placed wherever it was needed. In later times, the co-cathedrals had their own altars, as is the case, for example, in the time of Ambrose in Milan. Anyhow, mobility has

519 Palazzo 2008, 81 f.
520 See above p. 48 n. 99.
521 For Rome this is certain; for Carthage it is assumed.
522 S. Heid, in: Gnilka 2015, 187 f.
523 Cf. Kirsch / Klauser 1950, 335 f.
524 Cypr. ep. 59,18 (CSEL 3,2, 688).

525 Ibid. 66,5 (CSEL 3,2, 730): *sit antistes et rector altari eorum pariter et plebi.*
526 This is probably also how one would have to imagine it happening if Harnack or Stutz were right with their thesis that in pre-Constantinian times the bishop of Rome celebrated in alternating churches. See above p. 143.

nothing to do with profanity; on the contrary, the altar is transportable because, like the cathedra, it is, as it were, an insignia of office. At that time, bishops did not have a mitre or crosier as a sign of their dignity: the early Church was content with a seat and an altar.

On the whole, however, itinerant altars really must have been inconvenient if the altar had to be transported every time from the bishop's church. It is possible that the cathedral altar was permanently installed, while a smaller, lighter secondary altar was used outside the cathedral and was reserved for the bishop and his representatives. In this way, the unity of the main altar was preserved. Other churches will have gone over to setting up special altars in the cemeteries. It can only be a matter of speculation which solution was taken into consideration by the Syrian *Didascalia*, which is familiar with the bishop's altar fixed in the ground and at the same time speaks of services for the dead in the cemeteries.[527] Otherwise, the sources lead one not to expect fixed altars in suburban martyrs' churches until the second half of the fourth century. Such altars are at least attested under Emperor Julian in Asia Minor,[528] under Basil in Caesarea[529] and somewhat later under Emperor Theodosius outside the gates of Gaza.[530]

For Rome, information is available about the altar donations of the Emperor Constantine († 337), which raises a number of questions. As far as the Lateran is concerned, one wonders whether the seven silver altars he donated include the main altar.[531] This is probably not the case because the number seven is explained by the seven regions of Rome and the seven deacons. But if Constantine did not gift a main altar, then the reason might have been that Pope Sylvester had transferred the altar of the earlier bishop's church to the new church at the Lateran. Since this older bishop's church appears to have been demolished – it has so far not been possible to find any trace of it – the idea might have been to save at least the (mobile) altar and continue to use it in order to establish episcopal cultic continuity.[532] The first mention of an altar dedicated to St Peter in the Lateran Basilica – evidently the main altar – dates from the ninth century, by which time it must already have been venerated as such for a very long time. For only the pope was allowed to celebrate at it, and it was not until Stephen III (768–772) that the cardinal bishops of the seven suburbicarian sees were permitted to do so, too.[533] In the Middle

527 Didasc. syr. 26 (ACHELIS / FLEMMING 1904, 143).
528 Sozom. hist. eccl. 5,20,7 (SC 495, 206–208); BRAUN 1924a, 66.
529 Basil. hom. 18,2 (PG 31, 496A). Basil here undoubtedly assumes there to be altars in the martyrs' churches.
530 Sozom. hist. eccl. 5,9,9 (SC 495, 132).
531 So BRAUN 1924a, 69. It is indeed hardly conceivable that a different altar was used on every week-

day. At that time, the pope as a rule only celebrated on Sundays.
532 Aptly DE BLAAUW 1994, 118; *id.* 2001b, 971; cf. CLAUSSEN 2008, 184 f. Later DE BLAAUW 2006, 169 states less convincingly that Constantine did not donate an altar to the Lateran Basilica "most likely because an altar was installed here from an important house church."

Ages, people are convinced that Pope Sylvester brought the wooden altar to the Lateran Basilica.[534]

Something similar may apply to the nearby port city of Ostia. Here Constantine likewise built a basilica within the city and made extraordinary donations, but these did not include an altar.[535] This cannot have been due to a lack of money. Possibly Ostia had already a bishop's church with an altar, which was then used for the new church. Or alternatively, the church, as a station church of the Roman bishop, initially did not have its own altar.

All the same, in Rome the principle of the physical unity of the episcopal altar was broken by the donations of Emperor Constantine. For one thing, he also donated an altar to the Sessorian Basilica (*Santa Croce in Gerusalemme*).[536] Admittedly, this was a palace chapel, where the emperor could do whatever he wanted. Also it was probably looked after from the Lateran. On the other hand, Constantine donated altars for the suburban cemetery churches of *San Pietro in Vaticano* (Old St Peter's)[537] and Santi Marcellino e Pietro,[538] but not for *San Paolo fuori le mura*, *Sant'Agnese* and *San Lorenzo fuori le mura*. In the Greek East, altars in martyrs' churches cannot be attested to until a few decades later. The fact that Rome leads the way here is probably due simply to the high number of imperial interventions. They take place, even though they in part contravene the ecclesiastical norm, by virtue of the authority of a man who regards himself as "bishop".[539] Constantine probably donated the altars in *San Pietro* and *Santi Marcellino e Pietro* primarily in order to commemorate the dead of the Constantinian family,[540] in just the same way as he donated the altar of the imperial mausoleum in Constantinople.[541]

The situation is therefore unclear for the Constantinian period, i.e. up to the 330s. It is in any case by no means safe to assume that the pope found an altar in every church. It was only under Pope Damasus (366–384) that at least the cemetery churches outside the city had permanently installed altars.[542] However, this does not necessarily apply to the

---

533 LP 96,27 (DUCHESNE 1886, 478): *Hic statuit ut omni dominico die a septem episcopis cardinalibus ebdomadariis, qui in ecclesia Salvatoris observant, missarum solemnia super altare beati Petri celebraretur.*

534 DE BLAAUW 1994, 238; CLAUSSEN 2008, 187. The wooden altars in the Lateran Basilica, in *Sancta Sanctorum* and in Santa Pudenziana see BRAUN 1924a, 56–63.

535 LP 34,28 f. (DUCHESNE 1886, 183 f.). Nor did the benefactor Gallicanus donate an altar.

536 LP 34,22 (DUCHESNE 1886, 179): *altare argenteum.*

537 LP 34,18 (DUCHESNE 1886, 177): *ipsum alterem ex argento.*

538 LP 34,27 (DUCHESNE 1886, 183): *altare ex argento purissimo.*

539 Cf. J. VOGT, Constantinus der Große, in: RACh 3 (1957) 306–379, here 360 f., 363.

540 For SS Marcellino e Pietro this is obvious. Here, Constantine donates two altars, one for the basilica, the other for the adjoining Helena mausoleum. For San Pietro in Vaticano the inscription *Constantinus Augustus et Helena Augusta hanc domum regalem simili fulgore coruscans aula circumdat* points to a special interest on the part of the imperial family in this church.

541 See above p. 103 f.

542 This is attested to by five Damasan martyr inscriptions: FERRUA 1942, 120, 166, 167, 195, 229.

churches inside the city. The earliest buildings – the basilica of Pope Sylvester (314–335) (*San Martino ai Monti*),[543] the church of Pope Mark (336) (*San Marco*), the two basilicas of Pope Julius (337–352) at the *Forum Romanum* and in Trastevere, the basilica of Pope Liberius (352–366) on the Esquiline[544] and the city church of Damasus (*San Lorenzo in Damaso*)[545] – are evidently episcopal foundations and were therefore initially set up for papal worship, or were at any rate under papal supervision. With the exception of the last-named foundation, they were of modest dimensions,[546] were unlikely to have had their own clergy[547] and were possibly without a fixed altar. At that time, there was anyway not yet a daily celebration of mass, and the feasts of the martyrs during the week were, of course, celebrated not in the city but outside in the cemeteries and catacombs. The additional city churches were probably necessary at first for the simple reason that the pope had to stop off somewhere on his way across the city from the Lateran to Old St Peter's or to other cemeteries located in the north. So it is quite conceivable that on his irregular trips across the city he sometimes still used a portable altar for the celebration of the Eucharist.

A statement found in the *Ambrosiaster*, which was written in Rome around 400, is at all events remarkable. According to this document, in Rome and in all the other local churches the deacons carry the altar and the liturgical vessels for the bishop.[548] This certainly does not mean that in Rome, or even in Italy, they had only mobile altars. It merely clarifies the responsibility for transporting them: if an altar has to be carried or brought, this is the task of the deacons, not of other subordinate clerics.[549] What is important here is the fact that this service is related to the bishop. It is only the bishops who have, in addition to the fixed altar of their cathedral, a mobile altar that is reserved for them or their representatives. It is possible that it was deliberate that a fixed altar was not initially installed in the titular churches since at the beginning of the fifth century

---

543 LP 34,3. 33 (DUCHESNE 1886, 170. 187) does not mention an altar among the gifts for the church.

544 Also the *basilica Sicinini*; H. JORDAN / C. HUELSEN, Topographie der Stadt Rom im Alterthum 1,3 (Berlin 1907) 336.

545 LP 39,4 (DUCHESNE 1886, 212) does not mention an altar among the gifts for the church.

546 GUIDOBALDI 1993, 77 f.

547 LP 34,3 (DUCHESNE 1886, 170): *Hic* [Sylvester] *fecit in urbe Roma ecclesiam in praedium cuiusdam presbiteri sui*. This means, then, that only one "of his presbyters" made his private grounds available for the papal church building. Marcell. et Faust. lib. prec. 22,79 f. (CCL 69, 379): Damasus forbids the Roman presbyters from freely summoning the sacred gatherings of the people during the day, so

that the presbyter Macarius celebrates the holy sacraments secretly in a *domus*. The report is admittedly tendentious. It can be interpreted as saying that Macarius celebrated mass independently of the bishop, and what is more, in a profane location. It appears that none of the smaller churches, let alone the Lateran Basilica, are at his disposal for this. Macarius is banished. This is still a far cry from regular masses by presbyters in titular churches.

548 Ambrosiast. quaest. 101,3 (CSEL 50, 195): *nam utique et altare portarent et vasa eius, et aquam in manus funderent sacerdoti, sicut videmus per omnes ecclesias*.

549 WIELAND 1906, 123; *id*. 1912, 36 f.; BRAUN 1924a, 69 f.

the presbyters there still did not have permission to celebrate the Eucharist in their own right on Sunday, but instead distributed the portions of the Eucharist from the papal Mass, the *fermentum*, to the faithful within the framework of a shortened celebration of mass.[550] The presbyters installed at the suburban martyrs' churches, on the other hand, were permitted to celebrate the Eucharist independently (i.e. without *fermentum*) on Sundays as well.[551] This may explain why at the time of Damasus there are already altars (only?) in these churches. It might only have been in the course of the fifth century that the itinerant episcopal altar finally became redundant for the titular churches as well.

SUMMARY

The scholarly debate over the organisational shape of nascent Christianity, which can be paraphrased as "house churches versus bishop's church", ends on the side of the bishop's church and the unity of the city community. The popular thesis of a pluralistic urban Christianity fragmented into small cult groups must be radically called into question. Texts from the first three centuries and into the Constantinian period that comment on church buildings and altars in the various regions of the Roman Empire do not provide sufficient evidence for the existence of so-called house churches. Early Christian house churches exist only in the books of historians, not in reality. As a rule, every city has just one eucharistic meeting place under the leadership of the bishop. All the city's Christians, across every social class, gather on Sundays with the presbyterium and the bishop around one and the same altar. In Alexandria and Rome alone, there were probably other, decentralised assembly rooms before 300 in which deacons or presbyters exercised liturgical functions, but without celebrating the Eucharist in their own right. These rooms, which are purely hypothetical for Rome and also barely tangible for Alexandria, are probably without altars and are distributed round the various districts of the city to serve the pastoral ministry there. In both cities they are under the direction of the bishop.

550 It is unclear exactly how this celebration of the mass must be imagined. It cannot have been a full celebration of mass. The necessary quantity of species for the Communion of the faithful was probably produced by means of contact consecration with the *fermentum*. After daily mass celebrations arose in Rome, the titular presbyters are likely to have celebrated the Eucharist independently in the titular churches on most weekdays.

551 Innoc. I ep. ad Decent. 8 (FC 58,2, 496). Cf. SAXER 1989, 930. MARTIN 1989, 1137 n. 11 brings up an interesting consideration which might confirm that under Pope Leo the presbyters at the titular churches still did not celebrate an independent Eucharist on Sundays. Leo. I ep. 9,2 (PL 54, 626C) advises the bishop of Alexandria to have a second Mass read on feast days if there are large crowds. Around 400, the martyrs' churches in North Africa also have fixed altars; BRAUN 1924a, 68 f.

The principle of the one city church and the one city worship service survived in most cities up to the Middle Ages. It is always the bishop who is the primary celebrant of the city community; the presbyters merely assist or represent him. There is therefore only one genuine bishop's liturgy (in the style of the respective city), but no presbyteral or group liturgy.[552] Over the course of the centuries, however, the presbyters emancipated themselves from the bishop, but not without taking over the bishop's liturgy when they did so. But up to the Middle Ages, there was no question of a parish system. The cathedral continues to dominate as the centre of pastoral care and administration. The martyrs' churches in the cemeteries lie round the city wall like satellites, but they, too, are not parish churches and themselves serve the episcopal station liturgy in that the bishop presides at the Eucharist there on the feast days of each of the martyrs.

This basic picture calls for further delineation. From the second half of the fourth century on, the titular churches emerged in Rome's inner city, but these have no more to do with house churches than they do with parish churches. Nor did they contribute in any way to a disintegration of the unity of the city's worship since, although such churches were under the pastoral care of the titular presbyters, they still remained strictly dependent on the pope. Until the fifth century, the titular presbyters were not even allowed to celebrate the Eucharist independently (on Sundays) because this right belonged first and foremost to the pope, who probably visited the titular churches at irregular intervals for worship right from the start. Other special cases are constituted by churches at certain shrines, for example those built since Constantinian times at numerous biblical sites in the Holy Land. If they are not, like the Church of the Holy Sepulchre in Jerusalem, themselves bishop's churches, they initially function as dependent station churches (like the Church of the Nativity in Bethlehem), but can develop into church centres in their own right.

The question of the private oratories or house chapels of rich aristocrats is also another story. Researchers like to draw a direct line from the house churches to the private house chapels of the fourth and fifth centuries and claim that the early house churches still served as meeting places in the post-Constantinian period.[553] But just as the alleged house churches have nothing at all to do with the *domus ecclesiae*, they have even less of a connection with the house chapels. There are undoubtedly cases, in Rome as well, of mass being celebrated in the private houses of wealthy citizens.[554] But all the information on this dates back no further than the time of Pope Damasus (366–384). Such elite worship, which then also came to be combined with the private cult of martyrs, is a new

---

552 BOGUNIOWSKI 1987, 388–392 derives the justification of group masses for modern pastoral care from the alleged house churches.

553 Cf. ROBINSON 2017, 231.

554 SCHMITZ 1975, 248 f.; DASSMANN 1986, 893 f.; BRENK 2003, 75–128; KRITZINGER 2016, 144 f.; FUGGER 2019. Oratories in Augustine see ROETZER 1930, 72.

and distinct phenomenon.[555] It is not in opposition to the bishop's liturgy, nor does it challenge the principle of the one city church since it can be taken for granted that those involved in it would normally attend the bishop's liturgy. Whether the private oratories possessed altars is doubtful.

The question of the unity of the city's Christian community can appear in a completely new light again if it is seen in relationship to the Jewish communities. Here, too, the prevailing opinion is that there could of course have been several synagogues in every city, and this analogy is employed to try to justify the plurality of house churches.[556] But this threatens to be a circular argument. It still remains to be examined whether there is evidence of a plurality of synagogues in the cities of late antiquity (cf. Acts 9:2; 13:5) or whether the unity of the Jewish city community is more likely to have been the rule.[557] In Rome there seems to have been only one synagogue in around 220.[558] In a number of cities of late antiquity there is archaeological evidence of only one synagogue.[559] The Syriac *Didascalia* assumes that there was only one synagogue in which the Jews gathered.[560] The most famous example is probably Dura Europos, where *one* church and *one* synagogue have been excavated. The at-times violent confrontation between the Jewish and Christian communities in some cities, for example in Smyrna in the second century, is likely also to be connected with this concentration on the part of the two religions on each having one assembly room and one leadership.

---

555 This is to be stressed versus Bowes 2008, 71–84. The prohibition issued by the Synod of Laodicea around 363/64 is directed at this new phenomenon of private masses and has nothing to do with the alleged house churches.

556 Klauck 1981, 95–97.

557 Mk 1:21; 6:2; Mt 13:54; Lk 4:16; Jn 6:59; 18:20; Ac 13:14; 14:1; 17:1, 10, 17; 18:4, 19; 19:8. Cf. the synagogues of Tiberias, Dora, Caesarea Maritima and Antioch in Flav. Ios. vit. 277, ant. 19,300–305, bell. Iud. 2,285[14,4]–2,289[14,5], 7,44–47[3,3]. On the unity of the Jewish city community in Ephesus see P. Trebilco, The Jewish Community in Ephesus and its Interaction with Christ-Believers in the First Century CE and Beyond, in: J. R. Harrison / L. L. Welborn (eds.), The First Ur-

ban Churches 3. Ephesus (Atlanta 2018) 93–126. For Rome see also Domagalski / Mühlenkamp 2016, 458.

558 Hippol. ref. 9,11,7 (Marcovich 1986, 351) speaks of "the synagogue of the Jews". It is by no means certain that there were several synagogues in Rome as Klauck 1981, 26 f. thinks; cf. S. T. Katz (ed.), The Cambridge History of Judaism 4. The Late Roman-Rabinic Period (Cambridge 2006) 498.

559 E.g. in Dura Europos, Sardes, Priene, Ostia, Bova Marina, Gerasa, Stoboi. See also White 1996, 60–101; Robinson 2017, 237. Cf. Ac 14:1; 17:1, 10, 17; 18:4, 19; 19:8.

560 Didasc. syr. 13 (Achelis / Flemming 1904, 71).

IV. CULTUS

The people in the presence of God

So far we have been discussing the origin of the Christian altar and its exclusivity and uniqueness, but now let us turn to its function as a sacrificial table. Franz Wieland was bound to deny the existence of early Christian altars as the result of two errors. First of all, his understanding of an antique "altar" was exclusively of altars upon which sacrificial victims were slaughtered – and these were not to be found among the Christians (above Figs. 1, 4; below Figs. 119, 128). What escaped his notice, however, were the sacred tables (*mensae sacrae*) customarily used in the performance of rituals, which the Christians employed, too. Second, he understood sacrifice to mean the offering up of gifts and thought that nothing of this was to be found among the Christians, who allegedly knew only a purely spiritual sacrifice of thanksgiving (eucharist). This overlooks the fact that the early Christians did understand their concrete worship, with bread and wine standing on the table, as a cultic and sacrificial action.[1] And for this purpose they used an altar. In order to prove this, we have to take a look at the relevant texts from the second and third centuries that discuss the sacrifice and prayer of the Christians.

1. THE SACRIFICIAL SERVICE OF THE CHRISTIANS

Early Christianity certainly does not have an elaborated sacred law that is a linear continuation of the high religions of antiquity. In many respects, it cut itself off from the Greek and Roman religious cosmos and from Judaism, thus also ridding itself of associated sacred norms. Herein lies an act of liberation and emancipation. However, the very idea that the essence of Christianity lay in an elimination of everything ritual and cultic lacks all plausibility. Christianity is not called to a complete spiritualization but rather to a new classification of action and word. This goes for the liturgy as a communication

---

1   HANSON 1985, 83–112 does not discuss Wieland directly, but nevertheless contributes to correcting his interpretation of the Fathers.

event, too. The communication event of prayer cannot be sublimated into pure word (*sola scriptura*). For there is always the rite that forms the framework of the word. It is only in this embodiment that liturgy is passed on enduringly. Liturgy is acting word and verbal act. Even the earliest prayer formulae of the first and second centuries must be imagined as underlain with a rite that supports the memorization of what was known by heart. Here, however, the rite is on no account merely a support and handmaid of the word but rather a co-carrier of the message. After all, when speaking of the Eucharist, Jesus does not say: "Speak this in memory of me" but rather "Do this in memory of me."

The basic coordinates of the ancient worldview, such as above and below, God and man, taboo and *sacrum*, also form the framework of the words and actions of the early Christians. This also includes such powerful phenomena as guilt and sacrifice. An unbiased examination of the sources leads to the irrefutable conclusion that early Christianity understood itself as a sacrificial religion and thus as a cult (see above chapter I, 1).[2] It is not possible to shunt this off into a later period either, as if it was only the pressure exerted on the Christians by the Roman state authorities during the persecutions to participate in the public sacrifices that led them to reinterpret the Lord's Supper as a sacrificial act.[3] Markus Öhler considers it highly plausible in the context of ritual community meals that Paul already understands the blessing over bread and wine as a sacrificial rite.[4] But an even clearer testimony to the eucharistic sacrificial service is offered by texts dating from the period around the year 100. The "sense of duty towards the gods" (*pietas erga deos*) that is taken for granted in the ancient world and which consists in offering them acceptable worship, thus establishing a good relationship with them, is not something the Christians regard as fundamentally reprehensible (Fig. 17).

Nor is there a break between the Old Testament with its sacrificial cult and the New Testament with the cult of the new covenant.[5] Jesus himself declares the sacrificial service at the temple in Jerusalem to be legitimate and calls for its observance (Mk 1:44). So why should the Christians develop an aversion to sacrifice (cf. Lk 2:24)? If they refer to their own worship, like the temple service in the Old Testament before it, as "liturgy", this is anything but a weakening of the cult principle but rather a continuation of it.[6] In any case, the New Testament (Jn 4:23 f.: "worship in spirit and truth") does not imply any opposition between holiness and materiality, as if a real practice of cult could not and must not exist at all in Christianity.

---

2   See the fundamental analysis by NEBEL 2014. From the perspective of the history of religion see STROUMSA 2009, 63 f.: "To a certain extent rabbinic Judaism and Christianity would both remain sacrificial religions, but very special sacrificial religions because they functioned without blood sacrifice" (cf. ibid. 78).

3   So BURNS / JENSEN 2014, 233.
4   ÖHLER 2014.
5   Cf. BÖHLER 2013; DEIGHAN 2014.
6   People are fond of pointing to the profane meaning of λειτουργία as "work for the people" in order to prove an alleged lack of cult in primitive Christianity. The opposite is true.

Fig. 17: Personification of *PIETAS* (piety) standing in the orans posture at a round altar with a fire burning on it; KLAUSER 1959, Plate 8c.

The dispute between pagans and Christians on the question of worship does not revolve around the question of "cult: yes or no?" but solely around the right way of worshipping, i.e. around what is the *true* cult – a discussion with which paganism is already familiar. For example, Emperor Constantine († 337) rejected bloody sacrificial service even before his conversion to Christianity, showing himself to be influenced in this by the intellectual movement of Neoplatonism.[7] This is exactly what makes it easier for him to accept the Christian sacrificial service with its natural gifts of bread and wine. The religious environment of nascent Christianity resembles a pantheon of sacrificial cults. Hence the Christians do not have to justify themselves when they in turn speak of sacrifice and practise it. They merely have to explain in what way the Eucharist differs from the generally accepted sacrificial cult.

The fact that in the ancient religions wine and blood have been regarded since time immemorial as sacred gifts is undoubtedly well known to the Christians when they themselves celebrate the "cup of salvation" and the blood of the altar as ritual acts.[8] The break which, of course, comes despite all the continuity lies not merely in the new image of God but also in the outrageous act of drinking the blood that has been offered up. Both continuity and discontinuity are reflected in the writings of Bishop Eusebius of Caesarea († 339). For him, the Christian sacrificial service took the place in equal measure of the Jewish and the pagan sacrifices. With his prophecy about the altar in "the land of Egypt" (Is 19:19) Isaiah is, according to Eusebius, referring to the Christian altar at which the priests of the new covenant offer unbloody, spiritual sacrifices.[9] This Christian altar will then make the (legitimate) sacrifice in Jerusalem superfluous, but also put an

---

7 BLECKMANN 2012.
8 This cannot be treated in depth here. But see 1 Cor 11:24–26; Ph 2:17; Eph 5:2; Heb 13:10–12; Ign. ad Rom. 2,2 (SC 10³, 128).

9 Euseb. demonstr. 1,6,50 (GCS Euseb. 6, 30). Likewise (Ps.-)Aug. serm. 228/B,1 (DROBNER 2006, 452).

end to pagan idolatry. Every Christian will now offer the pure and bloodless sacrifice in his own country.[10] The memorial of Christ's sacrifice is now celebrated daily[11] on the table with the symbols of his Flesh and Blood. These, he says, are the sacred oblations of Christ's table: unbloody, reasonable, acceptable sacrifices.[12]

If, despite such testimonies, scholars still believe that the Christians rejected altars and material sacrifices, this is on account of certain statements by the Apologists, a group of philosophically educated Christian writers in the second and third centuries. They do, in fact, distance themselves sharply from the normal cultic practices with their temples and altars.[13] However, it would be taking it too far to see this as a total rejection on principle of any kind of ritual. The matter is not so simple. For every criticism presupposes what is criticised; polemics are accompanied by adaption.[14] Already in the pagan and Jewish enlightenment, fierce polemics related to sacrifice and the traditional practice of sacrifice can be found side by side.[15] The learned enlighteners among them may demand a spiritualization of cultic acts, but this nevertheless presupposes the worship that actually exists. The more strongly a cult flourishes and takes on popular characteristics, the more likely it is that there will be an elitist call for spiritualization.

The Plato-schooled defenders of Christianity – the Apologists – are fond of frequently contrasting the spiritualized sacrificial service of the Christians with the bloody cult of the Romans,[16] but it is necessary here to look closely at exactly where they draw the dividing line.[17] In opposition to the heretic Marcion, who rejects the Old Testament, they defend the sacrificial service of the Jews in the Jerusalem Temple, including their animal sacrifices.[18] It is only the pagan temples and altars that are rigidly rejected, especially animal sacrifices. The Christians do not, in fact, have temples and altars like the pagans. If you then add those texts in which the same authors talk about Christian wor-

---

10 Euseb. demonstr. 1,6,47. 57 (GCS Euseb. 6, 30. 32).

11 Ibid. 1,10,18 (GCS Euseb. 6, 46).

12 Ibid. 1,10,28 f (GCS Euseb. 6, 47 f.). Ibid. 5,3,18–20 (222) speaks of the immaterial spiritual sacrificial service performed by the Christian priests. However, the "immaterial" sacrifice actually consists in the gifts of bread and wine, indicating the mysteries of the Saviour's Body and Blood.

13 Cf. WIELAND 1906, 47–57; id. 1909, 61–133.

14 FINNEY 1984, 210–225. More cautious in his assessment of the criticism of early Christian cult also JUDGE 2008, 424 f.

15 BORNKAMM 1964, 54–59. The Old Testament is full of fierce criticism of both temple and sacrifice while the temple cult in Jerusalem blossoms: Theologisches Wörterbuch zum Neuen Testament

3 (1938) 186–189: criticism of sacrifice in the Old Testament does not intend to cast doubt on the temple cult on principle. The demand for a spiritualization of the sacrifice often refers only to the voluntary sacrifices performed on account of vows, etc., which should not be senselessly multiplied. On the criticism of pagan temple and sacrifice see CLARKE 1974, 343.

16 YOUNG 1972; FERGUSON 1980.

17 FINNEY 1984, 199 refers to "the false notion that the basic idea of the early Christian religion was the inward, self-isolating, cult-less and immaterial, rationalising and 'spiritual' tendency of late-Hellenistic philosophers' conventicles. This conclusion is simply not correct."

18 POORTHUIS 2014.

ship, then you can see that they by no means measure everything by the same yardstick. Rather, with their criticism of the pagan cult they want to safeguard the Christian altar and sacrificial service and emphasize what is special about it.

Their strategy is not to set a cultless fraternal meal of the Christians against the sacred sacrificial cult of the pagans. This would have resulted in the Christians losing all standing as a religion among their contemporaries. Furthermore, the Jewish and pagan sacrifices are always accompanied by a sacred meal (e.g. Lv 7:11–21; 1 Cor 10:18–21).[19] It would not be very credible to contrast the material sacrifice of the pagans with an allegedly spiritual sacrifice of the Christians when it is common knowledge that a meal, whether pagan or Christian, is something material. So the Apologists take a different route: starting from the spiritual idealisation of the material offering in ancient religious criticism, they interpret the material (thingly) sacrifice of the Christians, at which bread and wine are offered, as a "spiritual sacrifice" (θυσία λογική). So they develop a dialectical concept of sacrifice which does in fact fit into the religious practice of late antiquity. It will even be permissible to assume that the success of Christianity lies to no small degree in presenting itself as an enlightened sacrificial religion.[20]

The *First Letter of Clement* (c. 96 or c. 64–70 in Rome) can already say in the words of Psalm 50 that the sacrifice of God is a broken spirit.[21] At the same time and without any contradiction, it speaks of the "offerings" (προσφοραί) and "services" (λειτουρίαι) of the Christians[22] and further of the presbyters who "offer gifts" in a blameless and holy manner.[23]

The *Epistle of Barnabas* (c. 130–140 in the Alexandrian milieu) finds neither sacrifices nor burnt offerings nor oblations (προσφοραί) among the Christians. But it then qualifies this by stating that the Christians do not have any oblation "made by man".[24] Moreover, Christ offered the vessel of his spirit, his Flesh, as a sacrifice (θυσία) in the same way as Isaac was offered on an altar (θυσιαστήριον).[25] So it seems that the Epistle of Barnabas does indeed concede the Christians an oblation, one prepared by God himself, i.e. not one made by man: Christ's Eucharistic Flesh.[26]

19 LEONHARD / ECKHARDT 2010. During the persecutions, the Christians were still forced not only to sacrifice to the gods but also to eat of the sacrifices; Euseb. mart. Pal. 9,2 (SC 55, 148); GUYOT / KLEIN 1993, 124f.

20 Albrecht Dihle has shown how the spiritualization of traditional cultic actions among the Stoics is actually meant to enable and justify participation in the feasts of the gods; DIHLE 1980, 42–46. The

Christians promote their own feasts in a similar way.

21 1 Clem. 52,4 (SC 167, 184).
22 Ibid. 36,1 (SC 167, 158); 40,2 (166).
23 Ibid. 44,4 (SC 167, 172).
24 Ep. Barn. 2,4. 6 (SC 172, 82. 84).
25 Ibid. 7,3 (SC 172, 128–130).
26 Otherwise WIELAND 1909, 42–44.

The philosopher and martyr *Justin* (c. 160 in Rome) is even clearer. In his apologia addressed to the pagans he rejects material offerings (ὑλικὴ προσφορά) among the Christians and recognises only virtues as sacrifices.[27] His criticism is directed concretely at the pagan sacrifices of animals and flowers in honour of the images of gods set up in the temples.[28] However, in his *Dialogue with Trypho*, in which he is talking to Jews who are well-versed in the Bible, this same Justin, appealing to Malachi 1:11, refers to the "*bread* of the Eucharist" and the "*cup* of the Eucharist" as "sacrifices" that are offered to God in all places.[29] So these are material offerings. God gladly accepts the gifts (δῶρα) and offerings (προσφοραί) of the Christians.[30] He prefers their sacrifices to those of the Jews.[31]

There is no contradiction here between materiality and spiritualization. The Christians may only possess prayers and thanksgivings (eucharists) as sacrifices, but their priests[32] offer these spiritual sacrifices every time they celebrate Christ's Passion with bread and wine.[33] This is an example of dialectical theology that would do credit to any modern theologian: it cannot be resolved in favour of one side.[34] After all, the Eucharist consists of both linguistic and material elements. What is crucial here is not the sacrificial *theory* but rather the fact that the Eucharist is placed in the tradition of the Jewish sacrificial cult and that the Old Testament sacrificial terminology is eucharistically adapted.[35] All this must allow us to conclude that Justin was familiar with a Christian altar or sacred table.[36] Although he does not expressly mention one in his detailed description of the Eucharist, he describes bread and a drinking vessel being brought to the presider at the liturgy,[37] who will be standing at a (single!) table on which he sets down the gifts. It is probably a somewhat elevated table since those attending the worship will

27 Iustin. apol. 1, 10,1 (SC 507, 148–150); 1, 13,1 f (158–160).
28 Ibid. 1, 9 (SC 507, 146–148): It refers to the sacrificial animals hung with garlands of flowers which are then burnt along with the animals. Ibid. 1, 62,1 (292–294): κνῖσα – savour of a burnt sacrifice.
29 Iustin. dial. 41,3 (MARCOVICH 1997, 138).
30 Ibid. 28,4 (MARCOVICH 1997, 115).
31 Ibid. 29,1 (MARCOVICH 1997, 116).
32 Ibid. 116,3 (MARCOVICH 1997, 270).
33 Ibid. 117,1–3 (MARCOVICH 1997, 271 f.). Cf. apol. 1, 13,1 f (SC 507, 158–160). On Justin in general MOLL 1975, 123–142.
34 Correctly RAUSCHEN 1910, 86–88. WIELAND
1909, 87 on the other hand constructs a contradiction between
Iustin. dial. 41,3 and dial. 116 f. and regards only dial. 116 f. as correct.
35 Otherwise WIELAND 1906, 50 f.; id. 1909, 71–102. FERGUSON 1980, 1174 rightly recognises that Justin regards the elements of bread and wine as sacrificial offerings. Cf. DALY / NESSELRATH 2015, 177; LEONHARD / ECKHARDT 2010, 1079.
36 WIELAND 1908, 65–71 thinks that Justin cannot possibly have known a Christian altar, but here, too, he can only conceive of an altar as one on which animals are slaughtered.
37 Iustin. apol. 1, 65,3 (SC 507, 304).

1. THE SACRIFICIAL SERVICE OF THE CHRISTIANS

also be standing.[38] But it would be very odd if Justin quoted Malachi in speaking of the "pure sacrifice" of bread and cup "offered to God" yet refused to join that same prophet in speaking of the altar or sacred table as well (Mal 1:7, 10).[39] The fact that he does not mention it here should be seen as pure coincidence.

This impression is strengthened by a further statement of Justin's regarding the Christian sacrificial actions:

> We praise (God) to the utmost of our power by the exercise of prayer and thanksgiving
> (Eucharist) for all things wherewith we are supplied, as we have been taught that the only
> honour that is worthy of Him is not to consume by fire what He has brought into being
> for our sustenance, but to offer it for ourselves and those who need, and to send up to him
> with gratitude through the word solemn praise.[40]

Justin is undoubtedly talking here about the Eucharist, at which items of food are "offered" (προσφέρειν) for those present ("for ourselves"), while praise is at the same time being sent up to God.[41] When Justin says that the Christians do not burn their food, he is inveighing against the pagan sacrifices so far as they are burnt food on an altar. By contrast, he stresses positively the oblation of the eucharistic food, which is offered up – where else but on the altar? – but not burnt. Here the eucharistic oblation stands in one and the same cultural context as pagan sacrifices.

Not many decades later, Bishop *Irenaeus of Lyon* († c. 200) is able to state equally radically that mercy is worth more than (animal) sacrifices[42] and that God has need of nothing.[43] At the same time, however, referring to the Old Testament prophet Malachi (1:10), he calls bread and wine the first fruits of the gifts of the new covenant which the Church offers to God in gratitude.[44] Based on this statement, Wieland thinks that Irenaeus was the first theologian to understand the Eucharist as a material sacrificial oblation: "The Fathers before Irenaeus declared: we do not offer God a gift, for he is without needs.

---

38 Ibid. 1, 67,5 (SC 507, 308); O'LOUGHLIN 2014, 81. There is no longer any satiating meal at which people would have to recline.

39 Such terminology had already been introduced by Paul in 1 Cor 10:21, apparently alluding to Mal 1:7 (see below Indices). It can only be by chance that in his multiple quotations from Malachi Justin every time omits the verses with the "altar" and "table of the Lord". Around this time, the "altar" (θυσιαστήριον) is likely to have been something taken for granted in Rome. When Polyc. ad Phil. 4,3 (SC 10³, 208) calls the widows "the altar of

God", that is not an Old Testament way of talking but rather a Christian one which presupposes the Christian altar as an established reality. Polycarp (c. 130–150) knew Rome.

40 Iustin. apol. 1, 13,1 f (SC 507, 158). WIELAND 1909, 71–76.

41 The same in Iustin. apol. 1, 67,1–6 (SC 507, 308–310).

42 Iren. adv. haer. 4,17,4 (SC 100,2, 590).

43 Ibid. 4,18,6 (SC 100,2, 612).

44 Ibid. 4,17,5 (SC 100,2, 590–592).

Since the appearance of the idea of oblation, people said: we offer God gifts even though he is without needs."[45] In truth, Irenaeus is not so revolutionary at all, even the opposite: he is a strictly traditional theologian who does not proclaim anything novel but simply upholds Justin and, incidentally, says the same thing as Clement of Alexandria.[46] They all wish to understand the Eucharist as a sacrifice *sui generis*. Yet it is precisely the criticism of sacrifice in the Old Testament that opens the door to a Christian concept of sacrifice. Irenaeus puts it as follows:

> And the class of oblations (*oblationes*) in general has not been set aside (in the New Covenant); for there were both oblations there (in the Old Covenant), and there are oblations here (among the Christians). Sacrifices (*sacrificia*) there were among the people (of Israel); sacrifices there are, too, in the Church.[47]

Like Justin, Irenaeus, too, was probably familiar with a Christian altar or sacred table. He even has to insist on an altar in order to prevent there being any doubt about the sacrificial nature of the Eucharist. There are in fact statements to be found to this effect. For example, he speaks of David who, invoking his priestly dignity, went into the house of God (*domus Dei*) in Jerusalem, ate the showbread there, and gave it to those who were with him (Mt 12:13 f.; cf. 1 Sam 21:4–7) and continues:

> And all the disciples of the Lord are priests, who inherit here neither lands nor houses, but serve God and the *altar* (*altare*) continually.[48]

What Irenaeus is referring to is the scene in which David goes right into the Temple on account of the consecrated loaves, which he then eats there. Irenaeus associates these loaves with the Eucharist, which leads him to the altar. In fact, the biblical texts do not mention an altar or table at all. But Irenaeus is thinking of the showbread table, which was a sacred table, and associates it with the altar that the Lord's disciples serve. This can only refer to the celebration of the Eucharist at which the priests preside. Such a chain of associations actually only comes about if the term "house of God" is commonly used to refer to the Christian meeting room and if there is a real "altar" standing there.[49]

---

45 WIELAND 1906, 52 f.; *id.* 1908, 84 f.
46 See below p. 174–177.
47 Iren. adv. haer. 4,18,2 (SC 100,2, 598).
48 Ibid. 4,8,3 (SC 100,2, 472–474): *Sacerdos autem scitus fuerat David apud Deum, quamvis Saul persecutionem faceret ei: omnes enim justi sacerdotalem habent ordinem. Sacerdotes autem sunt omnes Domini discipuli, qui neque agros neque domus hereditant hic, sed semper altari et Deo serviunt. [...] Qui autem sunt qui dereliquerunt patrem et matrem et omnibus proximis renuntiaverunt propter Verbum Dei et testamentum ejus, nisi discipuli Domini?*
49 HARVEY 1857, 168 n. 1.

Elsewhere, too, Irenaeus speaks of the altar at which the faithful should offer their oblations (*oblationes*) without ceasing. This visible altar points to the heavenly altar for which the prayers and oblations are intended:

It is also his [God's] will that we, too, should offer the gift at the *altar*, frequently and without intermission. There is, then, an *altar* in heaven, for towards that place are our prayers and oblations directed.[50]

Here Irenaeus mentions the altar twice: first the earthly one at which "we" offer our gifts, and then the heavenly one. William W. Harvey and Franz Wieland are, however, of the opinion that Irenaeus is not talking about an earthly altar here[51] but only a heavenly one. It is impossible for us to concur. First of all, only a few sentences earlier Irenaeus speaks of the oblation of the Church (*Ecclesiae oblatio*), which is offered throughout all the world, and clearly offered on the altar, as is evidenced by the reference to Mt 5:23 f.: "So when you are offering your gift at the altar..."[52] Irenaeus is clearly thinking of the earthly altar on which the gifts lie. Furthermore, speaking of a heavenly altar presupposes an earthly one. After all, Irenaeus's teaching on the Eucharist is directed against the Gnostics, who declare the world to be evil and separate it from the creator God. Against this, he sets great store in the materiality of the oblations – bread and cup.[53] His whole theology is directed towards the fact that earthly things exist because they have a prototype in heaven. Hence he can say with respect to the Christian altar that because there is an altar on which the Church sacrifices, there must also be an "altar in heaven". For "the earthly things that were commanded with respect to us correspond as images to the heavenly things and are made by the same God."[54] All this leaves no room for any doubt that Irenaeus is familiar with the Christian altar as an indispensable furnishing for worship.

The Athens apologist *Athenagoras* responds in c. 177 to the accusation on the part of the pagans that the Christians "do not sacrifice". What the pagan critics miss among the

50 Iren. adv. haer. 4,18,6 (SC 100,2, 614): *nos quoque offerre vult munus ad altare frequenter sine intermissione. Est ergo altare in caelis, illuc enim preces nostrae et oblationes diriguntur.* On Christ's sacrifice in heaven see SYMONDS 1966, 280–285.
51 HARVEY 1857, 210 n. 1; WIELAND 1906, 109.
52 Iren. adv. haer. 4,18,1 (SC 100,2, 596): *Igitur Ecclesiae oblatio, quam Dominus docuit offerri in universo mundo, purum sacrificium reputatum est apud Deum et acceptum est ei, non quod indigeat a nobis sacrificium, sed quoniam is qui offert glorificatur ipse in eo quod offert, si acceptetur munus ejus. [...] quod in omni simplicitate et innocentia Dominus volens nos offerre praedicavit dicens:* Cum igitur offeres munus tuum ad altare et recordatus fueris quoniam frater tuus habet aliquid adversum te, dimitte munus tuum ad altare, et vade primum reconciliari fratri tuo, et tunc reversus offeres munus tuum. *Offerre igitur oportet Deo primitias ejus creaturae* [...]. The Church offers God the first fruits; ibid. 4,18,4 (606).
53 Ibid. 4,17,5 (SC 100,2, 590–592). Cf. FERGUSON 1980, 1179; DALY / NESSELRATH 2015, 177 f.
54 Iren. adv. haer. 4,19,1 (SC 100,2, 616).

Christians is animal and flower sacrifices. Athenagoras's reply is framed in the context of pagan sacrificial praxis. Naturally, as a Christian he wants nothing to do with hecatombs and holocausts. Rather, in his opinion the noblest sacrifice to God

> is for us to know who stretched out and vaulted the heavens, and fixed the earth in its place like a centre [...]. When, holding God to be this Framer of all things, who preserves them in being and superintends them all by knowledge and administrative skill, we lift up holy hands to him, what need has he further of a hecatomb? [...] And what have I to do with holocausts, which God does not stand in need of? – though indeed we must offer a bloodless sacrifice and worship in accordance with the Logos.[55]

This statement can on no account be invoked against the existence of an early Christian altar. For Athenagoras is talking about the service of prayer, at which those praying lift their hands (and eyes) heavenwards to God, who watches over everything from his throne. In so doing, the person praying offers up two things that belong together: a bloodless sacrifice and worship in accordance with the Logos. At all events, Christian worship is here characterized as a cultic and sacrificial event. But at the same time two elements of this sacrificial cult are described: the unbloody gifts and the oral prayers. Athenagoras specifically does not speak of a "spiritual" offering but rather of an "unbloody" one. He does not choose the adjective "immaterial" (ἀσώματος θυσία), nor does he speak of the "spiritual offering" (θυσία λογική); instead, he creates the neologism "unbloody" (ἀναίμακτος) because he is thinking here of the food offering of the Christians, namely bread and wine, which are unbloody but not immaterial. So Athenagoras is certainly referring to the Eucharist.[56] It is for him a sacrificial act and thus presupposes an altar.

Like all Christian apologists, *Clement of Alexandria* (c. 150–215) rejects the pagans' temples and statues of deities.[57] He even seems to deny the existence of a Christian sacrificial service when he says: "And for this reason we rightly do not sacrifice to God, who, needing nothing, supplies all men with all things."[58] On the other hand, Clement would like the Christian offering (προσφορά) to take place with bread and wine in accordance with Church law.[59] How can these two things be reconciled with one another? Here we

55 Athen. suppl. 13,2–4 (SC 379, 110–112): [...] δέον ἀναίμακτον θυσίαν καὶ λογικὴν προσάγειν λατρείαν.
56 So WIELAND 1906, 48; *id.* 1909, 67–71; RAUSCHEN 1910, 85 f. Differently MOLL 1975, 149–151.
57 Clem. Alex. strom. 7,5,28 (SC 428, 104–106).
58 Ibid. 7,3,14,5 (SC 428, 72).
59 Ibid. 1,19,96,1 (SC 30, 121). Cf. frgm. 24 (GCS Clem. Alex. 3, 204): *sacerdotium autem propter oblationem, quae fit orationibus et doctrinis, quibus adquiruntur animae, quae offeruntur deo.* That is an elitist interpretation of the Church's sacrificial celebration.

have the typical ambivalence that results from the criticism of sacrifice that comes from the philosophical enlightenment that says that God does not need food for the simple reason that he does not feel hunger. But Clement applies his verdict exclusively to pagan holocausts that are offered to the gods as food:[60] such sacrifices cannot be reconciled with God's lack of need and are therefore rejected by the Christians. It is only in this sense that the Eucharist is not a sacrifice, even though, in the Christian understanding, it definitely is an oblation with bread and wine.

This is consistent with another statement by Clement about the Christian altar:

> But if, by nature needing nothing, the deity delights to be honoured, it is not without reason that we (Christians) honour God in our prayer; and this sacrifice we send up to God as the best and holiest (sacrifice) with righteousness. We honour God with the most righteous Word, by praising through the word, that gives us knowledge, that which we have come to know. The *altar* (θυσιαστήριον) then, *that is with us here*, is the terrestrial congregation of those who devote themselves to prayers, having as it were one common voice and one mind. [...] Now breathing together is properly said of the Church. For the *sacrifice of the Church* is the word breathing as incense from holy souls, the *sacrifice* (of the Word) and the whole mind being at the same time unveiled to God.[61] But there has been a lot of talk that the very ancient *altar* (βωμός) in Delos is pure and holy; which alone, being undefiled by slaughter and death, they say Pythagoras approached. And will they not believe us when we say that the righteous soul is the *truly sacred altar*, and that incense arising from it is holy prayer?[62]

Here, too, the wider context is the polemics against pagan sacrifices and against the view that God's hunger could be satisfied with a burnt offering and a smoke offering on an altar.[63] Clement rejects this. On the other hand, he allows sacrifices that please and honour God, namely prayer. "The sacrifice of the Church" is nothing other than prayer

60 Clem. Alex. strom. 7,3,14,6 (SC 428, 72).
61 With the Roman sacrifice, on the other hand, the person offering the sacrifice veils himself.
62 Ibid. 7,6,31,7–7,6,32,5 (SC 428, 116–120): Εἰ δὲ τιμώμενον χαίρει, φύσει ἀνενδεὲς ὑπάρχον, οὐκ ἀπεικότως ἡμεῖς δι' εὐχῆς τιμῶμεν τὸν θεόν, καὶ ταύτην τὴν θυσίαν ἀρίστην καὶ ἁγιωτάτην μετὰ δικαιοσύνης ἀναπέμπομεν, τῷ δικαιοτάτῳ λόγῳ γεραίοντες, δι' οὗ παραλαμβάνομεν τὴν γνῶσιν, διὰ τούτου δοξάζοντες ἃ μεμαθήκαμεν. Ἔστι γοῦν τὸ παρ' ἡμῖν θυσιαστήριον ἐνταῦθα τὸ ἐπίγειον ἄθροισμα τῶν ταῖς εὐχαῖς ἀνακειμένων, μίαν ὥσπερ ἔχον φωνὴν τὴν κοινὴν καὶ μίαν γνώμην. [...] Ἡ

σύμπνοια δὲ ἐπὶ τῆς ἐκκλησίας λέγεται κυρίως. Καὶ γάρ ἐστιν ἡ θυσία τῆς ἐκκλησίας λόγος ἀπὸ τῶν ἁγίων ψυχῶν ἀναθυμιώμενος, ἐκκαλυπτομένης ἅμα τῇ θυσίᾳ καὶ τῆς διανοίας ἁπάσης τῷ θεῷ. Ἀλλὰ τὸν μὲν ἀρχαιότατον βωμὸν ἐν Δήλῳ ἁγνὸν εἶναι τεθρυλήκασι, πρὸς ὃν δὴ μόνον καὶ Πυθαγόραν προσελθεῖν φασι φόνῳ καὶ θανάτῳ μὴ μιανθέντα, βωμὸν δὲ ἀληθῶς ἅγιον τὴν δικαίαν ψυχὴν καὶ τὸ ἀπ' αὐτῆς θυμίαμα τὴν ὁσίαν εὐχὴν λέγουσιν ἡμῖν ἀπιστήσουσιν; Cf. DALY / NESSEL-RATH 2015, 182f.
63 Clem. Alex. strom. 7,6,31,2–4 (SC 428, 114–116).

or more specifically the prayer spoken together in the church gathering. The phrase "sacrifice of the Church" must be an already firmly established convention of speech. What Clement is actually engaged in is ultimately apologetics: he wants to explain why the Christians in Rome rightly speak of the "sacrifice of the Church". They are able to do so because it refers to the spiritual sacrifice of prayer. Clement also uses the phrase "the most righteous word" for this prayer.

Wieland interprets Clement's statements in an ambiguous manner: in the phrase "most righteous word" he sees the words of consecration at the Eucharist, i.e. in the "sacrifice of the Church"; on the other hand, he maintains that "the altar that is here with us" is to be taken metaphorically and does not denote a Christian altar.[64] For, he says, the sacrifice is understood precisely as a spiritual, not a material sacrifice. That, however, is once again modern theology, not Clement. The crucial point is that Clement speaks equally of the "sacrifice of the Church" and of "the altar that is here with us". Whether or not he means this metaphorically is of little interest to the faithful or to his audience.

It is necessary to take as a starting point the concrete situation that Clement had in mind: he is talking about the worship community gathered in a room and praying together which he identifies with the altar ("The altar then, that is with us here, is the terrestrial congregation of those who devote themselves to prayers"). And it is likely that what he meant by "our prayer", which is the "holiest sacrifice", is indeed the eucharistic "prayer" over bread and wine. For it says that God is honoured with "the most righteous Word, by praising through the word, that gives us knowledge, that which we have come to know." But for Clement "flesh and blood of the Word (Logos)" or "meat and drink of the divine Word (Logos)" are a sacrificial food, and whoever partakes of this food gains knowledge of the divine essence.[65] So the Eucharist is the Logos which imparts knowledge. It is precisely the unbloody nature of the sacrificial gifts of bread and wine that leads Clement in the passage that follows to note an association with the sacred altar in Delos, on which no animal blood is shed. He only brings himself to mention this astonishing elevation in rank of a pagan altar because it has two things in common with the Christian altar: it is unique – the Christians in Alexandria have only the one altar, that of the bishop's church[66] – and holy, i.e. undefiled by blood.

Nevertheless, there are still those who maintain that Clement is not talking about a Christian altar here but is in fact denying the existence of such a thing. This is impossible to understand. After all, Clement explains to the pagans that the Christians, too, have an altar and sacrificial service even though they do not share the pagan view that God is in need of sacrifices. The term "altar" has already become established to refer to the eu-

---

64 Wieland 1906, 49 f., 109 f.; *id*. 1908, 89 – 94; *id*. 1909, 106 – 121. A purely spiritual interpretation of Clement is also espoused by Camelot 1970, 4 – 6.

65 Clem. Alex. strom. 5,10,66,2 – 5 (SC 278, 134); Wieland 1908, 92.

66 See above, p. 148.

charistic table, which is precisely why Clement feels compelled to defend the Christian use of language. He distinguishes the "altar [...] that is with us here" from the altars of the pagans on which animals are slaughtered. For although the Christians have an altar, their sacrifice is not intended to satisfy God's hunger but solely to honour God. This is why the altar is spiritually elevated by Clement but in no way dematerialised: it stands for the terrestrial sacrificial community that has *one* common voice and *one* mind. Further, the idea is that there is just this one single altar on which the whole sacrificial offering lies. For him, this corresponds to the congregation, which speaks the prayers with *one* voice. Here we find the same equating of altar and worship community as is to be found in Ignatius of Antioch.[67]

Just as there is a line leading from Julian to Irenaeus, there is also one leading from Clement to *Origen of Alexandria* († 253/254). Here, too, there is no break to be found in it but rather increasing conceptual clarity. The pagan Celsus accuses the Christians of not erecting any altars, images of gods or temples.[68] This confirms once again how inseparably these three things that are flatly rejected by the Christians belong together. But it is far from saying that the latter do without altars in their own worship. Origen, based on Jn 4:23 f., rejects fleshly sacrifices such as are offered in certain places[69] and in his reply spiritualizes the altars, moralising them by relating the Christian sacrifice to the right life and the prayers of the Christians. But here again: spiritualization is not the same as deritualization, let alone the same as secularisation.[70] For example, Origen writes in the same work against Celsus:

> For this reason, then, let Celsus, as one who knows not God, give thank-offerings to demons. But we give thanks to the Creator of all, and, along with thanksgiving [Eucharist] and prayer for the gifts we eat the bread presented to us; and this bread becomes by prayer a sacred body, which sanctifies those who sincerely partake of it.[71]

This is talking about the transformation of the loaves into the sacred Body of Christ; these loaves are offered to God – as a sacrifice.[72] If Origen elsewhere points out to the pa-

---

67 See above p. 52. Elsewhere, too, Clement comes to speak of the idea of unity when he says that the Christians offered pleasing sacrifices by bringing together in prayer and praises the gift prepared in both Testaments; Clem. Alex. strom. 7,6,34,2 (SC 428, 126).

68 Orig. c. Cels. 7,62 (SC 150, 158): οὐκ ἀνέχονται νεὼς ὁρῶντες καὶ βωμοὺς καὶ ἀγάλματα. ibid. 8,17 (210). Correctly BARTH 1999, 59.

69 Orig. c. Cels. 6,70 (SC 147, 352–356).

70 HERMANS 1996, 99: "Cette herméneutique nous ouvre tout le 'sacramentalisme' origénien: la réalité historico-corporelle signifie toujours plus qu'elle-même." Cf. M. BACHMANN, Tempel III, in: TRE 33 (2002) 54–65, here 61.

71 Orig. c. Cels. 8,33 (SC 150, 246). Cf. the offering of the first fruits in the Eucharist ibid. 8,34 (248).

72 WIELAND 1908, 95 f.

gans with their so-called "holy sacrifices" and feasts that the Christian prays constantly, "offering up (literally slaughtering) continually bloodless sacrifices in prayer to God,"[73] then this is directed first and foremost against the sacrifice of animals. Like Athenagoras, Origen speaks of the Church's "bloodless" sacrifices and not, for example, of "spiritual" sacrifices. So the bloody sacrifices of the pagans are not replaced by some purely moral worship on the part of the Christians but rather by "loaves offered with thanksgiving (Eucharist) and prayer over the offerings." What the feasts are for the pagans is for the Christians the concrete worship gathering. For the "slaughter" of the unbloody sacrifice in prayer expressly includes the worship celebrated on the Lord's Day.[74] And naturally bread and wine or the Body and Blood of Christ are offered here.

The same is to be read even more clearly in Origen when he does not contrast himself with the pagans but rather seeks a connection with Jewish worship. In view of the destruction of the Jerusalem Temple in 70 A.D., he says:

> When you, however, see that pagan nations come to the faith, that churches (*ecclesiae*) are erected, that *altars* (*altaria*) are not sprinkled with the blood of sheep but are consecrated through the precious Blood of Christ, when you see that priests and Levites [= deacons] do not offer up the blood of bulls and rams but practise service to the Logos through the grace of the Holy Spirit, then Jesus has obviously received and assumed dominion after Moses.[75]

So for Origen churches with altars at which the eucharistic sacrificial service is performed are something to be taken for granted.[76] Like other authors, he finds it hard to speak of the Christian sacrifice in the context of pagan sacrifices, but in the biblical context these inhibitions disappear. The eucharistic table is irreversibly consecrated (*consecratio*) through the first celebration of the Eucharist, as it were through contact with Christ's Blood. With this Christian sacred law is made.

The church space is also something special for Origen. With their gifts the faithful contribute to the decoration of the altar and the church.[77] The priests and deacons are, according to Origen, positioned in the vicinity of the altar as a model of humility so that they are seen as if perched on an observation point. Yet, he complains, there is a stench

---

73 Orig. c. Cels. 8,21 (SC 150, 220–222): [...] καὶ ἑορτάζει γε κατὰ ἀλήθειαν ὁ τὰ δέοντα πράττων, ἀεὶ εὐχόμενος, διὰ παντὸς θύων τὰς ἀναιμάκτους ἐν ταῖς πρὸς τὸ θεῖον εὐχαῖς θυσίας.

74 Ibid. 8,22 (SC 150, 222).

75 Orig. in Iesu Nav. hom. 2,1 (SC 71, 116): *Cum vero videris introire gentes ad fidem, ecclesias exstrui, altaria non cruore pecudum respergi, sed pretioso Christi sanguine consecrari, cum videris sacerdotes et Levitas non sanguinem taurorum et hircorum, sed verbum Dei per sancti Spiritus gratiam ministrantes, tunc dicito quia Iesus post Moysen suscepit et obtinuit principatum.*

76 That is something WIELAND 1906, 116 also concedes. See also STEWART 2015, 121–123.

77 Orig. in Iesu Nav. hom. 10,3 (SC 71, 276). Text see above p. 109 n. 223.

of arrogance about them: whereas the "altar of the Lord" (*altare Domini*) should really burn with sweet incense, it shimmers in the hideous odour of arrogance.[78] Of interest here is not the moral homily but rather the description of the church space. Origen is likely to be thinking of the presbytery, which contains an elevated semi-circular bench for the priests (the "observation point"), in front of which stands the altar. The altar is possibly censed with incense.

The series of authors who allow criticism of sacrifice and the cult of sacrifice to validly co-exist continues with *Tertullian* († after 220) in North Africa. He categorically rejects temples, altars and sacrifices, but this verdict applies exclusively to pagan worship.[79] Naturally, there is, on the other hand, a Christian sacrifice (*sacrificium, oblatio*)[80] and a Christian altar. Franz Wieland tries to spiritualize the fair number of instances in which Tertullian speaks of the Christian altar,[81] but in so doing he violates the obvious meaning of the text. For example, Tertullian says that the faithful as true priests bring their spiritual oblations "to the altar of God" (*altare Dei*).[82] Like the "table of the Lord" in Paul, here the possessive used in the "altar *of God*" denotes the exclusivity of the piece of cultic furniture, which is used only for sacrifices to the Christian God. Although Tertullian does occasionally stress the spiritual character of this sacrificial service, this does not rule out the real oblation of bread and wine. Accordingly, he speaks of the eucharistic offertory prayers that are performed by the priest standing at the altar of God (*ara Dei*); the faithful, too, stand there for Communion.[83]

---

78 Orig. in Iud. hom. 3,2 (SC 389, 100): *Nonnumquam autem morbus iste superbiae penetrat non solum pauperes plebis, verum etiam ipsum sacerdotalem et leviticum ordinem pulsat. Invenias interdum etiam in nobis aliquos qui ad exemplum humilitatis positi sumus et in altaris circulo velut specula quaedam intuentibus collocati in quibus arrogantiae vitium fetet, et de altari Domini quod deberet incensi suavitate flagrare odor taeterrimus superbiae et elationis renidet.* WIELAND 1906, 104.

79 Tert. spect. 13,4 (CCL 1, 239): *Nec minus templa quam monumenta despuimus, neutram aram novimus, neutram effigiem adoramus, non sacrificamus, non parentamus. Sed neque de sacrificio et parentato edimus, quia non possumus cenam Dei edere et cenam daemoniorum.*

80 Tert. cult. fem. 2,11,2 (CCL 1, 366): *sacrificium offertur.* Cor. 3:3 (CCL 2, 1043*): Eucharistiae sacramentum* […]. *Oblationes pro defunctis, pro nataliciis annua die facimus.*

81 WIELAND 1906, 112–114.

82 Tert. or. 28,3 f. (CCL 1, 273): *Nos sumus veri adoratores et veri sacerdotes, qui spiritu orantes spiritu sacrificamus orationem hostiam Dei propriam et acceptabilem* […]. *Hanc* […] *cum pompa operum bonorum inter psalmos et hymnos deducere ad Dei altare debemus.* Ibid. 11,1 (263): *ascendamus ad altare Dei.* Pat. 12,3 (CCL 1, 312): *Nemo convulsus animum in fratrem suum munus apud altare perficiet.*

83 Tert. or. 19,1–4 (CCL 1, 267 f.): *Similiter et de stationum diebus non putant plerique sacrificiorum orationibus interveniendum, quod statio solvenda sit accepto corpore Domini. Ergo devotum Deo obsequium eucharistia resolvit an magis Deo obligat? Nonne sollemnior erit statio tua, si et ad aram Dei steteris? Accepto corpore Domini et reservato utrumque salvum est, et participatio sacrificii et executio officii.* RAUSCHEN 1910, 89. MOLL 1975, 102 (with n. 56) sees in Tertullian merely the "tentative beginnings" of a "concept of a material Christian altar standing in a cultic building."

In his dialogue Octavius (first half of the third century), the apologist *Minucius Felix* (in North Africa/Rome) reacts to the allegation that the Christians held secret meetings.[84] He asks his pagan interlocutor the rhetorical question: "But do you think we conceal what we worship if we do not have temples and altars?"[85] Many people understand this famous statement as a flat rejection of Christian shrines,[86] sacrifices and altars.[87] And in fact Minucius does radically moralise the concept of sacrifice: "the victim fit for sacrifice (*hostia*)" is "a good disposition, and a pure mind, and a sincere judgment."[88] The conclusion drawn from this is that from the very beginning Christianity understood itself as a fundamentally anti-cultic religion and that it was from conviction that it did not possess any altars.[89] However, this is wrong, not just because the Christians developed their own understanding of cult very early on[90] but also on account of the context in which these words were spoken. For the above-quoted statement continues with the words: "And yet what image of God shall I make, since, if you think rightly, man himself is the image of God?"[91] For Minucius Felix, temple and altar serve an idol. The Christians neither have nor need any of that. Their gatherings are not secret nor does the fact that they have no temples and altars mean that they conceal their image of God. What Minucius is rejecting here is exclusively the pagan cult with its temples (*delubrum*), public altars (*ara*) and statues (*simulacrum*), replacing it with a Christian moralism without uttering a single syllable about Christian worship.

The further text, too, shows how Minucius Felix truly labours over the pagan cultic terminology and moralizes it: the *hostia litabilis* (victim fit for sacrifice) of the pagans is for the Christians the good heart; the *supplicatio* (public submission to the divine will) is innocence; the *libatio* (drink offering) is justice; the *propitiatio* (propitiatory offering) is honesty; the *caesio* (slaughter) is the saving of a person – "These are our sacrifices (*sacrificia*), these are our offerings (*sacra*) for God; thus, among us, he who is most just is he who is most religious (*religio*)."[92] So the Christian interlocutor only goes into the morality of the Christians, not their worship. He is totally consistent in this, just as he never quotes the Bible or mentions Christ. To be sure, the dialogue takes an anti-cultic position, but this is directed exclusively against the pagan cult. Thus nothing is stated, either positively or negatively, about the Christian understanding of cult. Nevertheless,

---

84 Min. Fel. 31,5 (CSEL 2, 45).

85 Min. Fel. 32,1 (CSEL 2, 45): *Putatis autem nos occultare quod colimus, si delubra et aras non habemus?* Correctly BARTH 1999, 59.

86 LEPPIN 2018, 124.

87 WIELAND 1906, 110; *id.* 1909, 104 f.

88 Min. Fel. 32,2 (CSEL 2, 46).

89 WIELAND 1906, 50 and many others.

90 See above p. 167. FINNEY 1994, 41 f. correctly points

out the difference between apologetics and Christian reality.

91 Min. Fel. 32,1 (CSEL 2, 45): *quod enim simulacrum Deo fingam, cum, si recte existimes, sit Dei homo ipse simulacrum.*

92 Ibid. 32,3 (CSEL 2, 46). On *hostiae litatio* see SCHEID 1990, 576; on all technical terms *id.* 1998 (Index).

the dialogue is not completely silent on Christian worship – and it is the pagan inter-locutor of all people who brings it up when he refers to the cultic sites and altars of the Christians.[93]

As the last of those authors commonly cited in support of the thesis that the Christians did not have any altars, let us now turn to *Arnobius of Sicca*, who wrote in around 303–305 in Numidia. Previously a pagan himself, he relates shortly after his conversion of the pagans' accusation that the Christians, unlike them, do not erect either sacred cul-tic buildings (*aedes sacrae*) or altars (*altaria, arae*), do not shed blood and do not offer fruit or wine libations.[94] So the context is once again pagan religious practice. Arnobius confirms once more that the Christians, unlike the pagans, do not possess altars for slaughter and do not offer animal sacrifices, nor do they participate in the pagans' sacri-ficial acts. It would, however, be wrong to conclude from this that the Christian worship attended by Arnobius – which he calls *religio, actio, divina officia*[95] and *cultus*[96]– was not seen by those attending it as a sacrifice and that it did not have an altar.[97] For in Ar-nobius's North African home, Christian altars had at this time long since existed, as is witnesses by countless texts authored by Cyprian of Carthage. The reason Arnobius does not mention them is that – in a similar way to Minucius Felix – he abstains in general from describing Christian worship in his writings.[98]

In summary, it can be said that among the Christian apologists of the second and third centuries there is no rejection of cult on principle nor any elitist opposition to eccle-sial community worship. None of the early Christian writers quoted above denies the sacrificial nature – however this is to be understood – of Christian worship in general and of the Eucharist in particular. Quite the opposite: their efforts are directed towards establishing a differentiated link to the Jewish sacrificial service and rigorously distin-guishing their own worship from the pagan temple and sacrificial cult, with the aim of formulating a specific understanding of prayer and sacrifice that fits into the religious context of late antiquity and equally takes account of the Christian claim to truth and mission. And the crucial door to this understanding is the eucharistic offering of the bloodless gifts of bread and wine.

---

93 See below p. 197 f.
94 Arnob. adv. nat. 6,1. 3 (CSEL 4, 214 f.). On the re-jection of animal sacrifices ibid. 4,31 (166 f.).
95 Ibid. 1,27 (CSEL 4, 18). On Christian worship as *actio* see NEBEL 2014.
96 Arnob. adv. nat. 1,31. 36. 39 (CSEL 4, 21. 23. 26); 2,73 (108); 3,2 (112).

97 The Christians gather to make prayer to the Su-preme God: ibid. 4,36 (CSEL 4, 171): *cur immaniter conventicula dirui, in quibus summus oratur deus*. On *conventicula* see above p. 124 f.
98 He could have mentioned baptism, for example, when talking about the initiation celebration of the mystery cults; ibid. 5,18 (CSEL 4, 189 f.).

2. SACRALITY OF THE CHURCH SPACE

The question of the Christian understanding of cult arises once more with respect to the sacred quality of the rooms in which the faithful gather. Our earlier observations on the meaning of the altar (above chapter II) and of Christian sacrificial service (above chapter IV, 1) in themselves explode the cliché according to which the early Christians used only inconsequential and arbitrary rooms to gather in.[99] Despite this, the view expressed almost unanimously in the theological literature is that until the Constantinian shift, Christianity did not have any rooms specifically for worship. Post-Easter Christianity is seen as a spiritualistic movement without sacred rooms since God simply does not live in a temple and in statues (Acts 17:23–29).[100] What value can walls and buildings have for a religion whose worship takes place "in spirit and truth" (Jn 4:23 f.)?[101] Accordingly, there were initially only house churches.[102] It was only from about 180–200 onwards, so it is claimed, that these were replaced by buildings used exclusively for communal worship like that in Dura Europos.[103] But even these were still in the tradition of profane houses. It was only with the Constantinian shift that the final break came about from mere buildings for meetings (*domus ecclesiae*) to a sacred house of God (*domus Dei*), from domestic worship to temple cult.[104] In support of this thesis, its proponents point to Constantine's church buildings: he has the graves of the martyrs in Rome (from 312) and the places of Jesus's life in Palestine (from 324) converted into magnificent shrines. The churches are richly ornamented and decorated with pictures in the way the temples once were.

The discussion about the beginning of sacred assembly rooms has both an archaeological and a religious aspect. First, as far as the rooms themselves are concerned, the existence of house churches must be radically challenged (above chapter III, 1). Such a challenge largely collapses the contention that sacred rooms cannot have existed in the first Christian centuries. Indisputably, new spatial designs were added from Constantine

99 WIELAND 1906, 35: "The place where people gathered was completely inconsequential in the restricted circumstances of the times."

100 E.g. Iren. adv. haer. 3,12,9 (SC 211, 218); Clem. Alex. strom. 7,5,28,1 (SC 428, 104).

101 Accordingly only the congregation and the "house of God" can be called sacred. This is also the position of some Catholics: ADAM 1998, 296 f.

102 WIELAND 1906, 34. Just one example of the uncritical adoption of the house church and secularisation thesis is SHALEV-HURVITZ 2015, 29: "The first Christian gatherings were held in private residences. […] In this early period, it was the con-

gregation that was sacred and there is no evidence for the sanctification of churches before the reign of Constantine."

103 WHITE 1996, 102–139. Borrowed from among others STEWART 2015, 69–76; ROBINSON 2017, 228.

104 LARSON-MILLER 2006, 17; HARNACK 1924, 612; SNYDER 2003, 299; DE BLAAUW 2008, 283 f. The house churches are specially emphasized by SÜSSENBACH 1977, 108–117. For him there were no prestigious sacred church buildings up to Constantine, just house churches.

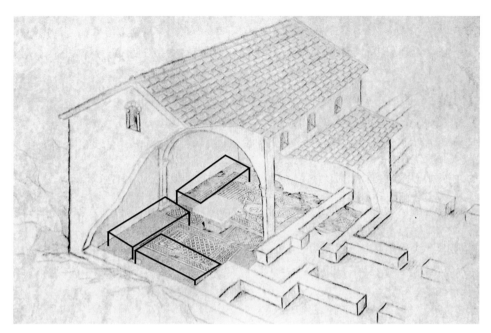

Fig. 18: Reconstruction of the Oratory at Megiddo near Nazareth, 3ʳᵈ century; S. Heid based on Tepper / Di Segni 2006, 25.

onwards with artistic pretentions that can be credited with having a sacred emphasis.[105] But church art existed before this, too, which makes it clear that the assembly rooms were not arbitrarily chosen but were designed to last and dedicated exclusively to Christian worship. In the church complex at Dura Europos, which dates from the middle of the third century, we find biblical frescoes, albeit only in the baptistery, not in the large hall where the Eucharist was celebrated. The frescoes are not chosen randomly for decoration but follow a programme linked to the baptismal rite.[106] They turn the room in question into a worship space. Jenn Cianca goes further and argues for the sacrality of the fresco-less assembly room, arguing that sacrality does not depend solely on the presence of wall paintings.[107]

Also of significance is the oratory at Megiddo, near Nazareth (Fig. 18). What is striking here is the carefully crafted mosaic floor in which seven people have been immortalised.[108] There is also a dedication inscription referring to the donation of the altar: "The

105 Cf. Schneider 2006.
106 Doig 2009, 13–17.
107 Cianca 2018, 99.

108 Among them are five women, which is not surprising in the civil settlement of a military camp.

God-loving Akeptous has offered the table to [the] God Jesus Christ as a memorial" (above Fig. 8). This is undoubtedly a sacred space. For when the neighbouring military camp was abandoned, the floor was not destroyed but instead was sealed off by being carefully covered with rubble.[109] Megiddo is also interesting as a sacred space since it is likely that both the Eucharist and the evening *agape* meal (love feast) were celebrated in it, which in no way detracts from the sacrality of the room.

Such a dual use is anyway strongly suggested by the design of the room. There are several mosaic panels in the inner area of the floor, where the altar also stands, whereas the floor along the walls is kept simple. This and the two fish in the centre of the largest mosaic provide an indication of what the room was used for.[110] It looks as if two triclinia, each with three large couches providing space for about twelve people, were placed along the walls, with their open sides facing each other in such a way as to leave a broad strip of floor between them marked by a mosaic pattern. In the middle of this strip stands the altar. It belongs, as it were, to both triclinia. But it does not serve as a place for the participants in the meal to put their food down since it is too far away from the benches for this. Hence it would be over-simplistic to think that the use of the word "table" instead of "altar" in the dedication inscription indicates that a symposium was celebrated here in memory of the Last Supper.[111] The dedication inscription simply means that this table is reserved for the Eucharist. If other foods are consumed as well, they just have to be placed on other tables.

The Christian community is likely to have celebrated both the Eucharist and the agape meal in this room. In the event that the Eucharist was not celebrated in the morning and the agape in the evening but instead both were celebrated together, special food tables were brought in for the agape and placed directly next to the couches (κλίναι), while the fixed altar served exclusively for the Eucharist. Then, when the agape meal was over and the food tables had been cleared away, the participants rose to pray and the Eucharist followed at the altar. The simple fact that there is only one fixed table in the room shows this to be an altar; this is confirmed by the inscription. For according to Christian tradition the altar is unique, whereas there can be a number of meal tables. The room's sophisticated décor reveals that the agape, too, was not celebrated as a normal meal but as a semi-ritual feast.

In view of the fact that, with the exception of the above-mentioned examples, the pre-Constantinian early Christian meeting places were almost completely destroyed,

---

109 TEPPER / DI SEGNI 2006, 42–44. Similarly, the church at Dura Europos was carefully emptied and filled in.

110 Cf. ibid. 39.

111 SASTRE DE DIEGO 2012, 1280f.

to pass any judgement regarding sacrality and profanity will inevitably amount to an arbitrary act. The simplicity-pomp interpretative model is in any case scarcely helpful. Any attempt to understand whether or not the early Christians perceived their meeting rooms to be sacred places will have to opt for a religious approach. A good starting point may be a comment by Luigi Canetti according to which there were no sacred places before Constantine but only "simple places of meeting and prayer."[112] A telling statement: for Canetti, prayer is not something sacred, and gathering for prayer is in fact a profane thing! What ultimately lies behind this is a Protestant Word of God theology. Put liturgically, the *pure* Word becomes *mere* prayer. In the wake of the Enlightenment and secularisation, the Word of scripture takes on an a-ritual and a-cultic edge. The same perspective has meanwhile been adopted on the Catholic side. For example, Franz Wieland sees the Eucharist as "just" prayer.[113] From this it follows, so he concludes, that the Christian assembly room is called simply a "prayer house" and is specifically not a sacred building (*aedes sacra*) like a Roman temple.[114]

Anyone who draws historical lines like this according to modern theological concepts blocks any insight into how late antiquity perceived itself. Paul Corby Finney quite rightly advocates for abandoning the ideal portrayal of early Christianity as a purely spiritual phenomenon. It is, he says, wrong to claim that the central idea guiding the early Christian religion was the inward, cultless, aniconic and immaterial thinking of the late Hellenistic philosophers' conventicles.[115] The Christians do actually spiritualize "temple", "altar" and "sacrifice", but spiritualization does not mean a dissolution of reality but instead its interpretation. Prayer is not spirituality without the senses or without space; rather, as a repetitive "conversation with God", it actually makes the meeting places into spaces of collectively experienced theophany.

Contemporary Christian criticism of the sacrality of worship buildings comes from the sort of authors and apologists who engage in elitist and anything-but-representative reflections. They claim that God does not dwell in temples because he is infinite and cannot be confined. This is to be understood in terms of religious apologetics: every ancient temple is built for the statue of a deity. If the deity lives in a statue, then the deity is only present in the respective temple in which the statue stands and is therefore locally limited. Worse still, the god in statues is the gateway to polytheism because every statue has a different god dwelling in it. Each of these deities watches jealously over his or her

---

112 L. CANETTI, Santuari e reliquie tra Antichità e Medioevo. Cristianizzazione dello spazio o sacralizzazione del cristianesimo? (2002, Internet-Publication): "Non più dunque semplici luoghi di riunione e di preghiera dei fedeli ma santuari che aprivano loro una porta sicura verso il cielo."

113 Cf. WIELAND 1906, 110; *id.* 1909, XI, 51, 94, 110 f.; *id.* 1912, 16 f.

114 WIELAND 1906, 105.

115 FINNEY 1984, 193–197. On the supposed aniconic nature of early Christianity see also BERGMEIER 2017, 72–75.

temple. This contradicts the omnipresence and unrivalled nature of God. Accordingly, the Christian God cannot live in a temple.

But does it follow from this that the omnipresent God is not present in, of all places, the gathering of Christians for worship? Or is he not rather *also* there in this space, and perhaps even particularly intensively so, experienceable in common prayer? Indeed, in the polemic of the apologists the two things always belong together. They speculate philosophically and systematically about the (im)possibility of the sanctity of walls and places,[116] but they are far from denying the experiential reality of the faithful, who – not unlike the pagans in their temples – seek God's presence and certainly experience it in their prayer houses.[117] For the faithful, the single most important thing is undoubtedly what they experience and what happens in the room where their worship takes place.

This is the precise point emphasized by Ann Marie Yasin in her seminal study: alongside the concept of the "place of the sacred", one must also speak of the concept of the "sacred space". For nascent Christianity the "sacred space" certainly does exist. God does not have a fixed place; the buildings of the Christians do not serve him as dwellings. Nevertheless, their meeting places are not profane but are perceived as sacred by virtue of the collective rites, prayers and experiences of God that take place there. As Yasin summarizes for the pre-Constantinian period: "Thus, regardless of their location or architectural form, as sites of ritual action, of community definition, and of prayer as a means of communicating with the divine, places in which Christians gathered to worship had been transformed into sacred spaces long before the developments of the Constantinian world."[118] What then happens from Emperor Constantine onwards is not a sudden, unprecedented sacralization, but merely a potentiation of holiness, for example, through the recovery of relics of all kinds and through holy images. Especially churches at the graves of martyrs[119] or places commemorating Christ become topographically fixed sacred places (*loca sancta*) of the divine.[120]

The sacredness of the spaces is initially not yet so materially fixed, but it is inseparably linked to the visible liturgy and what takes place at the altar. Neither the faithful nor the walls are, so to speak, statically loaded with sanctity. Rather, it simply becomes the practised conviction of Christians that God is reliably present at their places of as-

---

116 Clem. Alex. strom. 7,5,28,1 f (SC 428, 104).

117 Finney 1984. Received by Yasin 2009, 21; Perrin 2016, 209 f. The existential sense of the sacredness of space is also seen by archaeologists: Jäggi 2007; de Blaauw 2008, 277 f (inconsistent with 261 f.).

118 Yasin 2009, 44.

119 Cf. Bonfiglio 2010.

120 Yasin 2009, 14 – 45. Received by Czock 2012, 27 f. By contrast, Markus 1994 and Canetti 2002 think that it was only with the martyrs' churches that the sacred space entered Christianity.

sembly – Sunday after Sunday. When this experience stabilizes, when a certain space becomes for the faithful the embodiment of God's helping nearness, then this space has become a commemorative place, a *lieux de mémoire* (mnemotope) of sanctity and thus itself holy.

Yasin's assumption that the Christians might have perceived their meeting rooms as sacred spaces from the very beginning[121] gains in plausibility in the same measure as the house-church theory is discredited (above chapter III, 1). After all, the fragmentation of communities into domestic circles is bound to be accompanied by a profaneness of location. By contrast, having a special prayer room for the city's whole community is a sign of its sacredness. Even if the morning Eucharist is celebrated separately from the evening agape, it cannot be ruled out that in some places the two celebrations might have been held in the same hall.[122] And why shouldn't a meal be held in a room that is regarded as having been made sacred by the Eucharist? After all, the *agapae* are not profane feasts, but rather precisely regulated, semi-ritual events.[123] Nevertheless, it can be assumed that in most cases a special hall was used for the Eucharist – for practical reasons, too, since for an agape in a fairly small circle you need a kitchen and bathroom; for the Eucharist of the whole city community a fairly large room.

The sacrality also attaches itself to the altar. For this table serves the community for its encounter with God, thus becoming the point of contact for holiness (below chapter IV, 4). The prayers and offerings at the altar reach heaven.[124] This is also true in the physical-topographical sense: only where the altar is can the supreme form of contact be made with God in the offering up of the sacrifice. Christians make contact with God in prayer, and they are convinced that they can bring about this contact through the eucharistic oblation. For the transformation of bread and wine into the Flesh and Blood of Christ proves the power (δύναμις) of the priest's prayers.[125] But once this miracle has taken place – at the altar – then God can always be experienced there because he will always work the miracle. In this way the room itself becomes holy, a place where the miraculous presence of God is commemorated. This is a quite natural process since a collective meeting place cannot be constantly changed.[126] In this one room with its altar, the only one in a city, the faithful gather on Sundays over years and decades in order to experience their prayers being heard. What results is a sacred place that is dynamic in

121 YASIN 2009, 37.
122 Feasts (*agapae, convivia*) are still occasionally celebrated in church rooms in the fourth century; Synod of Laodicea, Can. 28.
123 LEONHARD / ECKHARDT 2010, 1067–1104. Cf. Apophth. (PG 65, 181AB). "Once there was an agape taking place; the brothers ate in the church and talked with one another." The critical edition does not have "in the church": Apophth. 12,8 (SC 474, 212).
124 Iren. adv. haer. 4,18,6 (SC 100,2, 614).
125 Iustin. apol. 1, 65,3 (SC 507, 304); 1, 66,2 (306); 1, 67,5 (310).
126 Cf. YASIN 2009, 35.

its materiality inasmuch as the commemorated presence of God has to be verified anew on each occasion.

The sacrality of the altar could then also provide an explanation for a question that arises in the context of the house-church theory. For if there are no such private house churches, but instead in every city only the one episcopal gathering, and if the place where this takes place is holy, then one wonders why there is practically no city in which these pre-Constantinian prayer rooms have been preserved or remembered, and why all that is known is without exception the fourth-century bishop's church. One attempt at an answer could lie in our reflections on mobile altars (above chapter III, 5). It is beyond doubt that the sacrality of the worship room culminates in the altar. Is it then not conceivable that during the building boom following Constantine's conversion the altar was regularly transferred from the older church to the new fourth-century building? Is this not all the more likely because an illiterate society is much more open to such material and haptic symbolism than to mere words? Through the transferring of the altar, the local community can proudly place itself in an unbroken continuity with the Church that suffered the persecutions. However, with the translation of the altar the thus-denuded cultic space is profaned. Since it does not contain any relics either, it loses significance and falls into oblivion. This is all the more the case if, as was not uncommon, it was destroyed in the Diocletian persecution.

There is nothing to justify arbitrarily setting a temporal limit as to when the Christian meeting place became a collective place of commemorating God's nearness and thus a sacred space. Going through the relevant texts and examining all the names given to this place – temple, house of God, sanctuary, church, house of prayer and basilica – gives the impression of there having been a seamless process, the beginnings of which are certainly already to be found in the second century.

There are early indications of the Old Testament temple terminology being adopted for the Christian gathering and its location. The idea connecting the two is that God is present in the Christian gathering just as he once was in the Jerusalem Temple.[127] The New Testament does not refer to any meeting room, but only to believers as the "temple of God" (ναὸς θεοῦ) (1 Cor 3:16f.; 2 Cor 6:16; Eph 2:19–22) and, in the same sense, as the "house of God" (Heb 3:6; 10:21).[128] The faithful themselves are, as it were, the cultic building – obviously not individually, but as a community (1 Cor 3:16; 2 Cor 6:16: "you", "we") – that has gathered to perform the sacrificial service (1 Pet 2:5). Access to this

---

127 On God's presence in the Jerusalem Temple see HEID 2001b, 31–35.

128 ADAM 1998, 296: "Although the New Testament writings often speak of worship gatherings, the place where they meet is never called a house of God, sanctuary or even temple."

house of God is only granted to those whose bodies have been washed with pure (baptismal) water (Heb 10:22). This is probably linked to the Mosaic regulations regarding the tent of the congregation (cf. Heb 3:3–5; 9:10). It is also known of the Jewish Essene community that they entered the dining room "after a pure manner […] as into a certain holy temple".[129]

When the assembly of the faithful becomes a temple, this is not meant as a spiritualization but is rather a relocation of the real presence of God. While the pagan gods are present in the temple statues,[130] now the presence of God shifts, as it were, from the anthropomorphous idol (2 Cor 6:16) to the faithful gathered for worship, in whom the Spirit of God dwells and who are therefore holy (1 Cor 3:16f.). This does not make God any less really present in the ecclesial gathering; indeed, his physical presence is even multiplied in the bodies of the Christians (1 Cor 6:19): the more faithful that are present, the more present is God and the more holy is the assembly. So however much the apologists stress that God cannot be enclosed in a temple made by human hands, this in no way prevents his almost quantifiable presence in the space once the faithful have gathered there.

This may sound abstract, but such considerations have a real background in the competition between religions. Christians should not feel inferior to pagans just because they do not have statues and temples where prayers are heard. God is no less present among them, their sacrificial cult is no less effective; on the contrary, here every Christian is, as it were, an image of God – here everyone is filled with the Spirit of God. This makes the church space holier than a temple can ever be. The presence of God can be experienced, for example, in various gifts of grace, as is already displayed in the congregation in Corinth (1 Cor 12:28–31). Above all, God rejoices in the numerous gifts and offerings of the Christians.[131] The place of assembly thus becomes a space where the nearness of God is experienced.

The *First Letter of Clement* (c. 96 or c. 64–70) emphatically applies the Old Testament sacred terminology "temple" (ναός) and "altar" to the Christians' place of worship and sacrificial table (above chapter II, 3). Above all, however, he regards the space in which a city's Christians gather as the place where they together, persistently and in harmony ("as with one mouth"), entreat God to fulfil his promises, in just the same way as tens of thousands of angels "stand around him" crying "holy, holy, holy".[132] The common gathering place of men and angels is thus the prerequisite for effective prayer; or put differently, the experience of God condenses in the place of the gathering.

129 Flav. Ios. bell. Iud. 2,129[8,5] (Niese 1955, 178).
130 Funke 1981, 713–716.
131 Iustin. dial. 28,4 (Marcovich 1997, 115).
132 1 Clem. 34,5–8 (SC 167, 154–156).

The same thought is encountered in around the same time period in the *Letter to the Hebrews*. Those who have gathered to hear the sermon (Heb 6:9; 10:39) – at the eucharistic assembly – "have come to Mount Zion and to the city of the living God, the heavenly Jerusalem, and to innumerable angels in festal gathering, and to the assembly (ἐκκλησία) of the firstborn […] and to Jesus, the mediator of a new covenant, and to the sprinkled blood" (Heb 12:22–24). This "coming to" does not take place in an abstract space, but rather in the assembly. The location where it takes place is sacredly charged through becoming a reliable meeting place and place of encounter between mortals, angels and God.

In his interpretation of *Ignatius of Antioch* (c. 110/20), Reinhard Messner goes so far as to say "that the most important root of Christian liturgy is not synagogue worship […] but the temple" in Jerusalem.[133] At the beginning of the second century, Ignatius relates the one Jerusalem "temple" (ναός) and "altar" unambiguously to the meeting place of the local church, to which the same uniqueness belongs. There can be no talk of a spiritualization here. On the contrary, through their physical presence the "temple" and "altar" not only create for the Christians a unity among the faithful of a city, but also bring about a unity in what they do, since it is only from here that prayers and intercessions are permitted to rise up to the Christian God.[134] Once again it is a question of, as it were, the concentrated power of the prayers at the altar, which are all the more effective the more completely "the whole Church" prays together with the bishop.[135] In other words, there God's powerful presence is experienced, and on this is the holiness of the meeting place ultimately grounded.

This resembles the way in which the Roman *Shepherd of Hermas* (c. 140/50) experiences the local church gathering (ἐκκλησία) and its location, the place in which his visions are read out in the presence of the presbyters and which is described in Old Testament temple terminology as a "sanctuary" (ἁγίασμα) and a "house of God" (οἶκος τοῦ θεοῦ).[136]

By taking this dynamic seriously it also becomes possible to understand the nomenclature of the church space better. Since about the year 200, the community's building has also been called a "church" (see below). Since the word *ecclesia*/ἐκκλησία actually means an "assembly", the church building is, in the literal sense of the word, simply the "assembly room" of the faithful. This sounds rather mundane, and people have indeed tried to infer the profanity of the space or building from the choice of word.[137] But this is too superficial. Different terms can emphasize different aspects of the same thing

133 Messner 2003a, 353.
134 Ign. ad Magn. 7,1 f (SC 10³, 100).
135 Ign. ad Eph. 5,2 (SC 10³, 72–74).
136 See above p. 130 f.
137 Cf. Wieland 1906, 100 f.; Claussen 2010a, 23 f.; Gerhards 2009, 115. Apart from the texts cited

without intending to exclude or contradict other aspects. For example, the Romans used both the religious term *templum* (temple) and the neutral term *aedes* (building) for the cultic building.[138] But this certainly did not make the temple of the gods half profane and half sacred; it was in any case something holy. So the seemingly neutral term *ecclesia*, too, can have a sacred connotation. For "church" naturally does not stand for just any gathering, but rather for the assembly that is regarded as the "house(hold) of God" (1 Tm 3:15). When a particular building in a city becomes the place of remembrance of the church that gathers there, then what the Christian of the time understands on hearing the word "church" is that God is reliably present there because it is the only place in which that congregation assembles which reliably establishes contact with God through its prayer and sacrifice.

Tertullian of Carthage († after 220) can use the term *ecclesia* to describe both the ecclesial assembly and the church building.[139] The latter he also calls the "house of God" (*domus Dei*); there the people raise their hands in prayer to God the Father.[140] Hence the term "church" is to be understood in just as sacred a way as "house of God". What this sacrality effects can be seen in Tertullian's treatise on prayer. Here he speaks of the pure sacrifice of the Christians, which consists in prayer:

> This offering […] we ought to escort with the pomp of good works, amid psalms and hymns, unto God's altar, and it will obtain for us all things from God.[141]

It is interesting to see how in the closer context Tertullian transfers the pagan sacrificial pomp, in which the fattened and decorated sacrificial animals are led to the altar for slaughter, to the Christian sacrificial celebration. For him the (eucharistic) sacrifice at the "altar of God" (*altare Dei*) guarantees the success of the prayer. Praying with outstretched hands resembles the imperial banner, so that the angels come and likewise pray.[142] In this logic, the church as a place of prayer must become the holy place of God's favour.

---

below, the first edict of Diocletian in the year 303 demands the destruction of the "churches"; Euseb. hist. eccl. 8,2,4 (SC 55, 7).

138 STAMBAUGH 1978, 557.

139 Tert. fug. 3,2 (CCL 2, 1139): *concurrimus in ecclesiam*; pud. 4,5 (CCL 2, 1287): *non modo limine, verum omni ecclesiae tecto submovemus*; ux. 2,8,3 (CCL 1, 392): *Sordent talibus ecclesiae: difficile in domo dei dives*; 2,8,8 (393 f.): *In ecclesia dei pariter utrique*. SCHÖLLGEN 1985, 210, 309; MOHRMANN 1962, 163; STEWART 2015, 37 f.; CIANCA 2018, 133 f.

140 Tert. idol. 7,1 (CCL 2, 1106): *in ecclesiam venire, de adversaria officina in domum dei venire, attollere ad deum patrem manus*. MESSNER 2003a, 362. Tert. Ux. 2,8,3 (CCL 1, 392): *Sordent talibus ecclesiae: difficile in domo dei dives*.

141 Tert. Or. 28,4 (CCL 1, 273): *Hanc […] cum pompa operum bonorum inter psalmos et hymnos deducere ad Dei altare debemus omnia nobis a Deo impetraturam.*

142 Ibid. 29,3 f. (CCL 1, 274): *Sub armis orationis signum nostri imperatoris custodiamus, tubam angeli expectemus orantes. Orant etiam angeli*

At the same time (200–204), *Hippolytus of Rome* speaks of the "house of God" as that meeting place where all pray and praise God.[143] Although he is also familiar with ἐκκλησία as the designation for the church building made of stone and clay that can be torn down, he prefers to use the syntagma "house of God" (οἶκος θεοῦ) for this. Naturally, he also spiritualizes both terms,[144] but this is precisely what shows how the mechanism of the place of remembrance works: for unlike the earthly building, the "spiritual house of God" and the (real) "church" are for him not the place and the building of stone and clay, nor the individual human being, but rather the congregation of saints standing together as one "in the same place" (ἐπὶ τὸ αὐτὸ).[145] And then he describes all the spiritual fruits and gifts of this assembly. In other words, the lasting experience of God's nearness in the same place makes it into a temple and house of God.

It is no different with *Clement of Alexandria* (c. 150–215). In his recommendations regarding correct behaviour during worship, he recalls Jesus's cleansing of the Temple (Mt 21:12–13) and continues:

> The avaricious, the liars, the hypocrites, those who make merchandise of the truth – the Lord cast out of his Father's court, not willing that the holy *house of God* (οἶκος τοῦ θεοῦ) should be the house of unrighteous traffic either in words or in material things.[146]

Now one might think that this is just about the historical episode of the cleansing of the Temple, but Clement in fact applies it explicitly to the right way to behave at the Christians' worship gathering. The sentence that immediately follows it deals first with the correct dress for attending church, then with seemly behaviour during the sermon and when exchanging the fraternal kiss.[147] If Clement had seen the church space not as a holy

---

omnes. On sacred space in Tertullian see also STEWART 2015, 36–42.

143 Hipp. Comm. In Dan. 1,21,2f. (GCS Hipp. 1,1², 48); BOGUNIOWSKI 1987, 100; MESSNER 2003a, 362. BRANDENBURG 2013, 12 mentions for 201 also Chron. Edess. (CSCO 2 / Syr. 2, 3): *in templum* (h.e. partem ecclesiae ubi populus locum habebat) *aedis sacrae Christianorum,* but that could, of course, be later terminology dating from the time when the chronicle was written.

144 Cf. WIELAND 1906, 101f.

145 Hipp. comm. in Dan. 1,18,4–6 (GCS Hipp. 1,1², 42): [...] ὥστε ἔστι νοῆσαι τὸ σύστημα

τῶν δικαίων τόπον εἶναι ἅγιον, ἐν ᾧ ἡ ἐκκλησία ἐφυτεύετο. οὔτε γὰρ ψιλὸς τόπος δύναται καλεῖσθαι ἐκκλησία, οὔτε οἶκος διὰ λίθου καὶ πηλοῦ ᾠκοδομημένος· [...] οἶκος γὰρ καταλύεται [...]. τί οὖν ἐστιν ἐκκλησία; σύστημα ἁγίων ἐν ἀληθείᾳ πολιτευομένων. ἡ οὖν ὁμόνοια καὶ ἡ ἐπὶ τὸ αὐτὸ τῶν ἁγίων ὁδὸς τοῦτο γίνεται ἐκκλησία, ‚οἶκος' θεοῦ ‚πνευματικὸς' ἐπὶ τῷ Χριστῷ ὡς ‚ἐν τῇ ἀνατολῇ' πεφυτευμένος.

146 Clem. Alex. paed. 3,11,79,2 (SC 158, 152).

147 Ibid. 3,11,79,3 (SC 158, 152–154); 3,11,80,4 (156); 3,11,81,2 (156).

house, but merely as a hall like any other, his rules of conduct could have been immediately rejected as unfounded. But his whole concern is that the holiness of a room calls
for special behaviour. No matter whether or not the term "house of God" was already
generally adopted terminology for the church building, this building was for Clement,
and probably for his audience too, a sacred space.[148]

Elsewhere, Clement talks about the ancient temples in general and, directly connected with this, about the place of assembly of the Christians:[149]

> And if "the sacred" has a twofold application (among the pagans), designating both God
> himself [= the holy] and the structure raised to his honour [= the sanctuary], how shall
> we (Christians) not with propriety call the *church*, made holy through knowledge for the
> honour of God, sanctuary of God? It is of great value, and not constructed by ordinary
> craftsmanship, nor poorly embellished, but by the will of God fashioned into a temple.
> For it is not now the place, but the assembly of the elect, that I call *church*. This temple is
> better suited to receive the greatness of the dignity of God.[150]

The language used by the Christians in Alexandria is evidently unfamiliar with the words
"temple" (νεώς) and "sanctuary" (ἱερόν) for the church. However, in the penultimate
sentence – "For it is not now the place, but the assembly of the elect, that I call church" –
Clement indirectly indicates that he is familiar with the term "church" (ἐκκλησία) used
for the building that is now dedicated entirely to worship.[151] In fact he on one occasion
says that what the Pythagoreans call their "auditorium" (ὁμακοεῖον) is for Christians
the "church" (ἐκκλησία).[152] For Clement the word "church" has a dual meaning: it is
the assembly room of the community and at the same time the local church assembly
(ἄθροισμα),[153] and thus the liturgical assembly. The church building made of stone can
be no more something holy than can a stone temple. Clement is completely clear on this,

148 Cf. Cianca 2018, 134. Unlike Origen later, in his discussion of the place of (private) prayer Clement does not go into the church space; Clem. Alex. strom. 7,7,35,3 (SC 428, 128–130).

149 Ibid. 7,5,28 (SC 428, 104–106).

150 Ibid. 7,5,29,3 f. (SC 428, 108–110): Εἰ δὲ τὸ ἱερὸν διχῶς ἐκλαμβάνεται, ὅ τε θεὸς αὐτὸς καὶ τὸ εἰς τιμὴν αὐτοῦ κατασκεύασμα, πῶς οὐ κυρίως τὴν εἰς τιμὴν τοῦ θεοῦ κατ᾽ ἐπίγνωσιν ἁγίαν γενομένην ἐκκλησίαν ἱερὸν ἂν εἴποιμεν θεοῦ τὸ πολλοῦ ἄξιον καὶ οὐ βαναύσῳ κατεσκευασμένον τέχνῃ, ἀλλ᾽ οὐδὲ ἀγύρτου χειρὶ δεδαιδαλμένον, βουλήσει δὲ τοῦ θεοῦ εἰς νεὼν πεποιημένην; Οὐ γὰρ νῦν τὸν τόπον, ἀλλὰ τὸ ἄθροισμα τῶν ἐκλεκτῶν ἐκκλησίαν καλῶ. Ἀμείνων ὁ νεὼς οὗτος εἰς παραδοχὴν μεγέθους ἀξίας τοῦ θεοῦ.

151 SC 428, 110, n. 2; Harnack 1924, 614 n. 5; Koch 1917, 93 f.; Deichmann 1964, 56; Klauck 1981, 75; Messner 2003a, 362; Cantino Wataghin 2014, 574.

152 Clem. Alex. strom. 1,15,66,2 (SC 30, 98). Ibid. strom. 1,19,96,1 f. (121): "church" is the place of assembly of the Christians, not the heretics.

153 O. Stählin, in: BKV II Clem. Alex. 5, 35 translates ἄθροισμα in Clem. Alex. strom. 7,5,29,4 (SC 428, 110) with the German "Gemeinschaft" [community/communion] (of the church), A. le Boulluec, in: SC 428, 111, on the other hand,

as he is, too, with the statement that God cannot be locked up in a space as in a temple. Rather, God fills the heavens and the whole cosmos.[154]

With this he is naturally not claiming that God is not to be found in the church space; he is, of course, everywhere, i.e. there too. Therefore Clement can say of the church assembly that it is the real sanctuary: "How shall we not with propriety call the […] church (assembly) (ἐκκλησία) sanctuary (ἱερόν) of God?" This again implies a potentiation of God's presence in the church space inasmuch as a temple building cannot enclose God whereas the church assembly can: "This temple is better suited to receive the greatness of the dignity of God." For here every believer, not just a hand-made statue of a deity, is the holy dwelling place of God.[155] Now this might be dismissed as an elitist theology for Gnostics, one that does not allow any insight into the life of the community. The normal churchgoer will have experienced the "house of God" as a sacred space without being in any way impressed. But the question is: Will he really? If so, why? Fortunately, Clement does occasionally come down from his ivory tower and offer some insight into what really happens. This passage has already been quoted in connection with the altar question:

> But if, by nature needing nothing, the deity delights to be honoured, it is not without reason that we (Christians) honour God in prayer; and this sacrifice we send up to God as the best and holiest (sacrifice) with righteousness. We honour God with the most righteous Word, by praising through the word, that gives us knowledge, that which we have come to know. The *altar* (θυσιαστήριον) then, *that is with us here*, is the terrestrial congregation of those who devote themselves to prayers, having as it were one common voice and one mind.[156]

Clement sees the altar strictly in conjunction with the worship community of the faithful. The altar is its centre. Here the faithful attain contact with God through prayer and sacrifice. They pray with *one* voice. This is associated with a potentiation of the power of the worship and thus an increase in its effectiveness. For those speaking with one voice are pursuing the same purpose, which gives them the greatest chance of being heard by God. In addition to the earthly community praying at the altar, there is evidently also a heavenly community of spirits and angels; these angels join in praying over the concerns

renders it correctly as "rassemblement". It is, after all, referring to the assembly of the local church. This is confirmed by the concept of church in Clem. Alex. strom. 1,19,96,2 (SC 30, 121); quis div. salv. 42,3 (SC 537, 210); frgm. 36 (GCS Clem. Alex. 3, 218). Also strom. 3,18,108,2 (GCS Clem.

Alex. 2, 246) is thinking of the church gathering at which the bishop presides.
154 Clem. Alex. strom. 7,5,28,1 f (SC 428, 104).
155 Ibid. 7,5,29,5–7 (SC 428, 110).
156 Ibid. 7,6,31,7 f (SC 428, 116–118).

of humans,[157] thus once more increasing the efficacy of the prayer. Moreover, the sacrifice performed at the Christian altar is the "best" and "holiest", which can only mean that it has maximum efficacy. With this, Clement is undoubtedly expressing in theological language the basic experience of worship by "normal" churchgoers. It is because of their hope in the near and helping God that they come to the assembly at all. The lasting experience of the sacred nearness of God makes the space a place to remember holiness and thus a holy place.

Origen of Alexandria († 253/254) points in the same direction. He, too, sees in the liturgical assembly a potentiation of holiness and thus of the efficacy of prayer due to the sheer number of God-filled participants praying there; to this he adds the invisible powers, thus doubling the size of the assembly.[158] God bestows on such a great gathering his oversight,[159] and with it the prospect of its prayers being heard. It is these merits of the place of assembly, namely the experience of prayer being heard and of protection, that impress themselves on the faithful when they always meet "in the same place" (ἐπὶ τὸ αὐτό).[160] Although it may seem that Origen is only according holiness to the assembled community,[161] liturgical praxis in fact lies behind it: the experience of potentiated holiness in the worship attaches itself to the place itself.

As with Clement before him, Origen takes "church" (ἐκκλησία) as the technical term not only for the church assembly, but also and even more clearly for the meeting room in which, for example, the readings are read aloud[162] and the faithful lift up their hands and eyes in prayer and receive bread and cup, but also from which the penitents should keep away. This church, like the Jerusalem Temple before it, is a "sanctuary" (ἱερόν) and "house of God" (οἶκος τοῦ θεοῦ).[163]

In his treatise on prayer, Origen unfortunately does not deal with the church building, but only with the place of prayer.[164] Nevertheless his instruction is remarkable that

157 Ibid. 7,7,39,3 (SC 428, 140).
158 Orig. orat. 31,5 (GCS Orig. 2, 398 f.); YASIN 2009, 35.
159 Orig. orat. 31,4 (GCS Orig. 2, 398).
160 Ibid. 31,7 (GCS Orig. 2, 400).
161 CZOCK 2012, 30 f.
162 Orig. in Ex. hom. 12,2 (SC 321, 358): *lectiones in Ecclesia recitentur. Alii vero […] in remotioribus dominicae domus locis saecularibus fabulis occupantur.* In Iesu Nav. hom. 2,1 (SC 71, 116): *ecclesias exstrui.* Ibid. 10,3 (276): *ad ornatum quoque altaris vel ecclesiae aliquid conferant.* Comm. ser. in Matth. 39 (GCS Orig. 11, 75): *et persecutiones passae sunt ecclesiae et incensae sunt.* In Ps.

36 hom. 3,11 (GCS Orig. 13, 570): *Et si quidem peccator es, egressus ecclesiam inseris te negotiis saecularibus.* In my opinion, in Lev. hom. 9,9 (SC 287, 114) also refers to the church building: *Prima aedes ista puto quod intelligi possit haec, in qua nunc sumus in carne positi Ecclesia, in qua sacerdotes ministrant ad altare holocaustorum.* See also in Ps. 67 hom. 1,10 (GCS Orig. 13, 199): gathering of the Christians in the same place and house of God (the house of God can hardly be understood purely spiritually here). On sacred space in Origen see STEWART 2015, 139–143.
163 Orig. comm. in Ioh. 28,27–30 (SC 385, 72).
164 Orig. orat. 31,1 (GCS Orig. 2, 395).

for private prayer at home the holiest place must be chosen where nothing unclean has taken place. For in his opinion, sin desecrates the place where it is committed. God no longer looks at this place,[165] i.e. he does not answer prayers offered there. This basically means that holy people also sanctify the physical place, just as conversely an idol makes the temple an unclean and godless place (2 Cor 6:16; cf. 2 Kings 23:6; Dn 9:27). It is then possible to draw conclusions from this about what Origen thinks of the church's common prayer room: obviously this place really must be holy if all the faithful gather there to pray.

The so-called *Traditio Apostolica*, a treatise dating from the beginning of the third century, speaks of the "church" (*ecclesia*) as the building where people gather for worship, and also speaks of the *sanctuarium* or *sanctum sanctorum*, an indication of the sacredness of the church space.[166] If *sanctuarium* or *sanctum sanctorum* means only the area round the altar, then this reflects the belief that the altar sanctifies the space. The sacrality and special protective power of the assembly room is also indicated by the invitation to pray in the church because in this way or in this place people "will be able to avoid all the evils of the day."[167]

Even pagan observers ascribe a sacred character to Christian meeting places. This is testified to by the dialogue Octavius by the apologist *Minucius Felix* (first half of the third century), in which a Christian and a pagan engage in a discussion with each other. In it the Christian states quite unambiguously that the Christians possess neither temples nor altars nor images of deities.[168] But this is said in response to his interlocutor's claim that the Christians are secretly engaged in subversive and immoral activities. While the Jews have public temples, altars, sacrifices and ceremonies,[169] the Christians, he claims, must be accused of shunning publicity. "They despise the temples as tombs, spit on (images of) the gods, laugh at the sacrifices."[170] They themselves have no temples, images of gods or outdoor altars where the cult takes place before the eyes of a large audience (Fig. 19).[171] Instead, they hold their conspiratorial gatherings in wicked "sanctuaries" (*sacraria*), the number of which is growing all over the

165 Ibid. 31,4 (GCS Orig. 2, 397 f.).
166 Trad. Apost. 8 (FC 1, 236), 21 (264), 35 (292) and 41 (298).
167 Ibid. 41 (FC 1, 298): *Qui enim orat in ecclesia poterit praeterire malitiam diei.* BRANDENBURG 2013, 12.
168 Min. Fel. 32,1 (CSEL 2, 45).
169 Ibid. 10,4 (CSEL 2, 14): *sed palam, sed templis, aris, victimis caerimoniisque coluerunt.*
170 Ibid. 8,4 (CSEL 2, 12): *templa ut busta despiciunt, deos despuunt, rident sacra.*
171 Ibid. 10,2 (CSEL 2, 14): *cur nullas aras habent, templa nulla, nulla nota simulacra, numquam palam loqui, numquam libere congregari* [...]. C. SCHUBERT, Minucius Felix "Octavius" (Freiburg i.Br. 2014) 586.

Fig. 19: Relief from the tomb of the Haterii, detail with the temple of Jupiter Stator: the image of Jupiter, recognisable by the thunderbolt in his right hand, stands behind a cubic altar, late 1st century, Capitoline Museums; LIBERATI / BOURBON 1996, 61.

world.[172] Their "religion" (*religio*), their "cult" (*colere*), their "ceremonies" (*ceremoniae*) and their "sacrifices" (*sacra*) are secret and so immoral that one conjures up the most terrible ideas – for example of child sacrifices – about their "altars" (*altaria*).[173]

Surprisingly enough, then, the pagan has no problem speaking of the Christians' "sanctuaries" (*sacraria*) and "altars" (*altaria*). He perceives their assembly rooms as sacred places with altars even though they bear no resemblance to normal temples and their altars. He dislikes the Christians' places of worship because they are closed spaces and "nooks". For a traditionally minded pagan, only the outdoor spaces of temples can

---

172 Min. Fel. 9,1 (CSEL 2, 12): *per universum orbem sacraria ista taeterrima impiae coitionis adolescunt. eruenda prorsus haec et execranda consensio.* LAMPE 2003, 369: Minucius Felix "is the first to document the use of the term 'sacraria' (9.1) for the Christian places of assembly."

173 Min. Fel. 9,4 (CSEL 2, 13): [...] *congruentia perditis sceleratisque tribuit altaria, ut id colant quod merentur.*

be considered as possible cultic locations.[174] And yet the *sacraria* of the Christians must also already be of some size, or at least be perceptible from outside, if even a pagan remarks that they are multiplying all over the globe.[175] He would hardly have noticed this if they had been meeting places in the style of private house churches.[176]

Unfortunately, *Octavius* does not follow the polemical description of the Christian places of worship and altars, whose existence is undeniable, with a response on the part of the Christian interlocutor.[177] But nor does the author correct the imputation of clandestine, immoral cultic activity. He concentrates exclusively on confirming that the Christians do not possess temples and sacrificial altars in the manner of the traditional cults. Here he shares Clement's view that God cannot be enclosed exclusively in a temple space or in an image or idol, but that every Christian is the image of God.[178] All in all, the *Octavius* dialogue cannot be adduced as a witness to the anti-cultic nature of Christianity; on the contrary, it points to the existence of Christian places of worship.

In the middle of the third century, the emperors, too, understand the Christians' places of assembly to be places of worship. For in the year 260, after the Valerian persecution, Emperor Gallienus has the confiscated "places of worship" (τόποι θρησκεύσιμοι) and cemeteries returned to the Christians.[179] These were the inner-city and suburban *loca religiosa* of the local churches, which were in principle entitled to own and acquire property.[180] Their immovable property could only be confiscated as a punishment, and then apparently only such property as was of relevance in sacred law. The bishops reacted to this with a petition in which they probably seized on the concept of "places of worship" so as to derive from it the special protection accorded to *loca religiosa*.[181] The authorities

174 NESTORI 1999, 707.
175 See above n. 172.
176 BOGUNIOWSKI 1987, 97–99, on the other hand, thinks *sacraria* refers to the Christians' private houses.
177 Even Wieland thinks that Minucius might have no hesitation in speaking of the altars of the Christians (WIELAND 1906, 110; *id.* 1909, 104 f.). It is only his own premises that lead Wieland to rule out the possibility of Minucius's having known a Christian altar.
178 Min. Fel. 32,1 (CSEL 2, 45 f.): *quod colimus, si delubra et aras non habemus ? Quod enim simulacrum Deo fingam, cum [...] sit Dei homo ipse simulacrum? templum quod ei extruam, cum totus hic mundus eius opere fabricatus eum capere non possit? [...] hostias et victimas Deo offeram,* *quas in usum mei protulit, ut reiciam ei suum munus?*
179 Euseb. hist. eccl. 7,13 (SC 41, 187); MOLTHAGEN 1975, 98 f.
180 HERRMANN 1980, 185–187. Cf. WISSOWA 1971, 477 f.
181 JUDGE 2008, 427. θρησκεία denotes the cult owed to the Roman gods (cf. the inscription from Arycanda appealing to the emperor to protect the cult of the gods before 312 [VON GEBHARDT 1902, 184]). From the first century on, this term became established for Christian worship, too, and can thus build a bridge to Roman sacred law. Later, Julian the Apostate still seems to confirm that according to ancient Roman sacred law the place of worship is defined by the building and altar; Sozom. hist. eccl. 5,20,7 (SC 495, 206–208).

did in fact recognise the status of the church buildings as (private) cult sites, meaning that their restitution actually took place. So the churches are by no means mere assembly rooms.[182] In the eyes of the authorities, it is probably precisely the altars that make them into genuine places of worship.[183] This is also hinted at in a remark by Lactantius at the beginning of the fourth century. He rebukes the pagans for disregarding the holiness of their own altars[184] and also indicates that the Christians call their meeting places "temples of God".[185]

In the Constantinian period, the nomenclature of Christian meeting places was extended to include the term "basilica",[186] which tended to focus on architecture. The basilica building itself is derived from the secular basilica, in which markets and courts were held. Here, too, people have felt bound to conclude from the technical terminology that this must be a profane building and space.[187] Similarly to the use of the term "basilica", so the argument goes, the simple word "table" was also used.[188] But the word "altar" (both *altare* and *ara*) had become established usage long before the term "basilica" appeared. Furthermore, the architecture of the basilica as such signalizes neither profanity nor sacrality.[189] It is the use the building is put to that is the decisive factor here. On this, all you need to read is the sermon Eusebius delivered in Tyre sometime in the period 314–321,[190] in which he offers an interpretation of a basilica church in terms of the theology of worship. The basilica churches that come into being in large numbers from the Constantinian period onwards are from the outset built exclusively for worship, and so people do not hesitate to use sacred expressions in reference to them insofar as, for example, the "worship owed" and the "Christian rite" are celebrated there.[191]

182 Cf. Judge 2008, 429.
183 Min. Fel. 9,1 (CSEL 2, 12) and 9,4 (13) on the *sacraria* and *altaria* of the Christians. Cf. Cyprian's terrifying vision of the replacement of the Christian altar in the apse with pagan *arae*; Judge 2008, 427f. Nevertheless in 303 the soldiers look for the image of the deity in the church of Nicomedia; Lact. mort. pers. 12,2 (SC 39, 91).
184 Lact. div. inst. 1,21,12 (CSEL 19, 80): *aut quid in profanis locis faciant qui inter aras deorum summa scelera committunt ?* Already Orig. c. Cels. 8,21 (SC 150, 220) knows that the pagans speak of "holy (animal) sacrifices".
185 Lact. mort. pers. 15,7 (CSEL 27, 189): *Nam Constantius […] conventicula id est parietes […] dirui passus est, verum autem dei templum, quod est in hominibus, incolume servavit.* So Lactan-

tius distinguishes between the temple of God made of walls that *surrounds* the people and the true temple of God that is *in* the people.
186 Voelkl 1954, 121; Mohrmann 1962, 169–173. Cf. de Blaauw 2008, 263.
187 Cf. Sotinel 2010c, 4f.
188 Sternberg 2003, 39f., borrowed from Kopp 2011, 21f.
189 Correctly Brandenburg 2013, 34.
190 See below p. 395f.
191 Constant. Aug. ep. ad Aelaf. (CSEL 26, 206): *debito cultu catholicae religionis.* Constant. Aug. ep. ad Cels. (CSEL 26, 212): *qualis divinitati cultus adhibendus sit. […] meritam omnipotenti deo culturam praesentare.* Ammian. Marc. 27,3,13 (Seyfarth 1986, 60): *in basilica Sicinini, ubi ritus Christiani est conventiculum.*

There is a different term that is more revealing about the sacred connotation of the Christian assembly room. From the mid–third century,[192] and increasingly in the following century, Christians began to speak of the *prayer house* or *house of prayer*.[193] Some see this as evidence of the profane character of the early church buildings since they consider prayer to be something profane. But this is wrong. For the Jerusalem Temple, a sacred space par excellence, is already a "house of prayer" for both the Old and the New Testament (Is 56:7). What Jesus is defending in his cleansing of the temple is precisely the sacred dignity of the place, which is to be a "house of prayer" and not a den of robbers (Mt 21:13). Pagans, too, see their temples as places of prayer,[194] as the Jews do their synagogues (cf. Acts 16:13, 16).[195] The service of chanting of the Torah celebrated there – the cult of the Logos – is the highest form of the presence of God in the world after the destruction of the Jerusalem Temple,[196] so certainly not a profane thing.[197] In Islam the place of ritual prayer, the mosque, is a holy place.

The earliest literary evidence of the Christian "house of prayer" (τὸ εὐκτήριον) is found in the mid–third century in Gregory Thaumaturgus, who in the same breath calls this house of prayer a "temple" (ὁ ναός).[198] Although Christians distinguish their prayer from that of the pagans, which is addressed to the false gods, every prayer is and

192 Commod. instr. 2,31[35] (CCL 128, 68): *Et, de domo Dei ceu nundinas facitis, astent. / Terruit hinc Dominus: Domus orationis adesto!*

193 Didasc. syr. 12 (ACHELIS / FLEMMING 1904, 68) speaks of the "house (of the Lord)" and ibid. 6 (27) quotes Mt 21:13 ("house of prayer"); on the sacred space in the Didascalia see STEWART 2015, 102–108. Ps.-Cypr. sing. cler. 13 (CSEL 3,3, 187): *ergo nec ad domum orationis debemus pariter convenire, ne aliquis aliquem scandalizet?* Act. purg. Fel. (CSEL 26, 199): *ad locum, ubi orationes celebrare consueti fuerant.* Cf. DUVAL 2000, 364–368; further evidence: Basil. ep. 94 (PG 32, 488B); 164,2 (637A); 243,2 (905B); hom. 18,2 (PG 31, 496A); Joh. Chrys. in act. apost. hom. 9,6 (PG 60, 83); Aug. ep. 22,3 (CSEL 34, 57); Sozom. hist. eccl. 2,3,8 (SC 306, 240); 5,9,9 (SC 495, 132); 5,20,7 (206). Rufin. hist. eccl. 2,10 (GCS Euseb. 2,2, 1018): orationum loca; Zen. Ver. tract. 2,6,6,11 (CCL 22, 170): *sacrae orationis iste locus novus.* It was thought that the "houses of prayer" merely denoted the small assembly halls of the third century in comparison to the large "churches" of the Constantinian era. But this is wrong for the simple reason that the enormous church buildings of the fourth centuries are still called "prayer houses." So the term "house of prayer" has nothing to do with

either a specific (hall) architecture or with the dimension of the church interior, but only with its functional definition: "a house of prayer." It is clear that the third century churches were smaller than those of the fourth. But both are called alternately "house of prayer" and "church". Erroneously DE BLAAUW 2008, 262 and JUDGE 2008, 428 invoking Euseb. hist. eccl. 8,1,5 (SC 55, 4) (text see above p. 125 n. 338). There Eusebius speaks of the fact that before the great persecution thousands were already gathering in the prayer houses, meaning that these rooms were already enormous. The new, large "churches" he also immediately afterwards calls "prayer houses"; hist. eccl. 8,2,1 (SC 55, 6). Not even the prayer houses of the heretics are necessarily smaller; cf. Euseb. vit. const. 3,65,3 (SC 559, 452).

194 Porphyr. adv. Christ. frgm. 76 (HARNACK 1916, 93).

195 STAMBAUGH 1978, 600.

196 L. BOUYER, Liturgie und Architektur (Einsiedeln 1993) 25–28; HEID 2001, 52–59.

197 MESSNER 2003a, 350 n. 63.

198 Greg. Thaum. ep. canonica, can. 11 (PG 10, 1048AB): τὸ εὐκτήριον. Dazu YASIN 2009, 37 n. 75.

remains a sacred act. For example, Christians and pagans alike perform the prayer for the emperor (at their sacrifices).[199] Furthermore, for the Christians the eucharistic sacrifice is a prayer,[200] even prayer par excellence (Gk. [προσ-]εὐχή,[201] Lat. *prex*,[202] *oratio*[203]). So everything points to the fact that an anti-cultic meaning is the very thing that must not be imputed to the concept of prayer. Christian cult is certainly spiritual: it is prayer, sacrifice of praise, etc. But the reverse is also true: this prayer is true and real cult!

If to this we then add the manner in which the prayer of the Christians actually takes place, namely in community, and not in just any house church but rather in the one meeting place of a city shared by them all, then it soon becomes clear that, on account of the prayer, this space becomes the place where God's presence can be and is experienced. All we need to do is take up what has already been said about the sacrality of the assembly room as a place of remembrance of God's holy presence.[204] The building is so strongly identified with the prayer performed in it that it is called a house of prayer – and this not in a neutral sense, as if people gathered there in exactly the same way to pray as they would to eat or do anything else.

On the contrary, the Christians are deeply convinced that their communal prayer guarantees the presence of God. The term "house of prayer" promises the sacrality and holiness that can only be reliably found in the place where Christians gather steadfastly for prayer. For, unlike in the temples of the pagans, whose gods see no one and hear no one, here is a God who answers prayers. The holiness of the Christian worship space is grounded in God, i.e. it is based on the conviction of the believers that they experience God's faithful presence here, not only from time to time during prayer, but permanently, reliably.

Since Ignatius of Antioch, the Christians' meeting place with its altar has been regarded as a space for communal prayer. Clement of Alexandria considers prayer at the altar to be the best and holiest sacrifice.[205] He and Origen see the advantage of the church space in the fact that the success of prayer is potentiated by the number of those, both visible and invisible, praying there.[206] In the same way, Athanasius says that the fact that the entire community of the city of Alexandria gathers in one and the same church guarantees the immediate answering of their prayer because they all pray with one voice.[207]

---

199 Duval 2000, 368. Cf. Guyot / Klein 1993, 210–221.

200 For the identification of prayer and sacrifice in the Didache and in Justin see Klinghardt 1996, 403 f., 507.

201 In any case, "Eucharist" and "prayer" are inseparable: Ign. ad Smyr. 7,1 (SC 10³, 160) – cf. Wieland 1909, 51 f. – und Iustin. apol. 1, 13,1 (SC 507, 158); 65,3 (304); 66,2 (306); 67,5 (310); dial. 117,2 (Marcovich 1997, 271).

202 E.g. Innoc. ep. ad Decent. 5 (FC 58,2, 492).

203 E.g. OR IV,56 (Andrieu 1948, 164). Vgl. Opt. Mil. 6,1,1. 7 (SC 413, 164): *Illinc enim ad aures Dei ascendere populi solebat oratio.*

204 See above p. 186 f.

205 Clem. Alex. strom. 7,6,31,7 f (SC 428, 116–118). Text see above n. 62.

206 See above p. 195.

207 Athan. apol. ad Const. 16 (SC 56², 120).

This is confirmed by Eusebius of Caesarea, who frequently speaks of the "houses of prayer"[208] and at the same time, in his sermon for the dedication of the new Basilica of Tyre (c. 314–321), gives the perfect example[209] of an interpretation based on the sacred theology of the "holy temple of God".[210] There is no contradiction here. The community gathered for prayer in this "sanctuary"[211] and "house of God"[212] is the guarantor of sacrality because it is loved by God and can achieve everything through its prayers. It is with the common prayer of the holy, pure Church in view that the miracles recounted in the old covenant really happen.[213] The destroyed Church of Tyre, the "sanctuary of God" that had been profaned to the ground,[214] was rebuilt before their eyes, thus attesting to the quite locally concentrated power of God.[215] The consecrated oblations in the Temple also make manifest the irresistible power of God at work there.[216] In the same vein, Augustine can say that the faithful sought the purity and beauty of the church space in the conviction that God heard their prayers there.[217]

As an interim taking stock, the following can be noted: from the end of the second century, there were already premises that were exclusively or at least predominantly intended for worship.[218] Hugo Brandenburg is correct in saying that from the early third century on the meeting place of the Christians possessed a sacred dignity.[219] Only a superficial approach regards the variety of terms used for the Christian assembly room – sometimes house of God[220] sometimes church (from the third century), sometimes basilica (from the fourth century) – as proof of its being understood as a profane space. In any case, "house of God" and "house of prayer" both have an eminently sacred connotation. On the one hand, the syntagma "house of God" expresses its character as a place where God's presence and holiness are remembered: God dwells in the "*house* of God" inasmuch as he shows himself reliably at work there when the faithful pray to him. On the other hand, there is an exclusiveness to it: the "house *of God*" belongs to God and

---

208 Euseb. hist. eccl. 10,4,14 (SC 55, 85); vit. Const. 1,53,2 (SC 559, 256); 3,43,3 (404) and more.; laud. Const. 17,3 (GCS Euseb. 1, 254). BARTELINK 1971.

209 It is intended as a model sermon. Its full title is: "Panegyric upon the building of the churches, addressed to Paulinus, Bishop of Tyre"; Euseb. hist. eccl. 10,4,1 (SC 55, 81).

210 Euseb. hist. eccl. 10,4,2 (SC 55, 81). Euseb. laud. Const. 17,3 (GCS Euseb. 1, 254) calls the churches "holy temples". Cf. DEICHMANN 1964, 58.

211 Euseb. hist. eccl. 10,4,66 (SC 55, 102).

212 Ibid. 10,4,2 (SC 55, 82). According to theoph. syr. 3,20 (GCS Euseb. 3,2², 135) the churches are also called "house of the Lord".

213 Euseb. hist. eccl. 10,4,54 (SC 55, 98 f.).

214 Ibid. 10,4,33 (SC 55, 91).

215 Ibid. 10,4,5 f (SC 55, 82).

216 Ibid. 10,4,20 (SC 55, 87).

217 Aug. enn. 33,2,8 (CCL 38, 287): *Oremus hic, dicis; et delectat te compositio loci, et credis quod ibi te exaudiat Deus.* On church furnishings see ROETZER 1930, 75–83.

218 BRANDENBURG 2013, 11.

219 Ibid. 12.

220 The beginning of this usage certainly does not lie in the fourth or fifth century, a time when it was extremely widespread; SOTINEL 2010b.

may therefore only serve the worshipping assembly. Here, using the term "house of God" for the building in which the worshippers gather does not mark the beginning of a sacralization, but instead merely manifests a process that began earlier, in principle as soon as the Christians began to gather in the same place to pray around the altar.

3. OFFERTORY TABLE FOR THE SACRIFICE

The sacred centre of every church space is the altar. What does it look like and what is it for? The Church Fathers speak either of the "table" or the "altar" irrespective of its concrete form. The same author calls an altar sometimes a table, sometimes an altar.[221] Neither term implies an opposition between meal table and sacrificial table; rather, they both designate the same object in the same way, namely the Christian sacred table (above chapter II).

All the same, it might not be a coincidence that its archaeological distribution as well as the patristic, especially Byzantine, sources indicate that the *table altar* (*mensa altar*) was the primary altar type and for a long time the dominant one. It is always a medium-sized, rectangular table on four solid legs. Often the legs are sunk into holes in a base plate to prevent it from moving. The altar always comes up to about belly height, which means that you stand and not sit at it. The oldest images of altars dating from the sixth century onwards depict tables of this precise kind, almost always covered by an altar cloth with a deep drop (below Figs. 26, 42, differently Fig. 50). Although the table is not recognizable as such and, with its massive side covers, can take on the form of a box-shaped altar (below Fig. 152),[222] it is still widely referred to as a table. This form of altar is also encountered in literature; for example, when someone is said to cling to the pillars of the altar seeking protection[223] or to seek asylum under the "holy table".[224]

---

221 BRAUN 1924a, 26. E.g. Aug. serm. 227 (SC 116, 234): *mensa dominica* und *altare*. Serm. 229A,3 (PLS 2, 555): *mensa domini* und *altare dei*. Ambr. myst. 8,43 (SC 25², 180): *sacrosanctum altare* und *mensa*. Joh. Chrys. in Eph. hom. 3,4f. (PG 62, 29): θυσιαστήριον und τράπεζα. Greg. Naz. or. 18,10 (PG 35, 996C). Further examples VAN DE PAVERD 1970, 52f.

222 Sozom. hist. eccl. 9,1,4 (SC 516, 372) speaks of an altar table with an inscription mounted on the front of it. This can doubtlessly be assumed to be a box-shaped altar with an inner structure that probably still resembles a table.

223 Synes. catast. (PG 66, 1573B): "I shall cling fast to the sacred pillars which hold up the consecrated table from the ground. There will I stand while I live, and sink down when I am dead. I am a priest of God, and perhaps he will demand the sacrifice of my life. God will certainly look graciously upon that unbloody altar reddened with the blood of the priest." Translated from the German version in O. BARDENHEWER, Geschichte der altkirchlichen Literatur 4 (Freiburg i.Br. 1924) 112. On the asylum of the altar see DÖLGER 1930, 170.

224 Sozom. hist. eccl. 8,7,4 (SC 516, 268). Cf. Socr. hist. eccl. 1,37,7 (SC 477, 254).

It would be misleading to claim that the Christian table altar is derived from the ancient dining- room table.[225] Early Christian art contains numerous depictions of meal scenes with dining tables, but without any recognisable reference to the celebration of the Eucharist or any resemblance of the tables to altars (below chapter VI, 1). Nor does the table altar belong in the tradition of the ancient altar of burnt offerings or blood sacrifices.[226] Here, too, although early Christian art does portray sacrificial altars, this is only when recalling biblical scenes such as Abraham preparing to sacrifice his son Isaac (Fig. 20).[227] The only plausible connection to be found for the Christian table altar in the history of religion is one to the sacred table of antiquity.[228] The Christians chose the sacred table because in the religious context of the time it was the customary piece of furniture used for a meal offering. Its primary function was to be simultaneously somewhere to place the offerings and a sacrificial table.

Besides the table altar form, there is also the *stipes* altar (Fig. 21) in which the mensa rests on a central support (masonry or monolith).[229] It is found in Italy, North Africa, southern Spain, southern Gaul and northern Jordan. If the oratory at Megiddo near Nazareth really does date back to the third century (before 230 or after 250), it would show the oldest (partially) preserved altar to be of this type with a masonry *stipes* (above Figs. 8, 18). What is left of it consists of blocks of stone with the mensa slab missing[230] and is called a "table" (τράπεζα) in the mosaic inscription belonging to it.[231]

Finally, there is the *box-shaped altar* (Kastenaltar). In this case, the altar slab rests on four corner feet, but these are connected with decorated side panels. This structure is mounted on a predella, thus creating a cavity. This category includes altars with a viewing aperture (*fenestella confessionis*) at the front if the altar contains relics (Fig. 22; below Fig. 74). This is referred to as a small *confessio* or altar-*confessio* (in contrast to the large *confessio* underneath the altar). The interior of the altar is hollow and contains relics either in the cavity itself or underneath it. The small door at the front allows access to the inside of the altar. In connection with the box-shaped altar, Yumi Narasawa also refers to an antependium altar in which the front stands out artistically from the other sides.[232] The box-shaped altar is mainly found in northern Italy and the northern Adriatic.[233]

---

225 CHEVALIER 1996, 135: "C'est pourtant paradoxalement la plupart du temps une table simple, […] héritière directe des tables de salle à manger antiques."

226 Their form varies greatly. REISCH 1894, 1669–1677.

227 LADERMAN 2014.

228 GOUDINEAU 1967; ThesCRA 5, 230–240.

229 BRAUN 1924a, 125–240; WIELAND 1912, 43–73; KIRSCH / KLAUSER 1950, 337–341. All three altar types also in NARASAWA 2015; DE BLAAUW 2017, 44. The traditional altar typography can in the

meantime be better determined chronologically and topographically on the basis of archaeological findings. SASTRE DE DIEGO 2013 defines six types of altars.

230 This type of construction does not indicate the base of a pillar but rather an altar; ADAMS 2013, 97; SHALEV-HURVITZ 2015, 29 f.; cf. REISCH 1894, 1672. Differently RIESNER 2007, 168 f.

231 TEPPER / DI SEGNI 2006.

232 NARASAWA 2015.

233 DUVAL 2005, 13.

Fig. 20: Ivory pyxis depicting the Sacrifice of Abraham (Gn 22): Abraham is about to slay his son Isaac with a sword in order then to carry him up the steps to the round altar and sacrifice him on it, c.400; Skulpturensammlung und Museum für Byzantinische Kunst, Staatliche Museen zu Berlin, inv. 563; photo: Jürgen Liepe 1992

No matter which of the three altar types it is, the altar, with its almost-always rectangular mensa stands crosswise in the church space. The fact that the altar slab is wider than it is deep probably has something to do with the need for not only the priest, but also the assistants (deacons) to stand at it.[234] The *mensae* present a smooth surface of by no means striking dimensions (up to approx. 1.20 × 0.80 m).[235] This may be why the surface is often sunken or has a raised edge.[236] Even though this may be a decorative

234 Orig. in Iud. hom. 3,2 (GCS 7, 481,23–25).
235 Duval 2005, 13 for North Africa. Cf. Metzger 1971, 143–145. Narasawa 2015, 464–470 (table with 425 different *mensae*): the length varies from roughly 1.00 to 1.60 m. Duval 2005, 13: the altar slab is (as a general average) c. 1.00–1.20 m wide and 0.70–0.80 m deep. The altar is 1.00–1.10 m high. On the size of the mensa see also Braun 1924a, 249–259.
236 Braun 1924a, 259–279.

Fig. 21: Reconstructed stipes altar (foot modern) with slab (mensa) from the 5ᵗʰ century, Marseille, Abbey of St Victor; M. Kroker / W. Walter (eds.), *Credo* 1 (Petersberg 2013) 68 Fig. 10.

element,[237] its practical usefulness cannot be denied. For if a large number of gifts are to be placed on the altar,[238] the raised edge prevents them from falling off.[239] An altar slab never rests completely flat on its base, so the rim can prevent the gifts from rolling off[240] (Fig. 23).[241]

237 Ibid. 276 f.
238 According to Weckwerth 1963, the texts distinguish between oblation tables (*altaria*) on which the gifts of the faithful are placed and the actual celebration altar (mensa). If this were correct, the gifts of the faithful would never have been collected at the main altar but only ever at side altars.
239 Cf. Reisch 1894, 1661. Differently Kirsch / Klauser 1950, 350. Altars with a sunken mensa see Braun 1924a, 259–279; Orlandos 1954, 444–454; J. Sirat et al., Recueil général des monuments sculptés en France pendant le Haut Moyen Age (IVᵉ–Xᵉ siècles) 3. Val-d'Oise et Yvelines (Paris 1984), Pl. LIV, Fig. 264 (Altar from Saint-Marcel-de-Crussol). Evidence of such *mensae* can be found particularly frequently in Gaul,

where they do not disappear in favour of the flat surface until the thirteenth century; Narasawa 2015, 451–470.
240 Kirsch / Klauser 1950, 343; Nussbaum 1961a, 112; Jeličić-Radonić 2005. Greg. I reg. past. 3,9 (SC 382, 298) interprets the rim round the altar in Ezek 43:13 as the soul, which lays down many good oblations before God's eyes. Slabs with raised edges served on tomb altars as places to put food for the dead (e.g. Fiocchi Nicolai 1998, 46 Fig. 49: Mensa in the Praetextatus catacomb) or as tabletops for reclining meals. In both cases, they were intended to prevent the food from falling off.
241 Apart from the sacrificial offerings, the altar could also – like the sacred table of antiquity (above Fig. 4, below Fig. 24) – serve as a place to put the

Fig. 22: Drawing of the box-shaped altar of *San Giovanni Evangelista* in Ravenna with a small *confessio* or aperture (*fenestella confessionis*) on the front for relics, 5th century; C. Rohault de Fleury, La messe. Études archéologiques sur ses monuments 1 (Paris 1883), Plate XXXIII.

The details of what gifts were placed on the altar when and by whom is difficult to establish. Regional and seasonal differences in customs are to be expected, for example, in the case of first fruits, depending as they do on the harvest. In addition to bread and wine, there is a tendency towards a greater variety of fruits. Money is not excluded either.[242] High feasts are marked by special customs. In Syria, for example, it seems that, in addition to bread and wine, milk, honey and water were also blessed on the altar at the Easter Vigil: the offerings of the newly baptised.[243] In the course of the fourth century, attempts were made to regulate practices that were getting out of hand.[244] In any event, it is hardly possible to make such an apodictic statement as Theodor Klausner's: "Throughout antiquity, the altar served only as a eucharistic sacrificial table; only the elements of the Eucharist together with the vessels for it (chalice and paten) were placed

cultic instruments down on. Accordingly, in the Christian Middle Ages the sacramentary can be laid on the altar (below Fig. 152) if it is not held up for the bishop by a cleric (BnF, Ms. lat. 9428, fol. 46v; below Figs. 91, 92).

242   Ps.-Cypr. aleat. 11 (CSEL 3,3, 103): *pecuniam tuam* [...] *super mensam dominicam sparge.*
243   Trad. Apost. 21 (FC 1, 266–268).
244   Rouwhorst 2015.

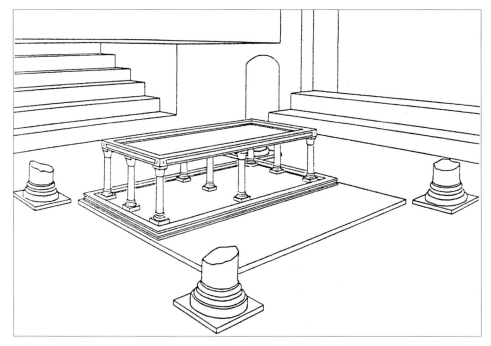

Fig. 23: Reconstruction of the main altar of Basilica B at Nikopolis. The priest stands on the podium in front of the altar and looks east towards the apse; Chevalier 2005, 70 Fig. 7.

on it, as well as the Gospel book and probably also the *libellus* containing the liturgical texts; other objects were not tolerated on the altar."[245]

Needless to say, at all times the altar serves primarily as the place where the bread and wine used in the eucharistic rite are set down. This alone requires a good deal of space in order to accommodate the leavened loaves and several chalices.[246] The gifts offered are so generous that the faithful can take a portion of them home with them, and some of the food can be taken to those who are not present.[247] In addition, items are donated for the poor and for other church concerns. Since for them love of God and love of neighbour are inseparably linked, the Christians, as it were, accord the collection the dignity of worship.[248] It is possible that the charitable gifts are also placed on the altar. The widows who are supported by the community are, in fact, identified with the altar:[249] it is as if the Christians place calves, tithes and voluntary donations

245 Kirsch / Klauser 1950, 350.
246 On the chalices see Trad. Apost. 21 (FC 1, 268).
247 Stuiber 2001, 520 f.

248 Care for the poor in worship: Heb 13:15 f.; Iustin. apol. 1, 13,1 f. (SC 507, 158–160) and 1, 67,6 (310).
249 Polyc. ad Phil. 4,3 (SC 10³, 208).

on them as the living altar of God.[250] Even the formulation that the clergy live from the altar (cf. 1 Cor 9:13)[251] could originate from the faithful offering their gifts for the upkeep of the clergy at the altar.

The visible placing of gifts on the altar is a public legal act according to sacred law: in front of witnesses, they are thus transferred to God and turned irrevocably into sacrificial offerings (cf. Mk 7:11; Mt 23:18–20).[252] Origen says that those who take a vow to offer fruit and wine to the Church or to the poor and to strangers but then take some of this for themselves violate God's holy thing.[253] The point here is that what is laid on the altar no longer belongs to the giver, but rather to the altar and sanctuary.[254] The "altar of God"[255] is not only a place where the eucharistic offerings are consecrated, but also the place that betokens God's exclusive claim to ownership. For this reason, the gifts of the faithful lying on the altar alongside the eucharistic gifts can also be called votive offerings (*vota*).[256]

Similarly, when the sacrificial offerings are placed on the altar, the idea of sanctifying them through contact with the altar might have a role to play.[257] The intention is for the gifts to share in the sacrality of the transubstantiation of bread and wine, so they should be as close as possible to the sacred Body and Blood of Christ. This, so to speak, applies the rule "*ad sancta*" analogously to burials "*ad sanctos*". The pious gifts are to be introduced into the epicentre of the fulness of spiritual power. This may be the reason why in the Roman Canon the priest asks God to accept the *dona, munera, sancta sacrificia illibata*. It can be understood additively: all the gifts, not just bread and wine, are to share in the priest's power.[258] Conversely, ecclesiastical regulations in Syria and North Africa

---

250 Method. symp. 5,8,130 (SC 95, 160).

251 Cypr. ep. 65,3 (CSEL 3,2, 724); Ps.-Cypr. sing. cler. 38 (CSEL 3,3, 213 f.); Euseb. comm. in Is. 23,18 (GCS Euseb. 9, 152 f.); Greg. Naz. or. 2,8 (SC 247, 98); Joh. Chrys. in 1 Cor. hom. 22,1 (PG 61, 181); 43,1 (PG 61, 369); Aster. hom. 8,31 (DATEMA 1970, 104); Hieron. ep. 52,5,2 (CSEL 54, 422); Max. Taur. serm. 26,4 (CCL 23, 103).

252 In the Jewish tradition, sacrificial offerings were deposited in front of the altar: Lv 6:7; Nm 7:10; Mt 5:24. It is unclear to what extent the deposition of votive offerings or gifts was associated with the altar of the respective deity in antiquity. Cf. Thes-CRA 1, 327–450.

253 Orig. in Lev. hom. 11,1 (SC 287, 148): *volo tantum offerre Ecclesiae vel in usum pauperum aut peregrinorum tantum praebere; sie postea ex eo modo, quem vovit, aliquid ad usus proprios praesumat, iam non de suis fructibus praesumpsit, sed sancta Dei violavit.*

254 Joh. Chrys. in 1 Cor. hom. 22,1 (PG 61, 181).

255 Polyc. ad Phil. 4,3 (SC 10³, 208): θυσιαστήριον θεοῦ; Actus Petri cum Simone 2 (LIPSIUS / BONNET 1891, 46): *altarium dei*; Cypr. ep. 62,2 (CSEL 3,2, 696): *altare dei*; Method. symp. 5,8,130 (SC 95, 160): βωμὸς θεοῦ. Cf. Past. Herm. 42,2 (SC 53², 190); Orig. in Iud. hom. 3,2 (SC 389, 100).

256 Opt. Mil. 6,1,1 (SC 413, 160): *altaria Dei [...], in quibus et vota populi et membra Christi portata sunt.*

257 The consecrated altar is sacrosanct; everyone who touches it becomes holy in the sense that he now belongs to the sanctuary (Ex 29:37; 40:10).

258 The bread and wine of the faithful that had been on the altar but had not been consecrated for Communion were thus something very special and treated accordingly: Theophil. Alex. can. 7 (PG 65, 41AB). In Egypt, only bread and wine were permitted on the altar, albeit in large quantities.

condemn it when priests fail to make any distinction and use the Eucharistic Prayer of Blessing over all the natural gifts on the altar instead of blessing the latter individually.[259] Accordingly, there are special prayers of blessing. They vary according to the gift but are all called "eucharist".[260] The formulae for such exceptional blessings have been preserved in the Roman Rite, for example for the blessing of the palms on Palm Sunday. They largely follow the Order of the Mass, except that at the high altar special prayers of blessing are said instead of the Canon Romanus.[261]

A statement by Cyprian of Carthage († 258) is particularly revealing. He speaks of the compelling need for an altar in order to sanctify the baptismal oil[262] because a blessing can only take place on the altar. The act of blessing is again called "eucharist". *Eucharistía*, like the other Greek word *eu-logía*, not only means thanksgiving, but also denotes the blessing, i.e. the prayer of benediction. For purely practical reasons, the altar is needed to put the oblations on since the priest spreads out his hands for the blessing and is therefore unable to hold them. The church order of the *Traditio Apostolica* has diverse "eucharists", namely over the oblations of bread and wine,[263] over the oil offered (by one of the faithful),[264] over the cheese with olives offered (by one of the faithful),[265] over the baptismal oil[266] and over milk with honey at the baptismal Eucharist.[267] Even if the church order does not mention an altar, the bishop[268] will certainly be standing at one[269] when – presumably within the celebration of the Eucharist and after the oblation of bread and wine[270] – he lays his hands on the other gifts or spreads them over them.[271] The altar as such has long since been a sacrosanct object, requiring sacred acts to be performed at it and not in some less holy place.

The texts from the third and fourth centuries do not, however, provide a clear picture of the extent to which the blessing of natural gifts takes place within a celebration of the

259 Trad. Apost. 5 f. (FC 1, 228); Const. Apost. 47,2 f. (FUNK 1905, 564); Conc. Hipp. a. 393, can. 23 (CCL 149, 40). On the *Concilium Quinisextum* can. 28 see ROUWHORST 2015, 70.

260 DÖLGER 1930, 187.

261 For example, at the blessing of the palms to be found in every missal prior to the reform of the liturgy for Holy Week and Easter under Pius XII.

262 Cypr. ep. 70,2 (CSEL 3,2, 768). Text see above p. 116 n. 265.

263 Trad. Apost. 4 (FC 1, 222). This speaks of thanksgiving.

264 Ibid. 5 (FC 1, 228). This speaks of thanksgiving.

265 Ibid. 6 (FC 1, 228). This speaks of *benedictio*.

266 Ibid. 21 (FC 1, 258). This speaks of thanksgiving.

267 Ibid. 21 (FC 1, 266). This speaks of thanksgiving.

268 The bishop is per se the one who offers up the gifts of the faithful (on the altar); ibid. 3 (FC 1, 218).

269 Perhaps not, however, for the blessing of the baptismal oil, which might have taken place in the baptistery; ibid. 21 (FC 1, 258).

270 ROUWHORST 2015, 62–64. This is the case for the blessing of oil, cheese and olives. For the blessing of gifts within the eucharistic celebration see also Can. Hippol. arab. 3 (PO 31, 354).

271 Trad. Apost. 4 (FC 1, 222). It is expressly stated that the blessing of the oil takes place in the same manner as the oblation of bread and wine: ibid. 5 (228). The eucharist should be spoken *super oleum, super panem et calicem*: ibid. 21 (258. 266).

Eucharist. For example, in the *Traditio*, the first fruits are handed to the bishop, who offers them to God and blesses them using a prayer of thanksgiving, but this is apparently not done during a celebration of the Eucharist.[272] It is possible that various "eucharists", i.e. blessings, are performed outside the celebration of mass, but nevertheless at the altar. In any case, acceptance as a sacrificial offering of the Church will have demanded a certain formality. The fact that deacons in Gaul "offer" (*offere*) – which is forbidden them[273] – is occasionally applied to the celebration of the Eucharist as if deacons presided at mass.[274] This is erroneous. "Sacrificing" applies to any form at all of sacrificial offerings by the faithful. It is possible that deacons accept them outside the eucharistic celebration,[275] but with a formal oblation or blessing at the altar.[276] This is now forbidden them. Other regions of the Church are more generous. In the Canons of Hippolytus, written in Egypt in the middle of the fourth century, it says: "If anyone wishes to make a sacrifice while no presbyter is present in the church, the deacon should always take his place, with the sole exception of the offering of the great (i.e. eucharistic) sacrifice and prayer."[277] This, so to speak, small oblation by the deacon seems nevertheless to have taken place at the altar. Similarly, the priest receives the first fruits of the faithful in the church in front of the curtain, but the bishop speaks the blessing[278] inside the presbytery, i.e. at the altar, with the gifts likely to be lying on the altar.

It is possible that in some churches the natural gifts of the faithful are placed on tables next to the altar, whereas bread and wine are brought to the main altar. Separate oblation or gift tables are undoubtedly found in the early Church,[279] although archaeological evidence is difficult to establish. Such tables will have been found in the chancel, in the side aisles and in niches or side chapels. But the transition to genuine side altars or tables, which in the Byzantine Rite are used for the prothesis, is fluid. In Rome, Emperor Constantine has seven side altars erected in the Lateran Basilica (above Fig. 16). These

272 Trad. Apost. 31 f. (FC 1, 284–288); ROUWHORST 2015, 59 f., 64 f.

273 Conc. Arel. a. 314, can. 16 (CCL 148, 12): *De diaconibus quos cognovimus multis locis offerre, placuit minime fieri debere.*

274 R. BARCELLONA / M. SPINELLI (eds.), I canoni dei concili della chiesa antica 2,2,1 (Rome 2010) 41.

275 Cf. Did. 10 (FC 1, 240): *Non autem imponetur manus super eam, quia non offert oblationem neque habet liturgiam.* This is said about the widows. Here the oblation seems to be conceivable outside the Eucharist, too: see NICKL 1930, 42 f.

276 Cf. Trad. Apost. 4 (FC 1, 220): *Illi (sc. episcopo) vero offerant diacones oblationes.* Ibid. 8 (236):

diaconus sit in tua ecclesia et offerat in sancto sanctorum tuo quod tibi offertur a constituto principe sacerdotum tuo. Cf. Didasc. syr. 9 (ACHELIS / FLEMMING 1904, 45). On the deacons' sacrificing see also LIETZMANN 1926, 182–186.

277 Can. Hippol. arab. 32 (RIEDEL 1900, 220 f. [PO 31, 404]). The term "great sacrifice" for the Eucharist performed at the "table" (Greg. Naz. carm. de seipso 79 [PG 37, 1260A]) presupposes small sacrifices, which are perhaps not performed at the altar.

278 Can. Hippol. arab. 36 (PO 31, 408–410). See RIEDEL 1900, 223 n. 4.

279 NUSSBAUM 1961a, 112.

are doubtlessly intended for the gifts of the faithful from the seven church regions of the city.[280] These additional places to set things down on are needed because in principle all the faithful of the city participate in the episcopal liturgy, which means that in Rome an incomparably large number of gifts arrive due to the sheer number of the faithful; in addition, the main altar already has to accommodate numerous loaves of bread and chalices for Communion. Interestingly, these are referred to as "altars" (*altaria*).[281] They are probably located to the right and left of the main altar, thus sharing its sacrality.[282] Their holiness is indicated by a candelabra on each of them.[283] Positioning the altars at which the seven regional deacons probably received the gifts in such a way that they are visible to all has the ancillary effect of leading the different parts of the city to compete for the fullest table.[284] The faithful got to their tables at the end of the side aisles. This creates an interesting parallel to the pagan *Basilica sotterranea* at *Porta Maggiore* in Rome, where sacred tables are likewise to be seen as stucco reliefs at the front end of the "side aisles" (Fig. 24).

Given the significance of the faithful going up to present their offerings, it is surprising that there is no depiction of an altar overflowing with offerings in early Christian art. Nevertheless, an illustration is found in the Ashburnham Pentateuch, a Vulgate dating from the sixth or seventh century and probably written in Africa.[285] It shows the construction and consecration of the Old Testament tabernacle by Moses (Ex 35 – 40). After he has built an altar with stones, he offers the full sacrifices and reads out the tablets of the covenant to the people. Priests dressed in white place numerous offerings, especially large round loaves, on the altar, which has several steps leading up to it (Fig. 25). The "laity" present – aristocrats with the lowly folk behind them – are not bearing gifts but rather listening to Moses. The representation shows a certain *interpretatio christiana* of the Old Testament events portrayed:[286] the layout of the picture suggests two-phase worship, the celebration of the word and the celebration of the sacrifice. In the middle

280 Joh. Diac. ep. ad Senar. 11. 13 (WILMART 1933, 177, 178). Cf. JUNGMANN 1952b, 11; RIGHETTI 1966, 311 n. 17.

281 LP 34,10 (DUCHESNE 1886, 172): *altaria VII ex argento purissimo.*

282 The *Sacramentarium Veronense* likes to use the term "table" (*mensa*) for the main altar; WECKWERTH 1963, 215 – 217. This is, of course, a convention of liturgical language. "Altar" and "table" are always used synonymously.

283 LP 34,11 (DUCHESNE 1886, 173).

284 Sacr. Veron. 1261 (MOHLBERG 1994): the faithful "gather joyfully at the venerable altars with their gifts." Ibid. 238, 1165 and Sacr. Greg. 575 (DESHUSSES 1971): *Tua, domine, muneribus altaria*

comulamus [!] and similar. The story of the raising of the bones of St Wulfram in the Abbey of Fontanelle (Saint-Wandrille de Fontenelle) in the year 772 urges the monks to pile the divine altar with the due votive offerings (Acta Inventionis 2 [ActaSS March 3, 148A]): *divinum altare congruis votorum donariis cumulemus.* Still in the High Middle Ages (votive) offerings are laid on the altar for the Offertory: ActaSS April 3, 339B. 872E; June 4, 309D.

285 On the codex see K. GAMBER, *Codices liturgici latini antiquiores* 1 (Fribourg ²1968) 33 – 35. Cf. SCHUBERT 1992, 235 – 260.

286 ZIMMERMANN 2010, 1125.

Fig. 24: Top end of the right-hand aisle of the underground basilica at the *Porta Maggiore* in Rome with a stucco image of a sacred table; C. Mocchegiani Carpano *et al.*, Unter den Strassen von Rom (Freiburg i.Br. 1985) 86.

of the altar, a large chalice is to be seen, together with two fairly large vessels and five round loaves. The artist may well have had the Offertory at a Eucharist in mind here.[287]

An offertory procession of all the faithful, or at least a few representatives of them, is known in all liturgical families as a separate liturgical act in the celebration of mass and was common practice at least until the Middle Ages.[288] There are two types to be distinguished: those of the West and of the East.

287 The idea of an *interpretatio christiana* is also supported on the same page by a portrayal beneath it of a table altar covered with a cloth with candles beside it. BnF, NAL 2334, fol. 76r.

288 Righetti 1966, 299–305.

Fig. 25: Sacrificial scene (*Hic ubi offerent olocausta*) from the Book of Exodus in the Ashburnham Pentateuch, 6th/7th century, BnF, NAL 2334, fol. 76r; Wikimedia Commons.

In the first basic type the faithful bring their gifts – bread and wine – to the altar before the Eucharistic Prayer.[289] This is the case in northern Italy (Milan). In Ravenna, the altar is filled with offerings like a pantry.[290] In North Africa, the faithful bring their offerings (*oblatio*) to the church when they wish to communicate.[291] Besides bread and wine, they also bring votive offerings (*vota*) to the altar.[292] The Synod in Hippo (in 393) restricted such additional gifts to milk and honey in the baptismal Mass at Easter and otherwise to grapes and cereals.[293]

Rome belongs to the same basic type. The Roman prayer formulae use a variety of terms to refer to the gifts (*munera*/more rarely *dona*), oblations (*oblationes*) and votive offerings (*vota*) of the faithful that lie on the altar and which God is asked to accept.[294] The faithful, either themselves or through others, hand over the oblations to the deacon after the Liturgy of the Word.[295] There are, however, restrictions. Only beans and grapes are allowed to be blessed "*super altare*".[296] Such oblations do not necessarily have to take

---

289 ROUWHORST 2015, 65 f.

290 Petr. Chrys. serm. 103,7 (CCL 24A, 645): *Doleo, doleo, quando lego Christi cunabula magos rigasse auro, et video altare corporis Christi christianum vacuum reliquisse […]. Repleamus altare dei, ut nostra horrea repleat fructuum plenitudo.*

291 Cypr. op. et eleem. 15 (SC 440, 118): *quae in dominicum sine sacrificio venis, quae partem de sacrificio quod pauper obtulit sumis?* Opt. Mil. 6,1,1 (SC 413, 160): *altaria […], in quibus fraternitatis munera […] imponi.*

292 Opt. Mil. 6,1,1. 7 (SC 413, 160. 164): *altaria Dei, in quibus et vos aliquando obtulistis, […] in qui-*

bus et vota populi et membra Christi portata sunt […]. Illinc enim ad aures Dei ascendere populi solebat oratio.* JUNGMANN 1952b, 9.

293 Conc. Hipp. a. 393, can. 23 (CCL 149, 39 f.); KLAUSER 1974, 166; ROETZER 1930, 117.

294 RIGHETTI 1966, 368–382; KLAUSER 1974, 156 f.

295 Greg. I dial. 2,23,4 f (SC 260, 208).

296 LP 28,2 (DUCHESNE 1886, 159). Duchesne understands *super altare* with respect to the celebration of the Eucharist in the sense that only beans and grapes are permitted to be blessed during the Eucharist.

Fig. 26: Mass of Pope St Clement in the "lower church" of *San Clemente* in Rome, c. 1100; WILPERT 1917, Plate 240.

place during the celebration of mass. Altar oblations in any case exist outside mass in the Roman baptismal ceremonial.[297] In the fifth and sixth centuries, it is common for the faithful to make sacrificial offerings for liturgical use. For example, they offer wax for the Easter candle, on Maundy Thursday ingredients for the chrism and at Easter milk and honey.[298] Even though there is no pictorial evidence of candle oblations before the eighth century (Theodotos Chapel in Santa Maria Antiqua, Rome), they had certainly already been around for a long time. In San Clemente, the painting of the sponsors with the motif of the Mass of St Clement (c. 1100) shows candles being brought to the altar (Fig. 26). They are probably first placed on the altar so that they can be burned on the altar.[299]

Votive candles are first encountered at martyrs' graves.[300] The famous tomb mosaic *ECCLESIA MATER* from Thabraca/Tabarka (late fourth/early fifth century) probably

297 OR XI,32 f. (ANDRIEU 1948, 425): *Et offeruntur oblationes a parentibus* [...]. *Et ponat ipsas sacerdos super altare et dicit orationem secreto*
298 That is at least likely: KLAUSER 1974, 165 n. 7.
299 WILPERT 1917, Plate 241: Fresco in San Clemente,

c. 1100: Donor family with votive candles in their hands; above them, the altar of the shrine of St Clement in the Crimea with two votive candles burning on the altar.
300 See below n. 305.

Fig. 27: Mosaic on the tomb of Valentia from Thabraca with the *ECCLESIA MATER*, c. 400; BURNS / JENSEN 2014, Fig. 132.

does not depict an altar, as is often assumed,[301] but rather a martyr's grave with railings round it (Figs. 27 and 28).[302] Nor does it intend, in that case, to show a standard church, as if the altar had always stood in the centre of the church in North Africa,[303] but rather the church of a specific martyr whose more precise identity is unknown. Furthermore, the supposed altar is not in the middle of the church at all, but just one or at most two column positions in front of the apse.[304] However, within the composition of the picture the putative martyr's grave is indeed positioned in the middle as its sacred centre. This centre is additionally accentuated by the two birds below it, as it were lifting upwards their acclamation of the martyr's grave, and by the three candles at the grave. All this points to a martyr's grave. The deceased Valentia, on whose tomb the mosaic is located,

---

301 FREND 1996, 123; LANG 2003, 82 f.; JENSEN 2015, 105.

302 Recognised correctly by WIELAND 1912, 132. Dr Salomon (Cologne) sees three candles on the altar and a *fenestella confessionis* at the front of the altar, behind which a relic or the grave of a martyr is to be found; graves were often protected with railings; cf. GAIN 2001, 1020 (grave of Basil); DRESKEN-WEILAND 1998, No. 63 (sarcophagus with latticework relief). Privileged graves (martyrs' graves?) in the central nave of churches see MICHEL 2005, 98–100.

303 So ELLIGER 2004, 271.

304 Wrongly observed by BURNS / JENSEN 2014, 101.

305 The candles are certainly not standing on the supposed altar (so BURNS / JENSEN 2014, Fig. 133; JENSEN 2015, 105 Fig. 2) as the colour illustration shows (BURNS / JENSEN 2014, Fig. 132 = below Fig. 27). Candles next to a latticed martyr's grave (?) see the mosaic in the dome of the *Hagios Georgios* in Thessaloniki. Candles next to saints see the Proculus and Januarius fresco in the St Januarius catacomb in Naples (CRIPPA / ZIBAWI 1998, 223 Fig. 83; 229 Fig. 184). Lights in honour of the martyrs see LUCIUS 1904, 291 f. BRAUN 1932, 493 n. 5 considers the altar to be arbitrarily added. See

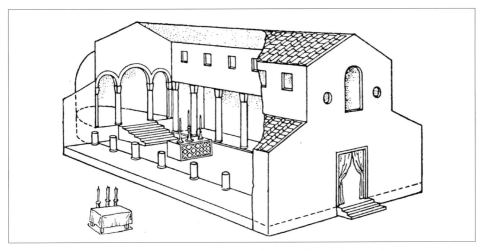

Fig. 28: Suggestive, but probably incorrect reconstruction of the church at Thabraca with an altar; PEETERS 1969, 278 Fig. 45.

hopes for the intercession of a particular saint or saints for whose tomb she has probably donated candles. The three candles stand behind, not on, the martyr's grave.[305] Numerous mosaic graves in North Africa prove that candles are put up for ordinary people who have died, too.[306] The votive candles later move from the martyrs' graves to the altars, probably because the latter contain martyrs' relics.[307] The candles customarily found on the altar today do not originate from bourgeois table decoration with a cloth, candles and flowers, but are devotional candles.[308]

In the second basic type of offering gifts, the faithful hand over their sacrifices to the deacons before the service. The latter collect them in a suitable place (Gk. *diakonikón, próthesis, pastophórion*, Lat. *sacrarium*) and bring only a portion of them to the altar after the end of the Liturgy of the Word. This type is common mainly in the East, but also in Gaul and perhaps in Spain,[309] although different customs are likely to exist. In Egypt

a photo of the mosaic on which the supposed altar is indeed missing: DE GRÜNEISEN 1911, 449 Fig. 357. Votive candles in the Demetrius cult in Thessaloniki (Pass. tertia s. Demetrii 7,61. 63 [PG 116, 1249B. 1252A]) as well as on Vatican devotional medals (GUIDOBALDI 2001, 182 Fig. 12).

306 CRIPPA / ZIBAWI 1998, 230 f.

307 In the two pictures of the donors in San Clemente the two candles stand only on the altar of Clement's burial church in the Crimea. However, the altar in the picture of the Mass of St Clement does

not itself have any candles on it even though there are candles being carried to the altar.

308 Such candles stood, for example, on the altar of the *Sancta Sanctorum* chapel in the Lateran; they burned day and night as votive candles of the fraternity for the highly venerated portrait of the Saviour there.

309 ROUWHORST 2015, 66–68; but see SMYTH 2003, 198. On Gaul: NICKL 1930, 37–44. Anon. de eccl. 101–105 (CSEL 16, 626): *onerantque altaria donis* […] *sic prior adgreditur mensas.*

at least, the faithful pile the altar high with gifts of bread and wine, only some of which are consecrated,[310] the rest being used to feed the poor.[311] The Syrian *Didascalia* (early third century) seems to be familiar with the placing of natural gifts – dues, tithes, first fruits – on the altar,[312] even if the usual offerings consist of bread (and wine) for the Eucharist.[313] In fourth-century Syria, honey, milk, vinegar, poultry, animals and vegetables are offered at the altar, but this encounters resistance, so the offerings are then limited to ears of grain, grapes, oil and incense.[314] John Chrysostom says that the table (of the altar) is full of a thousand goods, and from all sides abundant spiritual gifts flow to the faithful.[315] Although this is meant spiritually, it could be formulated with respect to the community's generous giving and an altar piled high with gifts. In Gaul, Caesarius of Arles asks the faithful to offer candles and oil as well.[316]

The altar is the primary place for the honouring of vows (*votum solvere/reddere*), not only in the Old Testament but for the Christians, too.[317] Already in antiquity, votive offerings are piled up on the altars.[318] The Christians do this in the context of the Eucharist, bringing to the altar what they have promised to God. Church leaders promote the practice of pious vows[319] and urge people to take the self-commitment associated with them seriously. For they are promising God that they will perform a particular service (a gift or donation) as soon as he has performed the hoped-for prior service (such as rescuing them from distress at sea). This is a religious legal act and both morally and ecclesially binding. The eucharistic celebration provides the space for this. Thus any kind of *oblatio altaris* can be a votive offering[320] given to either God or the Church. In the main these

310 Divine Liturgy of St Marc (BKV Griechische Liturgien [München 1912] 176); Ps.-Athan. in nativ. praec. 1 (PG 28, 908C); Theophil. Alex. can. 7 (PG 65, 41AB).

311 Leont. Neap. vit. Ioh. Eleem. 30 (Gelzer 1893, 63).

312 Didasc. syr. 9 (Achelis / Flemming 1904, 44–52). Schneider 1949, 49: "This means that the offertory procession of the faithful customary in Italy, Africa and Asia Minor is also attested for Syria." This Offertory was later replaced by the procession of the deacons (ibid. 51).

313 Didasc. syr. 11 (Achelis / Flemming 1904, 65); 12 (68).

314 Const. Apost. 47,2 f. (Funk 1905, 564); Jungmann 1952b, 14 f.; Klauser 1974, 166.

315 Joh. Chrys. cat. bapt. 2,4,27 (FC 6,1, 288).

316 Rouwhorst 2015, 69.

317 Earliest instance of vows at the Christian altar: 1 Clem. 41,2 (SC 167, 168); 52,3 (184): εὐχαί. Later

e.g. Opt. Mil. 6,1,7 (SC 413, 164): *Cur vota et desideria hominum cum ipsis altaribus confregistis? Illinc enim ad aures Dei ascendere populi solebat oratio.* Aug. ep. 149,16 (CSEL 44, 362): *voventur autem omnia, quae offeruntur Deo, maxime sancti altaris oblatio.* Aug. enn. 25,2,10 (CCL 38, 147): *altare Domini, ubi offers vota Domino, ubi preces fundis.* Also Valerian. Cem. hom. 4,6 (PL 52, 704D) points to the altar as the place for honouring vows within the Eucharist.

318 Virgil. Aen. 11,50: *fors et vota facit cumulatque altaria donis.*

319 Heid 2015b. E.g. Aug. civ. Dei 10,3 (CCL 47, 275): *ei dona eius in nobis nosque ipsos vovemus et reddimus.* Petr. Chrys. serm. 73,2 (CCL 24A, 448): *multo magis nos oportet laudis immolare sacrificium, vota solvere.*

320 Cf. Prud. c. Symm. 1, 397 f. (FC 85, 136): *ad aram Plutonis fera vota sui.*

are the oblations of bread and wine, but they can be special gifts as well. The eucharistic practice of vows is reflected in the Roman Canon of the Mass. Since the fifth century it has said in the prayer for the living:[321]

> Remember, O Lord, Thy servants and handmaids, N. and N. and all here standing around; whose faith and devotion (*devotio*) are known to Thee. They offer up to Thee this Sacrifice of praise: For themselves and all pertaining to them, for the redemption of their souls, for the hope of their salvation and safety they pay their vows (*reddunt vota sua*) unto Thee, the eternal God, living and true.[322]

In the official translations of the Roman Canon, the "vows" are discreetly discarded, being reinterpreted as "prayers" (the German translation has the equivalent of "prayers and gifts"): "They now send up their prayers to you."[323] The idea of "righteousness through works" in the form of pious vows no longer seems acceptable today. But *vota reddere* is a technical term that describes the fulfilment of vows. Devotion (*de-votio*) consists precisely in redeeming vows through sacrificial offerings in the celebration of the Eucharist.[324] In the Canon of the Mass, the vows are mentioned in the exact section in which the names of individual persons are singled out (*Memento Domine, famulorum famularumque tuarum N. et N.*), namely those who have offered gifts.[325] So from this, too, we can assume that the presenting of the offerings is the liturgical moment at which vows are redeemed. Salvian of Marseilles says that in times of need people honour their vows by filling the altars with gifts.[326] When the gifts are lying there, the vow they have offered is for them fulfilled and honoured.

---

321 BERGER 1964, 171.

322 *Memento domine famulorum famularumque tuarum N. et N. et omnium circumadstantium, quorum tibi fides cognita est et nota devotio. Qui tibi offerunt hoc sacrificium laudis: pro se suisque omnibus, pro redemptione animarum suarum, pro spe salutis et incolumitatis suae tibi reddunt vota sua aeterno deo vivo et vero.* Here according to the reconstruction by STUIBER 1954, 129f. See recently O'LOUGHLIN 2014, 69–91. The English translation from N. GIHR, The Holy Sacrifice of the Mass (St. Louis 1902).

323 The German quoted has "Gebete und Gaben" (prayers and gifts). In the Italian Missal, as in the English one, it is further reduced, having only "innalzano la preghiera". Along these lines also RIGHETTI 1966, 375. JUNGMANN 1952b, 211 certainly sees the possibility of genuine vows.

324 Cf. church foundation *ex devotione* (= *ex voto*) LP 42,3 (DUCHESNE 1886, 220).

325 *Oblationes et vota* in the prayer *post nomina*: Miss. Goth. 84, 207, 339, 416, 421. Paulin. Nol. ep. 32,8 (FC 25,2, 764): *Sic geminata piis adspirat gratia votis / Infra martyribus desuper acta sacris / Vota sacerdotis viventum et commoda parvo / Pulvere sanctorum mors pretiosa iuvat.* The *viventes* are then evidently the people making the offerings whose names are mentioned in the Canon. Cf. BERGER 1964, 170–175.

326 Salvian. gub. 6,17,94 (CSEL 8, 152): [...] *mixtis cum fletu gaudiis supplicamus inlustramus donariis sacra limina, aras muneribus implemus et, quia ipsi dono illius festi sumus, templis quoque ipsius vultum nostrae festivitatis induimus.*

It is of great importance in almost all families of rites that the names of those who are making the offerings – *nomina offerentium/viventium* – are made public when the gifts are presented. Such a reading aloud of the diptychs in association with the offering of gifts is known in the Old Gallic, Old Spanish and Roman liturgies.[327] It is possible that the gifts of the faithful lie piled up on the altar when this is done.[328] But the argument can also be made the other way round: the reading out of the names also makes sense if the faithful do not (any longer) bring their gifts visibly to the altar, for instance if they have already handed them over before mass. In Gaul, for example, the names of those who have handed over gifts before the mass are read out immediately after the liturgical preparation of the gifts by clergy.[329] In North Africa, however, no *recitatio offerentium* seems to have taken place.[330] Jerome makes the broad statement that the deacon reads out who has donated or promised to donate and how much it is.[331] Whether he is describing the conditions in Rome or has the Orient in mind is not clear. What is important, though, is that their gifts are also named alongside the donors. This leaves it open whether these gifts could be seen lying on the altar or not, especially since Jerome actually had offerings of money in mind.

In any case, this reading aloud makes the benefactors known, which, to Jerome's annoyance, harbours the danger of image cultivation and vanity. It seems to have happened that the faithful applauded during the recitation. This is probably why Pope Innocent († 417) insisted that the names should be read out not during the preparation of the gifts but rather within the Canon.[332] For in this way the donors are not so much praised for their generosity as commended to the prayers of the faithful.

327   KLÖCKENER 1992, 191. On the naming of those giving oblations and alms at the altar see Alcuin's *Missa pro salute vivorum et mortuorum* in DESHUSSES 1972, 27 f. An early example Trad. Apost. 31 (FC 1, 286).

328   Miss. Goth. 192 (MOHLBERG 1961): *Oblata munera superposita altario tuo* […]; 207: *Diversis oblationibus sacris altaribus una tamen fidei devotione conlatis*; 284.

329   K. BERG, Cäsarius von Arles. Ein Bischof des sechsten Jahrhunderts erschließt das liturgische Leben seiner Zeit (Thaur 1994) 185 f. The liturgical preparation of the gifts was probably carried out by the clergy alone by bringing the sacrificial offerings of the faithful from the sacristy to the altar; SMYTH 2003, 197–199.

330   KLÖCKENER 1992, 191 f.

331   Hieron. comm. in Hiez. 6,18 (CCL 75, 238): *publiceque diaconus in ecclesiis recitet offerentium nomina: 'Tantum offert illa, ille tantum pollicitus est'; placentque sibi ad plausum populi.* Comm. in Hier. 2,108 (CCL 74, 116): *At nunc publice recitantur offerentium nomina et redemptio peccatorum mutatur in laudem nec meminerunt viduae illius in evangelio, quae in gazophylacium duo aera mittendo omnium divitum vicit donaria.* STUIBER 1954, 138 f., 141.

332   Cf. CONNELL 2002, 26 f. R. BERGER, Die Wendung "offerre pro" in der römischen Liturgie (Münster 1965) 191–193 thinks that the reason for moving the diptychs was that it brings the names of those making the offerings closer to the consecration, thus making the prayer more efficacious for them.

The fact that the offerings on the altar are later formulaically called *vota*[333] and that the eucharistic celebration as such is understood to be a redeeming of vows[334] does not detract from the way things originally happened.[335] Accordingly, votive masses in the Latin Rite were originally masses on the occasion of (community) vows being made in specific urgent intentions; later they became devotional masses (Mass of the Sacred Heart of Jesus, etc.).

4. PRAYER POSTURE AT THE ALTAR

Prayer is the central act in the practice of the Christian faith. The celebration of the Eucharist is not one continuous prayer; rather, various prayers are embedded in the course of it. In the Latin-Roman liturgy there are four prayers that stand out: everything else leads up to them and they are always introduced with the solemn invocation "let us pray" (for the Collect, Offertory Prayer and Closing Prayer) or, in the case of the most important and longest prayer, the so-called Canon of the Mass, with the dialogue "lift up your hearts – we lift them up to the Lord" (*Sursum corda – Habemus ad Dominum*). All other liturgical families handle these in a similar way because it is important to make the faithful aware that something sacred, something special, is happening here, namely the making of direct contact with God, and that the words of prayer therefore require a certain inward and outward demeanour.

As soon as the priest or deacon has given the appropriate signals, all those present, except the penitents, assume the posture of prayer. This will be presented below with special reference to the priest at the altar. Ever since Paul spoke of the "table *of the Lord*" (above chapter II, 1), it has been surrounded by the ritual of prayer. Without this ritual, it is impossible to understand the function that the table has to fulfil. It is not just somewhere to put the offerings; it is also and above all a place of prayer (consecration and benediction). This is to be understood exclusively: the altar is removed from interpersonal dialogue and is consecrated to dialogue with the Lord. Thus it stands in the church space as both the starting point and the destination of a vertical axis.

---

333 Sacr. Veron. 115 (MOHLBERG 1994): *Da nobis quaesumus domine semper haec tibi vota deferre quibus sanctorum tuorum natalicia celebrantes tuam gloriam praedicemus.* Ibid. 375: *Intende, praecamur, altissime, vota quae reddimus.*

334 Aug. enn. 21,2,27 (CCL 38, 129): *Quae sunt vota sua? Sacrificium quod obtulit Deo.* Ep. 149,16

(CSEL 44, 363): *voventur autem omnia, quae offeruntur deo, maxime sancti altaris oblatio.*

335 Opt. Mil. 6,1,1. 7 (SC 413, 160): *altaria Dei [...] in quibus et vota populi et membra Christi portata sunt.* Here *vota* can only mean votive offerings, not merely prayers.

a. Standing upright

The early Church employed many prayer postures, including since biblical times kneeling (Eph 3:14; Phil 2:10).[336] But the dominant posture is standing,[337] which alone is suitable for prayer at the altar. Standing to pray is inseparably linked to two other elements, namely lifting up the hands and the eyes. This entire gesture has been practised by Christians for centuries, whether in the Latin, Greek or Oriental cultural spheres. It has been practised by men and women, clerics and laity, adults and children, alone or together, in private prayer or in the liturgy[338] (Fig. 29). The Christians did not invent this way of praying, but found it among pagans and Jews.[339] In the age of religious sensitisation in late antiquity, philosophers pondered the meaning of this traditional prayer posture, adopted instinctively by the majority of people, and sought explanations. Pagans and Christians recognise in a vertical, upwardly directed posture a meaningful expression of what prayer really is and what makes it the central human and religious act.[340] They see it as a profoundly appropriate and expressive language that in the truest sense of the word embodies the reverence owed to the deity.

Numerous portrayals in pagan art show sacrificial acts in which the person offering the sacrifice approaches a tripod or altar with incense or a libation bowl (*patera*) to perform the offering of wine (Fig. 30).[341] With this pre-sacrifice, which is followed by the slaughter of the sacrificial animal, he is inviting the deity and demonstrating his submission to divine sovereignty.[342] Those who allow themselves to be portrayed in this way at the sacrifice are intending to express their religious disposition and their attachment to tradition. Altar and sacrifice become the epitome of "piety" or a "sense of duty towards the gods" (*pietas erga deos*). This conviction finds its perfect expression on imperial coins showing a woman as the personification of *PIETAS* standing with raised arms next to an altar[343] (above Fig. 17). The same close connection between altar and prayer posture is shown in a third-century-A.D. votive altar from Palmyra (Fig. 31).[344] So in paganism already, prayer belongs to the sacrifice; both are expressions of the same *pietas* and cannot be played off against each other.[345] The same applies to the Christian priest at the altar. For the altar is not only the place of the most

---

336 On the significance of standing and kneeling when praying see Hvalvik 2014, 76–82.

337 Jungmann 1952a, 312 f.

338 Heid 2006, 356 f.

339 ThesCRA 3, 163 f.; Hamman 1980, 1212–1215; Suntrup 1978, 172 f.

340 On the anthropological and Christological interpretation of the orans position see Saxer 1980b.

341 For the same medal see ThesCRA 5, Plate 22,

Fig. 31. E.g. also Fless 1995, Plates 12,2, 15,2, 19,2, 24,2, 39,1 and 46,2.

342 Scheid 1990, 326–333.

343 Klauser 1959. Further pictorial illustrations in Donati / Gentili 2001, 92–96.

344 Crippa / Zibawi 1998, Plate 3; similarly an altar in the Vatican museums (JbAC 2 [1959] Plate 12a).

345 Iren. adv. haer. 4,17,6 (SC 100,2, 594).

Fig. 29: Ivory casket of Samagher (near Pola): two men and women, apparently clerics and consecrated women (widows), standing to the right and left of the Memoria of the Apostle erected by Constantine in St Peter's Basilica, Rome, and raising their hands in prayer, 1st half of the 5th century; Museo Archeologico Nazionale di Venezia; photo: Ministero della Cultura, Direzione regionale Musei Veneto.

exalted and the officially prescribed prayer of the Church[346] – it is also the place where each and every prayer (*oratio*) of the people is, as it were, gathered together and rises up to God.[347]

---

346 Actus Petri cum Simone 2 (Lipsius / Bonnet 1891, 46): […] *sacrificium* […] *et oratione facta* […]. Prud. c. Symm. 2, 712 (FC 85, 218): Prayer (= Eucharist) at the altar.

347 Opt. Mil. 6,1,7 (SC 413, 164): *Illinc enim ad aures Dei ascendere populi solebat oratio.* Athan. apol. ad Const. 16 (SC 56², 120). Countless further instances could be cited.

Fig. 30: Pre-sacrifice (wine offer) at the tripod and the slaughter of the sacrificial bull as the main sacrifice; bronze medal of Antoninus Pius, 158–159, Staatliche Museen, Berlin; F. P. C. KENT et al., Die römische Münze (München 1973), Plate 11, 324.

For the priest at the altar the rule is, without exception, that he must stand.[348] Not a single explicit reference to sitting at the altar exists, whereas every statement that is explicit stresses standing. There is not even a ban on seated celebration because it never crossed anyone's mind to do so. From the catacomb pictures depicting funeral banquets – which have been falsely interpreted as Eucharists (above Fig. 7, below Fig. 127) – scholars drew the conclusion that people were seated during the Eucharist, which is where the modern pastoral practice of seated masses comes from. But this has little to do with the historical facts. To be sure, for a while the Eucharist was celebrated within the context of meals. But even pagans and Jews stood up at meals for the actual prayer and sacrificial act.[349] The Christians[350] stood up and sat down again afterwards correspondingly.[351] It was impossible to pray on their cushions, if only because they propped themselves up on their arms when reclining. But you had to lift up your hands to pray. As long as the eucharistic rite was embedded in a reclining meal, there must therefore have

348 Already in paganism, sacrificing in a seated position is extremely rare, e.g. MATZ 1969, Suppl. 105. In pre-Christian Egypt, the prayer position seems to have been squatting, with outstretched arms and eyes raised; KAUFMANN 1913, Figs. 76–78. A. HERMANN, Die Beter-Stelen von Terenuthis in Ägypten. Zur Vorgeschichte der christlichen Oransdarstellung, in: JbAC 6 (1963) 112–128 does not deal with such terracottas.

349 See above p. 23 f.

350 Iustin. apol. 1, 67,5 (MARCOVICH 1994, 129); Trad. Apost. 25 (FC 1, 276); Orig. orat. 31,2 (GCS Orig. 2, 396); Pass. Sym. Bar-Sabbae 35 (Patrologia Syriaca 1,2, 761); Apophth. 12,17 (SC 474, 220); 19,18 (SC 498, 152); 20,3 (162). SAXER 1969, 207 f. To be sure, Aug. div. quaest. ad Simpl. 2,4,4 (CCL 44, 86 f.) stresses that one can pray seated, standing or reclining.

351 DÖLGER 1936, 116–137.

Fig. 31: Pagan votive altar from Palmyra with Orans, 3rd century AD; Institut du Monde Arabe, Paris, Foto: Ph. Maillard; CRIPPA / ZIBAWI 1998, 27 Tav. 3.

been a ritual change from meal to Eucharist in that the person presiding at the sacred rite approached the altar table (that had been fetched in) and those participating in the meal rose to their feet.

The Acts of Thomas (early third century) are revealing here. The story of the apostle relates how Thomas baptises, confirms and celebrates the Eucharist in the triclinium of a private house, during which he lays bread on the table.[352] From the location, i.e. the triclinium, interpreters conclude that the Eucharist was celebrated as a reclining meal. But "triclinium" here refers in the first instance merely to a room. A reclining meal is not mentioned. Furthermore, all those involved are certain to have stood at least for the baptism and confirmation. Even if they did lie down again afterwards, they will have got up again at the subsequent Rite of the Bread. For the Acts of Thomas describe a eucharistic celebration elsewhere, too, and there a bench is set up as a table, with Thomas

---

352 Acta Thomae 131–133 (LIPSIUS / BONNET 1903, 238–240).

approaching this table to say the blessing. The participants join him for the Eucharist, too, and are therefore not lying on cushions.[353]

There is no evidence that standing only becomes customary when the number of participants means that the Eucharist is no longer practised as a reclining meal.[354] Nor is it at all certain that people initially reclined at table simply because the Eucharist was understood as a meal, only generations later going over to standing worship when the Eucharist was celebrated in the manner of a sacrificial act. The truth is more complex: both reclining and standing, meal and sacrifice can have a place in one and the same gathering. In any case, the sacrificial rite requires standing even at reclining meals. So even if there were places in the second and third centuries where the Eucharist was still connected with dining, this would nevertheless have entailed a ritual transition which would have been clearly marked by the change of tables and posture.

In the case of those writers for whom it is not yet possible to completely rule out that reclining meals still existed in their day, all the indications point to a standing posture at the altar. Ignatius of Antioch mentions the choir at the altar.[355] But singing during the sacrifice and prayers takes place standing.[356] Ignatius speaks expressly of prayer at the altar,[357] and this too implies standing. Finally, he speaks of the believers gathering in a temple and at an altar. Even if the bishop "presides" over this gathering,[358] the expression (*prae* 'before' + *sedere* 'sit') makes it hard to imagine it as a reclining meal. Justin (c. 150) speaks explicitly of the whole community standing to pray at the Eucharist.[359] In his two descriptions of the eucharistic celebration there is no suggestion whatsoever of a reclining meal.[360] Tertullian of Carthage († after 220) says of the Christian love feast (agape) that those present stand up to pray.[361] Equally, he speaks of the *statio* at the Christian altar since priest and people stand at God's altar for the offertory prayers.[362] The *Traditio Apostolica*, which is likewise familiar with the communal reclining meal in the evening

---

353 Acta Thomae 49 (LIPSIUS / BONNET 1903, 165 f.). The Acts of Peter (c. 180–190) accord with this: Actus Petri cum Simone 2 (LIPSIUS / BONNET 1891, 46): *accedes ad altarium dei.* Although WIELAND 1906, 111 f. denies that the eucharistic table is being referred to here as an altar, it is obviously that he is wrong.

354 NUSSBAUM 1965, 379.

355 Ign. ad Rom. 2,2 (SC 10³, 128).

356 FLESS 1995, 32.

357 Ign. ad Eph. 5,2 (SC 10³, 72–74).

358 Ign. ad Magn. 6,1 (SC 10³, 98).

359 Iustin. apol. 1, 67,5 (SC 507, 308).

360 KLINGHARDT 1996, 502 f. interprets what Justin says about the Eucharist in the sense of an agape-Eucharist reclining meal in the evening, for which, however, he is forced to postulate an analogy between this and Sabbath worship, for the shape of which he admits there is no clear evidence. Cf. GRUNDEKEN 2015, 149. Here, too, most of it is pure hypothesis. Justin is more likely to be familiar with a Eucharist in the morning and agape in the evening (see above p. 137 n. 393).

361 Tert. apol. 39,17 (CCL 1, 152): *Non prius discumbitur quam oratio ad Deum praegustetur.* Ibid. 39,18 (153): *Post aquam manualem […] provocatur in medium Deo canere.*

362 Tert. or. 19,1–3 (CCL 1, 267 f.): *non putant plerique sacrificiorum orationibus […] ne sollemnior erit statio tua, si et ad aram Dei steteris.*

(*cena dominica*) alongside the (morning) Eucharist, veritably ritualizes standing up to pray at the Eucharist with the call to "lift up your hearts" (*sursum corda*).[363] At the agape, on the other hand, the "lift up your hearts" is omitted because people remain reclining during the thanksgiving. But after the meal, all rise for prayer, during which the bishop offers the mixed wine.[364]

b. Uplifted hands

In addition, when praying standing up, the hands are clearly upraised (with fingers together or spread).[365] A relict of this practice remains today in the priest's lifting up his hands after he has invited the people to pray ("let us pray").[366] This is the posture the priest has from time immemorial assumed at the altar, too (Fig. 32).[367] The precise moment in the rite when this happened must, however, remain open. This goes for the faithful, too, who – as testified to by John Chrysostom († 407) – also raised their hands. He regards precisely this as embodying the strength of the common prayer: "For when the whole people stands with uplifted hands, the whole priestly assembly, and that awful Sacrifice lies on the altar, how shall we not prevail with God by our entreaties?"[368]

All the same, the priest at the altar stands out with his posture. The apse mosaic of the sixth-century *Sant'Apollinare* in Classe (Ravenna) shows the titular saint, Apollinaris, in prayer posture (below Figs. 58 and 104). Apollinaris is held to be the first bishop of

363 Trad. Apost. 25 (FC 1, 276) and ibid. 4 (222). Standing to pray see also ibid. 18 (250). The priests stand at the Eucharist: ibid. 4 (226): *adstare coram te et tibi ministrare*. LIETZMANN 1926, 228–230 counts the *sursum corda* as among the oldest liturgical possessions, going back to the apostolic celebrations of the Lord's Supper.
364 Trad. Apost. 25 (FC 1, 276).
365 Cf. SITTL 1890, 190. On the sarcophagi the fingers are always together, probably for technical reasons, whereas in the catacomb paintings the fingers are often spread; WILPERT 1903, Plate 25; *id.*, Die gottgeweihten Jungfrauen in den ersten Jahrhunderten der Kirche (Freiburg 1892), Plate 1. Problematic is Ambr. sacr. 6,4,18 (SC 25², 146): *Volo autem viros, hoc est, qui possunt servare praeceptum, orare in omni loco levantes puras manus (1 Tm 2:8). Quid est levantes puras manus? Numquid debes in oratione tua crucem domini gentibus demonstrare? Illud quidem signum virtuti est non pudori. Est tamen quomodo pos-*

sis orare nec figuram demonstres, sed actus tuos leves: Si vis operari operationem tuam, levas puras manus per innocentiam. Levas eas non quotidie; semel levasti, non opus est ut iterum leves. Ambrosius seems to be saying that Christians only raise their hands at baptism and not again after that. That is, however, very unlikely. Ambrose speaks somewhat infelicitously only about praying outside the church (*in omni loco – gentibus demonstrare*). There the raised hands mean acting well (*purus – pudens – innocens*). People do not have to raise their hands daily (at most on Sundays) because they have raised them once (at baptism).
366 JUNGMANN 1952a, 476.
367 Greg. Naz. or. 18,29 (PG 35, 1020C–1021A); vgl. 13,3 (856A); Joh. Chrys. coem. et cruc. 3 (PG 49, 397 f.); cat. bapt. 2,4,26 (FC 6,1, 286).
368 Joh. Chrys. in Phil. hom. 3,4 (PG 62, 204). Ps.-Joh. Chrys. de circo (PG 59, 567–570) at the end of the sermon: "Lift up holy hands to the King."

Fig. 32: The Apostle Philip and the Ethiopian treasurer on the chariot (Acts 8:27f.); further, Philip as bishop in Tralles in Asia Minor: the Bishop approaches the altar from the front, facing east, and raises his hands and eyes to heaven; Menologion of Basil II (um 1000); BAV Vat. gr. 1613, fol. 107r, Ufficio Copyright.

Ravenna. The picture of him must be related to the church's altar, which is assumed to have contained relics of the saint.[369] The altar was probably originally located in the nave, below the steps of the podium (inside the lower enclosed choir, and not, as it is today, on the apse podium). That would result in the following disposition: the bishop celebrating the Eucharist at the altar and looking at the apse mosaic of the east-facing church sees there his holy predecessor Apollinaris, who continues his priestly prayer in heaven. How closely the apse mosaic is related to the altar is reflected in a remarkable incident: when Archbishop Theodor (seventh century) refused to celebrate the Christmas Mass in Classe, the faithful there called on the saint to help: "Saint Apollinaris, rise up (from your tomb) and celebrate Mass for us today, the day of the Lord's birth!"[370]

369 The highly problematic question of Apollinaris's tomb and the place of his relics cannot be discussed further here. On the connection of the saints in the apse mosaic to the altar relics see BRANDENBURG 1995b, 78f., 81f. (St Felix Basilica in Cimitile and the basilica in Fundi) and THUNØ 2015, 156–158. MICHAEL 2005, 222 with n. 1140 draws the wrong conclusions, as a result erroneously assuming a *celebratio versus populum*.

370 Agnell. Lib. Pont. Rav. 36,122 (FC 21,2, 450).

What meaning lies behind uplifted hands in the history of religion? This depends on how the hands are held. As a basic principle, the Christians simply adopted the usual prayer posture and did not develop one of their own. The variant of the wide "stretching out of the hands" (cf. Jn 21:18) is interpreted early on as a reference to the Crucifixion, but that is actually more of a spiritualization.[371] Nor is the arm position intended as a gesture of invitation in the sense of "be embraced, millions". Fundamentally, the real meaning of the prayer posture instead lies in the vertical lifting up of the hands, stretching them out to God,[372] just as the eyes are also directed upwards.[373] The faithful sometimes do this in an extreme manner, stretching out their hands, as it were, right up to heaven.[374]

The predominant prayer posture is with the arms close to the body and the hands held upwards (Fig. 33). The position of the hands is more important here than how wide the arms are. The hands are flat, not cupped; rather, the fingertips are bent slightly backwards (*manus supinas*) and the palms turned forward. Ancient texts speak not only of lifting up the hands (*manus*) but also of lifting up the palms (*palmae*).[375] This can be clearly recognised on numerous sarcophagi from Rome and Ravenna and in the Roman catacomb paintings.

Because the New Testament (1 Tm 2:8) and then the ecclesiastical writers repeatedly associate the lifting up of hands with purity, the idea suggests itself that it is a matter of showing God one's pure and innocent hands.[376] This, like looking heavenwards, dates back to a time when the people prayed outdoors. Impure hands must not be stretched out towards the pure heavens and the pure sun – which in itself presupposes that the person praying is facing east towards the sun.[377] Given their moral awareness, the idea of pure hands was bound to appeal particularly to the Christians. They examine their

---

371 Cf. Hvalvik 2014, 82–85. Stretching out the hands always also means lifting them up: Tert. or. 14 (CCL 1, 265): *Nos vero non attollimus tantum, sed etiam expandimus.* Orig. in Sam. hom. 1,9 (SC 328, 128): *si quis elevaverit vel extendit manus ad caelum – ut habitus esse orantium solet.* Aug enn. 62,13 (CCL 39, 802): *Levavit pro nobis Dominus noster manus in cruce, et extensae sunt manus eius pro nobis.* It is significant that ep. Barn. 12,2 (SC 172, 166) changes the ἐπῆρεν χεῖρας (Ex 17:11 LXX) into ἐξέτεινεν because both mean the same thing. Dölger 1972, 319; Heid 2006, 359f. n. 59.

372 1 Clem. 2,3 (SC 167, 102).

373 Tert. apol. 30,4 (CCL 1, 141): *Illuc sursum suspicientes Christiani manibus expansis, quia innocuis [...] oramus.*

374 Tert. or. 17,1 (CCL 1, 266): *manibus sublimius elatis, sed temperate ac probe elatis.* Cypr. or. dom.

6 (CSEL 3,1, 269f.): *manibus insolenter erectis*; Orig. orat. 31,2. 5 (GCS Orig. 2, 396. 398). Joh. Chrys. in Hebr. hom. 22,3 (PG 63, 158) encourages the faithful, if need be, to stretch forth their hands in supplication in order to grasp heaven.

375 Heid 2006, 360f.

376 1 Clem. 29,1 (SC 167, 146); Athen. suppl. 13,3 (SC 379, 112); Clem. Alex. strom. 6,3,28,5 (SC 446, 116); Pass. Serapiae 1,5 (BHL 7586); Ambr. sacr. 6,4,18 (SC 25², 146); Ps.-Basil. vit. Theclae 17 (BHG 1717–1718). Heid 2006, 359–366. A constricted view of the topics referred to here is found in Angenendt 2005, 245–267. I could not access M. A. Bellis, *Levantes puras manus* nell'antica letteratura cristiana, in: Ricerche di Storia Religiosa 1 (1954) 9–39.

377 Cf. Heid 2006, 364f.

Fig. 33: Roman sarcophagus lid showing Susanna praying in her need as she is importuned by one of the elders (Dan 13:42f), 1st third of the 4th century; Museo Archeologico Nazionale in Naples; DRESKEN-WEILAND 1998, Plate 74,2.

consciences since it would inevitably fill them with shame if they were to lift up tainted hands in prayer.[378] The person praying who sees himself as entitled to make contact with God shows his hands so that God might see them and confirm the person's worthiness. Tertullian claims that the Jews did not dare to lift up their hands in prayer to Christ because their hands were unclean, stained with the blood of the prophets.[379] Since prayer always takes place before the eyes of God, the person praying lets God see the open palms of his hands as evidence that there is no blood on them.[380] As we read in Isaiah 1:15 f.: "When you stretch out your hands, I will hide my eyes from you; even though you make many prayers, I will not listen; your hands are full of blood. Wash yourselves; make yourselves clean" (cf. Ps 26:6). So the Christian prays with a heavenward gaze and outstretched hands "because free from sin" and without blushing.[381] He worthily raises his hands to God and says with a clear conscience: "You, O Lord, know how holy, innocent and pure are the hands that I stretch out to you."[382] He does not need to hide his pure hands,[383] just as he does not cover his face but shows God his pure forehead.[384]

378 Aug. enn. 62,13 (CCL 39, 802): *ne erubescant levari ad Deum.*

379 Tert. or. 14 (CCL 1, 265). Iren. adv. haer. 4,18,4 (SC 100,2, 606): the Jews do not offer sacrifices anymore because their hands are full of blood.

380 HEID 2006, 362 n. 72. Euchologion of Serapion 19 (BKV Griechische Liturgien [München 1912] 140): "Pure hands we stretch out and our thoughts we lift up to Thee, O Lord." Cf. ibid. 28 (145): "We stretch out our hands, O Lord, and pray."

381 Tert. apol. 30,4 (CCL 1, 141): *Illuc (ad caelum) sursum suspicientes Christiani manibus expan-* *sis, quia innocuis, capite nudato, quia non erubescimus.* Epiph. pan. 26,4,5 (GCS Epiph. 1, 281) fiercely criticizes certain Gnostics for whom it is common practice for the man and woman to smear the emission on the palms of their hands after coitus and then, with hands uplifted, raise their eyes heavenward in prayer.

382 Aug. gest. Pel. 6,16 (CSEL 42, 68).

383 Cf. Min. Fel. 29,8 (CSEL 2, 43).

384 Tert. apol. 30,4 (CCL 1, 141); Cypr. laps. 2 (CSEL 3,1, 238).

This explains why only the baptised are allowed to raise their hands in prayer.[385] The washing of hands before entering the church, as practised by Christians,[386] also belongs in this context: the house of prayer can only be entered with pure hands. The hygienic act of washing is meant as a reminder of inner purification, but nevertheless retains its connection to the raising of hands in prayer.[387] Only non-penitents are permitted to enter the church space and raise their hands.[388] All this then applies all the more at the altar. It has already been shown in a different context that Christians, too, as a matter of course associate a sacred table with the idea of purity (above chapter II, 5). A further point of reference is offered by Psalm 26: the person praying resists murderers and deceivers, to whose hands injustice clings (26:10), and promises to wash his hands in innocence and to go around the altar of the Lord (*Lavabo in innocentibus manus meas et circumdabo altare Domini*) (26:6). In his commentary on this psalm, Augustine says that the altar stands before the eyes of God, hence one must approach it innocently.[389] Although he applies the rest of what he says to the faithful, it is nevertheless clear that the priest in particular, when he offers the sacrifice at the altar with uplifted hands, should also do so with a clear conscience.[390]

385 Ambr. sacr. 6,4,18 (SC 25², 146) to the newly baptized: *semel levasti, non opus est ut iterum leves.*
386 Trad. Apost. 41 (FC 1, 298. 302); Can. Hippol. arab. 25, 27 (PO 31, 392, 396); Basil. can. 28 (Riedel 1900, 246). Tertullian dislikes the washing of hands before prayer, but this is already an established practice; Tert. or. 13 (CCL 1, 264f.). Not only the hands but also the heavenward-gazing eyes should be pure; this explains why the face is also washed; Paulin. Nol. ep. 13,13 (FC 25,1, 326). On wells in the atrium see Orlandos 1954, 110–124; Severus 1972, 1226–1228; Testini 1980, 564f.; de Blaauw 2008, 358.
387 Tert. or. 13f. (CCL 1, 264f.); Joh. Chrys. exp. in Ps. 140,3 (PG 55, 430f.); in 1 Cor. hom. 43,4 (PG 61, 372); in Ioh. hom. 73,3 (PG 59, 398f.). Van de Paverd 1970, 19–21. The purity requirement undoubtedly exists to prevent the Eucharist from being received with dirty hands: Joh. Chrys. in

Eph. hom. 3,4 (PG 62, 28f.). But here, too, the connection to the prayer spoken at the altar is still recognisable.
388 Penitents must look at the floor and are not allowed to raise their hands for prayer: Lk 18:13; Euseb. hist. eccl. 7,9,3–5 (SC 41, 174f.); Siegert 1980, 34. Cf. Euchologion of Serapion 26 (BKV Griechische Liturgien [München 1912] 144). Dölger 1972, 310.
389 Aug. enn. 25,2,10 (CCL 38, 147).
390 Ibid. 25,2,10 (CCL 38, 147); 62,13 (CCL 39, 801f.); Roetzer 1930, 243f. Early on, there was already a liturgical washing of the priest's hands; B. Kötting, Handwaschung, in: RACh 13 (1986) 575–585, here 584; Lüstraeten 2014; Suntrup 1978, 350–355. Greg. Naz. or. 2,8 (SC 247, 98): The priest's ablutions at the altar; Dölger 1930, 171 n. 39.

Fig. 34: Fragment of a frieze sarcophagus with the deceased in the orans posture – hands raised and eyes looking up to heaven – between Peter and Paul, 4th century; Skulpturensammlung und Museum für Byzantinische Kunst, Staatliche Museen zu Berlin, inv. 6686; photo: Antje Voigt.

c. Eyes raised to heaven

It may sound banal, but you pray with your eyes open. This is already the case in Jewish and pagan antiquity.[391] It is only in elitist circles, under the influence of Neoplatonism, that people pray immersed in themselves.[392] Those praying alertly, on the other hand, have their eyes open (Fig. 34). They do not let curiosity make them wander, but rather direct them upwards in complete concentration. In the same way, the priest at the altar lifts up not only his hands, but also his eyes (above Fig. 32, cf. below Fig. 42).[393] This explicitly upward gaze enters various mass liturgies.[394] In the Roman Rite, the priest looks at the altar cross,[395] but this is already a later adaptation. Originally, the gaze was directed "heavenwards", even if the heavens cannot be seen in an enclosed space.[396] A relic of this

391 Min. Fel. 18,11 (CSEL 2, 25): *quid quod omnium de isto habeo consensum? audio vulgus: cum ad caelum manus tendunt* […]. W. Grunof dmann, Aufwärts-abwärts, in: RACh 1 (1950) 954–957, here 956; Severus 1972, 1230–1232; A. Lampe / H. Bietenhard, Himmel, in: RACh 15 (1991) 173–212, here 185 f.

392 Iulian. ep. 12, on this Weis 1973, 253 n. 5.

393 Both aspects, the lifting up of the hands and eyes, were already pointed out by Righetti 1964, 377–379.

394 Theod. Mops. cat. 16,15 (FC 17,2, 432).

395 Hartmann / J. Kley, *Repertorium Rituum* (Wien / Zürich ¹⁴1940) 386 f.

396 See below p. 360, n. 4.

Fig. 35: Decorated initial T (detail) from the beginning of the Canon of the Mass (*Te Igitur*) in the Drogo Sacramentary, showing the OT priest-king Melchisedek at the altar looking up to God, c. 835–855; BnF, Ms. lat. 9428, fol. 15v.

is retained when the priest looks up briefly as he prays the words: "With his [Christ's] eyes lifted up to heaven" (*elevatis oculis in coelum*) (Fig. 35).[397] This merely imitates and ritualises what Christ did at the Last Supper.[398] But looking heavenwards was originally an organic part of the eucharistic liturgy, not a brief looking upwards. Evidence of this is provided in the *Vita* of Pamphilus, the bishop of Sulmona (seventh century). As a guest at the Lateran Palace, during morning prayer he hears the angels in heaven celebrating mass. He calls the pope because it is now time to celebrate mass on earth, too. But the pope does not hear the angels. So he stands on Pamphilus's feet, raises his hands and eyes to heaven and then hears the angels.[399]

There is evidence that the celebrant looks up during the Offertory. A Roman-Franconian Order of Mass dating from the late eighth century explains that at the altar the bishop takes his own oblations (*oblationes*) in his hands and holds them up, at the same time looking up to heaven and praying silently to God.[400] Here it is necessary to recall

397 DÖLGER 1972, 302 f.; VOGEL 1962, 181 n. 15. Divine Liturgy of St James (BKV Griechische Liturgien [München 1912] 105): "lifting up his eyes to heaven."
398 Cf. Ambr. sacr. 4,5,21 (SC 25², 114).
399 Vit. Pamphili Sulmon. 6 (ActaSS Apr. 3, 592CD) (BHL 6418).
400 OR XV,33 (ANDRIEU 1961, 102). Likewise OR XVII,42 (ANDRIEU 1961, 181).

Fig. 36: Roman sarcophagus lid with the three men in the fiery furnace (Dan 3) in prayer posture: with outstretched arms and looking heavenwards, 1st third of the 4th century; Vatican Museums; PIAC Archivio Fotografico.

what has been said above about the altar as a table for gifts and sacrifices (chapter IV, 3). For the gifts are offered to God and must somehow reach him. For the priest, the altar is not a work table at which he performs certain manual acts, but rather it serves as a place to put the offerings, as a showbread table before God (cf. Ex 25:30), and is thus a visible part of a vertical line that leads from earth to heaven. Through the liturgist's prayer gesture, the altar enters into a three-dimensionality, into a spatial structure that extends right up to heaven.

Leaving the altar aside again, it remains to be noted that lifting up their eyes is something done by all Christians in their personal or communal prayer.[401] It is a common legacy of antiquity in that pagan and Jewish texts already stereotypically combine the raising of hands and eyes into one single gesture (cf. Ps 141:2, 8).[402] In early Christian funerary art, the deceased are often portrayed in a prayer posture gazing heavenwards (above Fig. 34).[403] Or you can see the three men praying in the fiery furnace (Dn 3:24), raising their arms and looking upwards (Fig. 36).[404] And the chaste Susanna, too, when

---

401 Cf. Pass. Potiti 6,32 (BHL 6911): *crediderunt ex eis circiter duo milia in Dominum Jesum, hujusmodi voces dantes ad caelum.* On communal prayer with uplifted eyes and hands see also Pass. Eustathii 21 (BHG 642); Pass. Piroou (HYVERNAT 1886, 161). On communal prayer with uplifted arms in prison see Pass. Sarapamon (HYVERNAT 1886, 313).

402 DÖLGER 1972, 305f.; HEID 2006, 352 n. 19. Jesus himself prays like this (Jn 11:41; 17:1), and Stephen, too, gazes into heaven (Acts 7:55f.).

403 HEID 2006, 352f. (with a picture of the velatio chamber in the Priscilla Catacombs). Occasionally the deceased is depicted in this posture at the centre of the front side of sarcophagi: CHRISTERN-BRIESENICK 2003, Plate. 114, No. 479; CRIPPA / ZIBAWI 1998, 89 Plate 82 (Sarcophagus of Velletri).

404 Further sarcophagus examples: DEICHMANN 1967, Nos. 121, 124, 162, 637, 750.

beset by the two elders, prays like this in her distress (above Fig. 33). Corresponding evidence can be found in a large number of texts from every ecclesiastical region right down to the Middle Ages.[405] Augustine urges the faithful particularly clearly to lift up their hearts ("*sursum cor*"): the Christian stands upright and looks towards heaven, that is towards God.[406] His whole posture should express how his heart is lifted up to heaven by God's grace, looking away from men and up to God.[407]

d. In the presence of God

It is only in combination with looking up to heaven that the meaning of lifting up the hands becomes clear at all. For the hands are raised in the direction in which the person praying is looking and speaking.[408] This obeys the rule of rhetoric which says that speech and gesture must match, or that you also look at the person you are talking to. In the Old Testament already, lifting up the hands is regarded as lifting them up "to God in heaven" (Lm 3:41). The lifting up of eyes and hands is due primarily to the fact that the deity is imagined as dwelling in heaven or enthroned on the vault of heaven (Ps 123:1: "To you I lift up my eyes, O you who are enthroned in the heavens!")[409]

The concrete background of this in the history of religion is clear to see. In antiquity, the point of reference was the images of deities, towards which they looked up[410] and stretched out their hands[411] because the deity was to a certain extent present in this figure.[412] It is the same during the sacrificial act. The altar is always dedicated to a particular deity or group of gods, whose name is usually mentioned in the inscription (cf. Acts 17:23). With many altars, a statue standing behind the altar and facing it makes it clear to which god the sacrifice may be offered (Fig. 37; above Fig. 19, below Figs. 39, 119).[413] Images of deities can also be found standing on sacred tables (above Fig. 9).[414] This means that the altar has a front and a back, it is orientated, even if it is possible to

---

405 Heid 2006, 256–258; Dölger 1972, 301–320; Radó 1961, 47 f.; Righetti 1964, 379; Hack 2006, 229 f. Ferner Theod. Mops. cat. 13,16 (FC 17,2, 355); 16,3 (FC 17,2, 424); Cyrill. Scyth. vit. Cyr. 17 (Schwartz 1939, 232).

406 Aug. ep. 120,14 (CSEL 34, 716); tract. in Ioh. 18,6 (CCL 36, 183 f.); 38,4 (339 f.); enn. 31,2,21 (CCL 38, 240); 68,2,8 (CCL 39, 923); serm. 227 (SC 116, 238–240).

407 Aug. pecc. mer. 2,19,33 (CSEL 60, 105); serm. 229A,3 (PLS 2, 555 f.).

408 The prayer is akin to the ascending incense (Ps 88:10; 141:2; Si 38:14; Ac 10:4; Rv 8:4). Heid 2006, 358 n. 49.

409 Heid 2006, 358 n. 47.

410 Dölger 1972, 318 f.

411 Vitruv. archit. 4,9 (Fensterbusch 1964, 200). Sittl 1890, 174 f. n. 5.

412 Dölger 1972, 309. Cf. Bergmeier 2017, 33–37.

413 Siebert 1999, 100, 102.

414 For images of deities on a Christian altar in a sacrilegious game see Dölger 1930, 179.

Fig. 37: Emperor Domitian offers the pre-sacrifice at a rectangular altar standing in front of the statue of Minerva, Roman sestertius, 85 AD; ThesCRA 1, Plate 52 Rom. 163.

walk round it from all sides (cf. Ps 26:6).[415] The person offering the sacrifice stands *in front of* the altar or sacred table looking towards the god.[416]

According to the Roman architect Vitruvius (first century B.C.), altars must stand in the open air to the west of the temple and face east so that during the sacrifice the per-

---

415 Reisch 1894, 1689; Kirsch / Klauser 1950, 326.
416 Reisch 1894, 1654 f. Prud. c. Symm. 1, 236 f (FC 85, 124). Didasc. syr. 26 (Achelis / Flemming 1904, 130): "they made themselves a cast calf and worshipped it and offered sacrifices to the statue" (cf. Ex 32:5). Opt. Mil. 3,12,2 (SC 413, 76): *cum altaria solemniter aptarentur, proferrent illi imaginem quam primo in altare ponerent, et sic sacrificium offeretur.* Marcellin. et Faustin. lib. prec. 20,76 (CCL 69, 378): *ipsum altare Dei de dominico sublatum in templo sub pedibus idoli posuerunt.* Sacrificing in the direction of the image of a deity see H. P. L'Orange / A. von Gerkan, Der spätantike Bildschmuck des Konstantinsbogens (Berlin 1939), Plate 39b; G. Kaschnitz-Weinberg, Sculture del magazzino del Museo Vaticano (Città del Vaticano 1936), Plate LXXVII, 417; Kirsch / Klauser 1950, 311 f. Fig. 11; 315 f. Fig. 12; ANRW 2,17,2 (Berlin / New York 1981) 1054; Heid 2014b, 370 n. 93; ThesCRA 2, Plate 16, Fig. 73; Plate 104, Figs. 268–269; Plate 105, Figs. 272–273; Plate 106, Figs. 332, 336; Plate 108, Fig. 390; Plate 110, Fig. 398; ThesCRA 4, Plate 36 (Taberna 18); Plate 54, Fig. 90a; Plate 55, Figs. 97a, 99b; S. Ciurca / G. W. Bologna, Die Mosaiken der "Erculia"-Villa von Piazza Armerina – Morgantina (Bologna no date) 43. Matz 1969, Suppl. 230 (No. 216); 237 (No. 218): Sacrifice scene with Dionysos. Baldini Lippolis 2001, 74 Fig. 14: Sacrifice scene of a mosaic in Piazza Armerina. Sacrifice in the direction of the image of the deity in the temple see ThesCRA 1, Plate 52, Rom. 163. Occasionally the position of the altar on the entrance steps of a temple and its standing space confirm that the priest looked towards the image of the deity when offering the sacrifice; ThesCRA 4, Plate 9, Aedicula, Rom. Imp. 3. See also U. Sinn, Der griechische Tempel: Kulisse für den Altar, in: N. Bock et al. (eds.), Kunst und Liturgie im Mittelalter (München 2000) 55–64. However,

Fig. 38: Sacrificial scene in front of a temple with the deity visible in its entrance. The steps in front of the altar show that the priest faces the statue as he approaches the altar; Codex Vergilius Vaticanus, BAV Vat. lat. 3225, fol. 45v; G. FRANZ (ed.), The Egbert Codex (Darmstadt 2005) 69.

son offering it looks up to the eastern sky and the image of the gods in the temple cella (Fig. 38).[417] He thus combines the two: looking heavenward and looking at the image of the deity, adding that the statue appears to be looking at the petitioners and sacrificers.[418] In fact, art often portrays the statue of the deity towering over the altar, sometimes inclining its head as if looking down at the altar (Fig. 39).[419]

there was also a fear of looking at the image of the deity; in such cases they are veiled, banished to dark cellulae, since God's gaze can kill; M. ROSENBAUM-ALFÖLDI, Bild und Bildersprache der römischen Kaiser (Mainz 1999) 16.

417 Vitruv. arch. 4,5. 9 (FENSTERBUSCH 1964, 188–190, 200); REISCH 1894, 1643, 1654 f.; DÖLGER 1972, 308 f.; KIRSCH / KLAUSER 1950, 320 f.; DE BLAAUW 2010a, 19. When there are deviations from the norm, the eastward orientation becomes even clearer: the two altars in the sacred area of Sant'Omobono in Rome are eastward oriented against the south-north axis of the temple itself;

F. COARELLI, Rom. Ein archäologischer Führer (Freiburg i.Br. 1975) 282 f. In *Felix Romuliana* (Serbia) the large and the small temple with the altar are east-oriented, i.e. the image of the god faces east, looking towards the hill of the tumuli of Galerius and his mother Romula. Sacrifices will certainly have been offered in both temples on the day of their apotheosis. Temple altars with steps on the western side NUSSBAUM 1965, 154.

418 Vitruv. arch. 4,5 (FENSTERBUSCH 1964, 188–190).

419 Pictorial examples: CRIPPA / ZIBAWI 1998, 33 Fig. 14; ANRW 2,17,2 (Berlin / New York 1981) 1052, 1058.

Judaism has rigorously rejected statues as idols and preached only the invisible God in heaven. But even there, in some formulations, a spatial, indeed even visual presence of God lives on, giving a direction to both prayer and altar. In the sacrificial service, eye contact occurs between man and God (Gn 4:4–6). The sacrifice is performed "in the presence of the Lord" (Jo 22:27; cf. Ex 29:42; 30:8; Lv 4:4, 7, 15, 24; 6:18; 1 Kgs 8:62; 1 Sm 2:30; Mal 1:9 f.). The Jerusalem altars stand "before the Lord", specifically "in the presence of the Lord". Of the cult table in the sanctuary it says: "This is the table that stands before the Lord" (Ez 41:22; cf. 1 Sm 21:7; Lv 24:7). The priests are to approach God, they are to come before him to offer the slaughter sacrifice; they are (then) to enter the sanctuary and approach "my [God's] table" (Ez 44:15 f.). This evokes the image of a statue of the deity looking (from the innermost part of the Temple) at the altar or cult table. The imageless cult of the Jews replaces this statue with the idea of the invisible face of God.[420] The offerings are brought to the tent of meeting "before the Lord" (Lv 1:3; 4:4; 5:6; 14:23), or more concretely "before the Lord, before the altar" (Lv 6:7 LXX).[421] Solomon approaches the altar of the Lord from the front in the presence of the whole assembly, spreads his hands towards heaven (1 Kgs 8:22, 54) and looks in the direction of the temple (cf. 1 Kgs 8:27–30). He prays that God may keep his eyes open towards the Temple and may hear the prayer of his servant there (1 Kgs 8:29, 52). It is significant that the prophet Ezekiel criticizes those men who place themselves between the Temple and the altar of burnt offerings, but with their backs to the Temple so as to worship the sun in the east (Ez 8:16). For Ezekiel it is clear that the sacrifice must be offered facing the Temple.[422]

When pagans convert to Christianity, they do not change their prayer posture, but they do change their deity. As Tertullian says, they run away from the graven images and into the churches, there to raise their hands to God the Father.[423] The raising of hands can also be called simply stretching out one's hands to the Lord or to God.[424] Marinus, for example, "stretched out his hands to heaven and looked up to his Father";[425] Simon prayed with his hands raised and his eyes lifted up to God's countenance;[426] Tryphon "lifted up his hands to the highest vault of heaven to our Lord Jesus Christ".[427] "Of course,

---

420 Lv 1:11: "It shall be slaughtered on the north side of the altar before the Lord." This does not mean that the animal should be sacrificed at the side of the altar; rather, it refers only to the slaughter, which takes place beside the altar yet still in the direction of the tent.

421 Lv 6:7 LXX: "bring near before the Lord, before the altar."

422 Cf. 1 Mc 7:36: "At this the priests went in and stood before the altar and the temple."

423 Tert. idol. 7,1 (CCL 2, 1106).

424 Tert. spect. 25,5 (CCL 1, 249); Cyrill. Alex. ep. fest. 8,3 (SC 392, 82); Pass. Ioh. et Pauli 1 (BHL 3237); Ps.-Gregent. disp. cum Herbano Iud. (PG 86,1, 724D); Pass. VIIdorm. 11 (BHL 2313).

425 Pass. Marini 2 (BHG 2256); Pass. Alexandri 2,21 (BHG 48–49): *oculos in caelum ad suum Dominum Jesum Christum erectos tenebat*.

426 Pass. Marini 2 (BHG 2256); Pass. Alexandri 2,21 (BHG 48–49): *oculos in caelum ad suum Dominum Jesum Christum erectos tenebat*.

427 Pass. Tryph. 10 (BHG 1856).

Fig. 39: Tondo from the time of Hadrian showing a sacrifice being offered to Apollo, Arch of Constantine in Rome; photo: D-DAI-ROM-32.54.

we can neither show nor see the God whom we worship".[428] But the invisibility of God is made up for by human imagination. Prayer is a gazing upon the Lord.[429] The monks of Pachomius should pray with outstretched arms, the eyes of the body and the spirit constantly lifted up to the Lord of the heavens.[430] Looking up to heaven means expecting God,[431] seeing Christ.[432] Conversely, God looks down from there upon the person praying.[433]

428 Min. Fel. 32,4 (CSEL 2, 46).
429 Pass. Fructuosi 2,3 (BHL 3196); Pass. Phileae 2,11 (BHL 6799); Pass. Conon. 5,1; 6,3 (BHG 361).
430 A. VEILLEUX, Pachomian Koinonia 2 (Kalamazoo 1981) 199.
431 Petr. Chrys. serm. 105,4 (CCL 24A, 652).
432 Prud. apoth. 502 (CCL 126, 94): *erigit ad caelum facies atque invocat Hisum* [!]. Seeing God's countenance as seeing Christ see G. BUNGE, "In Geist und Wahrheit." Studien zu den 153 Kapi-

teln *Über das Gebet* des Evagrios Pontikos (Bonn 2010) 228–239.
433 Philo. in Flacc. 14,121 (COHN / REITER 1915, 142); Pass. Martinae 2,17 (BHL 5587); Pass. Tarachi 3,32 (BHG 1574); Pass. Potiti 4,20 (BHL 6908); Pass. XXIII mart. romanorum 2 (BHL 16); Pass. Pisoura (HYVERNAT 1886, 116 f.); Pass. Tatianae 7 (BHG 1699); Sym. Metaphr. pass. Sergii 10. 19 (BHG 1625).

Fig. 40: Scene in the nave mosaics of St Paul Outside the Walls in Rome: Cain and Abel sacrificing grain and a lamb at the altar (Gn 4:3f); BAV Vat. Barb. lat. 4406, fol. 31; Proverbio 2016, 203.

The First Letter of Clement already says that the person praying stands before God, lifting up to him pure and undefiled hands.[434] By the High Priest Christ he offers sacrifices, by him looks up to heaven, by him sees God's visage.[435] Thus the Christian altar is also enlisted in the interaction between earth and heaven: to stand at the altar means standing in God's presence and looking into his face. The altar itself simply stands "before God's eyes".[436] Tertullian describes how those whose offerings (*oblationes*) a priest (at the altar) causes to ascend stand "facing the Lord", with the person praying (and the priest) looking upwards.[437] Even the earliest liturgical prayers already take up such ideas.

434 1 Clem. 28,3–29,1 (SC 167, 146–148). Cypr. or. dom. 4 (CSEL 3,1, 268): *cogitemus nos sub conspectu Dei stare.* Orig. orat. 9,2 (GCS Orig. 2, 318 f.): we lift up our eyes to heaven in prayer in order to see in the eyes of our heart the light of the Lord's face shining upon us (Ps 123:1; 4:7).

435 1 Clem. 36,1 f (SC 167, 158–160).

436 Aug. enn. 25,2,10 (CCL 38, 147): *est et altare coram oculis Dei, quo ingressus est sacerdos, qui pro nobis se primus obtulit. Est caeleste altare, et non amplectitur illud altare, nisi qui lavat manus in innocentibus.*

437 Tert. exh. cast. 11,1 f (SC 319, 106). Cypr. unit. eccl. 18 (SC 500, 228): *filii Aaron, qui inposuerunt altari ignem alienum quem non praeceperat Dominus, in conspectu statim Domini uindicantis extincti sunt.* Cf. Ps.-Cornel. I ep. 2,1 (PL 3, 846B): *Unusquisque enim sicut ante altare stans, Dei timorem habet prae oculis.* The author opposes making an eccesiastical vow (at the altar). Lib. Moz. 686 (Férotin 1995): *Adstantes ergo ante tuam Maiestatem […]. Prepara nobis mensam venerendi altaris, quam circumdemus velut mensam magnifici Regis.*

The Canon of the Mass of Pseudo-Hippolytus (early third century) mentions the bishop standing at the altar with his hands outstretched (raised?) and giving thanks to God for having "made us worthy to stand before you."[438] The *Traditio Apostolica* affirms this when it speaks of the bishop at the altar "incessantly making your face always favourable and offering the gifts of your Holy Church."[439] At the altar, the prayers ascend to heaven and beyond it to the countenance of God.[440]

During the Offertory the bishop looks up to God, who then turns his countenance towards the sacrificer in order to receive the propitiatory gifts. For example, in the so-called Clementine Liturgy (c. 380), the priest prays: "We give Thee (God) thanks, through Him (Christ) that Thou hast thought us worthy to stand before Thee, and to sacrifice to Thee; and we beseech Thee that Thou wilt mercifully look down upon these gifts (δῶρα) which are here set before Thee",[441] and elsewhere: "Do Thou now also look down upon us with gracious eyes, and receive our morning thanksgivings, and have mercy upon us; for we have not spread out our hands unto a strange God."[442] Similar formulations are also found in other liturgies,[443] for example, in the Roman Canon: "Be pleased to look upon these offerings with a favourable and gracious countenance; accept them as you were pleased to accept the offerings of your servant Abel the righteous (*Supra quae propitio ac sereno vultu respicere digneris, et accepta habere* [...])".[444]

Moreover, in the offertory prayers of the Roman-Franconian sacramentaries, the priest frequently says that he brings the oblations before the eyes of the Divine Majesty, asking God to turn his countenance and look down upon the gifts on the altar.[445] In the spirit of such liturgy, for Peter Chrysologus († c. 450), bishop of Ravenna, the dispenser of the divine Word always stands before God, and always does so facing the altar, i.e. facing east.[446] He never leaves God's sight and is incapable of sin in the Holy of Holies, where he stands before God.[447] Pope Gregory the Great (590–604) tells of Pope

---

438 Trad. Apost. 4 (FC 1, 220–222): *Illi vero offerant diacones oblationes quique inponens manus in eam* [sc. *oblationem*] *cum omni praesbyterio dicat gratias agens.* This probably means just a brief placing of the hands on the offerings when accepting them from the deacons, whereas at all other times the prayer posture was to be assumed; by contrast, RAFFA 1998, 697: "tutta l'anafora con le mani dei concelebranti stese sulle oblate".

439 Trad. Apost. 3 (FC 1, 218).

440 Joh. Chrys. in 2 Cor. hom. 20,3 (PG 61, 540).

441 Const. Apost. 8,12,38 f (FUNK 1905, 510). Cf. Prud. cathem. 7,4 f. (CCL 126, 35): Christ looks at the sacrificial offering.

442 Const. Apost. 8,38,4 (FUNK 1905, 548).

443 Offertory prayer of the Divine Liturgy of St James (in German: BKV Griechische Liturgien

[München 1912] 101): "and receive me graciously by Your goodness as I draw near to Your altar. [...] and cast me not away from Your presence."

444 Sacr. Greg. 12 (DESHUSSES 1971).

445 Miss. Goth. 339, 386, 412, 440, 505 (MOHLBERG 1961); Sacr. Veron. 10, 21, 43, 58, 131, 306, 309, 333, 347, 595, 1200 (MOHLBERG 1994); Lib. Sacr. 53, 518, 616, 629, 721, 865 (MOHLBERG / BAUMSTARK 1927); Sacr. Greg. 17,2; 23,2 (= 101,2; 134,2); 27,3; 48,2; 57,2; 116,2; 131,2; 132,2; 145,2 (LIETZMANN 1921b); Sacr. Greg. 125, 249, 313, 543, 608 (DESHUSSES 1971).

446 On the direction of prayer in Ravenna see below p. 279–283.

447 Petr. Chrys. serm. 26,3 (CCL 24, 149).

Fig. 41: Achilles sacrifices to Zeus: the god appears to him as a bust in the *clipeus*; Biblioteca Ambrosiana Cod. F. 205 inf., fragm. 47 pict., end of the 5th century; photo: Mondadori Media S.p.A.

Agapetus (535–536) coming to the altar to pray and offering the sacrifice "before God Almighty".[448] Elsewhere, he says emphatically: "Only when a sacrifice is set alight before his eyes with the flame of love on the altar of good works will God accept it."[449]

These contexts can be illustrated by a lost painting in the nave of the Roman basilica of St Paul Outside the Walls (mid–fifth century) which is known from a baroque water-colour (Fig. 40). It depicts Cain and Abel sacrificing their offerings, namely grain and a lamb (Gn 4:3 f.), which they are holding up. For iconographic reasons alone, they are standing at the narrow sides of the altar whereas they should in fact be standing in front of it. Hovering in a cloudy sky above the altar – which has the appearance of a Christian altar on account of the *fenestella confessionis* in the front of it – is the half figure of God. The design of the picture follows the biblical text, which says that God looked down with favour on Abel and his sacrifice, which he accepted, but did not look down on the sacrifice of Cain, which he rejected (Gn 4:4 f.). However, the way the watercolour depicts God with a triangular nimbus cannot be the way it looked in early Christian times. This nimbus at least must be considered a baroque addition, whereas a bust of God above the sacrificial

---

448 Greg. I. dial. 3,3,2 (SC 260, 268). Sacr. Veron. 160, 263 (Mohlberg 1994): *ut digna sint munera, quae oculis tuae maiestatis offerimus.* Cf. 411, 415. In Gregory's time, hands and eyes were still raised up to heaven when praying; Greg. I dial. 3,15,11 (SC 260, 322). Lifting up hands and eyes for the Lord's Prayer see Lib. Moz. 17, 53, 226, 1174 (Férotin 1995). Cf. 101.

Fig. 42: North wall of the presbyterium of the church of *San Vitale* in Ravenna, 6th century, showing the sacrifices of Abel and Melchisedek; Angiolini Martinelli 1997a, 238 Fig. 441.

altar may conceivably have been there from the start. Dating from the same period are not only a sacrificial scene in Santa Maria Maggiore, in which a bust of the nimbused Christ in heaven appears to the priest-king Melchisedek (below Fig. 118), but also a manuscript from the *Iliad* in which Achilles sacrifices to Zeus on an altar. The hero looks diagonally upwards over the altar, where the god appears to him as a bust in a *clipeus* (Fig. 41).[450]

Of course, there is also a possibility that in St Paul Outside the Walls it was not a bust, but rather the hand of God that was depicted pointing down out of heaven.[451] In any case, there is a similar scene in the chancel of the Church of *San Vitale* in Ravenna (sixth century) (Fig. 42). This time the mosaic shows Melchisedek (Gn 14:18) standing together with Abel (Gn 4:4) and performing a sacrifice at an altar which, on account of its form and the chalice and the round loaves, must be understood as Christian. Both Abel and Melchisedek are looking up to heaven and sacrificing their gifts to God by lifting them up and, as it were, offering them to God. From above, the hand of God emerges from the clouds to bless and receive the gifts.[452]

449   Greg. I reg. past. 3,9 (SC 382, 302).
450   Cf. Bergmeier 2017, 90 f.
451   Proverbio 2016, 204, 206.
452   In the Cod. Sinait. 1186, fol. 98r Abraham is to be seen looking up to heaven, to God's hand, at the very moment when he is about to sacrifice Isaac; Weitzmann / Galavaris 1990, Color plate XI. For a similar motif showing Job's sacrifice see Cod. Sinait. 3, fol. 9r (ibid. Plate CX, 302).

e. The diakonia of the angels

The vertical dynamics of the altar also include the idea of the heavenly altar, the heavenly sanctuary and the service of the angels – legacies of Jewish apocalypticism (e.g. Gn 22:11; Jgs 13:20; Lk 1:11).[453] Here the pious imagination richly embellishes the busy goings-on between heaven and earth. Already for Irenaeus of Lyon († c. 200), worship consists in offering up the gift (*munus*) at the altar without ceasing; and here the requests and offerings do not, as it were, remain lying on the altar, but are sent up to the heavenly altar.[454] John Chrysostom († 407) is of the opinion that when the double door or curtains open in front of the altar during the sacrifice, then the heavens, too, open and the angels descend.[455] The earthly altar on which the mystical sacrifice is performed thus turns into the heavenly altar at which the choirs of angels sing.[456] John Mandakuni († 499) asks the rhetorical question: "Don't you know that at the moment when the Holy Sacrament comes on to the altar, heaven above opens and Christ descends and arrives, that hosts of angels hover from heaven to earth and surround the altar?"[457]

At the Eucharistic Sacrifice, hosts of angels surround the priest and the altar to adore him who lies on the altar.[458] Gregory of Nazianzus († c. 390) thinks that the priest joins the angels and archangels on earth to send the oblations up to the heavenly altar and to participate in Christ's priesthood there.[459] Ambrose of Milan († 397) is also familiar

453 Past. Herm. 42,2 f. (SC 53², 190) is already likely to be speaking of a heavenly altar. Joh. Chrys. de inani gloria 39 (SC 188, 132): "upper altar". The eastern liturgies (of James, Mark, Chrysostom and Basil) speak repeatedly of the "heavenly altar": BKV Griechische Liturgien (München 1912) 90, 113, 166, 251, 266. 268. In the so-called Clementine Liturgy (c. 380) the priest beseeches God to take the gift that is offered through the mediation of his Christ upon his heavenly altar: Const. apost. 8,13,3 (FUNK 1905, 514). Similarly in the Divine Liturgy of St James (BKV Griechische Liturgien [München 1912] 95). Aug. enn. 25,2,10 (CCL 38, 147): Christ himself functions as a priest at the heavenly altar. Clem. Alex. strom. 7,7,40,1 (SC 428, 140–142): the person praying raises his eyes and hands to heaven and tries with his soul to reach the sanctuary there. See also two Victories at an altar on Augustan coins; H. MATTINGLY / E. A. SYDENHAM, The Roman Imperial Coinage 1 (London 1923), Pl. IV,66; STOLL 2000, 143 f. On

the whole complex see PETERSON 1935, 69–72; P. BROWE, Die eucharistischen Wunder des Mittelalters (Breslau 1938) 6–12.

454 Iren. adv. haer. 4,18,6 (SC 100,2, 614).

455 Joh. Chrys. in Eph. hom. 3,5 (PG 62, 29); in 1 Cor. hom. 36,5 (PG 61, 313). On the difficult question of exactly when the curtains open see VAN DE PAVERD 1970, 41–47, 340–344, 365 f.

456 Joh. Chrys. in Hebr. hom. 14,2 (PG 63, 111).

457 BKV Ausgewählte Schriften der Armenischen Väter 2 (München 1927) 226. Theod. Mops. cat. 15,27 (FC 17,2, 410): angels adore the Lord's Body on the altar. Ephr. Syr. paraen. (BOJKOVSKY / AITZETMÜLLER 1988, 26): during the Eucharistic Prayer the heavens are open and a fire and a crowd of holy angels descend.

458 Joh. Chrys. sac. 6,4 (SC 272, 316). Cf. VAN DE PAVERD 1970, 35.

459 Greg. Naz. or. 2,73 (PG 35, 481A). Cf. or. 45,23. 30 (PG 36, 656B. 664B).

with angels standing at the altar;[460] on their hands they carry the immaculate, bloodless offering up to the heavenly altar.[461] And for Peter Chrysologus († 450), the priest in the sanctuary becomes nothing less than an angel himself, that is, a messenger between man and God, when he accepts the concerns of the faithful, carries them to the altar and there offers them up with supplications, thereupon receiving what has been obtained, carrying it back and giving it to the faithful.[462]

A text that probably points to Egypt praises those who bring gifts to the altar and in return receive the seal, probably the sign of the cross, from the angels standing at the altar.[463] Here the angels receive the gifts from the faithful, like the deacons. Accordingly, the Liturgy of St Mark says that by no means only the Eucharist, but rather all the gifts of the faithful deposited on the altar are carried up by the angels. Thus, after reading out the names of the deceased (and those presenting the offering), the priest prays: "Accept, O God, by Your ministering archangels at Your holy, heavenly, and reasonable altar in the spacious heavens, the thank-offerings of those who offer sacrifice and oblation, and of those who desire to offer much or little, in secret or openly, but have it not to give. Accept the thank-offerings of those who have presented them this day."[464]

Gregory the Great writes: "What right believing Christian can doubt that in the very hour of the sacrifice, at the words of the Priest, the heavens be opened, and the quires of Angels are present in that mystery of Jesus Christ; that high things are accompanied with low, and earthly joined to heavenly, and that one thing is made of visible and invisible?"[465] The medieval legend of St Maurus tells of the vision of a monk who sees the saint at the high altar of the abbey church of St Maurus (Glanfeuil, *Saint-Maur-sur-le-Loir*) dressed as a deacon and with his arms raised, receiving the prayers of the monks, then turning to the east and handing the prayers on to an angel who is standing at the altar; the latter then carries the prayers up into God's presence.[466]

460 Ambr. sacr. 4,2,5 (SC 25², 104). An altar angel is also mentioned in Epiph. pan. 25,3,1 (GCS Epiph. 1, 269).

461 Ambr. sacr. 4,6,27 (SC 25², 116).

462 Petr. Chrys. serm. 26,3 (CCL 24, 149).

463 Ps.-Athan. in nativ. praec. 1 (PG 28, 908C). In any case, the faithful laid their oblations (*oblationes*) on an altar and these were then distributed to feed the poor; Leont. Neap. vit. Ioh. Eleem. 30 (GELZER 1893, 63). This is likely to have been a side altar. Can. Hippol. arab. 29 (PO 31, 400): powers reside behind the velum at the holy place of the altar.

464 Divine Liturgy of St Marc (BKV Griechische Liturgien [München 1912] 176).

465 Greg. I dial. 4,60,3 (SC 265, 202). Similarly Apophth. 18,48 (SC 498, 116).

466 Translatio S. Mauri 5,26 (ActaSS Jan. 2, 339) (BHL 5776). The Gallic Queen Bathilde († c. 680) sees a ladder standing in front of the Marian altar in the abbey church at Chelles, over which angels conduct her to heaven: Vit. S. Bathildis 13 (MGH.SRM 2, 498 f.). Opt. Mil. 6,1,7 (SC 413, 164): The altar is a ladder on which prayers rise up to God.

Fig. 43: Silver reliquary of Pope Paschal I
(817–824) for the Lateran's relic of the True
Cross; Vatican Museums; PIAC Archivio
Fotografico.

The angelic transport service of the Maurus legend was certainly inspired by the Roman Canon of the Mass (Canon Romanus). There, God appears, as it were, at the heavenly altar, served by an angel: "In humble prayer we ask you, almighty God: command that these gifts be borne by the hands of your holy Angel to your altar on high in the sight of your divine majesty (*Supplices te rogamus omnipotens Deus: jube haec perferri per manus sancti Angeli tui in sublime altare tuum in conspectu divinae majestatis tuae*)."[467] Accordingly, the silver reliquary of Pope Paschalis I (817–824) in the treasury of the *Sancta Sanctorum* shows two angels above Christ, who is standing at the altar (Fig. 43).[468] In the same way, there are two angels hovering over the ciborium on the well-known Frankfurt Mass ivory, bowing down as it were, to the altar (below Fig. 152). Even if the Roman Canon speaks of only one angel, this was not understood strictly numerically in Rome. The Ambrosian Canon anyway speaks of angels in the plural.[469] This may also be the case with the Ravenna liturgy. At all events, the ceiling mosaic above the altar of San Vitale in Ravenna shows four angels holding the Eucharistic Lamb of God[470] in their midst, evidently carrying it up from the earthly altar to heaven (below Fig. 56).[471]

Also noteworthy is a lost mosaic in the Church of *San Giovanni Evangelista* in Ravenna.[472] Exactly above the bishop's throne, the current bishop, Petrus Chrysologus († c. 450), is depicted standing at the altar with his hands raised and with the offering lying on the altar (Fig. 44). To the right and left of him, there are two imperial couples carrying gifts to the altar. Directly beside the priest, there is also an angel to be seen. At the time, the image was interpreted as showing the angel carrying the bishop's prayers (and gifts?) up to God.[473] Since the church has an east-facing apse, the celebrating priest standing in front of the altar can see in the picture in front of him an image of what he himself is at that very moment doing at the altar. It is also said that in the picture Peter has a look of surprise on his face at the presence of the angel. The whole thing is appar-

---

467 Sacr. Greg. 12 (DESHUSSES 1971). Vgl. 727; Sacr. Veron. 845 (MOHLBERG 1994).

468 GRISAR 1908, 99. Since the sixth century at the latest, we encounter veritable custodian angels that every altar possesses from the day of its consecration on; KIRSCH / KLAUSER 1950, 353. This may also be how the two majestic angels on the triumphal arch of *Sant'Apollinare* in Classe are to be interpreted (below Fig. 104). There is also mention of angels watching over altars in Ps.-Athan. nativ. praec. 1 (PG 28, 908C).

469 Ambr. sacr. 4,6,27 (SC 25², 116): [...] *incruentam hostiam, hunc panem sanctum, et petimus et precamur, ut hanc oblationem suscipias in sub-*

limi altari tuo per manus angelorum tuorum. Cf. Miss. Goth. 205 (MOHLBERG 1961): *ita offerentium famulorum suorum munera oblata benedicat, et per inlustrationem spiritus sancti deferentibus nuntiis odor suavitatis ascendat.*

470 The Eucharistic Christ Lamb as the food of angels see Agnell. Lib. Pont. Rav. 64 (FC 21,1, 286–288). On the Lamb of God as Eucharist see also Joh. Chrys. coem. et cruc. 3 (PG 49, 397 f.); Petr. Chrys. serm. 174,8 (CCL 24B, 1063).

471 DEICHMANN 1969, Figs. 311, 346.

472 IHM 1992, 170.

473 DEICHMANN 1974, 110; ZIMMERMANN 2010, 1125.

Fig. 44: Reconstruction of the artistic decoration of the apse of *San Giovanni Evangelista* in Ravenna, after 450; Rizzardi 2011, 59 Fig. 37.

ently intended as a pedagogical or devotional image: the priest celebrating at the altar should not fall into a routine, but should become aware of the heavenly reality when he sees the image.[474]

5. FACING EAST TO PRAY

In current usage, the word orientation means finding one's bearings spatially: you work out which way to go. It does not cause anyone to think of a particular direction, i.e. the east. But this is exactly what orientation originally meant, namely facing east (Lat. *oriens*), the preferred direction since time immemorial, and then also in Christianity, because the sun rises in the east. Orientation took on a new meaning for Christians, namely turning to Christ, the Sun of Righteousness. Probably at some point in the late Middle Ages, however, this original meaning was again lost. In the Renaissance, people no longer knew that the person praying actually "orients" himself and that the priest once looked up towards the eastern sky at the altar.[475] The term "orientation" continues to be used, but now without its original meaning.

East-facing prayer, or orientation, is a general inter-religious legacy of late antiquity, which the Christians already encountered among Jews and pagans and adapted for themselves.[476] Even in antiquity, temple, altar and priest were not independent entities that could be regrouped at will, but were related to each other in a certain spatial and directional structure. The altar, even though it may be free-standing and have no superstructure, nevertheless has a front (almost always decorated) and thus a direction, just like the temple. When offering the sacrifice, the priest looks at the image of the god to whom the altar is consecrated and which is located on the opposite side. The onlookers are not the addressee of the sacrifice and are consequently not who

474 Belonging to this kind of teaching are also the edifying stories of the miracles of the Sacrifice of the Mass in Greg. I dial. 4,55–58 (SC 265, 180–196); Ambr. sacr. 4,6,27 (SC 25², 116). Let it also be mentioned that in an important church in the Byzantine artistic sphere – in Jerusalem? – the Communion of the Apostles must have been depicted on the wall of the apse in the sixth century showing Christ standing behind the altar, albeit without angels (cf. Loerke 1975, 78–97; differently Wessel 1966c, 241). Despite all its dogmatic significance, such an image nevertheless still also possessed a pedagogical and edifying character

for the priest celebrating at the altar and facing eastwards.

475 This knowledge has only been regained by modern research; Heid 2006, 377–399. The historical recognition of an early Christian east-facing direction for prayer is, to be sure, unpopular with many a liturgist. The 2155-page lexicon by D. Sartore *et al.* (eds.), Liturgia (Cinisello Balsamo 2001) in fact ignores it altogether.

476 Lang 2003, 33–39. On pagan east-facing prayer see Tert. apol. 16,10 (CCL 1, 116); Reisch 1894, 1655 f.; Dölger 1972, 48–60. On Jewish east-facing prayer see Wallraff 2001, 61 f.

Fig. 45: Emperor Trajan with covered head offers the pre-sacrifice at the altar, facing him are the musicians; scene on Trajan's Column in Rome, beginning of the 2nd century; A. S. Stefan, Die Trajanssäule (Darmstadt 2020), Taf. 41.

the priest looks at.[477] Rather, numerous illustrations of sacrificial acts show the priest who offers the sacrifice approaching the altar from one side and the musicians from the opposite side.[478] Other participants usually stand behind the priest who offers the sacrifice, especially in sacrificial processions (Fig. 45; above Fig. 30). This arrangement is preserved and enters the Christian liturgy (below Figs. 91, 93).

Despite all the differences, the east-facing orientation of the altar on principle, which is as a rule approached from the front, also applies to the altar in early Christianity. The altar is functionally bound to prayer. Prayer, however, is intentionally and spatially oriented: one prays standing, hands raised to heaven and eyes to God. The direction is fixed. For although God is omnipresent, he is not placeless. Here the eastern sky comes into play as the seat of God's throne (Fig. 46). The origin of this is praying in the open

477 Fless 1995, 80. Further examples of musicians: Fless 1995, Plate 12,1–2; Plate 39,1; ThesCRA 1, Plate 46 Rom. 76; Plate 47 Rom. 88; Plate 48 Rom. 105; Plate 50 Rom. 138, 141; ThesCRA 5, Plate 17, Fig. 12; Stoll 2000, 43 No. 46; 44 No. 47.
478 Fless 1995, Plate 43,1.

Fig. 46: The prophet Isaiah at prayer, flanked by night (left) and sunrise (right) and looking up to the eastern sky, to God; Psalter, 9th century, BnF, Ms. grec 139, fol. 435v; photo: Wikimedia Commons.

air, which is where the looking upwards comes from that one would not initially expect inside a church. What is important in the prayer orientation is where the eyes are looking: they are directed upwards towards the rising sun, that is, towards the eastern sky. Nevertheless, the dominant idea in antiquity was that God is bound to an earthly location, for instance a temple, or to the cities of Jerusalem or Mecca.[479] This means that by looking up towards the eastern sky the Christians are for their part – and quite definitely with a polemical intention – expressing the omnipresence of the most high God, whom no temple can hold and who is concretely present wherever people gather for prayer.

Christian east-facing prayer is already heralded in the second century, and by about 200 it has become the undisputed practice.[480] It applies to both individual prayer and collective-liturgical prayer. For Christians, the East proves to be a theologically rich dimension, intimately linked to the veneration of Christ, and one that they can no longer do without when praying.[481] Hence it is possible for Martin Wallraff to sum up the first Christian centuries saying: "Christians pray towards the east. This principle was taken

479 VOGEL 1962, 175–178.

480 DÖLGER 1972, 136–149, 185–198; VOGEL 1962, 175; LANG 2003, 42 f.

481 LANG 2003.

for granted by the entire early Church. The testimonies to this are widely scattered in space and time. Nowhere is there any indication to be found of a Christianity without this custom or with the custom of praying in a different direction."[482]

Practising east-facing prayer is of direct relevance to the use of the altar, that is, to the location of the liturgist at the altar. For praying facing east gives the altar its orientation, too. This follows from the inner logic of the liturgy as well as from archaeological observations on church construction since the Constantinian shift (312). The altar is the ideal centre of every church; altar and church interior are strictly interrelated. The structure of the building therefore allows conclusions to be drawn about the meaning and use of the altar. Now, as Cyrille Vogel has observed, almost every church space, whether longitudinal or circular, has its longitudinal line on the west-east axis.[483] This makes it possible for Sible de Blaauw to summarize: "Basically, in the liturgical sense all churches are east-oriented."[484] The apse with the altar is usually in the east. If, exceptionally, the apse faces west, it is revealing that the written testimonies speak of the eastward orientation of the façade.[485]

The link between architecture and the direction of the action is also due to the parallel phenomenon of baptisteries.[486] In them, the entrance and exit to the baptismal font are preferentially located on the west-east axis, or there is an apse on the east side of the baptistery (for the bishop or as a place for the post-baptismal anointing).[487] This is not directly related to prayer, but rather to the profession of Christ as the sun rising in the east. All the same, the two are, of course, closely connected. It should also be noted that even if the structural and archaeological givens do not allow any conclusion to be drawn or if the entrance and exit deviate from the west-east axis, this in itself does not rule out east-facing baptisms. If need be, the descriptions of the rite are to be consulted on this. Interestingly enough, both Western and Eastern rites require the candidate, before the actual act of baptism, to turn to the east when confessing Christ so that he or she can, as

---

482 WALLRAFF 2001, 60. MESSNER 2003a, 356 f.: "Since the end of the 2nd century, testimonies to this custom are quite thick on the ground; their origins in different geographical regions and a variety of literary genres reveal its universality and great age. Whenever Christians pray, whether individually or in community, they observe the east-facing direction."

483 VOGEL 1964, 13–16.

484 DE BLAAUW 2008, 279.

485 DE BLAAUW 2006, 168; id. 2008, 279. With this Blaauw confirms what was already stated by NUSSBAUM 1965, 397: "When the communities were no longer dependent on rooms in Christian houses and on house churches, but were able to erect their own cultic buildings, when praying together they also adhered as a matter of course to the orientation that had so long been customary. The worship space was constructed as a longitudinal building with a west-east axis, which now offered two possibilities: the cult room could be east-oriented either with the entrance wall or with the narrow side opposite it or the later apse." With the exception of the house-church theory, this statement can only be accepted as correct.

486 Important notes on the orientation of baptism and Eucharist at CALABRESE 2021, 48–51.

487 RISTOW 1998 with the respective information in the catalogue.

Ambrose put it, look directly at Christ.[488] It is therefore possible that, on the one hand, the subsequent act of baptism is performed without facing east, or, on the other hand, that the candidate does not turn to face east until after climbing into the basin.

There must be a connection between the everywhere-observable building of churches on a west-east axis and facing east to pray. For the sake of simplicity, prayer should follow the longitudinal direction of the body of the space. Depending on where the east lies, the clergy and people should therefore look either towards the apse or towards the entrance of the church. For practical reasons, however, compromises may have been made with respect to having the entrance in the east. If the church did not lie exactly on a west-east axis, a corresponding deviation of the altar from the liturgical direction was deemed acceptable. For in Christian sacred architecture it is a principle set in stone that the altar always stands transversely at an angle of 90 degrees to the main axis of the church interior; it is never placed obliquely in order to follow the exact west-east axis.[489] Only occasionally are baptismal basins to be found which, as it were, correct the compass direction by being more exactly east-oriented than the church building itself.

For the early Christian altar the basic rule holds that the celebrant stands at it on the western side and faces east. In any case, he has to move in front of or behind it according to the demands of the concrete situation or custom. It is unthinkable that in a church lying on a north-south axis anyone would celebrate obliquely to the nave.[490] So in a church with an east-facing entrance the priest stands behind the altar; in a church with an east-facing apse the priest stands in front of it with his back to the people.[491] Joseph Braun already saw this to be the case.[492] Even though Otto Nussbaum follows Braun, he still thinks he can prove – in spite of very early evidence of east-facing prayer – that for the priest to face east at the altar was not the original practice, but only gradually established itself in the fourth and fifth centuries. However, the historical and archaeological untenability of his statements has been proved by Marcel Metzger and Klaus Gamber (see below chapter VI, 2).[493]

---

488 Ambr. myst. 1,2,7 (SC 25², 158). For the east see Joh. II cat. myst. 1,9 (SC 126², 98). Ps.-Dionys. Areop. eccl. here 2,6 (Heil / Ritter 1991, 72): "After he has called on him (the candidate for baptism) three times to profess his rejection and the latter has three times agreed, he leads him over to the east and asks him to profess Christ with his eyes lifted to heaven and his hands raised" (G. Heil, in: BGL 2, 103). On the theology of eastward-facing baptism see Dölger 1918; Wallraff 2001, 66–69.

489 The rare case of an altar standing diagonally on the main axis of the nave is as a rule due to topographical factors, e.g. in the case of the altar of the Basilica of St Alexander in the Via Nomentana.

490 On Cimitile see Heid 2006, 397–399; differently Wallraff 2004, 117 f.

491 Thunø 2015, 128–131; de Blaauw 2017, 45.

492 Braun 1924a, 412 f. Although Braun was familiar with Franz Joseph Dölger's fundamental studies on orientation in prayer (ibid. 414 n. 6), he no longer incorporated them into his altar book.

493 Metzger 1971; Gamber 1972. Cf. Lang 2003, 58–70.

The assumption that for the priest to face east when praying at the altar is a genuine practice, one that has always been followed and hence the rule, does in fact have the better arguments in its favour. Of the greatest significance in this respect is the Preface dialogue that has been in use throughout the Church since the third century: "Lift up your hearts – We lift them up to the Lord" (*Sursum corda – Habemus ad Dominum*). This is a stage direction (rubric): everyone should stand up, raise their hands in prayer and look up to heaven. Franz Joseph Dölger rightly points out that this implies turning eastward.[494] Through the change of body movement, turning to the east to pray dynamizes the liturgy and turns it into an expressive, even confession-like "play" as the sequence of readings, sermon, intercessions, Offertory, blessings and Eucharist unfolds.

Here a distinction must be made between the vectors of the different actors (principal celebrant, clergy, aristocracy, people).[495] Not all of them do the same thing; their movements are not identical. As a general rule, facing east to pray applies primarily to the priest: he has to face east at the altar, whereas the faithful probably only do so when this does not cause them to turn their backs on the altar.[496] So in a church with its entrance in the east, it would be hard to imagine the faithful looking towards the east rather than towards the altar.[497] A special form is to be assumed at most for North Africa.[498] In the priority given to the priest's facing east to pray it is possible to see a general liturgical principle at work: the reduction of more and more of the actions of the whole community to those of the priest. There then comes a point at which it is sufficient for the priest to face east when praying. In the case of the opening dialogue of the Eucharist, there is already a hint of this hiatus. The Latin *Sursum corda* speaks unspecifically of lifting up hearts. Looking up to God will certainly apply to everyone here, regardless of whether the church has its entrance or its apse in the east, but the priest at least must be facing east when he does so.

This then establishes the baselines of liturgical action in the church space and at the altar. Any study of early Christian church construction and any interpretation of archaeological evidence, especially regarding internal liturgical furnishings, must include in its deliberations the eastward direction of prayer as otherwise misinterpretations are inevitable. Precisely because not every church building is exemplarily identical to the next, it is imperative to look at individual cases. Although the principles are clear, there are many local factors determining how they are applied. One always has to reckon with exceptions or special cases, above all diachronic changes in liturgical disposition.[499] With the orientation of the building, account has to be taken of urban planning, which can

---

494   Dölger 1972, 301–336. He is followed by Vogel 1960, 450; id. 1962, 180 f.; id. 1964, 9–11; Gamber 1972, 49.

495   De Blaauw 2008, 280.

496   See below p. 296.

497   In itself turning towards the entrance door for prayer is not an unusual practice in antiquity; Wallraff 2004, 122–124.

498   See below p. 271 f.

499   Cf. Chavarría Arnau 2009, 82 f.

explain some deviations from the west-east axis, namely when a church complex draws on earlier building structures or makes allowances for where the roads run. It can be just as informative when churches observe the eastward orientation without paying any regard to urban planning.[500]

However, in all this, it must remain clear what is the rule and what is the exception. It is precisely not as if the priest at the altar always faced the people and only faced east in particular circumstances. Brown still held this view.[501] And then in 1965, in his postdoctoral thesis in Bonn, Nussbaum elevated front-facing celebration to the rule, irrespective of eastward orientation, and believed he could prove from literary and archaeological evidence that this was the case throughout the early Christian world.[502] However, the majority of scholars have long been convinced that facing east to pray is the genuine, valid rule for the priest and, as far as possible, for the faithful, too. For the concrete performance of the liturgy and for any assessment of the church space, this means that in the vast majority of churches the location of the liturgist is in front of the altar.

a. Byzantine cultural sphere

The entire eastern half of the empire, which was largely under Byzantine rule and which from the fifth century onwards became partly fragmented into autonomous church regions with their own liturgies in Syrian, Armenian, Coptic and other languages, offers the earliest and densest evidence of an eastward orientation of prayer as well as of the church space itself.[503] In principle, there was no difference in this respect between the various regional traditions, even if their architectural and liturgical solutions did differ. For Asia Minor, Cappadocia, Syria, Palestine and Egypt, the Greek church writers give clear indications of east-facing prayer, and there are also liturgical sources to back them up.[504]

---

500 The cave churches must have posed a special challenge. Unfortunately, N. B. TETERIATNIKOV, The Liturgical Planning of Byzantine Churches in Cappadocia (Rome 1996) does not go into the question of eastward orientation.

501 BRAUN 1924a, 412f.

502 NUSSBAUM 1965; again on a number of points id. 1971.

503 Socr. hist. eccl. 5,22,53 (SC 505, 230–232): Ἐν Ἀντιοχείᾳ δὲ τῆς Συρίας ἡ ἐκκλησία ἀντίστροφον ἔχει τὴν θέσιν· οὐ γὰρ πρὸς ἀνατολὰς τὸ θυσιαστήριον, ἀλλὰ πρὸς δύσιν ὁρᾷ. Socrates confirms that in general (in the Eastern Roman Empire) the altar "faces east" and only faces west in the Great Church (Domus Aurea) in Antioch (cf. G. DOWNEY, Antiocheia, in: RBK 1 [1966] 178–209, here 189). The formulation "faces east" indicates that the priest stands in front of the altar (looking east). It is impossible to clarify whether the priest stood behind the altar in Antioch. It is certainly conceivable that here, too, it was customary for him to stand in front of the altar and pray towards the west. Socrates is apparently not familiar with the cathedral of Tyre, which likewise has its entrance to the east.

504 DÖLGER 1972, 136–185, 320–336; VOGEL 1962, 179f.; NUSSBAUM 1965, 24–30, 62–64, 87–90, 117–120, 134–137; WALLRAFF 2001, 69–71;

In the church buildings, having the apse in the east is more or less continuously prevalent.[505] Even central spaces like the *Hagia Sophia* in Constantinople are directional: the altar is not located in the centre, but on the east side (Fig. 47). The importance of the eastward orientation of a church becomes obvious when in the Latin Empire, especially during the Justinian Restoration and expansion in North Africa (sixth century), churches that did not have their apse in the east were subsequently – under Byzantine influence – "turned around", i.e. the presbytery was moved to the east side of the church.[506] In numerous temple rededications in Cilicia (East Turkey) from the fifth century onwards, attention was paid to their orientation.[507] When, in the sixth century, the hexagonal triclinium in Constantinople was converted into the Church of *Hagia Euphemia*, the most eastern of the five apses was converted into the presbytery, which meant that the main entrance had to be moved.[508] There are churches that pay no attention to the urbanistic context and are located on an exact west-east axis.[509] The baptismal fonts, too, are designed in such a way as to ensure a passage from west to east. If a church itself deviates for any reason from this eastward orientation, the baptismal font or baptistery will be more exactly oriented.[510]

The purpose of the consistently east-facing orientation of the building is evidently to ensure that the faithful pray towards the east: as soon as they enter the church, they automatically look to the east. Only the priest has to turn round for the prayers. He positions himself not face-to-face with the congregation but rather as their prayer leader during the so-called Universal Prayer (General Intercessions) and during the eucharistic anaphora (Canon of the Mass).[511] Since the fourth and fifth centuries, in the context of the opening dialogue of the Canon ("The Lord be with you"), the deacon has invited

LANG 2003, 47–57; HEID 2006, 365, 378, 386–388; HVALVIK 2014, 64–72. For Cappadocia: Basil. can. 97 (RIEDEL 1900, 274): "The deacon should order those who are sitting to stand up, turn their faces to the east and be mindful of their sanctification." Greg. Naz. ep. 34,4 (GCS 53, 31): τὰς χεῖρας εἰς τὸν οὐρανὸν ἀνατείνας, πρός τε ἀνατολὰς οἷον βλέπων. For Syria: Didasc. syr. 20 (ACHELIS / FLEMMING 1904, 100 f.) on the phoenix: "[…] to the altar that is called of the Sun. […] as it prays towards the East, the fire kindles of itself, and consumes it, so that it becomes ashes." On east-facing prayer and altar 1252/53 in detail Theogn. thes. 11 (CCG 5, 53–61).

505 VOGEL 1962, 188; NUSSBAUM 1965, 24–117; DE BLAAUW 2008, 280. Macedonia: SOUSTAL 1995. Cilicia und Isauria: HILL 1996. Cyprus: NICOLAOU 2018. Palestine: OVADIAH 1970. Transjordan: HAMARNEH 2003. Ibid. 63 the compass rose is wrong. Church with its entrance in the east only

ibid. Fig. 76 (Huwara). The east-orientation of a church in Serbia is seen, for example, in *Felix Romuliana*.

506 DE BLAAUW 2008, 280. Cf. YASIN 2017.

507 R. BAYLISS, Provincial Cilicia and the Archaeology of Temple Conversion (Oxford 2004) 41–43.

508 DE BLAAUW 2008, 279.

509 For example, Serbian military camps exhibit churches that "break ranks"; POPOVIĆ / BORIĆ-BREŠKOVIĆ 2013, 42, 47.

510 For example, the bishop's church (octagon) in Philippi, the Episcopal and the North Basilica in Stoboi (SOUSTAL 1995, 1017 f., 1023 f.) and probably also the double basilica in Alyki in Macedonia (ibid. 1047 f.); the church in the Cartagenna quarter of Carthage (DUVAL 2008–2009, 135 f. Fig. 22a); basilica at Chersonesos (KHRUSHKOVA 2017).

511 VOGEL 1964, 9.

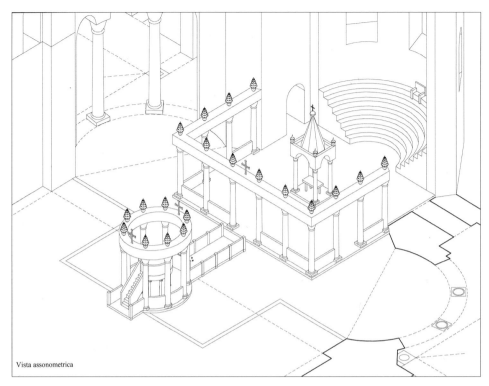

Vista assonometrica

Fig. 47: Axonometric view of the altar area of the *Hagia Sophia* in Constantinople, which has an east-end apse, 6th century. The ambo, free-standing altar and cathedra lie on the central axis of the church. The *Hagia Sophia* became the model church for Byzantium in a similar way to the Lateran Basilica for the West; LUIGIA FOBELLI 2005, Ill. 38.

those who are seated to stand up and turn their faces to the east.[512] This formulation is interesting. One might ask why the faithful should turn round since in a church with its apse in the east they are facing east anyway. But it seems that the deacon's call to turn their heads to the east only applies to those sitting on the benches along the walls of the church: they are to stand up and turn at least their heads towards the altar. The very thing that is not said is that they should look towards the altar; they are called upon to look towards the east. Exactly the same, of course, applies to the priest at the altar. Therefore he stands in front of the altar with his back to the congregation, as is still the case today in the Byzantine and Oriental Rites (Fig. 48).

Now one might think that the present position of the Orthodox priest in front of the altar is due to the introduction after the iconoclasms of the eighth and ninth centuries of the iconostasis, which thrusts itself like a wall between chancel and nave. Because the

---

512 DÖLGER 1972, 324–330.

faithful can anyway now no longer see the altar, it might be argued that the priest, who had previously celebrated *versus populum*, moved in front of the altar – not least of all for practical reasons – since he has already come out in front of the iconostasis several times in order to bless the faithful. With the introduction of the iconostasis, so this line of thinking goes, the cathedra at the apex of the apse had also become superfluous, so that in those churches where it still existed it was draped with icons.

Such a reconstruction, however plausible it may sound, nevertheless turns the historical development upside down. East-facing prayer is well documented centuries prior to the introduction of the iconostasis. Nor is the iconostasis an innovation that comes out of nowhere; rather, it goes back formally to the so-called templon (for the templon of the *Hagia Sophia* see above Fig. 47). Although these barriers with bricked-up columns and architraves (which were very common in early Byzantine churches) separate the chancel from the nave, they still permit the altar to be seen. Gradually, curtains and icons were added, so that the faithful were less and less able to follow what was happening behind them.[513] This would not have happened if celebration *versus populum* had been the norm and, as it were, what was required by the liturgy. Rather, it was possible to curtain off the templon because eye contact between priest and people was the very thing that did not matter in what went on at the altar and because the faithful could at least see the priest at the altar through the central door.[514]

It would in any case be extremely odd if, in the entire Byzantine cultural sphere, the eastward orientation of the faithful and the buildings was scrupulously observed, yet the priest at the altar, of all people, was permitted to face west. In fact, the sources show the priest to have stood in front of the altar.[515] On the other hand, it can be assumed that in the very rare churches with their entrance in the east the priest stood behind the altar.[516] Overall, it is therefore not very plausible when Nussbaum assumes that in the Byzantine sphere there were no rules and that the celebrant sometimes faced the apse and sometimes the people. On the contrary, there can be no reasonable doubt about a uniform east-facing celebration.[517]

---

513 Cf. Mathews 2016, 171–193.

514 The iconostasis (since the ninth century) makes the synthronon in the apse unusable (below Fig. 48). The clergy can no longer be seated there during the Liturgy of the Word. In fact, the Liturgy of the Word now takes place in front of the iconostasis. Bishop and clergy stand or sit in the middle of the nave, with the bishop looking eastwards towards the iconostasis.

515 Joh. Chrys. coem. et cruc. 3 (PG 49, 397 f.): Τί ποιεῖς, ἄνθρωπε; ὅταν ἐστήκῃ πρὸ τῆς τραπέζης ὁ ἱερεὺς τὰς χεῖρας ἀνατείνων εἰς τὸν οὐρανόν […];

Dölger 1972, 325; van de Paverd 1970, 51, 317. Joh. Chrys. in Hebr. hom. 22,3 (PG 63, 158): lift up hands to heaven to the Sun of Righteousness (i.e. to the east). Eger. itin. 48,2 (CCL 175, 89): *Salomon […] steterit ante altarium Dei et oraverit.*

516 In the church at Tyre with its east-end entrance (c. 314–321), the priest seems to receive the gifts of the faithful standing to the right of the altar and then to move behind it; Euseb. hist. eccl. 10,4,68 (SC 55, 102 f.).

517 Nussbaum 1965, 127, on the other hand, always assumes a "doubtlessly" west-facing celebration

Here one should not imagine just the priest at the altar – usually the bishop – but also the concelebrants. The bishop always celebrates the liturgy together with his presbyters, who take their seats on the synthronon to the right and left of him during the Liturgy of the Word (deacons, on the other hand, have to stand). The synthronon is the name for the benches along the apse wall (above Fig. 47, below Figs. 49, 86, 107, 108). It can be assumed from the outset that the concelebrating priests also face east at the altar. For the seats only have no purpose outside the Liturgy of the Word. During the celebration of the Eucharist, everyone must stand, and it can be ruled out that the priests stand on the sometimes very high steps of the synthronon while the bishop, as it were, celebrates mass down below at the altar. It is equally unlikely that they simply descend the steps of the synthronon and remain standing there in a confined space in the apse. Even though there is no proof of this, it can be assumed that the concelebrants stand in front of the altar with the bishop, thus also turning their backs on the people. It is interesting to note that the altar is sometimes in the middle of the enclosed presbytery, but frequently east of centre, so that there is now plenty of space in front of the altar (Fig. 49).[518] What was this space used for? For the choir? But this stands outside the presbytery by the ambo, just as it stands outside the iconostasis in the post-iconoclastic liturgy. If one were to assume with Nussbaum that the main celebrant stood behind the altar, then the concelebrants would have to have stood behind it, too, so as not to obstruct the view of the faithful. So why is the altar not moved closer to the nave? The fact that there is so much space in front of the altar is probably due to the staggered arrangement of the clergy resulting from the eastward orientation: the bishop stands in front of the altar with the concelebrants next to and behind him, and possibly other clergy behind them.[519]

There is also archaeological evidence of an east-facing celebration. The basilica in Aegina has a trapezoidal piece of flooring in front of the altar, which probably marks where the liturgist stood; furthermore, there is a relic shaft behind the altar.[520] Basilica B in Nikopolis also has a standing space marked in front of the altar.[521] In a number of

---

whenever the archaeological findings do not permit any direct clarification. By contrast, Priene, Korykos and Alahan advocate an east-facing celebration precisely on account of the clear eastern location of the altar within the presbytery (differently NUSSBAUM loc. cit. 126–129).

518 For Cyprus NICOLAOU 2018, 135: "In all the above-mentioned basilicas, the altar was located well in front of the apse, in the east part of the sanctuary, a fact which implies that the priest stood on its west side facing east." Cf. M. RESTLE,

Kappadokien, in: RBK 3 (1978) 968–1115. On the cathedral of Apamea see BALTY / BALTY 2011, 112 f. Fig. 7 f.

519 One must therefore assume for early Byzantine liturgy that there was a clear change of position for the clergy between the Liturgy of the Word (seated in the apse) and the Eucharist (standing at the altar), a change similarly to be observed in the Western liturgy (Rome, North Africa).

520 NUSSBAUM 1965, 141.

521 Ibid. 154 f.

Fig. 48: Apse of the Orthodox *Church of the Acheiropoietos* in Thessaloniki. The iconostasis, altar and covered cathedra. The celebrant stands in front of the altar looking east, i.e. towards the Cross in the apse calotte or the windows; photo: Beat Brenk.

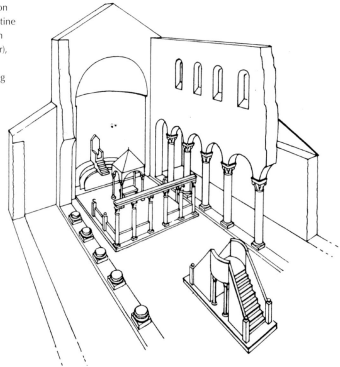

Fig. 49: Schematic representation of a standard 6th-century Byzantine church displaying an ambo with double stairs, a templon (barrier), altar (with ciborium) and the synthronos (with cathedra) along the apse wall; PEETERS 1969, 128 Fig. 20.

cases, a relic shaft in the floor behind the altar suggests an east-facing celebration.[522] In several basilicas, lack of space means that the priest can only have stood in front of the altar, for example when the altar stands directly in front of the apse step.[523] The layout of the basilicas of Laureotikos Olympos and the southern church of *Justiniana Prima* (Serbia) also suggests an east-facing celebration.[524] The altar of Pliska (Bulgaria) seems to have been surrounded on three sides by barriers, meaning that only an east-facing celebration was possible.[525] The Parthenon Basilica in Athens and the Basilica of Thasos have steps in front of the altar, which undoubtedly served as a place for the priest to stand.[526] Since the priest is known to not yet have genuflected at this time, he could

---

522 Ibid. 123 f., 138 f., 156 f.: Basilica of St John in Ephesus, Stoudios Basilica in Constantinople, Basilica A in Philippi, probably also Basilica B (P. LEMERLE, Philippes et la Macédoine orientale à l'époque chrétienne et byzantine [Paris 1945], Pl. LXXXI–LXXXII). A possible second altar in the actual apse of St John's also supports an east-facing celebration.

523 NUSSBAUM 1965, 141 f., 144 f., 152 f.: Basilica of Olympia, the Metochi chapel on Samos, the basilica in Sikyon. D'ANDRIA 2016–2017, 138 Fig. 7;182, Fig. 3: the Basilica of St Philip in Hierapolis. EEECAA 2, 445 Fig. 3: the Cathedral of Sagalassos.

524 NUSSBAUM 1965, 146. For the south church NUSSBAUM *op. cit.* 162 f. assesses the situation differently, but he is undoubtedly wrong here.

525 Ibid. 163.

526 Ibid. 142, 153 f.

Fig. 50: Altar in the cupola mosaic of the Orthodox Baptistery in Ravenna, 6th century (altar steps here largely reconstructed); Wilpert / Schumacher 1976, Plate 91.

easily have stood on a step at the altar. The mosaic of the dome of the Baptistery of the Orthodox in Ravenna shows altars with steps at the front, which there, too, have no purpose other than to indicate the position of the priest "with his back to the people" as is customary in the Ravenna liturgy (Fig. 50).[527] In several basilicas, the altar under the ciborium stands east of centre, meaning that there too the priest probably stood on the western side.[528] Although Nussbaum considers west-facing celebration to be proved for the *Hagia Sophia* in Nicaea, the latest archaeological findings show an east-facing celebration to be a possibility there as well.[529]

By contrast, there is not a single church in the regions we are dealing with that would from an archaeological point of view suggest a west-facing celebration.[530] The one verified west-facing celebration that Nussbaum finds in the Greek-Balkan area is in the Mastichari Basilica on the island of Kos since there the altar stands west of centre beneath

527 Sotira 2013, 105 f. Fig. 179–181. The altars and the area of the steps have been partially restored.

528 Nussbaum 1965, 142, 148–153: the Georgios Basilica in Athens, the Aphentella Basilica on Lesbos, the basilica in Klapsi, the basilica in Sikyon. Added to these, the East Basilica in Xanthos (R. Jacobek, Lykien, in: RBK 5 [1995] 856–902, here 889 f. Fig. 15).

529 On the Hagia Sophia in Nicaea (Nussbaum 1965, 120 f.) see S. Möllers, Nikaia, in: RBK 6 (2005) 976–1013, here 992–997.

530 Nussbaum 1965, 127 f. maintains a west-facing celebration for the "cathedral" of Korykos, but the description of the findings in E. Herzfeld / S. Guyer, *Monumenta Asiae Minoris Antiqua* 2. Meriamlik und Korykos (Manchester 1930) 98 f. does not offer any support for this.

the ciborium.[531] But once again his argumentation is not compelling. It is likely, instead, that this was simply an elegant solution enabling, on the one hand, the altar and, on the other hand, the square ciborium to be accommodated there in a very small space in such a way that neither the rear nor the front columns of the ciborium obstructed the clergy passing through. In this way the altar was freely accessible from the front. The floor covering there also indicates where the liturgist stood.[532]

b. Syrian region

Nussbaum provides all the literary and archaeological evidence with respect to Syria for the east-end location of the apse in all the churches and for the assumption that the priest faced east at the altar. Of outstanding significance here is the *Didascalia* (third century) as it describes the standard church interior for Syria. This resembles an elongated room, at the eastern end of which the bishop and priests are seated behind the altar during the Liturgy of the Word. In general, everyone stands to pray, both clergy and people, in a staggered formation and facing east: at the head are the clergy, behind them the men, then the women.[533] This clear rule applies even if different solutions were found as far as liturgical interior furnishings are concerned. On the one hand, there is the "concentrated disposition" (Sible de Blaauw) traditional in the Byzantine sphere in which the presbytery forms a unit with the apse, and, on the other hand – in northern Syria – there is the "spread disposition". In the latter case, the benches for the priests are not located in the apse, but rather stand isolated in the middle of the nave facing the apse (the so-called Syrian bema). In the apse itself, the altar is so close to the wall that there can be no reasonable doubt that the liturgist stood in front of it (Fig. 51).[534]

Nussbaum, however, indulges in numerous divergences so as to be able to find a celebration *versus populum* in individual cases. First of all, this must be countered by stating that there are a number of clear archaeological indications that the celebrant's place was to the west of the altar: the slabs he stood on or the lack of space on the east side.[535] Conversely, there is no case in which an east-facing celebration would have to be ruled out on archaeological grounds.

In view of the textual sources, which speak unanimously of east-facing prayer, it is unacceptable that Nussbaum leaves it open whether the direction of celebration was west-facing or east-facing. For him, there was no uniform practice; rather, in every church a particular direction of celebration established itself depending on whether the

531 Nussbaum 1965, 149, 168.
532 Gamber 1972, 54.
533 Messner 2003a, 363 f.

534 Wessel 1966a, 118; Comte 2012, 263–393.
535 See illustrations in Nussbaum 1965 II, 17–22
     Figs. 27, 30–35, 39.

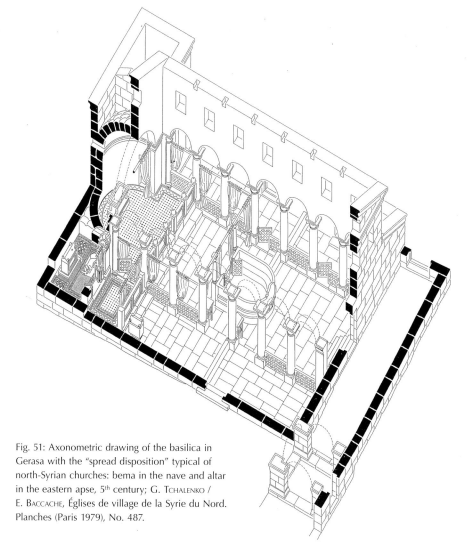

Fig. 51: Axonometric drawing of the basilica in Gerasa with the "spread disposition" typical of north-Syrian churches: bema in the nave and altar in the eastern apse, 5th century; G. TCHALENKO / E. BACCACHE, Églises de village de la Syrie du Nord. Planches (Paris 1979), No. 487.

old or the new practice was followed.[536] However, there is no evidence whatsoever of such a distinction. It becomes totally far-fetched when Nussbaum concludes from the presence of a Byzantine-style ambo that this indicates "with certainty" that the priest celebrated facing the people, whereas a Syrian bema points to an east-facing celebration.[537] Furthermore, it is hard to see what an ambo, which is used above all for readings, is supposed to have to do with the direction of prayer.

There is also no indication in the Syrian sources that the liturgical rule of facing east to pray applied only to certain types of churches or only to certain liturgies. Hence it is unconvincing to assume the existence of different celebrations in the city of Resafa, one facing east (Basilica of the Holy Cross) and one facing west (in the annex church adjoin-

---

536 NUSSBAUM 1965, 61. 537 Ibid. 50, 52, 59.

ing it to the east). Both churches have their apse at the east end. Both altars stand close to the synthronon, i.e. east of centre within the presbytery. Two things speak in favour of east-facing prayer: the Basilica of the Holy Cross has a round window (*oculus*) combined with a cross in the dome of the apse and the annex church displays a cross in a celestial sphere in the same place (below Figs. 116, 117; cf. above Figs. 27, 48).[538]

Nussbaum claims that the altar in the pilgrimage church of Kalat Siman is *versus populum*.[539] Its position is not certain, but archaeological evidence suggests that it stood so close to the synthronon within the apse that the celebrant was forced to approach it from the western side.[540] The same goes for the Church of Es-Sanamen, which has an altar that is a long way west of centre and was to all appearances used from the western side.[541] East-facing prayer at the altar might already have been the case in Dura Europos (mid–third century).[542] At all events, the large assembly room with its top end to the east points to where the "sacristy" is also located. In front of the east wall is a podium stretching 1.08 m from the wall to its front edge and offering enough space for both the altar and the celebrant since at the time he did not yet genuflect at the altar and therefore needed only a few centimetres to stand on. The podium marking the east side is the only indication that the space was used for worship at all.[543]

c. Palestinian-Transjordanian region

Wherever the altar is relatively free-standing in Palestine/Transjordan, Nussbaum makes the case for a celebration towards the people,[544] concluding that throughout the fourth and fifth centuries the liturgy was celebrated exclusively *versus populum*.[545] A number of observations contradict this. Once again, all the churches that are available to archaeology have their apses in the east; various patristic texts speak of "east-facing prayer";[546] and the liturgy of St James, which is widely used in Palestine, is familiar

538 IHM 1992, 209–211; HEID 2006, 371–373.

539 NUSSBAUM 1965, 51.

540 D. KRENCKER / R. NAUMANN, Die Wallfahrt-skirche des Simeon Stylites in Kal'at Sim'ân (Berlin 1939), Plate 1f.

541 NUSSBAUM 1965, 53 cites Kalat Siman, of all places, to suggest that here, too, the priest cele-brated *versus populum*.

542 VOGEL 1962, 184f.; *id.* 1964, 18f.; NUSSBAUM 1965, 32f. DE BLAAUW 2008, 278f., rightly points out that the baptistery lies on the west-east axis. The person being baptised steps eastwards out of the baptismal pool.

543 MESSNER 2003a, 363.

544 NUSSBAUM 1965, 62–87.

545 Ibid. 86.

546 Ibid. 62–64 does not see any literary sources for turning east in Palestine. This is false. Origen ex-presses himself very clearly on turning eastwards (DÖLGER 1972, 157–170; LANG 2003, 45–47), and he spent a long time living in Palestinian Caesarea. Further evidence is found in John II of Jerusalem, Jerome, Sophronius of Jerusalem and John Mo-schus: DÖLGER 1972, 234; WALLRAFF 2001, 66f.; HEID 2006, 378 n. 141. The clearest expression is to be found in Hieron. comm. in Am. 6,12–15 (CCL 76, 312): "'Glorify God, sing praises to the Lord, who ascended over the heaven of the heavens

with east-facing prayer inasmuch as the liturgist approaches the altar from the front.[547] Even though the cathedral in Tyre has its entrance in the east, the priest probably stood facing the people, which would confirm the principle of praying in the direction of the east.[548] From a purely archaeological point of view, it is striking that in Palestine the altar is practically always located in the eastern part of the presbytery, i.e. in the apse area. This means that the altar is not only a long way away from the faithful, but also that the priests and concelebrants are apparently located in the part of the presbytery that lies in front of it. Their seats are in the apse, but for the celebration of the Eucharist they move in front of the altar so as to pray facing east. Nussbaum himself mentions several cases in which an east-facing celebration must be assumed for archaeological reasons (altar in front of the apse step, altar directly on the apse wall, etc.).[549] In the Church of SS Lot and Procopius in Khirbet el-Mukhayyat there is a mosaic field showing a tree flanked by two sheep directly in front of the altar. Nussbaum rightly assumes that this is where the liturgist stood[550] since the altar is so close in front of the apse step that it can only be approached from the front.

While all the evidence suggests that the liturgist stood in front of the altar, there are no reliable archaeological indications of a west-facing celebration. In Gerasa, Nussbaum thinks that in the case of the synagogue church a west-facing celebration must be assumed. However, there is no evidence for this; on the contrary, the numerous churches in Gerasa all have their apses in the east;[551] and the baptismal route also runs from west to east.[552]

---

towards the east' (Ps 68:33 f.). Therefore, even in the celebration of the mysteries we renounce first him who is in the west and dies for us together with the sins; and so, turned eastward, we enter into a covenant with the sun of righteousness and promise to serve it." The text was written in 406 in Bethlehem (WALLRAFF op. cit. 67). On Jerome and the special case of praying facing east in Jerusalem see HEID 2001b, 150–159. Cyrill. Scyth. vit. Sab. 18 f. (SCHWARTZ 1939, 102–104): In the year 491, a church building in the Mar Saba monastery with its apse on the eastern side in which the altar stands ibid. 24 (SCHWARTZ 1939, 108): one faces east to pray. Cyrill Scyth. vit. Euthym. 28 (SCHWARTZ 1939, 45) suggests that the priest stands with his back to the people at the altar, otherwise Euthymius would not have permitted Sarazene to get into the habit of leaning on the altar railing during the sacred oblation. In Jerusalem, the priest once stood between the Temple, in which there was no cultic image, and the altar, thus looking eastwards in the sacrifice towards the Mount of Olives; Cypr. Fort. 11 (CCL 3,1, 204).

547 Divine Liturgy of St James (BKV Griechische Liturgien [München 1912] 87): "when about to stand at Your holy altar". Ibid. 97: "Let us bow our heads to the Lord [...] bowing their necks before Your holy altar". Ibid. 99 f.: "And for the offered, precious, heavenly, unutterable, pure, glorious, dread, awful, divine gifts, and the salvation of the priest who stands by and offers them". Ibid. 114: "To You, O Lord, we Your servants have bowed our heads before Your holy altar". Now definitive L. KHEVSURIANI et al. (eds.), Liturgia ibero-graeca sancti Iacobi (Münster 2011) 46, 58, 70, 72. See also RÜCKER 1923, 5: The priest stands in the face of the altar.

548 GAMBER 1972, 53.

549 NUSSBAUM 1965, 78, 80, 83, 84. Cf. OVADIAH 1970, Pl. 22, 26, 54 f.

550 NUSSBAUM 1965, 79 f. Cf. M. PICCIRILLO, The Mosaics of Jordan (Amman 1993) 215.

551 KRAELING 1938, 188.

552 M. RESTLE, Gerasa, in: RBK 2 (1971) 734–766. On the baptistery of the round church of St John the Baptist see ibid. 759 f. Fig. 8.

The synagogue church, which was originally a west-oriented Jewish house of prayer, had an eastern apse specially added in 530/31 for the Christian liturgy. Nussbaum has misunderstood the archaeological findings or the plan sketch. He believes that the altar stands at the front directly on a step, but this is not the case.[553] On the contrary, the priest has plenty of space in front of the altar.

The Basilica of Ein Hanniya is archaeologically problematic and does not in any case permit a decision in favour of a west-facing celebration.[554] On the other hand, the archaeological finds in the Church of the Multiplication of the Loaves and Fishes in Tabgha reveal that the church was east-oriented.[555] As in the Moses shrine at Mount Nebo, in St George's Church in Khirbet al Mukhayyat and in the monastery church of Ma'in,[556] this is indicated by the floor mosaics behind the altar: in each case they can be seen properly by the celebrant if he approaches the altar from the west.[557] Other Byzantine churches in Palestine and the province of Arabia display mosaic carpets in the presbytery that are uniformly to be viewed from west to east.[558] This is to name just a few cases, but they are sufficient to pull the rug out from under Nussbaum's statements. To be sure, they do not answer every question. It always comes down to the individual case. This is a matter of such things as the location of graves, depositories of martyrs and crypt steps in the altar area, all of which allow conclusions to be drawn. In many cases, however, the location and accessibility of the relics confirm that the direction of prayer was towards the east.[559]

d. Egyptian region

For Egypt, Otto Nussbaum likewise starts from a diffuse image and always assumes a front-facing celebration wherever a free-standing altar makes it impossible to establish anything archaeologically. Yet from the second century on there is clear evidence of

553 Nussbaum 1965, 77. Crowfoot 1938, 241 speaks only of the sanctuary being raised by one single step from the nave and of the altar being located on the apse chord, which is marked on the plan sketch Pl. XXXVI with a dashed line.

554 Nussbaum 1965, 75 is of the opinion, based on D. C. Baramki, An Early Christian Basilica at Ein Hanniya, in: The Quarterly of the Department of Antiquities in Palestine, Jerusalem 3 (1934) 113–117, that in the Basilica of Ein Hanniya the altar stood at the edge of the apse podium. But, first of all, this basilica, too, has its apse to the east and, second, Baramki speaks of the two steps of the apse podium not being preserved. Hence it is

impossible to decide what the floor level was like round the altar. Ovadiah 1970, 55 also assumes two steps, but says there "may be seen traces of the altar."

555 Differently Nussbaum 1965, 71 f. See below p. 445–447.

556 Hamarneh 2003, 126 Fig. 55.

557 Differently Nussbaum 1965, 79. The Moses shrine and St George's Church see M. Piccirillo, Madaba, in: RBK 5 (1995) 902–982, here 939 f. Fig. 12, 945 f. Fig. 14.

558 Comte 2012, 151, 180, 204, 206, 225, 240.

559 For particularly clear examples from Palestine and Arabia see Comte 2012, 151. 214.

east-facing prayer in the written sources for Egypt.[560] The priest goes in front of the altar behind the velum to pray.[561] From an archaeological point of view, all church buildings whose orientation can be verified are aligned with the chancel more or less exactly to the east.[562] The same applies to the orientation of the baptismal font and the direction the baptism follows from west to east.[563] Furthermore, the altar is located in the middle of the presbytery and otherwise somewhat more to the east.[564] The area in front of the altar evidently serves as a liturgical space as soon as the main celebrant, together with the concelebrants, approaches the altar from this side.

Sometimes an east-facing celebration is archaeologically very likely, for example in Basilica II of El Flusiye, where a band of mosaic leads from the entrance to the presbytery to the altar;[565] in Deir Abu Fana, where the altar stands almost directly against the apse wall;[566] in the Riverside Basilica at Faras and the monastery church on the site of the Isis sanctuary at al-Kubaniya, where the altar is located further to the east within the ciborium;[567] in Luxor and Amba Bishoi, where a highlighted section of floor in front of the altar may indicate where the liturgist stood;[568] in Hermopolis, where a large platform to the west of the altar indicates the location of the liturgist.[569] According to Nussbaum,

560 Severus 1972, 1225 f. Clem. Alex. strom. 7,7,43,6 (SC 428, 150); Orig. orat. 32 (GCS Orig. 2, 400 f.); in Lev. hom. 9,10 (SC 287, 122); in Num. hom. 5,1,4 (SC 415, 124); act. Phileae 9 (Bastiaensen 1987, 308); Pass. Piroou (Hyvernat 1886, 161); (Ps.-)Didym. Alex. trin. 3,2,28 (PG 39, 797); Sophr. vit. Mariae Aegypt. 1,9 (PG 87,3, 3704D); 2,15 (3708D); Pass. Mariae Aegypt. (Mombritius 1910, 2, 136. 137) (BHL 5417); Vit. Posthumii 3 (PL 73, 430A); Apophth. 12,1 (SC 474, 208): "Late on the evening of the Sabbath, when the Day of the Lord shines forth, he left the sun at his back, stretched out his hands to the (eastern) heavens and prayed until the sun shone in his face again, and then he sat down"; Vitae Patrum 1,36 (PL 73, 588C). Pass. Didymi (Hyvernat 1886, 285): the Roman persecution of the Christians consists precisely in making them now worship the idols facing west. T. Orlandi, Eudoxia and the Holy Sepulchre. A Constantinian Legend in Coptic (Milano 1980) 47: "He turned his face to the East, extended his hands, and prayed." The assertion in Nussbaum 1965, 89 that the literary sources for east-facing prayer in Egypt were "very scarce" fails to take into account the literary, non-liturgical evidence. Further Wallraff 2001, 66. See also Joseph and Aseneth 11,15 (Burchard 1983, 662):

"And she [Aseneth] stretched her hands out towards the east, and her eyes looked up to heaven".
561 Can. Hippol. arab. 29 (PO 31, 400). See already for the third century the Gnostic Coptic Gospel of Judas, in which the officeholders of the majority church are identified with the apostles who offer the sacrifice "before the altar".
562 Grossmann 2002, 13–15; id. 2014.
563 E.g. Grossmann 2002, Figs. 6, 14, 16, 20, 21, 27, 58, 68, 104, 111. Can. Hippol. arab. 19 (PO 31, 378–380): the baptismal candidate turns to the east for the exorcism, to the west for the renunciation of the devil, and to the east for the profession of Christ. Apophth. 18,17 (SC 498, 62–64): in the west are the demons, in the east the angels.
564 In this respect, the central church of Ayn Mahura and the church of the hermitage QIz 16 at Kellia support an east-facing celebration since the sanctuary is effectively separated from the nave and a celebration facing the people would make no sense; Grossmann 2002, Fig. 6, 114.
565 Nussbaum 1965, 93.
566 Ibid. 94 f.
567 Ibid. 96, 103.
568 Ibid. 100 f., 104 f.
569 Ibid. 101.

in the Menas sanctuary (Abu Mena) they celebrated facing east in one church and facing west in the other, even though both churches have their apses in the east.[570] Such arbitrary behaviour would have been completely absurd.

The Nubian churches, too, all have their apses in the east; the baptismal fonts are oriented accordingly.[571] As a rule, the altar is located in front of the apse chord within the enclosed presbytery, and clearly moved towards the east, sometimes right up to the apse steps.[572] To all appearances, the celebrant together with the concelebrants stood on the west side of the altar. This is confirmed by the Cathedral of Qasr Ibrim (Phase II): there the altar is located under the ciborium and shifted eastwards, so that the celebrant approaches the altar from the west.[573]

e. Maghreb region

In West North Africa (*Africa proconsularis*, Numidia, Mauritania), a distinction must be made between two historical phases: the Roman period with its Latin culture and the Byzantine conquest with the subsequent phase of a partial Hellenization of North African Christianity. In the second phase (from 533 on), it is to be expected that there will be a liturgical disposition like that generally observed in Byzantine churches (above chapter IV, 5a).[574] There we can consequently count on the altar having a clear orientation. However, in the preceding period, which is our primary concern here, determined as it was by Latin Christianity, the situation is less clear with regard to the eastward orientation of the church and how facing east to pray was handled. A clarification of this is not yet in sight in the research.

In the area of present-day Tunisia and Algeria, the churches frequently have their apses in the east, albeit not as consistently as in the Eastern Empire.[575] About a third have their entrance in the east.[576] Either way, however, the west-east axis is chosen, which is consequently of particular importance. The rule is confirmed by a few exceptions in which, due to external circumstances, the churches lie on a north-south axis:[577] for example, the Bellator Church (Basilica I) in Sbeitla (Sufetula), which was probably constructed within a former temple.[578] It was not until the Byzantine period that the apse there was moved from the southwest to the northeast.[579] The certain lack of concern

570 Ibid. 90 f.
571 M. RESTLE, Nubien, in: RBK 6 (2005) 1046–1258, here 1105 f. Fig. 26.
572 Ibid.
573 Ibid.1097 f. Fig. 22.
574 An instance of this is Basilica II in Sabratha, in which the floor shows beyond any doubt that the celebrant stood in front of the altar and looked east towards the apse; NUSSBAUM 1965, 209.
575 WARD PERKINS / GOODCHILD 1953, 62.
576 DUVAL 2008–2009, 73.
577 Ibid. 75.
578 Ibid. 73 f. Fig. 9; BURNS / JENSEN 2014, 91 n. 27.
579 DUVAL 1973, 165 f.

about orientation in pre-Byzantine times is shown in this case by the fact that the steps of the baptismal font also, quite unnecessarily, lie on a north-south axis. By contrast, in the Vitalis Church (Basilica II) in Sbeitla, which is likewise on a north-south axis, the baptismal font lies in a west-east direction.[580]

Sbeitla (Sufetula) is an instructive case overall. Noël Duval attempted to reconstruct the liturgical furnishings of the six churches in various building phases between the fourth and the seventh centuries.[581] It becomes clear how often churches could be fundamentally redesigned at that time. Nor should one rule out the possibility that the Catholic-Donatist controversy played a role in the alterations to the chancel, for it is well known that Donatists sometimes destroyed the altars of the Catholics. Perhaps they also did so when they took over a Catholic church, taking this opportunity to redesign the whole area surrounding the altar. But back to Sbeitla: in the various building phases, it is not always possible to say clearly where the altars were located, and even less where the liturgist stood at them. Ultimately, this lack of certainty also results from the fact that the two most important basilicas, I and II, lie on a north-south axis, and whether the north or the south was regarded as the liturgical east at the time – and thus as the direction of celebration – remains an open question.

Another problem is that it is often impossible to determine whether changes in spatial disposition still fall into the Latin period or already belong to the Byzantine period. This also goes for a number of instructive cases of the rededications of temples in which the spatial orientation is changed.[582] In the temple of Sbeitla, which lies on a north-south axis, Basilica III (Servus Basilica) is set up with its apse to the west as well as a chapel (*consignatorium*?) with its apse to the east.[583] In Thuburbo Majus, by contrast, although the west-east spatial axis is retained, the spatial orientation is reversed, so that the church's apse now points east.[584] This would suggest a liturgical motivation. In Tipasa, the church is put in the temple portico and rotated by 90 degrees: whereas the temple cell faces north, the apse of the church points east.[585] Again, praying towards the east is to be assumed as the crucial motive for this.[586]

For the whole of North Africa, standing to pray with hands raised and eyes looking east is in any case the usual practice.[587] The written evidence for this begins with Ter-

580 Duval 2008–2009, 83 f. Fig. 12.
581 Duval 1971a.
582 Cf. Burns / Jensen 2014, 91.
583 Duval 1971b, 268–276. Perhaps the chapel with its apse to the east dates from the Byzantine period.
584 Ibid. 277–290.
585 Ibid. 292–295.

586 A final case mentioned ibid. 290–292, the temple of Djebel Oust, is strikingly different. Here the church lies with its apse to the northwest, whereas the former temple cell points southwest.
587 Dölger 1972, 141–143, 330–333. Further evidence: Pass. Fructuosi 2,3 (BHL 3196); Pass. Montani 15,1 (BHL 6009). Aug. serm. 342,1 (PL 39, 1501) and enn. 62,13 (CCL 39, 801): raising hands. Enn. 122,12 (CCL 40, 1824): raising eyes.

tullian of Carthage († after 220).[588] The North African (?) writer Commodian (third century?) complains about improper behaviour in the "house of God" (*domus Dei*). Although when the priest at the altar utters the call to prayer with the words "lift up your hearts", the ladies answer in a high, clear voice, as soon as he begins to supplicate the Most High on behalf of the people, they turn to gossip with their neighbour and behave as if God were absent.[589] This rebuke only makes sense if the priest looks towards the people when he calls them to prayer and afterwards turns round to face the altar, so that the ladies feel unobserved and hold private conversations.

Special attention has always been paid to the liturgy of Bishop Augustine of Hippo (354–430), a North African coastal town in what is now Algeria. Augustine speaks of praying facing east as a custom through which the Christians distinguish themselves from the Manichaeans; the latter, for their part, go according to the position of the sun, thus performing a circular movement.[590] The North African baptismal rite probably has the symbolically significant act of the baptismal candidate turning round from facing west to facing east when making the baptismal promises.[591] A conscious turning of the body must also be assumed for the eucharistic celebration. Here the congregation, together with the bishop and clergy, turns to the east to pray, as is evidenced by the texts. Also to be pointed out in this context is the moment when Augustine, at the end of countless sermons, calls on the faithful to turn to the east with the words *conversi ad Dominum* – "turned to the Lord". This cue can be immediately followed by a freely formulated prayer. This might have to do with the dismissal of the catechumens. Ultimately, this invitation to turn to the Lord leads into the eucharistic prayer of thanksgiving at the altar,[592] and sets the congregation, so to speak, in motion from the locus of the sermon to the altar, where the prayer consciously takes place facing east.[593] Augustine therefore expects those present to turn round to pray[594] and probably also

---

588 Tert. apol. 16,10 (CCL 1, 116): *Denique inde suspicio, quod innotuerit, nos ad orientis regionem precari.*

589 Commod. instr. 2,31[35] (CCL 128, 67 f.): *Sacerdos Domini cum ‚Susum corda' praecedit* […]. Ibid. 2,23[27],5 f. (61): *Susum intendentes, semper Deo summo devoti / Tota Deo reddite inlaesa sacra, ministri.*

590 ROETZER 1930, 244 f.

591 VAN DER MEER 1951, 428. Cf. BURNS / JENSEN 2014, 208 f. n. 243. The baptismal fonts in Tunisia with entrance and exit on a west-east axis date from the fifth or sixth century; RISTOW 1998, 252–265.

592 Hence the frequent call of *"gratias agamus"* at the end of the sermon: Aug. serm. 34,5,9 (PL 38, 213);

67,5,10 (437); 141,4,4! (778); 183,10,15 (994); 272 (1248); serm. Guelf. 27,4 (MORIN 1930, 535).

593 VOGEL 1960, 449 f.; id. 1962, 182; id. 1964, 11 f.; M. KLÖCKENER, *Conversi ad dominum*, in: Augustinus-Lexikon 1 (1994) 1280–1282; LANG 2003, 52–54; DOLBEAU 2009, 173–175. In private prayer it is permissible occasionally to forget the direction in which you pray: div. quaest. ad Simpl. 2,4,4 (CCL 44, 87): *saepe etiam obliviscitur, vel ad quam coeli partem* […]. The word *converti* is also used by Ambrose for turning towards the east: Ambr. myst. 2,7 (SC 25², 158): *ad orientem converteris* […] *ad Christum convertitur.*

594 It refers to a physical turning round, as already in Ovid. fast. 4,777 f.: *conversus ad ortus* (SEVERUS 1972, 1227 f.). Aug. serm. Dolbeau 19,12 (DOL-

to raise their eyes.[595] The church buildings will therefore have lain on a west-east axis. This is confirmed by the archaeological findings: this orientation is indeed nearly always present, with the apse and altar located on either the west or the east side.

Since it is to be assumed that Augustine concluded his sermons with *conversi ad Dominum* in churches having both orientations, i.e. with either their entrance or their apse at the east end, there are two scenarios to be borne in mind as to how this instruction was concretely put into practice. In proconsular North Africa, the altar can be placed far forward in the nave or even in the centre of the church; it is then isolated from the apse. The best-known example of this is the Dermech I Basilica in Carthage, which has its apse at the east end (Fig. 52). Significantly, the altar there is clearly east-oriented; the celebrant must have turned his back to the people.[596] However, this cathedral already falls within the Byzantine period. In such churches, for the sermon the faithful apparently stood as best they could by the apse, where the seats of the bishop and priests were located, but afterwards moved to the altar, gathering round it on its south, north and west sides. During the Offertory they could all still look towards the altar. But for the *sursum cor*, their eyes turned eastwards towards the apse.

By contrast, in a church with its entrance in the east, everyone looks towards the entrance when praying. Augustine once said at the end of a sermon: *conversi mecum*.[597] This will probably have been in such a church. The location of the sermon is, as always, the apse. Augustine is already standing looking east and concludes by calling on those listening to him to turn to the east like him. Undoubtedly, he means this as a physical turning. What it comes down to is also significant here: clergy and people look in the same direction (*mecum*); it is a joint action, motivated by praying together to God. So the point is that when people pray, they are not face-to-face with one another as they are for the sermon. As a concrete illustration of a church with its entrance in the east, let us take the Basilica of St Cyprian in Carthage, where the altar stands isolated in the middle of the nave (Fig. 53).[598] There, the clergy do not need to turn round because they always look east in the direction of the church door, both when they are seated in the apse and

beau 2009, 164): *"Convertimini ad me"* […], *qui adtendebas occidentem, adtendas orientem*; cf. serm. Dolbeau 22,8 (Dolbeau 2009, 561): *aliae [partes caeli] sunt illae quas intuemur, cum orientem conspicimus, aliae partes quas intuemur, cum ad occidentem nos convertimus.* A turning round of the body at the transition from the sermon to the Eucharist is not unusual in liturgical history; it takes place in, for example, the Syrian liturgy, too; Schneider 1949, 61.

595 Heid 2006, 390 f. Aug. serm. dom. 2,5,18 (CCL 35, 108): *cum ad orationem stamus, ad orientem* convertimur, unde caelum surgit. See already Cyprian (Dölger 1972, 302). Pass. Dorothei 9 (*BHL* 3617): *Tunc sancti Martyres, laeto ad Dominum animo conversi, dixerunt.* Ibid. 7: *sancti Martyres laeto vultu ad Dominum suspicientes, dixerunt.*

596 Nussbaum 1965, 199. Cf. Elliger 2004, 272.

597 Aug. serm. 216,2 (PL 39, 2147).

598 Cf. Elliger 2004, 272 f. The cathedral church at Hippo, the entrance to which was at the east end, possibly also had its altar in the middle of the church; Burns / Jensen 2014, 157.

Fig. 52: Five-aisled
Dermech I basilica at
Carthage, 6th century; J.
CHRISTERN, in: RBK 3 (1978)
1166.

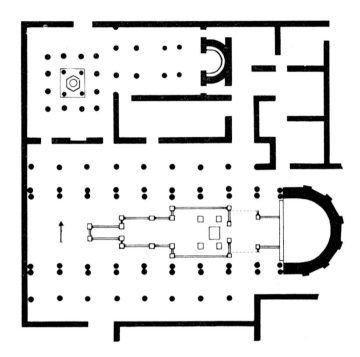

when they approach the altar.[599] During the Liturgy of the Word, the faithful stand in the front part of the church in front of the apse and look towards the apse where the Liturgy of the Word takes place. At the cue *conversi ad Dominum*, they turn round, move to the middle of the church and surround the altar on all sides during the Eucharistic Prayer.[600] At *sursum cor* they look towards the entrance door.[601] As they do so, they probably try not to turn their backs on the altar when praying. It is possible that the choir positions itself in the area in front of the altar.[602] In this case, it is liturgically justifiable for it to look towards the altar and thus face west.

Overall, however, such a scenario seems impractical. Of course, one must bear in mind that the churches have no seating and the faithful can move about freely.[603] Full churches cannot by any means be expected either. Nevertheless, inconvenience is inevitable in churches with their entrances in the east since the faithful have to turn round.[604]

599 NUSSBAUM 1965, 198.
600 For an Augustine sermon that sheds light on this movement in the church interior see DUVAL 2008–2009, 75; DOLBEAU 2009, 55. Aug. serm. 229A,3 (PLS 2, 555) distinguishes between prayer in the apse and at the altar.
601 WALLRAFF 2001, 73 f.; *id.* 2004, 117. The arguments advanced by NUSSBAUM 1971, 153 f. against this scenario are not compelling and can be in part refuted.
602 Cf. ROETZER 1930, 87.
603 The faithful stand: Aug. serm. de disc. crist. 14,16 (PL 40, 678): *Conversi ad Dominum* [...], *et pro omni plebe sua astante nobiscum in atriis domus suae.* Similarly serm. 100,3,4! (PL 38, 605); 362,30,31 (PL 39, 1634).
604 ROETZER 1930, 89.

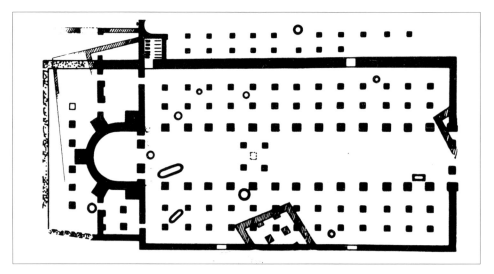

Fig. 53: Seven-aisled Basilica of St Cyprian at Carthage, 6th century; NUSSBAUM 1965, 101 Fig. 42.

This is only feasible with small congregations for which there is enough space behind the celebrant – between the apse and the altar – and next to the altar.[605] Through moving the altars far into the middle of the nave, the faithful are divided into two to the right and left of the altar, which also serves to separate the sexes. Since the churches often have multiple aisles, they offer the faithful a great deal of space across their width. Furthermore, during the Liturgy of the Word, the pagans wishing to be baptized and the catechumens are likely to have remained in the rear places of the nave, i.e. between the doorways and the altar; they then leave the church after the sermon, so that the church empties through its eastern exits and the space in front of the altar remains more or less free.

It might well have been precisely the disturbance of turning round to pray that made the central altars go out of fashion in the fifth century and led to a preference for having the apse in the east. At all events, most of the enclosed altar areas are located near the apse or directly adjoining the apse. From the fifth century onwards, most churches in North Africa have had their apses to the east,[606] a development that was further reinforced in the sixth century as a result of Byzantine influence. Cyrille Vogel conjectures that the east-end entrance still to be found in North Africa and Rome in the fourth century resulted from its being convenient for the clergy in that in such churches the

---

605 LANG 2003, 84 f.

606 PODOSSINOV 1991, 279. On the special problem of counter-apses, which will not be dealt with here but which forms the context for discussing the direction of prayer, see DUVAL 1971; *id*. 1973; T. ULBERT, Frühchristliche Basiliken mit Doppelapsiden auf der iberischen Halbinsel (Berlin 1978) 127–138.

celebrants could comply with facing east to pray without having to perform irksome body rotations. The price was, of course, that now the faithful had to do the turning round. It was, in fact, forbidden by religious law to turn one's back on the altar.[607] Hence the faithful will not have turned round in Rome. In North Africa, on the other hand, the altar was positioned so far forward in the nave that the faithful, too, could look east. However, the fact that from the fifth century on putting the apse at the east end becomes the dominant practice in Latin church building is probably ultimately due to pastoral considerations since the people, too, wish to and should face east to pray.[608]

Nussbaum also arbitrarily assumes for North Africa that in the case of free-standing altars the priest looked towards the people – even though no traces of any altars at all have survived. But almost every case in which it is in fact possible to draw archaeological conclusions as to the location of the liturgist confirms that the priest faced east. In a number of east-oriented churches in Numidia, the altar is located so close to the apse podium and so far to the east within the presbytery in front of it that an eastward celebration practically stares one in the face.[609]

In Mauritania, the Court Basilica at Tipasa has its entrance to the east; the way the altar is installed only permits a celebration towards the nave.[610] For the basilica of the Castellum Tingitanum, which has its apse to the east, the celebration facing east is probable on the basis of a floor mosaic.[611] The altar in the Basilica Maior at Tigzirt (Algeria), which has its apse to the east, is pushed so close to the apse wall that the priest must have celebrated facing the east.[612] The burial chapel of Asterius in Carthage also only permits facing east.[613]

In the province of Byzacena, in the Church of Henchir Haratt, the somewhat off-centre altar ciborium in the middle of the nave possibly indicates that the celebrant looked towards the western entrance to the church.[614] But that is by no means conclusive. For the central square (105 × 105 cm) of marble slabs need not necessarily be the location of the altar, of which nothing has been preserved. As a rule, the altars are rectangular, not square. The east-of-centre position of the ciborium on the central platform can just as easily mean that the altar was also located east of centre and that the celebrant approached it from the west.

607 VOGEL 1960, 454; *id*. 1962, 181 f. n. 15; 191 f.;
     id. 1964, 26; NUSSBAUM 1965, 398; DE BLAAUW
     1994, 96.
608 Cf. VOGEL 1962, 193 f.
609 Even Nussbaum concedes this in the majority of
     cases: NUSSBAUM 1965, 186–188, 192–196, 215.
     Cf. MICHEL 2005, 81 f., 88.
610 NUSSBAUM 1965, 178.
611 JENSEN 2015, 110.
612 NUSSBAUM 1965, 179 f.
613 Ibid. 210 f.
614 Ibid. 202.

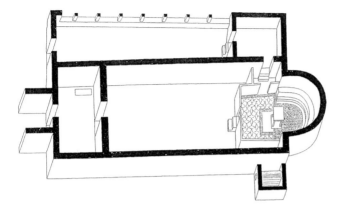

Fig. 54: Southern church of the western double church at Hemmaberg; F. GLASER, Frühes Christentum im Alpenraum (Regensburg 1997) 117 Fig. 44.

An analogous situation in the opposite direction is found in the Vitalis Church in Sbeitla. There the apse with the priests' benches lies to the west. In front of it, within the presbytery, there is a central podium on which the altar stands east of centre, meaning that the priest probably did look eastwards towards the nave.[615] By contrast, in Basilica I at Junca, which has its apse at the east end, the altar is located on the chord of the apse and has a very large presbytery extending in front of it.[616] Evidently the concelebrants and the choir position themselves there and, like the celebrant, look east towards the apse. In the larger church of the double-church in Bulla Regia, there is a floor slab on the west side of the altar[617] which possibly marks where the liturgist stood. In this case, he faced east.

In the church in Siagu, which has its apse exactly in the east, the altar is located far to the west.[618] Beneath it lies a relic grave. A prominent burial place on the axis between apse and altar did not protrude from the ground, so it does not give any indication of a possible direction of prayer. Given the disposition of the altar, one would imagine that the liturgist and concelebrants stood behind the altar looking towards the people. However, Noël Duval dates the church to the Byzantine period.[619] But is it conceivable that in such an ambitious church complex, which furthermore pays such meticulous attention to its eastward orientation, the celebrant at the altar, of all people, should face west? An east-facing celebration is certainly more likely.[620]

---

615 Ibid. 202 f.

616 Ibid. 206 f.

617 DUVAL 2008–2009, 87 f. Fig. 14.

618 On the plan in DUVAL 1984–1985, 168 Fig. 3 the altar appears to stand further to the west beneath the ciborium, which would once again suggest a celebration *versus populum*. In reality, the exact location of the ciborium is not known; ibid. 172.

619 DUVAL 1984–1985. Cf. *id.* 2008–2009, 93 f. Fig. 16.

620 There is a distance of 1 m between the altar and the barriers. However, the presbytery together with the barriers might possibly project further west.

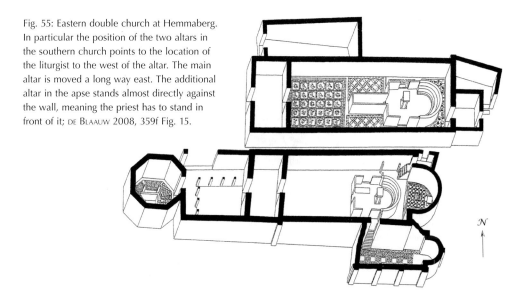

Fig. 55: Eastern double church at Hemmaberg. In particular the position of the two altars in the southern church points to the location of the liturgist to the west of the altar. The main altar is moved a long way east. The additional altar in the apse stands almost directly against the wall, meaning the priest has to stand in front of it; DE BLAAUW 2008, 359f Fig. 15.

f. Carinthia, Istria, Dalmatia

In the *Noricum* (Carinthia) all the churches have their apses to the east, and all the evidence points to east-facing prayer.[621] The disposition of the altar and sanctuary resembles that of Byzantine churches (Figs. 54 and 55).[622] In the western double-church at Hemmaberg the mosaic floor indicates the location of the liturgist in front of the altar, whereas in St Lawrence in Lorch this is marked by a step.[623] In a side chapel inside the enclosed presbytery at St Peter im Holz (Carinthia), the altar stands so close to the apse wall that the celebrant must have had to stand in front of it facing east.[624] Here, there would easily have been enough room for the altar to be further forward, which means they were absolutely intent on observing the east-facing prayer position. It is therefore to be assumed that east-facing prayer was also practised at the church's lost main altar. In the church on the Kirchbichl in Lavant (Tyrol) the altar is located in front of the apse and, for reasons of space, only allows an east-facing celebration.[625]

621 Cf. Pass. Floriani 4 (ActaSS Mai 1, 468B) (BHL 3054): *Rogabat autem B. Florianus milites qui eum tenebant, ut permitterent eum orare ad Dominum. Stans autem B. Florianus contra Orientem, extendens manus suas ad coelum, dixit* […].

622 Cf. the model of an ideal fifth- or sixth-century church complex in the Noricum-Pannonia region in F. HUMER *et al.* (eds.), A.D. 313. Von Carnuntum zum Christentum (Bad Vöslau 2014) 314–317.

623 NUSSBAUM 1965, 288.

624 Ibid. 290 f. Of course, the altar might also have served as a place to set down the sacrificial offerings.

625 Ibid. 292. Although Nussbaum assumes for the sixth century a change in favour of facing east, he does not offer any cogent reasons for this. For if, as he admits, east-facing celebration pertained in the sixth century, why would it not have done so in the fifth century, too?

The same picture emerges for *Istria/Dalmatia* (Croatia). It is a mystery how Nussbaum can conclude from his analyses of the findings that the priest there celebrated *versus populum* as a rule.[626] It must surely be obvious that almost without exception the churches have their apses to the east.[627] The steps to the baptismal fonts sometimes lie on the north-south axis, sometimes on the west-east axis.[628] A deviation from the west-east axis may, of course, have been adopted for practical reasons and does not rule out the possibility that the person being baptised is submerged facing east during the actual act of baptism.[629] In the churches of the region the early Christian altar has rarely been preserved, but where there is solid evidence, it indicates the prevalence of the liturgical practice of facing east to pray. For example, in the Basilica of St Anastasius in Salona-Marusinac, there is an (open) shaft behind the altar, which means that the celebrant probably stood in front of it.[630] Even for Nussbaum, the two churches of St Catherine and St Hermagoras (Samagher), both near Pola and both with east-end apses, allow only an east-facing celebration since the altar is located directly in front of the apse wall.[631] There is no doubt that the priest also stood in front of the altar in the chapel in Borasi as it is only 40 cm away from the cathedra.[632]

g. Northern Italy and Rome

In Italy and Rome, similarly to North Africa, the situation is complex. In the important church buildings in Aquileia (a cathedral complex) and Rome (the Lateran and *Santa Maria Maggiore* plus the martyr churches of *San Pietro, San Paolo, Basilica Apostolorum* [*San Sebastiano*] and others) no traces remain of an altar or ciborium dating from early Christian times. In order to arrive at an overall assessment, it is therefore necessary to carry out very detailed research into individual churches and to correlate archaeolog-

---

626 Ibid. 304.

627 Chevalier 1996, Pl. I–LXX.

628 Chevalier 1996, 169. The baptismal font in the cathedral of Salona is accessed via just one set of steps from the west; E. Dyggve, Le baptistère de la basilica urbana à Salone d'après les fouilles de 1949, in: Actes du Ve congrès international d'archéologie chrétienne (Città del Vaticano / Paris 1957) 189–198, here 195 Fig. 6. The direction of the baptismal font at Blagaj-Japra lies exactly on the west-east axis, whereas the nave of the church is, for reasons arising from the construction, only vaguely east-oriented; Chevalier 1996, Pl. XXVIII. Otherwise the steps to the baptismal fonts almost always follow the axis of the nave. Occasionally the steps lie on a north-south axis (ibid. Pl. XLI, XLVIII, XLIX, LVII).

629 Both the baptizing cleric and the person being baptized have to get into the pool and stand in it in such a way that the former can easily immerse the upper body of the latter. The neophyte must then be able to get out without the cleric being in the way.

630 Nussbaum 1965, 300 f.; Gamber 1972, 56.

631 In both cases all that can be detected is a depository for relics, above which the altar must have stood. Nussbaum 1965, 302; Gamber 1972, 58.

632 Differently Nussbaum 1965, 303. Cf. Chevalier 1996, Pl. LX,4.

ical with literary sources. Otto Nussbaum believes that up to the eighth century there is no evidence of an east-oriented altar and liturgy in Rome and Italy.[633] This view cannot be upheld in the light of the current state of the research. There is, to be sure, still a considerable gap in tradition, but where archaeological or literary evidence is available, it confirms the rule – albeit with significant exceptions – that in a church with its apse in the east, the celebrant stands in front of the altar, whereas in one with its entrance in the east, he stands behind it.

In northern Italy, as far as is archaeologically verifiable, the churches almost all have their apses to the east,[634] which is indicative of prayer at the altar also being east-facing. The altar is located in front of the apse within an enclosed presbytery, which, as far as one can tell, offers plenty of space in front of the altar (Grado,[635] Aquileia).[636] This indicates that during the eucharistic liturgy not only the main celebrant but also the concelebrants stand in front of the altar looking eastwards. Nussbaum always argues that the cathedra stands at the apex of the apse and that the celebrant, for the sake of convenience, takes the shortest route to the altar and celebrates facing the people. But he forgets the concelebrants. There is, in fact, no room for them behind the altar. Why do they go in front of the altar if it is all about convenience? If the intention were really for the clergy and people to face one another, the simplest solution would surely have been to move the altar a lot further forward so that the main celebrant and concelebrants would have a short approach to the altar from behind and thus not block anyone's view of the altar.

The eastward orientation is particularly noticeable in the Byzantine-influenced north of Italy, in the ecclesiastical provinces of Milan, Aquileia (Parenzo, Salona, etc.) and Ravenna.[637] Nussbaum, however, denies it in the case of Milan. He believes that Bishop Ambrose († 397) would have approached the altar from behind, at least in the *Basilica Ambrosiana*, his future burial church, which has its apse to the east. He points to the location of the double tomb of SS Gervasius and Protasius and the projected episcopal tomb underneath the altar, arguing that they lie at right angles to the altar and protrude beyond it at the rear. Because in relatively nearby Ravenna there are clear cases of the celebrant standing at the altar on top of the burial site of the bishops, Nussbaum concludes that Ambrose in Milan must also have stood on the protruding burial sites behind the altar and celebrated facing the people.[638] But that is untenable. More recent

---

633 NUSSBAUM 1965, 220, 284.

634 See, however, for southern Italy, Paulin. Nol. ep. 32,13 (FC 25,2, 774): generally churches have their entrances in the east. VOGEL 1964, 21 f. As far as archaeology is concerned, southern Italy does not, however, yield much information on early Christian church-building.

635 On Santa Maria delle Grazie in Grado see below p. 444.

636 The same is true of the church in Zitone on the island of Sicily. See the respective observations in NUSSBAUM 1965.

637 VOGEL 1964, 23.

638 NUSSBAUM 1965, 234 f.

reconstructions have the graves protruding beyond the altar on both sides,[639] so that the priest in theory stands on the graves whether he approaches the altar from the front or from behind. Furthermore, Ravenna actually speaks against Nussbaum's theory, for in Ravenna there are individual cases of the burial sites of bishops being located in front of the altar, with the celebrant only standing on them so as to be able to face east.

Although archaeology does not provide clear evidence of a particular direction of celebration in Milan's churches, written sources suggest that Ambrose practised east-facing celebration. In one psalm exposition he says that the Christian should always be like a house of God which has its windows standing open to the east so that the eyes of the Lord can see in.[640] It goes without saying that, conversely, the priest at the altar looks up to the face of God. In Milan, the eastward direction is also observed at the baptismal profession of faith.[641] Furthermore, all the churches in Milan have their apse in the east. It would therefore be peculiar if Ambrose had faced west to pray in his cathedral. It is not by chance that Ambrose, faced with the Arian persecution, throws himself to the ground *in front of* the altar of the Lord (*ante altare Domini*), weeping.[642]

For Ravenna, on the other hand, truly relevant literary, archaeological and iconographic evidence does exist to show the eastern location of the apse and a corresponding east-facing prayer direction of the priest.[643] There, the celebrant always approaches the altar from the west and stands *ante altare*.[644] The first *memoria* of *San Vitale* (fifth century) is already east-oriented: in the rectangular room (8,48 × 4,40 m) the altar stands on the narrow side so close to the wall that the priest undoubtedly looked east as he came before the altar.[645] The building that succeeded it in the sixth century, the round church that is still preserved today and famous for its mosaics, also has its apse to the east; here, too, the priest stands in front of the altar looking at the apse mosaic (below Fig. 108). It is almost certain that this is where he stood because directly above the altar there is a depiction of the Lamb of God (Fig. 56). The Lamb stands for the Eucharist, which is

---

639   S. DE BLAAUW, Il culto di Sant'Ambrogio e l'altare della *Basilica Ambrosiana* a Milano, in: Italian History & Culture 13 (2008) 43–62, here 54 Fig. 2.

640   Ambr. exp. in Ps. 6,19 (CSEL 62², 118).

641   Ambr. myst. 2,7 (SC 25², 158); J. SCHMITZ, in: FC 3, 34.

642   Paulin. vit. Ambr. 34 (PL 14, 39B).

643   In addition, the cathedral's baptistery suggests a west-east baptismal route. The mausoleum of Theodoric, too, was east-facing; the altar stood in the east.

644   Agnell. Lib. Pont. Rav. 23 (FC 21,1, 138): *ante altare subtus pirfireticum lapidem, ubi pontifex stat, quando missam canit.* Cf. ibid. 42 (214): *Sepulta est Galla Placidia […] ante altarium in-*

fra cancellos. Ibid. 65 (290): *Sepultusque est […] ante altarium.* Also ibid. 44 (218–220) proves that the priest stood in front of the altar, here in the Church of Sant'Agata (on this church with its apse at the east end see DEICHMANN 1976, 283 f.). Agnell. Lib. Pont. Rav. 52 (FC 21,1, 246–248): in the Church of San Cassiano in Imola, which also has its apse to the east, Peter of Ravenna (Petrus Chrysologus) goes onto the altar step and blesses the people, then he turns to the altar.

645   NUSSBAUM 1965, 273; DEICHMANN 1976, 47; DAVID 2013, 32 Fig 18; SOTIRA 2013, 31–35; JOHNSON 2018, Pl. 64, Fig. 7.1. There is a space of less than 50 cm between altar and wall. In addition, the mosaic field in front of the altar unmistakably marks where the liturgist stood facing east.

Fig. 56: Ceiling mosaic of the presbyterium of *San Vitale* in Ravenna looking east, mid-6th century; T. VERDON, L'arte cristiana in Italia. Origini e Medioevo (Cinisello Balsamo 2005) 101 Fig. 87.

borne by angels from the earthly to the heavenly altar. The priest would see this Lamb upside down if he were standing behind the altar. The Church of *Santa Croce* (first half of the fifth century) in Ravenna also has its apse to the east. In addition, the adjoining mausoleum of Galla Placidia to the right of the porch also has its apse to the east even though it has a cruciform and therefore basically directionless floor plan.[646] But the wall and ceiling mosaics point the visitors who enter the room through the only entrance to the north in the right direction: the apostles Peter and Paul, with upward gestures of acclaim, draw their gaze aloft to the starry heavens, in the middle of which shines a Latin cross; but visitors only see it the right way round if they stand facing east (Fig. 57).[647]

In some churches in Ravenna, the altar might originally have stood inside an enclosed presbytery at the foot of the apse podium, as in *Sant'Apollinare* in Classe (Fig. 58).[648] In this case, unlike today, only the Liturgy of the Word takes place on the podium, whereas the Eucharist is celebrated below. When the priest stands facing east in front of the altar there, he looks at the commanding apse mosaic. It shows the cross against a background of starry heavens. No doubt both priests and people looked up at this cross when praying since the cross is generally regarded as the point towards which prayers are to be directed.[649] This liturgical disposition can be compared with images on ancient coins showing an altar within a fenced area at the foot of the steps leading up to a temple.[650] In the temple, the statue of the deity is to be seen. All this presupposes that the pagan priest stood in front of the altar and performed his sacrifice looking towards the image of the deity.

There is probably just one exception to the rule of having the apse in the east in Ravenna: the Basilica of Probus in Classe, of which it is said that here alone among all the city's churches the priest celebrated mass above the people – "*super populum*".[651] Presumably, therefore, this no-longer-preserved church had its apse to the west, meaning that the celebrant stood behind the altar. This is, of course, the golden exception that confirms the rule. Although some Ravenna mosaics show the priest standing behind the altar and suggest a celebration *versus populum* even in churches with an east-end apse,

646 Cf. David 2013.
647 Podossinov 1991, 282 f.
648 The Basilica Ursiana can hardly possess an altar in the middle of the church (so Lang 2003, 86 f.). That notion goes back to a baroque sketch which is more like a reconstruction (Deichmann 1974, 5). Rather, in 1512 the altar along with the ciborium still stand "in mezzo il coro di sotto" = in the middle of the lower choir (ibid. 10).
649 Kopeček 2006, 197–201. Ephr. Syr. comm. in Ev. 20,23 (SC 121, 360): only those who spread out their hands (in prayer) towards the Cross are permitted to approach the table of the altar. Aster. Amas. hom. 11 (PG 40, 337B): Cross on the wall as the point towards which prayer is directed.
650 E. M. Steinby (ed.), *Lexicon Topographicum Urbis Romae* 1 (Roma 1993) 371 Fig. 27–28.
651 Agnell. Lib. Pont. Rav. 8 (FC 21,1, 108). I follow the interpretation of Gamber 1981, 120–124; differently Deichmann 1976, 355–359; C. Nauert, in: FC 21,1, 108 f. n. 25. The archaeological findings do not provide any clarity as to the west and east ends of the Basilica of Probus.

such a perspective is obviously due to the composition of the picture (above Fig. 44, below Fig. 148). Nussbaum also claims that the Ravenna altars with a *fenestella confessionis* at the front require the priest to stand behind the altar in order not to block the view of the relic window.[652] That remains pure speculation. Speaking against it are mosaics that show the altars completely covered with a cloth (only during the liturgy?), which means that any relic depository was inevitably concealed as well.[653] Apart from this, in pagan sacrificial practice, too, the priest stands in front of the altar, thus obscuring its visible and decorative front side.

In the case of churches with east-facing apses, even Nussbaum occasionally has to concede, on archaeological grounds, that the priest stood in front of the altar, for example, in the baptistery of the *Basilica Preeliana* in Grado (fifth century) and in *Sant'Andrea* in Rimini (fifth/sixth centuries).[654] On the other hand, in the basilica of the Temple of Augustus in Cuma (fifth/sixth centuries), which has its entrance in the east, the priest fairly certainly stood behind the altar and thus celebrated facing east.[655] The churches of *San Prosdocimo* in Padua (fifth/sixth centuries) and *San Salvatore* in Spoleto (eighth century) have their apses at the east end and their altars moved so far into the apse that an east-facing celebration is as good as certain.[656] Also in the church of *San Prospero* in Perugia (eighth century) with its east-end apse, the celebrant unquestionably stood in front of the altar.[657] All this confirms that in northern Italy both priests and people stand "*in front of* the altar of God".[658]

For *Rome*, as far as one can tell, there is no reliable witness to east-facing worship to be found in the patristic texts up to the sixth/seventh centuries. Surprisingly, the countless legends of Roman martyrs dating from this time speak of raising hands and eyes to heaven in prayer,[659] but do not mention turning to face the east, as is more frequently

652 NUSSBAUM 1965, 242 f.; of the same opinion GAMBER 1972, 52.

653 U. PESCHLOW, Altar und Reliquie. Form und Nutzung des frühbyzantinischen Reliquienaltars in Konstantinopel, in: M. ALTRIPP / C. NAUERT (eds.), Architektur und Liturgie (Wiesbaden 2006) 175–202, here 198.

654 NUSSBAUM 1965, 239 f.

655 Ibid. 240.

656 Ibid. 240, 246. Similarly the *Tempietto* at Clitunno; ibid. 246 f.

657 Ibid. 246.

658 Ps.-Maxim. Taur. tract. 2 (PL 57, 776): *Et quemadmodum nunc stamus in Ecclesia ante altare Dei* […]. Dated to the fifth or sixth century.

659 Pass. Eleutherii 10 (ActaSS April 2, 528A); 17 (529B) (BHL 2450); Pass. Aureae 1,4 (ActaSS Aug. 4, 758B); 2,18 (760E) (BHL 809); Pass. Macarii 15 (ActaSS Okt. 10, 569A) (BHL 5104); Pass. Serapiae 2,10 (ActaSS Aug. 6, 502F) (BHL 7586); Pass. Martinae 1,8 (ActaSS Jan. 1, 11); 5,39 (16) (BHL 5587); Pass. Priscae 3,13 (ActaSS Jan. 2, 550) (BHL 6926); Pass. Steph. 2,19 (ActaSS Aug. 1, 143C) (BHL 7845); Pass. Valentini (ActaSS Febr. 2, 754F) (BHL 8465); Pass. Nerei et Achillei 3,12 (ActaSS Mai 3,10A); 6,22 (12E) (BHL 6067); Pass. Caeciliae 6 (DELEHAYE 1936, 198) (BHL 1495); Pass. Anastasiae 27 (DELEHAYE 1936, 241 f.) (BHL 404).

Fig. 57: Ceiling mosaic of the mausoleum of Galla Placidia in Ravenna, 1st half of the 5th century; X. Barral i Altet, Alto medioevo dall'antichità all'anno mille (Cologne 1998) 83.

the case in Greek legends. This does not seem to be a coincidence, as the Latin legend of St Sylvester only speaks of the pope raising his hands and eyes to heaven when praying, whereas the Greek version adds turning east.[660] Naturally, the Greek legends are also read in Rome.

Few indications of east-facing prayer in Rome remain. The early work *The Shepherd of Hermas* (c. 140/50) seems to assume the practice of facing east to pray.[661] Hints of it can also be found in Hippolytus of Rome, who said in around the year 200 that the standing together of the saints in the same place as one was "church" and "a spiritual house of God" planted, as it were, on Christ in the east.[662] A note written by the southern French bishop, Guillaume Durand (1230–1296) points to the sixth century already in its reference to Pope Vigilius (537–555) having issued the instruction for the priest at the altar to pray facing east.[663] It is unclear whether such an instruction really ever existed.

660 Vit. Silv. (Mombritius 1910, 2, 528): *Sylvester episcopus expandit manus suas ad dominum.* Theogn. thes. 11,6 (CCG 5, 56).

661 Dölger 1972, 136 f.; Severus 1972, 1225.

662 Hipp. comm. in Dan. 1,18,4–6 (GCS Hipp. 1,1², 42). Text see above n. 145.

663 Durand. rat. div. off. 5,2,57, German Douteil / Suntrup 2016, 683: "Although God is every-

Fig. 58: Chancel of *Sant'Apollinare* in Classe; G. CORTESI, Classe e Ravenna. Origini cristiane e antichi edifici cultuali (Ravenna 1966), tav. 47.

It has been assumed, though, that if it did, it was because priests in Rome occasionally celebrated facing the people in churches with east-end apses, which displeased Vigilius.[664] But it is just as conceivable that the priests were in the habit of celebrating with their backs to the people, even in churches with their entrance to the east, and that this is what Vigilius was prohibiting. And finally, it is conceivable that such a decree was issued to a foreign church, for example in Gaul.[665] If that was the case, Vigilius merely wanted to make sure that the Roman practice of facing east to pray was adhered to there as well.

Alongside the written sources, there is archaeological evidence of east-facing prayer. A wooden door panel of the church of *Santa Sabina* on the Aventine in Rome (c. 431) shows, in the upper field of the image, Christ standing between Alpha and Omega as the eternal ruler of heaven against a background of the starry vault of heaven (Fig. 59). The cross falling from heaven heralds the eschatological coming (Parousia) of Christ. While Peter (left) and Paul (right) lift their arms upwards towards the cross in acclamation, the Church is personified in the middle as a woman praying, her hands raised eastwards and her head thrown back so as to look up at the bright rising Sun of Righteousness.[666] The praying Church awaits with longing the coming of Christ from the east.[667] Obviously the Church, when she prays towards the east, has this same Christ enthroned on the vault of heaven before her eyes.[668] If this small-format depiction of the Theophany actually reproduces a large apsidal mosaic that might once have been in the church itself,[669] the panel takes on a further special significance, for the church on the Aventine has its apse in the east. For that reason, the clergy and people really did turn to face the apse mosaic to pray.

where, 'the priest at the altar and during worship must, according to the decree of Pope Vigilius, pray in the direction of the rising sun (= east)'. Since we have the entrance from the west in our churches, during the celebration of Mass he turns towards the people when greeting because we present ourselves face to face with those whom we are greeting […]; and only then does he turn to the rising sun to pray. But in churches which, as in Rome, have their entrance door in the east no turning round is necessary for the greeting because in them the priest always stands facing the people when celebrating." VOGEL 1962, 183.

664   DÖLGER 1972, 333 f.

665   In Rome, however, Vigilius was himself the main celebrant; there he could have at most instructed the titular presbyters to pray towards the east. But it is actually unlikely that any dissent ever existed between pope and presbyters regarding the direction of celebration that made such a decree necessary.

666   The fact that the sun here represents the east becomes clear from the small moon behind the praying woman's back.

667   Cf. JEREMIAS 1980, 80–88; G. DE SPIRITO, Per interpretare la scena della c.d. "Seconda Parousia" sulla porta lignea di s. Sabina, in: V. RUGGIERI / L. PIERALLI (eds.), ΕΥΚΟΣΜΙΑ (Soveria Mannelli 2003) 189–200. Second Coming of Christ from the east see HEID 2001b, 153–155. I. FOLETTI, La porta di Santa Sabina, un'immagine in dialogo con il culto, in: *id.* / M. GIANANDREA, Zona liminare. Il nartece di Santa Sabina a Roma, la sua porta e l'iniziazione cristiana (Rome 2015) 95–199, here 167 considers the woman to be not the personified Church but instead St Sabina.

668   In a similar way, in the Ascension scene of the Rabbula Codex, Mary is depicted facing the viewer and praying upwards to Christ with raised hands; WEITZMANN 1979, 455 Fig. 68.

669   So SPIESER 1991, 79 f.

Finally, a mural from the church of *Santa Maria in Via Lata* dating from the sixth or seventh century needs to be mentioned (Fig. 60). It probably depicts an Old Testament scene, namely the Tent of the Covenant as a kind of temple which has a table standing in it with the Torah lying on it.[670] The concrete model for such a picture was evidently provided by the Christian church interior. That is to say, it is believed to depict a table altar with an altar cloth standing on a pedestal under a ciborium. Interestingly enough, the altar is only accessible from the front. This is exactly the same way as the priest is likely to approach the altar in the church of *Santa Maria in Via Lata*.

The fact that facing east to pray was already relevant in fourth-century Rome can basically be seen from the layout of the churches. Even the leading ancient Roman architect Vitruvius (first century B.C.) had the direction of prayer in mind when he insisted on building the temple cell with the image of the deity to the east.[671] If this is not possible, the entrance to the temple is put in the east.[672] Precisely this dual variant seems to have been adopted in Christian church-building in Rome. Contrary to the common opinion that an unregulated muddle prevailed here, Sible de Blaauw has drawn attention to the fact that not only the Constantinian churches[673] in Rome, but also almost all of the subsequent churches kept to the west-east axis. The occasionally considerable deviations can mostly be explained by urban planning constrictions.[674] Two conclusions can be drawn from this: Christian church-building deliberately places itself in the tradition of the ancient sacred building. The church space is therefore not simply a neutral space, but belongs to cultic architecture. Furthermore, the choice of the west-east axis in church-building probably results from liturgical necessity, namely the need to face east to pray.

The rising light is an important motif here. Since the Eucharist is normally celebrated in the morning, the idea of light also influences the layout of the churches (windows on the east side). De Blaauw therefore believes that especially in those Constantinian churches whose façade faces east, people pray towards the rising sun.[675] There is much to be said for this, even though it is ultimately scarcely possible to clarify the liturgical use of Rome's churches in any differentiated way before the time of Gregory the Great

670 WILPERT 1917, 699 f.

671 See above p. 236 f. Vitruvius's prayer regulations are adopted by Clem. Alex. strom. 7,7,43,7 (SC 428, 150–152).

672 MARQUARDT 1885, 156 f. The regulations required by Vitruvius are not permanently observed in Rome since the front of the temple is in many cases moved to the east. The question is then: In what direction does the priest sacrifice at the altar?

673 VOELKL 1949, 165 f.

674 DE BLAAUW 2006, 166–168; id. 2008, 279; id. 2010, 20–23. This 2010 publication is of funda-

mental importance for the question of architectural and liturgical facing east. It contradicts the older opinion (e.g. in GAMBER 1994, 49; also still HEID 2006, 381) that in Rome's early Christian basilicas the apse was located "practically in the direction of every point of the compass."

675 S. DE BLAAUW, Met het oog op het licht. Een vergeten principe in de orientatie van het vroegchristelijk kerkgebouw (Nijmegen 2000); id. 2008, 280; id. 2010a. Similarly WALLRAFF 2001, 77 f.; id. 2010, 115 f.; MONDINI 2016, 199. NUSSBAUM 1965 as a rule notes which churches have windows in the apse.

Fig. 59: Wooden panel from the main door of the church of *Santa Sabina* in Rome showing the Parousia of Christ, 5th century; PIAC Archivio Fotografico.

Fig. 60: Wall painting with table and Torah in the church of *Santa Maria in Via Lata*, Rome, 6th/7th century; Wilpert 1917, Plate 137.

(590–604). This applies particularly to the question of whether only the main celebrant faced east during the prayers, or whether the people did as well.

It is not possible to present all of Rome's churches here, so we shall restrict ourselves to the most noteworthy and frequently debated cases. Nor will there be any attempt to conceal the hypothetical nature of many of the reflections. In very few of Rome's early Christian churches has it been possible to prove archaeologically where the altar stood.[676] All the same, a sufficient number of elements can be brought together to reveal that facing east to pray was basically in force at least until the Middle Ages. A break with the Roman liturgical tradition did not come about until the "exile" of the popes in Avignon (1309–1378). The clergy who then returned to Rome were no longer familiar with the Roman traditions; they had lost any understanding of why the pope turned towards the nave in St Peter's and other churches with an east-facing entrance. Nor did they know why in St Paul's and the other churches with east-end apses it was customary to turn towards the apse. This process of alienation was reinforced by the numerous side altars, which were no longer characterised by any uniform direction.[677] In the end, they were simply no longer aware of the historical and liturgical meaning of prayer orientation, but the position of the priest in front of the altar was nevertheless retained. It was considered the norm at each and every celebration of mass with the exception of Pontifical Masses.[678]

Let us begin the series of churches with *Old St Peter's* (*San Pietro in Vaticano*), which dates from the fourth century. It is only since the Second World War that there has been a broad degree of clarity as to the basic archaeological set-up and the original furnishings of Old St. Peter's. It was during this period that the Venerable Fabric of Saint Peter carried out its spectacular excavations under the high altar of the Renaissance basilica.[679]

The findings regarding the building history of the church reveal that after 312 Emperor Constantine had the basilica built over the grave of the apostles, and that he did so in such a way that a high monument was now erected in the church (Fig. 61). The elongated basilica follows the west-east axis exactly. At the other end, opposite the entrance in the east, towers a majestic apse. Only a few metres in front of this rises up the aforementioned monument, the shrine of the apostle Peter. It is a masonry cube 2.90 m wide, 1.80 m deep and about 3.00 m high, designed to enclose and protect the ancient and highly venerated monument to the apostle. The monument contains the so-called Tropaion (Trophy) of Gaius (Fig. 62), the aedicule that was built on the site of the presumed tomb of St Peter as early as the second century. This aedicule essentially consists of a travertine slab resting on two columns at the front, lying horizontally at a height of 1.5 m and abutting a wall at the back.[680] The wall and the small column architecture

---

676 De Blaauw 2001b, 973.
677 Vogel 1960, 460f.
678 On the supposed papal privilege to celebrate *versus populum* see below p. 448.
679 Main documentation: Apollonj Ghetti 1951.
680 Not to assume that this is a slab on which to place

the sacrificial offerings, but to suppose it instead to be some sort of timberwork frame (Brandenburg 2017b, Plate 6) is unconvincing. This suggestion goes back to the fifth-century Terebinthus legend and a speculation by Francesco Tolotti based on it (cf. Arbeiter 1988, 45 Fig. 28).

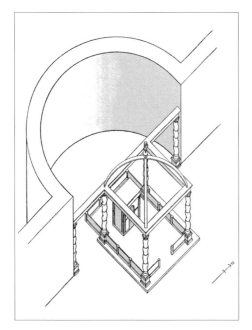

Fig. 61: Isometric reconstruction of the Memoria Petri in Old St Peter's after J. Toynbee / J. Ward Perkins, c. 320; LIVERANI 2006b, 142.

Fig. 62: Reconstruction of the "Tropaion of Gaius", the memoria of St Peter at the Vatican before the construction of Old St Peter's, c. 160; R. Gem, From Constantine to Constans. The chronology of the construction of Saint Peter's Basilica, in: R. MCKITTER-ICK et al. (eds.), Old Saint Peter's, Rome (Cambridge 2013) 35–64, here 45 Fig. 2.4.

joined to it were isolated for the Constantinian church building and encased with the apostle's shrine. The wall contains a 70-cm-wide niche (N²) rising vertically from the ground. It is no longer possible to tell how the wall ran above the slab as this zone was later lost as a result of the construction of the altar superstructure under Gregory the Great (590–604).[681] The excavators, however, assume a (conch-shaped) niche above a travertine slab measuring 1.05 m in width.[682]

The new tall shrine of the apostle is indisputably the sacred centre of the entire basilica (Fig. 63). It is enclosed by solid barriers with a surface area at the front of 6.70 m long and 5.40 m wide[683] and with a central opening left free at both the front and the back.[684]

681 Cf. ARBEITER 1988, 29 and the various reconstructions ibid. 30.
682 The excavators give the niche a hypothetical width of 1.05 m. See the dashed line N³ in APOLLONJ GHETTI 1951, 127, 138 Fig. 99, 141 Fig. 100, 143

Fig. 101; cf. 163 Fig. 116. The niche above the travertine slab must not be confused with the height of the later Niche of the Pallium (misleadingly marked in ibid. Fig. 91, 96). The two are correctly distinguished in ibid. Fig. 150.

In addition to this, Emperor Constantine endowed the church with a magnificent altar which with its gold and four hundred gems weighed a total of c. 106 kg.[685] It is generally thought that it was located inside the barriers.[686] Others, however, are content that there was not enough space there for the papal liturgy[687] and assume that the altar stood either a few metres in front of the enclosed area (under the triumphal arch)[688] or even further into the nave.[689] There are no literary or archaeological reference points for either solution. All the same, it is hard to imagine that in a church that possessed a sacred centre in the form of such a monumental martyr's tomb, the Eucharist would be celebrated outside this sacred area and further up the nave. Rather, the barrier enclosure (with its raised floor level) suggests more than anything else a space intended for the liturgy.

The contention that there is no room for an altar in the enclosed area is not convincing. First, the actual size of the barrier installation is not at all certain since its eastern end has not been archaeologically established.[690] Second, one must not overestimate the number of clergy directly involved in the liturgy.[691] The papal liturgy contents itself with such tiny rooms as *San Silvestro* on the *Via Salaria*[692] and *Sancta Sanctorum* in the Apostolic Palace (below Fig. 96). Even the Basilica of *San Clemente*, which with its furnishings (pulpit, cancelli, etc.) represents a medieval model church for the papal liturgy (below Fig. 88), offers little space for the clergy.[693] Moreover, one must always reckon with mobile furnishings being used to change the liturgical space as needed. Wooden barriers are still erected today for every Papal Mass at St Peter's. Hence one should not conclude from the bare archaeological findings for the Constantinian Basilica of St Peter that these already allow us to see the defined liturgical space. It is quite possible that

683 De Blaauw 1994, 481.
684 For the celebration of the liturgy an "invisible" 1.90-m-wide opening has been intentionally left in the barriers so that the altar ministers can come and go through it unimpeded to the area at the front.
685 LP 34,18 (Duchesne 1886, 177); Arbeiter 1988, 181 n. 365; de Blaauw 2001b, 970. A piano weighs about 170–190 kg.
686 Cf. Arbeiter 1988, 183.
687 Brandenburg 2017b, 44 speaks of a "cramped space". Similarly Lang 2003, 80, making reference J. Ward-Perkins.
688 Cf. Arbeiter 1988, 183 f.
689 Brandenburg 2005–2006, 264; id. 2011a, 243; id. 2017b, 44. Id. 2015, 33 thinks that Symmachus (498–514) moved the altar from the middle of the church to a position close to the shrine, meaning

that it had not stood there before. However, LP 53,10 (Duchesne 1886, 263 f.) speaks only of donations for the furnishing of the altar area. Tolotti 1986, 68 has different reasons for claiming the altar to have been in the middle of the nave, but that too is speculative. De Blaauw 1994, 481, based on the testimony of Agiulf, definitively rules out an altar in the nave.
690 Apollonj Ghetti 1951, 168.
691 De Blaauw 1994, 505 speaks of there being space for nine thousand people in the basilica, but no one knows whether the church was ever so full.
692 The reconstruction of the altar in San Silvestro in the middle of the space in Tolotti 1986, 64–66 is, however, unconvincing.
693 The Oratorio di San Silvestro chapel at SS Quattro Coronati was also sufficient for the medieval papal liturgy.

Fig. 63: Shrine of the Apostle and apse of Old St Peter's around 400, reconstructed after the ivory casket from Samagher. The apse mosaic shows the so-called Traditio Legis; with slight variation, according to Longhi 2006, Tav. 12.

the area surrounding the apostle's shrine that was enclosed with marble barriers was reserved for the higher clergy and that wooden barriers were erected ad hoc in the wider area, for example for the *Schola Cantorum*.[694] This is the case in the fifth century at the latest, when the floor around the apostle's shrine was raised and equipped with cancelli and possibly also a *Schola Cantorum* (Fig. 64).[695]

However, the ivory casket from Samagher dating from the early fifth century, which almost certainly depicts the Memoria Petri on one side, argues against the existence of a permanently installed altar within the barriers. It shows the barriers, but no altar (Fig. 65; above Fig. 29).[696] If we still assume that there was an altar in this area, it must have been a mobile one, put up just for the Eucharist.[697] This would not be in any way surprising since mobile furnishings must always be expected for the celebration of mass. There are two further arguments in favour of a mobile altar: on the relief in question, two pilgrims are to be seen right next to the Memoria Petri. This means that the faithful were permitted to enter the enclosed area inside the barriers.[698] There might even have been actual processions in which the pilgrims entered the area from the front and left it through the rear exit.[699] However, the magnificent Constantinian altar is far too valuable (with its gold and gems) to be left unprotected. After all, from 503 at the latest synods were held in the area known as the *ante confessionem*.[700] In all probability, this denotes the enclosed area. So seats were placed there, or else there were benches there at least for the Liturgy of the Hours.[701] There would hardly be any space left in between for a permanently installed altar.

694 This is what DE BLAAUW 2016, 98 Fig. 6 also seems to assume.
695 DE BLAAUW 1994, 478 f., 506 f., moves the date of these archaeologically proven extensions to the presbytery to under Symmachus (498–514).
696 ARBEITER 1988, 183.
697 On the mobile altar ARBEITER 1988, 183; DE BLAAUW 1994, 481 f.
698 BISCONTI 2009, 224 f.
699 This relative accessibility of the niche (RUYSSCHAERT 1954, 45) was probably ensured over centuries until the large *confessio* was then built in about 590, which itself also allowed the pilgrims to enter; Notitia eccl. urbis Romae 38 (CCL 175, 311): *Et exinde pervenies ad altare maius eiusque confessionem.*
700 DE BLAAUW 1994, 860. LP 57,3 f. (DUCHESNE 1886, 281): *Hic congregavit synodum in basilica beati Petri apostoli et fecit constitutum ut sibi successorem ordinaret. Quod constitutum cum cyrographis sacerdotum et iusiurandum ante confessionem beati apostoli Petri in diaconum Vigilium constituit. [...] ante confessionem beati apostoli Petri ipsum constitutum praesentia omnium sacerdotum et cleri et senatus incendio consumpsit.* There is also mention of a gathering of bishops directly at the altar of St Peter [Leo. I] ep. 56 (PL 54, 860C–862A).
701 DUCHESNE 1886, 422: *omnibus diebus dum vesperas expleverint ante confessionem.* See on the monks in San Pancrazio Greg. I ep. 4,18 (MGH. Ep. 1,1, 253): *ut ibidem ad sacratissimum corpus beati Pancratii cotidie opus Dei proculdubio peragatur.*

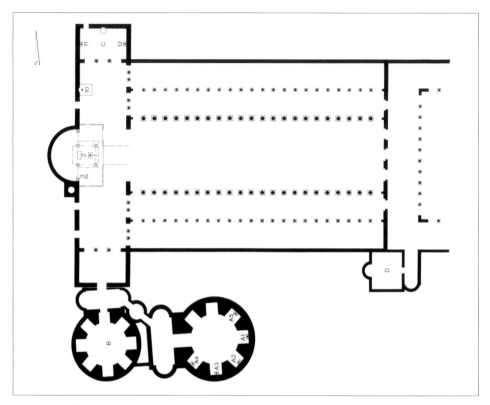

Fig. 64: Floorplan of Old St Peter's with a reconstruction of the liturgical furnishings under Pope Symmachus (498–514); 1 = mobile altar, 2 = Apostle's Shrine, 3 = cathedra; DE BLAAUW 1994, Fig. 19.

It is possible that as long as it was not needed in front of the tomb of St Peter, the magnificent altar was stored behind the tomb monument, where there is a passage through the barriers.[702] Only when the pope himself celebrates, and this is probably quite rare, is

702 APOLLONJ GHETTI 1951, 170 Fig. 121. This area is not just protected with curtains, as the ivory casket once again shows, but people were fundamentally convinced that the martyrs watched over their altars. Damas. epigr. 16, 32, 48, 61 (FERRUA 1942, 120, 166, 195, 229). See also the respective commentaries by Ferrua. So in this way the magnificent altar remains close to its protector, Peter. If the altar stands behind the apostle's shrine and is used for (non-papal) mass celebrations, the liturgist will look towards the tomb and thus towards the east. The faithful stand behind him in the curve of the apse. The genuine possibility of considering this location in the apse *retro sanctos* is revealed by Panvinio's drawings of San Paolo f.l.m. (below Fig. 79), in which an altar is to be seen in the apse. The later remodelling of the apse area of San Pietro (under Pope Gregory) also suggests that there have always also been celebrations *retro sanctos* there, for the annular crypt has a slype that leads to St Peter's tomb from behind. At the end of the slype, exactly behind the memoria, the altar stands *ad caput* (below Fig. 70). Cf. APOLLONJ GHETTI 1951, 177 Fig. 127; DE BLAAUW 1994, Fig. 21.

Fig. 65: Ivory casket from Samagher (Pola) with two persons at the Apostle's Shrine in Old St Peter's (detail), 5ᵗʰ century; Museo Archeologico Nazionale di Venezia; photo: SPIER 2007, 117 Fig. 85.

the altar moved to the front of the tomb monument and placed under the central chandelier (*corona*) (above Fig. 29).[703] But on which side does the celebrant stand? If he stands behind the altar so as to look east towards the nave, he turns his back on the apostle's tomb. So what is more important, seeing the apostle's tomb or facing east to pray? Surely the unique tomb of the apostle takes priority here.[704] An analogous case with regard to celebrating facing the tomb is provided by the Helena mausoleum at the Basilica of *Santi Marcellino e Pietro* on the *Via Labicana*. There, Constantine had the altar positioned "in front of the tomb" of the empress.[705] The imperial porphyry sarcophagus is probably in the eastern niche of the circular building,[706] meaning that the altar is on the west side. The celebrant thus approaches the altar facing the sarcophagus and at the same time facing east. In St Peter's, the celebrant will also look towards the tomb, albeit at the cost

703 ARBEITER 1988, 183; DE BLAAUW 1994, 481 f.; *id.* 2001b, 973.

704 DE BLAAUW 1995, 505 f. decides in favour of facing east. But when Leo I serm. 27,4 (CCL 137, 135) inveighs against the sun worshippers who bow low to the sun on the steps of Old St Peter's before entering the basilica, this gives the impression that he does not attach the greatest importance to facing east to pray. It is rather to be assumed that the people in the basilica in any case look west towards the apostle's memoria (VOGEL 1960, 450 f.; *id.* 1964, 27–29), and probably the pope does too.

705 LP 34,26 (DUCHESNE 1886, 182). Cf. DE BLAAUW 2001b, 974.

706 M. J. JOHNSON, The Roman Imperial Mausoleum in Antiquity (New York 2009) 117.

of now standing facing west.[707] At least he will see a cross above the double door of the apostle's shrine marking a kind of ideal east. It can be seen on the ivory relief (Fig. 66). The celebrant's turning towards the tomb of the apostle is also evident from the designation of the enclosed area as *ante confessionem*.[708] The view of the *confessio* of St Peter behind the double door determines the perspective here.

So much for a possible scenario as to where and how the Eucharist was celebrated in the Constantinian Basilica of St Peter. The basic idea is that the celebrant (the pope) stood at an altar specially erected at the memoria of St Peter, from where he could see the apostle's tomb. However, there is a further possibility that can be considered if one takes a closer look at the structure of the Constantinian shrine of the apostle. José Ruysschaert already suggested that the apostle's shrine itself, or more precisely the niche at the front, could be considered a kind of altar on which the Eucharist was celebrated.[709] Constantine's above-mentioned magnificent altar would in that case not have been used, at least not by the pope, or they would soon have dispensed with it. Even if a celebration directly at the niche of the apostle's shrine may at first seem far-fetched, this hypothesis nevertheless deserves closer examination. In the end it will even prove to be the more likely solution.

On the basis of the ivory relief (above Fig. 65) and the archaeological findings, there are two possible ways of looking from the front of the apostle's memoria into its inside and, as it were, seeing the archaeological monument to St Peter (the Tropaion of Gaius). The first possibility is to open the double door at the bottom, which enables a view of the rear wall of the former aedicula (the Red Wall). The door is indeed important: the person on the left seems to be pointing at it with his left hand.[710] The fact that it is a double door is in itself remarkable. If you follow the ivory relief, it cannot just be a small hatch. Rather, two door leaves are needed in order to offer access to a sufficiently large opening. Furthermore, it is not a door with a rounded top, but rather one that is straight along the top, apparently because it abuts a slab, the front edge of which is in fact visible on the ivory relief. The second way of looking inside the memoria is to look into the niche (concha) that opens above the travertine slab in question.

For the proportions here it is important to note that Constantine's original aedicula (the Tropaion of Gaius) was encased by the apostle's shrine in such a way that the

---

707 Jacobsen 2000a, 70 f.; *id.* 2000b, 66 f. Cf. Lang 2003, 80. A not completely comparable situation is found in the Crypt of the Popes in the Catacomb of Callixtus (de Blaauw 2016, 79 Fig. 1). Here the altar stands in front of the inscription wall. It is possible that the celebrant stood behind the altar here; since there are graves everywhere in the crypt, it makes no difference which he turns his back on. The fact that the altar stands away from the wall probably has to do with the desire to enable access to the graves lying behind it.

708 See above p. 293.

709 Ruysschaert 1954, 39–49.

710 Kalinowski 2011, 144.

Fig. 66: Drawing of the section above the double door of the Apostle's Shrine in Old St Peter's; Guarducci 1978, 41 Fig. 17.

adjacent floor level was raised by 35 cm. As a result, the aedicula lost height and the travertine slab now rose up only about 1.15 m (instead of the previous 1.50 m) above the ground.[711] It shrinks, so to speak, to the height of a table[712] and reaches to someone's stomach (Fig. 67). This suggests that the intention might have been to make the travertine slab more accessible for the faithful. This does not mean that it was designed from the start as an altar mensa. However, the opportunity to use it for celebration has de facto presented itself ever since.

Since the double door is probably mostly closed (the right leaf has a keyhole on the ivory relief?), the travertine slab is usually the only visible part of the historical monument of St Peter and therefore the precise thing that pilgrims want to touch. In any case, the travertine slab is considered particularly sacred and is therefore made accessible through a niche. So the two believers on the ivory relief are reaching into the niche to get to the slab. They probably want to lay cloths (*palliola*) on it and thereby sanctify them (make them relics *ex contactu*); the woman on the right does in fact seem to be holding a cloth. Perhaps because they are laity – privileged all the same[713] – only this kind of approach is permitted them, whereas for clergy the double door beneath the table slab is opened.[714] For the artist who created the ivory, the travertine slab is so important that he moves the two people outwards so that the front edge of it can be seen. But nor does

711 Calculated according to Apollonj Ghetti 1951, 125 Fig. 91.
712 Arbeiter 1988, 167.
713 Cf. Brenk 1995, 76.
714 Greg. Tur. lib. mirac. 1 in glor. mart. 27 (MGH. SRM 1, 504).

Fig. 67: Longitudinal section of the Apostle's Shrine in Old St Peter's, 4th century; CARANDINI 2013, Fig. 17.

Livello 123-130 d.C. ca.

0   2,5

** Tomba vuota di Pietro, 256-319 d.C. ca.
a. Edicola-trofeo di Pietro, 150-160 a.C.
b. Teca dell'edicola, 319 d.C.
c. Ciborio e lampadario, 319 d.C.

he want the two people to obscure the double door. Hence they are too small, giving the impression that the pilgrims had to climb onto a platform in order to reach the niche.[715] In reality, however, they are at ground level, and the supposed platform is actually the barrier that surrounds the apostle's shrine on all sides.

Not all researchers share the opinion that the semicircle on the ivory relief represents a conch-shaped niche. Some see it as a flat wall.[716] But in that case the builders could have saved themselves the trouble of enclosing the Tropaion of Gaius in an apostle's shrine that was about 3 m high. After all, the tall superstructure only makes sense if it

---

715 So erroneously KLAUSER 1956, 111; BRENK 1995, 76; KALINOWSKI 2011, 144.

716 CARANDINI 2013, Tav. III–IV.

was meant to display something. Furthermore, it would be pretty strange if it was just the upper wall that the people on the ivory were reaching for, seeing that the tomb of the apostle is undoubtedly to be found further down.[717] All these circumstances support the idea of a niche as the actual place of veneration. That is why the excavators themselves were right to reconstruct a niche even though there is no archaeological evidence for it.[718]

Therefore it would have been possible to stand at the niche and celebrate the Eucharist directly above the presumed tomb of the apostle. However, Ruysschaert's suggestion to this effect was rejected because there was said not to be enough space.[719] Such an objection is based on two erroneous scenarios. The first is based on the assumption that it was possible to enter the Constantinian apostle's shrine so that you could take a step inside it (cf. above Fig. 63).[720] But there was said to be far too little space inside the casing for any liturgy to be performed. However, this problem does not in fact arise at all: neither the measurements based on the archaeological findings nor the ivory casket leave any doubt that the front edge of the travertine slab and the double door are flush with the front wall of the Constantinian apostle's shrine (Fig. 68). So the double door is not moved inwards. The entire front side is flat – except for the niche. This means that it is only possible to approach the apostle's memoria, not to enter it.

In the second case, the niche itself is thought to be too small for a dignified celebration. Let us note here that the excavators assign the niche a hypothetical width of 1.05 m, which is not small. Archaeologically, however, an even wider niche is conceivable. It is necessary to distinguish precisely between the visible niche above the travertine slab and the hidden niche below, which is located in the Red Wall. From looking at the ivory relief, it seems that the upper niche is as wide as the double doors below it. If this is the case, its clear width may have been up to 1.40 m, which would make the niche of a considerable size.[721] But in this case, due to the archaeological shape of the tropaion (and unlike on the relief), the double doors cannot lie axially in the front of the apostle's shrine but must be offset by about 50 cm to the left. This is quite conceivable. An artist

717 There are ancient tomb altars with fake double doors; e.g. ALTMANN 1905, 103 Fig. 85.

718 KIRSCHBAUM 1957, 150; GUARDUCCI 1978, 40; ARBEITER 1988, 171 f.; LONGHI 2006, 60–65.

719 RUYSSCHAERT 1954, 37–49. Rejecting the proposal KIRSCHBAUM 1957, 228 n. 13; ARBEITER 1988, 182; DE BLAAUW 1994, 481 n. 169.

720 APOLLONJ GHETTI 1951, 170 Fig. 121; ibid. Tav. H; KIRSCHBAUM 1957, Plate 29, adopted, for example, by BRACONI 2016, 267 Fig. 111. BRANDENBURG 2017 similarly suggests in all the recon-

struction drawings that it was possible to enter the apostle's shrine. All this goes back to a false interpretation of the relief on the ivory casket from Samagher (above Fig. 65). It is clearly recognisable that the door leaves are covered up on the right and left; however, this is not due to the wall frame of the apostle's memoria, but rather to the cloaks of the man and woman standing there.

721 The measurements are calculated between the walls S and g in APOLLONJ GHETTI 1951, 143 Fig. 101; 163 Fig. 116; DE BLAAUW 1994, Fig. 20.

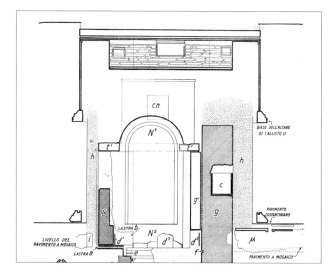

Fig. 68: Front (east side) of the
Memoria Petri on the Vatican
hill: g Red Wall, t travertine
slab, g¹ is later; APOLLONJ GHETTI
1951, 125 Fig. 91.

can overlook such a deviation for the sake of symmetry in the composition of the picture
(Fig. 69).

Thus, if we assume a double door that is offset to the left, this will, when open, make
it possible to look into the artificial cavity of the *confessio* or, if you like, into the lower
structure of the Tropaion of Gaius; above this – above the travertine slab – is the allegedly 1.40-m-wide niche.[722] The door is intended to afford access to the cavity since,
presumably from the very beginning, there was a libation hole or shaft there leading
down to what was presumed to be the tomb of the apostle (Fig. 70).[723] Pope Sixtus III
(432–440) lavishly embellished a pre-existing *confessio*,[724] which means that the apostle's memoria can be assumed to have possessed such a fixture right from the start.

There is a further reason why the niche located above it cannot have been small. On
the ivory relief, in the arched opening of the niche, there is a cross to be seen flanked
by two persons – probably Peter and Paul (above Figs. 65, 66).[725] This is probably a
mosaic.[726] The opinion is also expressed that a three-dimensional cross[727] and two stat-

722 Even the baroque columns in front of the Niche of
the Pallium still take exact account of the cavity of
the aedicula, that is, the clear width of walls S and
g (ibid. 163 Fig. 116; DE BLAAUW 1994, Fig. 20),
whereas since Gregory the Great the altars have
understandably been erected centrally on the
shrine of the apostle (ibid. Fig. 22).

723 ARBEITER 1988, 167. The shaft is marked in APOL-
LONJ GHETTI 1951, 201 Fig. 154; DE BLAAUW
1994, Fig. 22. For the earliest archaeological documentation of the *confessio* see GRISAR 1899, Tav.

VIII. In detail THÜMMEL 1999b, 62–68.

724 LP 46,4 (DUCHESNE 1886, 233): *Hic ornavit de
argento confessionem beati Petri apostoli.* Cf.
BRAUN 1924a, 550; DE BLAAUW 1994, 472f.

725 KLAUSER 1956, 111 speaks of apostles, GUAR-
DUCCI 1978, 43–58 of angels keeping watch. See
the redrawing ibid. 43 Fig. 18.

726 KALINOWSKI 2011, 144.

727 This might have been the gold cross donated by
Constantine: DE BLAAUW 1994, 475; against this
GUARDUCCI 1978, 41f. LP 34,17 (DUCHESNE

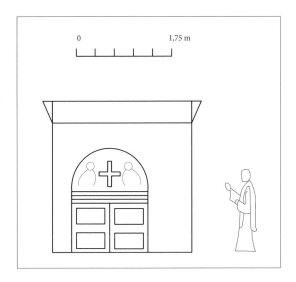

Fig. 69: Schematic drawing of the Apostle's Shrine in Old St Peter's. The double doors are moved to the left, so that the niche above them attains its maximal size; measurements after Apollonj Ghetti 1951, 124 Fig. 90, 125 Fig 91, 163 Fig. 116, 165 Fig. 118; drawing: Chiara Cecalupo.

0   1,75 m

uettes (of apostles) stood in the niche. However, this would increase the danger of theft by pious pilgrims and would therefore argue against it. In fact, David Longhi postulates a protective grille in front of the niche that was not reproduced on the ivory relief.[728] However, a grille would have largely obstructed the view of the mosaic behind it – or the artist would have depicted the grille rather than the mosaic unless the grille itself had been designed with a central cross and two figures. This, in turn, is completely illogical since the cross and the figures would have blocked the view into the niche. Whatever the case, if one assumes a grille, then the two pilgrims would be wanting to touch it. Yet that, too, seems illogical. For if it is correct that the front edge of the travertine slab is visible, then it is to be expected that the pilgrims would not touch an iron grille, but rather the front edge of the travertine slab. But they are not reaching out towards this front edge because they can apparently touch the slab from above.[729] This supports the idea of an open mosaic niche. It is even possible to recognise the mosaic from some distance; at least the ivory relief gives this impression. So it seems that the niche was quite spacious, large enough for a celebration.

1886, 176): *fecit crucem ex auro purissimo […] in mensurae locus.*

728   A grille in front of the niche as postulated by Klauser 1956, 111 and Longhi 2006, 62 f. would be a purely analogical conclusion from the Damasian monumentalising of the martyrs' tombs in the catacombs. But one cannot contend that "l'ar-

tista, che ha rappresentato con cura straordinaria le grate nella scena del pannello sinistro del cofanetto" (ibid. 58 f.) and at the same time say that the artist omitted the niche grille.

729   This corresponds to the situation in San Paolo, where the faithful are probably permitted to touch St Paul's sarcophagus or its cover. See below p. 316.

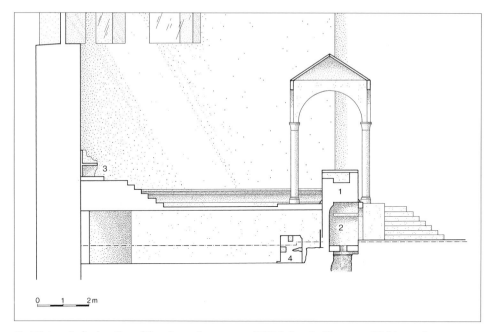

Fig. 70: Longitudinal section of the altar and apse area of Old St Peter's, 7ᵗʰ century. Visible are the passage-way of the crypt with the altar *ad caput*, the *Confessio*, and above it the main altar; DE BLAAUW 1994, Fig. 24.

If pilgrims venerated the mosaic niche or the travertine slab as much as the ivory relief shows, should it not then be the pope, and only him, who celebrated mass in this niche? As already stated, this may sound strange, but it is not unthinkable, especially since, al-though such celebrations were rare, they were significant for the sense of the Petrine office, for example on the Feast of SS Peter and Paul on 29 June. A comparable case can in fact be found for this: at the end of the fourth century, the bishop of Jerusalem once a year – on Holy Thursday – offered the sacrifice in the Church of the Holy Sepulchre in Jerusalem in a cramped room "behind the cross", apparently because the altar there stood directly on the rock of Golgotha, which was soaked with the true blood of Christ.[730] A modern example of a cramped celebration such as that in St Peter's is found in *San Giovanni Battista dei Cavalieri di Rodi* in Rome (*Piazza del Grillo* 1). Here an altar was built in the twentieth century into a doorway that was no longer in use, which gives an idea of the dimensions and practicality of a niche altar: a celebration at the door, as it were, is certainly not particularly uplifting, but nevertheless possible if the circumstances so require (Fig. 71).[731] So as early as the fourth century the pope presumably no longer

---

730 Eger. itin. 35,2 (CCL 175, 79).

731 A nineteenth-century cupboard chapel see DE PAULIS / MASCONI 2010, 46 f.

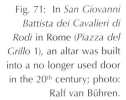

Fig. 71: In *San Giovanni Battista dei Cavalieri di Rodi* in Rome (*Piazza del Grillo* 1), an altar was built into a no longer used door in the 20th century; photo: Ralf van Bühren.

used the magnificent Constantinian altar in St Peter's, but celebrated at the niche of the apostle's shrine. There are, in fact, a number of reasons for making this assumption.

One crucial argument in support of it comes from a polemic written in around 400 by the presbyter Vigilantius, who is upset that – to put it dramatically – the popes say mass on top of corpses. His reproof is only preserved indirectly in Jerome's reply and has been frequently misunderstood even though the actual context can be very accurately reconstructed. It should be noted that there was no one was more suited to put Vigilantius in his place than Jerome since he had been a close collaborator of Pope Damasus (366–384) in the Curia and was therefore very familiar with the situation in Rome. Now (in 406) he says quite unequivocally that the pope himself uses the tombs of the apostles Peter and Paul as altars, i.e. he celebrates mass on their graves:

Does the bishop of Rome do wrong when he offers sacrifices to the Lord over the venerable bones of the dead men Peter and Paul, as we should say, but according to you [Vigilantius], over a worthless bit of dust, and judges their tombs worthy to be Christ's altars?[732]

This is mostly interpreted as if Vigilantius were simply accusing the popes of reading mass *in the vicinity of* the tombs.[733] In fact, for a long time the Christian cult of the dead was content to worship above the extensive catacombs in which the martyrs are here and there also buried.[734] But anyone who reads Jerome's words closely has to admit that he is by no means concerned merely with celebrating mass in the vicinity of a grave, for he unmistakably identifies altar and grave: the graves of the apostles themselves serve as altars. This is exactly the situation that Vigilantius knows and criticises: the apostles and martyrs are in their graves "under the altar" of God (cf. Rv 6:9) and therefore cannot be of any use.[735] Jerome, on the other hand, thinks that the martyrs are wherever the Lamb is (Rv 14:4), and this is undoubtedly true of the tomb altar on which the Lamb of God is sacrificed.[736] However, the polemic brings out a further crucial aspect and one that leads us further; namely, the fact that Vigilantius had only the graves of the Princes of the Apostles in mind. Concretely, he only complains about masses celebrated on the graves of SS Peter and Paul. Therefore the pope must already have celebrated at the niche of the apostle's shrine in St Peter's.

A letter written in the year 450 by Galla Placidia also suggests that from a specific time onwards the tomb of the apostle itself served as an altar in St Peter's. In it the empress describes how, accompanied by Pope Leo, she "desired to venerate the most blessed apostle Peter directly at the admirable 'martyr's altar'". While they were there, the pope withdrew from prayer for a moment and addressed the empress on urgent matters of faith, taking as his witness the Prince of the Apostles himself, on whom they had both just been calling in prayer. Numerous bishops were present.[737] Although this scene can

732 Hieron. c. Vigil. 8 (PL 23, 346B): *Male facit ergo Romanus episcopus, qui super mortuorum hominum Petri et Pauli, secundum nos ossa veneranda, secundum te vilem pulvisculum, offert Domino sacrificia, et tumulos eorum Christi arbitratur altaria?* LANG 2003, 78 n. 143 does not want to see this statement overworked. Yet it is so unambiguous that it can scarcely be left aside. BRANDENBURG 2017b, 45 thinks it only possible to apply the statement generally to churches built over the graves of the apostles.

733 KIRSCHBAUM 1957, 228 f. n. 13; BRANDENBURG 2017b, 45.

734 DECKERS 1987, 166.

735 Hieron. c. Vigil. 6 (PL 23, 344A): *Ais enim vel in sinu Abrahae, vel in loco refrigerii, vel subter aram Dei, animas apostolorum et martyrum consedisse, nec posse de suis tumulis, et ubi voluerint adesse praesentes.*

736 Ibid. 6 (PL 23, 344A).

737 [Leo. I] ep. 56 (PL 54, 860C–862A): Ὁπήνικα ἐν αὐτῇ τῇ εἰσόδῳ τῆς ἀρχαίας πόλεως ταύτην ἐτιθέμεθα τὴν φροντίδα ἀποδοῦναι τὴν προσκύνησιν τῷ μακαριωτάτῳ ἀποστόλῳ Πέτρῳ ἐν αὐτῷ τῷ προσκυνητῷ θυσιαστηρίῳ τοῦ μάρτυρος ὁ εὐλαβέστατος ἐπίσκοπος Λέων,

be imagined as taking place at an altar standing in front of the apostle's shrine, a different constellation is more plausible. The empress will hardly have come specially to Rome only to see the tomb of the apostle from a distance. Rather, as the highest representative of the Western Empire, she undoubtedly went right up to Peter's tomb. For her, the tomb is quite simply the "martyr's altar" at which the pope usually celebrates the Eucharist. The pope and empress now stand directly in front of the niche, at which they pray. Thereupon the pope addresses the empress in confidence without the bishops, who are standing behind them inside the enclosed area, able to hear what is said.

Finally, Gregory of Tours († 594) confirms the tomb altar for St Peter's basilica. Around 586–590 he describes in detail the church along with its main altar – not from seeing it himself but thanks to an eyewitness, the deacon Agiulf – as it was just before the alterations under Pelagius II and Gregory the Great.[738] Beat Brenk thinks that here the Constantinian apostle's shrine has now become an altar.[739] In fact, however, Agiulf still sees exactly the same thing as is depicted on the ivory casket and knows, like Vigilantius and Jerome, that the niche on the mosaic is used as an altar. In fact, Gregory of Tours states expressly that this is an example of the very rare case of a tomb lying underneath the altar (*sepulchrum sub altare collocatum*).[740] Of course, at the end of the sixth century such tomb altars existed all over the place in Rome, but for the pilgrim Agiulf this was probably something unusual. He may also have found it strange to celebrate on the altar in a niche. At all events, there is no disputing that altar and tomb are identical.[741] It cannot be claimed in contradiction to Jerome and Agiulf that an altar stood *in front* of the tomb. For there was nothing standing in front of the tomb monument. This is clear from Agiulf's description. He says that you open the door of the surrounding enclosure (the external barriers) and from there you reach the *confessio*, behind the *fenestella* of which you then enter the cavity above the tomb. He does not say that you have to pass the altar in order to reach the actual tomb. Rather, the pilgrim is fully aware that there is just a tomb and above it the altar. This does not, of course, exclude the possibility that a mobile altar was used during non-papal masses.

ὀλίγον ἐπισχὼν ἑαυτὸν ἀπὸ τῆς εὐχῆς, ἕνεκα τῆς καθολικῆς πίστεως πρὸς ἡμᾶς ἀπωδύρατο· αὐτόν τε ὁμοίως τὸν κορυφαῖον τῶν ἀποστόλων, ᾧ καὶ ἔναγχος προσείπμεν, μάρτυρα συλλαβόμενος, περιεστοιχισμένος τε πλήθει ἐπισκόπων.

738 De Blaauw 1994, 480 f.

739 Brenk 1995, 77.

740 Greg. Tur. lib. mirac. 1 in glor. mart. 27 (MGH. SRM 1, 504): *Habet etiam quattuor [columnas] in altare, quod sunt simul centum, praeter illas quae ciborium sepulchri sustentant. Hoc enim*

sepulchrum sub altare collocatum, valde rarum habetur. Sed qui orare desiderat, reseratis cancellis, quibus locus ille ambitur, accedit super sepulchrum; et sic fenestella parvula patefacta, inmisso introrsum capite, quae necessitas promit efflagitat. [...] Sunt ibi et columnae mirae elegantiae candore niveo quattuor numero, quae ciborium sepulchri sustenere dicuntur. The account given by deacon Agiulf after visiting Rome dates from the years 586–590; de Blaauw 1994, 480.

741 Ruysschaert 1954, 44.

Many archaeologists react sceptically to the statements of Jerome and Agiulf and re-interpret them accordingly. Their main objection can be found in the sixth-century *Liber Pontificalis* (Book of the popes), which states that Pope Gregory the Great (590–604) ordered masses to be celebrated over the bodies of Blessed Peter and Paul: *Hic fecit ut super corpus beati Petri missas celebrarentur; item et in ecclesiam beati Pauli apostoli eadem fecit.*[742] The archaeologists conclude from this that Pope Gregory was the first to desire a celebration above the tombs of the apostles and that he had the sanctuary in both St Peter's and St Paul's raised for this purpose, so that there was now an altar above the tombs of both Peter and Paul. They regard this interpretation as doubly confirmed by the archaeological evidence that shows the sanctuary to have been raised in both ba-silicas under this pope (Figs. 72 and 73 and below Figs. 81 and 83). The question is only whether the *Liber Pontificalis* necessarily contradicts Jerome.

There is only a contradiction if one assumes that the *Liber Pontificalis* intended to make an archaeological statement.[743] On the other hand, the contradiction vanishes when the papal chronicle is interpreted liturgically, which is something that certainly suggests itself in the case of a book such as this written by clerics. In other words, the *Liber Pontificalis* is not talking about a building measure at all, even though there really was one.[744] It is only talking about masses over the two tombs of the apostles. And that brings us back to the controversy between Jerome and Vigilantius. This, too, is exclu-sively about the tombs of the apostles. In the eyes of Vigilantius, a particularly reprehen-sible practice is taking place at mass in St Peter's and St Paul's. What he criticises is the practice of celebrating directly over the tomb and in the immediate vicinity of the bones (*super ossa*), which he regards as a kind of necrophilia,[745] and besides, at that time such altars apparently only existed in St Peter's and St Paul's. As far as the concrete situation in St Peter's is concerned, this can only mean that the celebrant used the travertine slab as an altar mensa. It is easy to understand how outrageous it must have seemed for mass to be celebrated directly on a grave, especially if such a practice only arose at a later date. Vigilantius will have been by no means the only one to have taken offence at this practice.

---

742 LP 66,5 (DUCHESNE 1886, 312).

743 This is rightly pointed out by DE BLAAUW 1994, 533 f.

744 Here BRANDENBURG 2005–2006, 266 is wrong: "The Liber Pontificalis reports that the Pope undertook building alterations at the respective tombs of the apostles in both St Paul's and St Pe-ter's so as to be able in future to celebrate Mass over the grave", *Id.* 2011a, 245 and 2011b, 380: "Af-ter all, we know from the *Liber Pontificalis* that

Gregory the Great put a raised podium round the memoria here in St Paul's as well as in St Peter's." Similarly SPERA 2007, 67.

745 Hieron. c. Vigil. 8 (PL 23, 346B): […] *super mortu-orum hominum Petri et Pauli, secundum nos ossa veneranda* […]. *Super* certainly does not mean a vague "somewhere above it" but rather "in contact with it". That is how *super altare* continues to be understood later, namely in the sense of "directly on the altar slab"; OR I,31 (ANDRIEU 1948, 77).

It is further striking that Jerome speaks only of the pope saying mass over the apostles' graves, not of other priests doing so. This has been interpreted as meaning that the right to celebrate in the basilicas of the two apostles was reserved solely to popes.[746] This may well have been the case in the beginning. At that time they possibly still celebrated at the magnificent Constantinian altar in St Peter's. But it is likely that from the time of Pope Damasus (366–384) onwards, as a result of the increased veneration of martyrs and a greater awareness of the primacy of the *sedes apostolica*, the popes reserved for themselves the right to celebrate directly over the tombs (*super corpus*) in St Peter's and St Paul's. There are several reasons why such a time frame fits. Under Damasus, Jerome was a secretary, which means that he may have defended the tomb altars because it was his own superior who had introduced celebration *super corpus*. In addition, Damasus was involved in the initial planning of the new Basilica of St Paul's, which further underlines his special relationship to the two Princes of the Apostles.[747] For St Peter's, this means that he had the niche set up as the place of celebration for the papal liturgy.[748] For iconographic reasons, the niche mosaic – showing the apostles to the right and left of a triumphal Cross – is generally dated to the second half of the fourth century.[749]

All this indicates that since the time of Damasus presbyters probably celebrated at the magnificent Constantinian altar, whereas the pope reserved for himself the right to celebrate the Eucharist at the apostle's memoria. This may have remained the accepted state of affairs for centuries. It was not until Gregory the Great that the right to celebrate at the apostle's memoria was extended to presbyters as well. This, and this alone, is the correct interpretation of the controversial statement in the *Liber Pontificalis* that Gregory "brought it about (*hic fecit*) that Masses are celebrated over the body of blessed Peter." *Hic fecit* does not refer to a building measure but rather simply to permission or an instruction: he is now giving other chosen (titular) presbyters the privilege of celebrating *super corpus* as well.[750]

This describes the historical development. But is a papal celebration directly on the tombs of the apostles really conceivable for the fourth century? Achim Arbeiter rejects such a notion because he considers Friedrich Wilhelm Deichmann to have proved that the tomb altar was still alien to early Roman martyrs' churches. He contends that they did not exist in Rome until the fifth or sixth century.[751] Hugo Brandenburg, too, cate-

---

746 Brandenburg 2015, 33.

747 Löx 2013, 64–68.

748 Damasus in any case had building work conducted at San Pietro (baptistery), see Löx 2013, 68–70.

749 Brenk 1995, 76.

750 Fürst 1967, 28 seeks to apply this privilege to the titular priests. At the cemeteries – probably not at St Peter's – there are permanently installed presbyters: Innoc. ep. ad Decent. 8 (FC 58,2, 496).

Under Gregory III (731–741) the hebdomadary priest still officiates at the high altar of San Pietro: *post prima quae in sacro corpore beati Petri fecerit missa* (Duchesne 1886, 422 n. 13). Cf. Chavasse 1958, 86; de Blaauw 1994, 533 f., 592. The papal prerogative may have been relinquished earlier at other cemetery churches. Cf. LP 27,2 (Duchesne 1886, 158): *Hic constituit supra memorias martyrum missas celebrare.*

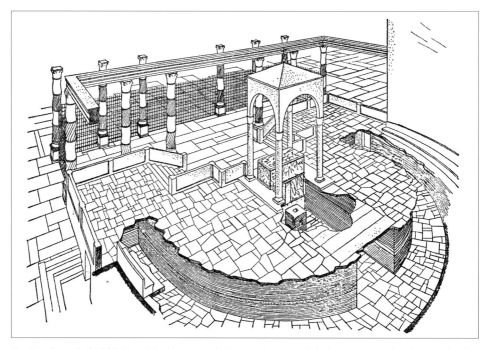

Fig. 72: Chancel of Old St Peter's looking towards the nave (eastwards) In the ring-crypt, the altar stands *ad caput*; Kirschbaum 1957, 163 Fig. 41.

gorically rules out the possibility of tomb altars in Rome in the fourth century.[752] But the situation is by no means as clear as is claimed. There is no conclusive evidence against tomb altars in Rome as early as the fourth century; on the contrary, archaeological and historical evidence rather indicates the opposite. And this applies not least of all to St Peter's and St Paul's since these are the two most important tombs of all: those of the apostles Peter and Paul, from whose veneration the Roman Church has derived her authority and primacy since the early second century.[753] These two graves appear to have remained until the Decian persecution of the Christians (250) the only martyrs' tombs in Rome. It is, therefore, unsurprising that special forms of cultus were created

751 Deichmann 1970, 144–146; Arbeiter 1988, 182. The box-shaped altar of St Felix in Cimitile/Nola is also unlikely to date from before 480–520; T. Lehmann, Eine spätantike Inschriftensammlung und der Besuch des Papstes Damasus an der Pilgerstätte des hl. Felix in Cimitile/Nola, in: Zeitschrift für Papyrologie und Epigraphik 91 (1992) 243–281, here 251.

752 Brandenburg 2011a, 245, *id*. 2011b, 379 f. and *id*. 2017b, 44 f., even though *id*. 1995b has a lengthy discussion of tomb altars in the fourth and fifth centuries – including in Rome.

753 Gnilka 2015.

Fig. 73. Rekonstruktion des Altarraums von Alt-St. Peter zur Zeit Gregors des Großen. Vor der großen *Confessio* führen Stufen rechts und links auf das Apsispodium; Apollonj Ghetti 1951, Tav. 1.

here early on. Hence it must be regarded as a special custom, and, what is more, a papal prerogative, to celebrate directly over the tombs of the apostles. Another reason this is unsurprising is that in 356 Emperor Constantius II had the relics of Peter's brother Andrew and Paul's disciple Timothy buried beneath the altar of the Church of the Holy Apostles in Constantinople.[754] Bishop Ambrose of Milan also has the relics of the apostles (Thomas, John and Andrew? Peter and Paul?) buried (before 386) beneath the altar of the suburban Church of the Holy Apostles in Milan.[755] Are they possibly already imitating the altar installations of the Roman churches of the apostles?

754 Cf. Brandenburg 1995a, 71–74.

755 Brandenburg 1995a, 83 f.; Bonetti 1997, 70–73; Löx 2013, 94–105.

If it was not already the case in the first half of the fourth century, a celebration *super corpus* is nevertheless likely in Rome by the end of the century at the latest, when there was a marked intensification of the liturgical veneration of martyrs. This same mentality of identifying tomb and altar is displayed in the inscriptions that Pope Damasus had put in the vaults of the martyrs in the catacombs.[756] Here it is to be assumed that mass was celebrated in the immediate vicinity of the tombs, that is, no longer only in the church spaces above ground.[757] The simultaneous phenomenon of privileged burials near the tombs of martyrs – *ad sanctos* or *retro sanctos* – will be connected with the masses that are now also celebrated in the catacombs.[758] In individual cases, the architectural monumentalising of the tombs[759] suggests that the intention was possibly to enable mass to be celebrated directly over the grave.[760] The cubiculum of SS Nereus and Achilles in the Catacombs of Domitilla[761] and the Catacomb of St Hippolytus on the *Via Tiburtina* were probably given altars over the martyrs' tombs under Pope Damasus.[762] In around 370–410 the tomb of St Alexander on the *Via Nomentana* was used as an altar. It has a *fenestella confessionis* at the front for the veneration of relics (Fig. 74).[763]

In the mentality of the time, celebrating mass on the grave of a martyr was probably also seen as potentiating the consecration of bread and wine. It is in the nature of things that the purpose of a *confessio* is to benefit from the immediate holiness of the place by, on the one hand, guarding and almost enclosing this holiness and, on the other hand, making it accessible in privileged moments. This is also true of the apostle's shrine in St Peter's. Archaeological evidence shows that behind the double door there is a cavity in the floor of which a libation channel led down to the presumed tomb of St Peter. The power centre is thus the tomb of St Peter itself, which radiates through the said cavity of the *confessio* to the travertine slab. Like Ambrose,[764] Paulinus of Nola († 431) also

---

756 Damas. epigr. 16, 32, 33, 48, 61 (FERRUA 1942, 120, 166, 167, 195, 229). Cf. TOLOTTI 1986; SPERA 2007, 55 f.

757 Cf. FIOCCHI NICOLAI 2001, 123.

758 Cf. ibid. 88.

759 Löx 2013, 193–214.

760 TOLOTTI 1986 discusses several vaults, but always pronounces against tomb altars. His individual arguments are not particularly convincing and are based on traditional hypotheses that are themselves doubtful.

761 BRANDENBURG 1995b, 96.

762 Ibid. Prud. peristeph. 11,169–173 (CSEL 61, 418): *Talibus Hippolyti corpus mandatur opertis, / propter ubi adposita est ara dicata deo. / Illa sacramenti donatrix mensa eademque / custos fida*

sui martyris adposita / servat ad aeterni spem vindicis ossa sepulcro, / pascit item sanctis Tibricolas dapibus. Prudentius was in Milan in about 384–404 and visited Rome from there. The grave of the martyr Cassianus in Imola is also a martyr's tomb: Prud. peristeph. 9,99 f. (CSEL 61, 370): *pareo, complector tumulum, lacrimas quoque fundo, / altar tepescit ore, saxum pectore*; DÖLGER 1930, 212 f.

763 FIOCCHI NICOLAI 2009, 305–318; cf. CAMERLENGHI 2018, 90.

764 Ambr. ep. 77[22],13 (CSEL 82,3, 134): *Succedant victimae triumphales in locum ubi Christus est hostia. Sed ille super altare qui pro omnibus passus est, isti sub altari qui illius redempti sunt passione.*

Fig. 74: Reconstructed tomb altar of St Alexander in the Catacomb of St Alexander on the *Via Nomentana*, looking east; PIAC Archivio Fotografico.

believes that a dual source of power emanates from the *mensa divina*: from below that of the martyr's relics, from above that of the priest's prayers.[765] This dual power makes the altar mensa, as it were, glow: in the church at Fundi, a "burning" porphyry mensa covers the relics of the apostles. Paulinus probably relates this on the one hand to the blood of the martyrs and on the other to the combined power of the relics and the grace of God.[766] So if all sorts of objects are sanctified through the *confessio*, why not then also do this for the Eucharist by placing the bread and chalice on the travertine plate? These are mechanisms that are deeply rooted in the history of religion. People think in these haptic-concrete categories, just as contact relics are created through touching the tomb or the Eucharist is consecrated through touch.[767]

765 Paulin. Nol. ep. 32,8 (FC 25,2, 764): *Sic geminata piis adspirat gratia votis, / Infra martyribus, desuper acta sacris.* Joh. Chrys. coem. et cruc. 3 (PG 49, 397 f.): the Holy Spirit coming down from heaven "touches" the bread and wine at the consecration. In the Jewish grave cult, the vertical radiation of power is in evidence, but exactly the other way round: if a pious person walks or puts his hand over a grave, this ritually contaminates him in a vertical direction. (S. HEID, in: GNILKA 2015, 123–126).

766 Paulin. Nol. ep. 32,17 (FC 25,2, 784).

767 J. SCHMITZ, in: FC 3, 54.

Finally, there remains the question of the direction of celebration in St Peter's to examine. If things developed as described above, between the fourth and the sixth centuries the pope did not adhere to an east-facing direction when celebrating *super corpus*. For the faithful, too, it is taken for granted that they look towards the apostle's shrine in St Peter's and do not turn to face east to pray.[768] In the late sixth century, this will have been the main reason for raising the sanctuary and creating a crypt[769] (Fig. 75; above Figs. 72, 73, below Fig. 86). This raising of the sanctuary allows a large *confessio* to be created, making it easier to go right up to St Peter's tomb from the front. Above it stands the new altar of Gregory the Great. It lies just a few centimetres above the old travertine slab, which is now broken, so that physical contact remains possible upwards from the tomb. Now the pope also observes east-facing prayer as the new altar can only be approached from the west.

It has been claimed that a celebration *super corpus* could not have taken place at all before Gregory the Great since otherwise Gregory could have saved himself the trouble of raising the sanctuary and gone on as before.[770] But after three hundred years, a modernisation was anyway due.[771] In addition, the reconstruction allows a number of liturgical improvements, such as placing the cathedra in the apex of the apse.[772] The introduction of a *super corpus* celebration is the least of the concerns here; the intention is merely to maintain the existing practice in an improved form, which includes correcting the direction of celebration so as to face east. This does not present any problems because it does not change the liturgy or the liturgical disposition at the altar: the pope now stands behind the new Gregorian high altar, whereas before he stood in front of the niche of the Constantinian apostle's shrine. But in both cases, all the assistants and officiants have to stand behind him. Consequently, from the pope's point of view there is scarcely any change in how the liturgy proceeds; it is simply rotated by 180 degrees.

No less controversial than St Peter's is *St Paul Outside the Walls* (*San Paolo fuori le mura*).[773] The first, quite small, Basilica of St Paul on the *Via Ostiense*, which once again was built by Emperor Constantine after 312, may not have had its own altar; at least, according to the list of gifts in the *Liber Pontificalis*, Constantine did not donate one. So does the pope celebrate over the apostle's tomb? Archaeologically, it can be assumed that, as in St Peter's, a tomb containing the bones of the apostle is clearly visible in front of the

---

768 See above n. 701.

769 Apollonj Ghetti 1951, 193 sees the reconstruction of *San Pietro* as beginning under Pelagius II, but says that the altar was built by Gregory the Great.

770 Brandenburg 2011a, 245; *id.* 2011b, 380.

771 The chancel in *San Paolo* was fundamentally re-

modelled at considerably shorter intervals than that in *San Pietro*, already under Leo and then under Gregory.

772 On all the liturgical advantages of the new disposition see de Blaauw 2001b, 978–980.

773 Heid 2017c, 143–151.

Fig. 75: Fresco in the *Sala di Costantino* of the Vatican Palace (detail) with a depiction of the Donation of Constantine (Donation of Rome) in Old St Peter's, 16th century. The great *Confessio* can be seen beneath the main altar. The *Schola Cantorum* is already dismantled by the 16th century, so the choir now stands on the altar podium to the right. The two busts on the altar (Peter and Paul) are seen from behind because the celebrant faces the nave when standing at the altar; photo: Vatican Museums.

apse. In addition, there is a golden cross "over the place of the blessed Apostle Paul".[774] But nothing more can be said on this, especially since this first church with its east-end entrance had such a short lifespan.

It was demolished and replaced at the end of the fourth century with a huge new basilica, the so-called Basilica of the Three Emperors. Its orientation is significantly changed in that the apse is moved to the opposite side, i.e. to the east.[775] The question of the direction in which the pope should celebrate the eucharistic liturgy certainly played a part in this switch.[776] It must therefore not be neglected in the further course of our argumentation. The Basilica of the Three Emperors was initiated by Pope Damasus,[777] but was consecrated under his successor Siricius (384–399). If you think of the controversy between Vigilantius and Jerome, the desire to celebrate on the tombs of the apostles (*super corpus*) must already have been quite virulent at the time. They will have been anxious to avoid from the outset a liturgically unsatisfactory situation such as that in St Peter's, where the pope has to stand looking west at the apostle's shrine. So is the apostle's tomb in the new Basilica of St Paul already set up in such a way that the pope can celebrate *super corpus* facing east?

It is only recently that archaeological surveys have succeeded in clarifying the situation at St Paul's tomb sufficiently to be able to roughly determine the original appearance of the Basilica of the Three Emperors and the later designs of the chancel. Nicola Maria Camerlenghi has recently made further reconstruction proposals.[778] It is clear that in the first basilica the apostle's sarcophagus was located higher than his original tomb and in the new basilica was placed in a central position that was clearly visible from the nave. It now stood at ground level a few metres behind the triumphal arch which separates the nave from the somewhat higher transept (Fig. 76). According to the excavator Giorgio Filippi, this free-standing sarcophagus also served as an altar.[779] This must be accepted as correct. The mere fact that St Paul's sarcophagus is placed transversely in a position where one would actually expect to find the altar offers sufficient support to the assumption that it was also intended from the outset to serve as an altar. So once again Jerome is to be taken at his word when he defends the papal practice of using the tombs of the apostles as altars.[780]

---

774 LP 34,21 (Duchesne 1886, 178): *crucem auream super locum beati Pauli apostoli posuit.*

775 Panvinio: *Basilicae absida versa est ad orientem, prospiciunt (?) ianue ad occidentem.* Quoted from Pesarini 1913, 420.

776 Mondini 2016, 200 sees the switching round of the layout as resulting primarily from topographical and legal considerations determined by the right of way of the *Via Ostiense*.

777 Löx 2013, 64.

778 Camerlenghi 2018. Descriptive, without making a choice between Hugo Brandenburg and Giorgio Filippi: F. Bisconti / G. Ferri, La strada di Paolo. La via Ostiense dalle origini alla cristianizzazione (Padova 2018) 101–119, esp. 110.

779 Filippi 2004, 217–220; *id.* 2005–2006, 282–284.

780 See above p. 304.

By contrast, Filippi is unconvincing when he says that the celebrant stood behind this altar and looked west towards the nave because there was not enough space in front of the altar.[781] That is not true. Camerlenghi has the sarcophagus standing free within a set of barriers. Access to it from the nave is provided by a central flight of steps, and there is also enough space in front of the altar for the liturgist.[782] So nothing stands in the way of assuming that the pope approached the altar from the front. There is also good reason to believe that the slabs bearing the dedicatory inscription *[SIRICIUS] PAVLO / APOSTOLO MART[YRI]* ("[Siricius] to Paul, Apostle, Martyr") could be seen from the nave. Filippi wants to reconstruct them as encasing the sarcophagus; Camerlenghi sees them as the front of the set of barriers. Whatever the case, the letters are very large because they are meant to be read at a distance from the nave.[783]

The tomb altar of the apostle Paul is 1.27 m high, plus the assumed altar slab, giving a total height of 1.30 m. This seems too high for an altar, which is why the theory of a tomb altar has been contested.[784] But the objection is not very well founded. Paul's sarcophagus is by no means a regular altar, but serves as one solely at rare papal liturgies. On such occasions, a wooden podium may have been placed in front of the altar, possibly draped with carpets (below Fig. 94). Such improvised installations are still today customary at papal Masses; there are even special staff responsible for this (the so-called Sanpietrini).[785] This results in a liturgical disposition similar to that of St Peter's: the celebrant stands at the tomb altar with his back to the people. In St Peter's he faces west; in St Paul's he looks in the liturgically correct direction, namely eastwards. Outside the papal liturgies, the sarcophagus is clearly visible to its full height to visitors to the church and probably also accessible to them.[786]

781 Filippi 2004, 219. Here Filippi reconstructs the altar in such a way that it is surrounded by barriers on the north, south and west, thus standing under a double ciborium (Filippi 2009, 41 Fig. 15 A). Such a reconstruction suggests that the altar is only accessible from the west, so that the priest at the altar looks towards the nave, i.e. to the west. For this there is neither any archaeological evidence nor any external necessity.

782 Camerlenghi 2018, 75. However, like Brandenburg, he rules out the use of the sarcophagus as an altar in this early period.

783 A parallel case is a church in Constantinople (the *Hagia Sophia*), which has a (side-)altar with an inscription on the front that is expressly intended to be seen; Sozom. hist. eccl. 9,1,4 (SC 516, 372).

784 Brandenburg 2005–2006, 266 f.; id. 2011a, 245; Spera 2007, 56 f.; Camerlenghi 2018, 77.

785 Wooden steps insulating against the cold marble or stone were quite indispensable for elderly dignitaries. Brandenburg 2011a, 245 and id. 2011b, 380 draws attention to the supposedly excessive height of the altar. But in antiquity and the Middle Ages, altars were likely to have been considerably higher than today's standard altars. This is all the more so in unusual situations such as of the high tomb altar of the Catacomb of St Alexander on the *Via Nomentana* (Fiocchi Nicolai 2009, 273 Fig. 250: 1.30 m from floor to mensa). However, where the liturgist stood here was in front of the altar facing east, and not, as the drawing suggests with its stepped podium, behind the altar. Michael Brandt (Hildesheim) draws attention to the fact that the signs of wear on the front caused by historical chasubles show that the edge of the altar was definitely at chest height.

786 Cf. Löx 2013, 68.

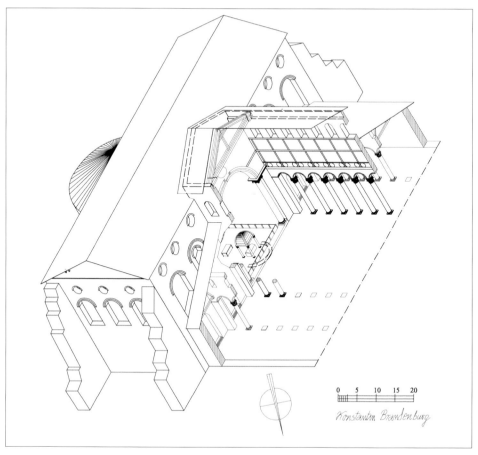

Fig. 76: Reconstruction of the chancel of the so-called Three Emperors Basilica of St Paul Outside the Walls, end of the 4th century; BRANDENBURG 2011a, 239 Fig. 14.

In contrast to Filippi, Hugo Brandenburg reconstructs a duplication of sarcophagus and altar in the Basilica of the Three Emperors. He believes that the sarcophagus could not have served as an altar because there is not enough space in front of it for a celebrant. So he concludes that a separate altar was therefore placed between Paul's sarcophagus and the cathedra, which is located at the apex of the apse (Fig. 76). But this is unconvincing, first of all because there is in fact enough space in front of the sarcophagus altar, as much as 3.80 m from the triumphal arch,[787] which is more than enough for the

787 BRANDENBURG 2005–2006, 267.

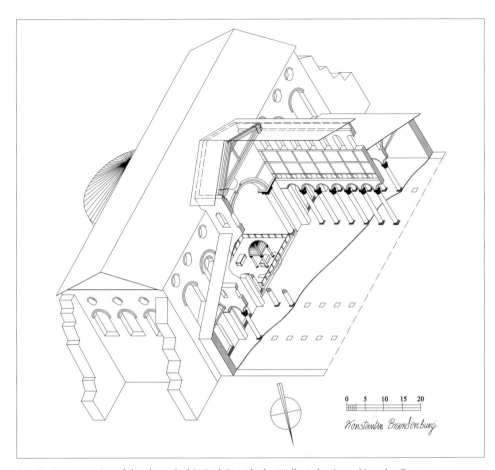

Fig. 77: Reconstruction of the chancel of St Paul Outside the Walls at the time of Leo the Great (440–461) with a raised presbyterium; BRANDENBURG 2011a, 246 Fig. 16a.

celebrant. Secondly, Brandenburg rightly assumes an east-facing prayer position,[788] but this then leads to the celebrant turning his back on the apostle's tomb. Furthermore, Paul's sarcophagus interposes itself between him and the people like a screen. Even if the celebrant stands the other way round and faces west towards the apostle's tomb,[789] this does not improve things. For then, despite a costly reconstruction of the basilica, the liturgically unfortunate situation of St Peter's would be replicated. Everything supports the idea that Paul's sarcophagus served as a tomb altar.

788 BRANDENBURG 2005–2006, 266–268, 271; *id.* 2011a, 244 f.; *id.* 2011b, 379. Similarly CAMER-LENGHI 2018, 77.

789 So now BRANDENBURG 2017d, 147 Fig. 8.

This situation will have remained essentially the same under Pope Leo the Great (440–461) (Fig. 77). Only a spacious podium was created round the sarcophagus, which possibly extended as far as the apse and was elevated by one step (16 cm) from the right and left transepts.[790] Paul's sarcophagus was itself left untouched when the floor was raised. But since this dropped it 16 cm into the ground, it was built up accordingly. The marble slabs with the inscription *PAVLO / APOSTOLO MART* were dismantled, cut to size and placed on top as a cover (Fig. 78).[791] In the middle of the slab, but slightly towards the front, a round opening was cut leading down into the sarcophagus itself via a pipe and doubtlessly used for pouring in spices or producing contact relics.

This sarcophagus, which was given new surrounding railings under Leo, must at the least have served as an altar.[792] This may have been unusual in Jerome's day, but in the middle of the fifth century such a solution certainly no longer presented any theological or ritual problems.[793] The careful reuse of the marble slabs with the inscription and their smooth pointing indicate that they were used as an altar mensa. The pope approached the altar from the front and thus celebrated in the liturgically required direction, facing east.[794] This is also evident from the position of the circular opening in the mensa, which, due to the depth of the altar (1.75 m), can only be reached from the front, in fact from the middle, just where the pope stands to celebrate.[795] The round hole is fitted with a lid in such a way that it is flush with the surface. So the hole is meant to be closed when the pope celebrates on this altar. The pope stands at the front so that the bread and the cup are, if possible, placed over this opening and are thus in contact with the grave when they are consecrated. The martyr's relics become, as it were, co-consecrators of the eucharistic gifts.[796] It has been objected that the *PAVLO / APOSTOLO MART* inscription slabs are laid exactly the other way round, so that they can only be read when one is standing behind the altar. But is it at all likely that the cover of the sarcophagus is meant to be seen? Is it not possible that the mensa was only shown on very specific occasions

790 Camerlenghi 2018, 85, Fig. 3.2.

791 Cf. a similar procedure – the reusing of the cancelli slab with its inscription as an altar slab with a relic depository – in *Santa Pudenziana* in Braconi 2016, 242.

792 Correctly Camerlenghi 2018, 86; still of a different opinion Brandenburg 2005–2006, 271.

793 On the tomb altar in *San Lorenzo f.l.m.* under Sixtus III (432–440) see de Blaauw 1994, 482.

794 In a church with an eastern apse it is to be expected at this time that the direction of prayer would be

eastward. The anonymous basilica of Castelfusano (Ostia) dating from the fifth or sixth century may serve as an example here. The altar stands on the chord of the apse. The *Schola Cantorum* lying in front of it was now extended in such a way that the celebrant and concelebrants had enough room in front of the altar. Buonaguro 2011, 291 Fig. 3.

795 Important for this is the reconstruction of the altar surface in Camerlenghi 2018, 86f.

796 On this haptic aspect see above p. 310f.

Fig. 78: Present situation of St Paul Outside the Walls: the base slab of today's high altar that lies between the ciborium columns has existed since Gregory the Great (c. 600) but was reduced in size after the fire of 1823 (east is at the bottom); FILIPPI 2005–2006, 280 Fig. 3.

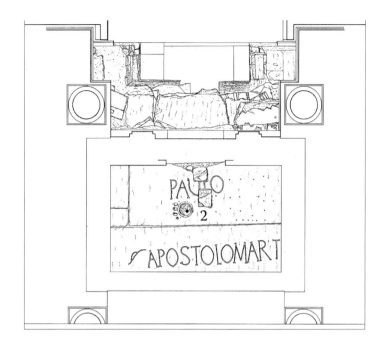

and was only meant to be read at such moments, whereas it was otherwise covered with a magnificent cloth?[797]

In the next phase of reconstruction, after 590 Pope Gregory the Great will have the entire altar area in St. Paul's, as in St. Peter's, raised once again and again reduced in size. Since Paul's sarcophagus again remains where it is, the resulting disposition is now the same as in St Peter's. For a new altar is built and stands exactly above the original tomb altar.[798] The Leonine altar loses its function, with the former altar mensa (*PAVLO / APOSTOLO MART*) now becoming the base slab of the new altar. Unlike in St Peter's, however, there is no change in where the liturgist stands in St Paul's: the pope or the presbyters continue to stand in front of the altar facing east.

This liturgical disposition is borne out by two absolutely key drawings by Onofrio Panvinio. The sketches, first published in 1913, show the ground plan and the interior furnishings of St Paul's Basilica in around 1570. Despite several alterations, this is still

797 Correctly CAMERLENGHI 2018, 89.

798 LP 66,4 (DUCHESNE 1886, 312): *Hic fecit ut super corpus beati Petri missas celebrarentur; item et in ecclesiam beati Pauli apostoli eadem fecit.*

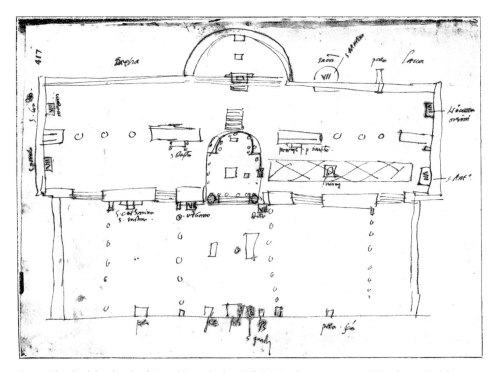

Fig. 79: Sketch of the church of St Paul Outside the Walls by Onofrio Panvinio, BAV Vat. lat. 6781, fol. 417, c. 1570. The altar stands free on the podium, the small ambo is in the nave on the left, the Gospel ambo on the right, the cancelli of the *Schola Cantorum* are already removed; Pesarini 1913, 394 Fig. 1.

the Gregorian state of the church (Figs. 79 and 80).[799] The sketches show that Gregory created an island-shaped podium behind the triumphal arch, in the middle of which stands the altar.[800] The width of the podium is disputed since the two drawings contradict one another. In the sketch reproduced here, it takes up the entire width of the triumphal arch, including the two columns (c. 16.50 m), whereas in the other sketch it is somewhat narrower (ca. 13 m).[801] Whatever the case, the sketches show the altar quite

799 According to Camerlenghi 2018, 129 the sketches reproduce the presbytery as it presented itself after renewed alterations under Leo III (795 – 816). But the disposition of the Gregorian presbytery is essentially retained. Both Panvinio sketches in Pesarini 1913, 394 f. Fig. 1 f.; Krautheimer 1980, 139 Fig. 125; Camerlenghi 2018, 130. A reconstruction of the elements of the furnishings of St Paul's Basilica after Panvinio's

sketches and descriptions is offered by Docci 2006, 103 Fig. 102.

800 Panvinio 1570a, 96: "In mezo [!] del choro, è l'altar maggiore di S. Pietro, & di Santo Paolo". *Id.* 1570b, 75: "*marmoreus chorus* […]. *In cuius chori medio est ara maxima sanctorum apostolorum*".

801 Even the archaeologists are not in agreement: Filippi supports the broad solution, Brandenburg the narrow.

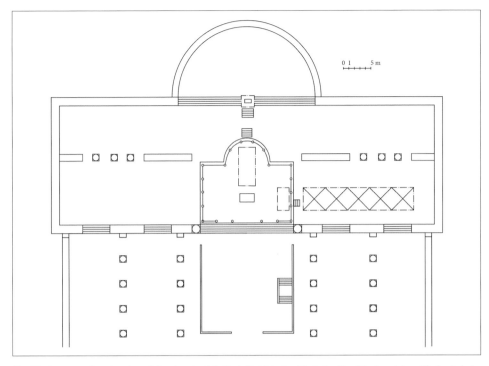

0 1   5 m

Fig. 80: Interpretative drawing of the sketch of St Paul Outside the Walls by Onofrio Panvinio with the *Schola Cantorum* as it probably was in the 7th century, BAV Vat. lat. 6781, fol. 417. The crypts are marked with dot-dash lines; drawing: Chiara Cecalupo.

clearly standing free in the middle; it can be walked round on all sides and there is plenty of space in front of it for the liturgist. Hence it is to be assumed that, in accordance with the liturgical rules, the celebrant stood at the front facing east.[802] A fourteenth-century *Book of Ceremonies* expressly confirms this for the papal liturgies in St Paul's,[803] and it remained so for centuries until the altar was redesigned after the disastrous fire of 1823.[804] It is only now that the pope celebrates – to date – liturgically in the wrong direction, namely facing west towards the people.

There is no large *confessio* beneath the altar in the Gregorian St Paul's Basilica as in St Peter's. There are three reasons for this: first, the Panvinio plans show the altar at ground level without any hint of a large *confessio*. Second, there is an unbroken flight of steps up to this podium, which once again rules out a large *confessio*. Third, the altar

802 HEID 2017c, 146; now also CAMERLENGHI 2018, 107 Fig. 3.18; 129 Fig. 4.8.

803 DE BLAAUW 1999–2000, 282 n. 77.

804 Correctly the reconstruction of the sanctuary around 1790 by CAMERLENGHI 2018, 242 Fig. 7.25.

must instead have had an aperture or door grille (*fenestella confessionis*) at the front since the altar slab of the Leonine altar with a round hole in it became the base slab of the new altar in the Gregorian basilica. So you have to lean into the new altar in order to reach the openings in the old altar slab if you want to introduce oil, incense or cloths for the production of contact relics. This makes it necessary to have an opening in the front of the altar. The square holes ("cataracts") created under Gregory in addition to the round hole are located on the western edge of the altar base. Hence there is no doubt that the *fenestella* of the Gregorian altar was located at the front of the altar.[805] Further proof is offered by a measurement taken in the course of the rebuilding of the basilica after 1823: the altar – not the base slab – was turned so that the writing on the *PAVLO / APOSTOLO MART* base slab can be read the right way round through the *fenestella*.[806] In other words, the *fenestella* was originally on the front of the altar, so that the inscription was upside down when read from that side. The *fenestella* must also have been at the front because it signals the sacred centre of the church (there are votive lamps burning in the *confessio*) and the faithful therefore want to be able to see it. Also the Papal Ceremonial (*Ordo Romanus* I) from c. 700 assumes that the *confessio* is on the front of the altar.[807] This means that the Gregorian altar at St Paul's must have been accessible from the front. This is also where it is to be assumed that the pope stood during the liturgy. The fact that in so doing he obscures the people's view of the *confessio* is not a problem. The crucial agent of the liturgy is the pope, not the people. The *confessio* is normally visible anyway during the liturgy, just not during the eucharistic act itself. For the latter, the pope must stand right at the sacred centre and participate in its sanctifying aura.

Panvinio's sketches play a key role in the reconstruction of St Paul's Basilica as it was at the time of Gregory the Great. This makes it all the more disastrous that they have been misinterpreted in several essential details ever since they were first published, partly because the liturgical functionality of the presbytery was not taken into account. The error begins with the way the Gregorian altar podium is interpreted. Since Santi Pesarini (1913), on whose authority everyone else relies, the altar podium was recon-

805 HEID 2017c, 147; now also CAMERLENGHI 2018, 108 Fig. 3.19.

806 G. AMATI, in: Mondo Illustrato. Giornale Universale 1 (1847) 762: "Sopra una gradinata di marmi bianchi sorge il tabernacolo, e sta nella sua prisca situazione: l'altare *è* stato nuovamente posto nella sua direzione antichissima, cioè che il sommo sacerdote, celebrandovi, sia volto al popolo adunato nella nave grande della basilica, secondo i riti della chiesa greca. Ora per la vera disposizione dell'altare si legge intera l'iscrizione di remotissima età.

PAVLO . APOSTOLO . MAR. che prima dell'incendio vedevasi in parte ed a rovescio nel piano della piccola cella destinata a custodire il turibolo." I wish to thank Andrea Venier (Rome) for pointing this out to me.

807 OR I,74 (ANDRIEU 1948, 92): *Pontifex* [...] *descendit ante confessionem et suscipit oblatas.* Only the Lateran Basilica probably still did not have a *confessio* around 700, but the OR I does not apply to the Lateran as it only describes the station liturgy (outside the cathedral).

structed without a central entrance, but rather with only a narrow entrance on the right-hand southern side (Fig. 81).[808] It is hard to accept such a reconstruction. As well as being based on Panvinio, who speaks of the *chorus solevatus*,[809] it also appeals to Pompeo Ugonio, who sees a "*choro antico cinto attorno di marmi*" during the reconstruction of the podium under Pope Sixtus V.[810] But this cannot mean that the presbytery was closed off with marble slabs all the way round except for a narrow side entrance on the right. If the nave under the great triumphal arch really did end in front of an insurmountable wall and the altar stood up above on the podium, then this would be something extremely unusual. It would make it the only church far and wide with an altar island that was isolated in such a way. Would Panvinio not have been bound to mention this curiosity in his three descriptions of St Paul's Basilica?

Rather than a wall, Panvinio's sketches contain several lines marking a central staircase level with the triumphal arch leading from the nave to the sanctuary and stretching across a broad part of the front of it.[811] But then he draws an equal number of steps in all five entrances from the nave to the transept, although more steps would have to be expected in the nave.[812] For this reason, Engelbert Kirschbaum assumes that there were steps leading up from the nave, but that these were no longer functional as they meet the podium wall halfway up (Fig. 82).[813] But whoever furnishes a church with a dead-ended flight of steps? Francesco Tolotti and Hugo Brandenburg ignore the steps completely.[814]

808 PESARINI 1913, 404, 410 f. Pertinent reconstruction drawings: KIRSCHBAUM 1957, 192 Fig. 50; APOLLONJ GHETTI 1969, 30 Fig. 20; TOLOTTI 1983, 96 f.; FILIPPI 2004, 223 Fig. 25; id. 2009, 36 Fig. 10; DOCCI 2006, 94 Fig. 94. In BRANDENBURG 2011a, 248 Fig. 16b and id. 2011b, 379 Fig. 19 there are no entrance steps at all; in id. 2005–2006, 269 Fig. 18 they lie on the south side of the podium. CAMERLENGHI 2018, 108, 129 does reconstruct the presumed altar area under Leo III with a central entrance to the presbytery podium, but then thinks that in c. 1140 this entrance no longer existed and that there was instead a narrow flight of steps on the right-hand side (ibid. 154 Fig. 5.10); so too in c. 1220 (ibid. 161 Fig. 5.15) and in Panvinio's day c. 1570 (ibid. 187 Fig. 6.3 and 188 Fig. 6.4). On the other hand, he nevertheless then postulates a central entrance again in c. 1280 (ibid. 158 Fig. 5.13). All this is inconsistent. There was no reason to close a central entrance stairway that once existed in favour of a side door. In this respect, Camerlenghi falls prey to the same misinterpretation of the Panvinio sketches as his predecessors.

809 Quoted from PESARINI 1913, 424.
810 UGONIO 1588, 237. PANVINIO 1570b, 75: "*marmoreus chorus* […]. *In cuius chori medio est ara maxima sanctorum apostolorum.*" PESARINI 1913, 404 overinterprets Panvinio's reference to "four gates" from the aisles to the transept as if the central triumphal arch had not provided access from the nave to the transept (ibid. 423). On original wooden constructions on the columns of the choir or the ciborium see DOCCI 2006, 70, 104.
811 The steps marked as lines are undoubtedly not to be taken "literally". In the two plans the number of steps between the nave and the transept varies between two and five. Although he mentions the three steps to the cathedra in his description (PESARINI 1913, 424), he does not adopt them in his sketches. In the reconstructions by Kirschbaum, Tolotti, Filippi and Brandenburg, the number of steps varies between two and four.
812 APOLLONJ GHETTI 1969, 32.
813 KIRSCHBAUM 1957, 192 Fig. 50. So also DOCCI 2006, 104.
814 TOLOTTI 1983, 97 Fig. 5; BRANDENBURG 2005–2006, 269 Fig. 18.

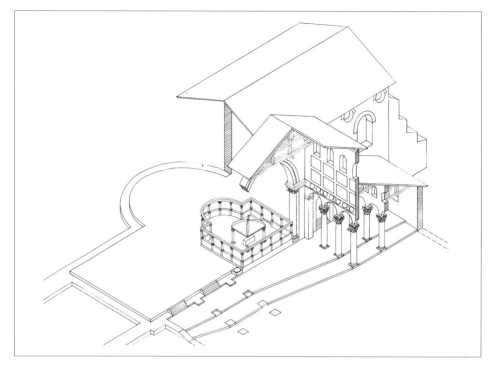

Fig. 81: Reconstruction – partly requiring correction – of the chancel of St Paul Outside the Walls under Gregory the Great (590–604): the altar area is closed off with barriers and can only be accessed via a narrow staircase on the right; Brandenburg 2005–2006, 269 Fig. 18.

But if one wants to do justice to both Panvinio and the liturgical requirements, it is necessary to assume a central stairway with more steps than in the transepts. Panvinio was not showing the exact number of steps with his lines but merely indicating the existence of "steps" – as evidenced by the difference in the number of steps shown in his two drawings.

Then what was the purpose of the narrow flight of steps to be seen on the right-hand side of the altar podium in Panvinio's sketches? It is either an additional side way up or the steps are in actual fact intended to mark a way down into a crypt.[815] Panvinio himself

815 There are two analogous examples of this in Panvinio's sketches (above Figs. 79, 80). Above all, the narrow steps directly behind the cathedra cannot be a way up onto the altar podium but instead lead into the *confessio* underneath it. Further, a continuous and a narrow flight of steps is to be seen on the chord of the apse in St Paul's. The end-to-end

one is the way up, the narrow one the way down into an oratory (of SS Celsus, Julian and Basilissa) underneath the apse.

816 Panvinio 1570b, 75 f.: *Paulo extra chorum, ab eodem latere* (south side of the altar podium)*, ubi in pavimento est pars quaedem opere vermiculato & teßellato strata cum altari quodam sanctae Lu-*

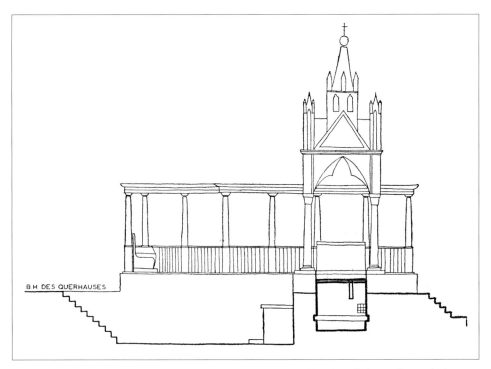

Fig. 82: Reconstruction – partly requiring correction – of the podium-like chancel of St Paul Outside the Walls at the time of Gregory the Great (590–604), in longitudinal section, looking south (so the east-end apse of the church is on the left); KIRSCHBAUM 1957, 192.

more or less clearly confirms this second option. He speaks of an obstructed underground access to the crypt of Lucina, which once led through the Chapel of Julianus.[816] The Lucina crypt is marked in his plans by a chequered strip in the south transept. This

cinae extat eiusdem divae coemeterium sub terra effoßum, ad quod antiquitus iter erat per oratorium S. Iuliani, nunc obserato aditu impervium est, in quo iacent multa sanctorum martyrum corpora. Panvinio according to PESARINI 1913, 425: *Sub confessione, sive capella, sive oratorio s. Iuliani, sunt due porte nunc murate, per quas iter erat per cemeterium in quo iacent multa millia martyrum* [...]. The problem is that Panvinio knows of a subterranean oratory of St Julian in the middle of the steps leading into the apse of the basilica (PANVINIO 1570a, 97); elsewhere he speaks only of the altar there of SS Celsus, Julian und Basilissa (PANVINIO 1570b, 76; PESARINI

1913, 424). BOSIO 1632, 147 thinks Panvinio must be understood to be indicating that a way led from this oratory to the Lucina crypt, but that would have been a 25-m-long tunnel. There must have been a second Julian chapel on the south side of the altar podium, perhaps dedicated to a different Julian. This would explain the steps. The formulation "*Sub confessione, sive capella, sive oratorio s. Iuliani* [...]" is to be translated as follows: "Behind the confessio [of St Paul under the main altar] or (behind) the chapel or oratory of St Julian there are two now-walled-up doors through which a way led to the cemetery (of Lucina), where many thousand martyrs lie."

square abuts the flight of steps in question. So the most likely solution is that the steps lead down into a small chapel under the altar podium, from which it was once possible to access the crypt of St Lucina.[817]

This results in a different reconstruction of the sanctuary of St Paul's in the seventh century from that previously proposed (Fig. 83). The upper edge of the altar podium is lined with columns. However, Panvinio's sketches do not reveal whether there was a barrier between the columns. A continuous barrier can in any case be ruled out since there have to be ways through, at least at the front.[818] One would expect three passages between the columns.[819] Such a central flight of steps providing access to the chancel is a liturgical imperative as long as the papal liturgy is celebrated according to the *Ordo Romanus* I. This includes the two ambos that are clearly visible in the sketches.[820] They would be useless in that position if there were no direct access from there to the altar area.[821] It does not need to be taken into consideration here that for the seventh century one can assume that there was just one ambo on the right-hand side since it was not until the twelfth century that the readings were divided between two ambos. The ambos in any case mark the area for the *Schola Cantorum*, around which the barriers had already been demolished in Panvinio's day.[822] In this area, on both sides of the central aisle, stands the clerical choir of men and boys. In general, the *Schola Cantorum* always leaves a space free in front and behind for the pope to process through as he solemnly enters and exits the church. This processional route leads from the entrance of the church, from where the pope can already see the illuminated altar *confessio*,[823] straight ahead through the Schola, up the steps to the altar and from there to the cathedra.[824] A side entrance on the right-hand side of the altar podium, for which the pope would have to turn right behind the Schola and then take the back way into the chancel would go against the requirements of medieval liturgy.

A final proof of there being a central flight of steps leading up to the chancel is provided by Attilio Serrano, who visited St Paul's Basilica in around 1575. He walks from the ambos to the choir and then to the altar without ever mentioning that he has to

817 This eliminates the need for an extensive system of passages underneath the altar podium as assumed by Tolotti 1983, 96 Fig. 4, 100–103. Critical of this also Docci 2006, 70.

818 The suggested reconstructions since Kirschbaum have a balustrade topped with cancelli all the way round it, but that would obstruct any view of St Paul's sarcophagus and the *confessio* of the altar from the nave. What purpose is it meant to serve?

819 This results from liturgical considerations. The central entrance is reserved for the pope. Cf. OR I,69 (Andrieu 1948, 91), 74f. (92). LP 95,3 (Duchesne 1886, 464), 97,58 (503): three *rugae* at the entrance to the presbytery of St Peter's.

820 These are also mentioned by Panvinio 1570a, 94, Serrano 1575, 35 and Ugonio 1588, 237. On Panvinio further Pesarini 1913, 423.

821 The nonsensical nature of a closed-off presbytery with a *Schola Cantorum* in front of it can be seen in Camerlenghi 2018, Fig. 5.15.

822 Pesarini 1913, 400f.

823 The line of sight from the entrance of the church to the *confessio* can still today be verified in *San Clemente*.

824 OR I,49–51 (Andrieu 1948, 83). OR XXXB,7 (Andrieu 1961, 468): *transierit per medium scolae […] antequam ascendat ad altare.*

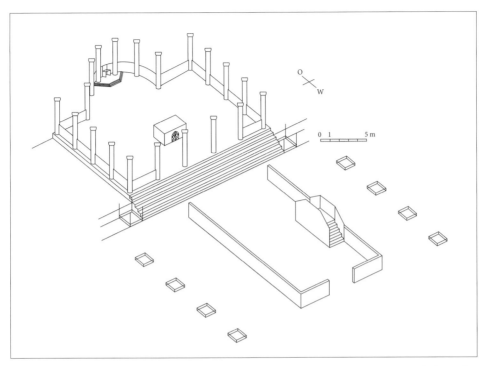

Fig. 83: Liturgically appropriate reconstruction (details simplified) of the chancel of St Paul Outside the Walls since about the 7ᵗʰ century based on Panvinio's sketches. Below the central steps leading up to the altar podium lies the *Schola Cantorum* with the ambo; drawing: Chiara Cecalupo.

make a detour before he can get to the altar. First he venerates the Eucharist kept on the podium, then he venerates the relics in the altar, apparently standing in front of the altar at the *confessio* to do so. Then he then turns right to the monumental crucifix that is permanently installed there.[825] It may come as a surprise that the faithful were allowed to set foot on the podium, but it cannot be denied. This is probably why the altar has heavy barriers all round it for the sake of security.[826] Furthermore, clinging to the crucifix is the memory that St Bridget frequently prayed "before it" – on the podium – and that Christ turned his head towards her.[827]

Of interest for the fifth century is the church of *Santo Stefano Rotondo* on the Celian Hill, which was probably consecrated under Pope Simplicius (468–483). Being circular,

825 SERRANO 1575, 35–37. This crucifix can also be seen in a sixteenth-century image: DE BLAAUW 1999–2000, 281 Fig. 8.

826 UGONIO 1588, 237.
827 PANVINIO 1570b, 75; SERRANO 1575, 37.

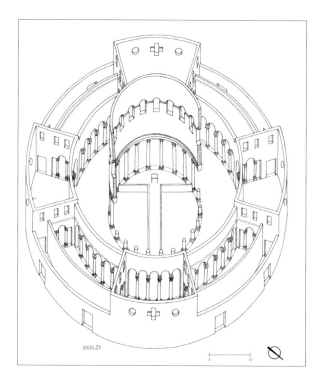

XXXI.23

Fig. 84: Reconstruction of the church of Santo Stefano Rotondo in Rome, 5th century; Brandenburg 2013, 337.

Fig. 85: Apse mosaic of the eastern chapel of Santo Stefano Rotondo, Rome, mid-7th century; Andaloro / Romano 2002, 79 Fig. 59.

this church does not, in principle, have a specific orientation, but the *Schola Cantorum* was placed roughly on a west-east axis, thus giving the church an interior direction (Fig. 84). Whereas there is archaeological evidence of the Schola, no trace has been found of the site of the altar. It must have been located at the western end of the Schola, either in the central area or in the adjoining ambulatory, where the cathedra probably also stood.[828] It is reasonable to assume that the celebrant stood behind the altar and looked east towards the Schola. So why was the altar not put on the east side to begin with? Apparently both altar solutions were possible in Rome. At all events, an east-facing orientation was observed at the time. This is confirmed by new findings about the Chapel of the Greek Martyrs by the *Basilica Marci* on the *Via Ardeatina*, which had an east-end entrance. From about 500, it had a *confessio* altar. The celebrant stood behind it (in front of the *fenestella*) looking towards the entrance.[829]

But back to *Santo Stefano*, it is also conceivable that the church remained unused for decades and was only reactivated under Byzantine influence.[830] In any case, it is certainly

828 As is suggested by the findings related to the foundation, the *Schola Cantorum* may have extended over the whole central area. The small apse built into the outside colonnade on the west under

Pope Theodore might indicate the traditional location of the cathedra.

829 Oral information from V. Fiocchi Nicolai. Cf. Fiocchi Nicolai 2002, 1192 Fig. 12 f.

not by chance that Pope Theodore (642–649), coming as he did from Byzantine Jeru-salem, had the relics of SS Primus and Felician transferred to the eastern chapel area of the church, which he furnished with an apse and an apse mosaic, in the centre of which a golden cross can be seen (Fig. 85). By doing this, the pope is clearly accentuating the eastward orientation of the church space. There is no doubt that the cross is to be under-stood as a liturgical point of orientation: it fixes the celebrant's direction of vision at the church's high altar. This then also establishes where the liturgist stands at the additional altar that Theodore is likely to have built in the chapel in question in order to keep the relics of the two martyrs in it.[831]

The significant alterations made to Rome's *major and titular basilicas* under popes Pe-lagius II and Gregory the Great and their successors also provide for east-facing prayer. In an ever-increasing number of martyr's churches outside the city gates, the apse area

830 So VOLLMER 2017.
831 LP 75,5 (DUCHESNE 1886, 332): [...] *basilica beati Stephani protomartyris, ubi [Theodorus] et dona obtulit: gabatas aureas III, tabula ex argento ante confessionem.* The *confessio* probably refers to the main altar, which in that case contained Stephen's

relics. LP 98,47 (DUCHESNE 1892, 13): *Fecit [Leo III] et in ecclesia sancti Stephani in Celio monte vestes de staurace II, e quibus una in altare maiorem alia vero super corpora sanctorum mar-tyrum Primi et Feliciani.*

is raised and a crypt created underneath it. This makes it possible to approach the martyr's tomb lying beneath the altar from both the crypt and the nave. Here, the way this was done in St Peter's served as a model for those churches in Rome and Latium that had their entrances at the east end. In St Peter's, the altar stands on the front edge of the apse podium above the large *confessio* (Fig. 86; above Figs. 73, 75). One can imagine it as being similar in design to the altar still to be seen in *San Clemente* today (below Fig. 88). A *confessio* is a chamber-like room belonging to a tomb altar and offering the visitor a chance to come close to the tomb without, so to speak, disturbing the peace of the grave.[832] Access is either through a *fenestella* on the front of the altar itself (small *confessio*) or through an opening below the altar, both of which have a grille over them. For Rome, there is evidence at the latest from the fifth century onwards of a small altar *confessio* in churches with east-end entrances and apses.[833] It is, on the other hand, only since Pelagius II/ Gregory the Great that a large *confessio* has been found in churches with their entrance to the east, and this initially only in St Peter's.

The raising of the altar is undertaken not just for practical reasons, i.e. to ensure easy and direct access to the *confessio*, but also out of liturgical considerations, namely to facilitate east-facing prayer.[834] In St Peter's, the aim is, on the one hand, to enable the pope to celebrate over the tomb, as was already common practice before this, and, on the other hand, also to ensure east-facing prayer. It should be borne in mind that Pope Vigilius (537–555) allegedly decreed that the priest should celebrate facing east at the altar.[835] One reason this came to be doubted may have been that the pope himself faced west when celebrating at the shrine of St Peter. The decree might have had the effect of remedying irregular situations in Rome. The altar in St Peter's that was newly created in around 600 is now only accessible to the liturgist from behind, so that the priest automatically faces east. It is no coincidence that this model is followed by almost all the Roman churches that had their entrance to the east (*San Clemente, San Pancrazio, San Crisogono, San Marco, Santa Cecilia, Santi Giovanni e Paolo, Santa Prassede, San Martino ai Monti, Santa Maria Maggiore, Santa Maria in Trastevere, Santa Maria in Domnica, Santi Quattro Coronati, Santa Balbina, Santi Marcellino e Pietro*).[836] Nevertheless, little clarity exists about exactly when the alterations were carried out. There was no

---

832 BRAUN 1924a, 551.

833 ORLANDOS 1954, 455. The church of *Santa Pudenziana*, which has its entrance to the east, appears to have possessed an altar with a small *confessio*: PETRIGNANI 1934, 10: "*Altaria sunt 3. omnia fere antiquo more facta, plena reliquiis martyrum*" (Panvinio). In the Church of *Santi Cosmae Damiano* such an altar with a *fenestella* on the visible side still exists (the so-called lower church dating from the sixth century); CLAUSSEN

2002, 367 Fig. 295; 369. BRANDENBURG 2013, 341 mistakenly reverses the north and south directions.

834 CLAUSSEN 2002, 17. Different again HEID 2006, 393f.

835 See above p. 286.

836 See the *Corpus Basilicarum* by Krautheimer and the "Kirchen der Stadt Rom" by Claussen. On *Ss. Marcellino e Pietro* see ANGELELLI 2002, 1022–1028.

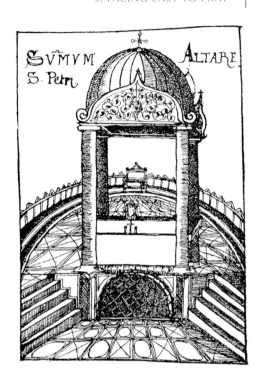

Fig. 86: Chancel of Old St Peter's with cathedra, seats of the cardinals and altar after Sebastian Werro, 1581; clearly visible is the large, grille-covered *Confessio* beneath the altar; BALLARDINI 2016, 54 Fig. 23.

reason, especially in the urban churches which did not contain a martyr's tomb, to install a large *confessio*, something that involved a considerable outlay because of the need to raise the sanctuary. There is much to suggest that such measures were not undertaken until the Carolingian period, i.e. not before the ninth century.

In churches with an east-facing apse, on the other hand, such an altar arrangement is avoided.[837] Instead, although here too the altar is elevated, it is free-standing, so that

---

837 CLAUSSEN 2002, 17. Corresponding churches: KRAUTHEIMER 1937, Tav. I (*Sant'Agata dei Goti*); Tav. VI(*Sant'Agnese f.l.m.*); Tav. IX (*Sant'Ana-stasia*); Tav. XXVIII (*Santa Croce in Gerusa-lemme*); Tav. XL (*San Giovanni a Porta Latina*); id. 1962, Tav. XX (*Santa Maria in Cosmedin*); id. 1971, Tav. VIII(*San Pietro in Vincoli*); CLAUSSEN 2002, 367 Fig. 295 (*Santi Cosma e Damiano*); 448 Fig. 361 (*Sant'Eusebio*). As late as 1829, it was still the practice to celebrate facing east at a free-stand-ing altar in *San Pietro in Vincoli* (KRAUTHEIMER 1971, 209 Fig. 177). In my opinion, it is fairly un-likely that the Church of *San Lorenzo in Lucina* with an east-end apse really had a large *confessio* and counted liturgically as having an east-end en-trance (CLAUSSEN 2010b, 288); the preserved con-*fessio* slab may simply have formed the front of the altar itself (small *confessio*). If this is the case, here too the altar stood free on the apse podium, meaning that the celebrant stood on the west side. There are also churches with their entrance in the east that have what is presumed to be a free-stand-ing altar (see n. 896 below). Also the church of *San Menna* in *Sant'Agata de' Goti* (near Naples), which was consecrated by Paschal II in 1110, has a free-standing altar on the apse podium; the priest went in front of the altar facing east – there is a central window in the apse wall – even though there is not much space there between the altar and the steps. This was still how it was done until the Second Vatican Council; LONGO / ROMAG-NOLI 2014, 111 Fig. 47.

the priest can get in front of it and it is possible to celebrate facing east. Even if a crypt is constructed in a church with an east-end apse, the altar is probably then moved so far to the east that the celebrant approaches it from the front.[838] In the first phase of the martyr's church of *San Valentino* on the *Via Flaminia*, which goes back to Pope Julius (337–352), the altar was located in the eastern apse of the single-nave church, so far back that only about 80 cm were left between it and the wall. The celebrant therefore stood in front of the altar *versus orientem*. This was confirmed by the new, three-nave church that replaced the previous building in the first half of the seventh century. It has a side altar at the end of the north aisle that is a mere 50 cm from the apse wall. The main apse of the new church is, on the other hand, greatly enlarged. Steps lead up from the nave onto the wide podium. There, the altar probably stands above its old location, which brings it to the middle of the sanctuary.[839] But here, too, the priest will have celebrated in accordance with the hitherto accepted custom, namely *versus orientem*. In the church of *San Gregorio al Celio*, with its east-end apse, there is an apse podium (without an annular crypt) with a free-standing altar, which the priest apparently approaches from the west. The side altars standing along the entrance wall of the church are moved away from the wall, apparently to enable an east-facing celebration.[840] In the church of *Santi Filippo e Giacomo* (*XII Apostoli*), likewise with an east-facing apse, the altar was also used in the sixth century to store the martyrs' relics and therefore had a small *confessio* (*fenestella*) at the front (Fig. 87). In this enormous church, the altar is located so far into the apse that for this reason alone a celebration *versus populum* seems nonsensical. In addition, the Byzantine context of the church building supports the idea that the priest stood in front of the altar.[841] Two frescoes dating from the end of the sixteenth century showing Pope Sixtus V(1585–1590) in the Church of the Apostles offer further proof that east-facing celebration was regularly practised there.[842]

East-facing prayer shapes the Roman liturgy according to the orientation of the church space. Visitors know exactly which way a church is oriented, i.e. whether the sanctuary lies to the west or the east.[843] They do not have to wait to see the liturgy being celebrated, but can tell this already from the arrangement of the church, namely from the position of the ambo. Like the *Schola Cantorum*, the ambo has belonged to the basic furnishings of

---

838 For example, in *Sant'Adriano*; CLAUSSEN 2002, 35. Here the altar will have had a small *confessio* (*fenestella*).

839 ASCIUTTI 2019, 140f., 186, 192f. In the eighth century the church was given a crypt and a (new) *Schola Cantorum*.

840 CLAUSSEN 2010b, 200–205.

841 My thanks to Simone Schiavone (Rome), who is performing archaeological surveys in the church.

842 DE BLAAUW 1999–2000, 294–298. Cf. CLAUSSEN 2002, 111 Fig. 71.

843 Notitia eccl. urbis Romae 35 (CCL 175, 310): *pervenies ad basilicam beati Petri* [...], *in cuius occidentali plaga beatum corpus eius quiescit*; LP 103,32 (DUCHESNE 1892, 80); Durand. rat. div. off. 5,2,57, German DOUTEIL / SUNTRUP 2016, 683 (see above n. 663).

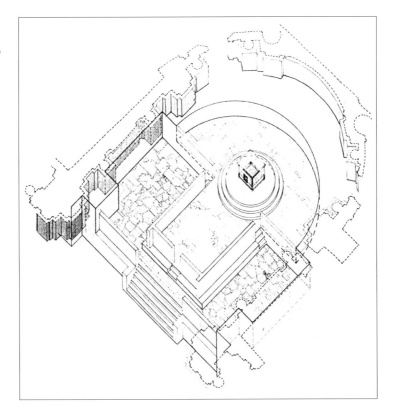

Fig. 87: Reconstruction of the church of *Ss. Filippo e Giacomo* in Rome, 6ᵗʰ century; Goodson 2007, 64 Fig. 2.5.

all station churches since the end of the seventh century at the latest.[844] It is accessed from the *Schola Cantorum*. Initially, there was just a single ambo from which all the readings were read. It was only in the High Middle Ages that a second ambo was added. The later Gospel ambo corresponds to the location of the original single ambo. It is always located on the south side of the *Schola Cantorum*, which means that it changes depending on the orientation of the church. In churches with an east-end entrance the ambo is on the left: this is the case in St Peter's, *Santa Maria Antiqua*, *Santa Maria in Trastevere*, *San Clemente* (Fig. 88), *Santa Pudenziana* and the *Basilica portuense*. In churches with an east-end apse, however, the ambo is on the right: this is the case in St Paul's Outside the Walls (above Fig. 83), *San Lorenzo fuori le mura*, *Sant'Agnese fuori le mura*, *Sant'Adriano* and *Santa*

---

844 The ambo and the *Schola Cantorum* are taken for granted as standard in the station churches, as is a (small or large) *confessio* (OR I [c. 700]).

Fig. 88: Interior of *San Clemente* in Rome, the 11th-century liturgical model church, looking west. At the front is the *Schola Cantorum* with the Gospel ambo on the left and the Epistle ambo on the right; further, the great *Confessio* beneath the altar and the bishop's seat behind the altar against the apse wall; PIAC Archivio Fotografico.

Maria in Cosmedin (Fig. 89).[845] The side on which the men and women stand in the nave changes accordingly, too: the men are always on the ambo side, i.e. on the right in a church with its apse to the east[846] and on the left in one with its entrance to the east.[847] Accordingly, the ivory casket from Samagher shows the men on the left and the women on the right in

845 HEID 2017b, 94 f. This is pointed out by PESARINI 1913, 401. On Santa Pudenziana see PETRIGNANI 1934, 17; on *Santa Maria in Trastevere* see KINNEY 1975, Plate. 6; COCCIA 2000; BULL-SIMONSEN EINAUDI 2000. The presbytery of Santa Maria Antiqua does not lie slightly to the southeast (as BRANDENBURG 2013, 342 mistakenly claims), but to the southwest; E. TEA, La basilica di Santa Maria Antiqua (Milan 1937), Plan between 34–35; KRAUTHEIMER 1962, Tav. XVIII. Also in the churches of Ravenna, which all have their apses to the east, the ambo stands on the right.
846 OR I,113 with 115, 117 and 118 (ANDRIEU 1948,

103–105); OR XI,83 (ibid. 443); LP 103,32 (DUCHESNE 1892, 80). The same arrangement is found in the churches in Ravenna with their apse to the east, as the mosaic of the procession of men and women in the nave of Sant'Apollinare Nuovo shows: Agnell. Lib. Pont. Rav. 88 (FC 21,1, 346).
847 For St Peter's there is appropriate textual evidence. LP 92,6 (DUCHESNE 1886, 417): *Hic fecit oratorium intro eandem basilicam, iuxta arcum principalem, parte virorum, in quo recondivit in honore Salvatoris sanctaeque eius genetricis reliquias sanctorum* (cf. DUCHESNE 1886, 522 n. 113). ICUR N.S. 2, No. 4213: *Ad sanctum Petrum*

Fig. 89: Interior of *Santa Maria in Cosmedin* in Rome, looking east. In the front is the *Schola Cantorum* with the Gospel ambo on the right and the Epistle ambo on the left; further, the great *Confessio* beneath the altar and the bishop's seat behind the altar against the apse wall; PIAC Archivio Fotografico.

St Peter's (above Fig. 29).[848] This arrangement is relevant because the deacon proclaims the Gospel from the ambo towards the south, i.e. in the direction in which one can assume the male representatives of the city's aristocracy to have had their places.[849] The southern position of the ambo and the men's side is likely to date back to at least the sixth century and indicates a general directional relevance in the liturgy.

From the early Middle Ages (seventh/eighth century) onwards, liturgical sources are available on the subject of the direction of prayer. However, the information they give only applies to the pope; they provide only limited information about liturgical assis-

apostolum ante regia in porticu columna secunda quomodo intramus sinistra parte virorum (DE BLAAUW 1994, 504). Cf. PODOSSINOV 1991, 276 f. SEVERANO 1630, 129 f. confirms this disposition for St Peter and thinks this to be true of other churches in which the women stand on the right

and the men on the left. Whether he is just thinking here of the churches with east-end entrances is not clear.

848 BRENK 1995, 76.
849 HEID 2017b, 99.

tants and nothing at all about the behaviour of the faithful during worship.[850] Facing east to pray will probably only have remained binding on whoever was presiding at the liturgy, i.e. the bishop or priest (presbyter) celebrating the papal liturgy as his representative. The papal liturgy itself has long been a highly ritualised clerical liturgy in which the participation of the people is more as spectators. The enormous size of the major churches alone makes it scarcely possible without modern-day technical facilities to actively involve the people in the liturgical action. The concrete outcome of this is that in churches with an east-end apse the people automatically look in the right direction for prayer. In churches with an east-end entrance, on the other hand, the celebrant goes behind the altar and faces east, while the faithful continue to look towards the sanctuary.[851]

The oldest description of the rites for the celebration of a papal Mass dates from around 700 (*Ordo Romanus* I) and offers crucial indications that the bishop really did turn to face east to pray.[852] However, the interpretation of this book of ritual stage directions is disputed. It seems to be clear that the first version was in fact written in Rome and compiled by the papal master of ceremonies. No one else could have described the course of the Mass so precisely and at the same time use his long experience to strip it down to its essentials. It is also clear that the book does not introduce any innovations, but merely codifies a long-established liturgical practice that might easily go back to Gregory the Great.[853] In order to be able to put the critical passages that talk about facing east to pray into their correct context, two vital questions need to be answered: In the context of the *Ordo Romanus* I, in which Roman churches is the liturgy of the Mass being celebrated? And, are the passages that talk about facing east interpolated, i.e. do they originate from later Frankish editing, or do they really reflect a Roman practice?

Scholars are fairly unanimous in assuming that the Roman Ceremonial describes the papal Mass in churches with an eastern entrance, i.e. in the Lateran Basilica, in *Santa Maria Maggiore* and in St Peter's.[854] This is suggested by the long version of the *Ordo*, whose opening chapters (1–23) seem to restrict the papal liturgy to Easter week.[855] In these churches, so the argument goes, the priest speaks the prayers in the direction of the

---

850 DE BLAAUW 1994, 96.

851 This can be seen from LP 103,32 (DUCHESNE 1892, 80): the tombs of SS Callistus, Cornelius and Calepodius in *Santa Maria in Trastevere* lay behind the backs of the faithful in the east end of the church. Thus, it would not have been felt to be unseemly (*non condigne honorificabantur*) if the faithful had turned to face the church entrance to pray.

852 HEID 2006, 394 f. needs to be revised. *Oriens* in the liturgical sources means the physical east. However, in churches with entrances in the east it is quite possible for the apse to function as an

ideal east for the faithful. On the *Ordo Romanus* I see comprehensively NEBEL 2012 (with a German translation of the OR I).

853 VOGEL 1962, 183.

854 S. BEISSEL, Bilder aus der Geschichte der altchristlichen Kunst und Liturgie (Freiburg i.Br. 1899) 297, 301; GRISAR 1899, 215; ANDRIEU 1948, 54 f., 63 n. 1; NEUNHEUSER 1996, 425; SAXER 2001, 117; *id*. 2001–2002, 72; DE BLAAUW 1994, 77, 82 f.; LANG 2003, 95 f. Cf. NEBEL 2012, 64 f.

855 OR I,5 (ANDRIEU 1948, 69), 7 (69) and 18 (72) mention Pascha.

people – towards the east – and therefore stands behind the altar for the celebration of the sacrifice. In St Peter's, for example, the altar is located at the front edge of the apse podium above a large *confessio*, so that the only possible place for the liturgist to stand is behind it. This, they claim, is why the Ceremonial does not specifically require the liturgist to turn to the east. Moreover, the book does not have the liturgy in a church with its apse at the east end, such as St Paul's Outside the Walls, in mind at all. It was not until the Roman Ceremonials were edited in the Franconian Empire in the eighth century that additions were made in a number of manuscripts to make the rite usable not only in churches with east-end entrances but also in those with east-end apses, the reason being that in the Franconian Empire the churches by and large had their apses to the east.[856] In fact, in the Old Gallican liturgy the place where the liturgist stands is "in front of the altar".[857] The diptychs are read out before the altar (*ante altare*).[858] Hence it is not surprising that Gregory of Tours (538–594) repeatedly ascribes pre-eminence to the location *ante altare*.[859] So scholars believe that it was only because of the turning east to pray customary in Gaul that an express reference was added to the Papal Ceremonial mentioning the celebrant's turning to face east when singing the *Gloria*[860] and when praying at the altar.[861]

Cyrille Vogel and others who espouse such a view thus see facing east to pray as proved for Rome, but nevertheless claim that in the oldest Book of Ceremonies there is only evidence of it for churches with an east-end entrance, in which the pope stands behind the altar. Nonetheless, in their opinion the practice of facing east to pray must also have applied to churches with an east-end apse, in which the pope then turns round to face the apse to pray or stands *in front of* the altar. This conclusion must be accepted. However, the texts need to be interpreted differently in order to arrive at it. For the oldest Roman formulary, the original version of the *Ordo Romanus* I, was not designed for a church like St Peter's, but for any church at all with an east-facing apse and a free-standing altar that can be walked round on all sides. A series of reflections on content and methodology lead to this conclusion.

First of all, the text of the *Ordo Romanus* I does not offer any evidence to justify restricting the papal Mass to the basilicas with east-end entrances at the Lateran, the Vatican

856 VOGEL 1964, 31.

857 SMYTH 2003, 205. The Synod of Vaison decided in 529 to read out the name of the pope "before the altar of the Lord": *cum sanctus papa Urbis suam oblatam dederit, recitemus [nomen] ante altarium Domini* (CCL 148A, 80).

858 Miss. Goth. 198, 454 (MOHLBERG 1961); Sacr. Veron. 283 (MOHLBERG 1994); DESHUSSES 1972, No. 63 f.

859 Greg. Taur. hist. Franc. 2,6 (MGH.SRM 1, 68): *sacerdotes Domini ante sacrosancta altaria perimentes.* For Gregory the Great, too, the marble floor in front of the altar is a holy place: Greg. I dial. 4,53 (SC 265, 178).

860 OR I,53 (ANDRIEU 1948, 84 f.): *Quando vero finierint, dirigens se pontifex contra populum incipit* Gloria in excelsis Deo. *Et statim regerat se ad orientem [...].* VOGEL 1960, 455 f.; id. 1964, 30.

861 OR I,123 (ANDRIEU 1948, 107): *surgit pontifex [...] et veniens ad altare dat orationem ad complendum directus ad orientem; nam in isto loco, cum* Dominus vobiscum *dixerit, non se dirigit ad populum.*

and the Esquiline. Although the opening chapters do deal with Easter Week, this is not the case in the *Ordo* proper (24–126), which does not refer to Easter Week but instead speaks unspecifically of station churches which the pope visits on certain days of the year according to a fixed system. So it applies in principle to the main basilicas (St Peter's, St Paul's, etc.) and the city's approximately thirty title churches.[862] At all events, the Lateran Basilica is not included.[863] This means that churches with an east-end apse have to be reckoned with right from the start, even if they were a minority among the churches in Rome.[864]

The fact that the *Ordo Romanus* I describes the papal Mass for a church with its apse facing east is indicated right at the beginning by a brief instruction to the pope. It may seem unremarkable, but it is of fundamental importance for the entire further understanding of the how the Rite of the Mass proceeds. It says that when the pope reaches his official seat (*sedes*) after processing into the church, he remains standing facing east: *accedit ad sedem et stat versus ad orientem* (OR I,51).[865] This sentence has occasionally been misunderstood. It does not say that when the pope is seated on the cathedra, he faces east.[866] There is no mention of his sitting down. Rather, the pope remains standing at the cathedra because the *Gloria* and the Collect follow and he has to say these standing.[867] Facing east is here only mentioned because it leads in a church with an east-end apse to an unusual situation at the cathedra.[868] The normal way of behaving would be to turn round at the cathedra and face the people. So the master of ceremonies has the task of making sure that the pope goes up the steps and remains standing in the same way as he arrives at the cathedra, namely with his face to the wall, because the prayer to the east follows first. This strange situation is even documented in pictures, at least for the cathedral of Metz. An ivory relief of the *Drogo Sacramentary* (835–855) shows the bishop standing in front of and facing his cathedra during the *Gloria* (Fig. 90). A Franconian interpolation can be ruled out in OR I, 51 since all the manuscripts contain the same version.[869] The logical conclusion from this is that the *Ordo Romanus* I presupposes a church with an east-end apse.

---

862 OR I,24 (Andrieu 1948, 74): *Denuntiata statione diebus festis, primo mane praecedit omnis clerus apostolicum ad ecclesiam.* OR I,25 (75): *Sed dum venerit pontifex prope ecclesiam, exeuntes acolyti et defensores ex regione illa cuius dies ad officium fuerit.* So, the churches change from day to day (cf. OR I,1 [67]). It can also include a diaconia; OR I,26 (75). Lang 2022, 169.

863 OR I,7. 18 (Andrieu 1948, 70. 72): For the station mass the pope leaves the Lateran. OR I,65 (ibid. 90): The Evangelion is carried back to the Lateran. Furthermore, in the seventh century the Lateran Basilica probably does not yet have a *confessio,* but one is assumed by the OR I; LP 104,19 (Duchesne 1892, 91).

864 Cf. de Blaauw 2010a, 20 Fig. 7.

865 OR I,51 (Andrieu 1948, 83). Cf. OR IV,18 (ibid. 159); OR V,21 (ibid. 213).

866 Thus is misunderstood by de Blaauw 1994, 77. Lang 2022, 210 also thinks because of OR I,51 that "The more widely attested version [von OR I; S.H.] was evidently composed for a Roman basilica with the entrance at the east end".

867 He does not sit down until after the Collect: OR I,53 (Andrieu 1948, 85).

868 U. M. Lang now agrees with this interpretation (oral communication); cf. Lang 2022, 210.

869 Vogel 1964, 33.

Fig. 90: Ivory cover of the Drogo Sacramentary (detail), c. 835–855, with the bishop at the cathedra, facing east, BnF, Ms. lat. 9428; photo: Wikimedia Commons.

Fig. 91: Ivory cover of the Drogo Sacramentary (detail), c. 835–855, with the bishop at the altar, facing east; opposite him, on the far right, stands the monks' choir, BNF, Ms. lat. 9428; photo: Wikimedia Commons.

Michel Andrieu nevertheless tries to render the rubric in question ineffective by claiming that the Roman author was at least under Franconian influence here. His argument is that the rubric does not suit the Roman churches with their east-end entrances.[870] He probably also assumes that the churches have their entrance in the east because of the reference in the Ceremonial to an important piece of church furnishing, namely the *confessio*. This could be interpreted as a large *confessio* such as that in St Peter's, leading to the conclusion that the rite must have originally been written for churches with east-end entrances. But this is wrong, as can already be seen from how the liturgy proceeds, which is incompatible with an altar arrangement such as that in St Peter's[871] –

870 ANDRIEU 1948, 54 f. For no good reason, NUSSBAUM 1965, 218–220, too, wants to ascribe all the references to east-facing prayer in the Ordines to Franconian influence.

871 OR I,74 (ANDRIEU 1948, 92): *Pontifex vero, antequam transeat in partem mulierum, descendit ante confessionem et suscipit oblatas* [...]. The pope first receives the oblations of the (male) nobility, who have ascended the steps on the right for this. Then, on certain days, the pope goes straight down the steps level with the altar *confessio* to those privileged persons from whom he receives the oblations at the bottom. Afterwards he goes just as directly up the steps again as far as the altar *confessio* and now turns towards the women's side, i.e. to the left. There he waits for the other (female) nobles, who ascend the steps on the left to bring him their gifts. This scenario presupposes that the altar podium has three doors.

although scholars have repeatedly claimed the contrary. Moreover, there is no archaeo-logical evidence of a large *confessio* in other churches with an east-end entrance such as the Lateran Basilica and Santa Maria Maggiore. On the contrary, in the seventh century, the Lateran Basilica had an altar that the celebrant could approach from the front via a step, which rules out any possibility of a large *confessio*.[872] Even more important is the fact that the *Ordo* applies in principle to all station churches, most of which lie within the city. Since there were traditionally no burials within the city, the title churches do not have a martyr's tomb underneath the altar. In other words, a large *confessio* is only at all likely in the few cemetery churches (like St Peter's), but not within the city, at least not before the Carolingian period (ninth century). Instead, they contented themselves there with an altar *confessio* and placed secondary relics (contact relics) in it.

The fact that even the original Roman version of the *Ordo Romanus* I had only a church with an east-facing apse in mind becomes perfectly clear when it gives the lo-cation of the liturgist as explicitly in front of the altar (*ante altare*):[873] while the pope is seated on the cathedra, the archdeacon stands in front of the altar and looks at the pope.[874] A little later, the pope himself stands at the altar in the same place, i.e. in front of the altar, facing the subdeacons, who have meanwhile positioned themselves behind the altar (*retro altare*).[875] The unanimous tradition of the two passages rules out any claim of a Franconian interpolation in the text. Cyrille Vogel rightly concludes that the pope stands at the altar facing east, towards the apse.[876] The only reason that the Book of Ceremonies does not specifically mention facing east is that at the altar – unlike at the cathedra – turning to face east is in no way unusual, so there can be no ritual uncertainty that the master of ceremonies would have to watch out for.

In order nevertheless to be able to cling to their hypothesis that the ceremonial di-rections of the *Ordo Romanus* I applied to a church with its entrance in the east, its adherents argue that they were given from different perspectives: only in a church with an east-end apse is the *ante altare* really in front of the altar, whereas in a church with an east-end entrance it is behind the altar. This, they say, is a result of the structural situation; for example, in St Peter's the altar can only be approached from behind on account of the large *confessio*. However, a reversal of the meaning of "in front" and "be-

872 Chavasse 1955, 25: *stante ante altare pontifice, et elevata dicente voce:* Sursum corda [...]. *At ille paululum divertens se ab altare, stans in suo gradu.*

873 OR I,77 (Andrieu 1948, 92): *Archidiaconus stans ante altare* [...]. Cf. OR I,46 (ibid. 82): [...] *praecedunt ante pontificem usque ante altare.* So the assistants accompany the pope from the nave to in front of the altar.

874 There is no mention of his having to turn round to look at the pope.

875 OR I,87 (Andrieu 1948, 95): *Et subdiaconi re-gionarii, finito offertorio, vadunt retro altare, aspicientes ad pontificem.* Cf. OR III,4 (ibid. 132): *Stat pontifex ante altare.*

876 Vogel 1964, 31.

hind" would be such a radical reinterpretation that it would be vital to offer proof of it. But no such proof exists. Hence the terms must always be understood in the same way, especially since this allows an unproblematic performance of the liturgy of the *Ordo Romanus* I. The fixation on a large *confessio* like that in St Peter's is in every respect unfounded, as if there were only the one variant of a large *confessio* in Roman churches and as if it had already been the standard for all churches with an east-end entrance in 700. Instead, it can be assumed that at that time the altar was still free-standing in practically all churches, so that the pope could approach it just as easily from the front as from the back. If *ante altare* sometimes meant in front of and sometimes behind the altar, then every reader of the *Ordo* would have to know on his own what it concretely meant for which church. The *Ordo* would then actually be of no help and would have failed to achieve its purpose. In reality, however, there is no such change of perspective. In front of and behind the altar are specifications that always define the location in the same way, and do so from the perspective of the nave.[877] The same goes for the directional terms left and right.[878]

There is further evidence that the *Ordo Romanus* I not only describes the papal Mass in churches with east-facing apses, but also requires the liturgist to stand in front of the altar. It says that the pope must turn round briefly after the Offertory because the rite requires him to look back (*respicit*) towards the Schola in order to give the choir the sign for the beginning of the Canon.[879] This looking back is again revealing: since the Schola is known to be located in the central nave (the so-called *Schola Cantorum*), the pope's location must be in front of the altar, with his back to the people.[880] This also makes it clear why, after the reading of the Gospel, when the liturgy moves to the altar, the (seven) candles or torches are set up behind the altar (*retro altare*).[881] Undoubtedly a place is chosen for the lights where they are least in the way. If the pope and his concelebrants and deacons[882] stood behind the altar, it would have been more likely for the candles to have been placed in front of it.

Once the pope has turned briefly towards the choir, the regional subdeacons from the *Schola Cantorum*, which is located in front of the altar, go "behind the altar". There the seven clerics now stand beside the seven torches, which is certainly what the liturgy

877 NEBEL 2012, 64 f. n. 8. LP 86,4 (DUCHESNE 1886, 372): *ante sacrum altare et confessionem beati Petri*. In San Pietro "in front of the altar" and "in front of the confessio" are identical; they both lie on the nave side.

878 OR I,24 (ANDRIEU 1948, 74 f.).

879 OR I,85 (ANDRIEU 1948, 95): *Et pontifex, inclinans se paululum ad altare, respicit scolam.*

880 Only for the Preface dialogue to the Canon do individual singers (subdeacons) go up onto the apse podium behind the altar.

881 OR I,66 (ANDRIEU 1948, 90): *acoliti sumentes cereostata ponent ea retro altare per ordinem.*

882 Concelebrating bishops and deacons stand behind the pope. OR I,86 (ANDRIEU 1948, 95).

intends. They look at the pope to give him the responses to the opening dialogue of the Eucharist: *Dominus vobiscum – Sursum corda*.[883] So if the regional subdeacons stand "behind the altar" looking at the pope, the latter must be standing in front of the altar, that is, with his back to the people.[884] This, too, is demonstrated by the *Drogo Sacramentary* (Fig. 91). The bishop is to be seen standing at the altar, on which stand the bread and chalice. Behind him in a semicircle stand five deacons or concelebrants. The altar is at the far right of the picture, indicating that the celebrant is facing east. However, it is just possible to make out a few monks at the extreme right edge. They are looking in the direction of the altar. So the altar is definitely free-standing. It appears that located between it and the cathedra, which stands at the apex of the apse, is the monks' choir with the task of giving the bishop the liturgical responses. This exempts the choir from facing east to pray.

Thus, as far as the oldest preserved Ceremonial is concerned, Mass in a church with an east-end apse is the norm in Rome. So it would seem that the standard church is not St Peter's after all, but rather St Paul's, which, with its liturgical furnishings from the time of Gregory the Great, enables an ideal celebration of the papal liturgy (above Fig. 83). There, both the clergy in the *Schola Cantorum* and the bishop in front of the altar in the chancel face east. It is possible to picture the scene with the aid of a thirteenth-century mosaic in *San Marco* in Venice. All the members of the choir – on the outside the adults, on the inside the boys – are turned towards the altar, in front of which stands the bishop. To the right and left of the Schola stand the aristocracy (Fig. 92).[885]

As far as the subdeacons are concerned, who in the Roman liturgy position themselves opposite the pope for the Canon, confirmation of this for the church of *San Lorenzo fuori le mura* is to be found in frescoes dating from the thirteenth century. In one of these frescoes, Count Henry is presenting a chalice to an abbot during the celebration of Mass (Fig. 93). The layman approaches the altar from the back right, i.e. where in perspective the area for the laity lies. Opposite, facing the celebrant, is the monks' choir. For reasons of space in *San Lorenzo*, the choir can only stand in the elevated eastern part of the church. Accordingly, on the fresco the priest stands in front of the altar with

---

883 OR I,87 (Andrieu 1948, 95): *Et subdiaconi regionarii, finito offertorio, vadunt retro altare, aspicientes ad pontificem.* Looking across the altar in OR I,87 has an equivalent in the opposite direction in OR I,76f. (Andrieu 1948, 92). Here it is clear that the pope is seated on the cathedra. The archdeacon stands *ante altare* looking into the pope's face.

884 Vogel 1964, 31.

885 Interestingly, everyone bows or performs the *prostratio*. In the Middle Ages, praying with raised arms and heavenward gaze was in fact abandoned in favour of bowing, at least at the eucharistic act of sacrifice, including in the Roman Rite. It is further to be noted with respect to the *San Marco* mosaic in Venice that the men in it (among others, the Doge = *Dux*) stand to the left of the *Schola Cantorum*. Their place is actually on the right, but this could only have been represented in the mosaic if the scene had been conceived the other way round.

Fig. 92: Mosaic in *San Marco* in Venice depicting the pontifical liturgy to celebrate the rediscovery of the bones of St Mark in 1094. The barrier can be seen that surrounds the *Schola Cantorum*. The ambo is located, against the normal practice, outside the *Schola*; beginning of the 13th century; photo: Web Gallery of Art.

his back to the people and facing east (towards whoever is viewing the picture). This is confirmed by two further images in the St Lawrence cycle depicting a Mass, in both of which the laity are seen standing behind the priest to receive Communion (Fig. 94).[886] Finally, a fourteenth-century liturgical source explicitly states that the pope celebrates facing east in *San Lorenzo*.[887]

The mass celebrated by the titular priests also assumes that the priest stands in front of the altar, even though many title churches have their entrance to the east. These are the same churches in which the pope, too, celebrates the station liturgy. The rite of the presbyteral liturgy has not survived, but the texts of the mass are to be found in the Old Gelasian Sacramentary (c. 650). These contain the instruction to the celebrant to turn towards the people (*ad populum* or *ad plebem*).[888] This refers to the dismissal blessing at the end of mass, which is later reduced to a final prayer, above all in Lent.[889] *Ad populum* is not a formulaic designation of a particular prayer of the mass, but rather a rubric, i.e. an instruction on what to do. It tells the priest to turn "towards the people" for the

886 WAETZOLDT 1964, Fig. 204, 226; WILPERT 1917, 953 Fig. 449; 960 Fig. 458.

887 DE BLAAUW 1999–2000, 282 n. 77. Further evidence ibid. 288.

888 Lib. Sacr. Gelas. 162, 167 and frequently (MOHLBERG 1960).

889 CHAVASSE 1958, 189.

blessing, which he apparently does not otherwise do for the prayers. This confirms that the titular priests, too, turn their backs on the people for the official prayers, probably in order to face east to pray. In the liturgies of Maundy Thursday,[890] Good Friday[891] and the Easter Vigil,[892] too, their position is in front of the altar (*ante altare*).

Thus the Roman liturgical books do not give any indication of how the papal and presbyteral liturgy is to be imagined in churches with an east-end entrance. They do not in any case clarify the critical points at which changes are imperative compared to churches with east-end apses. But this is simply not what the books are concerned with. Such a result may be unsatisfactory. However, research to date has also held that the *Ordo Romanus* I only describes the liturgy for one type of church, namely one with its with its entrance to the east. Perhaps there was also a description of rites appropriate to churches like St Peter's, but if so, it has not survived. The Franks were in any case only familiar with the *Ordo Romanus* I in the eighth century, so from the very beginning they were attuned to churches with an east-end apse. From then on, they regarded these as

890 Lib. Sacr. Gelas. 381 (Mohlberg 1960): during the Canon of the Chrism Mass the celebrant turns *ad populum* to bless the oil of the sick brought along by the faithful (cf. Chavasse 1958, 139 n. 96). So during the Canon the celebrant normally stands with his back to the people and looks towards the apse. His location in front of the altar is explicitly confirmed by his going to his seat (in the apse) after the Our Father and there blessing the oils required for the baptismal liturgy (once again facing the people); Lib. Sacr. Gelas. 383 (Mohlberg 1960). Only then does he return to the altar, expressly *ante altare*; Mohlberg, Lib. Sacr. Gelas. 390 (Mohlberg 1960). Rubrics nos. 383 and 390 belong to the underlying Roman stratum of the *Gelasianum Vetus*; Chavasse 1958, 133.

891 Lib. Sacr. Gelas. 395, 418 (Mohlberg 1960). Cf. Chavasse 1958, 87 f.

892 Lib. Sacr. Gelas. 425 (Mohlberg 1960). Cf. Chavasse 1958, 96 f.

Fig. 93: Wall fresco dating from the 13th century depicting the chalice legend in *San Lorenzo f.l.m.*: Count Henry presents an abbot with a chalice dedicated to St Lawrence; BAV Barb. lat. 4403, fol. 24r, Ufficio Copyright.

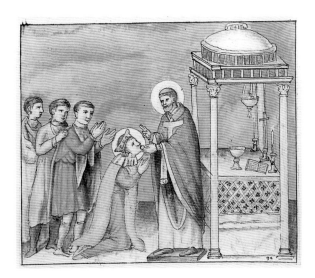

Fig. 94: Wall fresco in *San Lorenzo fuori le mura* showing St Hippolytus giving Communion and dating from the 13th century, watercolour in Windsor Royal Library 8993; OSBORNE / CLARIDGE 1996, 159, Plate 47..

the Roman norm. They did not make any changes to the text as far as orientation was concerned; they merely made it more precise based on the Roman practice to which they wished to be faithful in every respect.[893]

An astonishing exception to facing east to pray is found in the *Lateran Basilica* with its east-end entrance. At first, everything seems to have been done here, too, within the usual framework. Although the Lateran Basilica is the bishop's church and thus the main church of Rome, no detailed information is available on its chancel.[894] However, since the church did not have any altar relics in the early Christian period as it is located within the city, it did not have a *confessio* either.[895] There was therefore no need to raise the chancel, as was done in St Peter's and St Paul's in around 600. So the altar was probably free-standing and could be walked round from all sides.[896] A central flight of steps leads up to it

893 OR I,53 (ANDRIEU 1948, 84): *Quando vero finierint, dirigens se pontifex contra populum incipit* Gloria in excelsis Deo. OR I,123 (ibid. 107): *cum* Dominus vobiscum *dixerit, non se dirigit ad populum.*

894 CLAUSSEN 2008, 184.

895 OR I does mention a *confessio* as a standard installation in the station churches, but the Lateran is, of course, not one of them. Hence it cannot be concluded from the OR I that the Lateran possesses a *confessio*. See also the depiction of Sixtus V's Mass in the Lateran Basilica in a fresco in the Vatican's Salone Sistino: DE BLAAUW 1999–2000,

277 Fig. 6 (altar without *confessio*, but the entrance to a crypt can be seen in front of it).

896 LP 86,11 (DUCHESNE 1886, 375): *in circuitu altaris basilicae suprascriptae tetravela.* See the plans in KRAUTHEIMER 1980, 49–54; CLAUSSEN 2008, 168 f. The fresco mentioned in the previous footnote also suggests that the altar was suitable for a celebration from the front as well. It is likely that the so-called *confessio* likewise visible in the fresco was only installed (by Sixtus?) in the course of east-facing celebration; it was, however, in fact nothing more than a crypt accessed via a central flight of steps in front of the altar (UGONIO 1588, 41).

from the nave.[897] One must assume that the pope stands behind the altar, thus enabling him to pray facing east. This accords with the impression given by the ninth-century cruciform silver reliquary from the Sancta Sanctorum chapel (above Fig. 43). The lid has a remarkable pictorial decoration. It would not be unreasonable to see in it a reflection of the liturgical disposition of the Lateran Basilica. It depicts scenes of Christ, but these are clearly set fictionally inside a church. In fact, the longitudinal beam of the reliquary shows, from top to bottom, the liturgical furnishings of a church: at the very top stands the cathedra, in the middle the altar (without a *confessio*) and at the bottom the *Schola Cantorum*, indicated by the cancelli. Christ is portrayed in the central field presiding at a celebration of the Eucharist.[898] If this spatial arrangement alludes to the Lateran Basilica and the representation corresponds to liturgical reality, then the priest stands behind the altar, looking towards the Schola and in that case facing east.[899]

Surprisingly, though, it seems that in the sixth or seventh century at the latest there was a reversal of the direction of celebration in the Lateran Basilica, at least for the prayer at the altar. For in the papal liturgy of Holy Week, which was celebrated in the bishop's church, the liturgist stands in front of the altar (*ante altare*).[900] This probably also goes for all Masses celebrated by the pope in his cathedral outside Holy Week. So from a liturgical point of view, the Lateran was treated like a church with its apse facing east. This is also suggested by baptismal preparation. For the first and seventh scrutinies in the Lateran Basilica, the women stand on the left and the men on the right.[901] But then these are their places for churches with an east-facing apse.[902] A medieval fresco showing the consecration of the Lateran Basilica seems to confirm this (below Fig. 97). If the

897 See above n. 872. This disposition is also encountered in other churches in the city with their entrances to the east: SS Bonifacio e Alessio; Claussen 2002, 188. Santa Pudenziana; Petrignani 1934, 52.

898 E. Thunø, Image and Relic. Mediating the Sacred in Early Medieval Rome (Rome 2002) 82.

899 However, the silver reliquary probably originally belonged to Santa Maria Maggiore, which also an entrance to the east; Luchterhandt 2017, 389–393.

900 Chrism Mass on Maundy Thursday in the Lateran: seventh-century *Ordo* for Maundy (Chavasse 1955, 25): For the Canon the pope stands *ante altare* (cf. Chavasse 1958, 127). Good Friday liturgy in the Lateran around 750–800: OR XXIV,23, 26, 36 (Andrieu 1961, 292 f., 294): the celebrant stands *ante altare* to pray. Liber censuum 57,29 (Fabre / Duchesne 1910, 296): The pope *non communicat ad sedem, sed ante altare*. On the OR XXIV's relationship to the Lateran

see Chavasse 1958, 127; Vogel 1986, 170 f. It is unlikely to be a coincidence that in the Lateran Basilica there are lamps (*fara canthara argentea*) hanging *ante altare*; LP 48,6 (Duchesne 1886, 243). Innoc. III sacr. altar. myst. 2,22 (PL 217, 812AB), however, says that the priest (also at the altar) prays towards the east. He does not speak of an exception in the Lateran.

901 OR XI,2 (Andrieu 1948, 418); XI,83 (ibid. 443).

902 See above p. 332 f. There is some indication that the Gospel ambo, too, as would be expected (cf. Heid 2017b, 94 f.), stood on the right, i.e. on the north side, in accordance with this arrangement. De Blaauw 1994, Fig. 8 locates it hypothetically on the south side and Claussen 2008, 196 displays his agreement with this by locating the partially preserved paschal candelabrum (thirteenth/fourteenth century) on the south side. He would be right if the lion bearing the candelabrum really did have its front side facing the nave; this is, however, unlikely since the back of it is embossed

major papal basilica of all places is treated liturgically like a church with its apse at the east end, then it can hardly come as a surprise that the papal liturgical books only seem to be familiar with such church spaces.[903]

If the pope stands in front of the altar in the Lateran Basilica and, for example, consecrates the holy oils looking towards the nave,[904] then there must be sufficient space there. Interestingly, though, Pope Sergius II (844–847) had the cramped space round the altar extended so as to create more space for the clergy during the liturgy.[905] At the same time, he had a *confessio* built for storing relics.[906] One might think that the two things are connected: because Sergius possibly has a large *confessio* installed directly in front of the altar in the manner of St Peter's,[907] this would mean he had to create more space for the clergy behind the altar. But it is not that simple since the two measures were apparently carried out in reverse order: first the cramped area around the altar is extended, then Sergius has a *confessio* built. In principle, there is no reason at all that this *confessio*, if it is understood to be a kind of crypt, was necessarily positioned in the chancel. Nor, in fact, is this ever claimed. But even if it had been the case, it could have been an underground chapel with its entrance, as in St Paul's Outside the Walls, at some distance from the altar podium, so that the pope could continue to approach the altar from the front.[908]

and it would mean that the figure leaned lengthwise against the wall of the *Schola Cantorum*. It is therefore more likely that the candelabrum stood on the right, on the north side. In that way the lion would have its head turned towards the pope when he entered the *Schola Cantorum* and approached the altar.

903 To be sure, strictly speaking the Papal Ceremonial (*Ordo Romanus* I) is not talking about the Lateran at all but rather only about the liturgy in the station churches.

904 OR XXIV,16 f. (ANDRIEU 1961, 291): when consecrating the holy oils, the celebrant stands *ante altare* [...] *respiciens ad orientem*. Around 750– 800. Pontificale Romanae Curiae 42,11 (ANDRIEU 1940, 459): *ascendit sedem ligneam que est ante faciem altaris paratam* [...]. *Pontifex vero stans versa facie ad orientem.* Cf. app. II,31 (ANDRIEU 1940, 577): *pontifex ibi ante altare in mediocri sede* [...] *communicat.*

905 LP 104,19 (DUCHESNE 1892, 91): *Nam ambitus sacri altaris, qui strictim in ea fuerat olim constructus, largiorem proprio digito designans a fundamentis perfecit, pulcrisque columnis cum marmoribus desuper in gyro sculptis splendide decoravit, ubi nunc sacra plebs* (= the clergy) *in administratione sacri largiter consistit officii.*

906 LP 104,19 (DUCHESNE 1892, 91): *Ubi etiam confessionem mirificam, Christo cooperante, construxit, et argenteis tabulis auroque perfusis fulgide compsit; quam propriis manibus consecrans reliquias posuit.* This is presumably the first *confessio* since the altar does not seem to have possessed a small *confessio*.

907 So DE BLAAUW 1994, Fig. 8; CLAUSSEN 2008, 186.

908 DE BLAAUW 1994, 176 thinks the space in front of the altar might have been extended; cf. CLAUSSEN 2008, 186 f. Ibid. 188 maintains incorrectly that the fourteenth-century wall painting of the consecration of the altar of the Lateran Basilica (below Fig. 97) was on the east wall of the *confessio*; in that case the entrance to the crypt would have to have been located behind the altar. The crypt entrance must probably be imagined as resembling that in the fresco of the Lateran Basilica in the *Salone Sistino* of the Vatican Library (c. 1587) (cf. DE BLAAUW 1994, Fig. 11; id. 1999–2000, 277 Fig. 6). You can see the entrance to the crypt in front of the altar. The perspective might be compressed, so that in reality there was still space between the crypt entrance and the altar for the liturgist. Although the pope celebrates facing east here, i.e. standing behind the altar, that only allows conclusions to be made about the baroque practice.

What could have led to the pope's celebrating in the liturgically incorrect west-facing direction, i.e. towards the apse, in the Lateran Basilica? There is only one plausible explanation, namely the legendary image of Christ in the apse mosaic. This is the bust of the Saviour, still visible today in the calotte of the apse, apparently floating on clouds, which in its quasi-mystical iconography is considered an image of a divine theophany[909] (Fig. 95; below Fig. 111). The original apse mosaic with its bust of Christ dates from the fourth or fifth century.[910] It is important to note in this context that the Lateran Basilica, as an inner-city church, has no martyrs' relics and hence no real sacred centre, whereas the cemetery churches, first and foremost St Peter's and St Paul's, pride themselves on their martyrs' bones.[911] It is therefore conceivable that very soon, in order to compensate for this deficiency, this bust of Christ came to be seen as a wonderfully created, miraculous image.[912] There is an interesting remark in this respect by the Byzantine historian Sozomen (fifth century), who says that in Constantinople, God confirmed through apparitions that the city's prayer houses were holy and brought salvation.[913] In Rome, albeit not until the eleventh century, the rumour circulated that the image of Christ miraculously appeared on the wall of the Lateran Basilica when the church was dedicated by Pope Sylvester in the presence of Emperor Constantine (below Fig. 97).[914] Accordingly, Christ is believed to be present in his bust and thus in the church.

The conviction that the Lateran image of Christ works miracles is, of course, much older. The only part of the story that comes from the eleventh century are the alleged participation of Constantine and Sylvester and the timing of the apparition during the consecration of the church. But as early as the seventh century, a copy of the bust was made for the Venantius Chapel at the Lateran baptistery, where a very similar image was also included in the apse mosaic (below Fig. 112).[915] At the same time, the bust of Christ is copied in the Felicitas Oratory as well (below Fig. 113). The transferring of these images is most probably linked to the miraculous power of the original. In the Venantius Chapel and in the Felicitas Oratory, the apse and thus the image of Christ is on the east side, so that in all likelihood the celebrant turns towards the bust of Christ to pray.[916]

909 WARLAND 1986, 131.
910 WARLAND 1986, 38 f. opts definitively for the fourth century, BRANDENBURG 2013, 26 for the fifth. See also LEARDI 2006; CLAUSSEN 2008, 105.
911 CLAUSSEN 2008, 313.
912 Cf. generally SWEENEY 2018.
913 Sozom. hist. eccl. 2,3,8 (SC 306, 240); 7,5,1 (SC 516, 86). Pachomius's vision of the icon on the east wall of the chapel when he was praying see MATHEWS 2016, 137.
914 CLAUSSEN 2008, 106, 313.

915 BRANDENBURG 2013, 53 Fig. 26; IHM 1992, Plate 23,2. The dedicatory inscription in the apse mosaic of the Venantius Chapel reads: *QVO QVISQVIS GRADIENS ET XPM PRONVS ADORANS / EFFVSASQVE PRECES MITTAT AD AETHRA SVAS* (DUCHESNE 1886, 330 n. 3). So the image of Christ is worshipped.
916 The disposition of the altar in the Venantius Chapel is very similar to that in *San Paolo*. The altar is free-standing on a raised podium accessed via a central flight of steps: CLAUSSEN 2008, 383.

Fig. 95: The miraculous image of Christ the Saviour in the apse mosaic of the Lateran Basilica; photo by John Henry Parker, c. 1870, before the destruction of the mosaic; Fotothek RIGG, Rom 8049.

One can therefore assume an increasing veneration of the Lateran Basilica's image of Christ between the fifth and seventh centuries.[917] This, in turn, was probably reflected in the dedication of the church: since about 600, the church hitherto known as the Constantine Basilica (*Basilica Constantiana*) has been called the Church of the Saviour (*Ecclesia Salvatoris*).[918] From the point at which the bust of Christ began to be consid-

---

917 A further argument: if the Lateran Basilica had not had a holy image of Christ, and therefore no relic in the fifth century, it would not have surrendered the chains of Peter to the church later known as *San Pietro in Vincoli*, the relics of Stephen to the church later known as *San Stefano Rotondo*, and the crib relic to the church later known *Santa Maria Maggiore*. The cross relic in *Santa Croce in Gerusalemme* is a special case as Empress Helena was able to claim the relic for her palace chapel.

The fact that *Santa Maria Maggiore* possessed the crib relic in the fifth century seems to me to be compelling: it is the only reason this church was built at all, which in the sixth century was already called "*ad presepe*"; W. Buchowiecki, Handbuch der Kirchen Roms 1 (Wien 1967) 240.

918 De Blaauw 1994, 112. In the fifth century it is still called the *Basilica Constantiniana* (cf. ibid. 109 f.); in the seventh century *Ecclesia Salvatoris*; LP 76,3 (Duchesne 1886, 336).

ered miraculous, a reversal of the direction of celebration may have taken place in the Lateran Basilica. For if Christ is miraculously present in his image and it is Christ to whom the pope addresses his prayers, it would be absurd for him to turn his back on the image while he prays. So now the pope must approach the altar from the front.[919] This disposition is no different from that in the east-facing palace chapel of Sancta Sanctorum, where the pope likewise stands on the step in front of the altar, thus looking at the miraculous icon of the Saviour fixed to the wall opposite (Fig. 96).[920]

A medieval painting in the altar crypt of the Lateran Basilica shows the apparition of Christ at the consecration of the altar by Pope Sylvester as recounted in the legend (Fig. 97). It is no coincidence that in it the image of Christ occupies a central place above the altar. So Christ appears at the very moment when the pope is standing at the altar. Image and altar are inseparably interrelated. It was self-evidently the artist's intention that Sylvester should stand in front of the altar looking towards the apse and thus able to see the image of Christ. For the Christ who is appearing is nothing other than the bust of Christ in the apse mosaic. But while the pope is still occupied with anointing the altar, all the other people, including Emperor Constantine (with a crown), look up in astonishment at the image of Christ and point towards it.[921] Since the consecration takes place during the papal liturgy, it is possible that the spatial arrangement corresponds to the liturgical order. The old layout of the Lateran Basilica was as follows: on the longitudinal axis, in the nave, was the *Schola Cantorum*, behind it and a few steps higher stood the altar, and behind that lay the apse with the papal throne. First of all, it is to be noted that the picture does not show the clergy who stand in front of and behind the altar at every papal Mass, i.e. in the *Schola Cantorum* in front and between the altar and the apse behind. Also absent are the Lateran canons, who at the time of the creation of the picture formed the basilica's clergy, or actually any clerical dignitaries at all.[922] On the other hand, in the right half of the picture the virgins are to be seen to the left of the pope; on his right are what look like monks or clerics (with tonsure). Like Sylvester, they are standing in front of the altar, more specifically to the left and right of the *Schola Cantorum*. Opposite the virgins and monks, in the left half of the picture, is where the imperial court and nobility can be seen, apparently with men and women in both the

919 Greg. I ep. 9,147 (MGH.Ep. 2,1, 147f.) speaks of the significance of the image of the Saviour that one has before one's eyes in the church and before which one prostrates oneself in adoration.

920 Even though it was possible to go behind the altar, this area was nevertheless railed off for safety reasons. The barrier was apparently only opened when the icon was taken out for the procession on 14-15 August. See in general A. MATENA, Das Bild des Papstes. Der Lateransalvator in seiner Funktion für die päpstliche Selbstdarstellung (Paderborn 2016).

921 The apse is suggested by the upper curve of the picture, which follows the curve of the vault of the crypt.

922 The cleric opposite the pope, however, is possibly the donor of the picture and may be a Lateran canon.

Fig. 96: The *Sancta Sanctorum* chapel in the so-called *Scala Sancta* (Holy Stairs) at the Lateran; M. Cempanari / T. Amodei, Scala e Sancta Sanctorum (Città del Vaticano 2013) 51, Fig. 29.

Fig. 97: Watercolour after the former wall painting on the back wall of the crypt beneath the high altar of the Lateran Basilica, likely c. 1367. It shows the appearance of the Salvator image at the dedication of the basilica by Pope Silvester in the presence of Emperor Constantine, BAV Barb. lat. 4423, fol. 5r, Ufficio Copyright.

left and right wings of the transept.[923] So in the basilica no one stands with his or her back to the apse. Far from standing opposite the pope, the nobility are in the wings of the transept and look towards the image of Christ. The only problem is the central area of the transept between the altar and the apse. This is the place for the higher clergy, who, as already mentioned, are missing from the fresco. They, too, are certain not to stand with their backs to the apse, but will instead position themselves on two sides facing each other, leaving the space in between free for the pope's processional route from the cathedra to the altar and back. The fact that the virgins stand on the left and the monks on the right corresponds to the distribution of the sexes in a church with an east-end apse and confirms the liturgical reversal of direction in the Lateran Basilica.

923 On the location of the aristocracy in the wings
of the transept in *San Paolo* see CAMERLENGHI
2018, 85, 91.

When Sergius III (904–911) had a ciborium erected over the altar of the Lateran Basilica,[924] care will have been taken to ensure that the celebrant could still see the image of Christ. In the baroque period, the direction of celebration was once again reversed: the pope then stood behind the altar and the area around it was redesigned accordingly. This has nothing to do with a rediscovery of turning east to pray, but arises instead from the idea that the pope has the privilege of celebrating facing the people at the altar.[925]

SUMMARY

There is no radical, absolute suppression of cult and religion in nascent Christianity; nor can there be, inasmuch as the new movement arises within the sphere of Judaism. Only the pagan realities of altar, sacrifice and temple are rejected. The Eucharist, embedded as it is in the history of religion, reveals itself and is performed as a sacrificial activity – with an enlightened distancing from the pagan cult, but also with a biblical link to the sacrificial service of the old covenant, the Eucharist is understood as a sacrificial act. Performed at the sacred table, it stands out from the assembly's other meals and very soon becomes an independent cultic act (the celebration of the Eucharist). What the nature of sacrifice consists in theologically is of secondary importance for an assessment from the point of view of liturgical history; the crucial factors here are solely the contemporary sacrificial terminology and a corresponding performative ritual language.

The rejection of the pagan temple and the simplicity of early Christian assembly rooms are not an expression of programmatic profanation, just as spirituality and otherworldliness in Christian preaching cannot be equated with desacralisation. Although the terms "church" (= assembly room) and "basilica" have no sacred connotations, the terms "house of God" and "house of prayer" that were used at the same time do. Through the Sunday prayers of the faithful, the assembly room becomes a place where God's helping power is experienced and thus a *lieu de mémoire* of holiness and the presence of God.

Since it first came into existence, the altar has been the centre of the experience of holiness. It is the privileged negotiating space between heaven and earth. Here holiness culminates and is condensed in the powerful effect of prayer. At the same time, it is God's sovereign territory: the altar serves as a place to deposit the offerings that are irreversibly consecrated to God in a public act. The altar becomes a coveted place for blessing a wide variety of natural gifts over which the priest speaks specific prayers of blessing. Last but

---

924 CLAUSSEN 2008, 186 f.

925 On this phenomenon see DE BLAAUW 1999–2000.

not least, the altar is the place where vows are taken and redeemed, which is the origin of votive Masses.

The altar is a privileged place of prayer. All the gestures that accompany it emphasize the vertical dimension. The priest stands upright at the altar, raising his hands and eyes as he prays. Whole-body prayer is always directed to God in his sovereignty, not to the individual or the congregation, on which the priest literally turns his back. He extends his hands towards God, hands whose visible and moral purity empowers him to pray. As he does so, he looks up towards the One with whom he is speaking. He seeks eye contact; he seeks "God's countenance". Even inside the church, he looks up "to heaven", which he imagines opening up above the altar.

Like the ancient altar before it, the Christian altar is also directional: it stands "before God" (Rv 9:13),[926] who shines as the Sun of Righteousness in the east. The habit of turning towards the east to pray began to come into use everywhere from the second century on and became a firm rule. Although an individual is permitted to dispense with turning towards the east for private prayer, for liturgical prayer at least it amounts to an obligation that is even traced back to the apostles.[927] In the liturgy, of course, facing east is something that ultimately only the presider is required to practise, whereas exceptions are allowed for the faithful and the liturgical assistants.

The preference for churches to lie on a west-east or east-west axis, which has existed since monumental churches began to be built in the fourth century, results from the long-established practice of facing east to pray. Most of these churches have their apse at the east end, others at their entrance. From the fifth and sixth centuries onwards, having the apse at the east end came to prevail completely, apparently for practical reasons – to make the sequence of movements easier for the clergy and people when they prayed together facing east. All in all, the impression remains that right from the start the Orient was more consistent than the Occident in matters of facing east to pray, which is presumably explained by its different religious landscape: in the Orient, there was a strong presence of Jews, Manicheans and later Muslims, making the direction of prayer an important distinguishing feature.

The meaning of east-facing prayer, its Christological reference and its mystagogical embedding in latreutic activity are not subjects to be investigated here. There is, however, no denying that its significance faded as a result of the ritualisation and rubricization that took place in the Middle Ages. Of course, this is not per se an undesirable development, but it lies in the nature of ritualisation that it preserves certain procedures even if they are no longer understood by everyone. Nor, though, is there any mistak-

---

926 Cf. Tycon. expos. Apoc. 3,38 (CCL 107A, 160);   927 Severus 1972, 1226; Lang 2003, 48 f.
Caesar. Arel. expos. in Apoc. 7 (PL 35, 2430).

ing that the multiplication of side altars in Western churches and the discontinuation of liturgical practice in Rome as a result of the papacy's exile in Avignon meant that knowledge of the original, i.e. the geographical, turning east to pray was lost during the Renaissance. But facing east nevertheless lived on and still does insofar as in the Latin liturgy (Tridentine Rite) the priest always stands in front of the altar, i.e. looking not at the people, but at the Lord or the Cross.[928]

928 Cf. HEID 2009a.

V. IMAGE

Seeing while praying

Christ opened the eyes of the blind and enabled them to see things and people in every colour. For this reason alone, Christians are not hostile to images. Nor do they close their eyes when they pray – quite the opposite. The sources speak almost stereotypically of people looking up to heaven when they pray, which, of course, means that their eyes are open and they are seeing. But what? Perhaps the external things are not so important. For it is clear that there was an inner seeing long before the images moved inside the church. In the Bible, there are pre-formulated patterns of thought and language that have become adapted through centuries of prayer and are so interwoven with images that the latter stand before the inward eye of the people praying. These were then merely made visual in church art from the fourth century on, i.e. from when Christian worship created a stage for itself in monumental church architecture. The new, sublime church interior, be it a basilica or a rotunda, offered manifold opportunities for this.

If this is so, then early Christian church art must be regarded as an emanation of the liturgy, or at least as liturgy-related art. What has been said above about altar and sacred space, about prayer posture and facing east, has already incorporated many findings of archaeological research. Now all of this is to be placed in the context of the three-dimensional, dynamic spatial events of the liturgy, paying special attention to pictorial art.[1] What this means is examining the significance for the liturgy of the images to be found in an early Christian church interior.

---

1 On the following HEID 2016b. For a long time there was reticence in this area. Protestant researchers traditionally had little interest in images, whereas on the Catholic side the dominant interest was in their theological-iconological aspect. It is only in more recent publications that a growing sensitivity has been shown to the liturgical context of the images. Foundational PIVA 2008. See further JOUNEL 1984; HELLEMO 1989; VERSTEGEN 2002; id. 2009, 595–597 (with literature); YASIN 2012 (also ritual). On church architecture see the overview in DE BLAAUW 2008.

1. SPACE AND LITURGY

Referring to the meeting place in the fourth and fifth centuries primarily as a house of prayer is making a lofty and exclusive claim: church space is sacred, for nothing is more sacred than prayer. Then the space must also be suitable for prayer. White walls are not ideal for this; at least, there was no opposition to the increasingly sophisticated decoration of churches with images until the Iconoclastic Controversy. The images enfold and simultaneously create the sacred space. They are directly related to the liturgy and to the prayer of the congregation. Here the connection to the image is initially established non-verbally through posture: the congregation rise to pray, stand upright and look upwards, to the very place where they come upon images. It is these images (paintings, mosaics) that we shall look at in what follows in this chapter. Although we must remember that many churches also have artistically designed floor mosaics that give the space a sacred structure,[2] these are not considered here because they do not catch the gaze of those who are raising their eyes to pray.

It is significant that those wall decorations in the churches that are not purely decorative, but rather figurative, are not found at the bottom of the walls, where one might expect them and where they would be easy to look at from close up. Instead, they are higher up. According to modern nudge theory, the high position of the pictures is meant to arouse curiosity about what is above: they involuntarily draw the inert gaze upwards into the sphere of God, who is enthroned above the heavens. The images direct the gaze to "the things that are above" (Col 3:1) and help those gathered in the church to glide over into prayer mode through this external lifting-up.

Its visual aspect influences the perception of the church interior as a sacred place. Whereas ancient worshippers stood outside the temple looking up to heaven (Fig. 98), the Christians rejected traditional temples and gathered in halls. Ever since Paul's words at the Areopagus in Athens, apologists have emphasised that God does not dwell in a temple made by human hands (cf. Acts 17:23 f.)[3] but is instead enthroned above the heavens (cf. Acts 7:47–50). This does not, however, desacralize the meeting rooms of the Christians; on the contrary, heaven is brought into the churches, and the imaginations of those praying there experience all the more strongly that heaven and God are really present inside the church. When the Christians seek the protected space of the church, they do not intend to shut themselves off from the public sphere or from heaven; on the

---

2 JÄGGI 2007, 75–89; WATTA 2018.

3 E.g. Iren. adv. haer. 3,12,9 (SC 211, 218); Clem. Alex. strom. 7,5,28,1 (SC 428, 104).

Fig. 98: Figure of the praying prophet Jonah, Asia Minor, 3rd century; The Cleveland Museum of Art, John L. Severance Fund 1965.240.

contrary, they constantly look up "to heaven" or "towards the face of God" as they pray (above chapter IV, 4d). Numerous texts offer a pertinent description of the Christian prayer posture, i.e. that involves, even when they are in church, raising their hands and eyes *to heaven*.[4] This, of course, applies to all prayer, but most expressly to the central place of Christian prayer, the altar. "The altar is the place where heaven is opened up. It does not close off the church, but opens it up."[5] This statement by Joseph Ratzinger cannot be emphasized enough. The heavens lying open above the altar is the crucial key to understanding Christian liturgy and art. The priest stands before the altar and raises his hands to heaven.[6] Upon his prayer, the heavens open.[7] The Eucharistic gift comes down from heaven like manna when the priest at the altar lifts up his hands to heaven.[8]

The large, magnificent houses of prayer were built during the Constantinian period, a fact that contemporary victory propaganda made much of. It is not, though, as if Emperor Constantine († 337) had set out to impose sacred buildings on the Christians against their religious convictions. Rather, he wanted to provide them with a suitable space for prayer, which in fact meant paying the greatest attention to their posture when praying. As in the open air, when those who are praying look upwards in the new churches, they must see the heavens and the face of God – only much closer. The church interior, as it were, zooms in on heaven. The Christians experience it as a privilege to pray inside the church and to experience heaven, and therefore the sacred sphere, so closely. Constantine makes those of his soldiers who still serve the old gods feel this: on Sundays, they are required to recite the emperor's prayer on an open plain, raising their hands to heaven

---

4   Tert. idol. 7,1 (CCL 2, 1106): *in ecclesiam venire, de adversaria officina in domum dei venire, attollere ad deum patrem manus*. Orig. comm. in Ioh. 28,28 (SC 385, 72): raising eyes (in the house of God); Pass. Macarii (HYVERNAT 1886, 45): prayer in a room with raised hands. Apophth. 20,3 (SC 498, 162): prayer in a monastic cell with hands raised to heaven; the roof opens and it receives light. Greg. Naz. ep. 34,4 (GCS 53, 31): prayer in a room with hands raised to heaven and eyes towards the east. Joh. Chrys. in act. apost. hom. 18,5 (PG 60, 148 f.): hands raised in prayer inside a church. Athan. apol. ad Const. 16 (SC 56², 120): everyone inside the church raises their hands. Greg. Tur. lib. mirac. 3 de virt. Mart. 7 (MGH.SRM 1,2, 593): […] *in loco illo sancto* (St Martin's basilica) *venit ante sanctum altare; et stans oculis ad caelum elevatis et manibus* […]. […] *elevans se et erigens iterum oculos ac manus ad caelum*. A. BERGER, Leontios Presby-

teros von Rom. Das Leben des heiligen Gregorios von Agrigent (Berlin 1995) 321, 324: prayer with eyes and hands raised to heaven in the church of St Hippolytus in Rome (cf. 283, 289, 302, 314). Anon. de eccl. 8 (CSEL 16, 621): *sacra canunt pariterque oculos ad sidera tollunt* (inside the church). A. VEILLEUX / A. DE VOGÜÉ, Pachomian Koinonia 1 (Kalamazoo 1980) 300: Pachomius raises his hands to heaven in gaol and prays. Pass. Pisoura (HYVERNAT 1886, 116–119): Bishop Pisoura raises his eyes to heaven in prayer and then celebrates the Eucharist with the congregation. Further instances HEID 2006, 366 f.
5   RATZINGER 2000, 71.
6   Joh. Chrys. coem. et cruc. 3 (PG 49, 397 f.).
7   Expos. brev. antiquae liturgiae gallic. (PL 72, 94 AB): *Sursum corda ideo sacerdos habere admonet* […]. […] *ad orationem sacerdotis caeli aperiuntur*.
8   Joh. Chrys. cat. bapt. 2,4,26 (FC 6,1, 286).

Fig. 99: The Colossus of Constantine, which once crowned his statue in the Basilica of Maxentius near the Forum Romanum, shows him as someone inspired by God looking upwards; Capitoline Museums; Foto: Universität zu Köln, Archäologisches Institut, Forschungsarchiv für Antike Plastik, Hannes-tad-90-A0112_16567.

and looking up to the King of Heaven, whereas the Christians go to church.[9] Maybe as a tit-for-tat response, in the Eastern Empire the anti-Christian emperor Licinius sends the Christians out of the city churches and into the open fields.[10] Basil of Caesarea once said that the Christians persecuted by the Arian Goths were driven out of their churches and now had to raise their hands to their Lord in heaven in the open air.[11]

9   Euseb. vit. Const. 4,18f. (SC 559, 474–476); Döl-
    GER 1972, 304. Athan. apol. ad Const. 16 (SC 56²,
    120): prayer for the emperor with raised hands.

10 Euseb. vit. Const. 1,53,2 (GCS 1,1², 43).
11 Basil. ep. 164,2 (PG 32, 637A).

With his Sunday decree urging pagans as well as Christians to pray, Constantine practically elevated the prayer posture described above to an imperial law. And so it will have to be understood as propaganda for prayer when Eusebius praises the gold coins depicting Constantine with his eyes turned upwards and a picture in the palace at Constantinople showing him standing upright "in the manner of a praying man, his eyes turned to heaven and his hands outstretched"[12] (Fig. 99). Art shows how important prayer posture was seen to be in Rome. In countless variations, it depicts the deceased and saints, women, men and children as praying in this way (above Figs. 33, 34, 59, below Fig. 113).[13]

If the full prayer posture is practised by the entire worshipping community more or less as an imperial decree, then this has consequences for church-building. In fact, Constantine's trend-setting foundations are inexplicable without the Christian image of God and the corresponding prayer posture. The modern prejudice that in the beginning the assembly rooms were marked by poverty and austerity is untenable. Hugo Brandenburg wrote an essay on this with the programmatic title "Prachtentfaltung und Monumentalität als Bauaufgaben frühchristlicher Kirchenbaukunst" (Splendour and monumentality as the building tasks of early Christian church architecture).[14] The love of splendour is not the result of vain megalomania, but arises from the desire to pay homage to God – the Constantinian church building is anything but neutral and profane. In their designs, the architects are responding to the emperor's new image of God: the Most High God must be worshipped in the only appropriate prayer posture.[15] The gaze is therefore deliberately directed upwards in the church interiors. This is apparent in the height of the interior spaces, which people found impressive.[16] It has to do with the verticality of prayer. Flat and low buildings and in fact anything that is oppressive and gives the impression of being walled in all the way round are all inappropriate for the Christian church interior.

The prescribed prayer posture must, of course, be specially observed in the imperial capitals.[17] This is why Constantine first designed the Lateran Basilica in Rome as a model. After all, it is located close to the imperial residence (*Sessorianum*, near *Santa Croce in Gerusalemme*), and is more or less oriented towards it: the Lateran Basilica ex-

---

12 Euseb. vit. Const. 4,15 (SC 559, 476); DÖLGER 1972, 303; WALTER 2006, 14. Gelas. Cyz. comm. act. conc. Nic. 2,28 (MANSI 2, 884A): Constantine himself prays with hands raised and eyes looking heavenwards to God. On the emperor's preference for this prayer posture see K. M. GIRARDET, in: FC 55, 158 f. n. 89.

13 Cf. RUBERY 2014.

14 On early Christian "baroque" see BRANDENBURG 2004.

15 Euseb. vit. Const. 4,18 f. (SC 559, 474 – 476).

16 Euseb. hist. eccl. 10,2,1 f. (SC 55, 79 f.); 10,4,43 (95); vit. Const. 3,43,3 (SC 559, 404); cf. Procop. aed. 1,1,27 f. (HAURY / WIRTH 1964, 10).

17 The prayer regulations are closely linked to the palace regulations: Euseb. vit. Const. 4,18 (SC 559, 474 – 476).

tends in an east-west direction, with the entrance façade facing east towards the *Sessorianum*, so that there is a direct processional route from the palace to the bishop's church. Constantine had the church erected, as it were, as a new and protective building over the demolished barracks of the bodyguard of his adversary Maxentius.[18] The Lateran Basilica was given a precious gilded ceiling,[19] probably so that it would be as if the Christian soldiers and civil servants were looking up at the sun during their Sunday prayers.[20]

Constantine's architects took further subtle measures to allow the Christians to pray inside the church as if they were actually praying outside. By dispensing with architectural decoration, the interior walls are, as it were, dematerialised. Instead, the flat surfaces were decorated with polychromatic marble incrustations and mosaics. The walls rise up extremely high and are pierced by large windows. The thinning of the external walls by the windows makes the building appear less massive when one looks out of them. Columns connected by arches open up the space into the width of the adjoining side aisles.[21] The gilded roof truss gives the illusion of dizzying heights,[22] suggesting, particularly in artificial light, a star-spangled firmament and drawing the gaze upwards.[23] Everything is designed to convey a light, sublime impression.[24] Praying in the early Christian basilica allows one to forget the heaviness of this world and enter the immaterial sphere of the divine.

It is true that the architecture itself has little to do with the liturgy; the actual structure of a church initially only provides a space, albeit always a lofty and also directional space. Its floor plan can be round, square or rectangular, and its elevation can end in a dome or a flat roof. Such elements have no influence on whether a liturgy of the Western or Eastern type is celebrated there. It is the furnishings and artistic decoration that make the space in the full sense capable of liturgy.[25] In other words, the adaptation of the space for the liturgy takes place on a horizontal level through the altar, ambo, cathedra and

---

18 ZIMMERMANN 2017, 118.

19 LP 34,10 (DUCHESNE 1886, 172): *camaram ex auro purissimo*. Cf. DE BLAAUW 2008, 365.

20 Looking towards the sun also has a role to play in Constantine's Sunday prayer call; cf. Lact. div. inst. 6,8,4 f. (CSEL 19, 507 f.). Euseb. vit. Const. 4,19 (SC 559, 476); Lact. div. inst. 6,8,4 f. (CSEL 19, 507 f.). Method. symp. 5,8,131 (SC 95, 162): Gold shines like the sun. D. IOZZIA, Aesthetic Themes in Pagan and Christian Neoplatonism (London 2015) 57–76: Gold and light.

21 BRANDT 2016, 65–70.

22 Paulin. Nol. ep. 31,6 (FC 25,2, 742): gilded coffered ceiling in the Church of the Holy Sepulchre;

LP 34,17 (DUCHESNE 1886, 176): gilded ceiling in *San Pietro in Vaticano*; Euseb. vit. Const. 4,58 (SC 559, 524): gilded ceiling of the Church of the Holy Apostles in Constantinople. Further evidence see BRANDENBURG 2004; *id.* 1995a. On the ceiling as an image of heaven see WARLAND 1986, 134. Cf. VAN DER MEER 1951, 426.

23 H.-J. HORN, Gold, in: RACh 11 (1981) 895–930, here 926. Prud. cathem. 5,141–146 (CCL 126, 141–146): the church interior lit up at night seems like the firmament of heaven.

24 BRANDENBURG 2002, 1539; GUIDOBALDI 2004; CARILE 2016.

25 BRANDT 2016, 71–74.

other furniture, and on a vertical level through the images. Permanently installed images forming an integral part of the church furnishings are not placed arbitrarily, but, like the liturgical furniture, each have their respective meaningful locations finely tuned to the liturgy. Conversely, the liturgy is oriented towards these images, or at least supported by the images. The concrete implementation of the relationship between image and liturgy depends on a number of factors, above all on whether the church has its apse or its entrance at the eastern end.

Images inside the church are complex. There are not just those in the apse, but a whole series of image locations and image types. In the discussion that follows, various groups of images will be presented, most of them from the fifth and sixth centuries, which differ in type and location within the church. The main focus will be on church interiors in Rome and Ravenna. Much from this period has been lost and can only be partially reconstructed, but the early Christian spirit still lives on in some medieval pictorial decorations. Anyone visiting such Roman churches as *Santa Pudenziana*, *Santa Maria Maggiore*, *Santi Cosma e Damiano* and even St Paul Outside the Walls today, but also *San Clemente*, *Santa Prassede*, *Santa Maria in Domnica* and *Santa Cecilia*, can relive in situ what is described below. The same goes for *Sant'Apollinare in Classe*, *Sant'Apollinare Nuovo* and *San Vitale* in Ravenna. In these churches, it is possible to recognise well-rehearsed, albeit not yet canonically established, classifications of the images. The size, arrangement, selection and function of the images influence the shape of the space as well as of the liturgy. Lines of sight, spatial axes and actors can be clearly distinguished. For space and liturgy are three-dimensional: liturgy is not the performance of a rite on just one level, but fills the entire space of the church.

The following sections will deal with the groups of images in a church interior as they enter the field of vision during the course of the celebration of the liturgy. Although the individual elements have been archaeologically authenticated, the overall picture is to be understood in terms of ideal types. Hardly surprisingly, high-quality art is found in the bishop's churches and papal station churches. It must be considered an unwritten rule that the liturgical furnishings and pictorial decoration of a church regularly visited by the bishop – for example, in the course of the station liturgy – is designed for the solemn pontifical liturgy, even if this is only rarely celebrated there. Hence the reference point for any spatial interpretation is the episcopal liturgy. This ultimately corresponds to the hierarchical structure of both the Church and the liturgy, whose defining local protagonist is always the bishop. He, along with his clergy and the participating faithful, contemplate the images in the church interior; these, in turn, have their own special function and meaning within the pragmatic context of the liturgy.

Rainer Warland speaks fittingly of the "goal-oriented conception space in early Christian churches, which starts from the entrance and accompanies the space to culminate in the apse".[26] This applies to the vast majority of churches, whether they are elongated basilicas or rotundas.[27] The church space extends along the west-east axis between the entrance wall and the round of the apse, in front of which lies the chancel (presbytery). This is the axis followed by the liturgical entry of the celebrant and his assistants from the entrance to the cathedra at the apex of the apse. So, as they enter, the clergy pass through a church space that grows in sacrality with every step they take.[28]

The thresholds that have to be to be surmounted are the church door and the step into the sacred precinct of the chancel.[29] Immediately on entering the church, one is already in a sanctuary since the demons cannot enter here; they must wait outside the door.[30] On the other hand, the power of the Lord and the spirits of the saints and the angels are present.[31] First, one enters the nave for the faithful (sometimes called the *Quadratum Populi*), which, seen from the entrance, is in turn divided into sections for the penitents, the catechumens, the rest of the people and finally for the widows, virgins, monks and aristocrats, although nothing much can be said for certain about the more precise distribution of the ecclesial estates. All the same, it is clear that the closer one comes to the area around the altar, the higher the social-ecclesial rank becomes. When the celebrant enters the chancel with his entourage, he is coming into the actual sanctuary, the Holy of Holies, which in principle only the clergy enter. This ideal sacred dynamic of the church interior has to be borne in mind as we now take a look at the sequence of images found in the various sections of this space.

26 WARLAND 1986, 131. DE BLAAUW 2008, 373 speaks of spatial hierarchy. Illuminating on the graduated divine presence in the Christian sacred space now BERGMEIER 2017, 239–246.

27 The northern Syrian churches constitute a special case.

28 In antiquity already, there is a spatial axial progression from the altar, which stands in front of the temple, to the temple, the cell and the statue standing at the end in the temple niche; cf. Min. Fel. 10,2 (CSEL 2, 14).

29 Maxim. Conf. myst. 8 f. (PG 91, 688D), 23 f. (697C–705C) describes the entrance: clergy and people enter the church simultaneously in the form of a procession: first the high priest, then the people; the people go into the nave, the priest goes up to the sanctuary, where he sits down on the cathedra. Cf. E. AYROULET, Mouvement, espace architectural, et temporalité liturgique dans la célébration de la sainte synaxe. Le regard théologique de Maxime le Confesseur dans la Mystagogie (unpublished lecture).

30 Prud. peristeph. 10,101–105 (CCL 126, 333). Gen 4:7: Demons lie in wait at the doors.

31 Orig. orat. 31,5 (GCS Orig. 2, 398 f.).

Fig. 100: St Paul Outside the Walls after a painting by Giovanni Paolo Panini, 1741, Private collection. Easily recognisable are the biblical images on the walls of the nave; SPIER 2007, 115 Fig. 83.

2. HISTORY OF THE PEOPLE OF GOD

The entry of the clergy from the main entrance through the centre of the church into the chancel is a solemn act in both Western and Byzantine liturgy. The dignified progress, during which the already-waiting congregation are graciously greeted, transforms the entire nave into a liturgical stage deserving its own decoration. Since the fourth or fifth century, there are known to have been cycles of pictures on the nave walls of basilicas showing scenes from the Old and New Testaments; for example in St Peter's, St Paul Outside the Walls (Fig. 100), *Santa Maria Maggiore* and probably also in the Lateran Basilica in Rome,[32] as well as in *Sant'Apollinare Nuovo* in Ravenna.[33] To be admired there were, for example, the experiences and deeds of Abraham, Isaac and Jacob, and Moses and

32 On Maria Maggiore see GEYER 2005–2006, WAETZOLDT 1964, 49 f. and BRANDENBURG 2013, 196 Fig. 125. On San Paolo see PROVERBIO 2016, WAETZOLDT 1964, 56–61 and BRANDENBURG

2013, 312 Fig. 7. On the Lateran see CLAUSSEN 2008, 177.

33 DEICHMANN 1995, Figs. 98–107.

Joshua and Jesus's healings of the sick and raisings from the dead. Such pictures were scarcely intended to be didactic in the sense of a poor man's Bible (*Biblia pauperum*) for those who could not read. Both their relatively small format and the considerable height at which they hang in themselves rule this out as the scenes as such can hardly be recognised. Nor is the purpose of such elaborate cycles merely to serve as decoration. Rather, they are meant to proclaim salvation in Jesus Christ and to reveal the Divine Logos at work in both the old and the new covenants.[34] So their message is: it is always the same Lord working wonderfully throughout the whole of salvation history. What can be said, though, is that they constitute a series of images and that this makes them, in a sense, processional images: you have to walk the full length of them if you want to view them. There is actually pictorial support for this interpretation in *Sant'Apollinare Nuovo*, where two extremely solemn processions of holy women and men move from west to east – in the direction of the altar – along almost the entire length of the nave below the biblical picture cycles (Fig. 101).

Thus, the procession of the clergy during the liturgical entrance and exit is meant to walk the full length of the rigid cycles of biblical images in the nave. It is, as it were, narrative-processional art in the sense that when, for example, the bishop and his entourage pass by the picture gallery in the nave, even without looking at it, this ritual takes on a higher meaning: the bishop takes with him the entire history of salvation from Adam and Eve through the story of the patriarchs and Moses down to the appearance of Jesus Christ – and makes himself its spokesman. This correlation is confirmed inasmuch as the main entrance of *Santa Sabina* in Rome possesses an elaborate wooden door depicting numerous Old and New Testament scenes.[35] There is, however, one curious image, the so-called acclamation scene, that is strikingly different. It does not depict a biblical motif, but instead possibly the election of Pope Celestine as bishop in the year 422 (Fig. 102).[36] The church was built under this pope and therefore was also consecrated by him. So if his election as bishop of Rome is depicted in the midst of the biblical cycle, then the pope himself becomes a part of salvation history. The same thing happens in the liturgy when Celestine passes through this church portal. It is possible that the church originally had another series of biblical images decorating the walls of the nave and corresponding to the entrance.[37] Whatever the case, as soon as the bishop passes through the main portal, he enters the whole history of God with his people as he processes in.

---

34 Inspiring Spieser 2012, 101 f. Cf. Deichmann 1974, 156 f.

35 Jeremias 1980. For further wooden church doors decorated with biblical images see de Maria 2002, 1689 f. The church in Tyre possessed a central "royal gate"; Euseb. hist. eccl. 10,4,65 (SC 55, 102).

36 Jeremias 1980, 96 also speaks of an episcopal election.

37 Spieser 1991, 78 f.

Fig. 101: Processions of saints on the left and right lateral walls of the nave of *Sant'Apollinare Nuovo* in Ravenna; above them, (biblical) figures; above these, a cycle of new Testament scenes, 6th century; Dresken-Weiland 2016, 120f.

Fig. 102: Wooden panel of the main door of the church of *Santa Sabina* in Rome showing the election of Pope Celestine as bishop in 422 (?), 5th century. What is to be seen in the background would in that case not be two church towers but rather the papal Lateran Palace; below are applauding aristocrats and clerics; PIAC Archivio Fotografico.

In any event, the bishop is at the head of the people of God. Nowhere is this more evident than in the dedicatory inscription on the apex of the mosaic on the triumphal arch of *Santa Maria Maggiore* in Rome; it reads *XYSTVS EPISCOPVS PLEBI DEI*, which means "Bishop Sixtus (donates this church) to the people of God (in Rome)". Every local church represents a part of the people of God, whose history goes back to the time of the old covenant. The bishop at its head benefits from God's mighty acts (*magnalia Dei*) in the Bible and is at the same time their herald, since he himself possesses the miraculous power of Christ the eternal Logos. In his panegyric at the dedication of the church in Tyre (314 – 321), Eusebius of Caesarea († 339) attributes to the bishop the same power to raise the dead as that possessed by Christ.[38] The miraculous power of bishops becomes a topos, and not only in hagiography. In Old St Peter's, the correlated images of the Old and New Testaments signal that the apostle Peter, as a second Moses, leads his people to salvation.[39] Extended to the present, this means that, as Peter's successor, every incumbent bishop of Rome also leads God's people to salvation.

The scene is already set for the biblical miracle galleries on the nave walls of the basilicas in Eusebius's above-mentioned panegyric. For he says of the Liturgy of the Word that God's mighty acts of old towards his people Israel are read out and heard during worship. But when they are read aloud, they are merely apprehended with the ears as far-off events. Now, however, through the splendour of the new church, the assembled congregation *see* with their own eyes the credibility of what has been handed down from ancient times: what they have heard in the holy scriptures as something past, they now see as something present (Ps 48:9).[40] What Eusebius is referring to here is not just the church community that has, so to speak, been restored by God after the persecutions, but rather the concrete church building in which his listeners can physically see God's wondrous deeds.[41] This seeing invites the faithful to offer liturgical praise to the mighty God who works such wonders.[42] The same goes for Christ, who not only performed miracles in the past, but whose surpassing power can now be seen in the treasures and votive offerings of the Church.[43] The votive offerings undoubtedly also include the artistic accoutrements.

For Eusebius, then, seeing both architecture and sacred art is nothing less than a proof of reality that makes the past true in the present. Based on this premise, it is logical to include artistic images of Old and New Testament miracles. In fact, as already noted, scenes from the Old and New Testaments are depicted on the nave walls of many later cathedral churches. There are two reasons for this. First, the nave is the location of the readings and the accompanying psalm chants, hymns and canticles.[44] What is related in the readings is portrayed in the same place in pictures, namely in the nave.[45] Secondly, based on Eusebian theology, the narrative images contain the catechetical-apologetic statement that the same God who back then worked the miracles seen in the images celebrates victories in his miracles right here and now and is therefore worthy of all praise. So the images encourage us not only to accept what we have heard as a distant message, but also to celebrate it as a visible present.

---

38 Euseb. hist. eccl. 10,4,12 (SC 55, 84);10,4,36 (93); 10,4,54 (98 f.).
39 BRANDENBURG 2013, 102.
40 Euseb. hist. eccl. 10,4,6 (SC 55, 82).
41 Ibid. 10,4,7 (SC 55, 82 f.). Up to 10,4,21 (88) Eusebius is concerned with visible church-building.
42 Ibid. 10,4,9 (SC 55, 83 f.).
43 Ibid. 10,4,10–20 (SC 55, 84–87).

44 Ibid. 10,4,5 (SC 55, 82).
45 Although only two readings are customary in Rome, the first reading before the Gospel can be taken from either the Old or the New Testament (mainly Paul's epistles); P. JOUNEL, La Bible dans la Liturgie, in: Parole de Dieu et Liturgie (Paris 1958) 17–49, here 20.

3. HEAVENLY LITURGY

As Eusebius again says in his dedication panegyric, at the head of the nave or the space for the faithful, the bishop enters the chancel (presbytery) as the new priest-king Melchisedek, similar to the Son of God.[46] In so doing, he enters the sphere in which what is seemingly the past history of salvation enters its *hic et nunc*: here at the altar, God will work the new miracle of the Eucharist through the priest-bishop; he will bestow the true manna that comes down from heaven. This also explains why in the nave cycles of *Santa Maria Maggiore* in Rome and of *Sant'Apollinare in Classe* the priest-king Melchisedek (below Fig. 118) and the Last Supper (below Fig. 130) are positioned at the head of the sequence of images close to the altar.

In the early Church, the chancel is separated from the rest of the church with barriers made of wood or marble, marking it off as a sacred space that not everyone is permitted to enter.[47] At the front, this area is often separated from the nave by a wall arch that rises up like a great gate, through which the faithful look into the chancel. In this way, this so-called triumphal arch in a sense frames the liturgical stage, the chancel. The faithful have it before their eyes throughout the entire liturgical celebration. The pictorial decoration on the triumphal arch or behind it on the front wall of the apse is not chosen at random. Motifs from the Apocalypse of John are preferred, namely the description of the heavenly liturgy (Fig. 103; below Figs. 120, 121). The seer of Patmos describes in vivid, moving images the – actually invisible – liturgy of the world to come, the contemplation of which arouses in him the most sublime feelings (Rv 4–7).[48] Some impressions of the heavenly cult that have become important for iconography are set forth here:

> And I saw in heaven a throne, with one seated on the throne! And the one seated there looks like jasper and cornelian […]. Around the throne are twenty-four thrones, and seated on the thrones are twenty-four elders, dressed in white robes, with golden crowns on their heads […] and in front of the throne burn seven flaming torches […]. Around the throne, and on each side of the throne, are four living creatures, full of eyes in front and behind […]. And the four living creatures, each of them with six wings, are full of eyes all around and inside. Day and night without ceasing they sing, 'Holy, holy, holy, the Lord God the Almighty' […]. […] the twenty-four elders fall before the one who is seated on

---

46 Euseb. hist. eccl. 10,4,23 (SC 55, 88). Christ as Melchisedek see Cypr. ep. 63,4 (CSEL 3,2, 703 f.).

47 The purpose of the *cancelli* is to prevent the masses from entering the chancel; Euseb. hist. eccl. 10,4,44 (SC 55, 96).

48 PRIGENT 2000 (deals mostly with the apses); NILGEN 2000; *id.* 1999. On the triumphal arch mosaic in *San Pietro* see LIVERANI 2006a; KOLLWITZ 1947–1948, 104 f.

Fig. 103: Triumphal arch mosaic in St Paul Outside the Walls restored after the 1823 fire according to the old design, originally 5th century; photo: Armin Bergmeier.

the throne and worship the one who lives for ever and ever; they cast their crowns before the throne, singing, 'You are worthy, our Lord and God, to receive glory and honour and power' […]. […] Then I saw in the right hand of the one seated on the throne a scroll written on the inside and on the back, sealed with seven seals […]. […] He [the Lamb] went and took the scroll from the right hand of the one who was seated on the throne. […] After this I looked, and there was a great multitude that no one could count, from every nation, from all tribes and peoples and languages, standing before the throne and before the Lamb, robed in white, with palm branches in their hands. They cried out in a loud voice, saying, 'Salvation belongs to our God who is seated on the throne, and to the Lamb!' […] Another angel with a golden censer came and stood at the altar; he was given a great quantity of incense to offer with the prayers of all the saints on the golden *altar* that is before the throne.

Those mosaic artists who translated such texts into images and, as it were, framed the chancel with them were convinced that the liturgy celebrated by the bishop is not simply either a community gathering or a mere moral edification for sinful people, but is instead a gripping participation in the cosmic liturgy that carries them along with it. In the bishop's Mass, the *sacrum*, which can only be seen and portrayed through grace, is truly touched. Among the elements of this image-rich celestial liturgy are the apocalyptic throne, the winged creatures, the sacrificial lamb, the sealed scroll, the seven candlesticks and the twenty-four elders prostrating themselves in a gesture of homage and adoration. Such motifs are perhaps first portrayed in churches in Spain,[49] then in Ravenna in *San Giovanni Evangelista* (c. 424–434),[50] then in Rome in St Paul Outside the Walls (c. 440–461) (Fig. 103)[51] and *Santi Cosma e Damiano* (sixth century) (below Fig. 121),[52] and further in Naples in *Santa Restituta*.[53]

It would undoubtedly be problematic to interpret the individual pictorial elements on the triumphal arches and front walls of apses based on patristic commentaries on the Book of Revelation (Apocalypse of John).[54] For this would fragment the large-scale mosaics into a jigsaw puzzle of exegetical opinions. The interpretative framework for the apocalyptic pictorial world is not learned theological commentaries, but rather the liturgies celebrated in the church itself. It is important to note that the Apocalypse of John does not draw on earthly models, but looks into heaven in a visionary way: "After this I looked, and there in heaven a door stood open! And the first voice, which I had heard speaking to me like a trumpet, said, 'Come up here, and I will show you what must take place after this'" (Rv 4:1). The Apocalypse is regarded as that scripture which makes manifest, i.e. shows, the heavenly mysteries.[55] The less visionary faithful are offered the opportunity, through both the church's images and the liturgy that goes with them, to, as it were, stretch their heads into the heavens and catch a glimpse of the unseen.

Concrete examples: the seven torches of the Apocalypse (Rv 4:5) are found on the triumphal arch, but seven torches are also carried during the liturgical entrance of the Roman bishop and during the Liturgy of the Word in the nave; during the actual celebration of the Eucharist they stand behind the altar.[56] Later, in the Tridentine Rite, these lamps flank the cross on the high altar, signalling that the cross has eschatological significance as the focal point of the liturgy: it is the sign that will appear at the Second Coming of Christ (Mt 24:30). The twenty-four elders on the triumphal arch carrying wreaths with covered hands (Rv 4:10) are echoed in the liturgical hand-covering when,

---

49 Iʜᴍ 1992, 136.

50 Ibid. 170.

51 Wᴀʀʟᴀɴᴅ, 1986, 41–46; Wɪʟᴘᴇʀᴛ / Sᴄʜᴜᴍᴀᴄʜᴇʀ 1976, 87 f. The front wall of the apse in the Lateran Basilica also quotes motifs from the liturgy in the Apocalypse of John (ibid. 28).

52 Iʜᴍ 1992, 137 f. The mosaics on the triumphal arch may have to be dated to as late as 700. Nɪʟɢᴇɴ 2000, Fig. 4 (Apse and triumphal arch).

53 Iʜᴍ 1992, 136. The apocalyptic motifs can also ex-tend over both triumphal arch and apse, e.g. in *San Giovanni Evangelista* in Ravenna.

54 So in Wɪssᴋɪʀᴄʜᴇɴ 1990, 114–119.

55 Caes. Arel. expos. in Apoc. 1 (PL 35, 2417). On John's vision of the throne in the pictorial decoration on the front walls and triumphal arches see Bᴇʀɢᴍᴇɪᴇʀ 2017, 170–179.

56 OR I,54 (Aɴᴅʀɪᴇᴜ 1948, 85); I,66 (ibid. 90). Bᴇʀɢ-ᴍᴇɪᴇʀ 2017, 157 f.

Fig. 104: Front wall and apse calotte of *Sant'Apollinare* in Classe. Central jewelled Cross against a starry circle of sky; below it, the title saint Bishop Apollinaris in prayer posture. To the left and right on the front wall are the archangels Michael and Gabriel, 6th century; photo: Armin Bergmeier.

for example, clergy take hold of the Evangelary with the fabric of their vestments.[57] The white colour of the vestments of the saints (cf. Rv 7:9) can also bring to mind the white vestments of the liturgical assistants.[58] Connections are evident here without liturgy simply being a re-enacting of Sacred Scripture.

The beholder in the nave sees the heavenly liturgy depicted on the triumphal arch or on the front wall of the apse. These frame the earthly worship going on at the altar and signal that here, in this zone, is holy ground![59] This is particularly clear in the case of the angels Michael and Gabriel, who, wearing magnificent courtly robes stand guard, as it were, to the right and left of the apse of *Sant'Apollinare in Classe*. They hold a standard in their right hand on which the word "holy" (ΑΓΙΟC) is written three times (Fig. 104).[60] In the chancel, both the visible and the invisible take place in equal measure. Corresponding to the actions of the priest is the diaconal ministry of the angels. A world opens up of saints and heavenly beings, who participate in their own way in the earthly liturgy (above chapter IV, 4e). The beholder of the images in this way becomes a viewer of a double liturgy: what he hears in the liturgy, he sees. The duplication of sensual perception increases the excitement and consolidates active participation in the liturgical action.

In his study on the visualisation and experience of the presence of the divine in late antiquity, Armin Bergmeier rightly rejects an overly narrow Eucharistic-sacramental interpretation of the early Christian pictorial decoration of the chancel, beginning with the triumphal arch and ending with the apse image.[61] It would be wrong to read an incarnational interpretation of the Eucharistic transubstantiation into these pictures. In general, one should not apply too much theology (dogmatics) to early Christian art. Nevertheless, a mystagogical-liturgical-pragmatic interpretation of church decoration in the way outlined above certainly is justified, indeed practically compelling. The connection between the wall paintings and divine worship and the cult of Christ is in a quite fundamental sense nothing less than essential: the images in the chancel are meant to evoke the heavenly liturgy in the presence of God. It is first and foremost a matter of the real presence of the invisible God in the image. Hence the pictorial decoration is essentially theophanic in nature, which in turn accords with

57 The Gospel Book is carried on the planeta: OR I,30f. (Andrieu 1948, 77); I,64 (89), likewise the skyphos (OR I,70 [91]) and the paten (OR I,91f. [97]).

58 Cf. Braun 1907, 754–760; Hermann 1969, 421 f.; S. Ristow, Kleidung I (Mode u. Tracht), in: RACh 20 (2004) 1263–1274, here 1269–1271. White-clad (Old Testament) priests are shown in the Ashburnham Pentateuch.

59 On the sacrality of the apse see de Blaauw 2008, 365.

60 Warland 2002a, 56. Cf. Michael 2005, 119–128, 189–212; Rizzardi 2011, 160f. (with illustrations).

61 Bergmeier 2017, 156–166.

62 Only the deacons did not have places to sit in the early Church.

the claim of the liturgy. For services of divine worship do not first and foremost serve man, but really and truly serve *God*, an awesome service since it always expects of the servants that they will experience a theophany in the here and now, will encounter God face to face in his holiness.

4. AUTHORITY OF THE APOSTLES

After entering the sacred precinct of the chancel, the bishop takes his seat on his throne (*cathedra, sedes*) at the apex of the apse, i.e. at the far end of the church interior. The assisting priests sit on the benches to his right and left.[62] Like the entrance, sitting down on the chair of office is a liturgical act. This later becomes particularly clear in the Roman liturgy in that when the bishop has arrived at his seat, i.e. before he sits down, the "Glory to God in the Highest" (*Gloria*) is sung. This hymn is regarded as a kind of papal throne hymn and is therefore reserved for the bishop's Mass[63] and audience ceremonial.[64]

In the dedication panegyric that we have already referred to several times, Eusebius reveals the truly outstanding importance of the throne. According to this, behind the altar in Tyre there are lofty thrones and seats "arranged in proper order"[65] (cf. above Figs. 47, 49). They appear to stand in a semicircle on a podium with steps leading up to it and can be easily seen by the faithful. Eusebius compares the bishop's cathedra and the clergy seats to Christ in the midst of the college of apostles.[66] He is thinking of the Pentecost event, when the disciples receive the Holy Spirit while seated (Acts 2:2).[67] Eusebius says that the bishop, in whom Christ dwells in his fulness, is enthroned on the highest chair. The lower levels are occupied by the subordinate clergy, who have a proportional share in the miraculous power of Christ and the Holy Spirit.[68] So the seating arrangement is not randomly chosen, but rather makes visible the hierarchical structure of the

63 OR I,53 (ANDRIEU 1948, 84).

64 Significantly, the *Gloria* is written on the front wall of the apse of Leo III's triclinium in the Lateran. C. STIEGEMANN / M. WEMHOFF (eds.), Kunst und Kultur der Karolingerzeit 2 (Mainz 1999) 603 Fig. 3.

65 Euseb. hist. eccl. 10,4,44 (SC 55, 95 f.). Official seat behind (not at!) an official table, possibly as an apse image, see WEITZMANN 1975, Fig. 6 (Christ before Pilate in the Codex Rossanensis).

66 Germanus of Constantinople still sees it thus: the bishop's bema is the throne on which Christ presides in the midst of the apostles. MATHEWS 1971, 150 f.

67 Eusebius does not relate the priests' seats to the Last Supper, which was thought of as a reclining meal (Mt 26:20). This means that the altar is also not conceived of as the table at a reclining meal. Cf. HEID 2014b, 355 f.

68 Euseb. hist. eccl. 10,4,66 f. (SC 55, 102). For Paulinus bearing the whole Christ in him see also ibid. 10,4,26 (89).

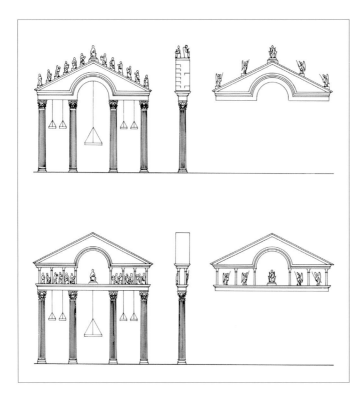

Fig. 105: Reconstruction of the *fastigium* of the Constantinian Lateran Basilica with the statues on it, 4th century; DE BLAAUW 1994, Fig. 3.

clergy.[69] The prominent seats of the "overseers" signal simultaneously official power and liturgical competence.

In saying that with his new church building in Tyre the local bishop, Paulinus, has reproduced an exact likeness of the heavenly sanctuary,[70] Eusebius is suggesting that a corresponding seating arrangement exists in heaven. In fact, this idea is translated into art in at least two Roman churches. In the Constantinian Lateran Basilica (early fourth century), at a certain distance in front of the altar, there was a monumental architectonic structure of columns, the so-called *fastigium*, a sort of triumphal gateway into the chancel, the remains of which could, despite all the looting and destruction, still be seen for several centuries (above Fig. 16).[71] At the top of this column structure there stand large silver statues, namely the seated figures of Christ and the twelve apostles on the

69 Thus already Past. Herm. 9,7–10,4 (SC 53², 100–102).

70 Euseb. hist. eccl. 10,4,25 (SC 55, 89).

71 LP 34,9f. (DUCHESNE 1886, 172). GEERTMAN 2001–2002. This could possibly have been an ornamental roof (*baldachino*) over the altar sup-

ported by four columns. CLAUSSEN 2008, 184 does not, however, intend to equate the *fastigium* with a ciborium. In fact, LP 87,3 (DUCHESNE 1886, 383) refers to an altar ciborium using different terminology as *super altare* [...] *coopertorium*.

side facing the nave[72] (Fig. 105). Thus the faithful can see the bishop and clergy sitting below in the apse and Christ and the apostles enthroned above in the form of statues. They are bound to relate the two to one another, which was certainly intended.[73] For the pope sees himself as the vicar of Christ, while the Roman presbyterate identifies itself with the college of apostles. Its members act as representatives of the apostles in the local church, the Sancta Ecclesia Romana.[74]

It is interesting that, immediately after interpreting the priests' seats as relating to the college of apostles, Eusebius says that Christ himself, as the High Priest, receives the offerings at the earthly altar with bright eye and extended hand and bears them to God in heaven.[75] It is now striking that on the *fastigium* of the Lateran Basilica the apostles carry wreaths of pure gold, doubtlessly in order to offer them, as it were, to Christ. Thus the group of figures representing the college of apostles affords a liturgical interpretation as well as an imperial one. The crowns or *aurum coronarium* of the apostles can be related to the liturgy of the Offertory: as the martyr apostles in heaven present Christ with their victory wreaths, so the concelebrants and the faithful present the bishop with their gifts and votive offerings for the altar.

One last observation regarding the *fastigium*: on its rear side there was also a group of figures, but this time they are comprised of a seated statue of Christ flanked by angels. The fact that it has two display sides makes it obvious that the *fastigium* had a liturgical function. The intention was for the bishop to still be able to see Christ even when standing at his throne.[76] This, of course, goes especially for the liturgical moments of prayer when the bishop looks up to heaven. He was not meant to look into empty space. Since the Lateran Basilica has its entrance at the east end, the bishop stands facing the nave when he prays, thus looking at the enthroned Christ.[77] It is worth noting that in his description of the priests' seats in the Cathedral of Tyre, Eusebius compares the clergy not only with the apostles but also with the angels.[78]

Something similar can be said about the church of *Santa Pudenziana* in Rome (early fifth century) (Fig. 106).[79] Here, too, the twelve apostles play a prominent role, albeit not

---

72 J. ENGEMANN, Fastigium, in: P. C. FINNEY (ed.), The Eerdmans Encyclopedia of Early Christian Art and Archaeology 1 (Grand Rapids 2017) 529 f. thinks it impossible for the adornment with figures to date from earlier than the sixth century. Such an adornment with figures makes it reasonable to doubt whether, as Tilmann Buddensieg suggests (cf. WARLAND 1986, 31–41), the apse mosaic shows the group of apostles as well.

73 DE BLAAUW 2001a, 144; BRENK 2010, 52.

74 Correspondingly, the seven Roman deacons see themselves as successors to the seven deacons of the apostles (Ac 6:3).

75 Euseb. hist. eccl. 10,4,68 (SC 55, 102 f.).

76 DOIG 2009, 26; BRENK 2010, 51 f.

77 From the sixth or seventh century on, there seems to have been a change of direction, so that the celebrant, at least at the altar, now looks towards the apse (see above p. 346 and below p. 387).

78 Euseb. hist. eccl. 10,4,67 (SC 55, 102).

79 WILPERT / SCHUMACHER 1976, Taf. 20–22; IHM 1992, 130–132. Further apse images with the college of apostles: dated c. 460–470, the lost apse mosaic of *Sant'Agata de' Goti* with Christ enthroned on the cosmos among the twelve standing apostles (IHM 1992, 153 f., Plate IV,1). Dated to the fourth

Fig. 106: Apse mosaic of *Santa Pudenziana* in Rome, beginning of the 5th century: Christ among the Twelve Apostles against the background of the Heavenly Jerusalem; photo: Armin Bergmeier.

as a group of sculptures in front of the altar, but rather in the apse mosaic behind the altar. In the centre of this, Christ sits enthroned with an imperial habitus (gold robe, nimbus, jewelled throne); around him sit the college of apostles, attired like Roman senators. Here, too, the martyrs' crowns or the *aurum coronarium* are present, being presented to Christ not by the apostles themselves, but rather by two female symbolic figures standing behind the apostles Peter and Paul.[80] Such pictorial decoration is only conceivable if the church was already a papal basilica at that time, i.e. a station church in which the bishop celebrated together with the presbyters on certain days of the year. It was for these solemn Masses that the pictorial decoration was created. The position of the mosaic makes its relationship to the bishop's throne and the bench for the presbyters obvious since both must have been located underneath the mosaic (Fig. 107).[81] The

or fifth century, the college of apostles in an apse of *Sant'Aquilino* in Milan (ibid. 158 f., Plate I,1). Kollwitz 1936, 54 considers the college of apostles to be an early Christian apse motif.

80 Here, too, these wreaths being handed to Christ are the victory wreaths of the apostles since they are

held directly over the heads of Peter and Paul by the two women depicted in the form of aristocratic matrons.

81 However, in contrast to Mathews's drawing, one should not imagine a closed apse but rather a set of columns in front of which the cathedra and pres-

Fig. 107: Reconstruction of the original interior of the church of *Santa Pudenziana* in Rome, beginning of the 5th century; T. F. MATHEWS, The Clash of Gods (Princeton ²1999) 93 Fig. 70.

scene with the apostles in *Santa Pudenziana* brings out more clearly an aspect of the mosaic that might also have been present in the *fastigium* mentioned above: the book and the appearance of speaking depict Christ as a teacher.[82] Matching this is the bishop's cathedra below it, which is also a teaching chair: seated on it, the bishop listens to the readings from the Gospels in order then to interpret them authoritatively in the name of Christ through his preaching.

5. THE LORD OF HEAVEN

It is an almost standard feature for the church interior to end in an apse at the front. This then brings us to by far the most important zone for images in early Christian churches, spreading as it does across the curved wall behind the altar.[83] It is possible to assume that the apses were adorned with images – mostly in mosaic technique – from as early

byters' benches are arranged. The disposition of the presbyters' bench and the college of apostles can be confirmed by the lost oratory at *Monte della Giustizia* (end of the fourth century?); IHM 1992, 16 Fig. 1. See also HEYDEN 2014, 302–304.

82 Cf. Euseb. hist. eccl. 10,4,25 (SC 55, 89). Cf. KOLLWITZ 1936.
83 Euseb. vit. Const. 3,38 (SC 559, 400) calls the apse the most important place in the basilica of the Church of the Holy Sepulchre.

as the fourth century on.[84] The large-scale image in the upper vault (calotte) embraces from behind both the priests' seats and the altar, shedding, as it were, its radiance over the whole chancel.[85]

Seen from the perspective of the people, the church interior flows towards the apse image. In moments of liturgical prayer, intercessions and litanies, the congregation do not look straight ahead; for example, towards the altar or the cathedra, but instead lift up their hands and eyes in the same way as the celebrant and his assistants do. They do not look at each other as they pray, but all orientate themselves upwards towards God. This makes the apse calotte the most important element of the pictorial decoration at the most intimate, most sacred moment of liturgical activity, namely during prayer.[86] It is obvious from the outset that such images – unlike those in the catacombs or on small objects – bear a pragmatic relationship to the liturgy and are, as it were, liturgically interactive. The connection between apse and prayer also leads to a specific choice of images.

For all the diversity of the apse images, it is striking that, to the extent they have survived or are known, they almost never depict biblical events, for example a healing miracle or the crucifixion of Christ. This distinguishes them fundamentally from the biblical or apocalyptic scenes portrayed in the nave or on the triumphal arch or the front wall of the apse. Instead, for the apse calotte the choice always falls on free pictorial creations, images representing the idea of a timeless, heavenly reality, namely the powerful presence of the God-Logos in past, present and future, in heaven and on earth.[87] These are actually theophanies: the apse image is the unveiling par excellence of the invisible God. The eternal Christ appears as the divine Lord of his congregation.[88] So the focus is always on Christ. In most cases, he is portrayed in the centre as the heavenly Ruler of the World.[89] Christ is the visually dominant main figure of

84 IHM 1992; BRENK 2010; ANDALORO / ROMANO 2002, 73–102; V. BLANC-BIJON / J.-M. SPIESER, Mosaik, in: RACh 25 (2013) 1–58, here 41 f. These publications do not ask about the liturgical value of the apse images. On Brenk see the review by N.-G. WEISS, in: RQ 107 (2012) 130–135. Brenk denies that the apse images have any liturgical significance – an untenable position. KOLLWITZ 1936, 59 assumes San Pietro to have already had an apse mosaic in the late Constantinian period (motif the Traditio Legis).

85 Paulin. Nol. ep. 32,10 (FC 25,2, 770): *Absidem solo et parietibus marmoratam camera musivo inlusa clarificat.*

86 HEID 2006, 366–377; now also THUNØ 2015, 131 f. APOSTOLOS-CAPPADONA 2014 fails to notice this

central connection. HELLEMO 1989 interprets the apses correctly in relation to the liturgy, but misses the basic premise that the praying congregation look "towards heaven" and thus always upwards towards the apse. The call to the faithful to lift up their hearts (*Sursum corda*) in the opening dialogue of the Canon interprets spiritually what they automatically do with their eyes when praying. Cf. NILGEN 2000, 79.

87 ENGEMANN 1976.

88 SPIESER 1998, 65, with interesting comments on the origin of the Christian apse image.

89 Images of Christ in *Santa Pudenziana* (Rome), *Santi Cosma e Damiano* (Rome), *Sant'Andrea in Catabarbara* (Rome), *San Vitale* (Ravenna), *San Giovanni Evangelista* (Ravenna), *Sant'Agata*

Fig. 108: Chancel of *San Vitale* in Ravenna, 6th century, with largely modern reconstructions of the interior furnishings. The location of the altar is below the bottom edge of the picture; Angiolini Martinelli 1997a, 198 Fig. 376.

the apse which can ultimately be detached from the wider pictorial context. The apse images in *Santa Pudenziana* in Rome (above Fig. 106) and *San Vitale* in Ravenna (Fig. 108) are examples of this. The only historical depiction in this location is, significantly enough, that of the Transfiguration of Christ (Mk 9:2–10) in St Catherine's Monastery at Sinai.[90] Such a motif is possible by way of an exception because the Transfiguration, in which Christ appears to three apostles on the mountain in his divine glory, is itself quite plainly a theophany (Fig. 109).

The striking difference between the apse images and the rest of the pictorial decoration of the church interior has to do with their location and the strictly liturgical function that this gives them. They are not to be understood as decoration or illustration, but rather as a template for prayer and an image offering orientation. Christ faces the liturgist and the praying congregation as a God with a face and wishing to be worshipped. Christ becomes and is present in his image and thus very really present.[91]

Images are by their very nature a visualisation, and the very fact of there being a representation of Christ in his heavenly glory in the apse carries a theophanic message: God is no longer hidden, but shows his face.[92] The effect of this is likely to be that everyone looking at the apse from whatever angle has the impression that Christ is looking at him or her. So it is possible to state here what Hans Belting says of Middle Byzantine apse decoration: "The frontality guarantees direct cultic contact."[93]

When, from the fifth century on at the latest, Christ is graphically portrayed in a large-format apsidal image, this may indeed be an artistic innovation, but it is not one in substance. For it merely translates into a physical image what has long been a certainty in the mind's eye of the faithful: the God of heaven is personally present and shows his face (above chapter IV, 4d). Those who pray there not only want to speak to him, but also hope to see him. So if a heavenly Cross or Christ in heavenly glory glows out from the apse mosaic, then it is because this is exactly what those looking upwards as they pray, like the prophets of old before them, are actually expecting: that heaven will open and

---

Maggiore (Ravenna), *San Michele in Africisco* (Ravenna), *Hosios David* (Thessaloniki), St. Katharina (Sinai) and elsewhere (IHM 1992). Petrus Chrysologus might have been looking at an apsidal image of Christ when he preached that Christ, the Saviour of the World, who shines in heaven like the sun, is, as it were, the heavenly ornament of the altar (serm. 149,1 [CCL 24B, 927 f.]). In the nave, Christ can be portrayed more than once depending on which New Testament scene he appears in, but in the apse he appears only once, large and central.

90 HEID 2003.

91 This is very clear, partly due to the inscriptions, in the case of the apse mosaic of *Hosios David* in Thessaloniki; IHM 1992, 182–184; C. STEPHAN-KAISSIS, Zwei byzantinische Damen und das Gottesbild des Klosters Latomou in Thessaloniki. Neues zum Mosaik von Hosios David und der Ikone von Poganovo, in: M. PANAGIOTIDE-KESISOGLU (ed.), E gynaika sto Byzantio (Athen 2012) 87–105.

92 In detail BERGMEIER 2017. WARLAND 2002b, 155: "The revealing theophany image of the apses anticipates the vision of the Exalted Christ."

93 H. BELTING, Bild und Kult (Munich⁵ 2000) 197.

Fig. 109: Apse mosaic of the basilica of St Catherine's Monastery on Sinai, Transfiguration of Christ, 6th century; Coche de la Ferté 1982, Fig. 43.

Christ will appear.[94] Peter, while praying on the roof, sees heaven open (Acts 10:9–11), as does Stephen immediately before his stoning (Acts 7:55 f.).[95] Irenaeus of Sirmium "lifts up his eyes to heaven, right up to God," and then prays with uplifted hands that the heavens may open so that the angels might receive his soul.[96] In a Christian-Jewish dispute, the Jewish interlocutor demands that Christ, if he lives in heaven, should descend so that he can be seen. Thereupon Gregentius kneels down three times, then stands still, raises his hands to heaven and prays. Then thunder is heard in the east, the gates of heaven open and a cloud of light stretches down from heaven like a flat road upon which Christ descends to them from the gates of heaven.[97]

94 Hieron. ep. 18A,2,2 (CSEL 54², 76): *propheta oculos non levavit ad caelum, non ei sunt reserata caelestia, non apparuit dominus.*

95 Ps.-Cypr. dupl. mart. 14 (CSEL 3,3, 229): *stabat placido angelicoque vultu et ad Domini exemplum orat pro lapidantibus nec alibi habet oculos quam in caelum. illic videre meruit, cuius praesidio superior erat persequentibus.*

96 Pass. Irenaei 4,7; 5,3 f. (BHL 4466).

97 Ps.-Gregent. disp. cum Herbano Iud. (PG 86,1, 773C–777A).

Of course, this only goes for churches with an east-end apse, and thus, for instance, always in Ravenna with its magnificent mosaics. In Rome, however, the situation is more differentiated. Here, especially in churches with their entrance to the east, it has to be envisaged that the celebrant will face the nave since he at least has to maintain the liturgically correct direction of prayer (east). The faithful, on the other hand, are of course permitted to look up towards the apse mosaic when they pray even though it lies to the west. The mosaic then becomes for them, as it were, the ideal east. Origen said that one should not go to any unnecessary trouble in order to face east.[98] It could, for example, be difficult to pray towards the east in an enclosed space; hence some people preferred to look up to heaven through the door or window instead of facing east to pray. Admittedly, Origen himself wants the practice of facing east to be observed even if this means praying facing a wall.[99] Augustine, who likes to speak of Christ as the "inner teacher", also relativises prayer posture: the only important thing, he says, is that one prays inwardly in the presence of the Lord – then it is of no consequence whether one prays standing, sitting, lying down or facing east.[100]

Impressive apse images are, in fact, known in churches with their entrance at the east end, for example in *Santa Pudenziana* (above Fig. 106). Although not for the celebrant, who faces east when praying, these apse images nevertheless serve as a focus of attention for the faithful.[101] Everything in this image is aligned towards the central figure of Christ, with the apostles depicted on both sides as sitting lower and lower the further they are from Christ. From the enthroned Christ, his divine power embodied in his sweeping gesture, all the lines radiate outwards in the shape of a star, most clearly upwards towards the colossal Cross. Since time immemorial, the Cross has served as a focal point for prayer.[102] Thus, in this mosaic, too, the towering jewelled Cross that shines forth upon Golgotha in the heavenly Jerusalem has a clear liturgical function: it marks the ideal east for the faithful, who are at that moment actually looking towards the west.[103]

In the Church of St Peter in Rome, which likewise has its entrance in the east, it is possible that in Constantinian times already there was an apse mosaic above the memoria area containing the tomb of St Peter (above Fig. 63).[104] It shows the princes of

98 Orig. orat. 31,1 (GCS Orig. 2, 395).

99 Orig. orat. 32 (GCS Orig. 2, 400 f.). Cyrill. Hier. cat. 2,15 (PG 33, 420C): one can even pray to heaven through walls.

100 Aug. div. quaest. ad Simpl. 2,4,4 (CCL 44, 86 f.).

101 A clue to the fact that the faithful see the apse as the (ideal) east might be provided by the occasional presence in the apse mosaic of a phoenix sitting on a palm, as legend has it that it worships the rising sun (Const. Apost. 5,7,15 [SC 329, 230]; cf. WALLRAFF 2001, 170–172). It figures in the

apse images of *San Pietro* (probably, see IHM 1992, 36), SS Cosma e Damiano and the oratory of Felicitas, which lie to the west or vaguely to the east.

102 PETERSON 1959, 31–33. Cf. LANG 2003, 48 f.

103 The heavenly Jerusalem lies in the east: Euseb. mart. Pal. 11,11 (GCS Euseb. 2,2, 938); Vit. Epicteti 18 (PL 73, 405B–406A) (BHL 2568); Agathangel. vit. Greg. Ill. 81 f. (ActaSS Sept. 8, 357AC) (BHG 712); Pass. Pamphili 10 (ActaSS Juni 1, 66DE) (BHG 1406).

the apostles Peter and Paul receiving the scroll containing the Law from Christ, who is standing on the Mount of Paradise; what this depicts is nothing other than the New Testament (*Legisdatio / Traditio Legis*). Here, too, this is not an historical image since the New Testament contains nothing about Christ ever handing over a scroll containing the Law to Peter and Paul. What the mosaic offers is rather a free depiction of an epiphany of Christ: the eternal Ruler of the World is portrayed with an imperial gesture which itself indicates his interactive, real presence to the faithful. He speaks with the full authority of the lawgiver, as if directing his words into the church. This is the promise to the faithful that, through the mediation of the apostles, they will be permitted to enter paradise if they obey the New Law.

Even the Gregorian remodelling of the area surrounding the memoria in St Peter's, with the raised area around the altar and the row of columns in front of it, did not disrupt the pictorial unity of the presbytery and the apse mosaic. The positioning of columns in front of the apse podium (above Fig. 73), to which a second row was added under Gregory III (731–741), severely obstructed the view into the chancel (Fig. 110). This is consistent with the early medieval papal liturgy, in which the pope is at quite a distance from the people and performs the cult almost exclusively with the clergy. The sacred event takes place as if on a stage, but it is largely hidden behind columns and curtains. For the faithful, however, this makes the apse image towering over it all even more defining and necessary as a focus of attention and point of orientation for prayer.

The Lateran Basilica, which likewise has its entrance at the east end, represents a somewhat different case. The bust of Christ floating on clouds has already been mentioned (Fig. 111; above Fig. 95).[105] It is the visualisation of what those who are praying see in their mind's eye: the face of God. This demonstrates both the epiphanic nature of the apse image and the almost tangible connection with prayer posture. The people always looked towards the image of Christ and are hardly likely to have turned to face east, i.e. towards the entrance doors, to pray. Only the pope as the main liturgist is obliged to face east, so he stands behind the altar looking towards the people. But – and this is astonishing – from about the sixth or seventh century on, when the image of Christ in the apse mosaic came to be regarded as miraculous, the pope started to celebrate at the altar likewise looking west, towards the apse. There was probably a jewelled Cross below the image of Christ with the apostles on the right and left. If such a triumphal Cross was meant as an allusion to the vision of the Emperor Constantine before the Battle of the Milvian Bridge and his victory over Maxentius, the persecutor of the Christians, then it reinforces the epiphanic message of the mosaic. At the same time, the Cross, like the image of Christ, serves as a point of orientation for prayer.

---

104 LIVERANI 2005, 77 f.; BRANDENBURG 2013, 102.   105 See above p. 348.

Fig. 110: Reconstructed chancel of Old St Peter's after the addition of a further row of columns in front of the altar area under Pope Gregory III (731–741).

Another east-end apse image that belongs in this context is that of *Santo Stefano Rotondo* in Rome, which not only has a central triumphal Cross, but also the face of Christ in a *clipeus* above it (above Fig. 85). In the apse mosaic of the likewise east-facing church of *Sant'Apollinare in Classe*, the triumphal Cross shines out majestically from the starry firmament (above Figs. 58 and 104). Here, too, the "face of God" is not omitted – if you look closely, you will discover the bust of Christ in a central position. It is, admittedly, very small, but that is because it is fitted into the centre of the Cross.[106]

Other apse designs show literally in the image itself that they are intended as orientation images for prayer since they depict people looking straight at the viewer.[107] Usually this is Mary or another saint. But although they seem to be looking at the viewer, this is an illusion. They have their hands raised: so they are praying, which is precisely why Christ or the Cross is portrayed above them. For in reality they are not praying in the

106 Dresken-Weiland 2016, 264.   107 Thunø 2015, 131.

Fig. 111: Detail of the apse mosaic of the Lateran Basilica, restored in 1884 according to the medieval design; W. OAKESHOTT, The Mosaics of Rome from the Third to the Fourteenth Centuries (London 1967) 71, Plate VIII.

direction of the congregation, but rather vertically upwards to Christ, thus in a sense acting as prayer leaders for the faithful, who are also looking up towards the image of Christ. The best example of this is once again provided by the church of *Sant'Apollinare in Classe*: beneath the firmament with its Cross rising up in the eastern apse stands the church's titular saint Apollinaris, bishop and martyr, who is stretching his hands upwards in prayer and directing his prayer vertically towards the celestial Cross. Thus he is praying in exactly the same way as the congregation gathered in the church.[108] The situation is similar in the oratory of St Venantius by the Lateran Baptistery (Fig. 112), which has an east-end apse, and in the no-longer-extant oratory of St Felicitas in the Baths of Titus, likewise east-facing with its image niche (Fig. 113): there the praying Mary or Felicitas faces upwards looking towards the bust of Christ floating on clouds.[109]

---

108 MICHAEL 2005, 55–59 without pointing to the vertical direction of prayer but with further examples of orans images.

109 Similarly, in the Ascension scene of the Rabbula Codex, Mary looks straight at the viewer as she prays with uplifted hands upwards to Christ; WEITZMANN 1979, 455 Fig. 68. In this tradition are also the Byzantine churches that show Mary praying below the Pantokrator, e.g. the apse mosaics in the cathedral at Cefalù (I. HUTTER, Früh-

Fig. 112: Chapel of St Venantius at the Lateran Baptistery with 7th-century mosaics; the Baroque altar conceals Mary, who is standing in prayer posture below the bust of Christ that floats on clouds above her; photo: Armin Bergmeier.

The vertical direction of prayer is made emphatically clear in the Parousia wood panel of *Santa Sabina* (above Fig. 59) and in an apse mosaic of the Monastery of Apollo at Bawit (Fig. 114):[110] in both cases Mary stands in the centre as a woman praying with uplifted hands, literally throwing her head back so as to look upwards to Christ.[111]

A particularly important detail of the apse images, namely the illusion of heaven, reinforces the connection between prayer and image. For when texts speak of prayer, they stereotypically say that the worshippers raise their hands "to heaven" and look up "to heaven". Some of these phrases may be literary set phrases, but even that still reflects a genuine feeling. Somehow the person praying wants to come into contact with heaven – especially inside the church.[112] This inner vision of heaven also influences the artists who

christliche Kunst – byzantinische Kunst [Stuttgart 1968] 150), or which show Maria Orans in the apse and Christus Pantokrator in the apex of the cupola. This makes it immediately clear that the direction of prayer for the congregation is ultimately not the apse but rather heaven. See aslo J. Pascher, Der Christus-Pantokrator in der Liturgie, in: Jahresbericht der Görres-Gesellschaft 1939 (Cologne 1940) 42–57. On the Felicitas Oratory see also Heid 2015b, 240.

110 Ihm 1992, Plate XXIV,1.
111 Even if at Bawit Mary is raising her hands to heaven more in astonishment than in prayer, just as the apostles surrounding Mary are very moved, it is nevertheless clear that the people in the lower register are turning to face upwards towards Christ.
112 See above n. 4.

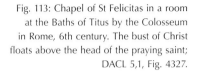

Fig. 113: Chapel of St Felicitas in a room at the Baths of Titus by the Colosseum in Rome, 6th century. The bust of Christ floats above the head of the praying saint; DACL 5,1, Fig. 4327.

make heaven visible in the apse mosaic. There are six possible ways of doing this, some of which have already been indicated:

1. A layer of clouds: *Santa Pudenziana*, Rome (above Fig. 106); *Santa Costanza*, Rome; the basilica in Fundi; the *Basilica Nova* in Cimitile; *Santi Cosma e Damiano*, Rome (below Fig. 121); *San Teodoro*, Rome; *San Venanzio*, Rome (above Fig. 112); *San Vitale*, Ravenna (above Fig. 108); *Sant'Apollinare in Classe* (above Fig. 104); the *Basilica Eufrasiana*, Parenzo

2. A segment of heaven at the top edge of the apse vault: Lateran Basilica, Rome (at least in the medieval mosaic, the bust of Christ floats in the segment of cloud) (above Fig. 111); *San Pietro*, Rome (?) (above Fig. 63); *Sant'Agnese fuori le mura*, Rome; *Santo Stefano Rotondo*, Rome (above Fig. 85)[113]

3. A circle of starry heavens in the centre of the apse: *Sant'Apollinare in Classe* (above Fig. 104); the *Basilica Nova* in Cimitile; the apse hall of the Basilica of the Holy Cross, Resafa-Sergiupolis (below Fig. 117)[114]

---

113 On the apse decorations mentioned see IHM 1992.

114 IHM 1992, 76–80, 244f. The likelihood of such crosses being very widespread in the apse calottes of Byzantine-Syrian churches is supported by the portrayals of the council churches in the Church of the Nativity in Bethlehem (ibid. 77). See also R. GARRUCCI, *Storia della Arte Cristiana nei primi otto secoli della Chiesa* 3 (Prato 1876) 129–138.

Fig. 114: Niche fresco of Chapel XLVI of the Monastery of Apollo in Bawît (Egypt): Mary and the apostles, with Christ enthroned above them; A. Iacobini, Visioni dipinte. Immagini della contemplazione negli affreschi di Bawit (Rome 2000) 55 Fig. 27.

Fig. 115: Apse mosaic in *Sant'Andrea in Catabarbara* in Rome, around 470–480, showing Christ on Mount Zion, surrounded by apostles; watercolour in Windsor Royal Library 9172; Osborne / Claridge 1998, 81 Fig. 178.

4. A circular opening (*oculus*) in the calotte of the apse:[115] Basilica of the Holy Cross, Resafa-Sergiupolis (below Fig. 116); church mosaic *ECCLESIA MATER*, Thabraca[116] (above Fig. 27). Even in the Middle Ages, the apse of some churches and chapels has a central window, if not in the calotte, then in the apse wall.

5. A blue background: the Sylvester chapel in *San Martino ai Monti*, Rome.[117]

6. A gold background, which is to be understood as a pure, sunny sky ("cielo d'oro"):[118] *San Michele in Africisco* and *San Vitale* (above Fig. 108), Ravenna; St Catherine's Monastery church, Sinai (above Fig. 109);[119] *Sant'Andrea in Catabarbara*, Rome (Fig. 115);[120] possibly the original apse decoration of the Lateran Basilica[121]

115 This recalls the antique temples which allow the sky to be seen through an open roof so that people can turn towards it when praying
116 Possibly it is not an *oculus* that is depicted but rather a circle, but then presumably a circle of heaven with the Cross.
117 Osborne / Claridge 1998, 81 Fig. 178.
118 Bodonyi 1932. See above n. 22.
119 Heid 2003.
120 Osborne / Claridge 1998, 81 Fig. 178.
121 Brandenburg 2013, 26. The medieval mosaic in the Lateran Basilica still combines a large gold background with a segment of heaven lying above it. See further Ihm 1992, 78. For an apse completely lined in blue and with a golden Cross see ibid. 77.

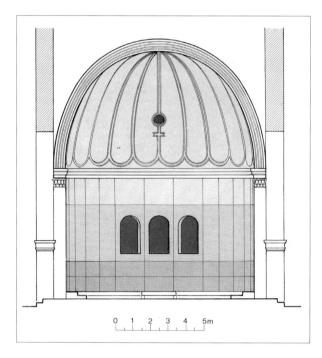

Fig. 116: Apse of the Church of the Holy Cross in Resafa-Sergiupolis (Syria) with a small Cross and above it a hole in the wall; T. Ulbert, Resafa II (Mainz 1986) 37 Fig. 20.

Fig. 117: Apse fresco in the south-eastern extension of the Church of the Holy Cross in Resafa-Sergiupolis (Syria) showing a Cross in a starry sky; T. Ulbert, Resafa II (Mainz 1986) 87 Fig. 52.

So heaven is always present in the Christian church interior, whether in reality through a window or fictively through an image. People who are praying should turn and look upwards towards heaven. The Church of the Holy Cross in Resafa-Sergiupolis in eastern Syria, which has its apse to the east, is particularly revealing. In the first phase of its construction (559), the calotte of the apse had an *oculus* with a Cross below it (Fig. 116). In addition, the basilica had large windows in the apse wall, which is precisely why the *oculus* seems to have had the specific function of being an opening to the sky. When the faithful look up to the Cross and thus to the vault of the apse, they are meant to see the real sky. Ambrose's words have already been quoted saying that the Christian should be like a house of God with the windows open to the east so that the eyes of the Lord can look in.[122] The *oculus* with the Cross in Resafa is to be understood in exactly this sense. The church hall that was added a little later to the southeast provides convincing proof of this since it has a fake *oculus* in the calotte of the apse (end of the sixth century). Here a painted jewelled Cross in the starry sky simulates a circular opening in the wall[123]

---

122 Ambr. exp. in Ps. 6,19 (CSEL 62², 118).
123 Cf. Ihm 1992, 245. A rayed Cross against a starry sky similar to that in the southeast apse hall is to be found in the Hagia Sophia in Thessaloniki

and in Mar Gabriel (Kartmin); H. Torp, Mosaik-kene i St. Georg-Rotunden i Thessaloniki (Oslo 1963) 38. For the apse hall in Resafa the jewelled Cross was probably chosen because Justinian and

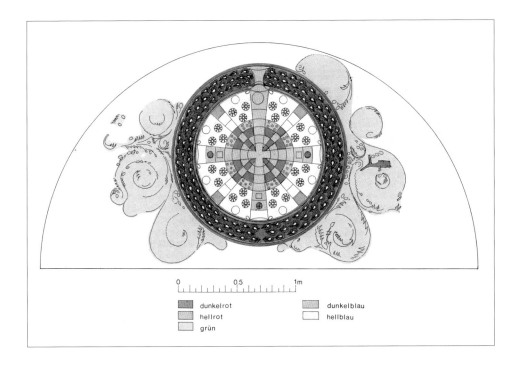

0   0,5   1m

☐ dunkelrot   ☐ dunkelblau
☐ hellrot   ☐ hellblau
☐ grün

(Fig. 117). Those praying are thus led to believe that they are looking through a circular window at the celestial Cross shining forth outside.

These reflections do not exhaust the liturgical function of the apse mosaic in early Christian churches. What remains to be considered is its special relationship to the altar. Within the topography of the sanctity of the Christian house of prayer, the altar is the point at which it culminates, where the God and Father of all graciously hears the prayers of his faithful people.[124] Bishop Eusebius of Caesarea, in his panegyric at the dedication of the church in Tyre, puts it as follows:

> But the great and august and unique *altar*, what else could this be than the pure holy of holies of the soul of the common priest of all [= Bishop Paulinus of Tyre]? Standing at the right of him, Jesus himself, the great High Priest of the universe, the Only Begotten of God, receives with bright eye and extended hand the sweet incense from all, and the bloodless and immaterial sacrifices offered in their prayers, and bears them to the heav-

Theodora had donated one to the church; it had come into the possession of the Persians but was restored to the church by Chosroes II (HEID 2002, 248 f.). A rayed jewelled Cross see also C. PRA-

SCHNIKER, Forschungen in Ephesos 4,2 (Baden 1937) 214 Fig. 128.

124   CZOCK 2012, 34.

enly Father and God of the universe. And he himself first worships him, and alone gives to the Father the reverence which is his due, beseeching him also to continue always kind and propitious to us all.[125]

The most important place of priestly prayer is the altar. The priest stands, if the church's east-facing orientation permits, in front of the altar and looks at the apse image. It has already been pointed out that this arrangement of altar and image is not new in the history of religion.[126] There may be a formal link between the image of Christ and the raised, colossal statues of gods in temple niches.[127] The Christian apse images, as it were, replace them functionally.

In a remarkable passage, Cyprian of Carthage († 258) expresses his fear that a church might be, as it were, converted into a temple: the clergy leave their seats in (the apse of) the church and take with them the altar of the Lord that stands in front of it, whereupon pagan altars are erected instead and the corresponding statues of gods are placed on the priests' bench.[128] But Cyprian does not say here that the pagans reversed the direction of prayer in order to set themselves apart from the Christians. Rather, all they did was exchange the altar and set up their own images of gods so that these were what they looked at during the sacrifice. Where do the Christians look? Cyprian says elsewhere that when praying, even when celebrating the divine sacrifice together with the priest, one must call to mind that "we stand in God's presence".[129] So the Christian altar is orientated towards this presence, and everyone, both priest and faithful, look towards it together. Cyprian probably assumes that for the sacrifice the people face in the direction of the apse even though in his time there was not yet an image of Christ or a Cross to be seen there.

---

125 Euseb. hist. eccl. 10,4,68 (SC 55, 102 f.); DE BLAAUW 2008, 288. CZOCK 2012, 34 at least concedes: "It follows from Eusebius's description of the altar that his interpretation, despite its massive spiritualisation of its subjects, may not completely rule out a localisable sanctity" (cf. ibid. 37).
126 See above p. 235.
127 DECKERS 1992; SPIESER 2012, 99 f.; BERING 2012, 154 f.; THUNØ 2015, 134 f. Images of gods in niches see DOIG 2009, 22; BRENK 2010, 31–50.

128 DÖLGER 1930, 161 f. For a reverse case see Marcellin. et Faustin. lib. prec. 20,76 (CCL 69, 378): *ipsum altare Dei de dominico sublatum in templo sub pedibus idoli posuerunt.*
129 Cypr. or. dom. 4 (CSEL 3,1, 268): *cogitemus nos sub conspectu Dei stare. placendum est divinis oculis […]. et quando in unum cum fratribus convenimus et sacrificia divina cum Dei sacerdote celebramus […].*

6. NOT WITH EMPTY HANDS

When the priest and the faithful look upwards towards the image of Christ in the apse, this accords with the dynamic of the sacrifice. The gifts of the altar are offered to the divine recipient. The priest may simultaneously elevate the gifts.[130] This is also suggested by mosaics depicting Old Testament sacrifices found in St Paul Outside the Walls (above Fig. 40), *Santa Maria Maggiore* (Fig. 118) and *San Vitale* (above Fig. 42). For there Cain, Abel and Melchisedek hold up their offerings at the altar. Through their motifs (e.g. altar shape, round loaves, chalice) and location (close to the altar), the images are directly related to the Eucharistic sacrifice taking place in the church itself. The priest must never stand at the altar with empty hands; his office demands this.

The altar as an offertory table laden – at least rhetorically – with an overabundance of gifts has already been discussed (above chapter IV, 3). Ancient representations of sacrifices also have the motif of an abundance of gifts when they show fruits being brought to the altar from all sides and animals being led to up it (Fig. 119). Behind this lies the primordial religious act of offering gifts to God. Already in the Old Testament it says: "No one shall appear before me empty-handed" (Ex 23:15; Dt 16:16).[131] The significance of the gifts is obvious: in the heavenly audience, God needs to be put in a good mood. According to an anonymous text, Christ himself brought gifts to his Father in heaven before he took his seat at his right hand.[132] Thus the gifts at mass are part of a concerted action by clergy and people made in the hope of receiving something in return.[133]

Irenaeus of Lyons (c. 200) already relates this scriptural reference (Ex 23:15; Dt 16:16) to the gift offered to the Heavenly King at the Eucharist, adding:

> The oblation (*oblatio*) of the Church [...] is accounted with God a pure sacrifice (*sacrificium*), and is acceptable to Him, [...] because he who offers is himself glorified in what he does offer, if his donation (*munus*) be accepted. For by the donation (*munus*) both

---

130 The elevation of the gifts at the Offertory – already suggested by the sacrificial term ἀναφέρειν (cf. Heb 7:27; 13:15; Jas 2:12; 1 Pt 2:5) – was common early on in the liturgy of Asia Minor and Palestine; JUNGMANN 1960, 366–372. Cf. Greg. Naz. or. 13,3 (PG 35, 856A). See further above p. 233 n. 400.

131 Cf. W. SCHWER, Armenpflege, in: RACh 1 (1950) 689–698, here 695. BAUER 2009 does not go into any detail regarding gifts in the religious-liturgical context; nor does SOTINEL 2010a. See also the issue titled "Die Gabe: Geschenke, Opfer und Tribute" in: Archäologie Weltweit 3,2 (2015).

132 Anon. de eccl. 85–88 (CSEL 16, 625).

133 Sacr. Veron. 91 (MOHLBERG 1994): *Altaribus tuis, domine, munera terrena gratanter offerimus, ut caelestia consequamur.* Cf. 253, 494, 575; Sacr. Greg. 560, 620 (DESHUSSES 1971).

Fig. 118: Scene in the nave mosaics of *Santa Maria Maggiore* in Rome showing the sacrifice of Melchisedek, who is offering bread and wine (Gen 14:18). Melchisedek is elevating the basket of bread; at his feet stands a cup. Above the scene floats the bust of Christ with a nimbus; WILPERT / SCHUMACHER 1976, Plate 28.

Fig. 119: Dionysian sarcophagus with a sacrifice scene: the pre-sacrifice inviting the god is already performed. The god shows himself and looks down graciously from out of the temple onto his altar. Approaching this from the left are a boy with a bread basket, a woman bearing a tray of fruit and a man slaughtering a ram; 3rd century AD; Vatican Museums; MATZ 1968, Plate 35.

honour and affection are shown forth towards the King [...] so that man, being accounted as grateful, by those things in which he has shown his gratitude, may receive that honour which flows from Him.[134]

Gifts thus give material form to gratitude. For its part, the gesture of thanksgiving has the desired result as it brings the giver acknowledgment from God. An ancient Roman prayer over the offerings runs: "Grant, we beseech Thee, O Lord, that we may serve freely with Thy gifts (*donis*), so that the donations (*munera*) we offer with the help of your saints may bring us salvation and honour."[135] In other words, a gift is a *captatio benevolentiae* that opens doors by disposing God to turn towards the supplicant.[136] When Totila was approaching Otricoli with his army, the bishop there had honorary gifts sent to him, possibly in order to appease the conqueror's anger with such donations (*munera*).[137] The code of honour requires that gifts must not be rejected. This accords with the ancient gift culture, which was cultivated especially at the royal court. One text from late antiquity says that if the king accepts the supplicants' gifts during an audience, this is a sign of grace,[138] i.e. that the king will hear the supplicants' requests. The giver thus hopes for an advantage, a favour, from the gift.[139]

In the offertory procession of the mass, the gifts of the faithful are carried to the altar, marking the beginning of the celebration of the sacrifice proper. There is always an offertory procession; it is an indispensable element, no matter whether it is performed by the clergy alone or by the faithful as well. In the Roman, Gallic and Spanish liturgies, those making the offerings as well as the apostles and martyrs (of the day) are named at the *offertorium*,[140] and here too the gifts repeatedly have a special role to play. In one Gallican offertory prayer, after the reading out of the names of those offering their gifts, it says:

134 Iren. adv. haer. 4,18,1 (SC 100,2, 596). Ex 23,15 also applied to the offerings at the Eucharist in Didasc. syr. 9 (ACHELIS / FLEMMING 1904, 52) and Greg. Naz. or. 19,9 (PG 35, 1053A).

135 Sacr. Veron. 66 (MOHLBERG 1994): *Tribue, quaesumus, domine, donis tuis libera nos mente servire, ut intervenientibus sanctis tuis munera quae deferimus et medellam nobis operentur et gloriam.*

136 Sacr. Greg. 626 (DESHUSSES 1971): *Munera tibi domine dicata sanctifica, et intercedente beato stephano martyre tuo atque pontifice, per eadem nos placatus intende.* Cf. 764.

137 Greg. I dial. 3,12,2 (SC 260, 296).

138 SIEGERT 1980, 20.

139 Cf. Euseb. vit. Const. 4,7,3 (SC 559, 464).

140 Miss. Goth. 294 (MOHLBERG 1961): *Auditis nominibus offerentum, debita cum veneracione beatissimorum apostulorum et martyrum omniumque sanctorum commemoracione decursa, et offerentum et pausancium commemoremus nomina [...],* 365, 421, 427; Lib. Moz. 66 (FÉROTIN 1995): *Nominibus sanctorum martyrum offerentiumque fidelium [...] a ministris iam sacri ordinis recensitis [...],* 239, 248.

> Let us ask the Lord to accept their offerings (*oblationes*) together with the gifts (*dona*) of the saints whose memory we celebrate, so that they too may graciously remember us.[141]

So the martyrs are mentioned in the Offertory because the faithful in a sense join their heavenly offertory procession. Even more frequently, however, another aspect is formulated in the prayers, namely that through their intercession with God and through their merits the martyrs assist in the acceptance of the gifts of the faithful.[142] The martyrs ask God, as the Mozarabic liturgy puts it, to look upon, accept and receive the gifts and offerings placed on the altar on their feast day.[143] Their intercession is auspicious since on the feast of their crown of immortality[144] they also win God's favour with their own gifts, namely their merits.[145] Pope Damasus (366–384) already speaks of the altar (in the church of *San Lorenzo fuori le mura*), which, looking up to the merits of the martyr Lawrence, he heaped with gifts.[146] An old Roman offertory prayer for the feast of Pope St Clement and St Felicitas similarly says:

141 Miss. Goth. 534 (Mohlberg 1961): *Offerentum nominibus recensitis […] dominum dipraecimur, ut eorum oblacione<s> inter sanctorum dona suscipiat.*

142 Miss. Goth. 392 (Mohlberg 1961): *Accipe, quaesomus, domine, munera dignanter oblata et beati Sixti episcopi et martyris suffragantibus meritis ad nostrae salutis augmentum prouenire concide.* 421: *[…] omnipotentem dominum depraecemur, ut plebis suae ministrorumque uota suscipiens oblationis nostras […] in odorem bonae suauetatis accipiat. Unde supplecis simus, ut beatissimorum patriarcharum, prophetarum, apostolorum et martyrum omniumque sanctorum piis praecibus adiuuemur.* 434: *Adesto, domine […] intercessione beatissimi martyris tui […] et munera superinposita dignanter adsume.* Similarly 445, 449, 470, 501; Sacr. Veron. 28, 281, 309, 313, 511, 759 (Mohlberg 1994); Sacr. Greg. 43, 103, 109, 611, 646, 675, 737 (Deshusses 1971); Lib. Sacr. 838, 841 (Mohlberg / Baumstark 1927); Lib. Sacr. Gelas. 887, 962 (Mohlberg 1960). Sacr. Greg. 88 (Deshusses 1971): *Ecclesiae tuae quaesumus domine dona propitius intuere. Vota* siehe auch Miss. Goth. 84, 207, 339, 416 (Mohlberg 1961); Heid 2015b, 238 f.

143 Lib. Moz. 311 (Férotin 1995): *Suscipite, gloriosissimi Martyres sancti, offerentium nomina sancto altario recitata et eorum devotionem auribus divine pietatis ingerite, atque pro eisdem affectu intentissimo Trinitatis omnipotentiam implorate: ut nomina suorum coram altario recensita viventium inserat libro septem signaculis presignato, eorumque oblationem placida serenitate respiciens, ratam acceptamque suscipiat.* Sacr. Veron. 819 (Mohlberg 1994): *Sanctorum tuorum nobis, domine, pia non desit oratio, quae et munera nostra conciliet […].* Cf. 286, 1191, 1194; Sacr. Greg. 608 (Deshusses 1971): *Offerimus tibi domine quaesumus praeces et munera quae ut tuo sint digna conspectui, apostolorum tuorum praecibus adiuuemur.* Cf. 492, 563, 566, 569, 572, 626, 650, 694, 724, 740, 743. Lib. Sacr. 819 (Mohlberg / Baumstark 1927); Lib. Sacr. Gelas. 820, 862, 976, 983, 1004, 1089 (Mohlberg 1960).

144 The saint's feast day is the *solemnitas coronae*; Lib. Moz. 886 (Férotin 1995).

145 Sacr. Veron. 338 (Mohlberg 1994): *Suscipe […] munera plebis tuae, que pro beatorum apostolorum Petri et Pauli nataliciis obtulerunt, et eorum tibi placita meritis propitius esse concede.* Sacr. Greg. 584 (Deshusses 1971): *Hostias tibi domine sanctorum martyrum tuorum iohannis et pauli dicatas meritis benignus adsume.* Lib. Sacr. Gelas. 874 (Mohlberg 1960): *Sanctorum tuorum, domine, Nerei et Achillei tibi grata confessio et munera nostra conmendent […].*

146 Damas. epigr. 33 (Ferrua 1942, 167): *Haec Damasus cumulat supplex altaria donis, / martyris egregii suspiciens meritum.* Löx 2013, 158.

In the precious sufferings of Thy saints, O Lord, we praise Thy wonders and bring votive offerings (*munera votiva*). We pray that as Thou hast gratefully received their merits [= the precious sufferings], Thou wilt also receive the works of our service.[147]

The martyrs thus also function as heavenly intercessors with vows made to God. Martyrs' feasts are so popular as days for making vows that in Rome they are called votive days or votive feasts (Lat. *votum* = vow).[148] In fact, the *vota* of those offering the sacrifices are often mentioned in the offertory prayers (*super oblata, post nomina*) on the feasts of martyrs in Roman sacramentaries, both those originating from the Roman tradition and those in Mozarabic sacramentaries.[149] A prayer of blessing on the feast of St Felix expresses this particularly clearly: "All of you who, on account of the victories of the Maccabean martyrs and the martyr Felix, make your vows today to Eternal God, may you receive the reward of your vows."[150] The Mozarabic liturgy has its own mass formulary for those offering vows to the Lord on the feast day of a martyr.[151] Of course, martyrs are not merely helpers with the vows one makes to God; they also have vows made to

147 Sacr. Veron. 1210 (Mohlberg 1994). Similarly Lib. Sacr. Gelas. 842 (Mohlberg 1960). Sacr. Greg. 697 (Deshusses 1971): *Praesta quaesumus domine deus noster ut sicut in tuo conspectu mors est pretiosa sanctorum ita eorum merita, venerantium accepta tibi reddat oblatio.*

148 Sacr. Veron. 771. 791. 1236 (Mohlberg 1994): *natalicia votiva.*

149 Sacr. Veron. 100. 127. 365. 821. 1210 (Mohlberg 1994); vgl. 603. 750. 1170. Ibid. 265: *Adesto domine quaesumus aeclesiae tuae votis, adesto muneribus.* Ibid. 1191: *tuorum vota fidelium munera suppliciter oblata concilient.* 1261: *Exultantes domine cum muneribus ad altaria veneranda concurrimus: quia et omnium nobis hodie summa votorum et causa nostrae redemptionis exhorta est.* 1348 (Christmas): *pia vota solvere cupientem.* Lib. Moz. 57 (Férotin 1995) (Mass of St Saturninus): *Tu eius meritis et offerentium suscipe vota et omnes in commune pro tua miseratione letifica.* Ibid. 79 (Mass of St Clement): *sanctifica hec munera [...] per que et offerentium suscipias vota.* Ibid. 130 (Mass of St Eugenia): *Intuere propitius, Domine, offerentium vota.* Ibid. 202 (Mass of St Julian): *Tu pietate solita et offerentium suscipe vota.* Ibid. 230 (Mass of St Agnes): *Tu pius offerentium accipe vota.* Ibid. 247 (Mass

of St Vincent): *Alius ovans vota persolvit; alius plorans mestitudinis questus exponit. Tua sanctitas et vota suscipiat et tediosis succurrat.* Ibid. 257 (Mass of St Babylas): *offerentes tibi, Christe, sacrificium humiliati cordis, et vivorum vota offerimus, et sepultis requiem flagitamus.* Ibid. 1044 (Mass of the Saints): *Votorum nostrorum studia vincunt negotia meritorum.* Cf. ibid. 282 (Mass of St Dorothea): *abdita vulnerum curans, preces supplicantes iustificans ac vota nostra Salvatori nostro commendans.* Ibid. 920 (Mass of St Cyprian): *supplices postulemus ut populorum concurrentium suscipiat vota ac singulis quibusque propria desideriorum sperata distribuat; hodierno die votis adtollimus, sacrificiis honoramus.* Ibid. 939 (Mass of St Matthew): *dum eius meritis vota famulantium suscipis.* Ibid. 1296bis (Mass of St Felix): *et per illos votum nobis tribuas tolerandi adversa.* Miss. Goth. 84. 207. 339, 416, 421, 512 (Mohlberg 1961).

150 Lib. Moz. 1298 (Férotin 1995): *Omnes qui, ob triumphos Maccabeorum atque Felicis martirum, hodie eterno Deo vota persolvitis, votorum vestrorum premia capiatis.*

151 Férotin 1904, 319–322: *missa pluralis pro eis qui in natalicia martirum vota sua domino offerunt.*

them. This practice is extremely widespread, especially at the tombs of the martyrs,[152] so it cannot come as a surprise if the bishops prefer to cast God as the recipient of vows in the liturgical texts whereas the martyrs appear "merely" as their sponsors. This at the same time integrates the votive offerings made at the martyr's grave into the offertory procession of the liturgy.

Here, on the altar, is where all the gifts must come together because the saints in heaven, too, present their gifts here. They, too, do not approach God's throne with empty hands. All these gifts are for God in heaven and are offered for his honour and glorification.[153] This is why the Fathers attach such great importance to the gifts of the altar not merely being looked upon by God, but also being accepted, in fact borne up to heaven by the angels and brought to him (above chapter IV, 4e). The central task of the priest is to mediate all the gifts to God through prayers of thanksgiving (eucharists). The priest (through the deacon) receives the offerings from the people because he alone stands at the altar and offers up the gifts for the people.[154] Tertullian, following Mt 5:23, speaks of the faithful bringing their gift (*munus/oblatio*) to the altar,[155] which the priest then offers there.[156] Augustine of Hippo († 430) complains that the virgins captured by the Vandals can no longer bring their offerings to the altar and can no longer find a priest there to offer the gifts to God for them.[157] So laypeople cannot approach the altar themselves, but are dependent on a priest to offer their gift.[158] Only the latter performs the actual act of sacrifice, although the act of bringing their offering to the altar by the faithful is an integral part of the whole sacrificial act. The same practice obtains in the East.[159]

The central mediating function of the priest for the gifts of the people is grounded in his incomparable spiritual authority. The fact that the priest has the power to consecrate

152 Grisar 1901, 788–794; Lucius 1904, 288–297, 318 f.

153 Miss. Goth. 315 (Mohlberg 1961): *Exaudi nos, domine, sancte pater, omnipotens deus, et his oblacionibus praecibusque susceptis praesenciae tuae uirtutis intersere, ut quod singuli ad maiestatis tuae obtulerent honorem, cunctis proficiat ad salutem*. Similarly Miss. Franc. 143 (Mohlberg 1957); Sacr. Veron. 131, 353, 463 (Mohlberg 1994).

154 Didasc. syr. 9 (Achelis / Flemming 1904, 45): "For as it was not allowed for the stranger, that is to say for him who was not a Levite, to approach the Altar, nor to offer anything apart from the High Priest, thus do ye naught apart from the Bishop. [...] Present, therefore, your offerings to the Bishop, either ye yourselves, or by means of the Deacons."

155 Tert. pat. 12,3 (SC 310, 100): *Nemo convulsus animum in fratrem suum munus apud altare perficiet nisi prius reconciliando fratri reversus ad patientiam fuerit*.

156 Tert. exh. cast. 11,1 f. (CCL 2, 1031): [...] *Stabis ergo ad dominum cum tot uxoribus, quot in oratione commemores? et offeres pro duabus et commendabis illas duas per sacerdotem de monogamia ordinatum* [...].

157 Aug. ep. 111,8 (CSEL 34, 655).

158 Already in pagan antiquity, anyone wanting to offer a sacrifice to a particular god as a rule brings the oblation to the altar and is permitted to be present at the ceremony performed by the priest (Reisch 1894, 1686). It is also the same in Judaism (Mt 5:23).

159 Didasc. syr. 9 (Achelis / Flemming 1904, 45): see above n. 154.

bread and wine and thus make them an offering pleasing to God gives the faithful the certainty that their gifts will also find favour and acceptance with God. John Chrysostom testifies to the boundless confidence that the faithful have in priestly authority when he says that the priest performs the ministry of angels, as it were, bringing down the pillar of fire of the Holy Spirit from heaven upon the gifts.[160] Gregory the Great's thinking is no different when he asserts that the heavens above the altar only open at the word of the priest.[161]

Among the church art that has survived, no image exists, as one might expect, of an altar overflowing with gifts; rather, there is at best a depiction of bread and chalice.[162] It is always these same elements that are shown (above Figs. 42, 43, 91–94, below Figs. 137, 148) while the occasional and seasonal gifts are omitted. The real altar at the centre of the church is better than any image: here the gifts and offerings are to be seen that are brought in ever new acts of giving. And yet even church art cannot completely avoid the theme of the abundance of gifts. An excellent example is found in the church of *Santa Prassede* in Rome, whose medieval mosaic decoration draws on the style of older art (Fig. 120).[163] The triumphal arch and the front wall of the apse, including the apse calotte, depict the heavenly liturgy (Rv 4–7). Numerous characters from the world of the Bible and the saints populate the walls. What is striking about it is that almost none of them stands empty-handed: in the apse calotte, St Pudentiana and St Praxedis carry martyr's wreaths, Deacon Zeno carries a precious Gospel book, and the founding bishop Paschalis holds a model of the church. On the front wall of the apse, the twenty-four elders (twelve apostles and twelve prophets?[164]) carry wreaths. On the triumphal arch, the host of martyrs carry palms and wreaths; above them, the blessed and the apostles likewise carry wreaths. The wreaths or other objects are not so much attributes of the saints as gifts being presented to Christ.[165] This adds a dynamic to the images: all the representatives of this heavenly court are waiting to be allowed to present their gifts. Similar examples of veritable processions of martyrs and saints bearing gifts can be found in the Venantius Chapel of the Lateran Baptistery (above Fig. 112) and in the churches of Ravenna.[166] Particularly impressive is the procession of saints with wreaths and at the head the three Magi bearing gold, incense and myrrh on the

160 Joh. Chrys. sac. 3,4 (SC 272, 142–146).
161 Greg. I dial. 4,60,3 (SC 265, 202).
162 See above p. 212.
163 Wisskirchen 1990.
164 Cf. Nilgen 2000, 81.
165 Klauser 1950. Klauser thinks that models of churches might still be seen as gifts, whereas

scrolls or codices are attributes. Nevertheless, Gospel books also can be donated; LP 54,10 (Duchesne 1886, 271).
166 See also the processions of apostles in the two baptisteries in Ravenna. Klauser 1950; Bauer 2009, 36f.

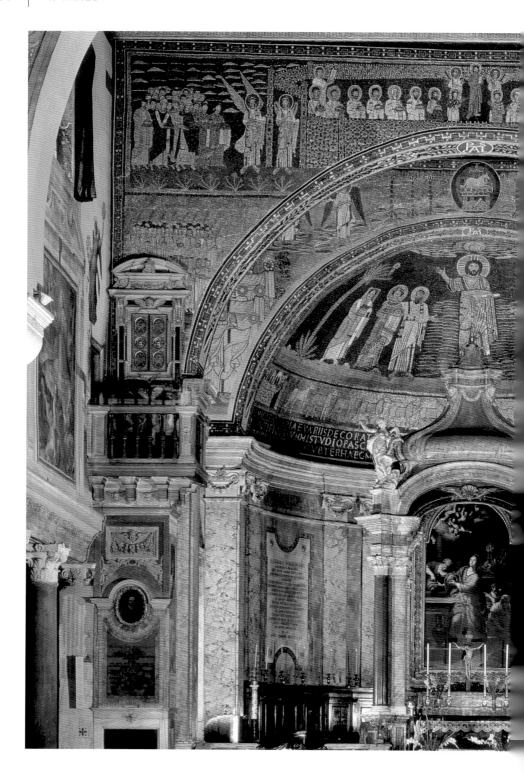

Fig. 120: Chancel of the church of
Santa Prassede in Rome, mosaics
9th century; photo: Franz Schlechter,
Deutsches Archäologisches Institut
Rom, D-DAI-ROM F90.1; photo:
Franz Schlechter.

Fig. 121: Apse mosaic of the church of *Santi Cosma e Damiano* in Rome, 6th century; photo: Armin Bergmeier.

nave walls of the basilica of *Sant'Apollinare Nuovo* (above Fig. 101).[167] This church was dedicated at the beginning of the sixth century to Christ the Redeemer. Naturally, the gifts are being offered to him – and to his mother Mary.

In every case the abundance of gifts expresses the maxim: "No one shall appear before me [God] empty-handed" (Ex 23:15; cf. Dt 16:16). The saints of heaven do not behave any differently from the faithful at worship: they bring their gifts to the (heavenly) altar. In the apse mosaic of the Roman church of *Santi Cosma e Damiano* by the *Forum Romanum*, its founder Pope Felix IV(526–530) is seen on the left side holding a model of the church that he wants to present to Christ (Fig. 121). An inscription explains his

---

167 The original pictorial decoration shows further persons against the silhouettes of the palace and the city wall. Since the church also functioned as a court church, these could be officials and senators, who probably form the beginning of the proces-sion. DRESKEN-WEILAND 2016, 181. However, the posture of the figures and their empty hands, which are still preserved in part, are more likely to indicate that these persons do not belong to the procession.

intention: the gift of the basilica is to guarantee him that heavenly life which is represented in the mosaic by the landscape of paradise.[168] For the people, on the other hand, the inscription says that the doctor-martyrs Cosmas and Damian, who are depicted on the mosaic and whose relics are contained in the altar holds, guarantee eternal salvation.[169] This guarantee is represented iconographically by the wreaths in their hands. For the martyrs are admitted to an audience with Christ. They are led to him by Peter and Paul because they bring with them gifts that the Ruler is disposed to accept. The wreaths represent the merits of the martyrs,[170] their victory in persecution. They bring these victories and triumphs to Christ, who has won the greatest victory of all time.[171] Christ will undoubtedly accept the gifts of his heroes. But if he accepts the gifts of the martyrs, he will also answer their petitions on behalf of the faithful.

It is against the background of this wider iconographic context that the altar is to be understood. Now it is possible to understand why, in addition to bread and wine, the altar is also laden with all kinds of gifts and votive offerings of the faithful during the Offertory. The liturgy of the early Church stages the oblation of the gifts in the expansive rite of the Offertory.[172] In the papal liturgy, it is primarily the Roman aristocracy who participate in this rite, solemnly bringing round loaves and little jugs of wine up to the chancel and presenting them to the pontiff.[173] The higher clergy, right up to the pope himself, also join in with their own offerings of bread and wine. It is not simply just the consecration that takes place at the altar, but before that also the oblation of the gifts and offerings. Hundreds of offertory prayers in all the Latin rites verbalise this very process, which is a genuine part of the act of sacrifice.

The practice of offering extraordinary gifts involves the highest representatives of Church and State. For example, the Byzantine emperors offered precious gifts at solemn acts of worship, as is seen in the mosaics in the church of *San Vitale* in Ravenna: Justinian († 565) and his wife Theodora are portrayed holding a precious paten and chalice (Figs. 122 and 123). It is no coincidence that these images are in the chancel since the imperial couple no doubt enjoyed the privilege of presenting their gifts there to the bishop, who then placed them on the altar. Emperor Valens already brings gifts to the "holy table" on the feast of the Epiphany in 371,[174] and similarly Theodosius († 395)

---

168 *Optulit hoc Dno Felix antistite dignum / Munus ut aetheria vivat in arce poli* (Ihm 1992, 138).

169 *Martyribus medicis populo spes certa salutis / Venit* (Ihm 1992, 138).

170 Petr. Chrys. serm. 135,1 (CCL 24B, 821); Miss. Goth. 25 (Mohlberg 1961); Sacr. Veron. 673 (Mohlberg 1994).

171 Petr. Chrys. serm. 79,3 (CCL 24A, 485): *apostoli diabolo superato et victis hostibus Christo et victoriam referunt et triumphum.* Victorin. Petav.

comm. in Apoc. 4,7 (CSEL 49, 58): [...] *coronas, proiecerunt eas sub pedibus eius: id est propter eminentem victoriam Christi omnes victorias sub pedibus eius.*

172 See in general Jungmann 1952b, 3–34; Sternberg 2006.

173 Lang 2022, 192–194.

174 Sozom. hist. eccl. 6,16,7 (SC 495, 320); Greg. Naz. or. 43,52 (PG 36, 564A).

Fig. 122: Mosaic with Emperor Justinian on the northern apse wall in *San Vitale* in Ravenna, 6th century; Angiolini Martinelli 1997a, 190 Fig. 358.

Fig. 123: Mosaic with Empress Theodora on the southern apse wall in *San Vitale* in Ravenna, 6th century; Angiolini Martinelli 1997a, 190 Fig. 357.

places gifts on the "holy table" inside the cancelli.[175] In the Byzantine tradition, 6 January must have been a very special gift-giving day, with the emperors in particular putting on a great show.[176] It is no coincidence that on the mosaic in question the Empress Theodora is wearing a magnificent robe with the image of the three Magi on its hem (Fig. 124). But the popes, too, bring gifts to their festive Masses. Whenever he celebrated at the main altar of St Peter's, Pope Eugene III (1145–1153) offered precious ornaments for this very altar: "And whenever he came to celebrate the festive Mass in this holy basilica of God and Blessed Peter, he did not come with empty hands," but offered a papal gift on the altar.[177]

SUMMARY

Seeing belongs to praying, and so it can come as no surprise that Christian pictorial art very soon captured the "house of prayer". From the very beginning, the pictorial decoration of early Christian churches had a function that was closely related to liturgy and prayer. Here the content of the prayers is less important than the prayer posture and the interior world of images that the person praying has internalized through practised traditions. In the course of the liturgy, from the solemn entrance to the final prayer, the church interior can be divided into different image zones, all of which differ in their relevance and expressiveness. The biblical picture cycles in the nave are to be understood differently from the pictorial decoration of the triumphal arch and the apse. The topography of sanctity grows progressively stronger and culminates in the chancel. Here, images take on a different quality as soon as they depart from the level of salvation history and typology and become genuine liturgical images with a direct function in relation to the act of prayer. When prayer is performed standing by

175 Theodoret. hist. eccl. 5,18,24 (SC 530, 412). Cf. RIGHETTI 1966, 310 f.; VAN DE PAVERD 1970, 469–471; DOIG 2009, 75.

176 Cf. Petr. Chrys. serm. 103,7 (CCL 24A, 644 f.); Agnell. Lib. Pont. Rav. 42 (FC 21,1, 216). J. DURAND, Byzantium and Beyond. Relics of the Infancy of Christ, in: C. HAHN / H. A. KLEIN (eds.), Saints and Sacred Matter (Washington 2015) 253–288, here 280 f.

177 Petr. Mall. descript. basil. vatic. 2,13 (ActaSS Juni 7, 36*B). Cf. JUNGMANN 1952b, 15. Agnell. Lib.

Pont. Rav. 52 (FC 21,1, 244–246): Bishop Peter of Ravenna (Petrus Chrysologus), who as a bishop had free access to the altar, lays a golden crater, a silver plate and two magnificent diadems on the altar of the cathedral of San Cassiano in Imola after he has touched them to the relics of the titular saint. Through both the contact and depositing them on the altar he undoubtedly wishes to dedicate the objects to this church and make this visible to all.

Fig. 124: Mosaic with Empress Theodora on the southern apse wall in *San Vitale* in Ravenna, with the Three Magi on the hem of her robe, 6th century; Coche de la Ferté 1982, Fig. 38

all the faithful, with arms raised and with their gaze lifted up "to heaven", this prayer is removed from all human interaction. It requires no human addressee, for it is directed solely to God, who dwells in heaven and yet is near, who is not merely seen in the apse image, but is also powerfully present and addressed in it.

VI. EPILOGUE

When Pope Julius II began to demolish the twelve-hundred-year-old St Peter's Basilica – known as Old St Peter's – in 1506 so as to make way for the massive new Renaissance cathedral, a world fell apart in the face of such sacrilege. Bramante even planned to excavate and move St Peter's tomb itself in order to rotate the axis of the new cathedral by 90 degrees (the new main entrance was to be on the *Campo Santo Teutonico* side).[1] The result is well known: all the historical papal tombs that once stood in the basilica were demolished, their altars and works of art destroyed and only the sarcophagi saved, which then disappeared into the inaccessible grottoes. The new cathedral was thus emptied of all memory, devoid of history, cold. If such a thing can be done to the sanctuary and to sacrosanct tombs, then the Church herself along with her doctrines and traditions can also be relocated wherever one pleases. That is what many fear. And with Luther, a redesigned Church does indeed come into being, even if, paradoxically enough, the reformer himself initially numbered among the conservatives who, in the face of the brutal innovations of the pope's Church, wanted to preserve and, if need be, restore the old, the early Church. But in his search for the old and the original, Luther himself got caught up in a dynamic that ends up with a different church, the Protestant Lutheran Church.

On the Catholic side, there was a surprising turn of events during the agonisingly long demolition of Old St Peter's. Now that it is already too late, people want to know everything about the old cathedral. During the demolition and excavation work, early Christian sarcophagi and other antiquities came to light. An interest in Christian archaeology was awakened,[2] and the Council of Trent (1545–1563) began to attach great importance to the "norm of the fathers" (*norma patrum*) and thus to the old traditions against which every reform must be measured. However, where the living tradition is broken off, there is a danger of making up one's own image of the early Church. Trent

---

1 H. Bredekamp, Sankt Peter in Rom und das Prinzip der produktiven Zerstörung (Berlin 2008) 28. C. Thoenes, Der Neubau, in: H. Brandenburg *et al.*, Der Petersdom in Rom (Petersberg 2015) 165–299, here 172: "The tomb of St Peter no longer appears as its given centre; Manetti does not mention it at all, Bramante will see it as a piece of furniture that can be moved at will within the new building." The remarks that follow were inspired by Martin Mosebach.

2 Cecalupo 2020, 26–28.

did not entirely escape this danger. This did not so much affect the liturgy itself, which the council largely renewed within the framework of the medieval books,[3] but there were drastic alterations to the chancels. Very many medieval church furnishings, such as the *Schola Cantorum* and the ambos, were destroyed (they are, however, still preserved in Rome in *San Clemente* [above Fig. 88] and *Santa Maria in Cosmedin* [above Fig. 89]). Alongside this, many historical altars were "renewed". This, so it was believed, would do justice not only to the early Church but also to modern needs.

History repeats itself, but differently. The Second Vatican Council (1962–1965) also issued the watchword of a renewal based on the "norm of the fathers" (*norma patrum*) (Constitution *Sacrosanctum Concilium*, no. 50). But now a new liturgy (Ordo Novus) is created at a "new altar" (Josef Andreas Jungmann SJ).[4] What is now called the "people's altar" (*Volksaltar*) is installed everywhere. Of course, this is not intended to be seen as an innovation but rather as a return to the early Church. The belief at the time was that scholars were in general agreement that the altar was originally a meal table and that the priest stood behind it. While the council was still in session, the Sacred Congregation of Rites already issued an instruction to the effect that the altar should henceforth be free-standing so that it could be used for celebrations *versus populum*.[5] In practice, this enforced the removal of tabernacles, retables and other altar superstructures. The new style was prescribed not just for new buildings but also for historical church interiors, which led to an iconoclasm and cultural loss of historic proportions, with altars that had existed for centuries being dismantled, mutilated, converted into flower shelves, robbed of their superstructures, moved forward or obscured by additional altars.[6] Such encroachments on the sacred structure of the church interiors alone gave the impression that the previous altars were wrong and that a wrong liturgy had been celebrated at them for centuries.

Today, the people's altar, along with the vernacular, is considered the hallmark of Vatican II's liturgical reform. Initially, it may have been thought in Rome that celebrating *versus populum* was not a serious encroachment since the pope had already celebrated the Tridentine liturgy at the supposed people's altar in St Peter's (below Fig. 145) as well as at the wall altar in the Sistine Chapel (below Fig. 144). It seemed, then, that all that was needed was to detach the altar from the wall and turn the liturgy round 180 degrees, and the rest could stay the same. In reality, however, the new altar became the motor and monument of a newly conceived liturgy in which everything is designed to portray the mass as a religious meal.

---

3   Heid 2014b, 352 f.
4   Jungmann 1967.
5   Instruction *Inter Oecumenici* (1964), No. 91. See Pacik 2012, 357–386; López-Arias 2021, 218–220.

6   Cf. Odenthal 2006, 10. Josef Andreas Jungmann had already warned of this, quoted in Nussbaum 1971, 150. Yet despite all the efforts being made to preserve historical monuments, the destruction of historical church furnishings and architecture still goes on today in every European country.

Once again, the risk of archaeologism becomes apparent: old practices are copied simply because they are thought to be original. In reality, however, when isolated from their historical context, they can take on a life of their own and set in motion something completely different from what was originally associated with them and intended. This happens when scientific artefacts are catapulted at high speed from the past into the present. The discussions regarding the round altar and the people's altar may serve as an example of this. The extensive introduction of the people's altar is the product of modern science and of pastoral concerns, but certainly not a return to the early practice of the Church.[7]

1. THE ROUND TABLE AS A MEAL SURROGATE

The invention of the people's altar is closely linked to the idea that the Eucharist is a meal and was initially celebrated as such. This led to the astonishing assertion that the round shape of the altar *mensa* was the genuine and correct one. The leading altar scholar Joseph Braun SJ noted that in the pre-Constantinian period, i.e. in the first three centuries, there probably were also round altars, "but even then the round table was scarcely the normal form of the altar, indeed not even the usual one. For such altars were not particularly practical for their purpose – or at least square ones were far more practical."[8] Today, on the other hand, the round altar is becoming increasingly popular in Catholic church architecture. There is more behind this than fashion, such as when long skirts are followed by short ones. What actually lies behind it is something more fundamental: the belief that it brings us closer to the original eucharistic meal. The idea of the round table is derived from the Last Supper or from the ancient meal in general, for which round tables were indeed also used. From this comes today's preference for a round table as a piece of eucharistic furniture because of its association with food, with being brothers and sisters, and with a meal of sinners, as well as with equality and democracy since the "round table" has at most an honorary chairperson[9] or a seat for a moderator, but no hierarchical seating arrangement opposite one another. Alongside this, theosophical-symbolic interpretations are mooted, such as the circle or hemisphere as symbols of eternity.

The discussion about the round altar goes back to a particular twentieth-century field of research that had its roots in Christian archaeology. Its main proponent in the 1960s was Otto Nussbaum, who drew on his teacher in Bonn Theodor Klauser.[10] Nussbaum reached out far afield in his altar studies: he began with the Last Supper, which Jesus celebrated together with the apostles as a reclining meal on cushions at a dining

7   GAMBER 1994, 7.
8   BRAUN 1924, 245.
9   ENGEMANN 1982.
10 NUSSBAUM 1961b.

table,[11] as was the general custom at a more formal meal. Although this was extremely uncomfortable, it was considered sophisticated. Usually there was a separate room, the so-called *triclinium*, reserved for these meals in a Roman home and equipped with suitable individual couches (κλιναί) (above Fig. 3) or with a semicircular communal sofa. On such a sofa, people lay crowded quite close together (Fig. 125). The side tables required for eating were usually low pieces of furniture with round or semicircular (sigma-shaped) tops,[12] which were often made of wood or – if they were permanent installations – of stone.[13] For this reason Franz Wieland already regarded the round three-legged (tripod) table and not a rectangular or cubic piece of furniture as the archetype of the Christian altar.[14]

Otto Nussbaum now claimed to know the precise details: for him, the original form of the Christian altar was not the round table, but the semicircular one, the so-called sigma table (D-shaped). For such a table, he says, generally went with the *stibadium*, the horseshoe-shaped couch with cushions (above Fig. 2, below Figs. 130, 131; differently Fig. 125). When the house churches grew too large for a reclining meal and the participants therefore had to stand during the gathering, the low sigma table was raised, which meant that the priest, too, now distributed the eucharistic food standing up. Nussbaum asserts further that the priest approached this sigma table from behind, on the round side.[15] Some people even think that the incorporation of an apse at the front in the building of early Christian churches is in fact a reflection of the original reclining meal: instead of the sigma couch (*stibadium*), the apse now contains the semicircular priests' bench (*synthronon*), in front of which again stands the eucharistic table (below Fig. 135).[16] It was not until the third or fourth century, so they claim, that a new theology of sacrifice led to the original (semi-) circular altar being replaced by a rectangular one, which then permanently shaped the image of the Christian sacrificial altar.

Nussbaum did not content himself with referring back to the Last Supper, but asserted further that the eucharistic reclining meal had continued to be practised for centuries. He felt justified in making this assumption since at that time the numerous depictions of reclining meals in the Roman catacombs and on sarcophagi dating from the third and fourth centuries were still interpreted as celebrations of the Eucharist, e.g. a famous painting in

---

11 Mt 26:20, Mk 14:18 and Lk 22:12, 14 all agree in speaking of a reclining meal that employed a table (Lk 22:21). The participants recline on the stibadium (Jn 13:23–25). The meal at Emmaus is also a reclining meal (Lk 24:30). Dölger 1943, 554 f., 578 f.; Nussbaum 1961b, 24.

12 Nussbaum 1961b, 22.

13 Kruse 1932, 941.

14 Wieland 1906, 140.

15 Nussbaum 1961b, 26 f.; *id.* 1965, 113 f.

16 Gamber 1968, 33–62, 86–94; cf. Riesner 2007, 169. Critical Nussbaum 1965, 384; Brakmann 1970, 85. The earliest Christian churches (Dura Europos, Meggido, Aquileia) do not display an apse. However, the apse is already part of the architectural language of the profane basilica without being in any way connected with the *stibadium*. Nussbaum *op. cit.* 378 nevertheless assumes that the clergy presided at the Eucharist at, as it were, an honorary *stibadium*; the only thing he denies is the connection between the *stibadium* and the apse.

Fig. 125: Funerary monument from Sentinum: twelve persons on three couches arranged in the form of a sigma meal, in the middle a tripod table, mid-1st century AD, Museo Nazionale di Ancona, inv. 123; photo: neg. 11998, with permission of the Ministero della Cultura-Soprintendenza Archeologia, Belle Arti e Paesaggio per le Province di Ancona e Pesaro e Urbino.

the so-called Greek Chapel of the Catacomb of Priscilla (above Fig. 7).[17] In such depictions, there is usually a dining table, often a tripod with a round tabletop or a sigma table standing in front of those participating in the meal. Although such tables were actually low,[18] they are occasionally given prominence in the painting by their size, which could indicate their special function.[19] These items of furniture are claimed to have in fact been eucharistic tables.[20] There are even today those who adhere to Joseph Wilpert's assertion that a tripod in the Catacomb of Callixtus (Sacrament Chapel A³) with a loaf of bread and a fish lying on it was an altar at which the consecration was symbolically performed (Fig. 126).[21]

17 WILPERT 1895, 81. Wilpert is already refuted by DÖLGER 1943, 503–527; cf. ZIMMERMANN 2010, 1128. But SOTIRA 2013, 18 continues to speak of a depiction of the Eucharist.

18 R. HURSCHMANN, Tisch, in: Der Neue Pauly 12,1 (2002) 620 f., here 620.

19 E.g. J. G. DECKERS et al., Die Katakombe "Santi Marcellino e Pietro." Repertorium der Malereien, Tafelband (Città del Vaticano / Münster 1987),

Plates 24b, 55a, 63, 64ab, Colour plates 12a, 55b, 57b.

20 WIELAND 1906, 127–145; id. 1909, 54; id. 1912, 43 f. (his citation – Hippolytus of Rome – is not authentic); BRAUN 1924a, 54; id. 1926, 164, 167; SAXER 1992, 554.

21 WILPERT 1903, 46; WIELAND 1906, 128; MAZZA 2005, 59; DRESKEN-WEILAND 2010, 197; SOTIRA 2013, 17 f. Cf. ZIMMERMANN 2010, 1125; id.,

Fig. 126: Portrayal of the gift of food (probably fish and bread) for the dead in the so-called Cubicle of the Sacraments A³ in the Catacombs of St Calixtus, 3ʳᵈ century; according to Wilpert, a "rappresentazione eucaristica"; photo: PCAS.

So it is thought to be possible to form an accurate idea of the early Christian eucharistic table based on numerous catacomb images. Catholic archaeologists before the Second Vatican Council did their utmost to prove, against the Protestants, that the sacrament of the Eucharist already existed in catacomb art in the second and third centuries. For this reason, they interpreted the Eucharist into the images of the reclining meal despite the fact that it is actually not depicted there at all. Instead, what really is to be seen there is loaves and fishes (Figs. 126 and 127; above Fig. 7), which do not go with the Eucharist at all, but rather with a funerary banquet (*refrigerium*).[22] Scholars are in the meantime no longer in any doubt that all the depictions of reclining meals in the catacombs and on sarcophagi are simply funerary meals such as were common among pagans and Christians alike.[23] There is not a single case in which the image itself can be used to plausibly justify a eucharistic interpretation. Nor is it tenable to assert that the Eucharist was already referred to early on as a banquet (*convivium*) and that the depictions of meals in the catacombs can therefore be interpreted eucharistically.[24]

Lebendige Bilder. Unbekannte Foto-Dokumente aus der Forschungsgeschichte der römischen Katakomben, in: Mitteilungen zur Christlichen Archäologie 19 (2013) 69–92, here 83 f.

22 ENGEMANN 1969, 1060; VOGEL 1976, 225–247; ThesCRA 2, 293. The equation of fish = Christ has only been made since the fourth century; DÖLGER 1922, 448–453.

23 KIRSCH / KLAUSER 1950, 335; ENGEMANN 1969, 1015–1017, 1060; ENGEMANN 1982, 248; JENSEN 2008, 123 f.; ZIMMERMANN 2010, 1127–1133; id., Zur Deutung spätantiker Mahlszenen. Totenmahl im Bild, in: G. DANEK / I. HELLERSCHMID (eds.), Rituale, identitätsstiftende Handlungskomplexe (Wien 2012) 171–186. On the antique funeral banquet see ThesCRA 2, 288–297.

24 DRESKEN-WEILAND 2010, 199.

Fig. 127: Funerary banquet with seven persons on a *stibadium*, two trays (*repositoria*) with fish and eight baskets of bread in the so-called Cubicle of the Sacraments A³ in the Catacombs of St Calixtus, 3ʳᵈ century; according to Wilpert, a "rappresentazione eucaristica"; photo: PCAS.

The *convivium dominicum* in Tertullian and Cyprian refers not to the celebration of the Eucharist, but rather to the community's evening *agape*.[25]

All this makes clear that there is absolutely no archaeological basis for maintaining that the Christian altar is derived from the profane dining table. However, in order nevertheless to rescue the idea of the early Christian round altar, Nussbaum relinquishes the meal images in the catacombs and on the sarcophagi, while continuing to assert that the early Christians practised the reclining eucharistic meal in the cemeteries in order to deliberately supplant the pagan practice of the feast of the dead. This idea is not new;[26] rather, it is in line with a particular research trend which sees the origin of the liturgy as lying more in the cult of the dead and the martyrs in suburban cemeteries than in the Sunday worship community in the city. Via this circuitous route, it is then said to be possible to trace the eucharistic table back to the round dining table of the funerary meal.[27] But is it really desirable to see the central act of Christian worship, the celebration of the Eucharist, as a product of the pagan cult of the dead in the cemeteries (Fig. 127)? For such a construction, especially if it is supposed to be a rule that applies to the entire Christian world, there would actually need to be some sort of concrete evidence.

Nor does it ultimately make any difference whether one imagines the Eucharist to be celebrated at a round or at a semicircular table. For according to the current state

25 See above p. 113.

26 RÜCKER 1920, 209–215 sees the origin of the medieval Coptic sigma altars as lying in the contemporary Christian funerary meal and not in the early Christian altar.

27 NUSSBAUM 1961b, 19, 29, 35 f., then above all JENSEN 2008. DÖLGER 1922, 571–573 already points in a similar direction.

Fig. 128: Altar of the Temple of Vespasian in Pompeii; L. Santini, Pompeji. Die Ausgrabungen (Narni / Terni no year).

of research, there is no literary[28] or archaeological evidence for either. All the known altar slabs of the early Church, whether actually preserved or merely depicted in art, are rectangular. Not a single altar takes the form of a round table on three legs.[29] Even if a church were to be excavated in which a tripod table was used for the Eucharist, this would still in no way prove that a normal dining table was used there. For the high tripod with a round tabletop was equally used as an altar in the Roman religion. On such a *foculare* (*foculus*) was offered the pre-offering, which consisted of incense and wine (above Figs. 30, 37).[30] The affinity of the tripod with the sacrificial altar is displayed particularly clearly by the altar of the Temple of Vespasian in Pompeii, on the front of which a sacrificial scene is depicted showing the pre-sacrifice on a high tripod (Fig. 128). So roundness did not arouse any associations with a meal. And vice versa, the Christians certainly did not view the high tripod as a dining table, but rather precisely as a pagan altar. This is proved by a painting in St Paul Outside the Walls, dating from perhaps the fifth century (Fig. 129). Walking across the Areopagus in Athens, Paul comes across the

28 Nussbaum 1961b, 28: "However, a round or semi-circular altar is nowhere expressly mentioned." Ps.-Basil. Sel. vit. Theclae 1 (PG 85, 560A) does not speak of a round altar but rather of an altar surrounded on all sides by the ciborium (differently G.

W. H. Lampe, A Patristic Greek Lexicon [Oxford ⁴1976] 1399: "circular in form"; correctly Chalkia 1991, 114 n. 15).

29 Sotira 2013, 18.

30 On the *foculare* see Scheid 2014, 28 f.

Fig. 129: Nave painting in St Paul Outside the Walls: Paul comes across the altar to the Unknown God in Athens (Acts 17:23); BAV Vat. Barb. lat. 4406, fol. 120; Proverbio 2016, 388.

altar to the Unknown God (Acts 17:23), which is here depicted as, of all things, a tripod with a round top, such as is used at reclining meals.[31]

So although it is of no use whatsoever to point to round tables when attempting to reinterpret the sacrifice of the Eucharist as the early Christians celebrated it at an altar and to turn it into a mere meal, people still want to rescue the round table. Its proponents believe that the Christians continued to celebrate the Eucharist as a genuine everyday meal in their normal community worship right up to the third century, with up to a hundred participants.[32] In a daring study, Klaus Gamber claims to have evidence that the Eucharist-agape was celebrated as a reclining evening meal in the Alpine and Danube region right down to the fourth and fifth centuries. Heinzgerd Brakmann, on the other hand, has irrevocably refuted such excursions into the world of archaeological fantasy.[33]

31 The sacrificial altars of antiquity can also be round, as the Christians well knew (above Fig. 20).
32 Nussbaum 1961b, 25–27. Latterly, Klinghardt 1996 has espoused this theory.
33 Gamber 1968. Brakmann 1970. Cf. Nussbaum 1971, 160. More recently, R. Messner, Die Synode von Seleukeia-Ktesiphon 410 und die Geschichte der ostsyrischen Messe, in: id. / R. Pranz (eds.), Haec sacrosancta synodus (Regensburg 2006) 60–85, here 84f. has speculated on eucharistic symposia in eastern Syria in the fifth century.

But Nussbaum sticks to his guns. Unlike Gamber, he does not try to use the church building to argue his case but instead uses images dating from the sixth century that show Jesus at the Last Supper on a *stibadium* at a sigma table. These allegedly prove that "for a certain time, the form of the Christian altar, too, was modelled on the prototype and archetype of the table used at the Last Supper."[34] This, of course, presupposes that the depiction of the Last Supper is, so to speak, an historical reconstruction and that the table is deliberately portrayed as the kind of table (a sigma table) that was thought to have been used by Jesus. But Franz Joseph Dölger already points to the banal fact that the artists did not engage in historical research on the Last Supper so as to be able to reproduce it, as it were, in a historically correct fashion. Instead, they depict the Last Supper according to the dining conventions of their own day, i.e. the sixth century.[35] Anyone seeking a motif for a sophisticated meal at the time could only choose a reclining meal since that had always been the sophisticated way of dining. And conversely, what the image of Jesus at a reclining meal brought to mind for the viewer of the time was by no means the Eucharist, but simply a sophisticated meal such as they knew from their own banquets and from images of non-Christian reclining meals (funerary meals, festive banquets, etc.[36]). Moreover, there are almost never any references to the Eucharist of any kind to be found in the depictions of the Last Supper.

Not the earliest,[37] but the most important image for researching the history of Jesus's Last Supper is a mosaic in the *Sant'Apollinare Nuovo* in Ravenna (early sixth century) (Fig. 130). It is a mosaic at the very front right of the nave, i.e. relatively close to the altar, which has misled some people into giving the image a eucharistic interpretation. Jesus and the twelve apostles can be seen reclining in close order. On the sigma table in front of them lie seven loaves and two fishes. This is undoubtedly the meal that Jesus shared with his disciples on the eve of his arrest. What it depicts is simply a common meal, in the course of which fish and loaves or perhaps also pyramid-shaped cakes are eaten.[38] There is no chalice in sight that could be interpreted as indicating the Eucharist. Fish are not only typical of the funerary meal, but also serve as food for sophisticated banqueting parties.[39] In any case, the two (!) fishes have nothing to do with eucharistic symbolism

---

34 NUSSBAUM 1961b, 25. This is adopted by GAMBER 1968, 87: "Jesus' farewell meal was portrayed in the same way as its imitation in the celebration of the Eucharist". SOTIRA 2013, 18 f. points to two mosaics from the fifth or sixth century with what is presumed to be a tripod altar. Both are incorrect.

35 Cf. DÖLGER 1943, 601.

36 DRESKEN-WEILAND 2010, 183–210.

37 To be ascribed to the fifth century is a Milan ivory showing Jesus with three persons on a *stibadium*; DÖLGER 1943, 574; VOLBACH 1976, 84 f. No. 119

with Plate 63. One may ask whether this image actually depicts the Last Supper at all and not, for example, Jesus's visit to the home of the tax collector Matthew (who in this case is the person drinking from the cup). On no account does a eucharistic interpretation suggest itself; DEICHMANN 1974, 173.

38 DÖLGER 1943, 585.

39 It seems that, at the time, Church banquets were still held as reclining meals in Ravenna; cf. Agnell. Lib. Pont. Rav. 29 (FC 21,1, 150). The mosaic of the Last Supper in the chapel of John VII in *San*

Fig. 130: Scene from the New Testament cycle in the nave of *Sant'Apollinare Nuovo* in Ravenna, 6th century: Jesus and the Twelve Apostles reclining on a stibadium for the Last Supper, with seven bread cakes and two fish on the table; Dresken-Weiland 2016, 138.

(fish = Christ).[40] The tablecloth, too, is in keeping with the custom of the banquet.[41] In the original mosaic, there was apparently also a table servant with a jug, as is indispensable for a reclining meal.[42] This leads Friedrich Wilhelm Deichmann to conclude when summing up all the observations that this is clearly not a depiction of the institution of the Eucharist and therefore the image cannot be interpreted eucharistically.[43] This means that the mosaic is not a model for the Church's celebration of the Eucharist in the sixth

---

Pietro in Vaticano (early eighth century) showed a fish or a food dish on the table; de Grüneisen 1911, Pl. IC.LXVI and LXVII. An ivory in the Aachen cathedral treasury (ninth century) shows the non-eucharistic evening meal with fish on a low round table; Dölger 1927, Plate 277,2. On the other hand, an ivory from Berlin (ninth or tenth century) shows the institution of the Eucharist at a round table (Schiller 1968, 334 No. 75).

40 Dölger 1943, 604, 609 f.; Deichmann 1974, 173; Dresken-Weiland 2016, 137–140.

41 Dölger 1943, 584 f.

42 Ibid. 581. Deichmann 1974, 173 f. unfortunately does not go into this.

43 Deichmann 1974, 173. Comparable reclining meals are to be found depicted in Christian art in quite different contexts, without any reference to the Eucharist whatsoever: the reclining meal of Joseph's brothers in the picture cycle of the story of Joseph in the BnF, Ms. gr. 510, fol. 69v; Weitzmann 1975, Fig. 13. The reclining feast of Herod in the so-called synoptic Gospels; Dölger 1943, Plate 320,1.

century either.[44] The very fact that it is located close to the main altar makes it easy to understand why it cannot be a eucharistic image.[45] The Last Supper belongs to the past, but the Eucharist is present and takes place at the Church's altar.

Also one of the four columns of the altar ciborium in *San Marco* in Venice, which date to the beginning of the sixth century and are of Byzantine provenance,[46] also strikingly portrays a common meal for satisfying hunger. The title reads *CENA DOMINI*. Jesus and two disciples are sitting, or rather reclining, at a sigma table with numerous dishes on it, just like other representations of New Testament meals on the ciborium columns.[47] What is concretely depicted is probably Judas's betrayal during the meal.[48] In a similar way to possibly that of the *Sant'Apollinare Nuovo* mosaic, a table servant (an apostle?) is bringing in more food on a tray.[49]

The Last Supper in the Rossano Codex (second half of the sixth century) has just as little to do with the Eucharist. It depicts instead the moment when Judas dips his hand into the bowl from which all the participants in the meal are eating. In order to leave this in no doubt, the corresponding scriptural verse is written above the scene (Mt 26:21) (Fig. 131).[50] The Eucharist can also be ruled out on the grounds that in the same codex the artist decided to paint two pictures specifically of the Eucharist, but now not as historical pictures showing the institution of the Eucharist, but rather as liturgical pictures showing the so-called Communion of the Apostles.[51] In these, according to contemporary liturgical custom, the apostles approach Jesus standing and receive from him in one picture the eucharistic bread and in the other the eucharistic cup.[52]

A lost mosaic in the chapel of Pope John VII(705–707) in Old St Peter's shows the Last Supper as a reclining meal on a stibadium; on the table lies a fish.[53] An Egyptian wood relief dating from the eighth century which shows Christ and the apostles huddled round a sigma table does not depict the institution of the Eucharist either, but merely a supper with loaves and a large fish.[54]

---

44 The table is not made to resemble a Christian altar, which could easily have been done. For example, the altar at which Abel and Melchisedek are sacrificing in *San Vitale* (above Fig. 42) is modelled on the Christian altar.

45 Even the institution of the cup was no longer part of the Last Supper, but followed it (cf. Lk 22:20; 1 Cor 11:25).

46 T. Weigel, Die Reliefsäulen des Hauptaltarciboriums von San Marco in Venedig (Münster 1997).

47 The beading round the edge of the table on the round side shows that people actually reclined at it. It was only the narrowness of the relief that made it impossible to represent this as such.

48 Dresken-Weiland 2019.

49 Lucchesi Palli 1942, 38–43 with Tav. II.

50 Dölger 1943, 586. The Judas motif (i.e. not the Eucharist) is encountered very frequently in the depiction of the Last Supper at a round or sigma table: Schiller 1968, 333 Nos. 70–72; 334 No. 76; 335 No. 79; 336 No. 84; 337 No. 85; 338 No. 91.

51 Deichmann 1974, 174.

52 Schiller 1968, 327 Fig. 57 f.

53 Grimaldi 1972, 120 f. Fig. 39; McKitterick 2013, 208 Fig. 10.10; 255 Fig. 12.10. It may also be two fishes.

54 Dölger 1927, Plate 273.

Fig. 131: Jesus' Last Supper with the Twelve Apostles on a stibadium; Codex purpureus Rossanensis in the Rossano Diocesan Museum, 2ⁿᵈ half of the 6ᵗʰ century; Sᴏᴛɪʀᴀ 2013, 111.

We do not come across a historical picture depicting the institution of the sacrament of the Eucharist until around 600 in a unique illuminated manuscript, the St Augustine Gospels, which may have been produced in the monastery of Monte Cassino. The scene is entitled *C[O]ENA D[OMI]NI*: Supper of the Lord (Fig. 132).[55] Jesus and the apostles are not reclining at table here, but are instead seated at a table which is cut off at the lower edge of the picture but is in reality circular. Only eight apostles are depicted, meaning that one has to imagine the others sitting at the hidden side of the table. The six plates, which are empty, are meant to tell us that this is no longer the common meal for satisfying hunger, the *coena*. They are, as it were, an indicator of time: according to the Roman Canon, which is what the monk painting it may have been thinking of, the institution of the cup takes place after the meal: *postquam coenatum est* (cf. Lk 22:20; 1 Cor 11:25). The eucharistic cup stands directly in front of Jesus, and he is blessing a sort of host that he holds in his hand. So the subject here is first and foremost the institution of the Eucharist. It is interesting that some of the apostles are also holding hosts in their hands, blessing them and looking at Jesus as they do so. So what is going on is a kind of teaching session for the future apostle-priests: Christ says to the apostles, "Do this in remembrance of me", whereupon the apostles immediately "practise".

The fact that in the sixth century altars were not normally round is proved by the depictions of the so-called Communion of the Apostles. Here Christ himself gives the

---

55 For the whole Passion cycle on the page in question
    see Jᴇʀᴇᴍɪᴀs 1980, Plate 76.

Fig. 132: Institution of the Eucharist (*CENA DNI*), painting in the St Augustine Gospels, c. 600, perhaps Monte Cassino; Corpus Christi College, Cambridge, Ms. 286, fol. 125r.

Eucharist to the apostles, standing as he does so at a rectangular altar. The Communion of the Apostles in the Rossano Codex dispenses with an altar and so can be left aside here. Of greater importance in Byzantium is a second type of image which by adding an altar clearly hints at the liturgy of the time.[56] Famous examples of this type of image are found on two liturgical plates dating from the 570s, the Stuma and Riha patens (below Fig. 149).[57] The images they display lead the viewer into the sanctuary of a sixth-century Byzantine basilica. Behind the altar stands Christ, twofold: once he is distributing the eucharistic chalice to the apostles, once the eucharistic bread. Significantly, the altar is not a round table, but a rectangular one covered with an altar cloth. Here Christ is not celebrating the Last Supper reclining, but is presiding at the Eucharist at an altar of the kind common in the sixth century (but without priestly vestments).[58] In a modified form, the motif is also popular in the West. The silver reliquary of Pope Paschal I (817–824) in the treasury of *Sancta Sanctorum* shows Christ behind an altar surrounded by Peter, John and the other apostles (above Fig. 43).[59]

56 Wessel 1966c; Schiller 1968, 326–331; Warland 2002a, 53; Zimmermann 2010, 1124f.

57 E. Gagetti, "*Sanctum altare tuum domine sub-
nixus honoro.*" Preziosi vasi eucaristici tra IV e VI
secolo d.C., in: G. Sena Chiesa (ed.), Costantino
313 d.C. L'editto di Milano e il tempo della tolle-
ranza (Milan 2012) 129–133, here 131, 133. Nussbaum 1961b, Plate 1: Riha Paten.

58 Christ as a priest at the altar see Joh. Chrys. cat.
bapt. 2,4,26 (FC 6,1, 286).

59 Grisar 1908, 99. The only unusual feature is that
Mary is standing there with them. She is clearly set
apart in that she is approaching the altar from the
side, whereas Peter is standing behind it right next
to Christ.

So in the Byzantine tradition and in the West (Ravenna, Rome), it is possible to conceive of the Last Supper, but not Jesus's first celebration of the Eucharist, in the form of a reclining meal. Eating to satisfy hunger and sacrament are two totally different things. Contrary to what Nussbaum asserts, the ancient reclining meal does not offer a convincing model for the design of the Eucharistic altar. It is simply not the case that the portrayal of the Last Supper as a reclining meal in the sixth century prompted the artists producing sacred art to give the Christian altar the same circular form in the Byzantine churches, but the other way round – the type of rectangular table altar that actually existed did in fact influence early Christian art in many ways (above Figs. 40, 42, below Figs. 148, 149).

However, Nussbaum does not refer just to the images of the Last Supper; he also points to the (semi-)circular stones or marble slabs that have been found in large numbers in archaeological excavations and undoubtedly once served as tables or shelves (Fig. 133).[60] But this evidence does not hold water either since these slabs were found scattered around and broken up, practically never intact and in situ, least of all in churches, so that their origin and function remain unclear. Furthermore, it is scarcely possible to date the slabs exactly as they were used in a variety of different contexts over several centuries. Not one of the known slabs can be proved to have been used as an altar in early Christian times.[61] The conclusion Jutta Dresken-Weiland draws from taking stock of the datable fourth-century round and sigma-shaped slabs that are decorated with reliefs is that these particularly magnificent table slabs most likely had a profane use.[62]

The claim that there were sigma-shaped altars is also based on an ivory box dating from the sixth century. It is said to show a church with a sigma altar (Fig. 135).[63] The altar supposedly consists of a sigma-shaped mensa standing on three corkscrew columns and has a cross and a Gospel book on it. Viewed in isolation, this would immediately seem to be an acceptable interpretation. However, a comparison of this box with another

60 Already B. BAGATTI, Gli altari paleo-cristiani della Palestina, in: *Liber Annuus. Studii biblici franciscani* 7 (1956–1957) 64–94, here 67, considers Byzantine sigma-shaped slabs in Palestine to be altars, citing for this the Byzantine iconography of the Last Supper.

61 RÜCKER 1920, 211: "The oldest altar had nothing to do with the sigma; it was a simple wooden table." W. E. KLEINBAUER, in: WEITZMANN 1979, 637 f.: "Nussbaum's […] recognition of a few such slabs as the tops of the main altar is highly unlikely." Sigma-shaped *mensae* that were assumed with certainty in the past to be altar slabs are either not at all certain or date from a time well outside the Early Christian period; CHALKIA 1991, 24 n. 160.

Although DUVAL 2005, 12 claims to have proof of a sixth-century sigma table in Sbeitla, the fragments were not in situ here either; *id.* 1971a, 46 f. None of the Spanish sigma slabs can be said with certainty to have been altar *mensae*; SASTRE DE DIEGO 2012, 1283–1285; *id.* 2013, 12 f., 105 f., 124–128, 141 f.

62 DRESKEN-WEILAND 1991, 257–261. Cf. RAMISCH 2018, 29.

63 A. S. CLAIR, in: WEITZMANN 1979, 580; CHALKIA 1991, 105, 113, Fig. 73. VOLBACH 1976, 114: "Jerusalem in Form einer Kirche." F. MÜTHERICH, Une pyxide d'ivoire du Cleveland Museum of Art, in: *Cahiers Archéologiques* 10 (1959) 201–206 failed to understand the scene.

Fig. 133: Sigma-shaped table slabs from the Herodium and from Tel Masos, East Negev; on the left a polylobate slab; Y. Israeli / D. Mevorah (eds.), Cradle of Christianity (Jerusalem 2000) 74.

contemporary ivory pyx bearing the same motif teaches us otherwise: in both cases, the image is not of a church with an altar, but is rather an admittedly idiosyncratic depiction of Christ's tomb. For on the second pyx, the scene is enriched with people: the women at the empty tomb of Christ in Jerusalem (Mk 16:1–8). Here, too, an architecture is to be seen that constitutes a free imitation of the tomb aedicula in the Church of the Holy Sepulchre in Jerusalem. In it there is a kind of table, this time rectangular, standing on three corkscrew columns. Once again, there seems to be a book lying on the rectangular slab. But the presence of the women makes it clear that this is not an altar with a Gospel book on it at all, but rather Christ's tomb with the rolled away stone, which, not unusually for representations of the time, is angular in shape.[64] The oil lamp above the tomb is further evidence that this is a depiction of the sacred site of Christ's tomb and not of a church. This now makes it clear that the pyx with the alleged sigma altar actually also depicts the empty tomb with the rolled-away stone, over which here, too, hangs a (triangular) oil lamp. The Cross on the tomb symbolises the Resurrection. Once again, the context of the image is Jerusalem since next to the empty tomb there is Jesus's entry into Jerusalem with people carrying palm branches.

In spite of this, Nussbaum speculates: "One must, however, reckon with the possibility that one or other of these monuments was used as an altar."[65] Just two pages later he states: "The examination of the archaeological monuments has provided clear evidence that the round and sigma-shaped tables were not only used as altars for the celebration of the Eucharist, but also had other functions to fulfil."[66] A further five pages later, Nussbaum sums up: "One must reckon with the fact that, in accordance with the

64 Volbach 1976, 111 No. 177 with Plate 90. It could also be a tombstone.

65 Nussbaum 1961b, 29.

66 Ibid. 31.

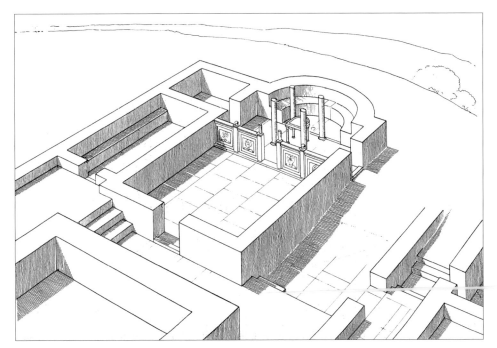

Fig. 134: Reconstruction of the Metochi basilica on Samos with a hypothetical sigma altar; A. M. Schneider, Samos in frühchristlicher und byzantinischer Zeit, in: MDAI.A 54 (1929) 96–141, here 96.

table forms in Jesus' day and in the first centuries of the Church, both the table at the Last Supper and the table used at the celebration of the Eucharist were as a rule round or sigma-shaped."[67] The name for this is "suggestive science," which, despite being ungrounded, continues to attract ever new adherents.[68]

In his sigma-altar thesis, Nussbaum juggles with the idea of the meal. He is fascinated by the idea that this typical form deliberately preserves the idea that the Eucharist was originally celebrated like a meal. However, this is already rendered implausible by the fact that the sigma slabs could be universally employed as building elements and were accordingly produced so as to be multifunctional and reused (as spolia) in both profane and sacred contexts: in private houses, in cemeteries, in baptisteries and in *pastophoria*,[69]

67 Ibid. 36. Reinforced by Gamber 1968, 87 referring to Nussbaum: "It is at all events certain that sigma tables were in use among the Christians at the sacred meal."

68 E.g. Gamber 1968. Volti 2005, 85 also aligns himself with the speculation about alleged sigma altars: "era largamente diffuso in tutto il mondo cristiano della tarda antichità."

69 Nussbaum 1961b, 29; *id.* 1965, 113; Wessel 1966a, 117; Chalkia 1991, 111–131.

and not least of all as Gospel ambos in north Syrian churches.[70] Because there was an abundant supply of high-quality slabs on the market, they were used just as shelves or as tables and even as flooring. It is therefore in principle conceivable that, being valuable materials, table tops once used in private houses were reused in churches, for example as oblation tables or side altars or, in individual cases, even as an altar mensa.[71] There is, however, absolutely no possibility that meal symbolism played any part in all this.

Alfons Maria Schneider has reconstructed the main altar of the Metochi chapel on Samos, which dates from the second half of the fifth century, with a sigma slab (Fig. 135).[72] Yet the exact location of the slab fragments is actually not known here either.[73] Since the altar in all probability stood on four little columns, it is likely to have been a rectangular table altar.[74] Nonetheless it is interesting to see how Nussbaum deals with this case.[75] He ought in fact to welcome such a reconstruction. But he rejects the case, citing the unclear circumstances of the find. His true reason for doing so is, however, that in this church, which has an east-facing apse, a step located directly behind the altar means that the priest can only have approached it from the front. But if the sigma slab possessed any meal symbolism, the priest would, in his opinion, have to stand at the round side.[76] In the Syrian monastery church of St Sergius in Maaloula, a sigma slab with a raised outer rim forms the mensa of the main altar. Its dating to the fourth century[77] is by no means certain as the church is medieval.[78] The altar stands behind the iconostasis, and the priest goes to the front, flat side of it for the liturgy, looking towards the east.

The same goes for a number of still functional sigma altars that have survived in Egypt[79] but are dated to not earlier than the post-iconoclastic period (ninth or tenth century).[80] The sigma-shaped *mensae* can be explained as an adoption from everyday life,[81] no doubt because such slabs are particularly valuable, and not out of a desire to

---

70 Duval 2005, 12.

71 Chalkia 1991, 113–120.

72 Nussbaum 1965, Volume of plates 66 Fig. 14.

73 Chalkia, 1991, 70, 183 (No. Gr. 2). W. Wrede, Vom Misokampos auf Samos, in: MDAI.A 54 (1929) 65–95, here 74, does not give an exact site for the find; the sigma slab can just as easily have been found in the northern annex (prothesis). M. J. Johnson, San Vitale in Ravenna and Octagonal Churches in Late Antiquity (Wiesbaden 2018), Pl.11, Fig. 3.4 offers a reconstruction of the Martyrium of St Philip in Hierapolis with a sigma altar as its main altar, the flat side facing east. There is, however, as far as I know, no archaeological evidence pointing to such an altar. The same goes for the reconstruction of a sigma altar in Veliko Tirnovo (Bulgaria) in Gamber 1994, 13 Fig. 1.

74 Heid 2014b, 362 needs to be corrected.

75 Nussbaum 1965, 144 f.

76 See also the justified criticism in Gamber 1972, 54.

77 Ramisch 2018, 27.

78 T. Ulbert, Zwei sigmaförmige Mensaplatten aus Syrien, in: E. Dassmann / K. S. Frank (eds.), Pietas, Festschr. B. Kötting (Münster 1980) 559–565, here 559.

79 Nussbaum 1961b; 30, id. 1965, 112.

80 Dölger 1927, Plate 274, 275,2; Kirsch / Klauser 1950, 343; Nussbaum 1965, 111–115; Chalkia 1991, 179–183 (Tipo C: Eg. 7–14, 16–17, 22–23). On two churches in Greece see Chalkia 1991, 193 f. (Tipo D: Gr. 9–10).

81 Dölger 1943, 502.

Fig. 135: Ivory pyxis with the Empty Tomb of Christ, 6th century; Museum of Art in Cleveland, 1951.114.

imitate the Last Supper.[82] Occasionally the round shape of the slabs is concealed by a box-shaped structure beneath them intended to make them more like the normal altar in shape.[83] The straight side of the sigma slabs is always at the front. Nussbaum sees this as confirmation of his view that it shows the continuing influence here of the ancient triclinium and that the liturgist must therefore have stood behind the altar, i.e. on the round side.[84] But in Egypt they have always faced east to pray.[85] The priest approaches the altar from the front, with his back to the people. How insignificant a role the idea of the meal plays in the Coptic liturgy is shown by the curtains concealing the chancel from the people.[86]

It becomes even more absurd when Nussbaum not only co-opts sigma slabs as early Christian altar *mensae*, but at the same time shows a bias towards polylobate slabs, i.e. sigma slabs with indentations or concave depressions round the edge (above Fig. 133). According to him, these particularly well illustrate the meal character of the Eucharist

82 The Last Supper is visualised as a sophisticated re-clining meal, with fish and bread (unrelated to the Eucharist); DÖLGER 1927, Plate 272, 273.

83 DÖLGER 1927, Plates 274, 275,2; cf. BRAUN 1924a, 99.

84 NUSSBAUM 1965, 113 f. His desperate arguments are: 1. the altar is always free-standing; 2. in depic-tions of the Last Supper Christ is seated (like all the rest) at the round side of the sigma table; and 3.

only the servers approach the sigma table on the straight side.

85 See above p. 267–269.

86 Can. Hippol. arab. 29 (PO 31, 400): no one enters the sanctuary behind the veil except to pray, genu-flect and prostrate themselves before the altar. Cf. DÖLGER 1943, 502; NUSSBAUM 1965, 117; *id*. 1971, 154 f.; METZGER 1971, 128; GAMBER 1972, 54.

since the depressions were used for the food or bowls of participants.[87] But even if an altar did ever have a polylobate slab in early Christian times, the idea that this indicates a meal situation is erroneous.[88] Or do we really want to believe that the priest placed the Eucharist in the depressions so that the faithful could take Communion from them?[89] But abstruse science bears strange fruit. In the Welsche Kirche in Graz, a replica of a polylobate sigma table has recently been installed as an altar (Fig. 136).[90] But who knows what to do with it today? It is a dead archaeologism, and a half-hearted one at that. For the priest should actually stand on the round side of the mensa – and it would be best to put a bed next to the altar, too, so as to make it clear that the table is actually intended for a reclining meal.

Practically no genuine Christian round altars have been preserved. There is a stone cylinder from Cappadocia, 90-cm high and 110-cm in diameter, which is dated to the sixth to eighth centuries.[91] But it is not known where it came from, so it is also unclear whether it is an altar or rather the main altar of a church at all. Even if this is the case, the imagery decorating the basalt stone gives no indication of its significance as the table of a meal fellowship. The mensa is dominated by a large cross with the apocalyptic symbols alpha and omega. The surface on the circular side depicts the ascension of the prophet Elijah and the Cappadocian martyr Mamas. Although a scene from Mamas's *passio* showing him milking a hind can be interpreted as a reference to the food of the Eucharist, the legend itself does not offer this interpretation, nor does the artist who carved the stone. He simply depicts Mamas surrounded by numerous animals in the midst of a lush landscape of vegetation. So his intention is to portray the paradisal scene spoken of in the legend according to which Mamas lived for many years in peace with the tame and wild animals and nourished himself from them.[92]

The apse mosaic in the church of *Sant'Ambrogio* in Milan, which has an east-end apse and probably dates from the Carolingian period (ninth century),[93] contains a re-

---

87 On such tabletops see CHALKIA 1991, 34–41; N. DUVAL *et al.* (eds.), Salona 1. Catalogue de la Sculpture architecturale paléochrétienne de Salone (Rome / Split 1994) 153–157. The depressions were used for safely putting down cups, bowls or dishes (that had a stand or were conical). At a reclining meal such bowls could be conveniently placed there and for the next course replaced with new dishes and other food. The participants in the meal, who could not eat directly from the table while reclining on their couches, could pick up the dishes and put them down again without them falling over the edge. The function of the depressions is made even clearer by those semi-circular tables where they are found only on the round side. There were no cushions on the straight side of the table; rather, this is where the servers approached the table.

88 No early Christian altar with a polylobate mensa is known. However, polylobate altars do appear in southern Gaul in the eleventh and twelfth centuries, but these are rectangular. A few round polylobate tables are also known which were reused as altars at this time. Here, too, the age of the slabs will have been the main motive for preserving them. In contemporary imitations, the impractical round shape is already avoided, whereas the decorative elements, which certainly have nothing to do with the early Christian sigma tables, are retained. NARASAWA 2015, 430–442.

89 Rightly sceptical NUSSBAUM 1961b, 31–33.

90 F.-R. PERGLER, Der Sigmaaltar als Volksaltar der Welschen Kirche; *id.*, Der Sigmaaltar als Altar der Urkirche (unpublished manuscripts).

91 RUGGIERI 2018.

Fig. 136: Modern altar design in the Welsche Kirche in Graz with a sigma-shaped mensa; photo: Alois Kölbl.

Fig. 137: Detail of the apse mosaic in the church of *Sant'Ambrogio* in Milan, which has an east-end apse, 9th century: Bishop Ambrose celebrating Holy Mass in the *Basilica Portiana*; PECKLERS 2012, 89 Fig. 7.

markable detail. It shows a legendary episode from the life of Bishop Ambrose. You can see the interior of the *Basilica portiana*. At the back of the nave, as it were, there are the people listening to the lector standing on the ambo. On the left, at the front of the church, Bishop Ambrose can be seen celebrating mass; he is standing at an altar which is striking because of its extremely rare circular shape (Fig. 137). Ambrose stands in front of the altar celebrating facing east. From behind, a deacon is tapping him on the shoulder. As a mirror image of this scene, there is another depiction of a church interior, this time the cathedral of Tours. Here, too, the altar stands at the top end, so that the celebrant approaches it from the front. Significantly, this altar is rectangular. So the circular shape of the altar in the *Basilica portiana* has no deeper meaning of any kind, but simply springs from the artistic imagination.

Equally, the claim that the "round table" stands for the equality of everyone at it is a modern projection. Such an association does not exist for antiquity. Franz Joseph Dölger

92 H. DELEHAYE, *Passio sancti Mammetis*, in: AB 58 (1940) 126–141, here 131.

93 Cf. BRAUN 1924a, 245. On the difficulty of dating the mosaic see C. BARTELLI, Percorso tra le testimonianze figurative più antiche. Dai mosaici di S. Vittore in Ciel d'oro al pulpito della basilica, in: M. L. GATTI PERER (ed.), La basilica di S. Ambrogio. Il tempio ininterrotto 2 (Milan 1995) 339–387, here 356–364.

already proved that the places at the sigma meal were by no means allocated randomly to the guests, but rather according to rank.[94] Alongside the seating arrangement, the accompanying ceremonial is also significant. Reclining meals very much serve to establish and represent the hierarchy of the participants through the allocation of places and the order of speaking and eating. The round table is therefore not even democratic at the Christian love feasts. For the agapes in the second and third centuries are not only hierarchically led by the clergy, but also follow a specific procedure, thus serving the well-ordered unity of the members and staff of the community.[95]

Occasionally, in addition to the round shape and the indentations of the mensa, the use of tablecloths is also cited in support of the claim that the Christian altar was originally a dining table. They are even seen as the main difference between a pagan and a Christian altar: the latter was, so it is claimed, always covered with a cloth, which was necessary for a dining table.[96] This connection is then said to be further reinforced by the table shape of the altar (in the case of a mensa altar). It is, of course, true that a tablecloth was not used for sacrificial altars (above Figs. 1, 19, 20, 37, 39, 119) and was also rarely found on sacred tables (above Figs. 4, 5, 9), whereas a cloth could be expected on a Christian altar from the third century on.[97] However, the type of altar covering used remains unclear until the sixth century; it is only then that images can be found providing sufficient indications. Here one thing becomes clear: the early Christian altar covering cannot be compared with today's bourgeois dining culture. For tablecloths in the modern sense were uncommon at ancient banquets.[98]

What one does come across, however, is table coverings as a sign of luxury at sophisticated reclining banquets.[99] Such drapery, falling as it does right down to the floor, is impossible at seated meals because it would get in the way of the diners' legs. Rather, the seated meal typically does not have a tablecloth, as can be seen in a mosaic in *Santa Maria Maggiore* in Rome. It shows Abraham welcoming the three mysterious men in Mamre (Gn 18:1 f.): the guests are sitting at a rectangular wooden table with their feet underneath it (Fig. 138).[100] Although round tables at reclining meals can do without

---

94 Dölger 1943, 575–578; Engemann 1982.

95 Cianca 2018, 115: "Banqueting in Roman tradition was a highly stylized, hierarchized affair." Very clear in Trad. Apost. 25–28 (FC 1, 274–282). The same is analogously true of pagan sacred meals: Scheid 1990, 661. On *sportulae* see Scheid 1990, 514–516.

96 Mazza 2005, 57.

97 Braun 1924b, 21 f.; Kirsch / Klauser 1950, 349; Nussbaum 1961b, 35; Wessel 1966b, 120–124; van de Paverd 1970, 55 f. Cf. Riganati 2002.

98 Marquardt 1886, 1, 312; Wieland 1906, 116; Kruse 1932, 942. 944; Nussbaum 1961b, 34.

99 Cf. Dölger 1943, 582–584.

100 Angiolini Martinelli 1997a, 210 Fig. 411 (three angels in Mamre, San Vitale); T. B. Stevenson, Miniature decoration in the Vatican Virgil (Tübingen 1983) Fig. 83 (Banquet scene in a mosaic, Bardo Museum in Tunis).

Fig. 138: Abraham entertaining the three angels in Mamre (Gen 18:1f), nave mosaic in *Santa Maria Maggiore*, Rome, 5th century; Wilpert / Schumacher 1976, Plate 29.

cloths,[101] they can equally well be draped with low-falling cloths. The cloths have no hygienic purpose because the food is not put on them but is instead served on a large round tray (*repositorium*) which is placed on the table.[102] Another alternative is just to cover the tables with hangings round the sides or merely at the front while leaving the

---

101 Funerary meals in catacombs: Deckers 1987, Plates 33c, 55a, Colour plates 12a, 55b, 57b. Funerary meals on the sarcophagi: Dölger 1943, Plates 306–311; the banquet of Dido and Aenaeas in the Vatican Vergilius Romanus codex: Engemann 1982, Plate 15d; Dresken-Weiland 2016, 139; tomb of the banquet in Constanta; *id.* 2010, 206 Fig. 95. Further examples: Dölger 1927, Plates 235 f., 240, 242, 246, 250–252.

102 Reclining meals with a round table and a large tray on the tablecloth see Volbach 1976, 77 f. No. 107 with Plate 57 (Brescia Lipsanotheca, fourth century); Deckers 1987, Plate 64ab (funerary meals); L. Pirzio Biroli Stefanelli, L'argento dei Romani. Vasellame da tavola e d'apparato (Rome 1991) 219 Figs. 229 and 239 Fig. 251 (silver plates from Seuso and Cesena). Using a tray placed on the table meant that the tablecloth did not get dirty. One server was sufficient as not everyone had to be served separately.

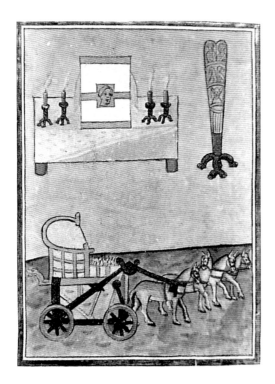

Fig. 139: Symbols of office (incl. official table with candles and codicil) of the Praetorian Prefect for Illyricum in der *Notitia Dignitatum*, 5th century; C. Neira Faleiro, La *Notitia Dignitatum* (Madrid 2005) 157.

Fig. 140: Christ before Pilate and the High Priests, Codex purpureus Rossanensis, 6th century, Museo Diocesano d'Arte Sacra in Rossano; Spier 2007, 163 Fig 121.

tabletop uncovered.[103] The sigma *mensae* often have a raised rim or also indentations or hollows round the circumference in which the participants can place their food (above Fig. 133). Such *mensae* are not covered with cloths.

But table coverings are not found only at luxurious banquets. They can also serve as an attribute lending dignity to official tables. The tables of Roman magistrates are depicted in the *Notitia Dignitatum* (fifth century) (Fig. 139). Pilate's official table in the scene of Jesus's interrogation in the Rossano Codex conforms to this (Fig. 140).[104] In each case the table is covered completely with a cloth, without this being intended to arouse any associations with a dining table. The Pilate scene is also interesting because it is pretty much identical to the situation in a church. Pilate is sitting in the apse. When he approaches the table of office, possibly to venerate the image of the emperor set up

103 This appears to be the case for the Last Supper in *Sant'Apollinare Nuovo* (above Fig. 130) and on the ivory in the Milan Cathedral Treasury (Dölger 1943, Plate 319,1; Engemann 1982, Plate 15a). Further examples of sigma meals with side hangings see Dölger 1927, Plate 272; Schiller 1968, 334 Fig. 76. People sitting at a round table

with side hangings see Jeremias 1980, Plate 31b (miracle of the quail). On *repositorium* see Nussbaum 1961b, 21–23.

104 Dölger 1930, 174 f. A further example see De Grüneisen 1911, Fig. 255 (Ivory pyx with St Menas).

there, he inevitably approaches the table from the front, as the priest does the altar. The chair of office is also covered with an equivalent cloth. The bishops' thrones (cathedra) may also be covered with linen.[105] Here the cloth signals authority and hierarchy.[106]

As far as the Christian altar is concerned, the priest *stands* at the altar, which means that it can be completely covered with a cloth without disturbing the liturgy. Pictorial evidence has been preserved mainly from the sixth-century Greek cultural sphere (above Fig. 32, below Figs. 149, 150). The altars of the Old Testament are also depicted in this way as Christian altars, for example the altar at which Abel and Melchisedek offer their sacrifice (above Fig. 42, below Fig. 148). But there are also occasions when the mensa remains uncovered while the sides are covered. This is probably done for practical reasons in the case of those altars that have a raised rim (below Fig. 149).[107] In any case, Christian altars should radiate luxury, dignity and sanctity. Or how else is it to be understood that although Emperor Constantine did not have the altars he donated in Rome furnished

---

105 Dresken-Weiland / Drews 2004, 635 f. Cf. Past. Herm. 9,4 (SC 53², 98). Sceptical Kritzinger 2016, 122 f.

106 Another different interpretation, and certainly a

singular one, is offered by Ambrose, who compares the altar cloth with a virgin's veil; Ambr. virg. 1,11,65 (PL 16, 206C).

107 Van de Paverd 1970, 56.

with cloths, he turned them into absolutely exquisite tables by covering them with gold, silver and precious stones?[108]

So it can be concluded that if there were ever round and sigma altars in the early Christian period, then these were completely isolated cases and did not belong to any superior context of meaning. In the design of Christian altars, there is no preference for sigma tables, not even as a speciality of a particular region. Still less is there a reconstructible historical line leading back to an original round altar which then went out of fashion over the course of later centuries. No one knows today, and no one knew back then, what the table used at Jesus's Last Supper looked like. There is no discernible link running from the table of the Last Supper to the early Christian altar. The only thing known for certain is that rectangular altars are attested in an overwhelming number of churches, meaning that they must be regarded as standard; all the same, neither the round nor the rectangular shape of the altar has any deeper significance – no more than the four legs of a table altar or the altar cloth are in any way intended to insinuate a meal situation. Therefore, as Johannes H. Emminghaus and Reinhard Messner have urged, we should put an end to the meal-table ideology.[109]

All this notwithstanding, a certain meal rhetoric is, of course, to be found among the Church Fathers. On the one hand, they are fond of talking about the "table" of the celebration of the Eucharist, but this table still always remains the "altar". It is not even the case that the Church Fathers associate the sacrificial *act* more with "altar" and the sacrificial *meal* more with "table".[110] Rather, it is simply a matter of a varying use of language. The fact that the term "holy table" has been in use since the fourth century is not the result of some Constantinian shift, as if dining tables were only now styled altars, but is simply a linguistic development. People revel in Byzantine hyperbole: altars and tables are not described just as holy, but also as immaculate, awesome, venerable, royal, divine, immortal and mystical.[111] Such epithets are not added in order to distinguish one's own piece of furniture from profane tables but rather in order to further honour one's sacred table.[112]

---

108 In the sixth century, the altar covers have an additional white cloth laid on top of them (above Fig. 42). Once again, this has nothing to do with being associated with a meal but instead shows reverence for the sacred food.

109 Messner 2003b, 34: "Behind the concept of the meal table is the inaccurate assumption of a continuity from the earliest Christian cult meals in the form of a Hellenistic symposium, where the participants reclined round low tables, to the form of the Mass we are familiar with, where the president *stands* at the *one* altar (at which no one eats or

drinks). Johannes H. Emminghaus put his finger on it: 'The "meal-table ideology" should be completely forgotten when considering the design of the altar.'" Gerhards 2009, 124f. also maintains that prior ideological decisions played a role in Nussbaum's altar studies.

110 E.g. Petr. Chrys. serm. 67,7 (CCL 24A, 404f.); 95,3 (587).

111 Dölger 1930, 171–173; Kirsch / Klauser 1950, 352; Weckwerth 1963, 220f.

112 Differently Reisch 1894, 1656–1659; Braun 1924a, 26, 29.

On the other hand, the Church Fathers like to identify the church altar with the table of the Last Supper. Only their intention here is not to conform the altar to an allegedly authentic communion table, but rather the other way round: the table of the Last Supper becomes the altar. Cyprian of Carthage († 258) quotes the biblical passage from Proverbs that speaks of the house (*domus*) with seven pillars, in which Wisdom has mingled her wine in the chalice and furnished the table (*mensa*) and invites the guests to lay down, to eat and to drink (Prv 9:1–5). Cyprian sees in this a prophecy of the celebration of "the Lord's sacrifice" in which Jesus offers bread and wine on the altar in the presence of the apostles during his Passion.[113] Although the biblical banquet is prophetically related here to Jesus's Last Supper, the reclining meal as such is not what matters at all. This is simply the normal way of taking a sophisticated meal in Jesus's day, and still in Cyprian's. The only thing that is important to Cyprian is the jug on the table in which she has mingled her wine. For this is the eucharistic chalice. Thus the table of the Last Supper becomes anachronistically the altar of the liturgy at which Christ himself offers the sacrifice.

Cyprian is not alone in this.[114] Other Church Fathers, and even art (below Fig. 149), already see the table of the Last Supper as an altar. And this does not have anything to do with a common meal either, but refers to the Eucharist: Christ himself offers the sacrificial food at the table or altar of the Church; he himself gives the nourishment there.[115] For example, Ambrose († 397) addresses the newly baptised, encouraging them to hasten to the altar of Christ (*altaria Christi*) in order to partake of the heavenly banquet (*caeleste convivium*) that Christ himself has prepared at the table (*mensa*) of the most holy altar (*sacrosanctum altare*).[116] Augustine († 430) urges the faithful when going to Communion to sit down at the table of the Last Supper of the Lord's Passion and approach his altar with humility.[117] By this he may possibly mean a physical act of self-humiliation, such as a deep bow.[118]

---

113 Cypr. ep. 63,5 (CSEL 3,2, 704): *Sed et per Salomonem spiritus sanctus typum dominici sacrificii ante praemonstrat, immolatae hostiae et panis et vini sed et altaris et apostolorum faciens mentionem […].*

114 Drawing on Prv 9:1–5, Ps.-Hippol. comm. in Prov. (PG 10, 628B) also identifies the "mystical and divine table" upon which the pure Body and Blood of Christ are daily sacrificed with "that memorable first table of the mystical divine supper (δεῖπνον)." Byzantine Communion hymn on Holy Thursday: "Receive me today, O Son of God, as partaker of thy mystical supper" (sixth century).

115 Aug. serm. 132,1,1 (PL 38, 735): *Christus quotidie pascit, mensa ipius est illa in medio constituta.*

116 Ambr. myst. 8,43 (SC 25², 178–180).

117 Aug. serm. Dolbeau 9,4 (DOLBEAU 2009, 32 f.): *Sede cenare ad mensam eius: humilis accede ad altare eius, sessio enim signum est humilitatis […]. Ad mensam pastoris tui sedisti: mortem enim invenis invitatoris tui […]. Haec est mensa illius potentis: ad hanc cenam venisti, si humilis sedisti; immo ad hanc cenam sedisti, si humilis venisti […]. Ecce potentis mensa, Christi mensa, plena gratia passionis dominicae.*

118 Cf. VAN DER MEER 1951, 208, 468. In the Byzantine liturgy, one bowed low as one approached the

For John Chrysostom († 407), too, the eucharistic table is the same table as that of the Lord's Supper.[119] He even compares the Eucharist to the wedding banquet (Mt 22:12), at which the guests recline to feast at the royal table. He calls on the faithful not just to wash their hands on entering the church and then stand idly by, but now also to lie down at the table. There at the royal table Christ and the angels serve. When the sacrifice is offered, Christ and the Lamb are slain; when all pray together, when the double door of the chancel is opened as a sign that the heavens are opened above the altar and the angels are descending, then the initiates must lie down at the table.[120] With these images, Chrysostom wants to prevail upon the faithful either to leave the church as sinners before the actual eucharistic rites begin or to confess and go to Communion.

The Syrian poet Balai († c. 460) has the following to say on the consecration of the church in Qenneschrin:

> His *altar* is ready, and he shares his supper with us; his glory is laid down for man, and they lie down at *table*; we dine with him at our *table*; one day he will dine with us at his. May his glory and majesty be worshipped![121]

So Balai draws a line from the reclining meal of the Last Supper to the celebration of the Eucharist in church. But this remains at the level of an historical construction. It might at first look as if the Eucharist really was held as a reclining meal, but in view of the large numbers of Christians thronging to the consecration of the church this is clearly wrong. Rather, Balai associates the proskynesis at the transubstantiation, when the faithful prostrate themselves in reverence of the "glory and majesty" of God, with "lying at table". The signal for the proskynesis is given by the liturgical Sanctus call. He says further: "The altar is ready, robed in truth; before it stands the priest and kindles the fire. He takes bread and gives the Body; he receives wine and distributes the Blood."[122] Despite all the meal rhetoric, the liturgical reality is that the faithful lie on the floor in deep reverence while the priest stands before the altar with his back to the people (above Fig. 92).

---

altar; GAMBER 1968, 88. In the Celtic liturgy, the communicants threw themselves to the ground three times on their way to the altar (HEILER 1941, 138). Theod. Mops. cat. 16,27 (FC 17,2, 442 f.) requires the reception of Communion with lowered eyes.

119 Joh. Chrys. in Matth. hom. 82,5 (PG 58, 744).
120 Joh. Chrys. in Eph. hom. 3,5 (PG 62, 29). Cf. Lib. Moz. 686 (FÉROTIN 1995): Altar as royal table.
121 BKV² Ausgewählte Schriften der syrischen Dichter 67.
122 Ibid. 65.

Agnellus of Ravenna (first half of ninth century) describes the sacrificial altar (*ara*) as a four-legged, explicitly square table and continues, "Have you reclined at it? Eat the bread!"[123] So the author associates it with a reclining meal, perhaps because he is thinking of depictions of the Last Supper in church art in Ravenna (above Fig. 130). But Agnellus does not present the celebration of the Eucharist as a meal any more than Balai does. For the mensa of the altar is in fact the Cross on which Jesus lay down and was offered as a sacrifice. He was sacrificed for the world, as the four table legs and table corners stand for the four points of the compass. The table of the Eucharist is and remains an altar at which, actually *in front of* which, the priest stands.[124] He does not look at the faithful, but instead turns towards the east, something incompatible with simulating a meal.

2. PEOPLE'S ALTAR WITH FRONT-FACING CELEBRATION

Much more fundamental to the modern altar than its circular form is its installation and use as a so-called people's altar. Shortly after the Second Vatican Council, the liturgist Josef Andreas Jungmann stated: "The often-repeated assertion that the ancient Christian altar regularly presupposed a turning towards the people proves to be a legend."[125] More recently, the Protestant historian Martin Wallraff has confirmed: "The idea of the congregation gathered around the altar and oriented towards the altar is a modern theologoumenon. [...] it can hardly claim patristic roots. The same goes for the *celebratio versus populum*, which has been discussed so intensively and sometimes emotionally in the Catholic Church since the days of the Second Vatican Council. Such an idea does not exist in the Early Church, even if some such arrangement may have de facto occurred in individual cases."[126] Such contributions give pause for thought. Why then has the so-called people's altar been introduced everywhere in the last fifty years? It would not be mistaken to see the reason as lying in the abandonment of essential principles of Christian liturgy as a result of the paradigm shift from sacrifice to meal.

---

123 Agnell. Lib. Pont. Rav. 64 (FC 21,1, 286): *Discu-buistis? Comedite panem.* Altar mensa as Cross and sacrificial table of the eucharistic *convivium* see also (Ps.-)Aug. serm. 366,6 (PL 39, 1649): *Mensa namque jucunditatis passio Christi est, qui se pro nobis in mensa crucis obtulit sacrificium Deo Patri, donans Ecclesiae suae catholicae vitale convivium.*

124 For Ravenna, the east-facing celebration is beyond doubt; see above p. 280–283.

125 Jungmann 1967, 376; in agreement Gamber 1994, 36.

126 Wallraff 2004, 116. Cf. Chavarría Arnau 2009, 96f.

The liturgical principles discussed in the preceding chapters were valid *mutatis mutandis* up to the latest liturgical reform. Leaving the early Church aside, from the Middle Ages until the Second Vatican Council, wall altars, i.e. altars against the wall of the church, and the corresponding Tridentine liturgy, characterised the Catholic church interior for a thousand years. When the priest stood at the altar, he looked at a Cross or altarpiece. The high altar at least also had a tabernacle in which to reserve the eucharistic sacrament. Everyone, both priest and faithful, stood at various intervals in front of the altar, all facing forwards together as if towards the ideal east. The one-sided reversal of the direction of prayer introduced after the council led to the priest standing behind the so-called people's altar and celebrating facing the congregation like a teacher standing at the front of the class (*Frontalunterricht*).[127]

In the meantime, even reform-minded liturgy professors regard the introduction of front-facing celebration (*Frontalzelebration*) as one of the most problematic measures of the post-conciliar reforms.[128] But instead of restoring the old order of a common prayer orientation, there is now a fondness for moving the altar even farther into the middle of the church and introducing a central celebration. This proposal is by no means new[129] and is once again linked with the sigma meal, at which the meal participants allegedly reclined in a semicircle at the Eucharist. If you turn this into a full circle, then you arrive at the altar in the middle of the church today encircled by rows of chairs. Its proponents seek to justify this with the claim that in the early Church the altar was seen as God's dwelling place and the location of his theophany, so that the faithful would have turned towards the altar. There may well be certain echoes of this in the Church Fathers, but they never led to a centring of the liturgy.[130] In fact, even in round churches the altar always stood non-centrally on the east or west side; this was the case, for example, with *Santo Stefano Rotondo* in Rome (above Fig. 84) and the *Hagia Sophia* in Constantinople (above Fig. 47). Central altars such as are found today in *Santo Stefano Rotondo* or in the round church of *Santa Costanza* (at *Sant'Agnese*

---

127 With disturbing consequences. A. LORENZER, Das Konzil der Buchhalter (Frankfurt 1984) 190: "Behind the empty altar table stands the priest, who cuts an absurd figure with his sacred vestments in this context since he after all no longer – at a symbolic distance in front of the congregation and as their representative – engages in a mystical dialogue with a transcendent being but instead functions as the dialogue partner of the congregation itself." MOSEBACH 2012, 84: "After the reform of the liturgy, the priest has turned round, looking at the congregation while affecting to be speaking with God. The model for the new liturgy is the chairman's table at a party or club meeting with a microphone and papers, an ikebana vase with an arrangement of old roots and a bizarre orange-coloured exotic plant to the left and two cosy candles in a hand-made pottery candlestick to the right."

128 MESSNER 2005. Even dogmatists are meanwhile speaking out against front-facing celebration; MENKE 2012, 301. See also A. STOCK, Liturgie und Poesie. Zur Sprache des Gottesdienstes (Kevelaer 2010) 113, 124.

129 GAMBER 1972, 63 f.; cf. NUSSBAUM 1971, 151 f.

130 NUSSBAUM 1971, 157 cannot find any evidence "which expressly refers to the altar as the focus of orientation."

fuori le mura) date from the baroque period. Originally, it was not the altar that was the point of orientation for the prayers of the faithful, but God in heaven, at whose altar the sacrifice was celebrated.[131] This can hardly be conveyed with the central celebration. The new design for worship is also more concerned with producing a meal simulation than the dimension of God.

As was already the case with the demand for round altars, the science of Christian archaeology was a driving force behind people's altars, too. In the twentieth century, archaeologists discovered churches in the formerly Christian areas of North Africa and present-day Turkey in which traces of the altar were still recognisable. Mostly it stood more or less in the middle of the presbytery and could be walked round on all sides. In a minority of cases, it was close against the (east) wall. It certainly had no superstructure and thus retained the shape of a table.[132] You could walk round it and look over it. In view of this finding, the idea spread that the early Church deliberately used tables for the Eucharist, around which the congregation gathered as if for a meal.[133] It was no coincidence that during the Second Vatican Council the Munich art magazine *Das Münster* reproduced the mosaic *ECCLESIA MATER* from Thabraca,[134] which seemed to show an altar in the middle of the nave (above Figs. 27, 28). Even renowned liturgical scholars expressed the opinion that the altar stood free in antiquity since the priest celebrated from behind it – facing the people.

The "new altar" (Josef Andreas Jungmann SJ) was so unanimously proclaimed by the experts as the restoration of an alleged original state that it became a self-fulfilling prophecy. Early Christian churches were restored in such a way as to give them a people's altar that they did not have before.[135] One example is the church of *Santa Maria delle Grazie* in Grado near Aquileia, which has an east-end apse and dates from the beginning

---

131 Already JUNGMANN 1966, 449, defends the traditional practice of priest and people facing in the same direction, even if facing east is scarcely understood any more today: "Nor, however, will it be possible to maintain that the bringing to God that lies in the *offere* can be expressed just as well by the more or less closed circle and the resultant upward direction as by the pathway. The closed circle speaks of community and emphasises the shape of the meal. In certain situations, this emphasis can be important and correct, but it would be paying homage to a contemporary trend if it were to be accorded sole legitimacy."

132 This is all the more the case when portable table altars were initially used.

133 GAMBER 1994, 28 f. *Id.* 1968, 94: "Die ursprüngliche Mahlgemeinschaft um den gemeinsamen Tisch." So also J. JUNGMANN, in: Lexikon für Theologie und Kirche², Suppl. 1 (Freiburg i.Br. 1966) 105 n. 5.

134 Frühchristliche Kunst gezeigt in Köln. Ausstellung von Mosaiken aus Tunesien (early Christian art on display in Cologne. Exhibition of mosaics from Tunisia), in: Das Münster 18 (1965) 25. On p. 50 of the same volume there is a presentation of the instruction *Inter Oecumenici* (1964), No. 91, see above n. 5.

135 Particularly instructive, but as yet little researched, is the influence of the demands made by liturgical reformers on altar designs in the historical churches of Ravenna long before the Second Vatican Council; see now M. VERHOEVEN, The Early Christian Monuments of Ravenna. Transformations and Memory (Turnhout 2011).

Fig. 141: *Santa Maria delle Grazie* in Grado, 5th century; modern placement of a people's altar, facing north west; G. Cuscito, Grado e le sue basiliche paleocristiane (Bologna 1980), Fig. 57.

of the fifth century (Fig. 141). The archaeologically confirmed location of the original table altar is immediately in front of the apse by the clergy seats. It was surmounted by a ciborium and stood offset to the east beneath it. This makes it clear that the priest stood in front of the altar looking east, especially since there was no room behind the altar for him and the concelebrants. In addition, a slab in front of the altar appears to mark where the liturgist stood.[136] Even in a second building phase, when the level of the entire church was raised in the sixth century, the altar remained above the old location and a wide set of barriers was erected in front of it. This space in front of the altar was undoubtedly intended for the choir and the concelebrating clergy, who, together with the main celebrant, faced east during the eucharistic liturgy. However, after the modern

136 Gamber 1972, 56 rightly corrects Nussbaum
    1965, 237; cf. *id*. 1996, 60 n. 58.

Fig. 142: Original situation of the holy rock, the table altar and the bread-basket floor mosaic in the Church of the Multiplication of the Loaves and Fish at Tabgha (east is at the top), 5ᵗʰ century; A. E. MADER, Die Ausgrabung der Basilika der Brotvermehrung und ihrer Mosaiken bei Et-Tabga am See Genesareth, in: Atti del III Congresso internazionale di Archeologia Cristiana (Rome 1934) 507–521, here 513 Fig. 4.

restoration of the church, in the spirit of the new liturgy, an antique-looking table altar was placed at the front towards the nave, thus suggesting that in the early Church the priest had celebrated facing the people.

Even more striking is the pilgrimage church of Tabgha on the Sea of Galilee, which was excavated by the Görres Society in 1932 (Fig. 142). The church has an east-end apse. The original table altar stood exactly above the revered rock on which, according to tradition, Jesus placed the bread and fish before their miraculous multiplication to feed the crowd (Mk 6:30 – 44). Two steps lead between the front table legs to the protruding rock. The priest undoubtedly stood on the step with his back to the faithful, which, as it were, granted him physical contact with the sacred rock.[137] This is supported by the fact

137 NUSSBAUM 1965, 71 f. maintains the opposite. But both the inscription and the mosaic of the fish and bread can be read from the west. Altar steps for pilgrims make no sense since they did not step up to the altar but rather crawled underneath it to venerate the sacred rock. For parallel examples of Byzantine churches with a step on the west side of the altar see ORLANDOS 1954, 447, 495, 528.

that at that time the Byzantine or Syrian liturgy was celebrated in this church, which was familiar with the practice of facing east to pray. As he did so, the priest would look at the famous floor mosaic with the bread basket and the two fish. It lay behind the altar, and in such a way that the priest saw it the right way round when standing in front of the altar. The mosaic was intended to establish a connection for the celebrating priest between the biblical multiplication of the loaves and the action of the Eucharist.[138] However, the restoration of the mosaic undertaken in the course of redesigning the church in 1984 followed Otto Nussbaum, who claimed against all the evidence that the priest had always stood behind the altar in this church and looked westwards towards the people (Fig. 143). Accordingly, the bread mosaic was moved directly in front of the new altar table, meaning that the priest is no longer permitted to stand there. In addition, the steps in front of the altar were covered by the new floor. Today's sanctuary gives the impression of an early Christian church, but is actually the result of a modern manipulation.

The following generalisation can be made with regard to the people's altar: it bears only an outward similarity to the altar of the first millennium. Certainly, both are sufficiently free-standing for it to be possible to walk round them, but that is almost as far as the similarity goes. The liturgical and theological meaning of the design of the altar in the early Church is almost diametrically opposed to the way the people's altar is used in the Roman Catholic world today. There is a vast and conspicuous disparity between the verbal appeal to the early Church and the actual reality. Werner Jacobsen observes on this:

The dominant idea today is that in early times the young community still sat (lay) harmoniously together round the table of the Lord's Supper and celebrated the Eucharistic sacrifice in their midst; such an ideal state with the liturgist behind the altar and the celebration facing the congregation across the altar is still preserved in an exemplary fashion in the Roman liturgy to this day, and so it is now a matter of restoring it as a spatial ideal for the other Christian churches, too. So the form of having congregation, liturgist and altar one behind the other on a single axis, an arrangement that had hitherto been common north of the Alps and meant that the liturgist stood between the congregation and the altar, i.e. with his back to the congregation, should be replaced by this 'communicative' form. The fact that in the early period the direction of liturgical celebration in those Roman churches that were east-oriented, for example San Paolo fuori le Mura or Santa Sabina, would have had to be towards the east, meaning that the liturgist would have stood, as was everywhere the case in the dioceses of the north, with his back to the congregation was a consideration that went unheeded amid all the enthusiasm for the newly discov-

138 MADER 1934, 513 Fig. 4.

Fig. 143: Present-day altar area of the Church of the Multiplication of the Loaves and Fish at Tabgha on the Sea of Galilee, looking east; photo: Georg Röwekamp.

ered form of liturgical 'togetherness'. Since almost all the churches here in the north are east-oriented – incidentally in Italy and, in many cases at least, in Rome itself as well – the current rearrangement of the sanctuaries after the Second Vatican Council has led to the liturgical furnishings of our historically grown church interiors being spoiled, abandoned and even devalued, right down to the profanation of former high altars. This astonishing phenomenon is actually not just an expression of cultural and historical indifference of the kind violently deplored by conservationists with an interest in art history, but also an expression of ecclesial disregard for its own hitherto traditionally hallowed locations of centuries of celebrating the Eucharist.

But with the current redesigning of the sanctuaries in the wake of the Second Vatican Council, the ideas that have existed since the early days of the Christian Church concerning the orientation of prayer and the liturgist celebrating towards the east as the location of the craved paradise, as the direction of God's coming, of the last day, of the final judgement and thus of the expected Christian redemption event – all these have been abandoned in favour of directional arbitrariness. The direction of prayer towards the east demanded in the Early Church has been replaced by a profane seating arrangement premised on being able to look at each other during the communal gathering.[139]

139 Jacobsen 2000a, 68 f.

Jacobsen sees the core problem as being the complete omission of facing east to pray in the latest reform of the liturgy. Since the early days of the Church, this orientation had led to the priest standing in front of the altar and praying in the same direction as the faithful. For by far the great majority of churches had their apse at the east end. The same was true of Rome, except that here the pope stood behind the altar in the fair number of churches that had their entrance to the east (above chapter IV, 5g). But either way, the rule of facing east to pray was observed. It was only after the long absence of the popes during the "exile" in Avignon (1309–1377) and the associated break with liturgical tradition that the understanding of facing east was lost in Renaissance Rome.[140] A paradigmatic example of this is the high altar of the Sistine Chapel, which stands against the west wall (Fig. 144). The pope celebrates with his back to the people and faces west. Many public station masses in the city are now also celebrated in a liturgically incorrect manner. The "people's altar" of St. Peter's plays a central role in this. Without yet understanding that here the correct place for the liturgist to stand is behind the altar and facing east, the popes claimed for themselves a general privilege to celebrate *versus populum*, whereas the Tridentine liturgy requires that all the other priests celebrate with their backs to the people. The papal master of ceremonies Paride Grassi († 1528) invoked the oldest customs of the Roman Church in order to justify this alleged privilege.[141] Consequently, Pope Sixtus V had the papal altars in Rome's great basilicas robustly remodelled so as to enable him to celebrate facing the people, regardless of whether he looked east or west when he did so. Thus it was not just in St Peter's and the Lateran with their east-end entrances that the pope looked towards the people, but also, for instance, in the church of *Santa Sabina*, which has an east-end apse. The liturgical experts of the time celebrated this as the restoration of the situation in the early Church.[142]

So facing east to pray had long since been abolished in the papal liturgy before the people's altar was introduced in the 1960s. Precisely because no one any longer had any concept of facing east, it proved possible in next to no time to turn the free-standing altar of the early Church into the people's altar. It is worth bearing in mind that the Second Vatican Council assembled in St Peter's Basilica, where the Synod Fathers could admire the supposed people's altar beneath Bernini's bronze baldachin at every session (Fig. 145).[143] What the pope can do, now everyone else should be able to do, too! The papal liturgy becomes the model for the liturgical reform *more romano*.[144] According

140 Cf. NUSSBAUM 1971, 160 f.
141 DE BLAAUW 1999–2000, 282 n. 78. The whole article is pertinent to the papal altar in the baroque period.
142 Ibid. 282, 286.
143 Only the pope celebrated at the high altar. On the other hand, beneath the Gloria of the *cathedra Petri* in the west apse of new St Peter's there stood an altar at which the celebrant had his back to the people (below Fig. 145). This altar formed a compositional unit with Bernini's artistic installation. But this did not save it. The altar was recently removed to make way for wooden stools.
144 Thus Theodor Klauser already in 1949; GAMBER 1994, 24, cf. 36 f. Cf. NUSSBAUM 1965, 284.

to the law of preservation of ancient practice in especially solemn celebration (Anton Baumstark),[145] it is believed that *versus populum* was the original way of celebrating in early Christian times. As early as 1912, Franz Wieland claimed that the priest celebrating with his back to the people was "completely unknown in the early Christian liturgy".[146] The Bonn liturgical historian Theodor Klauser adopts this verdict and provides a model for explaining the historical development: it was only at a later stage when east-facing prayer became a determining liturgical principle that there was any deviation from the original front-facing celebration; this then resulted in the priest moving to the side of the altar at the front.[147]

Although Franz Joseph Dölger and Erik Peterson had long since shown that facing east to pray was not something that only emerged in the fourth century, but had had a decisive influence on the liturgy since the second century, Otto Nussbaum still endeavoured during the council to help his teacher Klauser's theory to carry the day and to provide literary and archaeological evidence of the early Christian people's altar. He was concerned to show that the free-standing altar that the Congregation of Rites wanted was not mere archaeologism and also not the demand of modernist ideologues. He truly believed that the people's altar was restoring the original liturgy and thus making a genuine contribution to liturgical reform. He believed that the altar had been free-standing in the early Church precisely because it corresponded to the Last Supper and that since then the priest had stood behind the altar. In other words, he claimed that even the early Christian altars were people's altars in the sense of being tables for eating and fellowship.

Right on time for the end of the council in 1965, Nussbaum presented his post-doctoral thesis in Bonn on the "Position of the Liturgist at the Christian Altar before the Year 1000", thus enabling it to have the maximum effect.[148] With the assertion of an early Christian people's altar, he disqualified the Catholic and Eastern Church altars of the last one thousand years as an aberration which triggered an iconoclasm. The ready reception of Nussbaum's thesis and its widespread implementation in contemporary sanctuary designs have immortalised the myth of the people's altar. Instead of facing the (real or ideal) east, with the priest and people looking in the same direction towards the altar, the people's altar has brought about a new orientation: they all look towards the altar or rather look at each other. Newly built churches now also dispense with a sacred zone round the altar. The altar must once again be recognisable as a dining table, as at the Last Supper. This coincides with ecumenical interests: German

145 *Gesetz der Erhaltung des Alten in liturgisch hochwertiger Zeit.* Papal station masses are seen as such solemn celebrations.
146 WIELAND 1912, 146. Taken up by NUSSBAUM 1965, 251.
147 KIRSCH / KLAUSER 1950, 348; but, in a similar vein, already BRAUN 1930, 294f. See also RIGHETTI 1966, 374.
148 NUSSBAUM 1965.

Fig. 144: Papal Mass liturgy in the Sistine Chapel after a copperplate by Etienne Dupérac, 1578;
BAV Riserva Stragr. 7, tav. 116.

Fig. 145: St Peter's: in the foreground, Bernini's high altar ciborium and beneath it the papal altar, which is approached from behind. In the background, in the western apse, is the altar that stands under Bernini's *Cathedra Petri* installation; Satzinger / Schütze 2008, 327.

Fig. 146: The Last Supper, in the refectory of the Dominican convent and church of *Santa Maria delle Grazie* in Milan, Leonardo da Vinci, 1495–1498; photo: Wikimedia Commons.

Protestants have long spoken of the "Abendmahlstisch" (table of the Lord's Supper).[149] The idea of the Lord's Supper is the all-important key to the modern people's altar. The North American Benedictine and liturgist Godfrey Diekmann felt constrained to justify it as follows: "The head of the family does not usually preside at table by turning his back on the other participants."[150]

This conjures up an image of Leonardo's *Last Supper* (Fig. 146). Is this not proof enough that Jesus did not use an altar, but instead sat at a beautifully laid table offering bread and wine as food? Doesn't the altar have to look like a table and the priest have to stand, or preferably sit behind it?[151] Images are suggestive and shape perception. The idea is too lovely not to be turned into art. Since 2012, for example, a marble altar that replicates Leonardo's table has stood in the Catholic cathedral of St Ursula in Solothurn (Fig. 147). It does not seem to bother anyone that this is a gross misunderstanding, if not a deception. For Leonardo's painting is the mural of a monastic dining room in Milan (in the convent of *Santa Maria delle Grazie*). The table of the Last Supper is, as it were, the presidential table at which the abbot otherwise sits. Adjoining it to the right and left are the refectory tables of the monks. So what the image portrays – bread and chalice are both absent – is not the Eucharist at all but rather simply Jesus's last communal supper

149 E.g. Thümmel 1999, 495 f.

150 G. Diekmann, Liturgischer Kirchenbau, in: *Concilium* 1 (1965) 102–124, here 117.

151 Cf. Nussbaum 1971, 152, 160.

Fig. 147: Marble altar in the Catholic cathedral of St Ursula in Solothurn, which is modelled on the table of Leonardo da Vinci's Last Supper.

with the apostles, as seems fitting in a monastery refectory as an expression of fraternity and hospitality.[152]

But it was not such masterpieces that prompted the council's altar reform; once again, it was catacomb paintings that were the inspiration behind it. In 1894, the Silesian catacomb explorer and priest Joseph Wilpert discovered what he christened the *Fractio Panis* (Breaking of bread), in the "Greek Chapel" of the Catacomb of Priscilla in Rome (cf. Acts 2:42) (above Fig. 7).[153] After he had cleaned the completely sintered wall with acid, he brought to light an image, well preserved despite being seventeen hundred years old, which showed seven persons reclining on their stomachs on cushions in a semicircle, their legs, as it were, stretched out behind them. Among the six men there is probably also a woman. In front of them, the table companions have five loaves, two fishes and a drinking cup; to the right and left stand a total of seven baskets of loaves. The whole thing is taking place virtually in the open air, even though the picture itself is in a chapel-like room; below the picture, so Wilpert believed, stood an altar.[154] He interpreted the picture accordingly as a Eucharist: the "bishop" was sitting on the seat of honour on the

152 Other artists have indeed established such a connection, see SCHILLER 1968, 335 No. 81 (Stuttgart Psalter, c. 820–830). Juan de Juanes, basing his work on Leonardo's composition, portrayed the *Last Supper* as a Eucharist (oil painting c. 1562, in the Museo Nacional del Prado).

153 Cf. HEID 2009b, 191–194.

154 WILPERT 1895, 17–19 believes that a masonry tomb directly underneath the "triumphal arch" served as an altar. At it, the priest allegedly then had to celebrate "with his back to the people". Later a people's altar was put in the supposed chapel.

left and was breaking the eucharistic bread.[155] It seemed to him that the first Christians had celebrated the Eucharist as intimately and so close to nature as a picnic.[156]

Such ideas led to experiments even before the Second Vatican Council. Giulio Belvederi, the first secretary of the Pontifical Institute for Christian Archaeology in Rome, had the greatly enlarged depiction of the Eucharist mounted as a mosaic behind the altar in the monastery chapel of the Catacomb of Priscilla and himself celebrated facing the people. And it was no coincidence that Nussbaum began his altar studies with the reclining meal in antiquity.[157] He believed that he could deduce the form of the early Christian altar from Jesus's Last Supper (above chapter VI, 1), and felt bound to conclude from the reclining arrangement of the ancient symposium that the priest and the people faced each other.[158] For, he said, Jesus had lain at the edge and thus looked at the other participants in the meal. This was why the priest then stood behind the altar.[159] These are bold, highly constructed assertions that do not really need to be refuted. Let it suffice to point out that the place of honour at the sigma meal could also be in the middle of those gathered round the table,[160] which means not opposite the others, but more likely side by side.[161] Even with the best will in the world, there is no route from the ancient reclining banquet to front-facing celebration.

For this reason, Nussbaum attempted to prove in his post-doctoral thesis that, based on the archaeological findings, the altar was almost always free-standing and the priest stood behind it (above chapter IV, 5).[162] However, thanks to the studies by Dölger and Peterson, Nussbaum was aware of the extremely close connection between facing east to pray and the fact that the early Christian church interiors were oriented on an east-west axis.[163] It followed from this that the priest as a rule, and that means practically always, stood on the west side of the altar – with his back to the people – so as to face east. Nussbaum, however, continued undeterred, like Klauser, to maintain that facing east only became established from the fourth or fifth century onwards and did so at different speeds in the various Church regions.

Marcel Metzger, on the other hand, has calculated on the basis of Nussbaum's own data that in 31 percent of early Christian churches (with an east-end apse) the celebrant stood in front of the altar facing east; that is 88.8 percent of all churches for which it is at all possible to determine where the celebrant stood.[164] As we have seen above, this percentage

155 Ibid. 8–17.
156 The celebration of the Eucharist in the open air (in the cemeteries) remains speculation: ADAMS 2013, 181–197.
157 NUSSBAUM 1961b.
158 Cf. NUSSBAUM 1965, 373–377.
159 Ibid. 377. GAMBER 1994, 25, referring to the reclining meal, maintains the exact opposite.
160 ENGEMANN 1982.
161 METZGER 1971, 119.
162 NUSSBAUM 1965, 89: "original position of the liturgist behind the altar."
163 Ibid. 396.
164 METZGER 1971, 134, cf. 118 f.

is actually more likely to need setting higher. So Metzger is quite right when he says that the archaeological data do not support the hypothesis that celebrating *versus populum* was the original form and the norm – even less so since the hypothesis of a celebration *versus orientem* having been the norm is far better supported by textual sources.[165]

Other doubts also arise with regard to Nussbaum's view. For if facing east to pray did not establish itself until the fourth or fifth century, and then at different speeds in the different Church regions,[166] then how is it that no traces of such a change of sides is anywhere to be found in either sermons or synodal resolutions?[167] Would the conservatives not have had to defend the front-facing celebration as an apostolic heritage? And how is one supposed to concretely imagine this switch-over to a celebration "with one's back to the people"? According to Nussbaum, the priest could have celebrated in the same city in two churches with an east-end apse once *versus populum* and another time with his back to the people.[168] Yet he says the direction of celebration was fixed in every church. But why? The altars were almost always free-standing, meaning that they could be approached from either the front or the back. So one must, in all honesty, expect that every priest would choose the side according to his own personal taste: the conservative looks towards the people, the progressive looks east towards the apse. In fact, Nussbaum then abandons any kind of rule: "Since the erection of separate Christian cultic buildings, there has been no strict rule as to which side of the altar the place of the liturgist should be. He could stand sometimes in front of the altar, sometimes behind it."[169] And is it really likely that such a messy state of affairs would not have been discussed by the synods? A far more obvious assumption would be that there was neither any arbitrariness nor any switch-over, but rather that facing east determined the liturgy from the start.

Nussbaum sees it as an argument for a late dating of the triumph of east-facing prayer that an understanding of the Eucharist as a sacrifice came equally late: it was only then that people became inclined to regard the liturgist as a sacrificial priest as being, as it were, face to face exclusively with God.[170] Even today, this view still exerts an influence in that the prevailing theology regards the concept of the eucharistic sacrifice/sacrificial altar as obsolete within the history of religion and deems it necessary to use the people's altar as a way of correcting the earlier liturgy, which it feels is too sacrificial. But this is a misconstrual. For facing east and having priest and people looking in the same direction at the altar have essentially nothing to do with the sacrificial nature of the Eucharist. Turning towards the eastern sky, practised since the second century, concerns prayer

---

165 Ibid. 123 f.
166 NUSSBAUM 1965, 408–421.
167 Ibid. 409: "no concrete event and no decree [...] from which anything could be inferred about whether and when a change took place in the position of the liturgist at the altar."
168 Ibid. 50 (Resafa); 90 f. (Abu Mena).
169 Ibid. 408. This is rightly criticised by GAMBER 1972, 51.
170 NUSSBAUM 1965, 63; *id*. 1971, 150 f., 159; JUNGMANN 1967, 376 f.

in general, both within and outside the celebration of the Eucharist (above chapter IV, 4–5). So it makes absolutely no difference whether the Eucharist is understood as a sacrifice or not; it is enough that you pray during its celebration, since this already requires turning to face east.[171]

In truth, however, the sacrificial nature of the Eucharist is something people have been aware of since the second century, and this will inevitably reinforce the priest's habit of turning east to pray at the altar. There is no question of an allegedly original meal character of the Eucharist being replaced after the Constantinian shift by the vertical-latreutic dimension of worship.[172] Nor is there any break to be detected in the understanding of liturgy between the third and fourth centuries.[173] Furthermore, as has been shown above, the vertical dimension at the altar, demanded primarily by the prayer posture and then also by the sacrificial act, has been a continuous motif from as early as the second century,[174] one that continued seamlessly (above chapter IV, 4) and in the fourth century influenced church art as well (above chapter V). Everyone looks upwards, towards the eastern sky. The notion that priests and faithful should ideally stand face to face during the celebration of the mass is "complete nonsense" with respect to the early Christian church interior – so says Louis Bouyer, and Nussbaum even agrees with him on this.[175]

The free-standing altar of the early Church is not a people's altar in the modern sense since all the faithful, not just the priest, stand up to pray, raising their hands and eyes to the imaginary heavens. The fact that in early Christian times the liturgist was able to look upwards at all is, of course, connected with there not yet being any missals from which he is constantly reading.[176] Instead, the celebrant looks upwards while freely formulating the prayers, albeit according to traditional patterns. It would probably have seemed inconsistent to people in late antiquity if the priest were to raise his hands in prayer but not his eyes. What matters to the faithful is not at all that they see something, and the priest at the altar does not show them anything. In fact, he does not do anything worth seeing at the altar: no genuflection, no sign of the cross; at most he takes the gifts in his hand and elevates them.[177] It is only the ritual activities of the priest that developed in the High Middle Ages, in association with the modern people's altar and the *celebratio versus populum*, that have promoted a theatrical conception of liturgy in which the praying congregation is fixated on the priest's hand movements and eye contact.

Another weakness in Nussbaum's theory of the people's altar is his interpretation of the liturgical disposition of the early church interior. Basically, the circumstantial

---

171 See above p. 250.
172 Nussbaum 1965, 414–417.
173 Metzger 1971, 123.
174 Nussbaum 1965, 386f. does in fact also see the sacrificial dimension in the earliest Eucharist. Cf. Lang 2003, 66f.

175 Nussbaum 1965, 418 citing Louis Bouyer.
176 Cf. Heiler 1923, 426, 436f.; Budde 2001.
177 Jungmann 1952a, 95; Liccardo 2005, 148. OR I already contains bowing, signs of the cross and elevation of the gifts at the altar.

evidence he attempts to provide has three elements: (1) the early Christian altars are almost all free-standing; (2) they have no superstructures; and (3) the clergy seats are as a rule located at a certain distance behind the altar, mostly directly against the apse wall. The bishop sits in the centre, i.e. at the apex of the apse. On the basis of this disposition, Nussbaum assumes that the celebrant moves from his seat directly to the altar and looks at the people across the altar during the eucharistic liturgy. In this way, the people were able to observe what was happening on the altar. Here Nussbaum is basing himself on Joseph Braun. Braun had claimed that whenever the cathedra stood at the apex of the apse, it was "too awkward" for the priest to walk to the front of the altar.[178] Since practically all early Christian churches – with the exception of those in northern Syria – have the priest's seat at the apex of the apse, Braun has surreptitiously abolished facing east to pray.

Braun and Nussbaum are making use of modern plausibility categories that have little to do with the principles of liturgy. This is astonishing for two liturgy professors and priests who should know how many "awkward" rites the Roman Mass contains. From the outside, it may appear logical to proceed from the priest's seat to the altar by the shortest route. But what is liturgically logical? Do you ever see people lifting up their hands when they speak for a long time? And yet that is exactly what the priest does when he prays. Doesn't it take some getting used to when the pope stands at his cathedra with his back to the people in the medieval liturgy? And yet that is exactly what he did.[179] No doubt it would also be more practical not to walk round the altar and not to celebrate "with one's back to the people". But that is precisely what was done, as if it were the most natural thing in the world, so as to face east to pray.[180]

If it was not convenience, then one must ask what the underlying liturgical principle is supposed to have been that moved the priest in the first centuries to stand behind the altar. Nussbaum sees it as lying in the meal character of the mass.[181] But this does not hold water either. There is not a single early Christian text that, based on the meal character of the mass and possibly invoking the Last Supper, calls for a dining table or claims that the priest as the host must stand facing the congregation. There is no explicit and not even an implicit liturgical principle in the early Church that might have required a face-to-face celebration. What does exist, on the other hand, is the frequently, explicitly and universally attested liturgical principle of east-facing prayer and east-oriented churches, which leads us to assume, also based on archaeological facts, that the priest

---

178 BRAUN 1924a, 412.
179 See above p. 338.
180 There is not only clear evidence of the place of the liturgist in front of the altar, but liturgical sources

also exist according to which the celebrant walks to the altar from the cathedra (see above p. 340).
181 NUSSBAUM 1965, 387: "In early times the meal rite was in the foreground."

stood in front of the altar. When a church had its entrance to the east, the constellation of the priest at the altar looking towards the people came about more by accident and unintentionally.[182] This has nothing to do with the meal character of the Eucharist, let alone with the need for a pastoral liturgy for the people (*Volksliturgie*).[183]

It can certainly be regarded as a basic rule for the early Christian church interior that in most cases the main altar at least is free-standing[184] and can be walked round.[185] But this is a purely external feature shared with the modern people's altar. Nussbaum collected all the texts that speak of people standing round the altar on all sides. From this he drew the conclusion that the priest stood behind the altar, facing the congregation, and that the celebrant was concerned not to obstruct the people's view of the altar. But his assertions do not stand up to close scrutiny.

Origen of Alexandria († c. 254) preaches that the priests are located in a circle round the altar as if on a watchtower.[186] All this means is that during the sermon they sit behind the altar on the semicircular raised priests' benches.[187] John Chrysostom († 407) says that the table stands like a spring in the middle, so that the flocks may approach the spring from all sides and drink of the saving water.[188] This, too, is said as part of a sermon in which the preacher is seated on the cathedra at the apex of the apse, surrounded on the right and left by the college of priests. The altar stands in the centre of the chancel or presbytery. Thus it is indeed free-standing to the extent that both priests and laity are located on all four sides either inside or outside the enclosed chancel.[189]

This is confirmed by Bishop *John II of Jerusalem* († 417), who describes how the bishop and priest surround the altar and the deacon washes their hands. It is possible that the handwashing takes place at the priests' bench.[190] But it may also have taken place at the altar. In any case, during the eucharistic liturgy the presbyters stand with

---

182 Wallraff 2004, 119.

183 Vogel 1964, 13 n. 22; Nussbaum 1965, 448.

184 The so-called bema churches in Syria and several churches in North Africa are an exception to this rule.

185 Synes. catast. (PG 66, 1572B): κυκλώσομαι τὸ θυσιαστήριον; Nussbaum 1965, 87f.

186 Orig. in Iud. hom. 3,2 (SC 389, 100): *Invenias interdum etiam in nobis aliquos qui ad exemplum humilitatis positi sumus et in altaris circulo velut specula quaedam intuentibus collocati* [...] *et de altari Domini quod deberet incensi suavitate flagrare* [...] *ab omni hac sancta ecclesia et praecipue ab his qui ministrant in sanctis odor iste taeterrimus.* The phrase *in altaris circulo* makes

Wieland 1909, 54 think of a sigma-shaped table; that is incorrect.

187 Cf. Nussbaum 1965, 24.

188 Joh. Chrys. cat. bapt. 2,4,26 (FC 6,1, 286). Cf. in Eph. hom. 3,5 (PG 62, 30).

189 It is precisely this disposition that is also described in Euseb. hist. eccl. 10,4,44 (SC 55, 95f.) for the cathedral at Tyre: the altar stands in the middle of the presbytery, not of the church. The priests' benches are arranged to the right and left of the altar in an extension of the synthronos on which the bishops sit.

190 Joh. II Hieros. cat. myst. 5,2 (SC 126, 146–148); Nussbaum 1965, 62.

the bishop at the altar,[191] probably positioning themselves behind or beside the bishop, while the lower clergy can also stand opposite them, i.e. behind the altar. In the Liturgy of St James, the priest approaches the altar from the front,[192] and yet the priest prays for the deacons "surrounding your Holy Altar".[193] Here at the same time it becomes clear that lower clergy stand behind the altar and look westwards towards it; this means that for them the rule of facing east to pray is suspended.

Something similar is true of the Roman Rite, in which the bishop prays at the altar for the servants and handmaids and "*omnium circumstantium*" (round the altar).[194] The Spanish liturgy also has such formulations, and here, too, the location of the liturgist is in front of the altar.[195] The "servants and handmaids" of the Roman Canon embraces both clergy and laity.[196] However, it is only the clergy who in the strict sense stand round the altar. The bishop stands in front of the altar, while the lower clergy (regional subdeacons) stand opposite him on the east side. They look at the bishop because they give the responses in the Preface dialogue (*Dominus vobiscum – Et cum spiritu tuo*).[197] Later, it is the monks' choir that stands behind the altar with the same function (above Figs. 91, 93 and 152).

In support of his thesis that the priest stands behind the altar, Nussbaum also points to texts that speak of the faithful seeing the gifts on the altar. On closer analysis, however, all his texts prove not to be particularly valid. For example, in the week after Easter, Bishop *Ambrose of Milan* († 397) tells the newly baptised that they now have the opportunity "to come to the altar" and see the sacraments lying on there. Nussbaum thinks this to mean that the participants in the mass were able to see the altar and the bread and chalice on it from the nave.[198] But that is not what Ambrose is saying. He says several times quite clearly that only someone who comes to the front right up to the altar

191 Greg. Naz. or. 2,8 (SC 247, 98): The priests (clergy) jostle round the altar. Const. Apost. 8,12,3 (Funk 1905, 496): at the altar, the concelebrating priests stand to the right and left beside the bishop. See already the concelebration of the presbyters in Trad. Apost. 4 (FC 1, 222).

192 See above p. 266 n. 547.

193 Divine Liturgy of St James (BKV Griechische Liturgien [München 1912] 108).

194 See above p. 219 n. 322.

195 Lib. Moz. 686 (Férotin 1995): *Prepara nobis mensam venerendi* [!] *altaris, quam circumdemus velut mensam magnifici Regis*. Isid. eccl. off. 1,3,2 (CCL 93, 5): *Stantem sacerdotem ante aram, et in circuitu eius corona fratrum*. Conc. Tol. IV anno 633, can. 18 (Vives 1963, 198): *sacerdos et levita ante altare conmunicent*. Conc. Emer. anno 666, can. 19 (Vives 1963, 339): *nomina ... ante altare recitentur tempore missae*. Conc. Tol. XVII anno 694 (Vives 1963, 525): *ante sacrosanctum altare Dei ... missas ... dicere*.

196 The fact that the laity are also meant here becomes clear from Lib. Sacr. Gelas. 195 (Mohlberg 1960): Prayer for the godparents.

197 See above p. 342 n. 883. A speculative interpretation drawing in the second or third century is given by O'Loughlin 2014, 80–82. Cf. the Preface on the Feast of St Paul Lib. Sacr. 343 (Mohlberg / Baumstark 1927): *gratias agere circumdantes altaria tua*. Cf. Sacr. Gelas. 599 (Mohlberg 1971).

198 Nussbaum 1965, 216 f.

can see the sacraments.[199] If the bread and wine are now sacraments, namely the Body and Blood of Christ, then this can only refer to the reception of Communion. It appears that the baptised are given the bread and wine in which they recognise the Body and Blood of Christ with the eyes of faith[200] directly at the altar, inside the enclosed chancel (*cancelli*).[201] It is not immediately clear from the texts whether Ambrose stands in front of or behind the altar during the liturgy, but the whole thing is easier to imagine if he celebrates with his back to the people.[202] For he also says: "You came to the altar, you saw the sacraments laid upon the altar"[203] and further that the cleansed people (in baptism) make their way to the altars of Christ, "hastening to approach that heavenly banquet. It comes and sees the holy altar arranged."[204] This really only makes sense if the faithful cannot see the things on the altar properly from the *cancelli*, i.e. at some distance in front of the altar, evidently because the bishop and the concelebrants[205] block their view. At the Communion, the baptised then go behind the *cancelli*[206] and receive Communion at the altar.

---

199 Ambr. sacr. 3,2,11 (SC 25², 98): *Venire habes ad altare. Quoniam venisti videre habes quod antea non videbas.* Ibid. 3,2,12 (98): *Videbas quae corporalia sunt corporalibus oculis, sed quae sacramentorum sunt cordis oculis adhuc videre non poteras.* Ibid. 3,2,15 (100): *Isti, lavasti, venisti ad altare, videre coepisti quae ante non videras* […]. *Ergo, fratres dilectissimi, venimus usque ad altare* […]. It is possible that the catechumens do indeed already see with their eyes bread and wine on the altar during the Liturgy of the Word (*Videbas quae corporalia sunt*). That would mean that in Milan – as in Hippo (see further below) – bread and chalice are already standing on the altar. There is, at any rate, no sure evidence in Ambrose of a preparation of the gifts not taking place until after the sermon. The only possible instance (cf. SCHMITZ 1975, 374; *id.*, in: FC 3, 66 f.) is Ambr. exp. in Ps. 118 prol. 2 (CSEL 62, 4): […] *non offert sacrificium nisi octavum ingrediatur diem, ut* […] *suum munus altaribus sacris offerat.* But this speaks only of the handing over of the offering *for* the altar, not *at* the altar. Hence it may take place before or at the beginning of the mass. If this is the case, it becomes all the more likely that Ambrose stands in front of the altar for the Eucharist, meaning that those present cannot see the bread and chalice until they receive the sacraments directly at the altar.
200 Ambr. sacr. 4,2,5–7 (SC 25², 104): *Sequitur ut veniatis ad altare. Coepistis venire spectarunt an-*

geli […]. […] *veniebas desiderans ad altare, quo acciperes sacramentum.* Ibid. 5,3,12 (124): *Ergo venisti ad altare, accepisti corpus Christi.* Ibid. 5,3,14 (126): *Venisti ergo ad altare, accepistis gratiam Christi, sacramenta estis caelestia consecuti.* Myst. 9,50 (184): *Forte dicas: Alia video, quomodo tu mihi adseris quod Christi corpus accipiam?*
201 J. SCHMITZ, in: FC 3, 59 f. Ambr. Hel. 34 (CSEL 32,2, 430): *venit iam dies resurrectionis, baptizantur electi, veniunt ad altare, accipiunt sacramentum, sitientes totis hauriunt venis. merito dicunt singuli refecti spiritali cibo et spiritali potu: parasti in conspectu meo mensam, et poculum tuum inebrians quam praeclarum!* Ambr. exam. 6,9,69 (CSEL 32,1, 257) does not allow the conclusion that the faithful received Communion at the altar (differently J. SCHMITZ, in: FC 3, 60). Cf. Zen. Ver. tract. 1,32 (CCL 22, 83): *sacri altaris feliciter enutrit a cancellis.* It is unclear whether it means receiving Communion at or inside the *cancelli*.
202 See above p. 253, 280, 394.
203 Ambr. sacr. 4,3,8 (SC 25², 106): *Venisti ad altare, adtendisti sacramenta posita super altare.*
204 Ambr. myst. 8,43 (SC 25², 178–180): *His abluta plebs* […] *ad Christi contendit altaria* […]. *Venit igitur et videns sacrosanctum altare conpositum.*
205 On concelebration see SCHMITZ 1975, 299.
206 Ambr. sacr. 4,2,7 (SC 25², 104): *veniebas desiderans ad altare, quo acciperes sacramentum. Dicit anima tua: Et introibo ad altare dei mei.*

Nor does Bishop *Zeno of Verona* († 371) yield any evidence as far as front-facing celebration is concerned. In one sermon he compares pagan and Christian sacrifices. While the sacrifice of the pagan is public and can be touched by anyone, the sacrifice of the Christian (*tuum sacrificium*) is so secret that it may not even be looked at by the catechumens – let alone by pagans.[207] One might think that this refers to the dismissal of the catechumens at the beginning of the celebration of the sacrifice. From this it would follow that the faithful could see the Eucharist on the altar during the service.[208] However, that is wrong. For by "your sacrifice" Zeno does not mean the celebration of the Eucharist in church at all, but rather the eucharistic bread which the faithful keep in a box for domestic Communion or to take with them on a journey.[209] Zeno now constructs the case of a mixed marriage in which conflict arises with the pagan husband who for his part takes home with him the portion of food from the sacrifice to the gods. A sacrilege could occur if the pagan hits his Christian wife in order to snatch the Eucharist box and look into it. So in this text Zeno is not talking about either the altar or the location of the priest at the altar.

Augustine of Hippo († 430) notes in several sermons that the faithful see the food lying on the Lord's table. Nussbaum, for his part, thinks that the bishop stood behind the altar so that the faithful could, as it were, observe him at mass.[210] But that is not necessarily the case. Nussbaum fails to take into consideration the exact moment at which Augustine says this, namely during the sermon on Easter Sunday, more specifically during the sermon on the Eucharist preached to the newly baptised. He gives these sermons – unlike general ones – after the preparation of the gifts and before the Canon.[211] He was not necessarily standing at the altar to do so at all, but can just as easily have preached it from the ambo or from the apse podium.[212] At all events, what the newly baptised see at this moment is, as he puts it, the mere food on the altar, similar to how they have food standing on the table at home. But when the blessing is added, that bread and that wine – there on the altar! – become the Body and Blood of Christ.[213]

---

207 Zen. Ver. tract. 2,7,8,14 (CCL 22, 174f.): *Quid, quod illius sacrificium publicum est, tuum secretum? Illius a quovis libere tractari potest, tuum etiam a Christianis ipsis minime consecratis sine sacrilegio videri non potest?* [...] *tum tota mugiet litibus domus, blasphemabitur deus arreptoque forsitan ipso sacrificio tuo tuum pectus obtundet, tuam faciem deformabit.*

208 So NUSSBAUM 1965, 402.

209 Cf. O. NUSSBAUM, Die Aufbewahrung der Eucharistie (Bonn 1979) 268f. On the Eucharist outside the celebration see ID., Geleit, in: RACh 9 (1976) 908–1049, here 993f.; RACh 23 (2010) 1085f.

210 NUSSBAUM 1965, 175; id. 1996 (1967) 333.

211 DROBNER, 57f., and there the *sermones* 227, 229 and 229A Latin-German.

212 I thank Hubertus R. Drobner for pointing out these important considerations from liturgical history.

213 Aug. serm. 229A,1 (PLS 2, 554): *Quod videtis in mensa domini, quantum pertinet ad ipsarum rerum speciem* (sc. bread and wine), *et in vestris mensis videre consuestis.* [...] *Adhuc quidem, quomodo videtis, panis est et vinum: accedit sanctificatio, et panis ille erit corpus Christi, et vinum illud erit sanguis Christi.* Also ibid. 272 (PL 38, 1246) speaks of bread and chalice on the altar during the sermon: *Hoc quod videtis in altari Dei* [...]. *Quod ergo videtis, panis est et calix;* [...] *quod autem fides vestra postulat instruenda, panis est corpus Christi, calix sanguis Christi. Breviter quidem hoc dictum est, quod fidei forte*

John Chrysostom († 407) writes in his book on priesthood: "For when you see the Lord sacrificed and laid upon the altar, and the priest standing and praying over the victim, and all the worshippers empurpled with that precious blood [...]."[214] Although this seems to compel the priest to be standing behind the altar, in fact, according to Chrysostom's explicit testimony, the celebrant stands in front of the altar.[215] The short sentence is therefore to be understood differently. It describes three phases of the liturgy: the preparation of the altar by the deacons,[216] the prayer of the priest (the anaphora) and subsequently Communion. So during the course of the liturgy, the faithful first see the gifts on the altar, then the priest moves in front of the altar, so that they only see him praying, and finally they see the faithful receiving Communion from the chalice.[217]

This is confirmed by Bishop *Theodore of Mopsuestia* († 428/29). In his description of the mass (after 379) he speaks of the deacon's call: "Look at the sacrifice", which is addressed to the congregation before the Preface dialogue.[218] Nussbaum infers a celebration *versus populum* since the faithful could see what was happening at the altar.[219] But can this really be what is meant? After all, Nussbaum has to concede that the archaeological findings show that the liturgist looks eastwards towards the apse in the Syrian churches.[220] For this reason, Klaus Gamber thinks that the deacon's call has to be understood in the sense of "Look in the direction of the altar".[221] This then refers to the entire sacrificial act at the altar since the call is made at the beginning of the anaphora.[222] The faithful are exhorted not merely to look at the bread and wine or the altar, but also to follow the liturgical action as such.[223] This refers first of all to

---

sufficiat. In the same way ibid. 227 (1099) must be understood in a future sense: *Panis ille quem videtis in altari, sanctificatus per verbum Dei, corpus est Christi.*

214 Joh. Chrys. sac. 3,4 (SC 272, 142–144): Ὅταν γὰρ ἴδῃς Κύριον τεθυμένον καὶ κείμενον καὶ τὸν ἱερέα ἐφεστῶτα τῷ θύματι καὶ ἐπευχόμενον, καὶ πάντας ἐκείνῳ τῷ τιμίῳ φοινισσομένους αἵματι [...]; cautious Nussbaum 1965, 134, 416 n. 268.

215 Joh. Chrys. coem. et cruc. 3 (PG 49, 397 f.). Text see above p. 258 n. 515.

216 The "Lord sacrificed" is proleptic (differently van de Paverd 1970, 243). Theod. Mops. cat. 15,25 f. (FC 17,2, 408 f.) and describes how although at the offertory procession the deacons are still just bringing Christ to be sacrificed, when they place the gifts on the table, it is as if he were lying in the tomb having already completed the Passion.

217 Joh. Chrys. coem. et cruc. 3 (PG 49, 397 f.) describes this sequence exactly: first the priest stands in front of the altar during the Canon, but then,

when the faithful press forward for Communion, they see the sacrificed Lamb (i.e. the eucharistic food).

218 Theod. Mops. cat. 15,44 (FC 17,2, 419 f.).

219 Nussbaum 1965, 118.

220 Ibid. 61.

221 Gamber 1972, 50.

222 Theod. Mops. cat. 16,1 (FC 17,2, 422 f.): 'Look at the sacrifice' [...]. After that, the priest has to begin the sacrifice."

223 Ibid. 15,42 (FC 17,2, 422 f.): "Everyone [...] watches what is going on." Ibid. 15,44 (420): "And in this way he rouses everyone to look closely at the sacrifice since it is a shared matter that is to take place there." Ibid. 16,2 (423): "For after the deacon [...] has called 'Look at the sacrifice' – so everyone's gaze remains directed expectantly towards what is happening – the priest now begins with the oblation of the sacrifice, first blessing the people with the words [...]." Lang 2003, 51 sees the call as referring to facing east.

the preparation of the gifts by the deacons.[224] Here they then also see "the sacrifice on the altar [...] as if someone were laid in a certain tomb after death."[225] The faithful can therefore watch the deacons placing the bread and chalice on the altar. This, of course, lasts only a brief moment before the bishop comes up to the altar from the front. Then the faithful "offer up the sacrifice through the priest. For although he stands there (alone) to offer the sacrifice, he nevertheless offers it, like the tongue, for all the body."[226] The faithful see how "the acceptance [of the sacrifice] is displayed equally before all our eyes."[227] Apparently, then, the faithful see the priest standing in front of the altar for the oblation, but otherwise only hear his voice. Finally, during Communion the faithful are to "look attentively at the sacrifice presented."[228] What is now meant by the "sacrifice" is the Eucharistic species.

So the patristic texts adduced by Nussbaum to show that the altar was freely visible to the faithful basically controvert him. The preachers never say: "Look how the priest holds the Eucharist in his hands and shows you how he lifts up and blesses the chalice, how he mixes the bread and wine", etc. Yet such vital indications are essential if, like Nussbaum, you believe that the priest stands behind the altar precisely in order that the faithful can observe him and what is happening at the altar.[229]

Finally, a number of images remain to be discussed which appear to confirm Nussbaum's thesis of a front-facing celebration having existed since at least the sixth century. In most cases, however, it turns out that what is involved in these images is simply artistic freedom or compositional constraints, meaning that direct conclusions about the liturgical reality cannot be drawn from them. Some of them, however, have also been misinterpreted and cannot therefore be used in support of an alleged popular celebration (*Volkszelebration*).

A mosaic in the church of *Sant'Apollinare in Classe* (seventh century) shows the priest-king Melchisedek standing behind an altar, his gaze directed towards the observer (Fig. 148). Since the altar has the shape of a Christian altar, one might think that in Ravenna the priest celebrated *versus populum*. But this is obviously a case of creative freedom at work since the artist wants to bring together on one and the same altar three Old Testament sacrificial scenes as prefigurations of Christ's sacrifice: from the left Abel sacrifices a lamb, from the right Abraham his son Isaac, and from the back Melchisedek bread and wine. But the priest never approaches an altar from the side. So the artist was merely concerned to distribute the three persons on three sides of the

224 Theod. Mops. cat. 15,28 (FC 17,2, 411).
225 Ibid. 15,29 (FC 17,2, 411).
226 Ibid. 15,40 f. (FC 17,2, 417).

227 Ibid. 15,40 f. (FC 17,2, 417).
228 Ibid. 16,22 (FC 17,2, 437).
229 Nussbaum 1965, 380, 402 f., 448.

altar. Hence Melchisedek is not evidence of a front-facing celebration. It is more likely that the curtain in the background could be interpreted as separating the altar space from the worshippers' space. In that case, Melchisedek would have his back turned to the faithful. A similar mosaic in *San Vitale*, which is older and served as a model for the other one, shows only Abel and Melchisedek sacrificing at the altar, but here, too, for purely iconographic reasons, to the right and left of the altar, while the main sides remain empty (above Fig. 42).[230]

A number of pre- and post-iconoclastic pictorial documents, especially illuminations, show Christ at the Communion of the Apostles. For example, on the famous silver plate of Riha, Christ is seen standing behind an altar, facing the observer. He is giving the eucharistic bread and cup to the apostles to the right and left (Fig. 149).[231] So Christ appears as a priestly liturgist at a Christian altar. Once again, one might think that in Byzantium a front-facing celebration was normal, with the celebrant standing behind

230 The same solution is also found in pagan art, e.g. ANRW 2,17,2 (Berlin / New York 1981) 1054.

231 Schiller 1968, 326 Fig. 56; 328 Figs. 59–62; 329 Fig. 63; 330 Fig. 64; Loerke 1975, 85 f., 88, 90.

Fig. 148: Portrayal of the three Old Testament sacrifices of Abel, Melchisedek and Abraham at one altar, mosaic in *Sant'Apollinare* in Classe, 7th century; Dresken-Weiland 2016, 273.

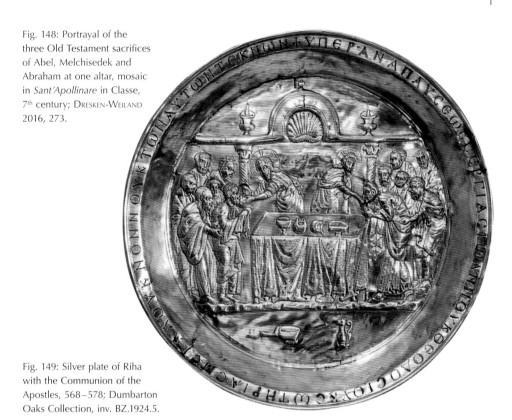

Fig. 149: Silver plate of Riha with the Communion of the Apostles, 568–578; Dumbarton Oaks Collection, inv. BZ.1924.5.

the altar. But the Byzantine liturgy only knows an east-facing celebration, which requires the liturgist to stand in front of the altar (above Figs. 32 and 48).[232] The composition and perspective of the images of the Communion of the Apostles are the result of artistic freedom alone, as can be seen from the mere fact that Christ is frequently depicted twice at the same altar: standing on one side, he distributes the eucharistic bread to some of the apostles; standing on the other side, he offers the chalice to other apostles. Also, the ciborium, which actually overarches the altar, is always moved behind the altar for compositional reasons. Occasionally, there are two angels standing behind the altar instead of Christ; they hold two fans (*rhipidion, flabellum*). In fact, in the Byzantine liturgy, the deacons performing the fanning ministry do stand behind the altar, whereas the liturgist's position is in front of the altar (Fig. 150).[233]

232 See above p. 255–263.
233 Schiller 1968, 329 Fig. 63; 330 Fig. 64. Where the deacons stand can vary, either beside or behind the altar; Nussbaum 1965, 30 f. n. 41. Occasionally the fan deacons stand beside the altar;

Theod. Mops. cat. 15,26 (FC 17,2, 409). Angel deacons with fans behind the altar are also to be seen in the St Sophia cathedral in Kiev (Schiller 1968, 329 Fig. 63).

Fig. 150: St Blaise at the altar, and behind the altar two deacons with fans; choir fresco in the *Hagia Sophia* cathedral of Ohrid; A. Grabar, La peinture byzantine (Geneva 1953) 140.

Fig. 151: D-initial of the Drogo Sacramentary allegedly showing a celebration of Mass, c. 835–855; BnF Ms. lat. 9428, fol. 87v.

A decorative initial in the *Drogo Sacramentary* (c. 835–855) appears to show a front-facing celebration of the mass (Fig. 151). The architecture framing it suggests the spatial arrangement of a church with the chancel on the left (under the dome) and the nave on the right, so you think you are seeing a church in longitudinal section. Accordingly, the bishop appears to be standing behind the altar and blessing the chalice that is standing on it. This seems to be supported by the fact that the crowd of people are bowing in reverence. The bishop, seemingly identified as a monk by his large tonsure, is performing the sacred act in the direction of the people. Charles Rohault de Fleury actually claims in his study of the Christian altar that the image shows the priest celebrating the mass facing the people as was customary in early Christian times.[234] This is, however, based on a misinterpretation. For what is portrayed here is neither a church nor a mass nor a bishop. A first clue is given by the text that the *D* initial decorates. It is the text of the prayers for the feast of the apostle Paul on 30 June. The Collect begins: "O God, who didst teach the multitude of the nations by the preaching of the blessed apostle, Paul […]." But what is to be seen inside the initial

---

234 C. Rohault de Fleury, La messe. Études archéologiques sur ses monuments 1 (Paris 1883) 68.

is not, as one might imagine, Paul preaching. Instead, the artist has chosen a quite specific scene from the life of the apostle which is found extremely rarely in Christian art. It is related in the Acts of the Apostles that Paul, along with four men, took a Nazarite vow in the Jerusalem Temple, that is, he had his head shaved (Acts 21:23–26). More specifically, it says that Paul chose four men who were to take this vow upon themselves with him. If we now look at the initial, we see four men standing upright in the front row of the crowd and led by a white-clad man with a tonsure, apparently Paul.[235] The crowd behind them is bowing. So what is depicted here is in reality Paul's Nazarite vow.[236] On the left is a man to be seen wearing a red robe; he is not a bishop but a Jewish priest standing in front of the altar of the Jerusalem Temple and turning towards the people. He, too, has a tonsure since he, too, has apparently taken the vow. He is not blessing the chalice, but rather greeting the five men who are taking their vows. The oversized chalice on the altar has nothing to do with the Eucharist, but is the

235 Paul also has a tonsure at his execution in the decorative initial on the Feast of SS Peter and Paul on 29 June: BnF, Ms. lat. 9428, fol. 86r.

236 This is confirmed for certain by another decorative initial, which shows the Jewish priest Zechariah in a similar building at an identical altar; here, too, it is the Jerusalem Temple and its altar (Lk 1:9–11). BnF, Ms. lat. 9428, fol. 83r: Vigil of the Feast of St John the Baptist on 23 June.

attribute of Paul, who is said in Acts to be a "chosen vessel" (Acts 9:15).[237] It does not really have to come as a surprise that such an unusual episode was chosen to decorate the initial. For the monks who produced the sacramentary, Paul's Nazarite vow could be compared to the great tonsure they received at their own investiture. Hence it is no coincidence that Paul is wearing a striking garment resembling a white dalmatic. What is actually meant, however, is probably a *cuculla* (monk's habit).

The famous ivory in the Liebieghaus in Frankfurt depicts the celebration of mass at the altar at the moment when the *Sanctus, Sanctus, Sanctus* is being chanted (c. 875) (Fig. 152). Here the word *"circumstantes"* in the Canon is quite accurate in that people are standing on both sides of the altar, and here, too, the priest appears to be celebrating "towards the people".[238] But this is once again a false conclusion. Even though the ivory does indicate the spatial depth of a church, in reality the whole church is not represented at all. The ciborium in the background, supported by four (corner) columns, is to be imagined above the altar. This enables one to understand better that the relief depicts only the chancel of a church, where the liturgy of the clergy takes place. In order to achieve an optimal perspective, the artist chooses the unusual view of the altar from the apse since this enables him to portray the bishop – who quite probably commissioned the ivory – from the front. So the bishop is not celebrating towards the people at all, but towards the apse, towards the east. There are two pieces of evidence for this. First, the medieval liturgy requires an east-facing celebration.[239] It also requires that the deacons stand behind the bishop at the altar.[240] On the relief there are indeed five deacons in dalmatics standing behind the celebrant. Second, the liturgy requires that the subdeacons stand facing the bishop and give him the liturgical responses.[241] Accordingly, on

Fig. 152: Celebration of Mass (*Sanctus* scene), ivory, c. 875; Liebieghaus Sculpture Collection, Frankfurt. photo: Liebieghaus Skulpturensammlung; photo: ARTOTHEK.

237 In the choral of the feast, Paul is lauded as *vas electionis*.

238 This is how VON EUW 1985, 404 interprets the ivory. It is no coincidence that Theodor Klauser, a zealous advocate of front-facing celebration, used this ivory as a frontispiece in his book *Kleine Abendländische Liturgiegeschichte* (Bonn 1965). The internet presentation of the Liebieghaus says of the ivory: "This relief depicts the Christian celebration of the Sacrifice of the Mass. In the centre, behind the altar, stands the priest, facing the faithful".

239 See above p. 337 f.

240 OR I,86 (ANDRIEU 1948, 95): [...] *stantes post pontificem* [...] *et archidiaconus* [...] *et ceteri* [*diaconi*] *per ordinem disposita acie.*

241 OR I,87 (ANDRIEU 1948, 95): *Et subdiaconi regionarii, finito offertorio, vadunt retro altare, aspicientes ad pontificem.* The regional subdeacons give the pope the liturgical responses and hence function as a choir. LP 16,2 (DUCHESNE 1886, 139): *ante se sacerdotes adstantes, sic missae celebrarentur.* Isid. eccl. off. 1,3,2 (CCL 93, 5): *Chorum autem ab imagine factum coronae et ex eo ita vocatum; unde et Ecclesiasticus liber scribit: "Stantem sacerdotem ante aram, et in circuitu eius corona fratrum."* Cf. Isid. etym. 6,19,5 (LINDSAY 1911a, 246): *dictus chorus quod initio in modum coronae circum aras starent et ita psallerent.* Isidor is not familiar with an eastward orientation for either churches or prayer: etym. 15,4,7 (LINDSAY 1911b, 168).

the relief chanting clerics are to be seen in front of the altar – but are in reality behind it. Their vestment, the *planeta*, identifies them as subdeacons (of the schola).[242] Hence the Frankfurt Mass ivory does not depict a front-facing celebration. Rather, the celebrant stands with his back to the people, who must be imagined as standing behind the ciborium. The same spatial arrangement is found in a scene of the *Drogo Sacramentary* (above Fig. 91) and in a thirteenth-century fresco in the church of *San Lorenzo* Outside the Walls with its east-end apse (above Fig. 93): in each case the choir of monks stands on the east side of the altar looking towards the celebrant.

The León Bible of 960, also known as the *San Isidoro Bible*, contains an illustration as the frontispiece to the Book of Leviticus which has recently been cited as key evidence for front-facing celebrations in Spain (Fig. 153). Isaac Sastre de Diego, in his study of late antique and medieval altars in Spain, discusses the position of the liturgist at the altar before the Gregorian reform of the liturgy (eleventh century).[243] Without any sound archaeological reasons for doing so, he argues in favour of a position of the priest behind the altar, i.e. facing the people. The Mozarabic liturgical books, however, leave no doubt that the liturgist always approaches the altar from the front, even if the altar is free-standing.[244] The priest's position in front of the altar is a liturgical requirement so that he faces east since the churches uniformly have east-end apses. Sastre points to the Leviticus frontispiece in the León Bible as a supposedly convincing argument for front-facing celebration because in it Aaron stands at the altar with a crowd of people (worshippers?) standing opposite him. But the proposed interpretation is wrong. Only a detailed description of the image allows a correct interpretation of it, and this makes it clear that, in a similar way to the *Drogo Sacramentary* (above Fig. 151), the illustrator wishes to depict something completely different from what modern viewers imagine. And once again, the image has nothing whatsoever to do with the position of the priest at the altar during the celebration of the Eucharist.

Since the Book of Leviticus deals primarily with Jewish worship, this is precisely what the artist is depicting in the image placed in front of it: priestly ministry in the Temple or in the Tent of Meeting. Specifically, what is shown here is the consecration of the sacrificial altar of the Old Testament Tent of Meeting and of the priests serving at this

---

242 OR I,44 (ANDRIEU 1948, 81): *subdiaconi de scola levant planetas cum sino*. The sole detail that deviates from the liturgical plan is the two candlesticks. From the viewer's perspective, they must stand in front of the altar. The chosen solution is artistic freedom since it is obvious that burning candles are not allowed to stand directly next to the celebrant. OR I,66 (ANDRIEU 1948, 90): *accoliti sumentes cereostata ponent ea retro altare per ordinem*.

243 SASTRE DE DIEGO 2013, 184–187.

244 See above note 195. FÉROTIN 1904, 229, 249, 270, 416 and *id.* 1995, 181, 335, 424: *ante altare*. FÉROTIN 1904, 236, 249, 252, 258, 283, 326, 411: *coram altario*. Ibid. 261 f.: *coram altaribus*. The altar stands facing east: ibid. 73. Behind the altar is the bishop's throne: ibid. 152, 212. Strong east symbolism in baptism ibid. 13–18. See also ibid. 503.

Fig. 153: Aaron at the altar of the Old Testament Tent of Meeting; illustration from the Visigothic León Bible, 10th century; © Museo San Isidoro de León, Real Colegiata de San Isidoro de León.

altar (cf. Ex 29:44). It is an artistic invention for which various Old Testament texts have to be consulted. The image shows a space created by a fictitious architecture. It is the Tent of Meeting. In it are the Ark of the Covenant, the mercy seat, a lampstand (Ex 25), a curtain (Ex 26:31–37) and a T-shaped altar of burnt offering (Ex 27:1–8). In front of it, outside the tent, stands the showbread table with a red cover and a circular loaf lying on it (Ex 25:23–30; Nm 4:7).

Inside and outside the Tent of Meeting, there are twenty-two persons to be seen. Judging by their garments (ephod, trousers, turban [Ex 28:40–43; 29:8 f.; Lv 8:13]), they must all be priests. The oversized main figure is probably Aaron. He stands on the left in front of the T-shaped altar and is looking at the seven priests standing at the bottom right. On the altar in front of him Aaron has a golden vessel with a long neck ending in two beak-shaped spouts. He is holding his hands under these spouts, apparently collecting in them anointing oil contained in the vessel. The group of people he is looking at are stretching out their huge hands towards him to catch the anointing oil. On the opposite side of the altar stand the four sons of Aaron (hence their small form) (Ex 28:1). They, too, are looking at the eight men at the bottom of the picture. The son at the front has stepped right up to the altar, on which stands a chalice. His large hand is not holding the chalice as it is in front of it. Apparently, the priest is letting blood from the chalice trickle down from his hand. The seven men are stretching upwards, or at least are clearly holding up their hands. Evidently they want to catch not just the oil but also the blood. For it is through both anointings that they are initiated into their priesthood. This must be the oil and blood with which the altar was previously anointed (Ex 29:20 f.).

So the image depicts neither a celebration of the mass nor any Christian liturgy at all, but rather an unique Old Testament act of consecration. Hence it is in no way possible to infer the position of the priest at the altar in the celebration of the Eucharist from the position of Aaron in this frontispiece.[245] Finally, the group of people on the right outside the Tent of Meeting still has to be explained. It, too, remains within the framework of the biblical narrative. It shows Moses at the head and behind him other priests.[246] The blue-and-red cloud above them offers the crucial clue as to the interpretation: as long as the cloud, which takes on a red colour at night, lies on the tent, Moses cannot enter it (Ex 40:34–38). But as soon as it lifts, the Levites, who alone are allowed to camp near the tent, have to take it down and move it on (Nm 1:49–53).[247]

245 This holds true in spite of the fact that Spanish theology sees in Aaron the prototype of bishops and in his sons that of presbyters.
246 Ps 99,6: Moses is, like his brother Aaron, a priest.
247 For important suggestions regarding the interpretation of the image, I am indebted to P. Augustinus Sander OSB. Sastre's supposed second piece of evidence for a front-facing celebration, the very late (eleventh or twelfth century?) bishop's sarcophagus from Dume in the Braga museum, shows a saint standing in the orans posture behind a block-shaped altar (without any liturgical objects

SUMMARY

The present people's altar, whether round or rectangular, is the product of historical mis-information or ahistorical archaeologism. The idea that it existed in the early Church as the centre of a eucharistic meal fellowship is a piece of scholarly fiction. The all-defining function of the early Christian altar was not to serve as a meal table for a congregation gathered round it in a circle and looking at each other; rather, its function from the outset was to be a place of prayer and at the same time also a place of sacrifice. Prayer is directed towards God and, according to a universal practice, is to be offered facing east. For the vast majority of churches in the early period and in the Middle Ages, this meant that the priest stood at the altar with his back to the people. This became so much the common practice that it was maintained even when churches were no longer built with east-facing apses or when side altars were erected facing in different directions.

This rule applied universally, i.e. in all the families of rites in both East and West (the special case of the Reformation churches is left out of account here). At all events, there is no family of rites known in the early Church to have had a people's altar. There was for a long time a de facto ecumenical consensus on this. In the churches of the Byzantine Rite and among the Old Orientals the worship spaces still continue as far as possible to have east-facing apses. The main altar is free-standing in them, but in such a way that the priest approaches it from the front.[248] The Latin Church alone has departed from the ecumenical consensus and gone its own way in the belief that it was restoring the origins: first, east-facing prayer was abandoned, then – after the Second Vatican Council – the location of the priest in front of the altar as well.

on it). The aim of this image is to depict with limited iconographic means the priestly dignity of the
saint. The artist has no alternative but to position
the saint behind the altar in order to provide a
front view of him (similarly above Fig. 44). This

in no way implies a celebration *versus populum*.
Cf. H. Schlunk, Ein Sarkophag aus Dume im
Museum in Braga, in: Madrider Mitteilungen 9
(1968) 424–458.

248 Gamber 1994, 29.

INDICES

SOURCE TEXTS

ACHELIS / FLEMMING 1904 H. ACHELIS / J. FLEMMING, Die syrische Didaskalia (Leipzig 1904).

ANDRIEU 1940 M. ANDRIEU, Le Pontifical Romain au Moyen-Age 2. Le Pontifical de la Curie Romaine au XIIIe siècle (Città del Vaticano 1940).

ANDRIEU 1948 M. ANDRIEU, Les *Ordines Romani* du haut moyen âge 2. Les textes (*Ordines* I–XIII) (Louvain 1948).

ANDRIEU 1961 Les *Ordines Romani* du haut moyen âge 3. Les textes (*Ordines* XIV–XXXIV) (Louvain 1961).

BASTIAENSEN 1995 A. A. R. BASTIAENSEN et al., Atti e passioni dei martiri (Roma ³1995).

BOJKOVSKY / AITZETMÜLLER 1988 G. BOJKOVSKY / R. AITZETMÜLLER, Paraenesis. Die altbulgarische Übersetzung von Werken Ephraims des Syrers 4 (Freiburg i.Br. 1988).

BROCK 2013 S. P. BROCK, The Martyrdom of St Phokas of Sinope. The Syriac Version (Piscataway 2013).

BROX 1991 N. BROX, Der Hirt des Hermas (Göttingen 1991).

BURCHARD 1983 C. BURCHARD, Joseph und Asenath (Jüdische Schriften aus hellenistisch-römischer Zeit 2,4) (Gütersloh 1983).

Chavasse 1955 A. Chavasse, A Rome, le jeudi-saint, au VIIe siècle d'après un vieil *ordo*, in: Revue d'Histoire Ecclésiastique 50 (1955) 21–35.

Clarke 1974 G. W. Clarke, The Octavius of Marcus Minucius Felix (New York 1974).

Cohn / Reiter 1915 L. Cohn / S. Reiter, *Philonis Alexandrini opera quae supersunt* 6 (Berlin 1915).

Cramer 1967 J. A. Cramer, *Catenae in Sancti Pauli epistolas ad Corinthios* (Hildesheim 1967).

Datema 1970 C. Datema, Asterius von Amasea Homilies I–XIV (Leiden 1970).

Delehaye 1936 H. Delehaye, Étude sur le légendier romain. Les saints de novembre et de décembre (Bruxelles 1936).

Deshusses 1971 J. Deshusses, Le Sacramentaire Grégorien 1 (Fribourg 1971).

Deshusses 1972 J. Deshusses, Les messes d'Alcuin, in: Archiv für Liturgiewissenschaft 14 (1972) 7–41.

Dolbeau 2009 F. Dolbeau, Augustin d'Hippone. Vingt-Six Sermons au Peuple d'Afrique retrouvés à Mayence (Paris ²2009).

Douteil / Suntrup 2016 H. Douteil / R. Suntrup, Wilhelm Durandus, *Rationale divinorum officiorum* 2 (Münster 2016).

Drobner 2006 H. R. Drobner, Augustinus von Hippo. Predigten zum österlichen Triduum (*sermones* 218–229/D) (Frankfurt a.M. 2006).

Duchesne 1886 L. Duchesne, Le *Liber Pontificalis* 1 (Paris 1886).

Duchesne 1892 L. Duchesne, Le *Liber Pontificalis* 2 (Paris 1892).

Fabre / Duchesne 1910 P. Fabre / L. Duchesne, Le *Liber Censuum* de l'Église Romaine 1 (Paris 1910).

Fensterbusch 1964 C. Fensterbusch, *Vitruvii de architectura libri decem* (Darmstadt 1964).

Férotin 1904 M. Férotin, Le *Liber Ordinum* en usage dans l'Église wisigothique et mozarabe d'Espagne du cinquième au onzième siècle (Paris 1904).

Férotin 1995 M. Férotin, Le *Liber Mozarabicus Sacramentorum* et les manuscrits mozarabes (Roma 1995).

Ferrua 1942 A. Ferrua, *Epigrammata Damasiana* (Città del Vaticano 1942).

Fischer 1986 J. A. Fischer, Die Apostolischen Väter (Darmstadt⁹ 1986).

Funk 1905 F. X. Funk, *Didascalia et Constitutiones Apostolorum* 1 (Paderborn 1905).

Von Gebhardt 1902 O. von Gebhardt, Ausgewählte Märtyreracten und andere Urkunden aus der Verfolgungszeit der christlichen Kirche (Berlin 1902).

Gelzer 1893 H. Gelzer, Leontios' von Neapolis Leben des heiligen Iohannes des Barmherzigen, Erzbischofs von Alexandrien (Freiburg i.Br. 1893).

Grenfell / Hunt 1898 B. P. Grenfell / A. S. Hunt, The Oxyrhynchus Papyri 1 (London 1898).

Guyot / Klein 1993 P. Guyot / R. Klein, Das frühe Christentum bis zum Ende der Verfolgungen 1 (Darmstadt 1993).

Hack 2006 A. T. Hack, *Codex Carolinus* 1 (Stuttgart 2006).

Harnack 1916 A. Harnack, Porphyrius „Gegen die Christen". 15 Bücher (Berlin 1916).

Harnack 1985 A. Harnack, Marcion. Das Evangelium vom fremden Gott (Darmstadt 1985).

Harvey 1857 W. W. Harvey, *Sancti Irenaei episcopi Lugdunensis Libros quinque adversus Haereses* 2 (Cantabrigiae 1857).

Haury / Wirth 1964 J. Haury / G. Wirth, *Procopii Caesariensis opera omnia* 4 (Leipzig 1964).

Heil / Ritter 1991 G. Heil / A. M. Ritter, *Corpus Dionysiacum* 2 (Berlin / New York 1991).

Hyvernat 1886 H. Hyvernat, Les actes des martyrs de l'Égypte 1 (Paris 1886).

Joannou 1962 P.-P. Joannou, Discipline générale antique (IVe-IXe s.) 1,2. Les canons des Synodes Particuliers (Grottaferrata 1962).

Krüger / Ruhbach 1965 G. Krüger / G. Ruhbach, Ausgewählte Märtyrerakten (Tübingen⁴ 1965).

Lietzmann 1921a H. Lietzmann, Das Muratorische Fragment und die monarchianischen Prologe zu den Evangelien (Bonn 1921).

Lietzmann 1921b H. Lietzmann, Das *Sacramentarium Gregorianum* nach dem Aachener Urexemplar (Münster 1921).

Lindsay 1911a W. M. Lindsay, *Isidori Hispalensis Episcopi Etymologiarum sive Originum libri XX*, 1 (Oxford 1911).

Lindsay 1911b W. M. Lindsay, *Isidori Hispalensis Episcopi Etymologiarum sive Originum libri XX*, 2 (Oxford 1911).

Lipsius / Bonnet 1891 R. A. Lipsius / M. Bonnet, *Acta Apostolorum Apocrypha* 1 (Leipzig 1891).

Lipsius / Bonnet 1903 R. A. Lipsius / M. Bonnet, *Acta Apostolorum Apocrypha* 2,2 (Leipzig 1903).

Mansi J. D. Mansi, *Sacrorum conciliorum nova et amplissima collectio* 1–53 (Florenz / Venedig 1759–1827).

Marcovich 1986 M. Marcovich, *Hippolytus, refutatio omnium haeresium* (Berlin / New York 1986).

Marcovich 1994 M. Marcovich, *Iustini Martyris apologiae pro christianis* (Berlin / New York 1994).

Marcovich 1997 M. Marcovich, *Iustini Martyris Dialogus cum Tryphone* (Berlin / New York 1997).

Mohlberg 1957 L. C. Mohlberg, *Missale Francorum* (Roma 1957).

Mohlberg 1960 L. C. Mohlberg, *Liber Sacramentorum Romanae Aecclesiae ordinis anni circuli* […] (*Sacramentarium Gelasianum*) (Roma 1960).

Mohlberg 1961 L. C. Mohlberg, *Missale Gothicum* (Roma 1961).

Mohlberg 1971 L. C. Mohlberg, Das fränkische *Sacramentarium Gelasianum* (Münster ³1971).

Mohlberg 1994 L. C. Mohlberg, *Sacramentarium Veronense* (Roma ³1994).

Mohlberg / Baumstark 1927 L. C. Mohlberg / A. Baumstark, Die älteste erreichbare Gestalt des *Liber Sacramentorum anni circuli* der römischen Kirche (Münster 1927).

Mombritius 1910 B. Mombritius, *Sanctuarium seu Vitae Sanctorum* 1–2 (Paris ²1910).

Morin 1930 G. Morin, Miscellanea Agostiniana 1. *Sancti Augustini sermones post Maurinos reperti* (Romae 1930).

Niese 1955 B. Niese, *Flavii Iosephi opera* 6 (Berlin 1955).

Paschoud 2002 F. Paschoud, Histoire Auguste 5,1 (Paris 2002).

Radó 1961 P. Radó, *Enchiridion liturgicum* 1 (Rom u. a. 1961).

Riedel 1900 W. Riedel, Die Kirchenrechtsquellen des Patriarchats Alexandrien (Leipzig 1900).

Rücker 1923 A. Rücker, Die syrische Jakobosanaphora (Münster 1923).

Rupp 1860 J. Rupp, *S. Patris nostri Cyrilli Hierosolymorum archiepiscopi opera quae supersunt omnia* 2 (München 1860).

Scheid 1998 J. Scheid u.a., *Recherches archéologiques à la Magliana*. Commentarii fratrum Arvalium qui supersunt (Rome 1998).

Schneemelcher 1989 W. Schneemelcher, Neutestamentliche Apokryphen 2 (Tübingen ⁵1989).

Schubert 2014 C. Schubert, Minucius Felix, „Octavius" (Freiburg i.Br. 2014).

Schuster 1933 M. Schuster, *C. Plini Caecili secundi, Epistularum libri novem, epistularum ad Traianum liber panegyricus* (Leipzig 1933).

Schwartz 1939 E. Schwartz, Kyrillos von Skythopolis (Leipzig 1939).

Seyfarth 1986 W. Seyfarth, Ammianus Marcellinus, Römische Geschichte 4 (Berlin ³1986).

Siegert 1980 F. Siegert, Drei hellenistisch-jüdische Predigten (Tübingen 1980).

Smith 2014 K. Smith, The Martyrdom and The History of Blessed Simeon Bar Sabba'e (Piscataway 2014).

Stern 1976 M. Stern, Greek and Latin Authors on Jews and Judaism 1 (Jerusalem 1976).

Vilella / Barreda 2002 J. Vilella / P.-E. Barreda, Los cánones de la Hispana atribuidos a un concilio iliberritano, in: Studia Ephemeridis Augustinianum 78 (2002) 545–579.

Vives 1963 J. Vives, Concilios visigóticos e hispano-romanos (Barcelona / Madrid 1963).

Weis 1973 B. K. Weis, Julian – Briefe (München 1973).

Wilmart 1933 A. Wilmart, *Analecta Reginensia* (Città del Vaticano 1933).

LITERATURE

Abyneiko 2014 R. Abyneiko, The sacrificial character of the eucharistic celebration in the Letter to the Hebrews, in: G. Deighan (ed.), Celebrating the Eucharist – Sacrifice and Communion (Wells 2014) 25–60.

Adam 1998 A. Adam, Grundriss Liturgie (Freiburg i.Br. 1998).

Adams 2013 E. Adams, The Earliest Christian Meeting Places. Almost Exclusively Houses? (London / New York 2013).

Aiello 2012 V. Aiello, Costantino, il vescovo di Roma e lo spazio del sacro, in: G. Bonamente *et al.* (eds.), Costantino prima e dopo Costantino (Bari 2012) 181–207.

Alikin 2010 V. A. Alikin, The Earliest History of the Christian Gathering (Leiden / Boston 2010).

Altmann 1905 W. Altmann, Die römischen Grabaltäre der Kaiserzeit (Berlin 1905).

Andaloro / Romano 2002 M. Andaloro / S. Romano, Das Bild in der Apsis, in: dies. (ed.), Römisches Mittelalter. Kunst und Kultur in Rom von der Spätantike bis Giotto (Regensburg 2002).

Andresen 1975 C. Andresen, Geschichte des Christentums 1. Von den Anfängen bis zur Hochscholastik (Stuttgart 1975).

Angelelli 2002 C. Angelelli, Nuove osservazioni sulle chiese siriaine di Roma, in: F. Guidobaldi / A. Guiglia Guidobaldi (eds.), Ecclesiae Urbis 2 (Città del Vaticano 2002) 1019–1031.

Angenendt 2005 A. Angenendt, „Mit reinen Händen". Das Motiv der kultischen Reinheit in der abendländischen Askese, in: *id.*, Liturgie im Mittelalter (Münster ²2005) 245–267.

Angiolini Martinelli 1997A P. Angiolini Martinelli, La Basilica di San Vitale a Ravenna. Atlante (Modena 1997).

Angiolini Martinelli 1997B P. Angiolini Martinelli, La Basilica di San Vitale a Ravenna. Testi (Modena 1997).

Apollonj Ghetti 1951 B. M. Apollonj Ghetti *et al.*, Esplorazioni sotto la confessione di San Pietro in Vaticano. Eseguite negli anni 1940–1949, 1 (Città del Vaticano 1951).

Apollonj Ghetti 1969 B. M. Apollonj Ghetti, Le basiliche cimiteriali degli apostoli Pietro e Paolo a Roma, in: *id. et al.*, Saecularia Petri et Pauli (Città del Vaticano 1969) 7–34.

Apollonj Ghetti 1978 B. M. Apollonj Ghetti, Problemi relativi alle origini dell'architettura paleocristiana, in: Atti del IX congresso internazionale di Archeologia Cristiana 1 (Città del Vaticano 1978) 491–511.

Apostolos-Cappadona 2014 D. Apostolos-Cappadona, „… decorated with luminous mosaics". Image and Liturgy in 5th/6th-Century Roman Church Apse Mosaics, in: Studia Patristica 71 (2014) 93–110.

Asciutti 2019 M. Asciutti, Il complesso monumentale di S. Valentino nell'area Flaminia a Roma (Foligno 2019).

Aubé 1881 B. Aubé, Les chrétiens dans l'Empire Romain de la fin des Antonins au milieu du IIIᵉ siècle (Paris ²1881).

Backhaus 2009a K. Backhaus, Der Hebräerbrief (Regensburg 2009).

Backhaus 2009b K. Backhaus, Der sprechende Gott. Gesammelte Studien zum Hebräerbrief (Tübingen 2009).

Balch 2008 D. L. Balch, Roman Domestic Art and Early House Churches (Tübingen 2008).

Ballardini 2015 A. Ballardini, Die Petersbasilika im Mittelalter, in: H. Brandenburg et al., Der Petersdom in Rom. Die Baugeschichte von der Antike bis heute (Petersberg 2015) 35–75.

Balty / Balty 2011 J. Balty / J.-C. Balty, L'autel majeur de la cathédrale d'Apamée, in: O. Brandt / Ph. Pergola (eds.), Marmoribus vestita, Miscellanea in onore di Federico Guidobaldi 1 (Città del Vaticano 2011) 103–117.

Barlea 1975 O. Barlea, Dai presbiteri ai sacerdoti, in: G. Concetti (ed.), Il prete per gli uomini d'oggi (Roma 1975) 159–192.

Bartelink 1971 G. J. M. Bartelink, „Maison de prière" comme dénomination de l'Église en tant qu'édifice, en particulier chez Eusèbe de Césarée, in: Revue des Études Grecques 84 (1971) 101–118.

Barth 1999 H.-L. Barth, Die Mär vom antiken Kanon des Hippolytos. Untersuchungen zur Liturgiereform (Köln 1999).

Batiffol 1910 P. Batiffol, Urkirche und Katholizismus (Kempten / München 1910).

Bauer 2003 F. A. Bauer, Stadtbild und Heiligenlegenden. Die Christianisierung Ostias in der spätantiken Gedankenwelt, in: G. Brands / H.-G. Severin (eds.), Die spätantike Stadt und ihre Christianisierung (Wiesbaden 2003) 43–61.

Bauer 2004 F. A. Bauer, Das Bild der Stadt Rom im Frühmittelalter. Papststiftungen im Spiegel des Liber Pontificalis von Gregor dem Dritten bis zu Leo dem Dritten (Wiesbaden 2004).

Bauer 2009 F. A. Bauer, Gabe und Person. Geschenke als Träger personaler Aura in der Spätantike (Eichstätt 2009).

Berger 2006 A. Berger, Konstantinopel, in: RACh 21 (2006) 435–483.

Berger 1964 R. Berger, Die Wendung „offere pro" in der römischen Liturgie (Münster 1964).

Bergmeier 2017 A. F. Bergmeier, Visionserwartung. Visualisierung und Präsenzerfahrung des Göttlichen in der Spätantike (Wiesbaden 2017).

Bering 2012 K. Bering, Die Ära Konstantins (Oberhausen 2012).

Betz 1955 J. Betz, Die Eucharistie in der Zeit der griechischen Väter 1,1. Die Aktualpräsenz der Person und des Heilswerkes Jesu im Abendmahl nach der vorephesinischen griechischen Patristik (Freiburg i.Br. 1955).

Bisconti 2009 F. Bisconti, La capsella di Samagher. Il quadro delle interpretazioni, in: E. Marin / D. Mazzoleni (eds.), Il cristianesimo in Istria fra tarda antichità e alto medioevo (Città del Vaticano 2009) 217–231.

Bleckmann 2012 B. Bleckmann, Konstantin und die Kritik des blutigen Opfers, in: G. Bonamente et al. (eds.), Costantino prima e dopo Costantino (Bari 2012).

Blue 1994 B. Blue, Acts and the House Church, in: D. W. J. Gill / C. Gempf (eds.), The Book of Acts in its Graeco-Roman Setting (Grand Rapids 1994) 119–222.

Bodel 2008 J. Bodel, From Columbaria to Catacombs. Collective Burial in Pagan and Christian Rome, in: L. Brink / D. Green (eds.), Commemorating the Dead (Berlin / New York 2008) 177–242.

Bodonyi 1932 J. Bodonyi, Entstehung und Bedeutung des Goldgrundes in der spätantiken Bildkomposition, Diss. Wien 1932.

Böhler 2013 D. Böhler, The Church's Eucharist, the Lord's Supper, Israel's sacrifice. Reflections on Pope Benedict's axiom „Without its coherence with its Old Testament heritage, Christian liturgy simply cannot be understood", in: J. E. Rutherford / J. O'Brien (eds.), Benedict XVI and the Roman Missal (New York 2013) 107–123.

Böhler 2022 D. Böhler, Volk Gottes vom Altar her. Die Konstituierung des Volkes Israel als Kultgemeinschaft, in: S. Heid / M. Schmidt (eds.), Kult des Volkes. Der Volksgedanke in den liturgischen Bewegungen und Reformen. Eine ökumenische Revision (Darmstadt 2022) 19–41.

Boguniowski 1987 J. Boguniowski, Domus ecclesiae. Der Ort der Eucharistiefeier in den ersten Jahrhunderten (Diss. Rom / Kraków 1987).

Boguniowski 1988 J. Boguniowski, ΕΠΙ ΤΟ ΑΥΤΟ. Die aelteste christliche Bezeichnung des liturgischen Raumes, in: Ephemerides Liturgicae 102 (1988) 446–455.

Bonetti 1997 C. Bonetti, La basilica Apostolorum. L'edificio, in: La città e la sua memoria. Milano e la tradizione di Sant'Ambrogio (Milano 1997).

Bonfiglio 2010 A. Bonfiglio, Presenza e attrazione del culto martiriale nei tituli romani, in: RACr 86 (2010) 195–242.

Bornkamm 1964 G. Bornkamm, Lobpreis, Bekenntnis und Opfer, in: Apophoreta (Berlin 1964) 46–63.

Bosio 1632 A. Bosio, Roma sotterranea (Roma 1632).

Bowes 2008 K. Bowes, Private Worship, Public Values,

and Religious Change in Late Antiquity (Cambridge 2008).

Bowes 2010 K. Bowes, Houses and Society in the Later Roman Empire (London 2010).

Braconi 2016 M. Braconi, Il mosaico del catino absidale di S. Pudenziana (Todi 2016).

Brakmann 1970 H. Brakmann, Die angeblichen eucharistischen Mahlzeiten des 4. Und 5. Jahrhunderts. Zu einem neuen Buch Klaus Gambers, in: RQ 65 (1970) 82–97.

Brakmann 1979 H. Brakmann, Alexandreia und die Kanones des Hippolyt, in: JbAC 22 (1979) 139–149.

Brandenburg 1995A H. Brandenburg, Kirchenbau und Liturgie. Überlegungen zum Verhältnis von Architektonischer Gestalt und Zweckbestimmung des frühchristlichen Kultbaues im 4. Und 5. Jh., in: C. Fluck et al. (eds.), Divitiae Aegypti. Koptologische und verwandte Studien zu Ehren von Martin Krause (Wiesbaden 1995) 36–69.

Brandenburg 1995B H. Brandenburg, Altar und Grab. Zu einem Problem des Märtyrerkultes im 4. Und 5. Jh., in: M. Lamberigts / P. van Deun (eds.), Martyrium in Multidisciplinary Perspective (Leuven 1995) 71–98.

Brandenburg 2002 H. Brandenburg, Die Basilica S. Paolo fuori le mura, der Apostel-Hymnus des Prudentius (peristeph. Xii) und die architektonische Ausstattung des Baues, in: F. Guidobaldi / A. Guglia Guidobaldi (eds.), Ecclesiae Urbis 3 (Città del Vaticano 2002) 1525–1578.

Brandenburg 2004 H. Brandenburg, Prachtentfaltung und Monumentalität als Bauaufgaben frühchristlicher Kirchenbaukunst, in: J. Gebauer et al. (eds.), Bildergeschichte, Festschrift K. Stähler (Möhnesee 2004) 59–76.

Brandenburg 2005–2006 H. Brandenburg, Die Architektur der Basilika San Paolo fuori le mura, in: MDAI.R 112 (2005–2006) 237–275.

Brandenburg 2009 H. Brandenburg, La basilica teodosiana di S. Paolo fuori le mura, in: U. Utro (ed.), San Paolo in Vaticano. La figura e la parola dell'Apostolo delle Genti nelle raccolte pontificie (Todi 2009) 13–27.

Brandenburg 2011A H. Brandenburg, Petrus und Paulus in Rom? Die archäologischen Zeugnisse, die Basilika S. Paul vor den Mauern und der Kult der Apostelfürsten, in: O. Brandt / Ph. Pergola (eds.), Marmoribus vestita, Miscellanea in onore di Federico Guidobaldi 1 (Città del Vaticano 2011) 213–262.

Brandenburg 2011B H. Brandenburg, Die Aussagen der Schriftquellen und der archäologischen Zeugnisse zum Kult der Apostelfürsten in Rom, in: S. Heid (ed.), Petrus und Paulus in Rom. Eine interdisziplinäre Debatte (Freiburg i.Br. 2011) 351–382.

Brandenburg 2013 H. Brandenburg, Die frühchristlichen Kirchen in Rom vom 4. bis zum 7. Jahrhundert (Regensburg ³2013).

Brandenburg 2015 H. Brandenburg, Die konstantinische Petersbasilika am Vatikan, in: id. et al., Der Petersdom in Rom. Die Baugeschichtc von der Antike bis heute (Petersberg 2015) 9–33.

Brandenburg 2017A H. Brandenburg, Die Paulsbasilika an der Via Ostiense, in: A. Wieczorek / S. Weinfurter (eds.), Die Päpste und die Einheit der lateinischen Welt, Katalog (Regensburg 2017) 141–147.

Brandenburg 2017B H. Brandenburg, Die konstantinische Petersbasilika am Vatikan in Rom (Regensburg 2017).

Brandenburg 2017C H. Brandenburg, Das Grabmal des Apostels Petrus, des ersten Vorstehers der römischen christlichen Gemeinde, in: A. Wieczorek / S. Weinfurter (eds.), Die Päpste und die Einheit der lateinischen Welt. Katalog zur Ausstellung (Regensburg 2017) 41–51.

Brandenburg 2017D H. Brandenburg, Die Paulsbasilika an der Via Ostiense, in: A. Wieczorek / S. Weinfurter (eds.), Die Päpste und die Einheit der lateinischen Welt. Katalog zur Ausstellung (Regensburg 2017) 141–147.

Braun 1907 J. Braun, Die liturgische Gewandung im Occident und Orient (Freiburg i.Br. 1907).

Braun 1924A J. Braun, Der christliche Altar in seiner geschichtlichen Entwicklung 1 (München 1924).

Braun 1924B J. Braun, Der christliche Altar in seiner geschichtlichen Entwicklung 2 (München 1924).

Braun 1926 J. Braun, Die Entwicklung des christlichen Altars bis zum Beginn des Mittelalters, in: Stimmen der Zeit 110 (1926) 161–172.

Braun 1930 J. Braun, Altar, in: LThK 1 (1930) 294–297.

Braun 1932 J. Braun, Das christliche Altargerät in seinem Sein und in seiner Entwicklung (München 1932).

Brenk 1995 B. Brenk, Der Kultort, seine Zugänglichkeit und seine Besucher, in: E. Dassmann / J. Engemann (eds.), Akten des XII. internationalen Kongresses für Christliche Archäologie 1 (Münster / Città del Vaticano 1995) 69–122.

Brenk 2003 B. Brenk, Die Christianisierung der spätrömischen Welt. Stadt, Land, Haus, Kirche und Kloster in frühchristlicher Zeit (Wiesbaden 2003).

Brenk 2010 B. Brenk, The Apse, the Image and the Icon. An Historical Perspective of the Apse as a Space for Images (Wiesbaden 2010).

Brent 1995 A. Brent, Hippolytus and the Roman Church in the Third Century. Communities in Tension Before the Emergence of a Monarch-Bishop (Leiden 1995).

Brent 1999 A. Brent, The Imperial Cult and the Development of Church Order. Concepts and Images of Authority in Paganism and Early Christianity before the Age of Cyprian (Leiden 1999).

Brent 2010 A. Brent, Cyprian and Roman Carthage (Cambridge 2010).

Brox 1995 N. Brox, Kirchengeschichte des Altertums (Düsseldorf ⁵1995).

Budde 2001 A. Budde, Improvisation im Eucharistiegebet. Zur Technik freien Betens in der Alten Kirche, in: JbAC 44 (2001) 127–141.

Bull-Simonsen Einaudi 2000 K. Bull-Simonsen Einaudi, L'arredo liturgico medievale di Santa Maria in Trastevere, in: MNIR 59 (2000) 175–194.

Buonaguro 2011 S. Buonaguro, La basilica paleocristiana anonima di Castelfusano. Nuovi dati dagli scavi 2007–2008, in: O. Brandt / Ph. Pergola (Hg.), Marmoribus vestita, Miscellanea in onore di Federico Guidobaldi, 1 (Città del Vaticano 2011) 287–303.

Burns / Jensen 2014 J. P. Burns / R. M. Jensen (eds.), Christianity in Roman Africa. The Development of Its Practices and Beliefs (Grand Rapids 2014).

Butzkamm 2011 A. Butzkamm, Kirchen in den Blick nehmen (Paderborn 2011).

Calabrese 2021 L. Calabrese, Il Sacerdózio filiale e prodromico di Gesù Cristo e la sua partecipazione, in: Guttadauro 21 (2021) 35–58.

Calder 1920 W. M. Calder, Studies in Early Christian Epigraphy, in: The Journal of Roman Studies 10 (1920) 42–59.

Camelot 1970 P.-T. Camelot, Handbuch der Dogmengeschichte, 3,3b. Die Lehre von der Kirche. Väterzeit bis ausschließlich Augustinus (Freiburg i.Br. 1970).

Camerlenghi 2018 N. M. Camerlenghi, St. Paul's outside the Walls. A Roman Basilica from Antiquity to the Modern Era (Cambridge 2018).

Canetti 2002 L. Canetti, Santuari e reliquie tra Antichità e Medioevo. Cristianizzazione dello spazio o sacralizzazione del cristianesimo? (2002, Internet-Publikation).

Cantino Wataghin 2014 G. Cantino Wataghin, Domus ecclesiae, domus orationis, domus dei: la chiesa, luogo della comunità, luogo dell'istituzione, in: Settimane di Studio della Fondazione Centro Italiano di Studi sull'Alto Medioevo 61 (2014) 565–604.

Carandini 2013 A. Carandini, Su questa pietra. Gesù, Pietro e la nascita della Chiesa (Roma / Bari 2013).

Carile 2016 M. C. Carile, Metafore di luce nelle architetture e nel decoro da Costantino a Costanzo II, in: T. Canella (ed.), L'Impero costantiniano e i luoghi sacri (Bologna 2016) 461–488.

Cattaneo 2017 E. Cattaneo, Les ministères dans l'Église ancienne (Paris 2017).

Cecalupo 2020 C. Cecalupo, Antonio Bosio, la Roma Sotterranea e i primi collezionisti di antichità cristiane 1 (Città del Vaticano 2020).

Chalkia 1991 E. Chalkia, Le mense paleocristiane. Tipologia e funzioni delle mense secondarie nel culto paleocristiano (Città del Vaticano 1991).

Chavarría Arnau 2009 A. Chavarría Arnau, Archeologia delle chiese. Dalle origini all'anno Mille (Roma 2009).

Chavasse 1958 A. Chavasse, Le sacramentaire gélasien (Vaticanus Reginensis 316) (Paris 1958).

Chevalier 1996 P. Chevalier, Salona II. Ecclesiae Dalmatiae 2. Illustrations et conclusions (Paris / Roma 1996).

Chevalier 2005 P. Chevalier, Les autels paléochrétiens des provinces d'Epirus Vetus, Epirus Nova et de Praevalis, in: Hortus Artium Medievalium 11 (2005) 65–79.

Christern-Briesenick 2003 B. Christern-Briesenick, Repertorium der christlich-antiken Sarkophage 3 (Mainz 2003).

Cianca 2018 J. Cianca, Sacred Ritual – Profane Space. The Roman House as Early Christian Meeting Place (London / Chicago 2018).

Clarke 2014 J. R. Clarke, Domus/Single Family House, in: R. B. Ulrich / C. K. Quenemoen (eds.), A Companion to Roman Architecture (Oxford 2014) 342–362.

Claussen 2002 P. C. Claussen, Die Kirchen der Stadt Rom im Mittelalter 1050–1300, 1 (Stuttgart 2002).

Claussen 2008 P. C. Claussen, Die Kirchen der Stadt Rom im Mittelalter 1050–1300, 2. S. Giovanni in Laterano (Stuttgart 2008).

Claussen 2010A J. H. Claussen, Gottes Häuser oder Die Kunst, Kirchen zu bauen und zu verstehen (München 2010).

Claussen 2010B P. C. Claussen et al., Die Kirchen der Stadt Rom im Mittelalter 1050–1300, 3 (Stuttgart 2010).

Coccia 2000 S. Coccia, Santa Maria in Trastevere. Nuovi elementi sulla basilica paleocristiana e altomedievale, in: MNIR 59 (2000) 161–174.

Comte 2012 M.-C. Comte, Les reliquiaires du Proche-Orient et de Chypre à la période proto-byzantine (IVᵉ–VIIIᵉ siècle) (Turnhout 2012).

Connell 2002 M. F. Connell, Church and Worship in Fifth-Century Rome. The Letter of Innocent I to Decentius of Gubbio (Collegeville 2002).

Connolly / Dodge 1998 P. Connolly / H. Dodge, Die antike Stadt. Das Leben in Athen & Rom (Köln 1998).

Crippa / Zibawi 1998 M. A. Crippa / M. Zibawi, L'arte paleocristiana. Visione e Spazio dalle origini a Bisanzio (Milano 1998).

Crowfoot 1938 J. W. Crowfoot, The Christian Churches, in: C. H. Kraeling (ed.), Gerasa. City of the Decapolis (New Haven 1938) 171–262.

Czock 2012 M. Czock, Gottes Haus. Untersuchungen zur Kirche als heiligem Raum von der Spätantike bis ins Frühmittelalter (Berlin / Boston 2012).

D'Andria 2016–2017 F. D'Andria et al., Hierapolis Alma Philippum. Nuovi scavi, ricerche e restauri nel santuario dell'apostolo, in: Atti della Pontificia Accademia Romana di Archeologia, Rendiconti 89 (2016–2017) 129–202.

Dal Covolo 1988 E. dal Covolo, Una „domus ecclesiae" a Roma sotto l'impero di Alessandro Severo?, in: Ephemerides Liturgicae 102 (1988) 64–71.

Daly / Nesselrath 2015 R. J. Daly / T. Nesselrath, Opfer, in: RACh 26 (2015) 143–206.

Dassmann 1986 E. Dassmann et al., Haus II (Hausgemeinschaft), in: RACh 13 (1986) 801–905.

Dassmann 2004 E. Dassmann, Ambrosius von Mailand (Stuttgart 2004).

David 2013 M. David (ed.), La basilica di Santa Croce (Ravenna 2013).

De Blaauw 1994 S. de Blaauw, Cultus et Decor. Liturgia e architettura nella Roma tardoantica e medievale 1–2. Basilica Salvatoris, Sanctae Mariae, Sancti Petri (Città del Vaticano 1994).

De Blaauw 1999–2000 S. de Blaauw, Immagini di liturgia. Sisto V, la tradizione liturgica dei papi e le antiche basiliche di Roma, in: Römisches Jahrbuch der Bibliotheca Hertziana 33 (1999–2000) 259–302.

De Blaauw 2001A S. de Blaauw, Imperial Connotations in Roman Church Interiors. The Significance and Effect of the Lateran Fastigium, in: Acta ad Archaeologiam et Artium Historiam Pertinentia 15 (2001) 137–146.

De Blaauw 2001B S. de Blaauw, L'altare nelle chiese di Roma come centro di culto e della committenza papale, in: Settimane di Studio del Centro Italiano di Studi sull'Alto Medioevo 48 (2001) 969–989.

De Blaauw 2006 S. de Blaauw, Konstantin als Kirchenstifter, in: A. Demandt / J. Engemann (ed.), Konstantin der Grosse. Geschichte – Archäologie – Rezeption (Trier 2006) 163–172.

De Blaauw 2008 S. de Blaauw, Kultgebäude (Kirchenbau), in: RACh 22 (2008) 227–393.

De Blaauw 2010A S. de Blaauw, In vista della luce. Un principio dimenticato nell'orientamento dell'edificio di culto paleocristiano, in: P. Piva (ed.), Arte medievale. Le vie dello spazio liturgico (Milano 2010) 15–45.

De Blaauw 2010B S. de Blaauw, Le origini e gli inizi dell'architettura cristiana, in: id. (ed.), Storia dell'architettura italiana da Costantino a Carlo Magno 1 (Milano 2010) 22–53.

De Blaauw 2016 S. de Blaauw, Die Gräber der frühen Päpste, in: B. Schneidmüller et al. (eds.), Die Päpste 1. Amt und Herrschaft in Antike, Mittelalter und Renaissance (Regensburg 2016) 77–99.

De Blaauw 2017 S. de Blaauw, Altar, in: The Eerdmans Encyclopedia of Early Christian Art and Archaeology 1 (Grand Rapids 2017) 43–45.

Deckers 1987 J. G. Deckers et al., Die Katakombe „Santi Marcellino e Pietro" (Città del Vaticano / Münster 1987).

Deckers 1992 J. G. Deckers, Konstantin und Christus. Der Kaiserkult und die Entstehung des monumentalen Christusbildes in der Apsis, in: G. Bonamente / F. Fusco (eds.), Costantino il Grande dall'antichità all'umanesimo 1 (Macerata 1992) 357–362.

De Grüneisen 1911 W. de Grüneisen, Sainte Marie Antique (Rome 1911).

Deichmann 1964 F. W. Deichmann, Vom Tempel zur Kirche, in: A. Stuiber / A. Hermann (eds.), Mullus (Münster 1964) 52–59.

Deichmann 1967 F. W. Deichmann, Repertorium der christlich-antiken Sarkophage 1 (Wiesbaden 1967).

Deichmann 1969 F. W. Deichmann, Ravenna Hauptstadt des spätantiken Abendlandes 3 (Wiesbaden 1969).

Deichmann 1970 F. W. Deichmann, Märtyrerbasilika, Martyrion, Memoria und Altargrab, in Mitteilungen des DAI Roem. Abt. 77 (1970) 144–169.

Deichmann 1974 F. W. Deichmann, Ravenna. Hauptstadt des spätantiken Abendlandes 2,1 (Wiesbaden 1974).

Deichmann 1976 F. W. Deichmann, Ravenna. Hauptstadt des spätantiken Abendlandes 2,2 (Wiesbaden 1976).

Deichmann 1995 F. W. Deichmann, Ravenna. Hauptstadt des spätantiken Abendlandes 3 (Wiesbaden 1995).

Deighan 2014 G. Deighan, Continuity in sacrifice. From Old Testament to New, in: id. (ed.), Celebrating the Eucharist. Sacrifice and Communion (Wells 2014) 87–99.

Dekkers 1948 E. Dekkers, L'église ancienne a-t-elle connu la messe du soir?, in: Miscellanea liturgica in honorem L. Cuniberti Mohlberg 1 (Roma 1948) 231–257.

Della Portella 2000 I. Della Portella, Das unterirdische Rom. Katakomben – Bäder – Tempel (Köln 2000).

de Maria 2002 L. de Maria, Il programma decorativo della porta lignea di S. Sabina: concordanza o casualità iconografica?, in: F. Guidobaldi / A. Guiglia Guidobaldi (eds.), Ecclesiae Urbis 3 (Città del Vaticano 2002) 1684–1699.

De Paulis / Masconi 2010 F. De Paulis / A. Masconi (eds.), Basilica di Santa Maria Maggiore. Fede e spazio sacro (Genova / Roma 2010).

Diefenbach 2007 S. Diefenbach, Römische Erinnerungsräume. Heiligenmemoria und kollektive Identitäten im Rom des 3. bis 5. Jahrhunderts n. Chr. (Berlin / New York 2007).

Dihle 1980 A. Dihle, Zur spätantiken Kultfrömmigkeit, in: E. Dassmann / K. S. Frank (eds.), Pietas, Festschr. B. Kötting (Münster 1980) 39–54.

Docci 2006 M. Docci, San Paolo fuori le mura. Dalle origini alla basilica delle 'origini' (Roma 2006).

Dölger 1918 F. J. Dölger, Die Sonne der Gerechtigkeit und der Schwarze. Eine religionsgeschichtliche Studie zum Taufgelöbnis (Münster 1918).

Dölger 1922 F. J. Dölger, IXΘYC 2 (Münster 1922)

Dölger 1927 F. J. Dölger, IXΘYC 4 (Münster 1927).

Dölger 1930 F. J. Dölger, Antike und Christentum 2 (Münster 1930).

Dölger 1934 F. J. Dölger, Antike und Christentum 4 (Münster 1934).

Dölger 1936 F. J. Dölger, Antike und Christentum 5 (Münster 1936).

Dölger 1943 F. J. Dölger, IXΘYC 5 (Münster 1943).

Dölger 1950 F. J. Dölger, Antike und Christentum 6 (Münster 1950).

Dölger 1972 F. J. Dölger, *Sol Salutis* (Münster ³1972).

Dörries 1954 H. Dörries, Das Selbstzeugnis Kaiser Konstantins (Göttingen 1954).

Doig 2009 A. Doig, Liturgy and Architecture. From the Early Church to the Middle Ages (Aldershot 2009).

Domagalski / Mühlenkamp 2016 B. Domagalski / Ch. Mühlenkamp, Pfarrei, in: RACh 27 (2016) 456–492.

Donati / Gentili 2001 A. Donati / G. Gentili, Deomene. L'immagine dell'orante fra Oriente e Occidente (Milano 2001).

Dresken-Weiland 1991 J. Dresken-Weiland, Reliefierte Tischplatten aus theodosianischer Zeit (Città del Vaticano 1991).

Dresken-Weiland 1998 J. Dresken-Weiland, Repertorium der christlich-antiken Sarkophage 2 (Mainz 1998).

Dresken-Weiland 2005–2006 J. Dresken-Weiland, Ein wichtiges Zeugnis zum frühen Kirchenbau in Kleinasien, in: JbAC 48–49 (2005–2006) 67–76.

Dresken-Weiland 2010 J. Dresken-Weiland, Bild, Grab und Wort. Untersuchungen zu Jenseitsvorstellungen von Christen des 3. und 4. Jahrhunderts (Regensburg 2010).

Dresken-Weiland 2016 J. Dresken-Weiland, Die frühchristlichen Mosaiken von Ravenna. Bild und Bedeutung (Regensburg 2016).

Dresken-Weiland 2019 J. Dresken-Weiland, Darstellungen neutestamentlicher Mahlszenen auf den Ciboriumsäulen von San Marco in Venedig, in: Antiquité Tardive 27 (2019) 241–253.

Dresken-Weiland / Drews 2004 J. Dresken-Weiland / W. Drews, Kathedra, in: RACh 20 (2004) 600–682.

Duval 1971a N. Duval, Les églises africaines à deux absides 1. Les basiliques de Sbeitla (Paris 1971).

Duval 1971b N. Duval, Église et temple en Afrique du Nord, in: Bulletin archéologique du Comité des travaux historiques et scientifiques, N.S. 7 (1971) 265–296.

Duval 1972 N. Duval, Études d'architecture chretienne nord-africaine, in: Mélanges de l'École Française de Rome, Antiquité 84 (1972) 1071–1172.

Duval 1973 N. Duval, Les églises africaines à deux absides 2. Inventaire des monuments – interprétation (Paris 1973).

Duval 1984–1985 N. Duval, Le choeur de l'église de Siagu (Tunisie), in: Felix Ravenna 127–130 (1984–1985) 159–199.

Duval 1991 N. Duval, Hippo Regius, in: RACh 15 (1991) 442–466.

Duval 1992 N. Duval, Church Buildings, in: A. di Berardino / W. H. C. Frend (eds.), Encyclopedia of the Early Church 1 (Cambridge 1992) 168–175.

Duval 2005 N. Duval, L'autel paléochrétien. Les progrès depuis le livre de Braun (1924) et les questions à résoudre, in: *Hortus Artium Medievalium* 11 (2005) 7–17.

Duval 2008–2009 N. Duval, Numidien, Mauretanien u. Africa proconsularis, in: RBK Lfg. 49f (2008–2009) 1–161.

Duval 2000 Y. Duval, Chrétiens d'Afrique à l'aube de la paix constantinienne. Les premiers échos de la grande persécution (Paris 2000).

Ebner 2012 M. Ebner, Die Stadt als Lebensraum der ersten Christen. Das Urchristentum in seiner Umwelt 1 (Göttingen 2012).

Elliger 2001 W. Elliger, Kaisareia II (in Palästina), in: RACh 19 (2001) 1026–1057.

Elliger 2004 W. Elliger, Karthago, in: RACh 20 (2004) 229–284.

Eltester 1937 W. Eltester, Die Kirchen Antiochias im IV. Jahrhundert, in: ZNW 36 (1937) 251–286.

Engemann 1969 J. Engemann, Fisch, Fischer, Fischfang, in: RACh 7 (1969) 959–1097.

Engemann 1976 J. Engemann, Auf die Parusie Christi hinweisende Darstellungen in der frühchristlichen Kunst, in: JbAC 19 (1976) 139–156.

Engemann 1982 J. Engemann, Der Ehrenplatz beim antiken Sigmamahl, in: Jenseitsvorstellungen in Antike und Christentum (Münster 1982) 239–250.

Feld 1985 H. Feld, Der Hebräerbrief (Darmstadt 1985).

Ferguson 1980 E. Ferguson, Spiritual Sacrifice in Early Christianity and its Environment, in: ANRW 2,23,2 (Berlin / New York 1980) 1151–1189.

Ferguson 1997 E. Ferguson, Sacrifice, in: E. Ferguson (ed.), Encyclopedia of Early Christianity 2 (²1997) 1015–1018.

Filippi 2004 G. Filippi, La tomba di San Paolo e le fasi della basilica tra il IV e VII secolo, in: Bollettino dei Monumenti, Musei e Gallerie Pontificie 24 (2004) 187–224.

Filippi 2005–2006 G. Filippi, Die Ergebnisse der neuen Ausgrabungen am Grab des Apostels Paulus, in: MDAI.R 112 (2005–2006) 277–292.

Filippi 2009 G. Filippi, Un decennio di ricerche e studi nella basilica ostiense, in: U. Utro (ed.), San Paolo in Vaticano. La figura e la parola dell'Apostolo delle Genti nelle raccolte pontificie (Todi 2009) 29–45.

Filson 1939 F. V. Filson, The significance of the early house churches, in: Journal of Biblical Literature 58 (1939) 105–112.

Finney 1984 P. C. Finney, TOPOS HIEROS und christlicher Sakralbau in vorkonstantinischer Überlieferung, in: Boreas 7 (1984) 193–225.

Finney 1994 P. C. Finney, The Invisible God. The Earliest Christians on Art (Oxford 1994).

Fiocchi Nicolai 1998 V. Fiocchi Nicolai *et al.*, Roms christliche Katakomben (Regensburg 1998).

Fiocchi Nicolai 2001 V. Fiocchi Nicolai, Strutture funerarie ed edifici di culto paleocristiani di Roma dal IV al VI secolo (Città del Vaticano 2001).

FIOCCHI NICOLAI 2002 V. FIOCCHI NICOLAI, *Basilica Marci, Coemeterium Marci, Basilica Coemeterii Balbinae*, in: F. GUIDOBALDI / A. GUGLIA GUIDOBALDI (Hg.), *Ecclesiae Urbis* 2 (Città del Vaticano 2002) 1175–1201.

FIOCCHI NICOLAI 2009 V. FIOCCHI NICOLAI, I cimiteri paleocristiani del Lazio 2. Sabina (Città del Vaticano 2009).

FLESS 1995 F. FLESS, Opferdiener und Kultmusiker auf stadtrömischen historischen Reliefs (Mainz1995).

FORNBERG 2023 T. FORNBERG, What is a Christian altar? Is it a βωμός, a τράπεζα or a θυσιαστήριον?, in: C. J. BERGLUND *et al.* (eds.), Why We Sing? (Leiden / Boston 2023) 393–408.

FRANK 1997 K. S. FRANK, Lehrbuch der Geschichte der Alten Kirche (Paderborn ²1997).

FRASCHETTI 2002 A. FRASCHETTI, Vom Kapitol zur Peterskirche. Aspekte der römischen Stadtlandschaft in der Spätantike, in: M. ANDALORO / S. ROMANO (eds.), Römisches Mittelalter (Regensburg 2002) 11–22.

FREND 1996 W. H. C. FREND, The Archaeology of Early Christianity (London 1996).

FÜRST 1967 C. G. FÜRST, *Cardinalis*. Prolegomena zu einer Rechtsgeschichte des römischen Kardinalskollegiums (München 1967).

FUGGER 2019 V. FUGGER, Hinter verschlossenen Türen. Häusliche Kultpraxis im frühen Christentum am Beispiel archäologischer Zeugnisse aus Kleinasien (4./6. Jahrhundert), in: JbAC 62 (2019) 118–157.

FUNKE 1981 H. FUNKE, Götterbild, in: RACh 11 (1981) 659–828.

GÄBEL 2006 G. GÄBEL, Die Kulttheologie des Hebräerbriefes (Tübingen 2006).

GAIN 2001 B. GAIN, Kaisareia I, in: RACh 19 (2001) 992–1026.

GALLEY 1987–1988 H.-D. GALLEY, Der Hebräerbrief und der christliche Gottesdienst, in: Jahrbuch für Liturgik und Hymnologie 31 (1987–1988) 72–83.

GAMBER 1968 K. GAMBER, *Domus ecclesiae*. Die ältesten Kirchenbauten Aquilejas sowie im Alpen- und Donaugebiet bis zum Beginn des 5. Jh. liturgiegeschichtlich untersucht (Regensburg 1968).

GAMBER 1972 K. GAMBER, *Conversi ad Dominum*. Die Hinwendung von Priester und Volk nach Osten bei der Meßfeier im 4. und 5. Jahrhundert, in: RQ 67 (1972) 49–64.

GAMBER 1981 K. GAMBER, *Sancta Sanctorum*. Studien zur liturgischen Ausstattung der Kirche, vor allem des Altarraums (Regensburg 1981).

GAMBER 1994 K. GAMBER, Zum Herrn hin! Fragen um Kirchenbau und Gebet nach Osten (Regensburg ²1994).

GEERTMAN 2001–2002 H. GEERTMAN, Il *fastigium* lateranense e l'arredo presbiteriale, in: MNIR 60–61 (2001–2002) 29–43.

GEHRING 2004 R. W. GEHRING, House Church and Mission. The Importance of Household Structures in Early Christianity (Peabody 2004).

GERHARDS 2009 A. GERHARDS, Vom jüdischen zum christlichen Gotteshaus? Gestaltwerdung des christlichen Liturgie-Raumes, in: R. VODERHOLZER (ed.), Der Logos-gemäße Gottesdienst (Regensburg 2009) 111–138.

GEYER 2005–2006 A. GEYER, Bibelepik und frühchristliche Bildzyklen. Die Mosaiken von Santa Maria Maggiore in Rom, in: MDAI.R 112 (2005–2006) 293–321.

GIELEN 1986 M. GIELEN, Zur Interpretation der paulinischen Formel ἡ κατ'οἶκον ἐκκλησία, in: ZNW 77 (1986) 109–125.

GIELEN 1995 M. GIELEN, Hausgemeinde, in: LThK³ 4 (1995) 1216.

GIELEN 2019 M. GIELEN, Zu Stefan Heids „Ende einer Legende", in: Herderkorrespondenz 73,8 (2019) 49–51.

GNILKA 2015 C. GNILKA *et al.*, Blutzeuge. Tod und Grab des Petrus in Rom (Regensburg ²2015).

GOODENOUGH 1953 E. R. GOODENOUGH, Jewish Symbols in the Greco-Roman Period 3 (New York 1953).

GOODENOUGH 1964 E. R. GOODENOUGH, Jewish Symbols in the Greco-Roman Period 9 (New York 1964).

GOODSON 2007 C. J. GOODSON, Building for Bodies. The Architecture of Saint Veneration in Early Medieval Rome, in: É. Ó. CARREGÁIN / C. NEUMAN DE VEGVAR (eds.), Roma Felix. Formation and Reflection of Medieval Rome (London / New York 2007) 51–79.

GOUDINEAU 1967 C. GOUDINEAU, ΙΕΡΑΙ ΤΡΑΠΕΖΑΙ, in: Mélanges d'Archéologie et d'Histoire 79 (1967) 77–134.

GRIMALDI 1972 G. GRIMALDI, Descrizione della basilica antica di S. Pietro in Vaticano. Codice Barberini latino 2733, ed. R. NIGGL (Città del Vaticano 1972).

GRISAR 1899 H. GRISAR, *Analecta Romana*. Dissertazioni, testi, monumenti dell'arte riguardanti principalmente la Storia di Roma e dei Papi nel medio evo 1 (Roma 1899).

GRISAR 1901 H. GRISAR, Geschichte Roms und der Päpste im Mittelalter 1. Rom beim Ausgang der antiken Welt (Freiburg i.Br. 1901).

GRISAR 1908 H. GRISAR, Die römische Kapelle *Sancta Sanctorum* und ihr Schatz (Freiburg i.Br. 1908).

GROSSMANN 2002 P. GROSSMANN, Christliche Architektur in Ägypten (Leiden 2002).

GROSSMANN 2014 P. GROSSMANN, Churches and Meeting Halls in Necropoleis and Crypts in Intramural Churches, in: E. R. O'CONNELL (ed.), Egypt in the First Millennium AD (Leuven 2014) 93–113.

GUARDUCCI 1978 M. GUARDUCCI, La capsella eburnea di Samagher. Un cimelio di arte paleocristiana nella storia del tardo impero (Padova 1978).

GUIDOBALDI 1993 F. GUIDOBALDI, Roma. Il tessuto abitativo, le *domus* e i *tituli*, in: A. CARANDINI *et al.* (eds.), Storia di Roma 3,2 (Torino 1993) 69–83.

GUIDOBALDI 2001 F. GUIDOBALDI, Strutture liturgiche negli edifici cristiani di Roma dal IV al VII secolo, in:

M. Cecchelli (ed.), Materiali e tecniche dell'edilizia paleocristiana a Roma (Roma 2001) 171–190.

Guidobaldi 2004 F. Guidobaldi, Caratteri e contenuti della nuova architettura dell'età costantiniana, in: RACr 80 (2004) 233–276.

Gutsfeld 2003 A. Gutsfeld, Kirche und *civitas* in der Spätantike. Augustinus und die Einheit von Stadt und Land in Hippo Regius, in: G. Brands / H.-G. Severin (Hg.), Die spätantike Stadt und ihre Christianisierung (Wiesbaden 2003) 135–144.

Hamarneh 2003 B. Hamarneh, Topografia cristiana ed insediamenti rurali nel territorio dell'odierna Giordania nelle epoche bizantina ed islamica, V–IX sec. (Città del Vaticano 2003).

Hamman 1980 A. Hamman, La prère chrétienne et la prière païenne, formes et différences, in: ANRW 2,23,2 (Berlin / New York 1980) 1190–1247.

Hanson 1985 R. P. C. Hanson, Eucharistic Offerings in the Pre-Nicene Fathers, in: *id.*, Studies in the Christian Antiquity (Edinburgh 1985) 83–112.

Harnack 1895 A. Harnack, Eine bisher nicht erkannte Schrift des Papstes Sixtus II. vom Jahre 257/8 (Leipzig 1895).

Harnack 1910 A. Harnack, Entstehung und Entwicklung der Kirchenverfassung und des Kirchenrechts in den zwei ersten Jahrhunderten (Leipzig 1910).

Harnack 1912 A. Harnack, Über den privaten Gebrauch der heiligen Schriften in der Alten Kirche (Leipzig 1912).

Harnack 1924 A. Harnack, Die Mission und Ausbreitung des Christentums in den ersten drei Jahrhunderten (Leipzig ⁴1924).

Heid 2001a S. Heid, Die gute Absicht im Schweigen Eusebs über die Kreuzauffindung, in: RQ 96 (2001) 37–56.

Heid 2001b S. Heid, Kreuz – Jerusalem – Kosmos. Aspekte frühchristlicher Staurologie (Münster 2001).

Heid 2002 S. Heid, *Vexillum Crucis*. Das Kreuz als Religions-, Missions- und Imperialsymbol in der frühen Kirche, in: RACr 78 (2002) 191–259.

Heid 2003 S. Heid, Der Sinai – Berg der Gottesschau in frühchristlicher Tradition, in: RACr 79 (2003) 313–358.

Heid 2006 S. Heid, Gebetshaltung und Ostung in frühchristlicher Zeit, in: RACr 82 (2006) 347–404 (in gekürzter Form: S. Heid, La preghiera dei primi cristiani [Magnano 2013] 7–94).

Heid 2009a S. Heid, Haltung und Richtung. Grundformen frühchristlichen Betens, in: Internationale katholische Zeitschrift *Communio* 38 (2009) 611–619.

Heid 2009b S. Heid, Joseph Wilpert in der Schule de Rossi's, in: *id.* (ed.), Giuseppe Wilpert – archeologo cristiana (Città del Vaticano 2009) 139–207.

Heid 2011 S. Heid (ed.), Petrus und Paulus in Rom. Eine interdisziplinäre Debatte (Freiburg i.Br. 2011).

Heid 2014a S. Heid (ed.), Operation am lebenden Objekt. Roms Liturgiereformen von Trient bis zum Vaticanum II (Berlin 2014).

Heid 2014b S. Heid, Tisch oder Altar? Hypothesen der Wissenschaft mit weitreichenden Folgen, in: *id.* 2014a, 351–374 (= The Early Christian Altar. Lessons for Today, in: A. Reid [ed.], Sacred Liturgy. The Source and Summit of the Life and Mission of the Church [San Francisco 2014] 87–114).

Heid 2015a S. Heid, Der christliche Altar im Hebräerbrief, in: G. Augustin / M. Schulze (eds.), Freude an Gott. Auf dem Weg zu einem lebendigen Glauben 1 (Freiburg i.Br. 2015) 409–421.

Heid 2015b S. Heid, Gelübde (*vota*) in der frühchristlichen Religionspraxis und Liturgie, in: L. Clemens et al. (eds.), Frühchristliche Grabinschriften im Westen des Römischen Reiches (Trier 2015) 227–246.

Heid 2016a S. Heid, Le origini della Chiesa romana e la questione delle cosiddette *Domus Ecclesiae*, in: RACr 92 (2016) 259–283.

Heid 2016b S. Heid, Das Sehen beim Beten. Visuelle Elemente in der frühchristlichen Liturgie, in: K. Dietz et al. (ed.), Das Christusbild. Zu Herkunft und Entwicklung in Ost und West (Würzburg 2016) 75–104.

Heid 2017a S. Heid, Der frühchristliche Altar als Sakralobjekt, in: A. Beck et al. (eds.), Heilige und geheiligte Dinge. Formen und Funktionen (Stuttgart 2017) 43–63.

Heid 2017b S. Heid, Funktion und Ausrichtung des Ambo in der byzantinischen und römischen Tradition, in: RQ 112 (2017) 76–102.

Heid 2017c S. Heid, Die päpstliche Liturgie in Sankt Paul vor den Mauern bis zu Gregor dem Großen, in: RQ 112 (2017) 143–159.

Heid 2018 S. Heid, Gab es „Hauskirchen"? Anmerkungen zu einem Phantom, in: Studia Teologiczno-Historyczne Śląska Opolskiego 38 (2018) 13–48.

Heid 2019a S. Heid, Altar und Kirche. Prinzipien christlicher Liturgie (Regensburg ²2020).

Heid 2019b S. Heid, Hauskirchen hat es nie gegeben. Das Ende einer Legende, in: Herderkorrespondenz 73,4 (2019) 37–39.

Heid 2019c S. Heid, Gab es in Rom eine Gemeinde der Quartodezimaner?, in: RQ 114 (2019) 5–26.

Heid / Dennert 2012 S. Heid / M. Dennert (eds.), Personenlexikon zur Christlichen Archäologie 1–2 (Regensburg 2012).

Heiler 1923 F. Heiler, Das Gebet (München ⁵1923).

Heiler 1941 F. Heiler, Altkirchliche Autonomie und päpstlicher Zentralismus (München 1941).

Hellemo 1989 G. Hellemo, *Adventus Domini*. Eschatological thought in 4th-century apses and catecheses (Leiden u. a. 1989).

Hermann 1969 A. Hermann, Farbe, in: RACh 7 (1969) 358–747.

Hermans 1996 T. Hermans, Origène – théologie sacrificielle du sacerdoce des chrétiens (Paris 1996).

Herrmann 1980 E. Herrmann, *Ecclesia in Re Publica* (Frankfurt a.M. 1980).

Heyden 2014 K. Heyden, Orientierung. Die westliche

Christenheit und das Heilige Land in der Antike (Münster 2014).

Hill 1996 S. Hill, The Early Byzantine Churches of Cilicia and Isauria (Hampshire 1996).

Hvalvik 2014 R. Hvalvik, Praying with Outstretched Hands. Nonverbal Aspects of Early Christian Prayer and the Question of Identity, in: R. Hvalvik / K. O. Sandnes (eds.), Early Christian Prayer and Identity Formation (Tübingen 2014) 57–90.

Ihm 1992 C. Ihm, Die Programme der christlichen Apsismalerei vom 4. Jahrhundert bis zur Mitte des 8. Jahrhunderts (Stuttgart ²1992).

Jacobsen 2000a W. Jacobsen, Organisationsformen des Sanktuariums im spätantiken und mittelalterlichen Kirchenbau, in: A. Gerhards / A. Odenthal (eds.), Kölnische Liturgie und ihre Geschichte (Münster 2000) 67–97.

Jacobsen 2000b W. Jacobsen, Altarraum und Heiligengrab als liturgisches Konzept in der Auseinandersetzung des Nordens mit Rom, in: N. Bock et al. (eds.), Kunst und Liturgie im Mittelalter (München 2000) 65–74.

Jäggi 2007 C. Jäggi, Die Kirche als heiliger Raum. Zur Geschichte eines Paradoxes, in: B. Hamm et al. (eds.), Sakralität zwischen Antike und Neuzeit (Stuttgart 2007) 75–89.

Jeličić-Radonić 2005 J. Jeličić-Radonić, Altar Types in Early Christian Churches in the Province of Dalmatia, in: Hortus Artium Medievalium 11 (2005) 19–28.

Jensen 2008 R. M. Jensen, Dining with the Dead. From the Mensa to the Altar in Christian Late Antiquity, in: L. Brink / D. Green (eds.), Commemorating the Dead (Berlin / New York 2008) 108–143.

Jensen 2015 R. M. Jensen, Recovering Ancient Ecclesiology. The Place of the Altar and the Orientation of Prayer in the Early Church, in: Worship 89 (2015) 99–124.

Jeremias 1980 G. Jeremias, Die Holztür der Basilika S. Sabina in Rom (Tübingen 1980).

Jounel 1984 P. Jounel, L'iconographie de Ravenne. Sa signification liturgique, in: La Maison-Dieu 158 (1984) 71–93.

Judge 2008 E. A. Judge, Kultgemeinde (Kultverein), in: RACh 22 (2008) 393–438.

Jungmann 1952a J. A. Jungmann, Missarum Sollemnia 1 (Freiburg i.Br. ³1952).

Jungmann 1952b J. A. Jungmann, Missarum Sollemnia 2 (Freiburg i.Br. ³1952).

Jungmann 1960 J. A. Jungmann, Liturgisches Erbe und pastorale Gegenwart (Innsbruck 1960).

Jungmann 1966 J. A. Jungmann, Rez. O. Nussbaum, Der Standort des Liturgen am christlichen Altar, in: Zeitschrift für katholische Theologie 88 (1966) 445–450.

Jungmann 1967 J. A. Jungmann, Der neue Altar, in: Der Seelsorger 37 (1967) 374–381.

Kalinowski 2011 A. Kalinowski, Frühchristliche Reliquiare im Kontext von Kultstrategien, Heilserwartung und sozialer Selbstdarstellung (Wiesbaden 2011).

Kaufmann 1913 C. M. Kaufmann, Ägyptische Terrakotten der griechisch-römischen und koptischen Epoche (Cairo 1913).

Khrushkova 2017 L. G. Khrushkova, The Bishop's Basilica [Uvanov's] of Chersonesos in the Crimea. The Modern View after a Century and a Half of Study, in: Archeologia Bulgarica 21,2 (2017) 27–78.

Kinney 1975 D. Kinney, Excavations in S. Maria in Trastevere 1865–1869. A Drawing by Vespignani, in: RQ 70 (1975) 42–53.

Kirsch 1918 J. P. Kirsch, Die römischen Titelkirchen im Altertum (Paderborn 1918).

Kirsch / Klauser 1932 J. P. Kirsch / T. Klauser, Altar III (christlich), in: RACh 1 (1950) 310–354; B. Kruse, Mensa, in: Paulys Real-Encyclopädie der classischen Altertumswissenschaft 15 (1932) 937–948.

Kirschbaum 1957 E. Kirschbaum, Die Gräber der Apostelfürsten (Frankfurt a.M. 1957).

Klauck 1981 H.-J. Klauck, Hausgemeinde und Hauskirche im frühen Christentum (Stuttgart 1981).

Klauck 1982 H.-J. Klauck, Herrenmahl und hellenistischer Kult. Eine religionsgeschichtliche Untersuchung zum ersten Korintherbrief (Münster 1982).

Klauck 1989 H.-J. Klauck, Thysiasterion in Hebr 13,10 und bei Ignatius von Antiochien, in: id., Gemeinde – Amt – Sakrament (Würzburg 1989) 359–372.

Klauser 1950 T. Klauser, Aurum coronarium, in: RACh 1 (1950) 1017–1019.

Klauser 1956 T. Klauser, Die römische Petrustradition im Lichte der neuen Ausgrabungen unter der Peterskirche (Düsseldorf 1956).

Klauser 1959 T. Klauser, Studien zur Entstehungsgeschichte der christlichen Kunst 2, in: JbAC 2 (1959) 116–123.

Klauser 1974 T. Klauser, Gesammelte Arbeiten zur Liturgiegeschichte, Kirchengeschichte und Christlichen Archäologie (Münster 1974).

Klinghardt 1996 M. Klinghardt, Gemeinschaftsmahl und Mahlgemeinschaft. Soziologie und Liturgie frühchristlicher Mahlfeiern (Tübingen / Basel 1996).

Klöckener 1992 M. Klöckener, Die Recitatio nominum im Hochgebet nach Augustins Schriften, in: A. Heinz / H. Rennings (eds.), Gratias Agamus (Freiburg i.Br. 1992) 183–210.

Kloppenborg 2017 J. S. Kloppenborg, Gaius the Roman Guest, in: New Testament Studies 63 (2017) 534–549.

Kloppenborg 2019 J. S. Kloppenborg, Christ's associations. Connecting and belonging in the ancient city (Yale University 2019).

Koch 1917 H. Koch, Die altchristliche Bilderfrage nach den literarischen Quellen (Göttingen 1917).

Kollwitz 1936 J. Kollwitz, Christus als Lehrer und die Gesetzesübergabe an Petrus in der konstantinischen Kunst Roms, in: RQ 44 (1936) 45–66.

Kollwitz 1947–1948 J. Kollwitz, Das Bild von Christus dem König in Kunst und Liturgie der christlichen Frühzeit, in: Theologie und Glaube 37–38 (1947–1948) 95–117.

Kopeček 2006 P. Kopeček, L'orientamento della preghiera liturgica nei primi secoli, in: A. Magris et al., Antiche vie all'eternità (Udine 2006) 192–208.

Kopp 2011 S. Kopp, Der liturgische Raum in der westlichen Tradition (Wien 2011).

Kraeling 1967 C. H. Kraeling, The Excavations at Dura-Europos, Final Report 8,2. The Christian Building (New Haven / New York 1967).

Krautheimer 1937 R. Krautheimer et al., Corpus Basilicarum Christianarum Romae 1 (Città del Vaticano 1937).

Krautheimer 1962 R. Krautheimer et al., Corpus Basilicarum Christianarum Romae 2 (Città del Vaticano 1962).

Krautheimer 1971 R. Krautheimer et al., Corpus Basilicarum Christianarum Romae 3 (Città del Vaticano 1971).

Krautheimer 1980 R. Krautheimer et al., Corpus Basilicarum Christianarum Romae 5 (Città del Vaticano 1980).

Kritzinger 2016 P. Kritzinger, Ursprung und Ausgestaltung bischöflicher Repräsentation (Stuttgart 2016).

Krönung 2008 T. Krönung, Vom Privathaus zum locus sacer. Die Entwicklung der römischen Titelkirchen in der Spätantike, Diss. theol. Jena 2008.

Kruse 1932 B. Kruse, Mensa, in: Paulys Real-Encyclopädie der classischen Altertumswissenschaft 15 (1932) 937–948.

Laderman 2014 S. Laderman, Models of Interaction between Judaism and Christianity as Seen Through Artistic Representations of the Sacrifice of Isaac, in: A. Houtman et al. (eds.), The Actuality of Sacrifice. Past and Present (Leiden 2014) 343–376.

Lampe 2003 From Paul to Valentinus. Christians at Rome in the first two centuries (Minneapolis 2003) (orig.: Die stadtrömischen Christen in den ersten beiden Jahrhunderten. Untersuchungen zur Sozialgeschichte [Tübingen 1987]).

Lancel 2004–2010 S. Lancel, Hippo Regius, in: Augustinus-Lexikon 3 (2004–2010) 351–363.

Lane 1991 W. L. Lane, Hebrews 9–13 Word Biblical Commentary 47B (Waco/Tex. 1991).

Lang 2003 U. M. Lang, Conversi ad Dominum. Zu Geschichte und Theologie der christlichen Gebetsrichtung (Einsiedeln / Freiburg i.Br. 2003).

Lang 2022 U. M. Lang, The Roman Mass. From Early Christian Origins to Tridentine Reform (Cambridge 2022).

Larson-Miller 2006 L. Larson-Miller, Does God Live Here? Lessons from History on domus ecclesiae and domus dei, in: M. Altripp / C. Nauert (eds.), Architektur und Liturgie (Wiesbaden 2006) 15–23.

Leal 2018 J. Leal, Los primeros cristianos en Roma (Madrid 2018).

Leardi 2006 G. Leardi, Il volto di Cristo della perduta abside di San giovanni in Laterano, in: M. Andaloro (ed.), L'orizzonte tardoantico e le nuove immagini 312–468 (Roma 2006) 358–361.

Leclercq 1907 H. Leclercq, Autel, in: DACL 1,2 (1907) 3155–3189.

Leonhard / Eckhardt 2010 C. Leonhard / B. Eckhardt, Mahl V (Kultmahl), in: RACh 23 (2010) 1012–1105.

Leppin 2018 H. Leppin, Die frühen Christen. Von den Anfängen bis Konstantin (München 2018).

Liberati / Bourbon 1996 A. M. Liberati / F. Bourbon, Rom. Weltreich der Antike (Erlangen 1996).

Liccardo 2005 G. Liccardo, Architettura e liturgia nella chiesa antica (Milano 2005).

Lietzmann 1926 H. Lietzmann, Messe und Herrenmahl. Eine Studie zur Geschichte der Liturgie (Bonn 1926).

Liverani 2005 P. Liverani, L'Edilizia costantiniana a Roma. Il Laterano, il Vaticano, Santa Croce in Gerusalemme, in: A. Donati / G. Gentili (eds.), Costantino il Grande. La civiltà antica al bivio tra Occidente e Oriente (Milano 2005) 74–81.

Liverani 2006a P. Liverani, L'architettura costantiniana, tra committenza imperiale e contributo delle élites locali, in: A. Demandt / J. Engemann (eds.), Konstantin der Grosse. Geschichte – Archäologie – Rezeption (Trier 2006) 235–244.

Liverani 2006b P. Liverani, La basilica costantiniana di San Pietro in Vaticano, in: Petros eni – Pietro è qui. Catalogo della Mostra (Roma 2006) 141–147.

Loerke 1975 W. C. Loerke, The Monumental Miniature, in: K. Weitzmann et al., The Place of Book Illumination in Byzantine Art (Princeton 1975) 61–97.

Löx 2013 M. Löx, monumenta sanctorum. Rom und Mailand als Zentren des frühen Christentums. Märtyrerkult und Kirchenbau unter den Bischöfen Damasus und Ambrosius (Wiesbaden 2013).

Lona 1998 H. E. Lona, Der erste Clemensbrief (Göttingen 1998).

Long 2018 F. J. Long, Ἐκκλησία in Ephesians as Godlike in the Heavens, in Temple, in γάμος, and in Armor, in: J. R. Harrison / L. L. Welborn (eds.), The First Urban Churches 3. Ephesus (Atlanta 2018) 193–234.

Longhi 2006 D. Longhi, La capsella eburnea di Samagher. Iconografia e committenza (Ravenna 2006).

Longo / Romagnoli 2014 R. Longo / G. Romagnoli, La chiesa di San Menna a Sant'Agata de' Goti, in: F. Iannotta (ed.), La chiesa di San Menna a Sant'Agata de' Goti (Salerno 2014) 73–111.

López-Arias 2021 F. López-Arias, El Concilio Vaticano II y la arquitectura sagrada. Origen y evolución de unos principios programáticos (1947–1970) (Roma 2021).

L'Orange 1995 H. P. L'Orange, Das römische Reich.

Von Augustus bis zu Konstantin dem Großen (Stuttgart / Zürich 1995).

Lucchesi Palli 1942 E. Lucchesi Palli, Die Passions- und Endszenen Christi auf der Ciboriumsäule von San Marco in Venedig (Prag 1942).

Luchterhandt 2017 M. Luchterhandt, Papst Paschalis I. (817-824), S. Prassede und die Reliquiare des Lateran, in: M. Liedmann / V. Smit (eds.), Zugänge zu Archäologie, Bauforschung und Kunstgeschichte (Regensburg 2017) 383–402.

Lucius 1904 E. Lucius, Die Anfänge des Heiligenkults in der christlichen Kirche (Tübingen 1904).

Lüstraeten 2014 M. Lüstraeten, „Ich will meine Hände waschen inmitten der Unschuld …". Liturgietheologische Anfragen an den Ritus der Händewaschung, in: D. Atanassova / T. Chronz (eds.), Synaxis katholike 2 (Wien / Berlin 2014) 419–440.

Luigia Fobelli 2005 M. Luigia Fobelli, Un tempio per Giustiniano. Santa Sofia di Costantinopoli e la Descrizione di Paolo Silenziario (Roma 2005).

MacMullen 2009 R. MacMullen, The Second Church. Popular Christianity A.D. 200/400 (Leiden 2009).

Mader 1934 A. E. Mader, Die Ausgrabung der Basilika der Brotvermehrung und ihrer Mosaiken bei Et-Tabga am See Genesareth, in: Atti del III Congresso internazionale di Archeologia Cristiana (Roma 1934) 507–521.

Markus 1994 R. A. Markus, How on Earth Could Places Become Holy? Origins of the Christian Idea of Holy Places, in: Journal of Early Christian Studies 2 (1994) 257–271.

Marquardt 1886 J. Marquardt, Das Privatleben der Römer 1 (Leipzig ²1886).

Martin 1984 A. Martin, Les premiers siècles du christianisme à Alexandrie. Essai de topographie religieuse (IIIᵉ–IVᵉ siècles), in: Revue des Études Augustiniennes 30 (1984) 211–225.

Martin 1989 A. Martin, Topographie et liturgie. Le problème des „paroisses" d'Alexandrie, in: Actes du XIᵉ congrès international d'archéologie chrétienne 2 (Città del Vaticano 1989) 1133–1144.

Mathews 1971 T. F. Mathews, The Early Churches of Constantinople. Architecture and Liturgy (University Park / London 1971).

Mathews 2016 T. F. Mathews, Alle origini delle icone (Milano 2016).

Matz 1968 F. Matz, Die dionysischen Sarkophage 1 (Berlin 1968).

Matz 1969 F. Matz, Die dionysischen Sarkophage 3 (Berlin 1969).

Mazza 2005 E. Mazza, Tavola e altare. Due modi non alternativi per designare un'oggetto liturgico, in: F. Debuyst et al., L'altare. Mistero di presenza, opera dell'arte (Magnano 2005) 57–79.

Mell 2011 U. Mell, Christliche Hauskirche und Neues Testament. Die Ikonologie des Baptisteriums von Dura Europos und das Diatessaron Tatians (Göttingen 2011).

Menke 2012 K.-H. Menke, Sakramentalität. Wesen und Wunde des Katholizismus (Regensburg 2012).

Messner 2001 R. Messner, Einführung in die Liturgiewissenschaft (Paderborn 2001).

Messner 2003a R. Messner, Der Gottesdienst in der vornizänischen Kirche, in: L. Pietri (ed.), Die Geschichte des Christentums 1 (Freiburg i.Br. 2003) 340–441.

Messner 2003b R. Messner, Gebetsrichtung, Altar und die exzentrische Mitte der Gemeinde, in: A. Gerhards et al. (eds.), Communio-Räume (Regensburg 2003) 27–36.

Messner 2005 R. Messner, La direzione della preghiera, l'altare e il centro eccentrico dell'assemblea, in: F. Debuyst et al., L'altare. Mistero di presenza, opera dell'arte (Magnano 2005) 201–212 (= Gebetsrichtung, Altar und die exzentrische Mitte der Gemeinde, in: A. Gerhards et al. [eds.], Communio-Räume [Regensburg 2003] 27–36).

Messner 2006 R. Messner, Die Synode von Seleukeia-Ktesiphon 410 und die Geschichte der ostsyrischen Messe, in: R. Messner / R. Pranzl (eds.), Haec sacrosancta synodus. Konzils- und kirchengeschichtliche Beiträge (Regensburg 2006) 60–85.

Metzger 1971 M. Metzger, La place des liturges à l'autel, in: Revue des Sciences Religieuses 45 (1971) 113–145.

Metzger 1998 M. Metzger, Geschichte der Liturgie (Paderborn 1998).

Metzger 2015 M. Metzger, L'Église dans l'empire romain. Le culte 1 (Roma 2015).

Meyer 1989 H. B. Meyer, Eucharistie (Regensburg 1989).

Michael 2005 A. Michael, Das Apsismosaik von S. Apollinare in Classe. Seine Deutung im Kontext der Liturgie (Frankfurt a.M. 2005).

Michel 2005 A. Michel, Aspects du culte dans les églises de Numidie au temps d'Augustin. État de la question, in: S. Lancel (ed.), Saint Augustin, la Numidie et la société de son temps (Bordeaux 2005) 67–108.

Mischkowski 1917 H. Mischkowski, Die heiligen Tische im Götterkultus der Griechen und Römer (Diss. Königsberg 1917).

Mohrmann 1962 C. Mohrmann, Les denominations de l'église en tant qu'édifice en grec et en latin au cours des premiers siècles chrétiens, in: Revue des Sciences Religieuses 36 (1962) 155–174.

Moll 1975 H. Moll, Die Lehre von der Eucharistie als Opfer. Eine dogmengeschichtliche Untersuchung vom Neuen Testament bis Irenäus von Lyon (Köln / Bonn 1975).

Molthagen 1975 J. Molthagen, Der römische Staat und die Christen im zweiten und dritten Jahrhundert (Göttingen ²1975).

Monachino 1947 V. Monachino, La cura pastorale a Milano, Cartagine e Roma nel sec. IV (Roma 1947).

Mondini 2016 D. Mondini, Drehmomente. Orientierungswechsel christlicher Kultbauten im mittelalterlichen Rom, in: M. Verhoeven *et al.* (eds.), Monuments & Memory. Christian Cult Buildings and Constructions of the Past (Turnhout 2016) 199–207.

Mosebach 2012 M. Mosebach, Häresie der Formlosigkeit. Die römische Liturgie und ihr Feind (München 2012).

Narasawa 2015 Y. Narasawa, Les autels chrétiens du sud de la Gaule (V^e–XIIe siècles) (Turnhout 2015).

Nebel 2012 J. Nebel, Die Entwicklung des römischen Messritus im ersten und zweiten Jahrtausend (Bregenz 2012).

Nebel 2014 J. Nebel, Von der *actio* zur *celebratio*. Ein neues Paradigma nach dem Zweiten Vatikanischen Konzil, in: S. Heid (ed.), Operation am lebenden Objekt. Roms Liturgiereformen von Trient bis zum Vaticanum II (Berlin 2014) 53–90.

Nestori 1999 A. Nestori, Riflessioni sul luogo di culto cristiano precostantiniano, in: RACr 75 (1999) 695–709.

Neunheuser 1996 B. Neunheuser, Eucharistiefeier am *altare versus populum*. Geschichte und Problematik, in: D. Gobbi (ed.), *Florentissima proles ecclesiae* (Trento 1996) 417–444.

Neusner 2001 J. Neusner, Sacrifice in Rabbinic Judaism. The Presentation of the atonement-rite of sacrifice in Tractate Zebahim in the Mishnah, Tosefta, Bavli, and Yerushalmi, in: Annali di Storia dell'Esegesi 18 (2001) 225–253.

Nickl 1930 G. Nickl, Der Anteil des Volkes an der Messliturgie im Frankenreiche von Chlodwig bis auf Karl den Großen (Innsbruck 1930).

Nicolaou 2018 D. Nicolaou, Liturgical Structures of the Early Christian Basilicas of Cyprus, in: M. Horster *et al.* (eds.), Church Building in Cyprus. Fourth to Seventh Century (Münster / New York 2018) 119–151.

Nilgen 1999 U. Nilgen, Die römischen Apsisprogramme der karolingischen Epoche. Päpstliche Repräsentation und Liturgie, in: C. Stiegemann / M. Wemhoff (eds.), Kunst und Kultur der Karolingerzeit 3 (Mainz 1999) 542–549.

Nilgen 2000 U. Nilgen, Die Bilder über dem Altar. Triumph- und Apsisbogenprogramme und ihr Bezug zur Liturgie, in: N. Bock *et al.* (eds.), Kunst und Liturgie im Mittelalter (München 2000) 75–89.

Nussbaum 1961a O. Nussbaum, De altarium ablutione, in: *Ephemerides Liturgicae* 75 (1961) 105–116.

Nussbaum 1961b O. Nussbaum, Zum Problem der runden und sigmaförmigen Altarplatten, in: JbAC 4 (1961) 18–43 (= Nussbaum 1996, 293–323).

Nussbaum 1965 O. Nussbaum, Der Standort des Liturgen am christlichen Altar vor dem Jahre 1000, 1–2 (Bonn 1965) (1965 II: Bildband).

Nussbaum 1971 O. Nussbaum, Die Zelebration versus populum und der Opfercharakter der Messe, in: Zeitschrift für katholische Theologie 93 (1971) 148–167 (= Nussbaum 1996, 50–70).

Nussbaum 1996 O. Nussbaum, Geschichte und Reform

des Gottesdienstes. Liturgiewissenschaftliche Untersuchungen (Paderborn 1996).

Oberlinner 2007 L. Oberlinner, Gemeindeordnung und rechte Lehre. Zur Fortschreibung der paulinischen Ekklesiologie in den Pastoralbriefen, in: Theologische Quartalschrift 187 (2007) 295–308.

Odenthal 2006 A. Odenthal, Raum und Ritual. Liturgietheologische Markierungen zu einem interdisziplinären Dialog, in: M. Altripp / C. Nauerth (eds.), Architektur und Liturgie (Wiesbaden 2006) 1–13.

Öhler 2014 M. Öhler, Cultic Meals in Associations and the Early Christian Eucharist, in: Early Christianity 5 (2014) 475–502.

Öhler 2016a M. Öhler, House Churches, in: Encyclopedia of the Bible and Its Reception 12 (2016) 488–492.

Öhler 2016b M. Öhler, Meeting at Home. Greco-Roman Association and Pauline Communities, in: W. E. Arnal (ed.), Scribal practices and social structures among Jesus adherents (Leuven 2016) 517–545.

Öhler 2017 M. Öhler, Die erste Gemeinde und ihr Ort. Beobachtungen zum lukanischen Doppelwerk, in: J. Verheyden (ed.), Luke on Jesus, Paul and Christianity (Leuven 2017) 257–280.

O'Loughlin 2014 T. O'Loughlin, The *Commemoratio pro vivis* of the Roman Canon. A Textual Witness to the Evolution of Western Eucharistic Theologies?, in Studia Patristica 71 (2014) 69–91.

Orlandos 1954 A. K. Orlandos, He xylostegos palaiochristianike basilike tes mesogeiakes lekanes 2 (Athen 1954).

Osborne / Claridge 1996 J. Osborne / A. Claridge, Early Christian and Medieval Antiquities 1. Mosaics and Wallpaintings in Roman Churches (London 1996).

Osborne / Claridge 1998 J. Osborne / A. Claridge, Early Christian and Medieval Antiquities 2. Other Mosaics, Paintings, Sarcophagi and Small Objects (London 1998).

Osiek 2002 C. Osiek, Archaeological and Architectural Issues and the Question of Demographic and Urban Forms, in: A. J. Blasi *et al.* (eds.), Handbook of Early Christianity (Lanham 2002) 83–103.

Ovadiah 1970 A. Ovadiah, Corpus of the Byzantine Churches in the Holy Land (Bon 1970).

Pacik 2012 R. Pacik, Einrichtung von Kirche und Altarraum in den Vor-Fassungen der Liturgiekonstitution, in: S. Haering *et al.* (eds.), In mandatis meditari, Festschr. H. Paarhammer (Berlin 2012) 357–386.

Padovese 2000 L. Padovese, Roma e la sollecitudine delle Chiese. Esspressioni di comunione ecclesiale nei primi due secoli, in: L. Pani Ermini / P. Siniscalco (eds.), La comunità cristiana di Roma. La sua vita e la sua cultura dalle origini all'alto medio evo (Città del Vaticano 2000) 65–82.

Palazzo 2008 É. Palazzo, L'espace rituel et le sacré dans le christianisme. La liturgie de l'autel portatif dans l'antiquité et au Moyen Âge (Turnhout 2008).

Panvinio 1570a O. Panvinio, Le sette chiese romane (Roma 1570).

Panvinio 1570b O. Panvinio, De praecipuis Urbis Romae sanctioribusque basilicis, quas Septem ecclesias vulgo vocant, Liber (Romae 1570).

Pecklers 2012 K. F. Pecklers, Atlante storico della liturgia (Milano 2012).

Peeters 1969 C. J. A. C. Peeters, Le liturgische dispositie van het vroegchristelijk kerkgebouw (Assen 1969).

Penna 2009 R. Penna, La chiesa di Roma (Brescia 2009).

Peppard 2016 M. Peppard, The World's Oldest Church. Bible, Art, and Ritual at Dura-Europos, Syria (New Haven / London 2016).

Perler 1955 O. Perler, L'église principale et les autres sanctuaires chrétiens d'hippone-la-Royale d'après les textes de saint Augustin, in: Revue des Études Augustiniennes 1 (1955) 299–343.

Perrin 2016 M.-Y. Perrin, À propos de la sacralité des lieux de culte chrétiens dans la première moitié du IVe siècle. Quelques observations, in: T. Canella (ed.), L'Impero costantiniano e i luoghi sacri (Bologna 2016) 191–211.

Pesarini 1913 S. Pesarini, La basilica di S. Paolo sulla via Ostiense prima delle innovazioni del sec. XVI, in: Studi Romani 1 (1913) 386–427.

Peterson 1935 E. Peterson, Das Buch von den Engeln. Stellung und Bedeutung der heiligen Engel im Kultus (Leipzig 1935).

Peterson 1959 E. Peterson, Frühkirche, Judentum und Gnosis (Freiburg i.Br. 1959).

Peterson 2010 E. Peterson, Ekklesia. Studien zum altchristlichen Kirchenbegriff (Würzburg 2010).

Petrignani 1934 A. Petrignani, La basilica di S. Pudenziana in Roma secondo gli scavi recentemente eseguiti (Città del Vaticano 1934).

Pietri 1997 C. Pietri, Christiana Respublica 1 (Rome 1997).

Pietri 2003 L. Pietri (ed.), Die Geschichte des Christentums 1 (Freiburg i.Br. 2003).

Piva 2008 P. Piva, Lo „Spazio liturgico". Architettura, arredo, iconografia (secoli IV–XII), in: id. (ed.), Architettura medievale. La pietra e la figura (Milano 2008) 221–264.

Podossinov 1991 A. Podossinov, Himmelsrichtung (kultische), in: RACh 15 (1991) 233–286.

Poorthuis 2014 M. Poorthuis, Sacrifice as Concession in Christian and Jewish Sources. The Didascalia Apostolorum and Rabbinic Literature, in: A. Houtman et. al. (eds.), The Actuality of Sacrifice. Past and Present (Leiden 2014) 170–191.

Prigent 2000 P. Prigent, La Jérusalem Céleste. Apparition et développement du thème iconographique de la Jérusalem céleste dans le christianisme, in: M. Hengel et al. (eds.), Die Stadt Gottes (Tübingen 2000) 367–403.

Proverbio 2016 C. Proverbio, I cicli affrescati paleoc-

ristiani di San Pietro in Vaticano e San Paolo fuori le Mura (Turnhout 2016).

Quacquarelli 1977 A. Quacquarelli, Note sugli edifici di culto prima di Costantino, in: Vetera Christianorum 14 (1977) 239–251.

Ramisch 2018 H. Ramisch 2018, Altar-Bilder im ersten christlichen Jahrtausend. Der christliche Altar und seine heilsgeschichtlichen Bildsysteme (München 2018).

Rapp 2005 C. Rapp, Holy Bishops in Late Antiquity. The Nature of Christian Leadership in an Age of Transition (London 2005).

Ratzinger 1966 J. Ratzinger, Das Problem der Dogmengeschichte in der Sicht der katholischen Theologie (Köln / Opladen 1966).

Ratzinger 2000 J. Ratzinger, The Spirit of the Liturgy (San Francisco 2000).

Rauschen 1910 G. Rauschen, Eucharistie und Bußsakrament in den ersten sechs Jahrhunderten der Kirche (Freiburg i.Br. ²1910).

Reisch 1894 E. Reisch, Altar, in: Paulys Real-Encyclopädie der classischen Altertumswissenschaft 1 (1894) 1640–1691.

Renaud 1971 B. Renaud, L'église comme assemblée liturgique selon Saint Cyrien, in: Recherches de Théologie ancienne et médiévale 38 (1971) 5–68.

Riesner 2007 R. Riesner, What does Archaeology teach us about early house churches?, in: Tidsskrift for Teologi og Kirke 58 (2007) 159–182.

Riesner 2012 R. Riesner, Zwischen Tempel und Obergemach. Jerusalem als erste messianische Stadtgemeinde, in: R. von Bendemann / M. Tiwald (eds.), Das frühe Christentum und die Stadt (Stuttgart 2012) 69–91.

Riganati 2002 F. Riganati, „… vestes super altare …" ed altri tessuti di uso liturgico nella Roma Carolingia, in: F. Guidobaldi / A. Guiglia Guidobaldi (eds.), Ecclesiae Urbis 3 (Città del Vaticano 2002) 1605–1628.

Righetti 1964 M. Righetti, Manuale di storia liturgica 1 (Milano ³1964).

Righetti 1966 M. Righetti, Manuale di storia liturgica 3 (Milano ³1966).

Ristow 1998 S. Ristow, Frühchristliche Baptisterien (Münster 1998).

Rizzardi 2011 C. Rizzardi, Il mosaico a Ravenna. Ideologia e arte (Bologna 2011).

Robinson 2017 T. A. Robinson, Who Were the First Christians? Dismantling the Urban Thesis (Oxford 2017).

Roetzer 1930 W. Roetzer, Des heiligen Augustinus Schriften als liturgie-geschichtliche Quelle (München 1930).

Roloff 1981 J. Roloff, θυσιαστήριον, in: Exegetisches Wörterbuch zum Neuen Testament 2 (Stuttgart 1981) 405–407.

Rordorf 1964 W. Rordorf, Was wissen wir über die christlichen Gottesdiensträume der vorkonstantinischen Zeit?, in: ZNW 55 (1964) 110–128.

ROUWHORST 2015 G. A. M. ROUWHORST, Oblation II, in: RACh 26 (2015) 47–74.

RUBERY 2014 E. RUBERY, From Catacomb to Sanctuary. The Orant figure and the Cults of the Mother of God and S. Agnes in Early Christian Rome, with Special Reference to Gold Glass, in: *Studia Patristica* 73 (2014) 129–174.

RÜCKER 1920 A. RÜCKER, Über Altartafeln im koptischen und den übrigen Riten des Orients, in: F. FESSLER (ed.), Ehrengabe deutscher Wissenschaft (Freiburg i.Br. 1920) 209–221.

RUGGIERI 2018 V. RUGGIERI, An altar in the archaeological museum of Kayseri. St. Mamas and the Prophet Elijah, in: *Orientalia Christiana Periodica* 84 (2018) 339–356.

RUYSSCHAERT 1954 J. RUYSSCHAERT, Réflexions sur les fouilles vaticanes, le rapport officiel et la critique, in: Revue d'Histoire Ecclésiastique 49 (1954) 5–58.

SAHAS 1997 D. J. SAHAS, Altar, in: Encyclopedia of Early Christianity 1 (New York / London ²1997) 30–41.

SASTRE DE DIEGO 2012 I. SASTRE DE DIEGO, Una nuova espressione del potere. Altari, martiri e religiosità. Il ruolo del Nord Africa nella Hispania tardoantica, in: M. BASTIANA COCCO et al. (eds.), L'Africa romana 2 (Roma 2012) 1279–1290.

SASTRE DE DIEGO 2013 I. SASTRE DE DIEGO, Los altares de las iglesias hispanas tardoantiguas y altomedievales. Estudio arqueológico (Oxford 2013).

SATZINGER / SCHÜTZE 2008 G. SATZINGER / S. SCHÜTZE (eds.), Sankt Peter in Rom 1506–2006 (München 2008).

SAXER 1969 V. SAXER, Vie liturgique et quotidienne à Carthage vers le milieu du IIIᵉ siècle (Città del Vaticano ²1969).

SAXER 1980A V. SAXER, Mort – martyrs – reliques en Afrique chrétienne aux premiers siècles (Paris 1980).

SAXER 1980B V. SAXER, „Il étendit les mains à l'heure de sa Passion". Le thème de l'orant/-te dans la littérature chrétienne des IIᵉ et IIIᵉ siècles, in: *Augustinianum* 20 (1980) 335–365.

SAXER 1988 V. SAXER, *Domus ecclesiae* – οἶκος τῆς ἐκκλησίας in den frühchristlichen literarischen Texten, in: RQ 83 (1988) 167–179.

SAXER 1989 V. SAXER, L'utilisation par la liturgie de l'espace urbain et suburbain. L'exemple de Rome dans l'antiquité et le Haut Moyen Âge, in: Actes du XIᵉ congrès internatinal d'archéologie chrétienne 2 (Rome 1989) 917–1033.

SAXER 1992 V. SAXER, *Mensa*, in: A. DI BERARDINO / W. H. C. FREND (eds.), Encyclopedia of the Early Church 1 (Cambridge 1992) 554.

SAXER 1994A V. SAXER, L'eucharistie chez Tertullian, in: *id.*, Pères saints et culte chrétien dans l'Église des premiers siècles (Hampshire 1994), V.

SAXER 1994B V. SAXER, Altare, in: Augustinus-Lexikon 1 (1994) 241–245.

SAXER 2001 V. SAXER, Sainte-Marie-Majeure. Une basilique de Rome dans l'histoire de la ville et de son église (Vᵉ–XIIIᵉ siècle) (Rome 2001).

SAXER 2001–2002 V. SAXER, Recinzioni liturgiche secondo le fonti letterarie, in: MNIR 60–61 (2001–2002) 71–79.

SAXER 2003 V. SAXER, Die Organisation der nachapostolischen Gemeinden (70–180), in: L. PIETRI (ed.), Die Geschichte des Christentums 1 (Freiburg i.Br. 2003) 269–339.

SCHEID 1990 J. SCHEID, Romulus et ses frères. Le collège des frères arvales, modèle du culte public dans la Rome des empereurs (Rome 1990).

SCHEID 2009 J. SCHEID, Rito e religione dei Romani (Bergamo 2009).

SCHEID 2014 J. SCHEID, Opferaltar und Weihaltar in Rom und in Italien, in: A. W. BUSCH / A. SCHÄFER (eds.), Römische Weihealtäre im Kontext (Friedberg 2014) 27–35.

SCHILLER 1968 G. SCHILLER, Ikonographie der christlichen Kunst 2. Die Passion Jesu Christi (Gütersloh 1968).

SCHLIER 1977 H. SCHLIER, Der Römerbrief = Herders Theologischer Kommentar zum Neuen Testament 6 (Freiburg i.Br. 1977).

SCHLOEDER 2012 S. J. SCHLOEDER, *Domus Dei, Quae Est Ecclesia Dei Vivi*. The Myth of the *Domus Ecclesiae*, in: Sacred Architecture 21 (2012) 12–15.

SCHMITZ 1975 J. SCHMITZ, Gottesdienst im altchristlichen Mailand. Eine liturgiewissenschaftliche Untersuchung über Initiation und Meßfeier während des Jahres zur Zeit des Bischofs Ambrosius († 397) (Köln / Bonn 1975).

SCHNEIDER 1949 A. M. SCHNEIDER, Liturgie und Kirchenbau in Syrien, in: Nachrichten der Akademie der Wissenschaften in Göttingen, Philol.-hist. Klasse 3 (Göttingen 1949) 45–68.

SCHNEIDER 2006 W. C. SCHNEIDER, Elemente der römischen Reichsreligion im christlichen Kultraum nach 313, in: R. HARREITHER et al. (eds.), Akten des XIV. internationalen Kongresses für Christliche Archäologie 1 (Wien / Città del Vaticano 2006) 947–964.

SCHOEDEL 1990 W. R. SCHOEDEL, Die Briefe des Ignatius von Antiochien (München 1990).

SCHÖLLGEN 1985 G. SCHÖLLGEN, *Ecclesia sordida*? Zur Frage der sozialen Schichtung frühchristlicher Gemeinden am Beispiel Karthagos zur Zeit Tertullians (Münster 1985).

SCHÖLLGEN 1988 G. SCHÖLLGEN, Hausgemeinden, OIΚΟΣ-Ekklesiologie und monarchischer Episkopat, in: JbAC 31 (1988) 74–90.

SCHÖLLGEN 1989 G. SCHÖLLGEN, Probleme der frühchristlichen Sozialgeschichte. Einwände gegen Peter Lampes Buch „Die stadtrömischen Christen in den ersten beiden Jahrhunderten"?, in: JbAC 32 (1989) 23–40.

SCHUBERT 1992 K. SCHUBERT, Jewish Traditions in Christian Painting Cycles. The Vienna Genesis and the Ashburnham Pentateuch, in: H. SCHRECKENBERG / K.

SCHUBERT, Jewish Historiography and Iconography in Early and Medieval Christianity (Assen 1992) 211–260.

SEELIGER / KRUMEICH 2007 H. R. SEELIGER / K. KRUMEICH, Archäologie der antiken Bischofssitze I. Spätantike Bischofssitze Ägyptens (Wiesbaden 2007).

SERRANO 1575 A. SERRANO, De septem Urbis ecclesiis una cum earum reliquiis, stationibus et indulgentiis (Romae 1575).

SESSA 2009 K. SESSA, Domus Ecclesiae. Rethinking a Category of Ante-Pacem Christian Space, in: Journal of Theological Studies 60 (2009) 90–108.

SESSA 2018 K. SESSA, Daily Life in Late Antiquity (Cambridge 2018).

SEVERANO 1630 G. SEVERANO, Memorie sacre delle sette chiese di Roma e di altri luoghi, che si trovano per le strade di esse 1 (Roma 1630).

SEVERUS 1972 E. VON SEVERUS, Gebet I, in: RACh 8 (1972) 1134–1258.

SHALEV-HURVITZ 2015 V. SHALEV-HURVITZ, Holy Sites Encircled. The Early Byzantine Concentric Churches of Jerusalem (Oxford 2015).

SIEBERT 1999 A. V. SIEBERT, Instrumenta Sacra. Untersuchungen zu römischen Opfer-, Kult- und Priestergeräten (Berlin / New York 1999).

SITTL 1890 C. SITTL, Die Gebärden der Griechen und Römer (Leipzig 1890).

SMITH 2003 D. E. SMITH, From Symposium to Eucharist. The Banquet in the Early Christian World (Minneapolis 2003).

SMYTH 2003 M. SMYTH, La liturgie oubliée. La prière eucharistique en Gaule antique et dans l'Occident non romain (Paris 2003).

SNYDER 2003 G. F. SNYDER, Ante pacem. Archaeological Evidence of Church Life Before Constantine (Macon 2003).

SOTINEL 2010A C. SOTINEL, The Christian Gift and its Economic Impact in Late Antiquity, in: DIES., Church and Society in Late Antique Italy and Beyond (Farnham 2010) IX.

SOTINEL 2010B C. SOTINEL, Locus orationis ou domus Dei? Le témoignage de Zénon de Vérone sur l'évolution des églises (tractatus II,6), in: DIES., Church and Society in Late Antique Italy and Beyond (Farnham 2010) X.

SOTINEL 2010C C. SOTINEL, Places of Christian Worhip and their Sacralization in Late Antiquity, in: DIES., Church and Society in Late Antique Italy and Beyond (Farnham 2010) XII.

SOTIRA 2013 L. SOTIRA, Gli altari nella scultura e nei mosaici di Ravenna (V–VIII secolo) (Bologna 2013).

SOUSTAL 1995 P. SOUSTAL et al., Makedonien, in: RBK 5 (1995) 982–1220.

SPERA 2007 L. SPERA, Hic constituit supra memorias martyrum missas celebrare. Interventi papali su tombe di martiri per la celebrazione ad corpus tra tarda antichità e altomedioevo, in: DIES. (ed.), Martiri ed Eucaristia nella civiltà cristiana (Città del Vaticano 2007) 43–69.

SPIER 2007 J. SPIER et al., Picturing the Bible. The Earliest Christian Art (Yale 2007).

SPIESER 1991 J.-M. SPIESER, Le programme iconographique des portes de Sainte-Sabine, in: Journal des Savants 1–2 (1991) 47–81.

SPIESER 1998 J.-M. SPIESER, The Representation of Christ in the Apses of Early Christian Churches, in: Gesta 37 (1998) 63–73.

SPIESER 2012 J.-M. SPIESER, Bildprogramm und Raumerlebnis in frühchristlichen und byzantinischen Kirchen, in: Boreas 35 (2012) 97–112.

STAMBAUGH 1978 J. E. STAMBAUGH, The Functions of Roman Temples, in: ANRW 2,16,1 (1978) 554–608.

STEIN 2008 H. J. STEIN, Frühchristliche Mahlfeiern (Tübingen 2008).

STERNBERG 2003 T. STERNBERG, Kirchenbau. Historische Vergewisserungen, in: A. GERHARDS et al. (eds.), Communio-Räume. Auf der Suche nach der angemessenen Raumgestalt katholischer Liturgie (Regensburg 2003) 37–69.

STERNBERG 2006 T. STERNBERG, Wie willst du deine Gabe Christus darbieten? Anmerkungen zur Praxis der frühchristlichen Gabenabgabe, in: B. KRANEMANN et al. (eds.), Die diakonale Dimension der Liturgie (Freiburg i.Br. 2006) 116–127.

STOLL 2000 R. STOLL, Architektur auf römischen Münzen (Trier 2000).

STUIBER 1954 A. STUIBER, Die Diptychon-Formel für die nomina offerentium im römischen Messkanon, in: Ephemerides Liturgicae 68 (1954) 127–146.

STUIBER 1978 A. STUIBER, Altar II. (Alte Kirche), in: Theologische Realenzyklopädie 2 (1978) 308–318.

SÜSSENBACH 1977 U. SÜSSENBACH, Christuskult und kaiserliche Baupolitik bei Konstantin (Bonn 1977).

SUNTRUP 1978 R. SUNTRUP, Die Bedeutung der liturgischen Gebärden und Bewegungen in lateinischen und deutschen Auslegungen des 9. bis 13. Jahrhunderts (München 1978).

SWEENEY 2018 C. R. SWEENEY, Holy Images and Holy Matter. Images in the Performance of Miracles in the Age before Iconoclasm, in: Journal of Early Christian Studies 26 (2018) 111–138.

SYMONDS 1966 H. E. SYMONDS, The Heavenly Sacrifice in the Greek Fathers, in: Texte und Untersuchungen 93 (Berlin 1966).

TABBERNEE 2014 W. TABBERNEE, Early Christianity in Contexts (Grand Rapids 2014).

TEPPER / DI SEGNI 2006 Y. TEPPER / L. DI SEGNI, A Christian Prayer Hall of the Third Century CE at Kefar 'Othnay (Legio). Excavations at the Megiddo Prison 2005 (Jerusalem 2006).

TESTINI 1980 P. TESTINI, Archeologia cristiana (Bari ²1980).

TESTINI 1989 P. TESTINI et al., La cattedrale in Italia, in: Actes du XIᵉ contrès international d'archéologie chrétienne 1 (Città del Vaticano 1989) 5–229.

THOMPSON 2015 G. L. THOMPSON, The *Pax Constantiniana* and the Roman Episcopate, in: G. D. DUNN (ed.), The Bishop of Rome in Late Antiquity (Farnham 2015) 17–36.

THÜMMEL 1999A H. G. THÜMMEL, Versammlungsraum, Kirche, Tempel, in: B. EGO *et al.* (eds.), Gemeinde ohne Tempel / Community without Temple (Tübingen 1999) 489–504.

THÜMMEL 1999B H. G. THÜMMEL, Die Memorien für Petrus und Paulus in Rom. Die archäologischen Denkmäler und die literarische Tradition (Berlin / New York 1999).

THUNØ 2015 E. THUNØ, The Apse Mosaic in Early Medieval Rome (Cambridge 2015).

THURÉN 1973 J. THURÉN, Das Lobopfer der Hebräer. Studien zum Aufbau und Anliegen von Hebräerbrief 13 (Åbo 1973).

TOLOTTI 1983 F. TOLOTTI, Le confessioni succedutesi sul sepolcro di S. Paolo, in: RACr 59 (1983) 87–149.

TOLOTTI 1986 F. TOLOTTI, Il problema dell'altare e della tomba del martire in alcune opere di papa Damaso, in: O. FELD / U. PESCHLOW (eds.), Studien zur spätantiken und byzantinischen Kunst 2 (Bonn 1986) 51–71.

UGONIO 1588 P. UGONIO, Historia delle stationi di Roma che si celebrano la Quadragesima (Roma 1588).

ULBERT 1986 T. ULBERT, Resafa II. Die Basilika des Heiligen Kreuzes in Resafa-Sergiupolis (Mainz 1986).

VAN DE PAVERD 1970 F. VAN DE PAVERD, Zur Geschichte der Messliturgie in Antiochia und Konstantinopel gegen Ende des vierten Jahrhunderts. Analyse der Quellen bei Johannes Chrysostomos (Rom 1970).

VAN DER MEER 1951 F. VAN DER MEER, Augustinus der Seelsorger. Leben und Wirken eines Kirchenvaters (Köln 1951).

VANHOYE 2015 A. VANHOYE, The Letter to the Hebrews (Mahwah/NJ 2015).

VERSTEGEN 2002 U. VERSTEGEN, Gemeinschaftserlebnis in Ritual und Raum. Zur Raumdisposition in frühchristlichen Basiliken des vierten und fünften Jahrhunderts, in: U. EGELHAAF-GAISER / A. SCHÄFER (eds.), Religiöse Vereine in der römischen Antike (Tübingen 2002) 261–297.

VERSTEGEN 2009 U. VERSTEGEN, Die symbolische Raumordnung frühchristlicher Basiliken des 4. bis 6. Jahrhunderts. Zur Interdependenz von Architektur, Liturgie und Raumausstattung, in: RACr 85 (2009) 567–600.

VOELKL 1949 L. VOELKL, „Orientierung" im Weltbild der ersten christlichen Jahrhunderte, in: RACr 25 (1949) 155–170.

VOELKL 1954 L. VOELKL, Die Konstantinischen Kirchenbauten nach den literarischen Quellen des Okzidents, in: RACr 30 (1954) 99–136.

VÖSSING 2004 K. VÖSSING, Vor dem Nachtisch oder nach Tisch? Zum Opfer beim römischen Bankett, in: Zeitschrift für Papyrologie und Epigraphik 146 (2004) 53–59.

VOGEL 1960 C. VOGEL, *Versus ad Orientem*. L'orientation dans les *Ordines Romani* du haut moyen âge, in: Studi Medievali 1 (1960) 447–469.

VOGEL 1962 C. VOGEL, *Sol aequinoctialis*. Problèmes et technique de l'orientation dans le culte chrétien, in: Revue des Sciences Religieuses 36 (1962) 175–211.

VOGEL 1964 C. VOGEL, L'orientation vers l'Est du célébrant et des fidèles pendant la célébration eucharistique, in: Orient Syrien 33 (1964) 3–37.

VOGEL 1976 C. VOGEL, Symboles cultuels chrétiens. Les aliments sacrés: Poisson et Refrigeria, in: Settimane di studio del centro italiano di studi sull'alto medioevo 23 (1976) 197–252.

VOLBACH 1976 W. F. VOLBACH, Elfenbeinarbeiten der Spätantike und des frühen Mittelalters (Mainz ³1976).

VOLLMER 2017 C. VOLLMER, Überlegungen zu Datierung, Auftraggeber und intendierter Funktion von Santo Stefano Rotondo in Rom, in: MDAI.R 123 (2017) 255–281.

VOLTI 2005 P. VOLTI, L'altare cristiano dalle origini alla riforma carolingia, in: F. DEBUYST *et al.*, L'altare. Mistero di presenza, opera dell'arte (Magnano 2005) 81–95.

VORHOLT 2012 R. VORHOLT, Alle Wege führen nach Rom. Die Hauptstadt im Blickfeld des Paulus, in: R. VON BENDEMANN / M. TIWALD (eds.), Das frühe Christentum und die Stadt (Stuttgart 2012) 208–218.

WAETZOLDT 1964 S. WAETZOLDT, Die Kopien des 17. Jahrhunderts nach Mosaiken und Wandmalereien in Rom (München 1964).

WAGNER 2011 J. WAGNER, Die Anfänge des Amtes in der Kirche. Presbyter und Episkopen in der frühchristlichen Literatur (Tübingen 2011).

WALLRAFF 2001 M. WALLRAFF, *Christus Verus Sol*. Sonnenverehrung und Christentum in der Spätantike (Münster 2001).

WALLRAFF 2004 M. WALLRAFF, Gerichtetes Gebet. Wie und warum richten Juden und Christen in der Spätantike ihre Sakralbauten aus?, in A. GERHARDS / H. H. HENRIX (eds.), Dialog oder Monolog? Zur liturgischen Beziehung zwischen Judentum und Christentum (Freiburg i.Br. 2004) 110–127.

WALTER 2006 C. WALTER, The Iconography of Constantine the Great, Emperor and Saint (Leiden 2006).

WARD PERKINS / GOODCHILD 1953 J. B. WARD PERKINS / R. GOODCHILD, The Christian Antiquities of Tripolitania, in: *Archaeologia* 95 (1953) 1–84.

WARLAND 1986 R. WARLAND, Das Brustbild Christi. Studien zur spätantiken und frühbyzantinischen Bildgeschichte (Rom 1986).

WARLAND 2002A R. WARLAND, Die Gegenwart des Heils. Strategien der Vergegenwärtigung in der frühbyzantinischen Kunst, in: *id.* (ed.), Bildlichkeit und Bildorte von Liturgie (Wiesbaden 2002) 51–74.

WARLAND 2002B R. WARLAND, Liturgien als Kommunikationsgeschehen, in: *id.* (ed.), Bildlichkeit und Bildorte von Liturgie (Wiesbaden 2002) 153–155.

WATTA 2018 S. WATTA, Sakrale Zonen im frühen Kirchenbau des Nahen Ostens (Wiesbaden 2018).

WECKWERTH 1963 A. WECKWERTH, Tisch und Altar, in: Zeitschrift für Religions- und Geistesgeschichte 15 (1963) 209–244.

WEIDEMANN 2014 H.-U. WEIDEMANN, Taufe und Mahlgemeinschaft. Studien zur Vorgeschichte der altkirchlichen Taufeucharistie (Tübingen 2014).

WEITZMANN 1975 K. WEITZMANN *et al.*, The Place of Book Illumination in Byzantine Art (Princeton 1975).

WEITZMANN 1979 K. WEITZMANN (ed.), Age of Spirituality. Late Antique and Early Christian Art, Third to Seventh Century (New York 1979).

WEITZMANN / GALAVARIS 1990 K. WEITZMANN / G. GALAVARIS, The Monastery of Saint Catherine at Mount Sinai. The Illuminated Greek Manuscripts 1 (Princeton 1990).

WESSEL 1966A K. WESSEL, Altar, in: RBK 1 (1966) 111–120.

WESSEL 1966B K. WESSEL, Altarbekleidung, in: RBK 1 (1966) 120–124.

WESSEL 1966C K. WESSEL, Apostelkommunion, in: RBK 1 (1966) 239–245.

WHITE 1990 L. M. WHITE, Building God's House in the Roman World. Architectural Adaptation among Pagans, Jews and Christians (Baltimore / London o.J. [1990]).

WHITE 1996 L. M. WHITE, The Social Origins of Christian Architecture 1. Building God's House in the Roman World. Architectural Adaptation Among Pagans, Jews, and Christians (Valley Forge 1990).

WHITE 1997 L. M. WHITE, The Social Origins of Christian Architecture 2. Texts and Monuments for the Christian Domus Ecclesiae in its Environment (Valley Forge 1997).

WHITE 1998 L. M. WHITE, House Church, in: E. FERGUSON (ed.), Encyclopedia of Early Christianity 1 (New York / London ²1997).

WHITE 2016 L. M. WHITE, Paul and *Pater Familias*, in: J. P. SAMPLEY (ed.), Paul in the Greco-Roman World (London / New York 2016) 457–487.

WIELAND 1906 F. WIELAND, *Mensa* und *Confessio*. Studien über den Altar der altchristlichen Liturgie (München 1906).

WIELAND 1908 F. WIELAND, Die Schrift „*Mensa* und *Confessio*" und P. Emil Dorsch S.J. in Innsbruck. Eine Antwort (München 1908).

WIELAND 1909 F. WIELAND, Der vorirenäische Opferbegriff (München 1909).

WIELAND 1912 F. WIELAND, Altar und Altargrab der christlichen Kirchen im 4. Jahrhundert. Neue Studien über den Altar der altchristlichen Liturgie, (Leipzig 1912).

WILPERT 1895 J. WILPERT, *Fractio Panis*. Die älteste Darstellung des eucharistischen Opfers in der „Cappella Greca" (Freiburg i.Br. 1895).

WILPERT 1903 J. WILPERT, Die Malereien der Katakomben Roms (Freiburg i.Br. 1903).

WILPERT 1917 J. WILPERT, Die römischen Mosaiken und Malereien der kirchlichen Bauten vom IV. bis XIII. Jahrhundert 2,1–2 (Freiburg i.Br. ²1917).

WILPERT / SCHUMACHER 1976 J. WILPERT / W. N. SCHUMACHER, Die römischen Mosaiken der kirchlichen Bauten vom IV.–XIII. Jahrhundert (Freiburg i.Br. 1976).

WISSKIRCHEN 1990 R. WISSKIRCHEN, Das Mosaikprogramm von S. Prassede in Rom (Münster 1990).

WISSOWA 1971 G. WISSOWA, Religion und Kultus der Römer (München 1971).

WRIGHT 2017 B. J. WRIGHT, Communal Reading in the Time of Jesus. A Window into Early Christian Reading Practices (Minneapolis 2017).

YASIN 2009 A. M. YASIN, Saints and Church Spaces in the Late Antique Mediterranean. Architecture, Cult, and Community (Cambridge 2009).

YASIN 2012 A. M. YASIN, Sacred Space and Visual Art, in: S. F. JOHNSON (ed.), The Oxford Handbook of Late Antiquity (Oxford 2012) 935–969.

YASIN 2017 A. M. YASIN, Renovation and the early Byzantine church. Staging past and prayer, in: B. BITTON-ASHKELONY / D. KRUEGER (eds.), Prayer and Worship in Eastern Christianities, 5th to 11th centuries (London / New York 2017) 89–115.

YOUNG 1972 F. M. YOUNG, The Idea of Sacrifice in Neoplatonic and Patristic Texts, in: F. L. CROSS (Hg.), *Studia Patristica* 11 (Berlin 1972) 278–281.

ZELLER 2002 D. ZELLER (ed.), Christentum 1. Von den Anfängen bis zur Konstantinischen Wende (Stuttgart 2002).

ZIEGLER 2007 M. ZIEGLER, *Successio*. Die Vorsteher der stadtrömischen Christengemeinde in den ersten beiden Jahrhunderten (Bonn 2007).

ZIEHEN 1950 L. ZIEHEN, Altar I, in: RACh 1 (1950) 310–329.

ZIMMERMANN 2010 N. ZIMMERMANN, Mahl VI (Räume und Bilder), in: RACh 23 (2010) 1105–1135.

ZIMMERMANN 2017 N. ZIMMERMANN, Inhalte und Intentionen bildlicher Kunst in Sakralräumen zwischen Damasus und Sixtus III. in Rom, in: *id. et al.* (eds.), Die Päpste und Rom zwischen Spätantike und Mittelalter (Regensburg 2017) 115–142.

ZIZIOULAS 2001 J. D. ZIZIOULAS, Eucharist, Bishop, Church. The Unity of the Church in the Divine Eucharist and the Bishop During the First Three Centuries (Brookline 2001).

ZORELL 1902 S. ZORELL, Die Entwicklung des Parochialsystems bis zum Ende der Karolingerzeit, in: Archiv für katholisches Kirchenrecht 82 (1902) 74–98, 258–289.

SACRED SCRIPTURE

ANCIENT WORKS

TERMS, SUBJECTS, PERSONS